The Standard
OLD BOTTLE
Price Guide

Carlo & Dorothy Sellari

This book is dedicated to Carlo Sellari who worked tirelessly to complete his manuscript during the last year of his life. In loving memory his family expresses this dedication for his endless enthusiasm and love for bottle collecting.

COLLECTOR BOOKS
A Division of Schroeder Publishing Co., Inc.

The current values in this book should be used only as a guide. They are not intended to set prices, which vary from one section of the country to another. Auction prices as well as dealer prices vary greatly and are affected by condition as well as demand. Neither the Author nor the Publisher assumes responsibility for any losses that might be incurred as a result of consulting this guide.

Bitters

In the days when Americans were attempting to cure their ailments by consuming the contents of patent (or non-prescription) medicine bottles, bitters were agreed to be the most potent of such cures. Though it is not known if bitters ever actually cured anything, they were indeed potent—one bitters product was calculated to be nearly 120 proof liquor. Unique bottles were designed to catch the eye and launch effective bitters marketing: In addition to the round, triangular and rectangular shapes, bitters bottles were also made in figural shapes of pigs, fish, cannons, drums, ears of corn and cabins.

Bitters manufacturing began when England's George II (reigned 1727-1760) tried to control overindulgence in the evils of gin through a heavy liquor tax. The gin sellers would not acquiesce: They added herbs to their commodity and called it medicine. American colonists began to drink the "medicine" to avoid the tax. Following an article published in 1785 by Dr. Benjamin Rush of Philadelphia entitled "Inquiry into the Effects of Ardent Spirits on the Human Mind and Body," it became socially acceptable to drink the patent medicine and leave the nastiness of gin and brandy alone. The Revenue Act of 1862 further stimulated bitters consumption by taxing liquor more than medicine. Bitters, of course, were taxed as medicine—strong medicine, to be sure, most with more than fifty percent alcohol, not to mention the strychnine and belladonna also contained.

Many Americans actually believed in the medicinal value of bitters. After all, nearly all of the manufacturers or endorsers were medical doctors, though their qualifications were rarely verified. Jacob Hostetter of Lancaster County, Pennsylvania, used his own bitters formula in his private practice. Upon his retirement in 1853, he granted his son, David, permission to manufacture it, and David established a partnership with George W. Smith. Their advertising budget was huge, but it paid off. "Hostetter's California Almanac of 1861" advertised Hostetter's Celebrated Stomach Bitters on every other page. The ads warned that the bitters was not a panacea. All it would cure is "dyspepsia, diarrhea, dysentery, general debility, chills and fever, liver complaint, bilious remittent fevers, and the pains and weaknesses which creep upon us in old age." The ads dramatic conclusion adds:

It lives, and continues to thrive and increase in popularity, with marvelous rapidity, simply because the world wants it, will have it, cannot do without it . . . Furnished with this preventative, the pioneer of California may fearlessly prosecute his search for gold and silver . . . He may sleep wrapped in his blanket or buffalo robe on the damp ground by night, and brave the hot beams of the sun by day without incurring the usual penalties.
. . provided he reinforces his constitution, his appetite and his strength by moderate and regular use of the Hostetter's Bitters.

David Hostetter always had an eye open for new markets. During the Civil War, he managed to convince the Federal Government to purchase the bitters as a before-battle invigorant. Following the war, one historian wrote, ". . .Many a frightened Yankee at Gettysburg knew he faced Pickett's charge as bravely as he did because of a swig of Hostetter's under his belt." Though Hostetter's Bitters practically guaranteed victory in battle and gold to California prospectors, it could not cure Hostetter's own kidney ailment from which he died in 1888.

There are over one thousand types of bitters bottles known, most of the collectables having been produced between 1860 and 1900.

Editors' Note: Words, letters and numbers embossed on the bottle or appearing on the label are indicated by bold typeface and italic typeface. Photographs of bottles are not shown to a consistent scale. For exact dimensions of bottles refer to individual entries. The height of the bottle is given in inches. Any other dimensions, such as diameter or length of neck, are so indicated. The original spellings or misspellings on the bottles have been kept and sometimes especially noted.

C. W. Abbott & Co., Baltimore; around shoulder; 8½"; amber: *C. W. Abbott & Co., Baltimore* on base............................**4.00-6.00**

Abbott's Bitters; on base; *C. W. Abbot & Co., Baltimore* on shoulder; machine made; 8"; amber...**4.00-6.00**

Abbott's Bitters; 6½"; machine made, $8.00-10.00

Dr. Abell's Spice Bitters; label; pontil; 7½"; aqua.................................**30.00-50.00**

Acorn Bitters; amber; tapered lip; 9"......**60.00-70.00**

African Stomach Bitters; in three lines near shoulder; 9½"; amber........................**30.00-40.00**

African Stomach Bitters; in three lines near shoulder; 9½"; amber; round; under Bitters small letters *Spruance Stanley & Co*....................**30.00 +**

Aimar's Sarracenia Bitters; on back
Charleston S.C.; **aqua; 7½", $25.00 +**

Aimar's Sarracenia Fly Trap Bitters; label; on back embossed *A. S. B. Charleston S.C.;* 7¼";
aqua **100.00-110.00**

Alex Von Humboldt's; on back *Stomach Bitters;* tapered neck; ring top; amber; 9¾" **85.00-125.00**

William Allen's Congress Bitters; rectangular bottle, deep green, clear, light amber, 10" . . . **80.00-100.00**
same except pontil, amethyst, 7¾" **80.00-100.00**

Alpine Herb Bitters; in two lines in front; in back in a shield *TT&CO;* amber; 9¾" **40.00-60.00**

Alpine Herb Bitters; label; *TT&CO.* in a shield on one side; other two sides plain; tapered top; square; 8½" **35.00-55.00**

Dr. Alther's Bitters; lady's leg shape; 5", clear **20.00-40.00**

Amazon Bitters; reverse side *Peter McQuade N.Y.;* **9¼";**
amber, $70.00-85.00

American Celebrated Stomach Bitters; amber;
9¼" **40.00-50.00**

American Life Bitters; back same; *P. Eiler Mfg. Tiffin Ohio;* log effect; cabin-type bottle; tapered lip; light amber to amber **135.00-155.00**

American Life Bitters; same as above except *Omaha, Neb* **135.00-155.00**

American Stomach Bitters: amber; 8½" . . . **40.00-65.00**

Dr. Andrew Munso Bitters; lady's leg shape; 11¼";
amber **50.00-100.00**

David Andrew's Veg. Jaundice Bitters; aqua;
open pontil **60.00-90.00**

Angostura; *Bitters* on back; *Rheinstorom Bros, N.Y. & Cin.* on bottom; amber **30.00-50.00**

Angostura Bark Bitters; 9½"; aqua or
clear **25.00-40.00**

Angostura Bark Bitters; figural bottle, Eagle Liquor Distilleries, amber, 7" **40.00-50.00**

Angostura Bitters; on base; 7¾"; green . . . **20.00-30.00**

Appetine Bitters Geo. Benz & Sons, St. Paul, Minn. Mfg.; label; 7¼"; amber **10.00-20.00**

Arabian Bitters; in back; *Lawrence & Weicesslbaum, Savannah, Ga.,* square, tapered top, amber, 9½" **50.00-100.00**

Argyle Bitters, E.B. Wheelock N.O.; tapered lip; 9¾"; amber, $40.00-80.00

Aromatic Orange Stomach Bitters; square bottle,
amber **30.00-50.00**

Arps Stomach Bitters; *Ernest L. Arp & Kiel,* label;
round; 11¼", aqua **20.00-30.00**

Asparagin Bitters Co.; 11"; clear to aqua . . **25.00-50.00**

Atherton's Dew Drop Bitters; on base *1866 Lowell Mass.;* ringed shoulder; short tapered top; 10";
amber **40.00-50.00**

Atwell's Wild Cherry Bitters; label; oval bottle,
aqua, 8" **10.00-15.00**

Atwood Genuine Phys. Jaundice Bitters, Georgtown, Mass.; 12-sided; 6½"; aqua **10.00-20.00**

Atwood Jaundice Bitter; *by Moses Atwood* on panels;
6"; clear or aqua **6.00-8.00**
same except pontil **60.00-100.00**

Atwood Jaundice Bitter; *formerly made by Moses Atwood;* 6"; clear or aqua **4.00-6.00**

Atwood Jaundice Bitter; machine made; 6"; clear
or aqua **2.00-3.00**

Atwood Jaundice Bitter; *formerly made by Moses Atwood;* 6"; clear or aqua; screw top **2.00-4.00**

Atwood's Genuine Bitters; round, aqua, 6½" **6.00-8.00**

Atwood's/Genuine/Bitters; marked on base; N. *Wood Sole Proprietor;* on domed shoulder;
aqua; 6" **10.00-25.00**

Atwood's/Jaundice Bitters/M.C. Arter & Son/ Georgetown/Mass; aqua, 12-sided, ring
top, 6" **8.00-20.00**

Atwood's Quinine Tonic Bitters; 8½";
aqua **40.00-50.00**

Atwood's Quinine Tonic Bitters, Gilman Bros. Boston,
label; 9"; aqua **40.00-60.00**

Atwood's Veg. Dyspeptic Bitters; pontil; short tapered
top; 6½" aqua **40.00-60.00**

Augauer Bitters; 8¼"; green **50.00-70.00**

Aunt Charitys Bitters; label; *Geo. A. Jameson Druggist, Bridgeport, Conn.;* 8½"; clear & amber . **10.00-20.00**

Dr. Aurent IXL Stomach Bitters; Barkers, Moore & Mein; *Mfg. Wholesale Merch. Phila;* 8½" **20.00-30.00**

Ayala Mexican Bitters; on back *M. Rothenberg & Co. San Francisco, Cal.;* long collar with ring; 9½";
amber **40.00-60.00**

Dr. M.C. Ayers Restorative Bitters; 8½";
aqua **50.00-60.00**

E. L. Bailey's Kidney and Liver Bitters; on back *Best Blood Purifier;* 7¾"; amber **50.00-125.00**

Baker's High Life Bitters; *The Great Nerve Tonic* embossed on back; tapered top; machine made; pint **18.00-20.00**

Bakers Orange Grove; on back *Bitters;* roped corners; tapered top; 9½"; amber **80.00-125.00**

same as above except yellow **100.00-200.00**

Bakers Stomach Bitters; label; lady's leg shape; 11¼"; amber **40.00-60.00**

E. Bakers Premium Bitters; *Richmond, Va.;* aqua, 6¾" **50.00-75.00**

Dr. Balls Veg. Stom. Bitters; pontil; 7"; aqua **60.00-70.00**

Balsdons Golden Bitters; *1856 N.Y.* other side; amber; 10½", $85.00-100.00

Barber's Indian Veg. Jaundice Bitters; 12-sided; 6¼"; aqua **50.00-75.00**

Bartlett's Excelsior Bitters; on bottom *Bartlett Bros. N.Y.;* 8-sided; 7¾"; aqua and amber . . . . **100.00+**

Barto's Great Gun Bitters; in circle in center *Reading, Pa.;* cannon shop bottles; amber, olive amber; 11" x 3¼" **100.00-200.00**

Bavarian Bitters; *Hoffheimer Brothers* other side; amber; 9½" **75.00-100.00**

Baxters Mandrake Bitters; *Lord Bros. Prop. Burlington, Vt.* on vertical panels; 6½"; amethyst . . . **12.00-25.00**

Beecham Bitters; *Woodward Drug Co. Portland, Org.,* label; 8¼"; amber **10.00-15.00**

Beggs Dandelion Bitters; *Chicago, Ill* other side; amber, 9" **50.00-60.00**

Begg's Dandelion Bitters; square bottle, 9¼"; amber **50.00-65.00**

Begg's Dandelion Bitters; (in 3 lines) tapered top, base to neck a plain band, amber, 7¾" **10.00-25.00**

Belle of Anderson Bitters; 7"; amber **40.00-60.00**

Dr. Bells Blood Purifying Bitters; 9¼"; amber, $30.00-60.00

Bells Cocktail Bitters; lady's leg shape; 10¾"; amber **60.00-100.00**

Belmonts Tonic Herb Bitters; 9½"; amber **50.00-100.00**

Ben-Hub Celebrated Stomach Bitters; *New Orleans* (in three lines), same in back; tapered top, 9" **60.00-100.00**

Benders Bitters; 10½"; aqua **50.00-60.00**

Bengal Bitters; 8½"; amber **40.00-80.00**

Bennetts Celebrated Stomach Bitters; 9¼"; amber **60.00-150.00**

Bennetts Wild Cherry Stomach Bitters; 9¼"; amber **50.00-100.00**

Berkshire Bitters, Amann & Co., Cincinnati, O.; ground top; dark amber; 10½" **600.00-1,000.00**

Berliner Magen Bitters; *S. B. Rothenberg sole agents S.F.,* label; 9½"; green **50.00-100.00**

Berliner Magen Bitters; 9½"; amber **40.00-60.00**

Berry's Vegetable Bitters; labeled only; square bottle, amber; iron pontil, 9½" **20.00-30.00**

Dr. L. Y. Bertrams Long Life Aromatic Stomach Bitters; 9"; aqua **30.00-60.00**

Billing's Mandrake Tonic Bitters; labeled only; rectangular bottle, aqua, 8" **10.00-20.00**

The Best Bitters of America; cabin shape; 9¾"; amber **80.00-110.00**

Big Bill Best Bitters; amber; 12" **60.00-100.00**

Bird Bitters; *Phila. Proprietor;* 4¾"; clear . . . **40.00-50.00**

Dr. Birmingham Anti Bilious Blood Purifying Bitters; 9¼"; round; green **60.00-90.00**

Dr. Bishops Wahoo Bitters; 10¼"; amber **80.00-100.00**

Bismarck Bitters; ½ pint; amber **20.00-30.00**

The Bitters Pharmacy; label; 4½"; clear **3.00-4.00**

Dr. Blake's Aromatic Bitters N.Y.; 7¼"; aqua; pontil **60.00-100.00**

Blake's Tonic & Dueretic Bitters; round; 10¼"; aqua **20.00-30.00**

Dr. Boerhaaves Stomach Bitters; 9¼"; olive amber **150.00-200.00**

Boston Malt Bitters; round; 9½"; green **20.00-40.00**

Botanic Stomach Bitters; same on reverse; paper label; 9"; amber, $40.00-80.00

same as above except back reads *Bach Meese & Co. S.F.*; 9"; amber **40.00-60.00**

Bourbon Whiskey Bitters; barrel; 9"; bright puce **100.00-200.00**

Bourbon Whiskey Bitters; barrel; 9″;
claret **100.00-200.00**

Bowes Cascara Bitters; *Has No Equal, P.F. Bowes,
Waterbury, Conn. U.S.A.;* 9¼″; clear . . . **40.00-60.00**

Dr. Boyce's Tonic Bitters; *Francis Fenn Prop. Rutland
Vt.* on panels; bottle has twelve panels; 7¼″; aqua
blue **40.00-50.00**

Dr. Boyce's Tonic Bitters; label; sample size; twelve
panels; 4½″; aqua **8.00-15.00**

Boyer's Stomach Bitters; bottle in shape of an arch;
fancy bottle; round; 11″; clear **50.00-85.00**

Boyer's Stomach Bitters Cincinnati; whiskey shape bottle; fluted shoulder and round base;
clear **60.00-90.00**

Brady's Family Bitter; on three sunken panels; amber;
9½″ **60.00-90.00**

Brophys Bitters; 7″; aqua **40.00-50.00**

Brown, N.K.; on other side *Burlington, Vt.* on front; *Iron
& Quinine Bitters,* ring top, aqua, 7¼″ . . **55.00-75.00**

Brown & Lyons Blood Bitters;
8″; amber **80.00-90.00**

Brown Chemical Co.; *Brown Iron Bitters* on other side;
8″; amber **10.00-20.00**

F. Brown Boston Sarsaparilla Stomach Bitters; pontil;
9¼″; aqua **50.00-90.00**

Brown's Aromatic Bitters; oval bottle,
aqua, 8½″ **40.00-60.00**

Dr. Brown's Berry Bitters; 8¼″; aqua
or clear **30.00-40.00**

Brown's Castilia Bitters; round; tapered; 10″;
amber **40.00-80.00**

Brown's Celebrated Indian Herb Bitters; amber;
12½″ **150.00-225.00**

Brown's Celebrated Indian Herb Bitters; in a shield
shaped panel at base on left side; on base *Patented-
Feb. 11-1867, Indian Maiden,* amber, golden amber,
other shades of amber which are common for this
bottle **150.00-225.00**

    Rare in green, clear, aqua . . . . **300.00 and Up**

Browns Indian Queen Bitters; 12½″; reddish
amber **150.00-300.00**

Bryant's; *Stomach Bitters* on 3
panels; green; small kick-up with
dot, **$200.00-600.00**

Bryants Stomach Bitters; on two panels; 8-sided; pontil;
11¾″; olive **100.00-200.00**

H.E. Bucklen & Co.; *Electric Brand Bitter* on each side;
amber; 9″ **10.00-20.00**

    same except no *Electric* **10.00-20.00**

Burdock Blood Bitters; Canadian type; early ABM; 8½″;
clear **8.00-15.00**

Burdock Blood Bitters; *T. Milburn & Co., Toronto, Ont.*
on back; tapered neck; 8½″; aqua
blue **20.00-30.00**

Burdock Blood Bitters; *Foster Milburn Co.* one side;
other side *Buffalo N.Y.;* clear; 8″ **10.00-25.00**

Professor Geo. J. Byrne New York; *The Great Universal Compound Stomach Bitters Patd 1870;* fancy
ware bottle; amber or clear; 10″ **50.00-150.00**

Bitters; label; *McC* on bottom; gold; 9½″ **4.00-6.00**

Bitters; label; amber; lady's leg
neck; 12″ **35.00-55.00**

Bitters; label under glass in circle; bar bottle;
12¼″ clear **10.00-25.00**

Bitters; label; crock; light olive, brown
trim; 10¼″ **10.00-25.00**

Bitters; label; different colors and sizes;
reproductions **4.00-10.00**

Bitters; or whiskey, label; green **40.00-70.00**

California Fig. Bitters; 9¼″; amber **60.00-70.00**

California Fig Bitters; square bottle, *California Extract of
Fig Co.,* amber, 9⅝″ **60.00-70.00**

    same as above except *Fig & Herb Bitters;*
black **100.00-200.00**

Caldwells Herb Bitters; 12¼″; pontil;
amber **100.00-200.00**

California Herb & Fig. Bitters;
9¾″; amber **60.00-80.00**

California Wine Bitters; *M Keller, L.A.* in shield on
shoulder; *M.K.* around bottle; 12¼″; olive
green **200.00-400.00**

Dr. Callender & Sons Liver Bitters; square bottle
Celebrated Liver Bitters, light
amber, 9⅝″ **50.00-80.00**

Canton (★) Bitters (★); all around
the shoulder; long bulged lady's leg
neck, round; amber; 12″ tall, 3½″
round, **$100.00-200.00**

Capital Bitters; one side; *Dr. M. M. Fenner's Fredonia,
N.Y.* on reverse side; 10½″; aqua **20.00-40.00**

Caracas Bitters; 8¼″; amber to emerald
green **20.00-30.00**

    same as above in dark green **25.00-50.00**

Carmelite Bitters; *for the Kidney and Liver Complaints*
on one side; on back, *Carmelite, Frank R. Leonori &
Co. Proprietors, New York;* square; 10½″; amber,
olive **40.00-60.00**

Carmeliter Kidney & Liver Bitters; square bottle,
"CARMELITER STOMACH BITTERS CO NEW
YORK", amber, 10⅝″ **35.00-45.00**

Caroni Bitters; pint; amber **12.00-25.00**

Caroni Bitters; ½ pint; green **12.00-25.00**

Carpathian Herb Bitters; ***Hollander Drug Co. Braddock P.*** **other side; amber, 8½", $20.00-50.00**

Carpenter & Burrows, Cincinnati, O.; (in 2 lines), cabin type bottle, tapered top, amber, label stated bitters-S is reverse in Burrows, 9½" **100.00-275.00**

Carter's Liver Bitters; oval bottle, w/label, amber, 8⅝" **40.00-80.00**

Cassins Grape Brandy Bitters; triple ringed top; 10"; dark olive green **200.00-400.00**

Castilian Bitters; in vertical lines, round shape and tapered from bottom to neck, narrow square top and ring in center of neck, narrow square top and ring in center of neck. Light amber, 10" **60.00-75.00**

Catawba Wine Bitters; cluster of grapes on front and back; 9"; green **100.00-200.00**

Celebrated Berlin Stomach Bitters; square bottle, light green, 9½" **75.00-100.00**

Celebrated Crown Bitters; *F. Chevalier & Co. Sole Agents;* 9¼"; amber **80.00-100.00**

Celebrated Health Restoring Bitters; *Dr. Stephen Jewetts;* pontil; 9½"; aqua **40.00-50.00**

Celebrated Parkers Bitters-Stomach; (in 3 lines), side mold, amber, tapered top, 8¼" **50.00-100.00**

Celery & Chamomile Bitters; label; square; 10"; amber **10.00-20.00**

Chalmer's; on shoulder; on base *Proprietors* in center, *Catawka Wine Bitters,* ¼ moon letters under it *Trade Mark,* center of it circle with mill tree, under it in ¼ moon letters *Sutters Old Mill. Spurance Stanley & Co.;* round, ring tapered top, aqua 11½₀" **65.00-85.00**

Chander's Dr., Jamaica Ginger Root Bitters (all in 4 lines), barrel type bottle; on shoulder in 2 lines *Chas. Nichols Jr. & Co. Props Lowell Mass.,* amber, double ring top, 10" . . . . **200.00+**

Christian Xander's Stomach Bitters, label; *Washington, D.C.;* 12"; amber **20.00-40.00**

Dr. E. Chyder Stomach Bitters, N.O.; 9"; amber **25.00-50.00**

Cintoria Bitter Wine; on shoulder; 11"; amber **15.00-30.00**

Clarke's Compound Mandrake Bitters; (in 3 lines) aqua, ring top, 7⅝" **30.00-40.00**

Clark's Giant Bitters; rectangular bottle, ring top, *Philada, Pa.* aqua, 6¾" **30.00-40.00**

Clarkes Sherry Wine Bitters; clear, blue green pontil, 8" **20.00-40.00**

Clarkes Sherry Wine Bitters; *Only 25¢;* pontil; 8"; blue green **60.00-100.00**

E.R. Clarke's Sarsparilla Bitters; *Sharon, Mass;* rectangular bottle, aqua, pontil, 7⅛" **70.00-90.00**

Clarkes Sherry Wine Bitters; clear, blue green pontil, 8" **20.00-40.00**

Clarks Veg. Bitters; *only 75¢;* 8"; pontil; aqua **80.00-100.00**

Claw Bitters; label; 4¾"; light amber **20.00-30.00**

Clayton & Russell's Bitters; labeled only; square bottle, *Celebrated Stomach Bitters;* label, amber, 8⅞" **15.00-20.00**

Climax Bitters; on back *S. F. Cal.;* 9½"; golden amber **60.00-100.00**

Clotworthy's; *Oriental Tonic Bitter* on back; amber; 10" **65.00-85.00**

Coca Bitters Andes Mts.; trademark; picture of Indian carrying man across stream; also *The Best Tonic* **90.00-100.00**

Cocamoke Bitters; *Hartford, Conn.;* square bottle, amber, tapered top, 9" **40.00-60.00**

Cocktail Bitters; ***Cribbs Davidson & Co*** **other side; 9¼", $75.00-125.00**

Dr. A. W. Coleman's Antidyspeptic Tonic Bitters; pontil; ground pontil; green **75.00-85.00**

Colleton Bitters; pontil; aqua; 6½" **50.00-65.00**

same as above without pontil **10.00-25.00**

Columbo Peptic Bitters; on back *L. E. June, New Orleans, La.;* square bottle; under bottom *SB&CO;* 8¾" amber **25.00-35.00**

Compound Hepatica Bitters; *H.F.S.* monogram, oval bottle, *"H.F. SHAW M.D.,"* aqua, ring top, *Mt. Vernon, Me.,* 8⅜" **65.00-85.00**

Compound Calisaya Bitters; in two lines; tapered top, square, amber, 9½" **14.00-18.00**

Comus Stomach Bitters; in two lines; *Back Clerc Bros & Co. Limited sole proprietors, New Orleans, La.* in three lines, tapered top, amber, 9" **70.00-90.00**

Congress; on other side, *Bitters*, amber or clear, tapered top, 9" **60.00-80.00**

Constitution Bitters 1880; *Bodeker Bros Prop. Rich. Va.;* 7"; amber **75.00-125.00**

Constitution Bitters; rectangular bottle, *Seward & Bentley,* Buffalo, N.Y., green, round. Below shoulder *A.M.S. 2;* at base *1864,* 9½" **90.00-115.00**

Corn Juice Bitters; flask-shaped bottle; quart; aqua **40.00-80.00**

Corwitz Stomach Bitters; 7½"; amber **25.00-50.00**

Crimean Bitters; under it on base, *Patent 1863*, on other side, *Romaines Crimena Bitters,* amber, 10¼" **175.00-225.00**

H.M. Crookess; Stomach bitters, letters separated from the mould seam, round big blob neck, long tapered top, small kick up olive green, 10½" **325.00-400.00**

Cunderango Bitters; same on back side; greenish amber; 7¾" **60.00-100.00**

Curtis Cordial Calisaya, The Great Stomach Bitters; tapered neck; 11½"; amber **100.00-150.00**

Damiana; *Baja, Calif.* on back; 8-pointed star under bottom, aqua, 11½" **20.00-40.00**

Damiana Bitters; *Baja, Calif.* on back; 8-pointed star under bottom; *Lewis Hess Manufr.* on shoulder; aqua; 11½" **30.00-40.00**

Dandelion Bitters; 7"; aqua or clear **40.00-60.00**

Demuth's Stomach Bitters; Philada.; square bottle, amber, 9⅝" **35.00-50.00**

Devil-Cert Stomach Bitters; Round bottle, clear, ABM, 8" **10.00-15.00**

DeWitts Stomach Bitters; *Chicago;* 8"; amber, **$40.00-50.00**

DeWitts Stomach Bitters; *Chicago;* 8"; amber **40.00-50.00**

DeWitts Stomach Bitters; *Chicago;* 9¾"; amber **40.00-50.00**

Dexter Loveridge Wahoo Bitters; *DWD 1863 XXX* on roof tapered top; Eagle faces down to left with arrow, dark amber, 10" **50.00-100.00**

same as above except Eagle faces up to right, light yellow **60.00-100.00**

Digestine Bitters; *P.J. Bowlin Liquor Co. sole proprietors-St. Paul, Minn.* in lines; tapered top, amber, 8½" **85.00-175.00**

Dimmitt's 50CTS Bitters; flask bottle, *St. Louis,* amber, tapered top, 6½" **50.00-70.00**

Doc Dunning Old Home Bitters; *Greensboro, N. Carolina;* 13"; dark red amber **40.00-80.00**

Doyle's Hop Bitters; cabin shape; *1872* **on roof; 9¼"; several shades of amber and many variants of colors, $40.00-60.00**

Doyle's Hop Bitters; cabin shape; *1872* on roof; 9¼"; several shades of amber and many variants of colors **40.00-60.00**

S. T. Drakes; on top of roof panel; *1860 plantation* on next panel: *Bitters* on next; reverse center panel *patented 1862* with six logs; front plain for label, other covered with logs; some have five logs and the earliest have four logs; 10"; amber the most common; others: citron, pale yellow, green, scarce in olive green.....................**50.00-85.00**

Eagle Aromatic Bitters; round bottle, *Eagle Liquor Distilleries,* yellow amber, 6¾" **10.00-20.00**

East India Root Bitters; *Geo. P. Clapp, sole Prop.;* gin shaped bottle, *Boston Mass,* amber, 9⅝" **95.00-110.00**

Emerson Excelsior Botanic Bitters; rectangular bottle, *E.H. Burns-Augusta-Maine,* amber, 9" ...**8.50-16.00**

Dr. E.P. Eastman's Yellow Dock; pontil, rectangular bottle, *Lynn, Mass.,* aqua, tapered top, 7¾" **40.00-80.00**

Electric Bitters; square bottle, *H.E. Bucklen & Co., Chicago, IL.,* amber, 9" **15.00-40.00**

Egon Braun Hamburs; embossed on shoulder, *Universal Mercantile Co. San Francisco, Original Amargo Bitters, etc.,* all on label, double ring top, green, 5", S20.....................**25.00-45.00**

English Female Bitters; on reverse *Dromgoole, Louisville, KY;* **8½"; clear or amber, $50.00-70.00**

Excelcior; on back *Bitters;* 9"; tapered top; amber **50.00-60.00**

Excelsior Herb Bitters; *J.V. Mattison, Washington, N.J.* rectangular, roofed shoulder, amber, 10" **115.00-145.00**

Favorite Bitters; *Powell & Stutenroth;* 9¼"; barrel shape with swirl ribbing; amber.........**60.00-100.00**

Feinster Stuttgaries Magen Bitters; *Brand Bros. Co.,* label; 3-sided bottle; long neck and ring top; 10"; amber **40.00-60.00**

Dr. M. M. Fenner's Capitol Bitters; 10½"; aqua **20.00-30.00**

same as above; green **30.00-40.00**

Fer-kina Galeno (Bitters) on shoulder; beer type bottle; 10⅛"; brown; machine made **8.00-20.00**

Fernet Gigliani Bitters; *San Francisco,* label; wine type bottle; kick-up bottom; green.........**20.00-25.00**

Fernet Gigliani Bitters; *San Francisco,* label; wine type bottle; kick-up bottom; green.........**20.00-25.00**

Ferro Quina Stomach Bitters Blood Maker; *Dogliani Italia, D.P. Rossi, 1400 Dupont St. S.E. sole agents, U.S.A. & Canada;* 9¼"; lady's leg type neck; amber **40.00-80.00**

Fischer's N.E., Cough Bitters; *Atlanta, Ga* (all in three lines) tapered top; aqua; 6" **45.00-60.00**

The Fishbitters; on side of eye; on reverse *W.H. Ware Patented 1866;* on base *W.H. Ware Patented 1866;* plain rolled top; 11½"; 3½" x 2½"; amber, rare in other color **100.00-250.00**
same as above except clear **200.00-400.00**

Fitzpatrick & Co.; shape of stubby ear of corn; 10"; amber, $150.00-250.00

A. H. Flanders M.D. Rush's Bitters; 9"; clear, amethyst, amber **20.00-30.00**

Dr. Flints Quaker Bitters; *Providence R.I.;* 9½"; aqua **40.00-70.00**

Dr. Formaneck's Bitter Wine; 10½"; amber; round **10.00-15.00**

Fowler's Stomach Bitters; fancy bottle, square, light amber, *Stomach Bitters,* 10" **110.00-140.00**

Frank's Laxitive Tonic Bitters; flask type, on bottom *502,* amber, tapered top, 6¼" **90.00-115.00**

Francks Panacea Bitters; *(Frank Hayman Rhine Sole Proprietors)* round, light house, amber, 10" **95.00-120.00**

French Aromatique; *The finest stomach bitters* in 4 lines on shoulder, ring top, aqua, 7⅜" **30.00-40.00**

Garry, Owen Strengthening Bitters; on one side *Sole Proprietor's;* on other side *Ball & Lyon's, New Orleans La.;* front plain; under bottom *W. McC & Co. Pitts.;* 9"; amber **50.00-100.00**

German Balsam Bitters, W. M. Watson & Co.; *sole agents for U.S.;* 9"; milk glass **100.00-200.00**

German Hop Bitters; square, amber, *Reading, Mich,* 9½", A65.00 . . . . **35.00-65.00**

German Tonic Bitters **60.00-80.00**

Dr. Gilmores Laxative-Kidney & Liver Bitters; oval bottle, amber, 10⅜" **90.00-115.00**

Globe Bitters; *Manufactured only by Byne Bros. & Co. New York;* fluted tapered neck; 11"; amber **90.00-150.00**

Globe Bitters; *Manufactured only by John W. Perkins & Co., Sole Proprietors, Portland Me.;* 10"; amber **100.00-200.00**

The Globe Tonic Bitters; tapered top, square bottle, amber, 10" **60.00-80.00**

Dr. Goddin's Bitters; square, aqua, *Gentian Bitters,* 10" **185.00-230.00**

Golden Seal Bitters; square bottle, amber, 9" **100.00-130.00**

Godfreys Celebrated Cordial Bitters; 10"; iron pontil; aqua **25.00-60.00**

Geo. C. Godwins; reverse *Indian Vegetable Sarsaparilla;* each side reads *Bitters;* all lettering reads vertically; 8¼"; pontil; aqua **60.00-125.00**

Goff's Bitters; label; *Camden, N.H.;* aqua . . **10.00-15.00**

Goff's Bitters; *H* on bottom; machine made; 5¾"; clear and amber **10.00-20.00**

Dr. Goodhue's Root & Herb Bitters; rectangular bottle, *JH. Russell & Co,* aqua, 10⅜" **65.00-85.00**

Gold Lion Bitters; round bottle, labeled, clear, 6" **10.00-20.00**

St. Gotthard Herb Bitters; *Mette & Kanne Pros. St. Louis, Mo.* in vertical line on front; tapered top; 8¾" **40.00-50.00**

Granger Bitters; clear, flask bottle, labeled, amber, anchor on front, 7⅞" **18.00-23.00**

W. H. Greeg Lorimer's Juniper Tar Bitters; *Elmira N.Y.;* 9½"; blue green **40.00-80.00**

Greeley's Bourbon Bitters; amber, olive; 9½" **100.00-150.00**
same as above except puce **100.00-150.00**

Greer's Eclipse Bitters; *Louisville Ky* on side; amber; 9", $80.00-100.00

Griel's Herb Bitters; Lancastle, Pa.; round bottle, *Griel & Young,* aqua, 9½" **40.00-60.00**

J. Grossman; *Old Hickory Celebrated Stomach Bitters* on back; amber; 4½" **30.00-65.00**

J. Grossman; *Old Hickory Celebrated Stomach Bitters* on other side; amber; 8¾" **40.00-60.00**

Dr. Gruessie Alther's Krauter Bitters, label; *B* under bottom; 10½"; amber **40.00-60.00**

Gunckels Eagle Bitters; square bottle, labeled only, amber, 9⅜" **15.00-20.00**

Hagans Bitters; amber; 9½" **30.00-40.00**

Dr. T. Hall's, Calif. Pepsin Wine Bitters; (in three lines) amber, tapered top, 9¼" **40.00-100.00**

Hall's Bitters; *E. E. Hall, New Haven, Established 1852* on back; amber; 9¼" **100.00-200.00**

E. E. Hall, New Haven; *established 1842* on base; amber; 10¼", $40.00-80.00

Hansards Hop Bitters; crock; 8″; tan and
green **20.00-40.00**

**Dr. Manley Hardy's Genuine Jaundice Bitters, Boston
Mass.;** long tapered neck; 7½″; aqua.**60.00-100.00**
same as above except **Bangor, Maine**.**60.00-100.00**
same as above except 6½″ **40.00-90.00**
same as above except no pontil **15.00-30.00**

Dr. Harter's Wild Cherry Bitters; *St. Louis or Dayton,
O.;* rectangular; 7¾″; amber **20.00-30.00**
same except miniature **20.00-30.00**

Dr. Harter's Wild Cherry Bitters; *St. Louis* (all in four lines)
embossed cherries on both side panels, two under bot-
tom, amber, 7¼″ **100.00-350.00**

Harts Star Bitters; *Philadelphia Pa.;*
9¼″; aqua, **$55.00-110.00**

Hartwig Kantorowicz; *Posen Germany;* 4″; case type
bottle; milk glass **45.00-95.00**
same as above except 9½″ **40.00-85.00**

Hartwig's Celebrated Alpine Bitters; base *Wm. Mc &
Co. Pittsburgh, Pa;* square bottle, *St. Joseph, MO.,*
golden amber, 9⅜″ **60.00-90.00**

Harzer Kranter Bitters; reverse *Herman C. Asendorf,
Brooklyn N.Y.;* 9½″; amber **25.00-50.00**

Havis Iron Bitters; in base the *Williamsburg Drug Co;*
square bottle, *Williamsburg, KY,*
amber, 8″ **65.00-85.00**

H.H. Hay Co.; *Selling Agents Portland Me.* on back; on
bottom *L.F. Atwood;* in center *L. F.;* 6¾″;
aqua **25.00-50.00**

Henderson's Carolina Bitters; *Trademark H.C.B.;*
square bottle, amber, 9⅝″ **65.00-85.00**

Dr. Henley's California IXL (in oval) Bitters; *W. Frank
& Sons Pitt.* reverse side; sky blue **60.00-150.00**

Dr. Henley's Spiced Wine; *OK* in a circle; Bitters label;
OK Bitters; round bottle; ring top; 12″; bluish
aqua **100.00-200.00**

Dr. Henley's Wild Grape Root; reverse *IXL* in an oval,
Bitters under it; tapered and ring top; square bottle;
under bottom *W.F. G. Sons;* 12″ amber.**50.00-60.00**

H.P. Herb Wild Cherry Bitters; *Reading Pa.;* in back
wild cherry and tree; *Bitter* on all four sides of the
roof; 10″; amber **50.00-100.00**
same as above except green **75.00-150.00**

Herkules Bitter; *Monogram, G.A.,* inside of circle;
figural-ball shape bottle, *1 Quart,* labeled, also 1 pint,
deep green, 7¾″ **65.00-85.00**

Hesters Bitter Monogram; *G.A.* inside of circle; figural-
ball shape bottle, *1 Quart,* labeled, also 1 pint, deep
green, 7¾ **65.00-85.00**

Dr. I. Hester's Stomach Bitters; 8¾″;
amber, **$60.00-80.00**

Dr. R.F. Hibbard's Wild Cherry Bitters; *Proprietor, N.Y.;*
round bottle, *C.N. Crittenton,* aqua,
8″ **80.00-95.00**

Hierapicra Bitters; reverse side *Extract of Fig, Botanical
Society;* other side *California;* 6½″;
aqua **50.00-75.00**

Highland Bitters & Scotch Tonic; barrel-shaped bottle;
ring top; 9½″; amber **100.00-175.00**
same as above except olive **125.00-200.00**

Hi Hi Bitter Co.; triangular shape;
amber; 9½″ **50.00-85.00**

Hill's Horehound Bitters; round bottle, labeled only,
Irish Moss, 6½″ **6.00-12.00**

Hill's Mountain Bitters; rectangular bottle, *Embossed Indiana Drug Specialty Company,* amber tapered top,
7¾″ **20.00-30.00**

Hoboken Avan Bitters; 9¼″; olive **20.00-40.00**

Hoffheimer Bros.; reverse Bavarian
Bitters; 9½″; amber, **$25.00-50.00**

Dr. Hoffman's Golden Bitters; label; *ACW* under bottom; amber; 9″ **10.00-15.00**

Holtzermann's Patent Stomach Bitters; on the roof of
cabin-shaped bottle; shingle roof; tapered top; 9¾″;
amber **100.00-160.00**

Holtzermann's Patent Stomach Bitters; label; 4¼″;
amber **100.00-150.00**
same as above except 9¾″ **100.00-150.00**

Home Bitters Company; *Home Stomach Bitters* one
side; *Proprietors St. Louis, Mo.* other side;
amber; 8¾″ . . . . **50.00 +**

Dr. Hoofland's German Bitters rectangular bottle, aqua,
pint, pontil, in back *C.M. Jackson,
Phila,* 4″ **25.00-50.00**

**Dr. Hoofland's German Bitters Liver Complaint
Dyspepsia;** *C.M. Jackson, Philadelphia* in sunken
panels; double ring top; pontil; 8″;
aqua **20.00-50.00**
same as above except light blue **30.00-60.00**

Hop & Iron Bitters; square bottle, in back *Utica, N.Y.,* amber, tapered top, 8⅜" **30.00-75.00**

Dr. Von Hopfs Curaco Bitters; in back *Chamberlain & Co. Des Moines Iowa;* 9¼"; tapered top; amber **80.00-90.00**

same as above in a flask type bottle **80.00-90.00**

Hops & Malt Bitters; roofed shoulder, *Trademark (Sheafil Grain),* square bottle, yellow amber, amber, tapered top, 9⅝" **60.00-85.00**

Dr. A.S. Hoppins; *Union stomach bitters,* in three lines; tapered top, off shade of amber, beveled corners, 9¾" **35.00-50.00**

Horse Shoe Bitters; *Horse Shoe Med. Co.,* Base *Pat. App. for;* Horseshoe shape, amber, *Collinsville, Il.* **75.00-150.00**

Dr. J. Hostetter's Stomach Bitters; square; 9"; light amber, amber **6.00-12.00**

same except yellow green **12.00-25.00**

same except machine made **4.00-6.00**

Dr. J. Hotsetter's; (sic); amber; 8¾" **15.00-30.00**

Dr. J. Hostetter's; amber, 8¾", $10.00-18.00

Dr. Hostetter's Stomach Bitters; on base *IG.L.;* square; amber; 9" **6.00-12.00**

same as above except on back *18 Fluid oz.;* 8¾" **6.00-10.00**

same as above, machine made **3.00-5.00**

Dr. J. Hostetter's Stomach Bitters; (J is backwards); 8½"; amber **40.00-65.00**

Dr. J. Hostetter's Stomach Bitters; *L & W 10* on base; 9½"; yellow amber **10.00-20.00**

same as above except dark amber **10.00-20.00**

same as above except *S. McKee & Co.; 2* on base **10.00-25.00**

same as above except *#2* on base **10.00-20.00**

H.U.A.; monogram on bottom; bitters label; lady's leg shape; 10½"; amber **25.00-55.00**

Geo. C. Hubbel & Co.; on each side; blank front and back; 10½"; tapered top; aqua **20.00-40.00**

Hutchins; on side; **Dyspepsia Bitters** on front; *New York* on other side; tapered top; aqua; 8½"; pontil **80.00-125.00**

J.W. Hutchinson's; reverse *Tonic Bitters, Mobile Ala.;* 8¾"; aqua **40.00-85.00**

Hygeia Bitters; square bottle, *Fox & Co,* amber, tapered top, base *L & W,* 9" **60.00-80.00**

Imperial Bitters; one side, *Victor Rivaud;* other side, *Louisville, KY;* amber, 10½" **75.00-85.00**

Imperial Russian Tonic Bitters; rope design on sides; 9¼"; clear or aqua **50.00-60.00**

I.N.C. Bitters; (Reedy, Pa.) round, long neck, barrel-shape, amber, 10½" **90.00-115.00**

Indian Vegetable Sarsaparilla; reverse *Bitters, Boston;* all vertical lettering; pontil; 8¼"; aqua . **60.00-100.00**

Iron Bitters; square bottle, *Brown Chemical Co.,* 8⅜" **17.00-23.00**

Isaacson Seixas & Co. Bitters; Co. with eye in center, monogram, square, light amber, *66 & 68 Common St.,* push up with five star pontil, etc. **160.00-210.00**

Isham's Stomach Bitters; square bottle, amber, 9⅜" **80.00-100.00**

Jacob's Cabin Tonic Bitters; cabin shape bottle, *Laboratory-Philadelphia,* clear glass, pontil, 7⅜" **175.00-225.00**

Dr. Jacob's Bitters; *S.A. Spencer;* rectangular bottle, *New Haven,* aqua, 10" **80.00-100.00**

Jenkins Stomach Bitters; in two lines; under bottom, *W. McC & Co;* tapered top, amber **50.00-70.00**

Jewel Bitters; reverse *John S. Bowman & Co.;* 9"; amber **75.00-100.00**

Jewel Bitters; on side; *John S. Bowman & Co., California* on back; tapered top; quart; amber . **75.00-150.00**

Jockey Club House Bitters; *J.H. Dudley & Co.,* 9½"; green **50.00-100.00**

Dr. Herbert John's Indian Bitters; *Great Indian Discoveries;* 8½"; amber **65.00-75.00**

A.H. Johnson & Co.; on the side, *Collingwood, Ont.,* on front, *Johnson's Tonic Bitters,* clear or amethyst, double ring top, 8¾" **45.00-60.00**

Johnson's Calisaya Bitters; reverse *Burlington Vt.;* tapered top; 10"; amber **20.00-40.00**

Johnson's Indian Dyspeptic Bitters; each on four sides, rectangular, aqua, tapered top, pontil, ring top, 6¼" **70.00-90.00**

Jones Indian Specific Herb Bitters; *S.W. Jones - Prop. Phila;* square, amber *Patent, 1868,* tapered top, 9" **50.00-70.00**

Johnson's Indian Dyspeptic Bitters; each on four sides; rectangular, aqua, tapered top, pontil, ring top, 6¼" **40.00-80.00**

Kaiser Wilhelm Bitters Co.; *Sandusky O.;* bulged neck; ringed top; round bottle; 10"; amber . . **100.00-200.00**

Kelly's Old Cabin Bitters; *Patd March 1870* on one side; olive; 10" **200.00-300.00**

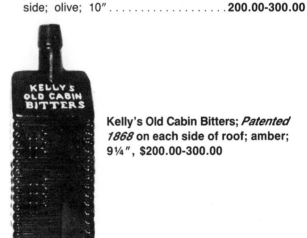

Kelly's Old Cabin Bitters; *Patented 1868* on each side of roof; amber; 9¼", $200.00-300.00**

Kennedy's East India Bitters; 6½"; clear . . **20.00-40.00**

Keystone Bitters; barrel-shaped bottle; ringed top; 10"; amber **50.00-70.00**

Kimball's (has backward S) **Jaundice Bitters;** *Troy N.H.* on side; tapered top; pontil; 6¾"; dark amber **100.00-200.00**

Kimball's Jaundice; on other side *Troy, N.Y.;* beveled corners, rectangular, olive green, tapered top, pontil, 7¼"x2¾"x2" **115.00-140.00**

King Solomon Bitters; *Seattle, Wash;* rectangular bottle, amber, 8½" **95.00-115.00**

King Solomon's Bitters; other side *Seattle, Washington;* rectangular, amber, 10 oz **45.00-60.00**

Klas's Oregon Peach Bitters; in large letters on shoulder; round; 11½"; aqua **30.00-50.00**

Koehler & Henrich Red Star Stomach Bitters; *St. Paul Minn* in a circle; label in red, black and white circle; *1908;* 11½" **100.00-200.00**

Koehlers Stomach Bitters Co.; 12½"; amber **20.00-30.00**

Landsberg's Century Bitters; (in three lines) over it a bird or eagle; in back *The Ader Company. St. Louis* also in three lines; 13 stars around shoulder, also *1776 & 1876;* corner diamond effect, very decorative bottle, tapered top and ring, 11½" ... **315.00-385.00**

Lacour's Bitters; *Sarsoparipher,* round fancy bottle, amber, yellow-green, 9⅛" **90.00-115.00**

Dr. Langley's Root & Herb Bitters; *76 Union St. Boston* on front; round; ringed top; 6¾"; light green **20.00-40.00**

Dr. Langley's Root & Herb Bitters; *99 Union St. Boston* on front; ringed top; 8½"; amber **25.00-50.00**

same as above, but embossing in indented panel **25.00-50.00**

Lash's Bitters Co.; *Chicago, San Francisco;* round, clear, dark amber, amethyst; 10¾" and 11" x 3" **5.00-10.00**

also with label *Cordol Bitter* **2.00-8.00**

Lash's/Bitters Co./New York, Chicago/San Francisco; amber, round, ABM only **10.00-14.00**

Lash's Bitters Co. N.Y. Chicago, San Francisco; round, fluted neck and shoulder, tapered top and ring, amber, 10½" **30.00-40.00**

Lash's Bitters; with circle between words *Kidney and Liver;* on back in two lines, *The Best Cathartic and Blood Purifier;* 2¾" x 2¾"; amber; 9½" **10.00-15.00**

same except 1" x 1" x 3" **8.00-20.00**

Lash's Liver Bitters; *Nature's Tonic Laxative* on back; machine made; amber; 7½", $4.00-10.00

Leak Kidney & Liver Bitters; reverse side. *The Best Blood Purifier and Cathartec;* 9"; amber **50.00-60.00**

Lediards; on side *Celebrated Stomach;* on back *Bitters;* tapered top; 10"; sea green **40.00-80.00**

Leipziger Burgunder Wein Bitters; all in a circle in center *A* around it, *The Hocktadter Co.* all under bottom, ring & tapered top. Round, 3pt. mould, green **25.00-40.00**

Dr. Leriemondie's Southern Bitters; 10"; dark green **35.00-65.00**

Lewis Red Jacket Bitters; around bottom; three-piece mold; 11"; amber **30.00-60.00**

Life Everlasting Bitters, Atlanta Ga.; 10" amber **40.00-85.00**

Lincoln Bitters; rectangular bottle, labeled only, clear glass, 9⅜" **10.00-25.00**

Lippman's Great German Bitters; other side *N.Y. & Savannah, Geo.* 9¾"; amber **80.00-125.00**

Litthauer Stomach Bitters; in center *Invented 1884 by Josef Lowenthal, Berlin* in vertical lines; tapered top; 9¾"; milk glass **80.00-100.00**

same as above except *Berlin* omitted ... **40.00-80.00**

Litthauer Stomach Bitters; round, fluted neck and shoulder, tapered top and ring, clear and "J" is backward, invented, 7" **85.00-100.00**

Dr. Loew's Celebrated Stomach Bitters & Nerve Tonic; 3½"; amber **40.00-50.00**

Dr. Loew's Celebrated Stomach Bitters & Nerve Tonic; reverse *The Loew & Son Co.;* tapered top and swirled ribbed neck; fancy bottle; 9½"; apple green **125.00-185.00**

Lohengrin Bitters; *Adolph Marcus, Van Buton German;* square-gin shape, milk glass, 9½" ... **175.00-200.00**

Lord Bros., Dr. Mandrake Baxto's Bitters; 12"; amber **10.00-30.00**

same as above except clear or amber ... **8.00-15.00**

Lorentz Med Co. Trade Mark; around shoulder; bitters label; 9¾"; amber **10.00-20.00**

Lorentz Med Co.; on bitters label; *Trade To-Ni-Ta Mark* around shoulder; amber; 10" **10.00-15.00**

Lorimer's Juniper Bitters; blue green; 9½"; 2¼" square **40.00-75.00**

Dr. XX Lovegoods Family Bitters; on roof of cabin-shaped bottle; tapered neck; 10½"; amber **60.00-100.00**

Dr. Lovegoods Family Bittrs (E left out of Bitters); 9½"; amber **100.00-300.00**

E. Dexter Loveridge Wahoo Bitters DWD; *1863 XXX* on roof; tapered top; eagle faces down and left with one arrow; 10"; dark amber **50.00-100.00**

same except eagle faces up to right; light yellow **50.00-100.00**

Lowell's Invigorating Bitters; square bottle, *Boston, Mass,* aqua, 8¼" **35.00-60.00**

Lutz Isaac D; *Reading, Pa;* red amber, double ring top, label stated bitters, 7¼" .... **50.00 +**

Dr. Lyford's Bitters; *C.D. Herrick, Tilton, N.H.;* on bottom *W.T. & Co. C;* ringed top; 8"; aqua **30.00-40.00**

E.G. Lyons & Co., Mfg. San F. CA.; (n in San in backward); tapered top; 9"; amber ... **100.00-250.00**

Mack's Sarsaparilla Bitters; in back *Mack & Co. Prop's S.F.;* 8½"; amber **100.00-150.00**

Magador Bitters; (E.J. Rose's) in back, superior tonic, cathartic and blood purifier, amber, 9" **50.00-100.00**

Magic Bitters; *prepared by Minetree & Jackson, Petersburg Va.;* two panels and rounded sides; tapered top; 14½"; olive **55.00-75.00**

Malarion Bitters; *Snyder Gue & Condell, St. Louis, Mo.;* 8½" amber **55.00-65.00**

Malt Bitters Co.; *Boston U.S.A.* under bottom; round; 8½"; emerald green **20.00-30.00**

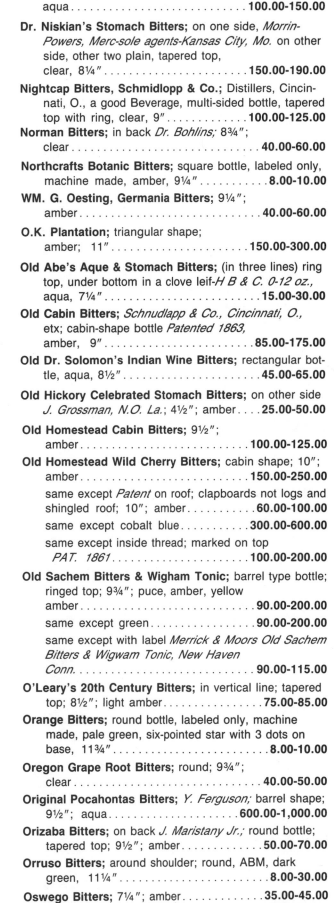

Mampe Bitters; label; back embossed same with *Carl Mampe, Berlin;* 6"; dark green, **$50.00-80.00**

Professor B.E. Manns Oriental Stomach Bitters; 10¼"; amber **20.00-40.00**

Mariani Coco Bitters; 7½"; green **15.00-30.00**

Marshall's Bitters; *The Best Laxative and Blood Purifier* on back; amber; 8¾" **25.00-40.00**

McKeever's Army Bitters; on shoulder; drum-shaped bottom; cannonballs stacked on top; tapered top; 10¼"; amber **400.00-600.00**

McNeil's Indian Vegetable Bitters; oval bottle, labeled only, aqua, 6¾" **18.00-24.00**

Mills Bitters; *A. M. Gilman, sole prop.;* lady's leg shape; ringed top; 6 ounce; amber **75.00-150.00**

same except sample size; 2 ounce **75.00-150.00**

Mishler's Herb Bitters; *S. B. Hartman & Co.* in back; under bottom *Stoeckels Grad Pat. Feb. 6, '66;* tapered top; 8¾" amber **40.00-60.00**

same as above except back reads *Wm. McC & Co.* **40.00-60.00**

Mohica Bitters; on back *Roth & Co. S.F.;* ringed top; 9"; amber **100.00-150.00**

Morning Star Bitters; (with Iron Pontil), fancy triangular, amber *Inceptum 5869, Patented (curve) 5869,* 13" **175.00-225.00**

same without pontil **90.00-115.00**

G.N. Morrison's; *Invigorating* - other side, *G.N. Morrison, New Orleans,* amber, tapered top, 9¼" **190.00-235.00**

Moultons Oloroso Bitters; trade (Pineapple) Mark, round, aqua, ribbed bottle, 11½" **80.00-100.00**

Murray's Purifying Bitters; rectangular bottle, labeled only, aqua, 8" **18.00-24.00**

National Bitters; *Patent 1867* under bottom; amber; 12¼", **$150.00-200.00**

National Bitters, Ear of Corn; *Patent 1867* under bottom, amber, corn, 12¼" **200.00-250.00**

New York Hop Bitters Co.; tapered top; 9"; aqua **100.00-150.00**

Dr. Niskian's Stomach Bitters; on one side, *Morrin-Powers, Merc-sole agents-Kansas City, Mo.* on other side, other two plain, tapered top, clear, 8¼" **150.00-190.00**

Nightcap Bitters, Schmidlopp & Co.; Distillers, Cincinnati, O., a good Beverage, multi-sided bottle, tapered top with ring, clear, 9" **100.00-125.00**

Norman Bitters; in back *Dr. Bohlins;* 8¾"; clear **40.00-60.00**

Northcrafts Botanic Bitters; square bottle, labeled only, machine made, amber, 9¼" **8.00-10.00**

WM. G. Oesting, Germania Bitters; 9¼"; amber **40.00-60.00**

O.K. Plantation; triangular shape; amber; 11" **150.00-300.00**

Old Abe's Aque & Stomach Bitters; (in three lines) ring top, under bottom in a clove leif-*H B & C. 0-12 oz.,* aqua, 7¼" **15.00-30.00**

Old Cabin Bitters; *Schnudlapp & Co., Cincinnati, O.,* etx; cabin-shape bottle *Patented 1863,* amber, 9" **85.00-175.00**

Old Dr. Solomon's Indian Wine Bitters; rectangular bottle, aqua, 8½" **45.00-65.00**

Old Hickory Celebrated Stomach Bitters; on other side *J. Grossman, N.O. La.;* 4½"; amber **25.00-50.00**

Old Homestead Cabin Bitters; 9½"; amber **100.00-125.00**

Old Homestead Wild Cherry Bitters; cabin shape; 10"; amber **150.00-250.00**

same except *Patent* on roof; clapboards not logs and shingled roof; 10"; amber **60.00-100.00**

same except cobalt blue **300.00-600.00**

same except inside thread; marked on top *PAT. 1861* **100.00-200.00**

Old Sachem Bitters & Wigham Tonic; barrel type bottle; ringed top; 9¾"; puce, amber, yellow amber **90.00-200.00**

same except green **90.00-200.00**

same except with label *Merrick & Moors Old Sachem Bitters & Wigwam Tonic, New Haven Conn.* **90.00-115.00**

O'Leary's 20th Century Bitters; in vertical line; tapered top; 8½"; light amber **75.00-85.00**

Orange Bitters; round bottle, labeled only, machine made, pale green, six-pointed star with 3 dots on base, 11¾" **8.00-10.00**

Oregon Grape Root Bitters; round; 9¾"; clear **40.00-50.00**

Original Pocahontas Bitters; *Y. Ferguson;* barrel shape; 9½"; aqua **600.00-1,000.00**

Orizaba Bitters; on back *J. Maristany Jr.;* round bottle; tapered top; 9½"; amber **50.00-70.00**

Orruso Bitters; around shoulder; round, ABM, dark green, 11¼" **8.00-30.00**

Oswego Bitters; 7¼"; amber **35.00-45.00**

Oxygenated Bitters; pontil; 6¾"; aqua **50.00-70.00**

Dr. Palmers Tonic Bitters; square bottle, labeled only, aqua, 8¾" **10.00-14.00**

Paine's Celery Compound Bitters; rectangular bottle, amber, 8"..............................**9.00-12.00**

same as above, clear glass...........**7.00-10.00**

Panknin's; *Hepatic Bitters N.Y.* on back; amber; 9".............................**60.00-85.00**

Parker R. Mason-Chicago; (in two lines) other side *Aromatic-Golden Bitters,* amber, tapered top, 9¼"...........................**110.00-135.00**

Patented Bitters; *(T. Pirters & Co. 31 & 33 Mich. Ave., Chicago),* square bottle *Chicago,* amber, 9¼"..................................**75.00-95.00**

Pawnee Bitters; *Indian Medicine Co. S.F.;* 11¼"; amber...............................**60.00-85.00**

Dr. Pelzolds Genuine German Bitters; cabin type bottle, amber..............................**90.00-130.00**

Penns Bitters For the Liver; on front panel; square; beveled edge; 6½" amber...........**40.00-60.00**

Pepsin Bitters; on one side; with *R.W. David Drug Co. Chicago, U.S.A.* in two lines on other side; shoulder and neck are raised, but not on ends; sunken panels on front and back; yellow green; 8¼" tall, 4¼" x 2⅛"........................**50.00-75.00**

Pepsin Calisaya Bitters; in two lines; opposite side *Dr. Russell Med. Co.;* rectangular; green, olive green; beveled corners with three vertical ribs; 7½" tall, 4¼" x 2¼".......................**15.00-30.00**

Perrins Apple Ginger, Phila.; embossed apple on front; cabin type bottle; 10¼"; amber.......**50.00-100.00**

Dr. D.S. Perry & Co.; on other side *New York, Excelsior Aromatic Bitters;* roofed shoulder; tapered top; 10½"; amber..........................**90.00-100.00**

John A. Perry's, Dr. Warren's Bilious Bitters; *Boston Mass.;* 10"; aqua....................**40.00-80.00**

Peter Vierling's Blood Purifying Bitters; *(Evansville, Ind.)* square bottle, amber, 10".......**50.00-75.00**

Dr. Petzolds Cabin Bitters; 11"; amber...**80.00-125.00**

Peychaud's American Aromatic Bitters Cordial L.E. Jung, Sole Prop. N.O.; round tapered top; 10½"; amber................................**30.00-40.00**

Philadelphia Hop Bitters; (in three lines) top of it a man holding a bottle, roof shoulder, tapered top, aqua, 10¼".............................**175.00-225.00**

Phoenix Bitters; on back *J.N. Moffat;* **on one side** *Price $1.00;* **other side** *N.Y.;* **pontil; 5"; dark olive, $40.00-60.00**

Dr. Geo. Pierces Indian Restorative Bitters; on side *Lowell, Mass.;* tapered top; 7½"; aqua..**40.00-60.00**

Pineapple Bottle; bitters label; 9¼"; light amber................................**90.00-125.00**

same except yellow green.........**200.00-300.00**

Piper Bitters; in a seal on shoulder, tapered top and ring, *Dr. Olive,* 3 Pt mold, 12¼".......**40.00-60.00**

Dr. Planetts Bitters; iron pontil; aqua; 9¾".............................**50.00-80.00**

Plow's Sherry Bitters; a large leaf on back for label; amber; 7¾".........................**200.00-400.00**

Pomlo Bitters Co.; *N.Y.* on back; tapered top and ring; 11½"; light green..............**40.00-70.00**

Pond's Bitters Co. Chicago, label; *Ponds Genuine Ginger Brandy* on back; clear; 11½"...**15.00-25.00**

Pond's Bitters; reverse side *Unexcelled Laxative;* on base 76; 9¾"; amber...........**25.00-50.00**

same except machine made.........**10.00-20.00**

Poor Man's Family Bitters; ringed top; 6½"; aqua..............................**20.00-30.00**

same except label reads **Poor Man's Bitters Co., Oswego N.Y.** *Entered according to the Act of Congress in 1870.*.....................**30.00-50.00**

Dr. Poter's Stomach Bitters; *(Dr. Poter New York),* rectangular bottle, labeled, clear glass, embossed, round boud top, 5½"...............**15.00-20.00**

R.W. Powers & Co. Aromatic Peruvian Bitters; *Rich. Va. 1881;* 10½"; amber.............**60.00-80.00**

Prickley Ash Bitter Co.; in two lines in sunken panel; other sides are flat for labels; beveled corners; 10"; 2¾" x 2¾"......................**25.00-35.00**

Prune Stomach & Liver Bitters (The best cathartic & blood purifier), square, amber, on base *2280,* tapered top, 9"...................**85.00-105.00**

Prussian Bitters; tapered top; 9½"; amber...............................**60.00-150.00**

The Quinine Bitter Co.; *184-196 Congress St. Chicago, Ill. U.S.A.;* diamond shape; concave sides; 8½"; clear...............................**40.00-60.00**

Ramsey's Trinidad Bitter; on shoulder; (*Bitters* misspelled on bottom); dark olive; 8¼".......**70.00-80.00**

Ramsey's Trinidad Bitters; round; dark olive; body 5"; 3¼" neck on a shoulder under bottom, *Ramsey Trinidad Bitter;* (no date)..............**25.00-60.00**

Dr. Miller's Ratafia; (Sphinx); under it, *Damiana Silbe Bros. Jr. Plagemann, S.F. sole agents, Pacific Coast;* round bottle; tapered and ringed top; 12"; amber...........................**200.00-300.00**

Red Cloud Bitters; square bottle, *Taylor & Wright Chicago,* green, also amber, 9½"....**100.00-120.00**

Red Jacket Bitters; square bottle, *Bennet & Pieters,* amber, 9½".......................**65.00-85.00**

Red Jacket Bitters; rectangular bottle, *Mon-Heimer & Co,* amber 9½".....................**50.00-65.00**

Reed's Bitters; (In back curved letters *Reed's Bitters),* round, lady's leg neck, on ring, 12½".......................**200.00-250.00**

Dr. Renz's Herb Bitters; tapered and ring top; 9"; light green...........................**85.00-150.00**

Rex Bitters Co., Chicago; whiskey shape; amber, clear; 10¼", $20.00-40.00

Red Kidney & Liver Bitters; square bottle; in back, *Laxative & Blood Purifier,* red amber, 10"..**55.00-75.00**

Richards, C.A. & Co.; *18 & 20 Kilby St., Boston, Mass.,* amber, label stated wine bitters, 9½", with label....................................**55.00-75.00**

same as above, without label.........**30.00-40.00**

S.O. Richardson; vertically on front; *Bitters So. Reading* on side; other side *Mass.;* flared top; pontil; 6½" light green..........................**50.00-65.00**

R.C. Ridgway & Phila.; big *3* under bottom; 11"; amber............................**60.00-85.00**

Rivaud's (reverse apostrophe) **Imperial Bitters;** *Victor Rivaud* on side; *Louisville Ky* on other side; amber, 10½".........................**75.00-85.00**

Dr. C.W. Robacks; *Cincinnati, O;* in small circle in center, *Stomach Bitters;* 9¾"; dark brown; barrel shape; ten ribs on top, ten ribs on base........................**85.00-150.00**

Rock City Bitters; 50¢ size in two lines; side mold, amber, 7½"......................**50.00-75.00**

Rohrer's; on one side *Lancaster Pa.;* on the other side *Expectoral-Wild Cherry Tonic;* 10½"; amber............................**60.00-100.00**

Romaines Crimean Bitters; fancy square, amber, *Patend 1863,* on base, 10".............**90.00-180.00**

E.J. Rose's; *Superior Tonic; Cathartic and Blood Purifier* on back; amber; 9", **$40.00-60.00**

Rosswinkle's Crown Bitters; square bottle, amber, tapered top, 8¾"..................**40.00-65.00**

S.B. Rothenberg; in a semicircle inside of which is *Sole /Agent/U.S./* the reverse has an applied blob seal stamped *Pat. Applied for;* bottle is in the shape of a square face gin, milk glass color, top, 8½" tall, 2" at base, 3" at shoulder.................**70.00-90.00**

Royal Italian Bitters; round, tall, red amber, wine type bottle, 13½"......................**85.00-105.00**

Royal Pepsin Stomach Bitters; 8½"; amber..............................**50.00-80.00**

W.L. Richardson's Bitters; pontil, rectangular bottle, *Mass,* aqua, 7"......................**60.00-80.00**
same except no pontil...............**20.00-40.00**

Rush's Bitters; square bottle, *A.H. Flanders, M.D.N.Y.* aqua, pint size......................**8.00-10.00**
same as above, amber, 9"............**20.00-30.00**

Russ's St. Domingo Bitters; square bottle, *New York,* amber, also olive green, 10"..........**40.00-50.00**

Dr. Russell's Angostura Bitters; round tapered top; 7¾"; amber, medium green, clear.....**40.00-60.00**
same except olive green (rare).......**60.00-100.00**

Saidschitser-Furstlich-Lobkowitz Bitter Wasser in circle; tan crock; four panels; round bottom; 9½"......................**50.00-100.00**

Sainsevins Wine Bitters, label; ringed top; 12"; aqua............................**10.00-20.00**

Salmon's Perfect Stomach Bitters; tapered top; square beveled corners; 9½"; amber........**40.00-85.00**

Sanborn's Kidney & Liver Vegetable Laxative Bitters; on bottom *B;* tapered bottle to paneled shoulder with fluted neck; 10"; amber............**50.00-100.00**

San Joaquin Wine Bitters; on back at bottom *B.V.C. Co.;* deep kick-up in base; 9¾"; amber, **$45.00-100.00**

Sarsaparilla Bitters; on side *E.M. Rusha;* back side *Dr. De Andrews;* 10"; amber................**30.00-60.00**

Sazerac Aromatic Bitters; in a circle on shoulder in monogram *DPH & CO.;* 12½"; milk glass; also in blue, green..........................**100.00-200.00**

Sazerac Aromatic Bitters; *D.P.H.* in seal; lady's leg shape; 10¼"; light amber..........**100.00-200.00 +**

Dr. S.B. & Co. ML; under bottom; clear or amethyst; 7¼".....................**4.00-6.00**

Schroder's Bitters; three-part mold; *KY CWC* under bottom; amber; 12".....................**150.00-200.00**

S.C. Smith's Druid Bitters; barrel shape bottle, brown, 9½"......................**165.00-200.00**

Schroeder's Bitters; *Louisville, KY* in three lines; base in one line; *Ky G.W. Co.;* lady's leg, ring top, amber, 11½", **$150.00-200.00**

same except tapered top and ring, 5½"**125.00-250.00**

Segrestat Bitters; in seal; kick-up on bottom; 11¾"; dark olive............................**50.00-75.00**

Segur's Golden Seal Bitters, Springfield, Mass; pontil; 8"; aqua............................**60.00-100.00**

W.F. Severa; on back *Stomach Bitters;* tapered top; 10"; red amber..........................**20.00-40.00**

Sherman Bitters; *Myer Bros. Drug. Co. St. Louis,* label; 7¾"; amber..........................**8.00-10.00**

Dr. B.F. Sherman's Prickly Ash Bitters; machine made; 10"; amber, **$4.00-8.00**

Simons Aromatic Stomach Bitters; 7¼"; clear or amber **50.00-75.00**

Simons Centennial Bitters Trade Mark; bust shape bottle; double ring top; 10¼"; amber, clear or aqua **150.00-300.00**

Dr. Sims Anti-Constipation Bitters; 6½"; amber **50.00-100.00**

Dr. Skinner's Celebrated 25 Cent Bitters; *So. Reading, Mass.;* pontil; 9½"; aqua **40.00-50.00**

Dr. Skinner's Sherry Wine Bitters; rectangular bottle, *So. Reading Mass,* aqua, pontil, 8½" **85.00-200.00**

Dr. Smiths Columbo Bitters, label and embossed; 9¾"; amber **20.00-30.00**

Snyder Bitters; *Jonesboro, Ark.* tapered top; 9½"; amber **40.00-60.00**

Solomon's Strengthening & Invigorating Bitter; on one sunken panel; on other *Savannah Ga.;* on other side, sunken panels; back flat; roofed shoulders; 2¾"x2¾"; 9½" tall; beveled corners; cobalt **85.00-250.00**

Dr. Sperry's Female Strengthening Bitters; *Waterbury, Conn.,* label and embossed; 10" **75.00-90.00**

Staake's Original Vital-Tone Bitters; around shoulder; ringed top; 8¼"; clear **35.00-55.00**

Standard American Aromatic Bitters Cordial; *Yochim Bros* in seven lines, New Orleans, round bottle, tapered top and ring, quart, amber, 10½" **18.00-24.00**

Standard American Aromatic Bitters Cordial; *Yochim Bros* in seven lines, *New Orleans;* round bottle, tapered top and ring, quart, amber, 10½" **10.00-20.00**

S. Stanley & Co. African Stomach Bitters; 9½"; amber **30.00-60.00**

Star Kidney & Livery Bitters; tapered top; 9½"; amber **20.00-35.00**

same as above with label **15.00-40.00**

Steinfield's Bitters; light amber, tapered top, in back on shoulder *First Prize-Paris,* 10" **100.00-125.00**

Steinfield's Bitters; light amber, tapered top, in back on shoulder *First Prize-Paris,* 10" **80.00-100.00**

Steketees Blood Purifying Bitters; 9½"; amber, $40.00-65.00

Dr. Stewarts Tonic Bitters; *Columbus Ohio* under bottom; amber; 8" **40.00-50.00**

St. Gotthards Bitters; 8½"; amber **60.00-75.00**

St. Gotthards Herb Bitters; 8½"; amber . . . **30.00-60.00**

Dr. Stoever's Bitters; established 1837, square, *Kryer & Co,* amber, 9" **75.00-95.00**

Stonghton Bitters; 7"; clear **20.00-40.00**

Suffold Bitters; other side *Philbrook & Tucker, Boston;* 9½" tall, 3½" wide; shape of a pig; ground lip; light amber **200.00-400.00**

Sumter Bitters; on front and back *Charleston S.C.;* on back *Dowie Moise & Davis Wholesale Druggist;* 9½"; amber **50.00-75.00**

Sun Kidney & Liver Bitters; square bottle, *Vegetable Laxative,* amber, machine made, 9½" **50.00-65.00**

Swan's, C.H.; on back *Bourbon Bitters,* square, tapered top, beveled corners, amber, 9" **70.00-90.00**

Dr. Sweet Strengthening Bitter; long tapered top; 8¼"; aqua **35.00-60.00**

Thorn's Hop & Burdock Tonic Bitters; square bottle, *Brattleboro, VT,* amber, label states this is a bitters, 8" **15.00-20.00**

Tip-Top Bitters; multi-sided bottle, labeled only, amber, 8½" **25.00-50.00**

Thorn's Hop & Burdock Tonic Bitters; square bottle, *Brattleboro, VT,* amber, label states this is a bitters, 8" **10.00-15.00**

Tip-Top Bitters; multi-sided bottle, labeled only, amber, 8½" **10.00-15.00**

Tippecanoe; amber, clear, aqua; 9" **60.00-80.00**

Tippecanoe; misspelled *Rochester* under bottom; 9"; amber **60.00-80.00**

Todd's Bitters; machine made; clear; 8¼" . . **8.00-10.00**

Toneco Bitters; clear; under bottom a diamond shape with number **25.00-35.00**

Tonola Bitters; trade mark *Eagle;* square, aqua, *Philadelphia,* 8" **40.00-60.00**

Toneco Stomach Bitters; square bottle, tapered top, *Appetizer & Tonic* clear glass, ABM **20.00-30.00**

Old Dr. Townsend Celebrated Stomach Bitters; in six lines; handled jug; amber; plain band; pontil; 8¾" **75.00-175.00**

Tufts Angostura Bitters; label; 9¾"; green . **10.00-15.00**

Tufts Tonic Bitters; rectangular bottle, labeled only, aqua, 9" **10.00-14.00**

Turner Brothers N.Y.; *Buffalo N.Y. San Francisco Calif* tapered top; pontil; 9½" amber **85.00-150.00**

Tyler's Standard American Bitters; square bottle, amber, 9" **65.00-90.00**

Turner's Bitters Travellers Bitters; a man with a cane standing up; oval, amber, *1834/1870,* 10½" **200.00-300.00**

Turner's Bitters; rectangular, clear glass, 8" **50.00-60.00**

The Ullman; *Einstein Co., Cleveland, O., Germania Mager Bitters* - back and front labels; complete label information; under bottom a diamond in center of it *#337;* golden amber, ring top, round shoulder, *3* blob in neck **75.00-125.00**

Ulmar Mt. Ash Bitters; 7"; aqua **40.00-90.00**

Uncle Tom's Bitters; square bottle' *Thomas Fould & Son,* Trevorton, Pa., pale amber, tapered top, 10" **75.00-95.00**

Universal Bitters; pontil; aqua **90.00-100.00**

Universal Bitters; *Mfg. by Aug Horstmann Sole Agent F.J. Schaefer, 231 Market St. Louisville, KY;* 12"; lady's leg shape; emerald green **100.00-250.00**

UNKA; within a ball on front, picture of an eagle on top of the ball, *Army & Navy* around all this, *Unka Bitters 1895* under all this, label; tapered and ringed top; amber; 8½" **18.00-25.00**

U.S. of Colombia; colon on bottom; *Bitters Colombian* around shoulder; tapered top and ring, 3-piece mold, black beer type bottle, 8½" **35.00-75.00**

U.S. Gold Bitters; (in center $20 Gold Piece, Marked on roof) square, aqua, *U.S. 1877,* (Reg in U.S. Patent Office), 10″ **75.00-200.00**

Usaacson Seixas & Co.; other side reads *66 & 68 Common St., C.O. Witheye;* bitters monogram under it; bulged neck; tapered and ring top; kick-up **40.00-80.00**

Usqebaugh Bitters; high domed, square tapered bottle, aqua, 10½″ **50.00-75.00**

Van Opsal & Co. Morning Dew Bitters, N.Y.; 10½″; amber **80.00-100.00**

Vegetable Stomach Bitters; reverse side *Dr. Ball's, Northboro, Mass.;* 7¼″; aqua **50.00-100.00**

Vermo Stomach Bitters; reverse side *Tonic & Appetizer;* tapered top; machine made; 9½″ **10.00-20.00**

Victoria Tonic Bitters; *(William & Ross, L & W),* square bottle, *Memphis, Tenn.,* pale amber, 9½″ **90.00-115.00**

Peter Vierling's Blood Purifying Bitters; square bottle, amber, 10″ **85.00-110.00**

Dr. Von Hopf's Curaco Bitters; *Chamberlain & Co. Des Moines, Iowa* on back; amber; 9¼″, $30.00-50.00

Von Humboldt; *German bitters* in two lines, on one side *liver complaint* other *dyspepsia & co.* domed panels on all sides, double rings top, pontil, 6¼″, aqua **120.00-165.00**

Alex Von Humboldt; on back *stomach bitters;* square beveled corners, base a dot, ring & tapered top, lt. amber, 10¼″ **75.00-95.00**

Alex Von Humboldt's Stomach Bitters; square bottle, pale amber, 10″ **80.00-105.00**

Wahoo & Calisaya Bitters; near shoulder on two sides, *Jacob Pinkerton,* on roofed shoulder *Y!!-Y!!, 1,M -ok,* amber, tapered top, 10″ **115.00-140.00**

Waits Kidney & Liver Bitters; in back (three lines) *Calif. own, true laxative and blood purifier* on bottom *P.C.G.W.,* amber, tapered top and ring, 9″ **45.00-60.00**

Wallace's Tonic Stomach Bitters; *(George Powell & Co., Chicago, Ill)* square bottle, amber, base *L & G,* 9″ **70.00-90.00**

J. Walker Vinegar Bitters; 8½″; aqua **10.00-20.00**

Wampoo Bitters; on other side, *Siegel & Bro. N.Y.,* amber, tapered top and ring, 10″ **50.00-65.00**

C.H. Ward's Excelsior Bitters; rectangular bottle, *C.H. Ward & Co,* clear glass, 8″ **45.00-60.00**

Warners Safe Bitters; figure of a safe in center; on base *Rochester N.Y.;* oval shape; round collar; 9¾″; amber . . . .**65.00 +**

Warner Safe Tonic Bitters; pint, various shades of amber **65.00-200.00**

same except ½ pint **50.00-175.00**

same except square ring top **50.00-100.00**

Warners Safe Bitters; ring top under bottom *A.U.D.H.C.* amber, 7¾″ **85.00-150.00**

same as above except plain smooth bottom, 7½″ **65.00-200.00**

same except square ring top **40.00-100.00**

Dr. Warren's Old Quaker Bitters; *Old Dr. Warren's* on one side; *Quaker Bitters* on other; aqua; 9½″; rectangular **50.00-100.00**

Weis Medicine Co.; *The Dr. H.F. Guard on the Rhine-Stomach Bitters-Dayton, Ohio* in four lines running vertically; ring top, amber, 9¼″ **40.00-90.00**

West India Stomach Bitters; *(W.I.M.C.);* square, amber, *St. Louis, Mo,* base 10″ **45.00-70.00**

Dr. Wheeler's Tonic Sherry Wine Bitters; round; pontil; 8¼″; plain or aqua **50.00-100.00**

Wheeler's Berlin Bitters; hexagonal, olive green, *Baltimore,* iron pontil, 9½″ **125.00-350.00**

White's Stomach Bitters; square bottle, amber, 9⅜″ **40.00-70.00**

Whitewell's Temperence Bitters; *Boston;* pontil; 7″; aqua **90.00-150.00**

J.T. Wiggins Gention Bitters; ribbed sides; 11″; amber **50.00-60.00**

Wild Cherry Bitters; *Mfg. by C.C. Richards & Co. Yarmouth N.W. L. & Co.;* 6¼″; aqua **40.00-60.00**

Wild Cherry & Blood Root Jaundice Bitters; round bottle, labeled only, aqua, 9½″ **10.00-20.00**

Edw. Wilder & Co.; *Edw. Wilder Stomach Bitters* on back; *Patented 5* on one roof; very light green; 10½″ **80.00-250.00**

Wilders Stomach Bitters; *(Edw. Wilder Co.);* square cabin shape bottle, *Wholesale Druggists, Louisville, Ky.,* clear glass, 10½″ **110.00-140.00**

Wilmerding & Co.; *Sole agents for Peruvian Bitters, 214 & 216 Front St. S.F.* in a circle; flask shape bottle; 6″; amber **200.00-400.00**

Dr. Wilson's Herbine Bitters; *Bragley Sons & Co. Montreal;* oval shape; 8½″ aqua **30.00-40.00**

same as above except 6″ **30.00-40.00**

L.Q.C. Wishart's; pine tree trademark on one side; *Pine Tree Tar Cordial Phila* on other side; different sizes and colors, $50.00-100.00

Dr. Wisters Oxygenated Bitters for Dyspepsia & General Debility; pontil; 6″; aqua **50.00-150.00**

Dr. Wonser's U.S. Indian Root Bitters; fancy round type bottle tapered top; 10½″; amber **175.00-300.00**

same as above except aqua **200.00-400.00**

Woodbury's Bitters; *Steinhardt Bros. & Co. N.Y.;* round bottle; tapered top; 8″; amber **30.00-60.00**

N. Wood's Bilous Bitters; rectangular bottle, labeled only, aqua, *Portland, Maine,* 6″ **10.00-12.00**

Wood's Tonic; *Wine Bitter* on side; *Cincinnati, Ohio* other side; aqua **40.00-60.00**

Woodcock Pepsin Bitters; (John Schroeder), rectangular, smoky amber **95.00-120.00**

Wryghte's Bitters; appears on all four sides; *London* also appears on four sides; ringed top; pontil; 5¾"; dark olive **50.00-100.00**

Yazoo Valley Bitters, Fulton M. McRae; 8¾"; amber **20.00-60.00**

Yerba Buena Bitters, S.F. Cal.; on each side; coffin-shaped flask; 8½"; amber **60.00-80.00**

same as above in quart size with *no. 2* on shoulder front and back **40.00-60.00**

Yochim Bros. Celebrated Stomach Bitters; 8¾"; amber **35.00-50.00**

Dr. Young's Wild Cherry Bitters; 8¾"; amber **40.00-60.00**

Zingari Bitters; *F. Rahter* on reverse side; lady's leg type bottle; ringed top; 11½"; amber **150.00-250.00**

Zoeler's Stomach Bitters; on one side *Zoeler Medical Co.; Pittsburgh Pa.;* deep V-like grooves on other side; long graduated top; amber, golden amber; 9½"; rounded corners **40.00-60.00**

Zu Zu Bitters; appears on all sides; medicine type bottle; ringed top; 8¼"; amber **40.00-60.00**

Cure

With undaunted determination medieval alchemists added varying proportions of a substance called elixir to metal in the hope that valuable gold would result. They were unsuccessful and elixir became known as a drug capable of prolonging life, presumably the next best thing to turning metal to gold. Thus Elixir was the name that Richard Stoughton chose for his patented medicinal concoction first produced in England in 1712.

In the age of patent medicines, some compounds were known as cures, and the people put their wholehearted faith in them. At the height of the nineteenth-century patent medicine fad, drugstores in the United States sold about 365 million bottles of the wondrous formulas a year. The reasons for the people's stubborn belief in self-prescribed remedies had much to do with the quality of medical care available.

Prior to 1730 most doctors in the New World were trained by apprenticeship. Though European training for doctors began to gain in popularity in the years that followed and medical colleges—however of inferior quality—began to be established, life expectancy in the United States in 1800 was only thirty-five years. Many medical advancements were made in this country during the first decades of the nineteenth century, and the profession of physician became a favorite. By 1850, practically any man could become a doctor after a mere year's training. Understandably, confidence in doctors was slight; trusting one's health to the contents of a patent medicine bottle made reasonable sense.

When American romanticists began to idolize the Indian as a symbol of strength and health, it was a simple step for the medicine hawkers to employ Indian names in the promotion of their products. Ka-Ton-Ka Cure was soon available, as was the Kockapoo Indian Cough Cure. To convince the public of their authenticity, many of these were endorsed by assumedly healthy Indians.

The intrigue of the Orient captivated the American people in the mid-1800's. Patent medicine soon stressed the wonders of Far Eastern health secrets with such products as Carey's Chinese Catarrh Cure, a remedy designed to eliminate the discomforts of the common cold.

Cures for diseases that puzzle scientists today could be found lining drugstore shelves in apothecary containers. W. Stoy of Lebanon, Pennsylvania, bottled his cure for hydrophobia in 1809 and J. Andrus of Hillsborough, New Hampshire, began selling his cancer cure in 1816.

Many collectable cure bottles are embossed with an owl and the traditional druggist tools of mortar and pestle. The Owl Drug Store, established in San Francisco, in 1892, became associated with Rexall in 1919. Owl Drug sold its rights to the parent firm of Rexall, the United Drug Company, in 1933, and the chain was known as Owl-Rexall Drug Company.

Interest in cures began to decline as higher standards in the practice of medicine were implemented. By the last decade of the nineteenth century, it was modern medicine that was promising cures. Following the passage of the Pure Food and Drug Act in 1907, which forced the disclosure of many worthless ingredients, many drug manufacturers supplanted the word "cure" with the less utopian word "remedy."

A No. 1 self cure; the specific (label), aqua, 5" **4.00-6.00**

Abbott-Bros. - Rheumatic Cure; *Estd. 1888* all in four lines one side; *Abbott Bros.* other; amber, 7¾" **10.00-20.00**

Acid Cure Solution, Empire Mfg. Co., Akron, Ohio; in a circle; crock; 4¾"; white **8.00-10.00**

Dr. Adams, Cough Cure; *prepared by E.J. Parker, Cortland, N.Y.* all in four lines, flat ring top, beveled corner, clear, 5½" **10.00-20.00**

Dr. Agnews Cure For The Heart; ring top; 8½"; clear **8.00-10.00**

Alexander's Sure Cure for Malaria, Akron Ohio; on side *Alexanders Liver & Kidney Tonic;* ring top; 8"; amber **8.00-10.00**

Alexander's Sure Cure For Malaria; ring top; 6½"; amber **8.00-10.00**

Alkavis Sure Cure for Malaria; label; ring top, amber, 8¼" **4.00-10.00**

Allcock's; on one side; other *Dandruff Cure;* ring top, clear, 6½" **8.00-10.00**

Almyr System of Treatment For Catarrh; *Almyr Catarrh Cure* in three lines; aqua, ring top, 8¼" **20.00-30.00**

Anchor Weakness Cure; amber, 8¼" **6.00-10.00**

Antibrule Chemical Co.; other side *St. Louis, Mo. U.S.A.;* on front *Antibule Cures Burrus-Wounds-Skin Diseases-And All Inflammation* in three lines, clear 6¼" **10.00-20.00**

Antimigraine Cure Every Variety of Headache; 5¼"; clear or amethyst **4.00-8.00**

Atlas Kidney & Liver Cure, Atlas Medicine Co., Henderson, N.C. U.S.A.; with fancy monogram; *AM Co.* in sunken panel; 9"; honey amber **6.00-10.00**

Ayers; in sunken panel; on side *Ague;* other side *Lowell, Mass.;* double ring collar; 7"; aqua **4.00-8.00**

B.H. Bacon, Rochester N.Y., Otto's Cure; 2½"; clear **4.00-8.00**

Baker's Blood & Liver Cure; large crown with a flag; 9½"; amber **40.00-65.00**

Bakers South American Fever and Ague Cure; ring top; 9¾"; amber **25.00-50.00**

Bauer's Cough Cure; on front; 2⅞"; clear **4.00-6.00**

Bauer's Instant Cough Cure; 7"; aqua **6.00-10.00**

P.A. Benjamin's Liver & Kidney Cure; tapered top, aqua, 7½" **4.00-8.00**

Benson's Cure for Rheumatism; in three lines; three ring top, pontil, aqua, 6½" **10.00-20.00**

Dr. Bennett's; other side *A.L. Scoville & Co.;* front, quick cure; aqua, 4½" **8.00-20.00**

Bird's Lung Cure; in two lines vertical; ring top, aqua, 2½" **10.00-20.00**

Bishop's Granular Citrate of Magnesia, San Francisco, Cough Cure; 6½"; blue **4.00-8.00**

Bliss Liver & Kidney Cure; 9¼"; aqua or clear **4.00-10.00**

Bliss Liver & Kidney Cure; 7"; clear **8.00-12.00**

The Bliss Remedy Co., Bliss Liver & Kidney Cure, Stockton, Cal.; 9¼"; aqua **8.00-10.00**

Boerike & Runyon, S.F. & Portland; 5½"; clear or amethyst **3.00-6.00**

Dr. Bosako's Rheumatic Cure; 5¾"; aqua . . . **4.00-8.00**

Breedens Rheumatic Cure, label; *Breeden Medicine Co., Chattanooga, Tenn.* on front; 6½"; aqua **8.00-10.00**

Briggs Tonic Pills, Never Fail to Cure; *Briggs, Valdosta, Ga.;* 3"; clear **3.00-6.00**

Brightsbane, The Great Kidney and Liver Cure; vertical on front; square beveled corners, 8⅞"; light amber **30.00-50.00**

Brown's Blood Cure, Philadelphia; 6½"; green **10.00-20.00**

Browns Household Panacea and Family Liniment; vertical on front panels; *Curtis & Brown* on side; *Mfg. Col'd. New York* on opposite side; rectangular; square collar; 5⅛" **4.00-8.00**

Buchan's Hungarian; *Balsam of Life, London;* vertical lines *Kidney Cure;* 5¾"; round short neck; green **3.00-5.00**

Dr. L. Burdick's Kidney Cure; in two lines, amber, ring top, 7¼" **10.00-25.00**

same except with *Lodewick* **10.00-20.00**

Dr. L. Burdick's Kidney Cure; in two lines, vertical; ring top, amber, 7¼" **15.00-30.00**

San Jak Burnham's; *Kidney cure* all in three vertical lines; on shoulder *Chicago,* ring top, clear, 7" . **10.00-20.00**

Dr. San Jak Burnham's; *Kidney Cure* in three lines vertical; on shoulder, *Chicago;* ring top, clear, 7¼" **10.00-20.00**

Buxton's Rheumatic Cure; 8½"; aqua **4.00-10.00**

The Dr. D.M. Bye Oil Cure Co.; reverse side, *316 N. Illinois St.;* side *Indianapolis Ind.;* ring top; 6½"; clear **4.00-8.00**

Campbell & Lyon; on one side; other *Detroit, Mich;* front *Umatilla-Indian-Cough Cure* in two lines, vertical, tapered top, aqua, 5½" **15.00-30.00**

Canadian Boaster Hair Tonic; reverse side *Dandruff Care;* 8¼"; clear **4.00-6.00**

Capudine Headache Cure; oval; 3⅜"; aqua . . **4.00-10.00**

Carson's Ague Cure; *Jamestown, N.Y.* in three lines vertical; ring top, aqua, 7¼" **10.00-20.00**

Certain Cure For Rheumatism; vertical on front in sunken panel; *Chas. Denin* on side; *Brooklyn* on opposite side; 6¾"; aqua **8.00-15.00**

Chamberlains Cure for Consumption; 5"; aqua **4.00-8.00**

Chase's Dyspepsia Cure; *Newburgh, N.Y.* in three lines vertical; double ring top, aqua, 8¾" **10.00-20.00**

Cill's Catarrh Cure; vertical on front; sheared top; round bottom; 3¼"; clear **8.00-10.00**

The Clinic Kidney & Liver Cure; in two lines; on back *M'frd by Foley & Co., Stubenville, O. & Chicago;* amber, tapered top, 9½" **18.00-25.00**

Dr. J.W. Coblentz Cure, Ft. Wayne, Ind.; label ; 7¾"; cobalt **4.00-8.00**

Coe's Dyspepsia Cure or Stomach Bitters, The C.G. Clark Co., New Haven, Conn. U.S.A.; 7½"; clear or aqua **8.00-15.00**

Coke Dandruff Cure; on bottom; large ring top; 6½"; clear **8.00-15.00**

Mrs. M.E. Converse's Sure Cure for Epilepsy; ring top; 6¾"; clear **8.00**

C.C.C. (Corn Cure) By Mendenhell Co., Evansville Ind.; ring top; 4½"; clear or aqua **10.00-20.00**

also *C.C.C. (Certain Cough Cure)* **10.00-20.00**

Dr. Costa's Radical Cure for Dyspepsia; in sunken panels; double ring top; 5½"; aqua **4.00-8.00**

Craig's Kidney; (C. 1887) in ½ moon circle; under it *Liver Cure Company;* amber, double ring top, bottle same as *Warner Safe Cure,* 9½" **20.00-30.00**

Craig's Kidney; in ¼ moon letters under it in 4 lines & *Liver Cure Company,* oval, double ring top, amber, 9¼" **10.00-30.00**

Dr. Craig's Cough & Consumption Cure; in four lines vertical; double ring top, amber, 8" **50.00-200.00**

Cramers Kidney & Liver, Cure; in three lines, ring top, aqua, 7" **10.00-15.00**

Cramer's Cough Cure; in two lines; ring top,
aqua, 6¼" **10.00-20.00**

Cramer's Kidney Cure Sample; *Albany, N.Y.* in four lines;
ring top, round bottle, aqua, 4½" **10.00-20.00**

Criswell's Bromo-Pepsin Cures Headache; vertical; round;
ring top; 2½"; amber **8.00-12.00**

Criswell's Bromo-Pepsin Cures Headache and Digestion
vertical on front; 4¾"; amber **8.00-12.00**

Crosby-5-Minute Cure; in three lines vertical; ring top,
amber, 2¾" **8.00-12.00**

Crow's Chill Cure; in two lines vertical; tapered top,
aqua, 9½" **10.00-15.00**

J.M. Curtis Cure For The Baldness; *Providence, R.I.;* flared
top; ½ pint; aqua **8.00-10.00**

Curtis Cough Cure; *C.C.C.* on each side, *J.J. Mack & Co.
- sole Proprietors, San Francisco, Cal.* ring top,
aqua, 7" **8.00-10.00**

Curtis Cough Cure; in two lines; on top *Ointment* in center
C.C.C., also on each side *C.C.C.;* ring top,
aqua, 7" **10.00-20.00**

The Cuticura System of Curing Constipational Humors;
on front of panel; *Potter Drug and Chemical Corp.
Boston, Mass. U.S.A.* on reverse of panel; rectangular;
9¼"; aqua **8.00-10.00**

Dr. Daniel's Colic Cure; ring top; 3¾"; clear or
amethyst **4.00-6.00**

Dr. Daniel's Colic Cure No. 1 on front; square; 3½";
clear **4.00-8.00**

Dr. Daniel's Colic Cure No. 2; same as
above **4.00-8.00**

Dr. Daniel's Veterinary Colic Cure No. 1; on front; square;
3½"; clear **4.00-8.00**

Dr. Daniel's Veterinary Colic Cure No. 2; same as
above **4.00-8.00**

DeCostas, Radical Cure; on three panels *Morris & Heritage*
on one side, other *Philadelphia, SSS* monogram at top,
in back panels, ring top, aqua, 8¼" **10.00-20.00**

Datilma - A Radical Cure for Pain; in three lines vertical;
clear, ring top, 4½" **5.00-10.00**

Dean's Kidney Cure; the *Langham Med. Co. Le Roy, N.Y.*
in 3 lines, ring top, aqua, 7¼" **8.00-15.00**

Deering & Berry - Great Kidney Cure; *Saco, ME* in three
lines vertical; ring top and ring on neck, clear,
6⅛" **6.00-12.00**

DeWitts Colic & Cholera Cure; 4½"; green . . .**4.00-6.00**

Dr. DeWitt's Liver, Blood, & Kidney Cure; 8½";
amber **25.00-30.00**

Dr. DeWitts; *Electric Cure, W.J. Parker & Co.
Baltimore Md.;* tapered top; aqua;
6½" **15.00-30.00**

E.C. DeWitt & Co., Chicago U.S.A., One Minute Cough;
tapered top; 4½"; aqua **4.00-8.00**

E.G. DeWitts & Co., Chicago; label; side mold; *Dyspepsia
Cure* on back; clear; 9¼" **10.00-20.00**

W.H. Dolfs Sure Cure for Colic; flat ring top; *T.C.W. & Co.*.
under bottom; 3½"; aqua **8.00-12.00**

Duffy's Tower Mint Cure (Trademark Est 1842); 6½";
tapered bottle; wide ring top; embossed tower & flag;
amber **75.00-100.00**

Electricity in A Bottle; around shoulder; on base *The West
Electric Cure Co;* ring top, blue or amber,
2½" **6.00-10.00**

**Elepizone, A Certain Cure for Fits And Epilepsy,
Elepizone, H.G.Root M.C.;** *183 Pearl St., New York* on
front; ring top; 8½"; aqua **25.00-35.00**

Ellis's Spavin Cure; in two lines vertical; ring top, aqua,
8" **10.00-20.00**

Emerson's Rheumatic Cure; *Emerson Pharmaceutical Company, Baltimore, Md* in five lines, ring top,
amber, 5" **6.00-12.00**

Faley's (sic) Kidney & Bladder Cure; on front; *Foley's & Co.*
on one side; *Chicago, U.S.A.* on reverse; 9½";
amber **4.00-8.00**

**Dr. M.M. Fenner's; amber; 10¼",
$12.00-15.00**

**Dr. M.M. Fenner's Peoples Remedies, N.Y., U.S.A.,
Kidney & Backache Cure 1872-1898;** all on front
horizontally; 10¼"; amber **25.00-45.00**

Fitch's Dandruff Cure, Ideal Dandruff Cure Co.; ring top;
6¼" **4.00-6.00**

Fitzgerald's Membrane Cure; vertical on front in sunken
panel; aqua **10.00-15.00**

Foley's Kidney & Bladder Cure; on front; on one side *Foley
& Co;* reverse *Chicago U.S.A.;* double ring top; 7½";
amber **8.00-10.00**

**Sample Bottle Foley's Kidney Cure, Foley & Co., Chicago,
U.S.A.;** vertical around bottle; 4¼";
aqua **4.00-8.00**

Foley's Safe Diarrhea & Colic Cure, Chicago; panels; 5½";
aqua **4.00-8.00**

Folger's Olosaonian; on front on one side, *Doct. Bobt. T.B.;*
deeply leveled corner, long neck, tapered top, pontil,
aqua, 7½" **10.00-20.00**

H.D. Fowle, Boston; in back, label; *Fowle's Pile & Humor
Cure;* ring top; 5½"; aqua **8.00-10.00**

**Dr. Frank, Turkey Febrifuge for The Cure of Fever and
Ague;** pontil; 6"; aqua **10.00-20.00**

Free Sample Cramers Kidney Cure; *Albany* and *N.Y.* are
reversed; 4¼"; aqua **10.00-12.00**

Frenchs; under it a crown; on each side *Trade Mark;* under
it *Kidney & Liver & Dropsy Cure Co.,* on base, *Price
1.00-*all on front, round corners double ring top, *Trade
Mark* in reverse, 9½", amber **15.00-30.00**

**Frog Pond Chill & Fever Cure; flat ring
top; 7"; amber, $25.00**

G.R. & H. Cure & Magical Pain Extractor; in three lines on
front; ring top, aqua, 4½" **10.00-15.00**

Ganter's L.F., Magic Chicken Cholera Cure; *L.P. Ganter Medicine Co., Glascow, N.Y., U.S.A.* in nine lines; ring top, amber, 6¼".....................**20.00-50.00**

Garget Cure, C.T. Whipple Prop., Portland, ME.; ring top; 5¾"; aqua.........................**4.00-6.00**

Dr. A.F. Geoghegan, Louisville Ky., Cure for Scrofula; graphite pontil; 9¼"; aqua, **$45.00**

Glover's Imperial Distemper Cure, H. Clay Glover, New York; vertical on front; 5"; amber.......**4.00-8.00**

Glovers Imperial Mange Cure; *H. Clay Glover Du's* on one side; *New York* on other side; amber, 7"..**4.00-6.00**

Gold Dandruff Cure; vertical on center front; ring top; 7½"; clear...............................**8.00-12.00**

Golden Rod Lotion, A Safe and Certain Cure; 6"; amber...**10.00-15.00**

Graham's Dyspepsia Cure; *S. Grover Graham Co., Newburgh, N.Y.;* 8½"; clear............**4.00-8.00**

S. Grover Graham's Dyspepsia Cure, Newburg, N.Y.; vertical on front in large letters; 8¼"; amethyst....................**12.00-15.00**

Dr. Graves Heart Regulator, Cures Heart Disease; ring top; 5¾"; aqua.........................**4.00-8.00**

The Great Dr. Kilmer Swamp Root Kidney Liver & Bladder Cure Specific; 8¼"; aqua or clear..................................**8.00-12.00**
same except **The Great & Specific**.....**8.00-12.00**

Gregory's Instant Cure; pontil; 4" and 6"; aqua..**10.00**

Grove's Chronic Chill Cure; all on front in 2 lines, ring top, clear, 7¼".....................**10.00-15.00**

Dr. B.W. Hairs Asthma Cure; 8"; aqua....**15.00-30.00**

Halls Catarrh Cure; aqua; 4½".............**6.00-8.00**

Hall's Catarrh Cure; aqua; 4½"...........**3.00-5.00**

Hall's Catarrh Cure; aqua; 4½"...........**3.00-4.00**

Dr. B.W. Hair's Asthma Cure; *Hamilton, Ohio* in three lines; tapered top, 8"................**10.00-15.00**

Hamilton's Medicines Cure; all inside of a 7 pts star, under it, *Auburn, N.Y.*, rectangular, ring top, aqua, 8½".........................**10.00-20.00**

Dr. Hanford's Celery Cure or Nerve Food Cure; *rheumatism - neuralgia - insommia & C & C* all in nine lines on front, double ring top, aqua, 7½"...........**8.00-10.00**

Dr. Harding's; *Celebrated, Catarrh Cure,* in three lines on front, ring top, clear, 3"..............**10.00-15.00**

Harts Honey & Harehound; *Cure, coughs, colds, group,* 4 lines on front; on one side *Lincoln, ILl. U.S.* other, *Harts Med. Co.,* ring top, clear 7".............**10.00-15.00**

Hart's Swedish Asthma Cure; *Buffalo N.Y.* on side; rectangular; beveled corners; 6⅝"; lt. amber.**4.00-8.00**
same as above except by **Indian Med. Co., Clintonville, Conn**.................................**4.00-6.00**

Healy & Bigelows Kickapp Indian Cough Cure; on panels; ring top; 6¼"; aqua..................**4.00-6.00**

Hebbard's, Dr. Cure For Fits; *New York* in three lines, vertical; ring top, clear, 8½"............**10.00-20.00**

Dr. J.B. Hemous; reverse side *Sure Cure For Malaria;* 6¼"; cobalt........................**8.00-10.00**

Hepaticure For Blood, Liver & Kidney; in two lines on front; on one side *Marshall Med. Co.;* other *Kansas City, Mo.;* ring top, clear or amethyst, 9½".......**10.00-30.00**

Dr. Herman's; *Vegetable, Catarrh Cure* on round type bottle in three lines, ring top, clear, 2¾".....**8.00-15.00**

Dr. Herndon's; on one side; other *Gypsey Gift Bank;* plain front. In overlap letter *H.G.G.* in side of a circle under it in five lines. *That is medicine which cures, Balt, DMD.;* rectangular, long neck and ring top, clear, 6½"..............................**10.00-20.00**

Herrick's Horehound Syrup; *cures all throat and lung infections* all in three lines, ring neck & top, aqua, 6".........................**10.00-20.00**

Hick's Capudine Cures All Headaches, Etc. amber, 5¼"............................**8.00-15.00**

Hillemans American Chicken Cholera Cure, Arlington, Minn.; flared top; 6½"; cobalt.........**30.00-50.00**

Dr. Hiller's Cough Cure; tapered top; 7½"; aqua...................................**8.00-10.00**

Hills; with block H letters and arrow; under it *Dys-Pep-Cu-Cures Chronic Dyspepsia, Indian Drug Specialty Co.; St. Louis, Indianapolis* on front; tapered top; 8½"; amber....................................**15.00-25.00**

Himalaya, The Kola Compound, Natures Cure for Asthma, New York, Cincinnati embossed horizontally on indented front panels; square; 7½"; amber**10.00-15.00**

Hires; *Cough Cure, Phila, Pa.* on sides; aqua; 4½".................................**10.00-15.00**

Hite's Pain Cure; *Staunton, Va* two lines on front, ring top, clear, 5½".....................**8.00-15.00**

Holloway's Corn Cure in two lines running vertically; ring top, clear, 2½".....................**4.00-8.00**

Hollensworth's Rupture Cure; in three lines, aqua, ring top, 6¼"...............................**10.00-20.00**

C.I. Hood & Co. *Lowell, Mass.* in back: *Tus Sano Cures Coughs* in three lines; aqua, double ring top, 2½"..............................**10.00-20.00**

Hood's Pills Cure Liver Ills; all in a circle; ring top, sim round bottle, 1"...........................**4.00-8.00**

Howard Bros.; on front; on one side *Cough Cure;* other side *Petit's American;* tapered top; 7"; aqua..**6.00-10.00**

Dr. S.D. Howe's Arabian Milk Cure For Consumption; 6"; clear.................................**8.00-10.00**
same as above except 7½".............**15.00-20.00**

C.H. Howe; on the other side *Cure;* ring top, aqua, 7¼"..............................**8.00-10.00**

Dr. Hoxsie's; on the side *Buffalo, N.Y. Certain Croup Cure* in 2 lines, clear, ring top, 4¾".........**4.00-10.00**

Huffman's in script; *Goitre Cure - Napanee, Ont.* in 3 lines vertical; ring top, clear, 4½"...........**8.00-15.00**

Hunnicutt's; reverse side *Rheumatic Cure;* ring top; 8"; aqua...............................**10.00-20.00**

Indian Med. Co., Clintonville Conn., Kickapoo Indian Cough Cure; 5¾"; aqua..................**4.00-8.00**

W.M. Johnson's Pure Herb Tonic, Sure Cure for All Malarial Diseases; vertical lettering; 6"; clear**8.00-12.00**

K.K. Cure's Brights Disease and Cystitis; all in six lines; one side *K.K. Med. Co.;* other side *New Jersey;* aqua, tapered top, 7½" **8.00-15.00**

K.K.K. Kay's Kentucky Kure or Liniment; vertical around bottle; 3¾"; aqua **15.00-25.00**

Dr. J. Kauffman's Angeline, Internal Rheumatism Cure, Hamilton, Ohio; vertical in three lines on front; flared top, 7⅞"; clear **15.00-30.00**

Dr. L.E. Keeley, Keeley's Cure For Drunkness; etc.; *Dwight, Ill.;* ring top; 5½"; clear or amethyst **15.00-35.00**

Keesling Chicken Cholera Cure C.C.C.; *Package 25 cents, B.F. Keeslings, Logansport, Ind.* **8.00-10.00**

Kellum's - Sure Cure for Indigestion and Dyspepsia; in 6 lines; ring top, clear, 6¾" **10.00-20.00**

Kendall's Spavin Cure for Human Flesh; vertical on two panels; ten vertical panels; 5¼"; aqua **4.00-8.00**

Kendall's Spavin Cure; around shoulders; *Enosburgh Falls, Vt.* on bottom; twelve vertical panels; 5½"; amber **4.00-8.00**

Kickapoo Cough Cure; vertical on indented panel; round; 6¼"; aqua **8.00-12.00**

E.J. Kieffer; amber; 8" **8.00-12.00**

E.J. Kieffer amber, 9" **8.00-12.00**

Dr. Kilmer's Sure Headache Cure; *25 doses in a box;* 5¼"; clear **8.00-10.00**

Dr. Kilmer's Indian Cough Cure Consumption Oil; vertical on front: *Binghamton, N.Y.* on side; rectangular, aqua, square collar, ball neck, 7¼" **8.00-10.00**

Kilmer's Dr. Sample Bottle Swamproot Kidney Cure; *London, E.C.;* aqua,double ringtop, 4½" **10.00-20.00**

Dr. Kilmer's Swamproot Kidney Liver and Bladder Cure; *London, E.C.* vertical on front, rectangular aqua, double band top, 5¾" **10.00-20.00**

Sample Bottle Dr. Kilmer's Swamproot Kidney Cure; *London, E.C.* vertical on front; aqua, cylindrical, square collar, 4½" **15.00-30.00**

Sample Bottle Dr. Kilmer's Swamproot Kidney Cure; *Binghamton, N.Y.* vertical on front, cylindrical, aqua square collar, 4¼", 3⅛", 4⅛", 4¼" **8.00-15.00**

Dr. T.J. Kilmer's Cough Cure; *Schohaire, N.Y.* vertical on front; rectangular, aqua, square band collar, 5¾" **8.00-15.00**

The Great Dr. Kilmer's Swamproot Kidney Liver and Bladder Cure; embossed kidney shape panel/*Specific,* front; *Binghamton, N.Y.;* aqua, double band collar, 8¼" 8¾", 8", 8½", 9" **8.00-20.00**

Dr. Kilmer's Swamproot Kidney Liver and Bladder Cure; *Binghampton, N.Y., USA* embossed on front; rectangular, aqua, double band collar, 7" . . . **5.00-10.00**

same as above only square band collaring neck 7¼" **4.00-10.00**

same as above only square band collar, 4¾" **4.00-10.00**

Dr. Kilmer's Indian Cough Cure Consumption Oil; vertical on front; *Binghamton, N.Y.* on side; rectangular, aqua, double band collar, 5¾" **15.00-20.00**

Dr. Kilmer's Cough Cure Consumption Oil; (in embossed lung shape panel) *Catarrh Specific* all on front: *Binghamton, N.Y.* on side; rectangular, aqua double band collar, 8¾" **40.00-70.00**

Dr. Kilmer's Swamp Root Kidney Cure, Binghamton, N.Y.; 1½"; aqua **4.00-6.00**

Kilmers, The Great; *Swamp-Root Kidney Liver and Bladder Cure Specific* on front; *Binghamton, N.Y.* on left; *Dr. Kilmer & Co.* on right; aqua, 8¼"; rectangular **5.00-10.00**

Dr. King's New Cure for Consumption; 6"; clear or aqua **4.00-6.00**

Kodol Dyspepsia Cure; on side; *E.C. DeWitt & Co., Chicago* on opposite side; rectangular; 6⅞"; aqua **6.00-10.00**

Langerbach's Dysentary Cure; vertical on front; *San Francisco, Cal.;* round; blob type; 6"; amber **15.00-25.00**

Lash's Kidney & Liver Cure; 9"; amber **20.00-30.00**

Jarabe De Leonardi; *para La Tos Creostodado, Leonardi Cough Cure Cresoted, New York and Tampa, Fla* in 4 lines in sunken panel; plain back; plain sunken side panels; 5¼"; aqua, under bottom *W.T. Co. 4 U.S.A.* **2.00-4.00**

Leonardi's Cough Cure, Creosoted; *N.Y. & Tampa;* 5½"; aqua **4.00-6.00**

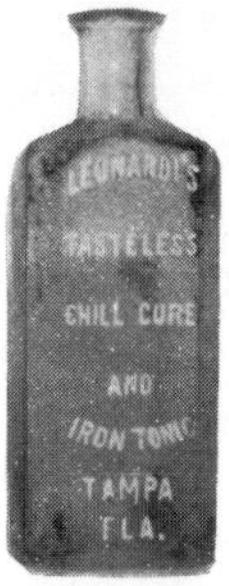

Leonardi's Tasteless; clear or amethyst; 6¼", $2.00-4.00

Liebig's Fit Cure - An English Remedy; *Dr. A. B. Meserole, 96 John St. N.Y.* in five lines; ring top, aqua, 5½" **8.00-12.00**

Lightning Kidney & Liver Cure, No. Relief, No Pay, Herb Med Co.; *Weston, West Va.;* 9½"; aqua **30.00-40.00**

Lightning Oil; on one side, other *Oil;* front *sure cure,* back plain, rectangular, ring top, aqua, 5½" . . . **8.00-15.00**

Little Giant Catarrh Cure; in two lines back, *Warsaw, N.Y.;* one side only *Mfd. by A. F. Mann,* ring top, amber, 3½" **10.00-20.00**

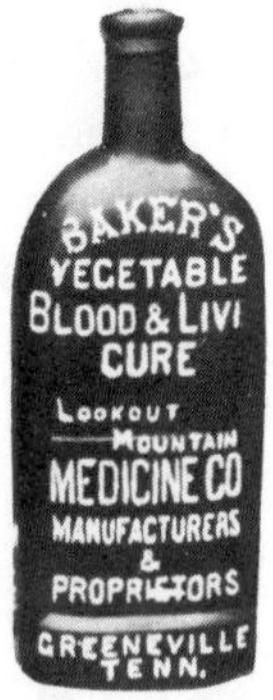

Lookout Mountain Medicine Co.; amber; 10½", $25.00 +

Lucas, D.D. Co. Vineland, N.J. Bohemian Catarrh Cure; ring top, clear, 3¼" **4.00-8.00**

J.J. Mack & Co., S.F. Cal., Curtis Cough Cure, C.C.C.; on both sides; 7" **8.00-10.00**

Magic Mosquito Bite Cure & Insect Exterminator, Sallade & Co., N.Y.; on front; oval; tapered collar; 7⅞"; aqua **10.00-20.00**

Maloy Oil H.F.M.; in leaf; *Instant Relief Cure Rheumatism;* 4¾"; clear **4.00-8.00**

Marne's Famous Aniseed Cure; in two lines, clear, ring top, 5".............................**10.00-20.00**

Marvinis Cherry Cough Cure; label; tapered top; 9½"; amber...........................**10.00-20.00**

Mayer's Magnetic Catarrh Cure; in two lines vertical; ring top, clear, 3½".......................**8.00-12.00**

Mertol Dandruff Cure; 5½"; clear...........**4.00-6.00**

Dr. Miles New Heart Cure; vertical on front in sunken panel; double band collar; 8½"; aqua.........**6.00-10.00**

same as above, 4¼"; free sample size..**8.00-15.00**

Miner's Damiana Nerve Disease Cure; embossed woman; 8¼"; amber......................**40.00-80.00**

Peter P. Miniottis - Rheumatism Cure; in center; in a circle man with a bear around it - *Great West Indian Discover,* etc. - *10 Wyckoll St. Brooklyn, N.Y.* registered; under bottom *21,* tapered top, aqua, label only, 10"**10.00-15.00**

Munyon's Inhaler, Cures Colds, Catarrh and All Throat & Lung Diseases; on front; *Patented, Fill to the Line* on back; round; 4⅛"; olive green.........**10.00-20.00**

Mystic Cure; other side *Mystic Cure;* on front *For Rheumatism and Neuralgia;* ring top, clear or Aut., 6¼"...........................**8.00-10.00**

Mysterious Pain Cure - A Scotch Remedy; in three lines, vertical; ring top, clear, 5½"...........**8.00-12.00**

Nau's Dyspepsia Cure; amber; 5", $6.00-8.00

No. 1 Laboree's Colic Cure; 3½"; clear.....**6.00-8.00**

One Minute Cough Cure; vertical on front in sunken panel; *E.C. DeWitt & Co.,* on side; *Chicago, U.S.A.* on opposite side; rectangular; 5½"; aqua.....................................**8.00-12.00**

same as above except 5"..............**4.00-8.00**

One Minute Cough Cure; vertical on front; *E.C. DeWitt & Co. Chicago, U.S.A.* vertical on back; rectangular; 4¼"; aqua.........................**4.00-6.00**

The Original Copper Cure; oval; flared lip; 7¾"; amber, $50.00-110.00

The Original Copper Cure; in two script lines, oval shape bottle, ring top, amber, 7¾".....**30.00-60.00**

The Original - Dr. Craig's Kidney Cure; (c. 1889) in three lines; on base *Rochester, N.Y.;* double ring top, amber, bottle same as *Warner Sale Cure,* 9½".........................**20.00-30.00**

Otto's Cure for the Throat & Lungs; on front indented panel; *B.H. Bacon* on right panel; *Rochester, N.Y.* on reverse side; 6"; aqua..............**4.00-8.00**

Otto's Cure for the Throat & Lungs; vertical on front indented panel; oval; 2¾"; aqua.........**4.00-6.00**

Park's Liver & Kidney Cure; in three lines; in back *Free Samples,* aqua, tapered top, 3".......**15.00-30.00**

same as 248 except aqua, 5".........**30.00-40.00**

Dr. Park's Cough Syrup; *Geo. H. Wells;* other side *Le Roy, N.Y.;* tapered top, label reads *The Throat & Lungs - A Positive Guarantee of Cure of Any Throat or Lung Disease,* etc.; aqua, 6¼".......**8.00-15.00**

Dr. Parker's & Sons Co. - Batavia, N.Y.; *Red Cherry Cough Cure for Consumption* all in 4 lines, running vertically; ring top, aqua, 5½".........**8.00-15.00**

Paris Med. Co., St. Louis, Grove's Chronic Chill Cure; 2¾"; aqua..............................**4.00-8.00**

Park's Sure Cure (Kidney Cure); 6½"; aqua....................................**8.00-10.00**

Dr. Parker's Cough Cure; ring top; 6"; aqua....................................**4.00-10.00**

Dr. Lee's Liniment, Packed by the Persian Balm Co. N.S. Pkg. Pr.; on front *Dr. Lee's Liniment;* on other side, *A Sure Cure For Quinsy Store Throat and Croup;* back *75 Years Before the Public a Sure Test;* ring top, ring neck, clear, 2½".........**8.00-10.00**

Peruviana-Nature's Kidney Cure; *Peruviana Herbal Remedy Co. - Cincinnati, Ohio* in four lines vertical; tapered top, amber, 8¼"...........**30.00-60.00**

S.K. Pierson, Gray's Balsam; *Best Cough Cure* in two lines, vertical; tapered top, clear, 5½"...**8.00-12.00**

Piso's Cure; on side; *For Consumption* on front; other side *Hazelton & Co;* 5"; emerald green...**4.00-6.00**

same as above except clear.............**4.00-8.00**

Polar Star Cough Cure; with embossed star in center, vertical on front in sunken panels; rectangular; 5¾"; aqua....................................**4.00-8.00**

same as above except 4"..............**4.00-8.00**

Porter's Cure of Pain, Cleveland, Ohio; 6½"; clear....................................**4.00-8.00**

Pratt Food Co.; *Phila. U.S.A.* in two lines vertical; *Pratt's Bloat Cure* in two lines vertical; double ring top and ring in neck, aqua, 6½"..............**15.00-30.00**

Pratts Distemper Cure, Pratt Food Co.; *Phila, U.S.A.;* ring top, amber, 7", $8.00-15.00

Pratts Distemper & Pink Eye Cure; 7"; amber...............................**4.00-6.00**

Pratts Distemper Cure, Pratt Food Co.; *Phila. U.S.A.;* ring top; 7"; amber.......................**25.00+**

Dr. Charles T. Price; *The Cure for Fit - 67 William St. New York* in 5 lines; ring top, clear, 8½".........................**20.00-40.00**

Primley's Iron & Wahoo tonic; all in four lines, tapered top & ring, back *Jones & Primley Co.; Elkhart, Ind.,* amber, 9½"......................**10.00-20.00**

Primley's Speedy Cure; *for cough and colds,* all on front, rectangular, ring top, aqua, 6½"..**10.00-20.00**

Quick Headache Cure, B.F. Keesling, Logansport, Ind.. . . . . **8.00-10.00**

W.M. Radamis; amber; 10½", $35.00+

Ray's Germicide Cures Many Diseases; on front in gold paint; hand painted flowers on top half; top half is white, lower half is brown pottery somewhat glazed; sheared type; handle; jug shape, 8½" . . **10.00-20.00**

Red Star Cough Cure; on one side; other side *The Charles A. Bogeler Co.; Baltimore; U.S.A.* on base; tapered top; 7½"; aqua **3.00-6.00**

Reddish & Co., Frank O.; on one side; other *LeRoy, N.Y.;* on front *Parker Liver & Kidney Cure* in three lines vertical; amber, tapered top, 9½" .**30.00-60.00**

Reeve's Comp. Terebene Cough Cure; 4"; clear **4.00-8.00**

same as above except 6" **4.00-10.00**

3913 - Rheumatism Cure; in two lines; ring top, clear or aqua, 5¾" **10.00-12.00**

Rhodes Fever & Ague Cure; 8½"; aqua . . .**30.00-60.00**

River Swamp, The; under it *chill and alligator, fever cure* under it *Augusta, Ga.* flat ring top, amber, 7" **50.00-100.00**

River Swamp Chill and Fever Cure; embossed alligator; ring top; 10¼" amber or clear **50.00-100.00**

Rock's Cough & Cold Cure, Chas. A. Darby, N.Y.; vertical on front in sunken panel; rectangular; 5⅝"; aqua **8.00-12.00**

Roll's Syrup Wild Cherry White Pine and Tar, Cure Coughs and Colds; flared top; clear **4.00-8.00**

A. Certain Cure for Fits and Epilepsy; ring top, amber, 8½" **15.00-25.00**

H.G. Root M.C., 183 Pearl St. N.Y., Elepizone, A Certain Cure for Fits and Epilepsy; ring top; 8½"; amber. **15.00-25.00**

Dr. Roper's; other side *Cure;* front, *Indian Fever;* clear, tapered top, aqua, 7" **8.00-10.00**

Rosewood Dandruff Cure, Prepared by J.R. Reeves Co., Anderson, Ind.; vertical on front; rectangular; paneling on collar; 6½"; amethyst **8.00-15.00**

Sample Shiloh's Cure; vertical on front; rectangular; 4¼"; aqua. **4.00-8.00**

Sanford's; on side; *Radical Cure* on opposite side; rectangular; 7¾"; cobalt blue **10.00-25.00**

Save-The-Horse, Registered Trade Mark, Spavin Cure, Troy Chemical Co., Binghamton N.Y.; on front; ring top; 6½"; aqua **4.00-8.00**

same as above except *Troy N.J.* **8.00-16.00**

Sawyer, Dr. A.P.; one side; other *Chicago;* front *Family Cure;* double ring top, aqua, 7½" **15.00-30.00**

Sayman's Vegetable Liniment; in two lines on one side *Cures Catarrh & Colds;* other side *Relieves All Pain;* tapered top, ring on neck, aqua, 6½" **8.00-15.00**

Shiloh's Consumption Cure; on front; *S.C. Wells* on side; *Leroy, N.Y.* on opposite side; rectangular; 6"; aqua **8.00-12.00**

same as above except *S.C. Wells & Co.* .**8.00-12.00**

Sample Shiloh's Cure; vertical on front; rectangular, aqua, 4¼" **4.00-10.00**

Dr. Shoop's Cough Cure; clear; 6½", $2.00-4.00

Simonds; other side *Pain Cure* ring top, aqua, 4¾" **10.00-15.00**

H.K. Smith Cure; all in two lines, ring top, aqua 5" **8.00-12.00**

Sloans Sure Colic Cure; ring top; 4¾"; clear or amber **4.00-6.00**

Sparks Kidney & Liver Cure; ring top; 9¾"; amber **40.00-80.00**

The Specific A No. 1, A Self Cure, Trade Mark; on front and bottom; 5½"; aqua **4.00-6.00**

Speedy Cure for Coughs and Colds; on one side *Jones & Primley Co.;* other side *Elkhart, Ind.;* ring top; 8"; clear **8.00-10.00**

Spohn's Distemper Cure, Spohn Medical Company, Goshen, Indiana U.S.A.; vertical on front in sunken panel; 5"; aqua **4.00-8.00**

Stewart D. Howe's - Arabian Milk Cure; in three lines, vertical; one side for *Consumption;* other *New York;* aqua, ring top, 7½" **15.00-30.00**

Dr. Strubles Kidney Cure; in a circle; under it *Himrode, N.Y.;* ring top, cobalt, 6½" **60.00-150.00**

Dr. Sykes Sure Cure for Catarrh; in four lines; aqua, 6½" **10.00-20.00**

Dr. Sykes Sure Cure for Catarrh; in front; four-part mold; aqua; 6¾"; round; short neck **6.00-10.00**

Sylvan Remedy Co.; Peoria, Ill. in back *Reids-German Cough & Kidney Cure;* one side *No Danger from Overdose,* other *Contains No Poison;* aqua, 5½" **8.00-10.00**

Ta-Ha Cough Cure; in two lines vertical; ring top and ring on neck, aqua, 6" **10.00-20.00**

Tamalon Safe Animal Cure; 11¼"; amber . . . .**45.00+**

Taylor's Hospital Cure for Catarrh; *N.Y. WT Co. U.S.A.* under bottom; 6¼"; clear or amethyst . .**10.00-20.00**

E.E. Taylor's Catarrh Cure; all in a circle; in center a star; ring top, clear, 2¾" **8.00-12.00**

Three-Nine-One-Three; in numbers, under it *Rheumatism cure,* rectangular, clear, ring top, 5½" **10.00-15.00**

Tiger Oil - Cure Pain; (in two lines vertical; ring top and neck, aqua, 4½" **6.00-12.00**

Dr. W. Towns Epilepsy Cure, Fond Du Lac, Wisconsin, U.S.A.; 7½"; amber **8.00-12.00**

Upham's Fresh Meat Cure; _Pat. Feb. 12, 1867 Phila;_
flared top; 6¾"; aqua **8.00-15.00**

Wadsworth Liniment; _Rheumatism_ on one side; _Cure_ on
other side; side mold; aqua; 5½" **10.00-15.00**

Wakefield's; other side _Bloomington;_ front _Magic Pain
Cure;_ all running vertically; ring top,
aqua **15.00-30.00**

Warner's Safe Animal Cure; 11¼"; amber . . . .**45.00 +**

Warner's Safe Cure; embossed; sample;
amber . . . .**15.00-20.00 +**

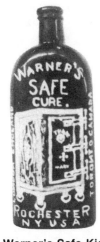

Warners Safe Cure; _London
England_ on side; _Toronto Canada_
other side; amber; 9½",
$40.00-80.00

Warner's Safe Kidney & Liver Cure; in center a safe;
under it, _Rochester N.Y.;_ various numbers under bottom; 9½"; oval; amber **6.00-10.00**
same except _Rheumatic Cure;_ amber **8.00-12.00**
same except 6½"; amber **6.00-10.00**
same except _Nervine;_ 6½"; clear **2.00-6.00**

**Warner's White Wind of Tar Syrup Consumption Cure,
C.D. Warner M.D;** _Coldwater Mich.;_ 4½"; and 6¼";
aqua **8.00-10.00**

Warner's White Wine of Tar Syrup-Consumption Cure
cures a cold in 24 hours on label; _Mfg. by C.D. Warner
M.D. Cold Water, Mich.;_ aqua,
7¼" **8.00-20.00**

The West Electric Cure Co., Electricity in a Bottle; ring
top; cobalt **10.00-20.00**

C.T. Whipple Prop., Portland Me. Garget Cure; 6";
aqua **4.00-6.00**

Faith Whitcomb's Balsam; in two lines on front; one
side _Cures Coughs & Colds;_ other _Cures Consumption;_ double ring top, 9½" **10.00-20.00**

A.J. White Curative Syrup; on sides in sunken panels;
rectangular; 5⅛"; aqua **8.00-10.00**

White's Quick Healing Cure; amber;
6¼", $2.00-6.00

Winans Bros., Indian Cure for Blood; _Price $1;_ 9¼";
aqua **40.00-100.00**

Wintergreen Great Rheumatic Cure, J.L. Filkins; 6";
aqua **3.00-6.00**

Wood Great Peppermint Cure for Coughs & Colds;
6½"; clear **4.00-6.00**

Dr. J.L. Woods Tasteless Chill Cure; _Wood Drug Co.,
Bristol, Tenn._ in four lines, vertical; ring top and
neck, aqua, 7" **10.00-20.00**

Wooldridge Wonderful Cure Co.; _Colum-
bus Ga.;_ amber; 8½", $25.00-50.00

Wykoop's Fever & Ague Cure; tapered top; pontil; 6½";
cobalt . . . .**75.00 +**

Dr. Yarnall's Gold Cure for Alcoholism; _prepared only by
the Yarnall Gold Cure Co.;_ ring top,
clear, 5½" **50.00-100.00**

Zemo Cures Eczemee; _E.W. Rose Med. Co. St. Louis_
on one side; reverse side _Zemo Cures Pimples and
all Diseases of the Skin and Scalp;_ fancy bottle; ring
top; 6½"; clear **7.00-10.00**

Medicine

Medicine is as old as history, but patent medicine
was first made in England and shipped to America in
1723. By mid-eighteenth century, Americans treated
themselves freely with ready-made cures for their
physical ailments.

All medicines were not patented; at first only a few
in America were. The U.S. Patent Office opened in
1790, but the first patent for medicine was not issued
until 1796. Only a few kinds were patented because

the maker would have had to disclose the alcoholic or
opiate components.

The well-known medicine salesman of the 1880's
in America was the show man, who, with his troupe in
a covered wagon, hawked his medicinal concoctions
from town to town. After passage of the Pure Food and
Drug Act in 1907, most patent medicine firms went out
of business. Because of the act, shocked Americans
learned that the nostrums they had been downing over

the last century—T.W. Dyott's, Swaim's Panacea, Kickapoo Medicines, Perry Davis' Pain-Killer, Lydia E. Pinkham's Vegetable Compound, to name a few—were largely liquor and opiates.

One of the oldest types of medicine bottles came out of England embossed *Turlington's Balsam of Life* between the years 1723 and 1900. The earliest truly American medicines came in plain bottles made in this country, and the first embossed bottles in the U.S. are dated around 1810. Medicine bottlemaking grew to an $80-million-a-year industry by 1906.

The P.L. Abbey Co.; 8¾″; clear **8.00-12.00**

The Abbott Aikal Co. Chicago; in vertical lines; ring top; 2⅝″; clear **3.00-6.00**

The Abbott Aiklord Co., Chicago; 2⅝″; clear or aqua **2.00-4.00**

Abbott Bros., Chicago; reverse side *Rheumatic Remedy;* 6½″; amber, $10.00-12.00

The Abner Royce Co.; 5½″; clear or amethyst **2.00-4.00**

Abrams & Corrolls Essence of Jamaica Ginger, San Francisco; 5¼″; aqua **10.00-20.00**

Absorbine; *Springfield, Mass. U.S.A.;* 7½″; amber **4.00-6.00**

A & Co.; under bottom; lable; amber; 5¼″ **4.00-8.00**

A.C. Co. Comfort, Jacksonville, Fla.; under bottom; clear; 5½″ **2.00-4.00**

Aceite Oriental Ressert; in back; cobalt; 3½″ **8.00-10.00**

Aceite Oriental Ressert; moon and star on back; 3½″; amber **6.00-8.00**

Acid Iron Earth; reverse side *Mobile, Ala.;* 6¾″; amber **6.00-8.00**

Dr. Acker's Ta-Ber-Ku; *Catarrh of the Head* other side; clear; 8″ **4.00-6.00**

Acker's Elixir, The Great Health Restorer; label; 6½″; amber **2.00-6.00**

Afflecks Drug Store, Washington, D.C.; 3¼″; clear or amethyst **2.00-6.00**

Africana; in script; 8″; amber **10.00-15.00**

Agua Perubinat Condal; label; round; 10½″ . . **6.00-8.00**

Aimars; reverse side *Charleston S.C.;* reverse *Sarsaparilla & Queens Delight;* 9⅝″; amber **30.00-60.00**

Albany Co. Pharmacy, Laramie, Wyo.; aqua . **4.00-6.00**

Dr. Alexander; on side; *Lung Healer* on opposite side; rectangular; square collar; 6½″; aqua blue **4.00-6.00**

Dr. W.H. Alexanders Wonderfull Healing Oil; label; aqua **4.00-6.00**

Allaire Woodward & Co.; Peoria, Ill.; reverse side *Elixir & Nutrans;* 10″; amber **8.00-10.00**

Allan Antifat Botanic Med Co., Buffalo N.Y.; 1895; 7½″; aqua **4.00-6.00**

Mrs. A. Allen's; *Worlds Hair Restorer* one side; *New York* other side; amber; 7½″ **4.00-6.00**

Mrs. S.A. Allen's; *Worlds Hair Restorer, 355 Produce St. N.Y.* on two panels; dark purple; 7″ . **10.00-20.00**

Allen's Essence of Jamaica Ginger; 5½″; aqua **8.00-12.00**

Allen's Nerve & Bone Liniment; vertical around bottle; square collar; round; 3⅞″; aqua **4.00-6.00**

Allen's Sarsaparilla; vertical on front; oval shape; narrow square; 8⅛″; aqua **10.00-20.00**

Alle-Rhume Remedy Co.; machine made; clear; 7¾″ **8.00-10.00**

T.C. Caulk Alloy; on bottom; sunken panel; 2¼″; clear **3.00-4.00**

American Drug Store N.O.; in center; tapered top; 9¼″; amber **20.00-40.00**

same except sample size; 4¼″ **25.00-50.00**

Amer's; in vertical writing; clear or amethyst; 1¾″ **2.00-4.00**

Sp. Ammon Ar; 9¼″; clear, $6.00-10.00

Ammonia; flask; all sizes; aqua **1.00-4.00**

Ammonia; label; aqua; 10½″ **2.00-6.00**

Spiritus Ammoniae; label; machine made; 6½″; amber **20.00-60.00**

Dr. H. Anders & Co.; on each side, picture of face of sun, under it *Hauriexhal Fontevitale;* ground top; pontil; 9″; aqua **25.00-40.00**

Angiers Emulsion; aqua; 7″ **2.00-4.00**

Angiers Petroleum Emulsion; under bottom in 3 lines; sunken panel in front; back side is rounded; 7″; aqua **2.00-4.00**

Angiers Petroleum Emulsion; aqua; 7″ **2.00-6.00**

Anodyne for Infants; vertical on front in sunken arch panel; *Dr. Groves* on side; *Philada* on opposite side; rectangular; 5⅜″; clear **3.00-6.00**

Anthony, 501 Broadway N.Y.; on front; *Flint Varnish for Negatives* on label on back; round; 5½″; clear **3.00-4.00**

E. Anthony, New York; vertical on front; oval; 6″; cobalt blue **4.00-8.00**

Apothecary Jars; open pontil; round; ground stopper; 8½″ and 10″; aqua **4.00-6.00**

Apothecary; (drug store); different sizes; 2″ and up; clear **2.00-8.00**

Apothecary; (drug store); different sizes; 2″ and up; green, amber, light amber, blue, etc. . . . . **4.00+**

Apothecary; (drug store); different sizes; 2″ and up;
pontil . . . . **6.00 +**

Apothecary; label; *100* under bottom; quart size;
amber **8.00-10.00**

Armour & Co.; 4″; amber **2.00-4.00**

Armour and Company, Chicago; in four lines on
cathedral type panels; round corner; lady's leg type
neck; taller than 5¼″; milk glass **10.00-20.00**

Armour Laboratories, Chicago; in egg shape circle in
center; 7¾″; amber **1.00-2.00**

Armour Laboratories, Chicago; on fancy oval panel;
rectangular; 5″; amber **2.00-4.00**

Armour's Vigorals Chicago; squat body;
amber **2.00-4.00**

Arnica Liniment, J.R. Burdsall's, New York; on front
and sides; flask; 5⅝″; aqua **4.00-6.00**

Arnica & Oil Liniment; vertical on two panels; eight vertical panels; 6½″; aqua **4.00-6.00**

Dr. Seth Arnold's Balsam, Gilman Bros., Boston; on
front and sides; rectangular; 3¾″;
amethyst **4.00-8.00**

Dr. Seth Arnold's Balsam, Gilman Bros., Boston; 7″;
aqua **8.00-12.00**

Dr. Seth Arnold's; on side *Cough Killer;* sunken panels;
rectangular; banded collar; 5½″; aqua **4.00-6.00**

Aromatic Schnapps; (S is backwards);
8″; dark olive, $20.00-40.00

Aster; in script running up; *The Puritan Drug Co. Columbus O.* on base; 8¾″; aqua **4.00-8.00**

Astyptodyae Chemical Co.; clear or
amethyst; 4½″ **2.00-4.00**

Astyptodyne Chemical Co.; in two lines; 3¾″ body, 1″
round, 1″ neck; clear or amethyst **2.00-4.00**

Athieu's Cough Syrup **4.00-6.00**

Dr. A. Atkinson, N.Y.; pontil; 8¼″; aqua **8.00-12.00**

The Atlanta Chemical Co., Atlanta, Ga U.S.A.; on side;
amber, 8½″ **4.00-6.00**

Atlas Medicine Co.; *Henderson N.C., U.S.A. 1898;* 9¼″;
amber . . . . **8.00-12.00 +**

Atrask Ointment; square bottle; 2½″; aqua . . . **1.00-2.00**

C.W. Atwell, Portland, Me; vertical on front in large letters; oval; 8″; light aqua **3.00-6.00**

C.W. Atwell; long tapered lip; vertical *C.W. Atwell
Portland Me;* oval shape; open pontil; 7½″;
aqua **10.00-30.00**

Atwoods Jannaice Laxative; machine made; 6″;
clear **4.00-6.00**

Ayer's Ague Cure, Lowell Mass; 5¾″; aqua . . **4.00-8.00**

Ayer's Cherry Pectoral, Lowell Mass.; 7¼″;
aqua **4.00-8.00**

Ayer's Concentrated Sarsaparilla; pontil;
aqua **10.00-30.00**

Ayer's Hair Vigor, label; aqua; 7½″ **8.00-12.00**
without label **2.00-6.00**

Ayer's; *Lowell Mass U.S.A.* on back; 8½″ . . . **3.00-6.00**

Ayer's Hair Vigor; square; 7¼″; peacock **6.00-8.00**

Ayer's Pills; square; 2⅜″; clear **1.00-2.00**

Ayer's Pills, Lowell Mass.; rectangular; 2″;
aqua **4.00-6.00**

Ayer's; in sunken panel; 6¼″; aqua **1.00-3.00**

Ayer's Sarsaparilla; *Lowell, Mass., U.S.A. Compound
Ext.,* 8½″; aqua **1.00-3.00**

Ayer's reverse side, *Lowell,
Mass.;* on side *Pectoral;* other
side *Cherry* 7¼; aqua, $6.00-8.00

**Elixir Babek For Malaria Chills Fevers, Washington,
D.C.;** vertical on front in sunken panel; rectangular;
6″; clear **4.00-6.00**

Baby Ease; aqua; 5½″, $2.00-4.00

Wm. A. Bacon, Ludlow, VT; pontil; 5½″;
aqua **10.00-15.00**

Dr. Baker's Pain Panacea 1855; pontil;
aqua; 5″ **15.00-35.00**

Dr. Ira Baker's Honduras Sarsaparilla; 10½″; aqua or
clear **12.00-18.00**

John C. Baker & Co., Cod Liver Oil; 9½″ **4.00-6.00**

JN. C. Baker & Co.; on one side *100 N. 3rd St.;* on
other side *Phild.;* pontil; 4¾″; aqua **8.00-10.00**

S.F. Baker & Co. Keokuk, Iowa; 8½″; aqua . . **4.00-6.00**

Ballard Snow Liniment Co.; clear or
amethyst; 4½″ **2.00-6.00**

Ball Balsam of Honey; ringed top; pontil; 3½″;
aqua **10.00-20.00**

Balm-Elixir Remedies, Ossipee, N.H.; 5¾″;
clear **2.00-6.00**

Balsam of Honey; pontil; 3¼″; aqua **6.00-10.00**

Balsam Vegetable Pulmonary; around bottle;
aqua; 5″ **2.00-6.00**

JNO. T. Barbee & Co.; 6″; clear or amethyst . . **4.00-6.00**

JNO. T. Barbee & Co.; 6″; clear or amethyst; machine
made **3.00-4.00**

Barber Medicine Co., Kansas City, MO.; label; 7½″;
aqua **10.00-20.00**

Barker Moore & Mein Medicine Co., Philadelphia; on
front and side; rectangular; 6⅜″; aqua . . . **3.00-4.00**

Barker Moore & Mein; vertical on front; *Druggist* on side; *Philadelphia* on opposite side; 5¼"; aqua **3.00-4.00**

Wm. Jay Barker, Hirsutus, New York; vertical on front in sunken panel; pewter stopper; square collar; ABM: 6⅝"; clear **8.00-10.00**

same as above except aqua; 5¼" **8.00-10.00**

Dr. Barkman's Never Failing Liniment; on front; 6¼"; light green **4.00-6.00**

Barnes & Parke, N.Y., Balsam of Wild Cherry & Tar, 7½" **8.00-10.00**

same as above except 6¼" **8.00-10.00**

Barry's Tricopherous For the Skin & Hair, N.Y.; pontil; 5¼" **4.00-18.00**

same as above except five other different sizes **4.00-18.00**

T.B. Barton; clear or amethyst; 4½" **2.00-4.00**

Bartow Drug Co.; clear or amethyst; 3½" **2.00-4.00**

Batchelor's; clear or amethyst; 3" **4.00-6.00**

Batemans Drops; vertical; cylindrical; 5¼"; amethyst **2.00-4.00**

Geo. H. Battier Druggist, 120 Beale St.; 5¼" **4.00-8.00**

J.A. Bauer, S.F. Cal.; 8¼"; lime green **8.00-15.00**

Bayer Aspirin; in circles; *Bayer Aspirin* run up and down as cross sign; screw top; machine made; clear, bubble-type bottle; 2½" **2.00-4.00**

X-Bazin Succrto, E. Roussel; *Philadelphia;* six panels; sheared top; 2¾"; clear **6.00-10.00**

B.B.B., Atlanta, Ga.; amber; 3¾" x 2¼", $6.00-10.00

Beason's Vego Syrup Compound; *Smith Chemical Corp. Johnson City, Tenn.,* label; 8½"; clear **2.00-4.00**

Bee-Dee Medicine Co., Chattanooga Tenn.; on one side *Bee Dee Liniment;* double ring top; 5½"; clear **4.00-6.00**

Beggs Cherry Cough Syrup; rectangular; 5¾"; aqua **3.00-4.00**

Beggs Diarrhoea Balsam; 5½"; aqua **4.00-6.00**

Dr. Belding's Medicine Co.; on one side of sunken panel; other side *Minneapolis, Minn.;* side sizes 1¾"; 3" wide panel; one side plain for label; other in script, *Dr. Belding's Wild Cherry, Sarsaparilla,* body 6", neck 3"; aqua **10.00-25.00**

Dr. Belding's Wild Cherry Sarsaparilla; in sunken panel in front; back plain; *Dr. Belding Medicine Co.* on one side in sunken panel; other side *Minneapolis, Minn.;* aqua; 10" **12.00-15.00**

Bell Ans; on both sides; round; ABM; 3¾"; amber **2.00-3.00**

Bell, Pa Pay Ans Bell & Co. Inc. Orangeburg, New York, USA; on opposite sides, rectangular; ABM; 2¾"; amber **2.00-3.00**

Dr. Bell's; *The E.E. Sutherland Medicine Co. Paducah, KY., Pine Tar Honey;* aqua, 5½" **2.00-3.00**

Belt & Son, Salem, Ore.; 5½"; aqua **3.00-6.00**

J.A. Bernard Druggist; *552 Westminister St. Providence, R.I.,* rectangular, clear, flared lip, 5½" **5.00-7.00**

Berry Bros., 323 E. 38th St. N.Y. in circle in front; aqua; 11¼" **2.00-4.00**

The Bettes Pharmacy, label; clear; 4½" **3.00-4.00**

El Bien Publico Drug Store, West Tampa, Fla.; 3¼"; clear **4.00-8.00**

Biokrene Hutchings & Hillyer, N.Y.; 7½"; aqua **2.00-4.00**

Dr. Birney's Catarrah All Power; 2¼"; clear . . **2.00-4.00**

Bism Subnitr; clear; 5¼" **8.00-10.00**

B-L Tonic, The B-L-Co Atlanta Ga.; label; *B-L Made in U.S.A.* embossed in back; 10"; amber **4.00-6.00**

H.C. Blair; *8th & Walnut Philada* on side of bottom; clear or amethyst; 6½" **4.00-8.00**

E. Bloch & Co.; *W.B.* under bottom; clear; 3½" **4.00-6.00**

Blood Balm Co., label; amber; 9" **4.00-12.00**

Dr. E. Blrickers Tonic Mixture for Fever and Chills; small tapered top; 6"; aqua **15.00-30.00**

Blud-Life; clear or amethyst; machine made; 8½", $2.00-4.00

Dr. A. Bochie's, German Syrup; in two vertical lines; 6¾"; square; aqua **2.00-3.00**

Boericke & Runyon Company; in script on front; 7¾"; clear **2.00-3.00**

Boericke & Runyon Co.; in large letters vertical on one panel; square; beveled corners; 8⅝"; amethyst **2.00-4.00**

same as above except sample size; 2½"; amber **2.00-6.00**

Boldwin Cherry Pepsin & Dandelion Tonic; 8"; amber **10.00-30.00**

W.H. Bone Co. C.C. Liniment, S.F. Cal. U.S.A.; 6½"; aqua **2.00-4.00**

Bon-Opto For The Eyes; clear or amethyst; 3¼" **2.00-4.00**

Booth's Hyomei; *Buffalo N.Y., Rorterie, Canada;* 3"; black **4.00-8.00**

Borax; clear; 5¼", $8.00-10.00

Dr. Bosanko's Pile Remedy; *Phila Pa.;* 2½";
aqua **2.00-4.00**

Dr. Bosanko's; *Trial Size* on one side;
aqua; 4" **2.00-4.00**

Dr. A. Boschees German Syrup; in vertical lines; long
neck; 6¾"; aqua **2.00-3.00**

Boston, Mass; on front panel; *Egyptian Chemical Co.;*
square; clear; 7½"; screw top; measured . .**2.00-3.00**

Dr. C. Bouvier's; clear; 4½" **4.00-8.00**

Bradfield's, Atlanta, Ga; 8¾"; aqua **3.00-6.00**

Brandriffs for Ague; on front; *Piqua, Ohio;* ring top; 8";
aqua or green **6.00-8.00**

Brandriffs Vegetable Antidote, Pique, O.; 8";
aqua **4.00-8.00**

**Brant's Indian Pulmonary Balsam, Mt. Wallace Pro-
prietor;** vertical on three panels; 8" wide vertical
panels; 6¾"; aqua **40.00-60.00**

Breig & Shafer; on bottom; on top of it a fish;
green **8.00-15.00**

G.O. Bristo; Backwar, Buffalo; six panels;
pontil; 4¾" **20.00-40.00**

Bristol's; on one side in sunken panel; other side, *New
York;* front panel plain for label; on back in sunken
panel *Genuine Sarsaparilla;* under bottom in circle
panel *#18;* 10¼" tall; 2¼" neck; 3¾" wide; 2¼"
thick; aqua **4.00-6.00**

Bristol's Sarsaparilla; pontil; green **20.00-30.00**

B & P; amber; *Lyons Powder* on shoulder of opposite
side; 4¼" **25.00-50.00**

B.P.Co.; on front, also *BP* back to back with circle
around it; cobalt; 3"; oval **8.00-12.00**

B.P. Co.; front, also *BP* back to back with circle around
it; cobalt; 1½"; oval **12.00-15.00**

**Bromated Pepsin, Humphrey's Chemical Co., New
York;** vertical on front; square; 3¾"; cobalt
blue **4.00-6.00**

Bromo Caffeine; 3¼"; light blue **2.00-4.00**

Bromo Lithia Chemical Co.; amber; 4¼" **3.00-4.00**

Bromo Lithia Checmical Co.; amber; 3¼" . . .**2.00-3.00**

Bromo-Seltzer; on shoulder; round; machine made
cobalt; under bottom *M1* in a circle; 5" **1.00-2.00**

Bromo-Seltzer Emerson Drug, Baltimore, MD; on front;
round; cobalt; 5" **2.00-4.00**

Bromo-Seltzer Emerson Drug, Baltimore, MD.; on
front; round; cobalt; machine made; 5" **1.00-2.00**

Bromo-Seltzer Emerson Drug, Baltimore, MD.; on
front; round; cobalt; machine made; 4" **1.00-2.00**

Bromo-Seltzer Emerson Drug, Baltimore, MD.; on
front; round; cobalt; 5" **3.00-5.00**

Bromo-Seltzer Emerson Drug, Baltimore, MD; on front;
round; cobalt; machine made; 6½" **1.00-3.00**

Bromo-Seltzer Emerson Drug, Baltimore, MD; on front;
round; cobalt; machine made, 8" **2.00-4.00**

Bromo-Seltzer Emerson Drug, Baltimore, MD; on front;
round; cobalt; machine made; 2½" **1.00-2.00**

Bromo-Seltzer Emerson Drug, Baltimore, MD; on front;
round; cobalt; machine made; screw
top; 4¾" **1.00-2.00**

Bromo-Seltzer; around shoulder; machine made; screw
top; cobalt **1.00-3.00**

The Brooks Drug Co., Battle Creek, Mich.; label; *887*
under bottom; clear; 8" **2.00-4.00**

Brooks & Potter Druggists, Senatobia, Miss.; 7¼";
clear or amber **2.00-6.00**

Brown Co., W.T. & Co.; 8"; cobalt,
$8.00-10.00

Dr. Brown's Ruterba; side mold; amber; 8" . . .**6.00-8.00**

Dr. C.F. Brown, Young American Liniment, New York;
ring top; 4"; aqua **6.00-10.00**

F. Browns Essence of Jamaica Ginger, Philada.;
tapered top; pontil; 5½"; aqua **10.00-20.00**
same except no pontil **4.00-8.00**
same except no pontil and has ringed top .**4.00-8.00**

F. Brown's; aqua, 5½" **3.00-6.00**

Brown-Forman Co.; clear or amethyst; 4½" . .**2.00-4.00**

Brown Household Panacea and Family Liniment; vertical on front in sunken panel; *Curtis & Brown* on
side; *Mfg. Co. L.D. New York* on opposite side; rectangular; 5⅛"; aqua **3.00-6.00**

J.T. Brown; 292 Washington St., Boston, Preparation;
pontil; 6"; aqua **8.00-10.00**

Dr. O. Phelps Brown; 3½"; aqua **2.00-4.00**

Dr. O. Phelps Brown; on side *Jersey City N.J.;* ring top;
2½"; aqua **2.00-4.00**

Brown Sarsaparilla; aqua; 3x1¾x9½" **4.00-6.00**

W.E. Brown Druggist, Manchester, Iowa;
clear **6.00-8.00**

W.E. Brown Druggist, Manchester, Iowa; mixing jar
and an eagle over it; 5½"; clear **3.00-6.00**

Brown's Instant Relief for Pain; aqua; 5¼";
embossed **3.00-4.00**

B.S. #30; under bottom; drop bottle; 3½";
clear **6.00-8.00**

Buchan's Hungarian Balsam of Life, London; vertical
lines *Kidney Cure;* 5¾"; round short neck;
green **3.00-5.00**

Buckingham; on one side; *Whisker Dye* on other side;
4¾"; brown **2.00-4.00**

Dr. Bull's Herbs & Iron; *Pat. Oct. 13, 85* on base;
9½" **15.00-20.00**

Dr. J.W. Bull's Veg. Baby Syrup;, trade mark; round;
5¼"; aqua **2.00-6.00**

W.H. Bull Medicine Co.; 9½″; amber, $4.00-6.00

W.H. Bull's Medicine Bottle; *Pat Oct 1885* under bottom; clear; 5¼″ 2.00-4.00

Dr. Bullocks Nephreticurn; *Providence R.I.;* 7″; aqua 10.00-20.00

Bumsteads Worm Syrup; *Phila;* 4½″; aqua . .8.00-10.00

Bumstead Worm Syrup; *Philad; #3* under bottom; ring top; aqua 4.00-6.00

A.L. Burdock Liquid Food, Boston, 12½ Percent Soluble Albumen; on four consecutive panels; twelve vertical panels on bottle; square collar; 6″; amber 4.00-6.00

J.A. Burgon, Allegheny City, Pa.; label on back; *Dr. J.A. Burgon* standing and holding a bottle and table; 8¼″; clear 10.00-15.00

Burke & James; *W.T. Co. A.A. U.S.A.* under bottom; clear or amethyst; 6¼″ 4.00-6.00

E.A. Burkhout's Dutch Liniment, Prep. At Mechanicville, Saratoga Co., N.Y.; pontil; 5¼″; aqua 100.00-150.00

Burlington Drug Co., Burlington Vt.; label; 5½″; clear 5.00-10.00

Burnam's Beef Wine E.J.B. & Iron; on front; thumb print on back; oval; 9¼″; aqua 3.00-6.00

Burt Smith Co.; aqua; 7″, $60.00-100.00

Burnett; clear; 6¾″, $2.00-4.00

Burnett; *Boston* on other side; clear; 4¼″ 2.00-4.00

Burnett; on side; *Boston* on opposite side; beveled corners; square collar; oval shape; 6½″ aqua .3.00-4.00

Burnetts Cocaine; vertical on front: *Burnetts* on side; *Boston* on side; *Boston* on opposite side; large beveled corners; tapered shoulders; aqua; 7⅜″ 4.00-6.00

Burnetts Cocoaine, Boston; ringed top; 7¼″; aqua 4.00-6.00

Burnetts Cocoaine, 1864-1900; ringed top; clear 8.00-12.00

Burnhams Beef Wine & Iron; 9½″; aqua 2.00-4.00

Burnham's Clam Bouillon, E.S. Burnham Co., New York; 5″; machine made; 4½″ 2.00-3.00

Burnham's; aqua; 4¾″ 2.00-4.00

Burringtons Vegetable Group Syrup, Providence, R.I.; vertical around bottle; ring collar; cylindrical; 5½″; clear 3.00-6.00

same as above except aqua 3.00-6.00

Burton's Malthop Tonique; label; three-part mold; dark olive; 7½″ 4.00-6.00

Burwell-Dunn; *R.S.J.; 969* under bottom; clear or amethyst; 3¾″ 2.00-4.00

Butler's Balsam of Liverwort; pontil; 4¼″; aqua 10.00-20.00

Cabot's Sulpho Napthol; vertical on front; oval back; beveled corners; square collar; 6½″ and 4¾″; amber 3.00-6.00

Cabot's Sulpho Napthol; written fancily; large beveled corners; oval back; square collar; 5⅛″; aqua 4.00-6.00

Caldwells Syrup Pepsin; *Mfd by Pepsin Syrup Co., Monticello, Ill.;* aqua; 3″; rectangular 3.00-4.00

Caldwells Syrup Pepsin; *Mfd by Pepsin Syrup Co. Monticello, Ill;* aqua; rectangular; machine made; screw top; all sizes 1.00-2.00

California Fig Syrup Co.; on front panel; *Louisville, Ky.* on left side; *San Francisco, Calif.* on right side; rectangular; amethyst; 7¼″ 3.00-4.00

California Fig. Syrup Co., San Francisco, Cal; vertical on front; *Syrup of Figs* on both sides; rectangular; square collar; 6½″; amethyst 4.00-6.00

California Fig Syrup Co.; *Califig, Sterling Products (inc) Successor* on front; rectangular; clear; 6¾″ 1.00-2.00

California Fig Syrup Co.; *Califig. Sterling Products (inc) Successor* on front; rectangular; machine made; screw top; all sizes and colors 1.00-2.00

California Fig Syrup Co.; on front; on side *Wheeling, W.Va.* 6″ ABM, clear 5.00-7.00

California Fig. Syrup Co., S.F. Cal.; *Syrup of Fig,* 6¾″; clear or amber 2.00-4.00

Prof. Callan's World Renowned Brazilian Gum; vertical on one panel; square collar; 4⅛″; aqua . . .3.00-4.00

Dr. Callan's World Renowned Brazilian Gum; 4½″; clear 3.00-4.00

Ext. Calumb, Fl.; cobalt; 9½″ 10.00-20.00

Calvert's; clear or amethyst; 8″ 8.00-12.00

The Campbell Drug Co., The General Store, Fostoria, Ohio; on back *Camdrugo;* 5¼″; green 4.00-8.00

Campbell V.V.; in script, *the genuine always bears this signature* in the front panel; diamond shaped base; 5⅛″; clear 2.00-4.00

Caplion; label; clear; 5″; *TCWCO. U.S.A.* on
bottom **2.00-6.00**

Capudine Chemical Co. Raleigh N.C.; in center; *G*
under bottom; label; amber; machine made;
7½″ **2.00-3.00**

Capudine for Headache; on front panel; amber; 3¼″;
oval **1.00-2.00**

Dr. M. Caraballo; *Vermicida* in back; aqua;
4¼″ **3.00-6.00**

Carbona; on the base; paneled; 5½″ and 6″;
aqua **2.00-5.00**

Carbona, Carbona Products Co.; *Carbona* in 3 lines;
hair oil; 6″; aqua **1.00-2.00**

Carbona, Carbona Products Co.; *Carbona* in 3 lines
running vertically; round; 6″; aqua; hair
dressing **2.00-3.00**

Carbona & Carbona Products Co.; *Carbona* on 3 vertical panels; twelve panels; square collar; 5⅛″;
aqua **3.00-4.00**

Carlo Erba Miano, Oleo Picino; 3¾″; clear or
amber **8.00-10.00**

Carlsbad; 5½″; clear **4.00-6.00**

Carlsbad AH; under bottom; sheared top; clear;
4″ **2.00-4.00**

Carlsbad RA; under bottom; sheared top; clear;
4″ **4.00-6.00**

Carpenter & Wood, Inc.; *Est. 1883 Providence, R.I.* with
eagle & shield on center front; glass stopper; round;
2¼″; clear or amethyst **2.00-4.00**

Carter's Spanish Mix; pontil; 8″; green **10.00-30.00**

Cary Gum Tree Cough Syrup; *S. Fran. U.S.A.;* 7½″;
aqua blue **8.00-10.00**

same as above except lime green **10.00-15.00**

Cassebeer; reverse side N.Y.; 7½″;
amber, **$8.00-10.00**

Castol Oil, Pure; *2 fl. oz. The Frank Tea & Co.;* cintion
front; clear; 5¼″; flask **4.00-8.00**

also machine made and screw top; all sizes and
colors **1.00-2.00**

Castol Oil; 4″ body; 3″ neck; 1¼″ round bottom; cobalt
blue **8.00-12.00**

same, except smaller, some in different
sizes **8.00-12.00**

Castor Oil; label; *W.C. 3oz* under bottom; cobalt;
8¼″ **8.00-10.00**

C.B. 6B; on bottom; green; 7¼″ **4.00-6.00**

C & C; inside two concentric circles; sides fluted;
amethyst; rectangular; 4½″ **2.00-4.00**

C.C.C. Tonic, Boericke & Runyon New York; vertical
on front in large letters; beveled corners; rectangular; large flared square collar; 8″;
clear **20.00-30.00**

C & Co.; 3½″; clear or amber **2.00-4.00**

Celery Medicine Co.; bitters label; clear or
amethyst; 9″, **$8.00-15.00**

Celery-Vesce, Century Chemical Co.; *Indianapolis, Ind.
U.S.A.;* 4″; amber **4.00-6.00**

Celro-kola, Phil Blumaur & Co., Portland, Or.; 10″;
clear **4.00-6.00**

Centour Liniment; ringed top; 5¼″; aqua **2.00-4.00**

Centour Liniment; on shoulder; 3½″; aqua . . .**1.00-2.00**

Centour Liniment; on shoulder; aqua; round,
5″ **2.00-3.00**

Centour Liniment; on shoulder; round bottle; machine
made; 5″; aqua **1.00-2.00**

Central Drug Co.; *Laramie Wyo.;* clear **4.00-6.00**

Certain Group Remedy; vertical on front in sunken
panel; *Dr. Hoxsie's* onside; *Buffalo, NY* on opposite
side; rectangular; 4½″; clear **4.00-6.00**

Chamberlain's; on side panel; *Bottle Made in America*
on opposite side; rectangular; 4½″; aqua . .**2.00-3.00**

Chamberlain's Colic Cholera and Diarrhea Remedy;
Chamberlain Med. Co. Des Moines, Ia. USA on front
and sides; rectangular; 4½″; aqua **4.00-6.00**

same as above except 6″ **4.00-6.00**

Chamberlain's Colic Cholera and Diarrhea Remedy; on
front; *Des Moines, Iowa US.A.* on side panel;
Chamberlain Med. Co. on opposite; aqua; 5¼″;
rectangular **2.00-4.00**

Chamberlain's Cough Remedy; on front; *Des Moines,
Ia. U.S.A.* on left side; *Chamberlain Med. Co.* on
right side; 6¾″; rectangular; aqua or clear . .**2.00-4.00**

Chamberlain's Cough Remedy; on other side
Chamberlains Med. Co.; 5½″; aqua **4.00-6.00**

Chamberlain's Pain-Balm; on front; *Des Moines, Ia.
U.S.A.* on left side; *Chamberlain Med. Co.* on right
side; aqua; 7″; rectangular **2.00-4.00**

Champlin's Liquid Pearl; on front; rectangular; square
collar; 5″; milk glass **4.00-8.00**

same as above except 6″ **3.00-6.00**

Dr. P.H. Chapelle, N.Y.; label; flask; 6¾″;
clear **8.00-15.00**

Chelf Chem. Co.; cobalt; machine made; 4″ . .**2.00-3.00**

Chemical Bottle; label; crystal glass; 6½″;
clear **6.00-10.00**

Chemical Co. D.D. N.Y. Sample; on the front panel;
amber; 5″; square **1.00-2.00**

Chesebrough; clear or amethyst; 3½″ **2.00-3.00**

Chesebrough Mfg. Co.; in horseshoe letters; under it
Vaseline; 2⅞″; clear **1.00-2.00**

Chesebrough Vaseline; 2¾"; clear **3.00-4.00**
    same except 3¾" **3.00-6.00**
    same except ABM; amethyst; thread top; 3¼" and
    2½" **2.00-3.00**
    same as above except ABM; amber **2.00-3.00**
    same as above; ABM; clear **2.00-3.00**
Chesebrough Vaseline Trade Mark, New York; on
    front; mold threads; pint size; amethyst . . . **2.00-3.00**
Prof Chevalier; clear; 4¼" **2.00-4.00**
Chinese bottle; clear; 2½" **2.00-4.00**

Chinidin; clear; 5¼", $8.00-12.00

Chlorate Potassique; pontil; 6½"; clear glass painted
    brown **10.00-20.00**
Christies Magnetic Fluid; flared top; 4¾";
    aqua **8.00-10.00**
Church, C.M.; in script in center on one side of it *Druggist,* other *Belvidere, Ill.* ring top, on bottom *A.M.F. & Co.* 6½" clear **5.00-8.00**

T.R. Cimicifug; clear; 7¾", $4.00-6.00

Circassian Bloom; 5"; clear or amber **2.00-6.00**
The Citizens Wholesale Supply Co.; label;
    clear; 7½" **2.00-4.00**
The Citizens Wholesale Supply Co.; *Columbus O. Camphorated Oil* on label; clear; 7½" **4.00-6.00**

Citrate Magnesia; clear or amethyst; 8", $4.00-6.00

Citrate Magnesia; clear or amethyst; three-ring top;
    8¾" **4.00-6.00**
Citrate Magnesia; in script around bottom; Sanitas bottle; 8"; clear or amethyst **2.00-3.00**

Citrate Magnesia; in script on bottom; Sanitas bottle; 8";
    clear or amethyst **1.00-2.00**
Citrate Magnesia; *National Magnesia Co. Inc.;* clear; 7";
    round **2.00-4.00**
Citrate Magnesia; in a sunken circle; in center *O Dot, 4T* around it; double-ring top; aqua; 7" **4.00-6.00**
Citrate Magnesia; embossed in indented curved bands;
    blob top; 8"; green **8.00-10.00**
City Drug Company; *103 Main St. Anaconda Mont.;*
    4¼"; clear **2.00-4.00**
City Drug Store; *Meridian, Tex.;* 3¼"; amethyst;
    rectangular **1.00-2.00**
Otis Clapp & Sons Malt & Cod Liver Oil Compound;
    vertical on front in fancy lettering; large square collar; 7¼"; amber **4.00-6.00**
C.G. Clark & Co.; *Restorative* other side; 7¾";
    aqua **6.00-10.00**
The C.G. Clark Co.; vertical on one panel; *New Haven, Ct* on third panel; twelve vertical panels; square collar; 5½"; aqua **3.00-4.00**
Clark's Cordial; on front in diamond shape panel; (note: you can see where the words *Clark's Calif. Cherry Cordial* were slugged out of the mold); 8¼"; amber **20.00-30.00**
Dr. J.S. Clark's, Throat & Lungs; reverse side *Balsam For The;* 8½"; aqua **8.00-12.00**
W.W. Clark, 16 N. 5th St. Phila.; pontil; 5⅜";
    aqua **8.00-15.00**
Clements & Co.; *Rosadalis* other side; aqua;
    8½" **4.00-6.00**
Clouds Cordial; on each side, tapered type bottle,
    tapered top, amber, 10¾" x 3" x 2" . . . **24.00-33.00**
Creme De Camelia for the Complexion; on side; *The Boradent Co. Inc., San Francisco* on opposite side; beveled corners; rectangular; flared collar; *New York* in slug plate; 5⅛"; cobalt blue **4.00-8.00**
    same as above except *San Francisco & New York* embossed **4.00-8.00**
Cod Liver Oil; aqua; 9¾" **2.00-6.00**
Cod Liver Oil; with fish in center; screw top; machine made; two sizes; amber; round **2.00-4.00**
Cod Liver Oil; in front with a fish in sunken panel;
    square; 9"; amber; screw top; machine made **2.00-4.00**
Cod Liver Oil; in front with a fish in sunken panel;
    square; 6"; amber; screw top; machine made **2.00-4.00**
Cod Liver Oil-Fish; different sizes and many different colors; some made in Italy **8.00-16.00**
Coffeen's Pain Specific; clear; 7¼" **6.00-8.00**
College Hill Pharmacy; clear or amethyst; 4½" **2.00-4.00**

N.A. Collings; *W.T.Co. U.S.A.* under bottom; clear; 6¼", $2.00-4.00

Coly Tooth Wash; backward S in Wash; 4½″;
clear **10.00-15.00**

Compound Elixir; aqua; 8¾″ **6.00-10.00**

W.H. Comstock; on back _Moses Indian Root Pills;_ onside _Dose 1 to 3;_ 2½″; amber **2.00-6.00**

Cone Asthma Conqueror Co.; _Cincinnati, O;_ 8″;
clear **4.00-6.00**

**Connell's Brahmnical Moon Plant East Indian
Remedies;** on base in back ten stars around a pair
of feet; under it trademark; 7″; amber . . **30.00-85.00**

Connell's Brahmnical East Indian Remedies;
amber **5.00-10.00**

Coope's New Discovery; tonic; 8¾″; label;
aqua **1.00-2.00**

Cooper's New Discovery; 9″; aqua **8.00-10.00**

Costar's; very light blue; 4″ **3.00-6.00**

Costar's, N.Y.; on shoulder; 4″; amber **8.00-10.00**

George Coster; side mold; aqua; 5½″ **2.00-6.00**

Crary & Co.; aqua; 4¼″ **2.00-3.00**

W.H. Crawford Co.; clear; 4¼″ **2.00-3.00**

**Creensfelder & Laupheimer Druggists,
Baltimore, MD;** on three panels; twelve
panels; on shoulder _A.R.B.;_ 8½″;
amber, $10.00-20.00

Creomulsion for Coughs Due to Colds; amethyst or
clear; 8¼″; rectangular **2.00-4.00**

Cresol U.S.P.; label; clear; 7¼″ **2.00-4.00**

Dr. Crossmans Specific Mixture; vertical around bottle;
square collar; 3¾″; aqua **4.00-8.00**

Crown Cordial & Extract Co. N.Y.; amethyst; 10¼″;
round **2.00-6.00**

The Crystal Pharmacy; clear or
amethyst; 7″ **2.00-4.00**

C.S. & Co. LD 6054; on bottom; 8¾″; aqua . . **3.00-4.00**

C.S. & Co. Ld 10296; on bottom; 9¾″; dark
green **4.00-8.00**

Dr. Cumming's Vegetine; aqua; 9¾″ **4.00-6.00**

Curlings Citrate of Magnesia; vertical on front; large
beveled corners; crude ring collar; 6⅛″; cobalt
blue **3.00-6.00**

Cushing Medical Supply Co., N.Y. & Boston, Full QT;
aqua; 10″ **4.00-8.00**

Cuticura Treatment For Affectations of the Skin; 9⅛″;
aqua **3.00-4.00**

Dad Chemical Co.; on the shoulders; amber; 6″
round **1.00-2.00**

Dalbys; _Carminative_ on back; _3751_ under bottom;
clear; 3¾″ **2.00-3.00**

Dalbys Carminative; pontil; 3½″; clear or
aqua **10.00-15.00**

Dalton's Sarsaparilla and Nerve Tonic; _Belfast, Maine
USA_ on opposite sides; rectangular; 9¼″;
aqua **8.00-10.00**

C. Damschinsky; aqua; 3¼″ **3.00-4.00**

Damschinsky Liquid Hair Dye, N.Y.; 3½″;
aqua **4.00-6.00**

C. Damschinsky Liquid Hair Dye, New York; in sunken
panels; 3½″; aqua **4.00-6.00**
same as above except 2¾″ **4.00-6.00**

Dana's; 9″; aqua **4.00-6.00**

Dana's Sarsaparilla; in two lines in a sunken panel; side
and back are plain sunken panels;
aqua; 9″ **8.00-12.00**

Daniel's; front side; other sides _Atlanta Ga.;_ 4½″;
aqua **2.00-6.00**

Dr. Daniel's Carbo-Necus; _Disinfectant Deodorizer
Purifier & Insecticide;_ clear; 6½″ **2.00-4.00**

Dr. Daniel's Veterinary; clear; 3½″ **3.00-4.00**

Dr. Daniel's Veterinary Colic Drops No. 1; square;
3½″; amethyst **6.00-8.00**

**Dr. A.G. Daniel's Liniment, Oster Cocus Oil, Boston,
Mass. USA;** vertical on front; oval back; beveled corners; 6¾″ clear **4.00-8.00**

Darby's Prophylactic Fluid; _J.H. Zeilen & Co.
Phila;_ 7½″; aqua, $4.00-8.00

Chas. F. Dare Mentha Pepsin; _Bridgetown,
N.J._ **4.00-10.00**

Davis; in an upper sunken panel; bottom of it flat; back
full sunken panel; on one side _Geoetable;_ other side
Pain Killer; 6″; aqua or light blue **2.00-4.00**

Davis; in sunken panel in front; medical; 6⅝″;
aqua **2.00-3.00**

Davis; in sunken panel in front; medical; 6½″;
blue **2.00-4.00**

Davis Vegetable Pain Killer; on front and sides; rectangular; sunken panels; 6″; aqua **2.00-4.00**

D.D. Chemical Co. N.Y. Sample; on front of panel;
amber; 5″; square **1.00-2.00**

D.D.D.; on front of panel; amethyst; square; 3½″
and 5½″ **3.00-6.00**

Dead Shot Vermifuge; pontil; amber or clear **10.00-25.00**

Prof. Dean's Barbed Wire Remedy; 5½″;
amber **2.00-4.00**

**Delavan's Syrup Whopping Cough Croup,
Philadelphia;** vertical on front; rectangular; square
collar; 6¼″; aqua **4.00-8.00**

Delavan's Whooping Cough Remedy; _Phila.;_ 6¼″;
aqua **2.00-4.00**

Dr. J. Dennis Georgia Sarsaparilla; _Augusta, Ga.,_
graphite pontil; tapered top; 10½″; aqua **50.00-85.00**

Derma-Royale for the Skin and Complexion; vertical
The Derma Royale Comp'y Cincinnati, O. also on
front, inside of circle; flared lip; square; 6⅛″;
clear **4.00-6.00**

Paul Devered & Co., Genuine C.V.E.; _Geo. Raphael &
Co. sole proprietor;_ pontil; flared top; 3½″; clear or
amber **8.00-12.00**

Dewitt's Soothing Syrup, Chicago; amethyst; round;
5″ **3.00-6.00**

Dewitts; aqua; 9″, $15.00-30.00

E.C. Dewitt & Co.; aqua; 9¼″ **4.00-8.00**

Diamond Oil; on two sides of panel; aqua; 5½″;
rectangular **2.00-4.00**

Diamond & Onyx; *Phila, U.S.A.;* 4¾″; aqua . . . **2.00-4.00**

Maximo M. Diaz; aqua; 7″ **2.00-4.00**

Dickey Chemist, S.F.; in center *Pioneer 1850;* 5¾″;
blue **10.00-15.00**

John R. Dickey's; *Old Reliable Eye Water, Mfg. by
Dickey Drug Co., Bristol, Va.;* aqua; 3¾″;
round **2.00-4.00**

Dill's Balm of Life; vertical on front; rectangular; AMB;
6″; clear **2.00-4.00**

Dill's Cough Syrup; vertical on front; *Dill Medicine Co.*
on side; *Norristown, Pa.* on opposite side; sunken
panels; rectangular; 5⅞″; clear **3.00-6.00**

**A.M. Dinimor & Co., Binningers Old Dominian Wheat
Tonic;** tapered top; 9½″; amber **10.00-20.00**

Mrs. Dinmore's Cough & Croup Balsam; vertical on
front in oval end of sunken panel; rectangular; 6″;
aqua **4.00-8.00**

Dioxogen; amber; 4″ **2.00-3.00**

Dioxogen; *The Oakland Chem Co.* on back;
amber; 7¾″ **2.00-4.00**

Dipper Dandy; on neck; sheared bottom; 10 to 60 cc
grad scale; metal shaker bottom; 6″;
clear **4.00-6.00**

**Dr. E.E. Dixon; clear or amethyst; 6½″,
$2.00-4.00**

Dodge & Olcott Co, New York, Oil Erigeron; label;
cobalt; machine made; *D & O* under
bottom; 7″ **4.00-6.00**

Dodson's; on one side of panel; *Livertone* on other side;
aqua or amethyst; 7″; rectangular **3.00-4.00**

Dodson & Hils, St. Louis U.S.A.; amethyst; 8¼″;
round **2.00-4.00**

Dolton's Sarsp. & Nerve Tonic; 9″; aqua . . . **8.00-15.00**

Donald Kennedy & Co., Roxbury Mass; label; aqua,
6½″ **4.00-8.00**

Donnell's Rheumatic Liniment; vertical on front; *J.T.
Donnell & Co., St. Louis, Mo.* on opposite sides; rectangular; 7¼″; aqua blue **3.00-6.00**

C.K. Donnell, M.D./809 Sabattus St., Lewiston, ME;
vertical on front in sunken panel; square collar; rectangular; 6¼″; amethyst **2.00-3.00**

George Dowden Chemist & Druggist; *No. 175 Broad
St. Rich. Va.;* pontil; 4½″; aqua **15.00-30.00**

Rev. N.H. Down's, Vegetable Balsamic Elixir; vertical
on four panels; twelve vertical panels in all; 5½″
aqua **3.00-6.00**

Dr. Doyen Staphylase Du; clear or amethyst;
8″ **3.00-6.00**

D.P.S. Co.; amber; 3½″ **2.00-3.00**

Dr. Drakes German Croup Remedy; vertical on front in
sunken panel; *The Glessner Med. Co.* on side;
Findlay, Ohio on opposite side; square collar; rectangular; 6⅜″; aqua **4.00-8.00**

Drexel's; clear; 4½″ **3.00-6.00**

Drop Bottle; *#45* under bottom; 4″; aqua . . . **8.00-10.00**

The Druggists Lindsey Ruffin & Co.; *Senatobia, Miss.;*
6¼″; clear or amber **2.00-6.00**

J. Dubois; on other panels around bottle; *Great Pain
Specific and Healing Balm, Kingston, N.Y.;*
aqua; 2¼″ **2.00-4.00**

Duch Poison, Zum K. Verschluss; under bottom; 8¼″;
clear or amber **8.00-10.00**

Dr. Duflot; clear or amethyst; 4¼″ **3.00-6.00**

S.O. Dunbar, Taunton, Mass.; 6″; aqua **4.00-8.00**

**T.J. Dunbar & Co.; on side *Cordial
Schnapps;* other side *Schiedam;* 10″;
green, $20.00-30.00**

Dutton's Vegetable; other side *Discovery;* 6″;
aqua **2.00-4.00**

E in square; very light green; 4″ **3.00-4.00**

The Easom Medicine Co.; on back a house in center of
trade mark; aqua; 2¼″ **4.00-8.00**

Eastman, Rochester, N.Y.; 6½″; clear or
amber **2.00-4.00**

A.W. Eckel & Co. Apothecaries; *Charleston, S.C.;* 4″;
clear **2.00-4.00**

Eddy & Eddy; clear; 5″; 1″ x 1¾″ **2.00-4.00**

Eddy & Eddy Chemist, St. Louis; round; 5″;
amethyst **3.00-5.00**

same as above except 6½″; clear **4.00-6.00**

Eddy's; round; 5¼″; green **2.00-4.00**

W. Edwards & Son; clear; 5″ **2.00-4.00**

**W. Edwards & Son, Roche Embrocation for Whooping
Cough;** 5″; clear **4.00-10.00**

Frank H. E. Eggleston; *Pharm. Laramie Wy.;* clear or
amber **4.00-6.00**

The E.G.L. Co.; aqua; 5¾″; sheared top **5.00-10.00**

E.H. Co. Mo Cocktails; same on reverse side; three-sided bottle; 10"; dark olive, $85.00+

Ehrlicher Bros. Pharmacists, Pekin, Ill; clear; 4¼" **4.00-6.00**

E.L. & Co.; under bottom; amber; 7¼" **2.00-3.00**

Electric Brand Laxative; label; 9¾"; amber . . **8.00-10.00**

Elixir Alimentare; on side; *Ducro A. Paris* on opposite side; beveled corners; large square collar; rectangular; 8¼"; light green **3.00-4.00**

Compound Elixir of Phosphates & Calisaya; 8¾"; aqua **6.00-10.00**

Elleman's Royal Embrocation for Horse; aqua; 7½" **8.00-12.00**

Charles Ellis, Son & Co., Philada.; vertical around bottle; round double band; 7"; light green **3.00-4.00**

Ely's Cream Balm; *Ely Bros. New York, Hay Fever Catarrh* on front and sides; sheared lip; rectangular; 2⅝"; amber **2.00-4.00**

same as above except 3¼" **3.00-4.00**

Elys Cream Balm; on front panel; rectangular; amber, 2½" **2.00-4.00**

C.S. Emersons American Hair Restorative, Cleveland, O.; pontil; 6½"; clear or amber **15.00-30.00**

Empire State Drug Co. Laboratories; aqua; 6½", $3.00-5.00

The Empire Med Co., Rochester N.Y.; blob-top; 8¼"; aqua **8.00-10.00**

Empress; written on front; round; flared lip; 3¾"; amber **2.00-3.00**

E.R.S. & S. 3; under bottom; label; amber; 7½" **2.00-4.00**

E.R.S. & S; under bottom; amber; 4½" **2.00-4.00**

Eschering; clear or amethyst; 5¼" **2.00-4.00**

Espey's; clear; 4½" **2.00-4.00**

C. Estanton; *Sing Sing, N.Y.* other side; *Prepared by Block Hunt's;* aqua; pontil; 5" **20.00-40.00**

Eureka Hair Restorative; *P.J. Reilly, San. Fran.;* dome-type bottle; 7"; aqua **8.00-10.00**

Eutimen; clear or amethyst; 5¼" **2.00-4.00**

D. Evans Camomile Pills; pontil; 3¾"; aqua **15.00-25.00**

The Evans Chemical Co.; clear or amethyst; round back; 6¼" **3.00-4.00**

The Evans Chemical Co. Proprietors, Cincinnati, O. U.S.A.; on front with big *G;* oval; 5"; clear **2.00-3.00**

Dr. W. Evans Teething Syrup; flared lip; pontil; 2½"; aqua **10.00-20.00**

Ewbanks Topaz Cinchona Cordial; 9½"; amber, $8.00-10.00

Eye Cup; *S* under bottom; clear or amethyst; 2" **3.00-4.00**

Eye-Se; around shoulder twice; on bottom *Gilmer Texas;* decorated; round; aqua; 9¼" **2.00-4.00**

G. Faccella; on bottom; aqua; 6" **2.00-6.00**

B.A. Fahnestocks; in back *Vermifuge;* pontil; aqua; 4" **6.00-8.00**

Dr. Fahrney's; *Uterine* other side; clear or amethyst; 8½" **2.00-4.00**

Dr. Peter Fahrney; *71* under bottom; clear; 6" **3.00-6.00**

Farbenfabriken of Elberfeld Co., N.Y.C.; label; *90* under bottom; amber; 4¼" **4.00-6.00**

Farr's Gray Hair Restorer, Boston, Mass.; 6 oz.; all on front at a slant; beveled corners; *AMB;* 5⅝"; amber **2.00-4.00**

H.G. Farrells Arabian Liniment; pontil; 4¼"; aqua **8.00-12.00**

Father Johns Medicine; *Lowell Mass.;* ring top; wide mouth; 12"; dark amber **4.00-10.00**

same as above except 8¾" **5.00-10.00**

Febrilene Trade Mark; on front; aqua; 4½"; rectangular **1.00-2.00**

Fellows & Co.; aqua; 7¾" **3.00-4.00**

Fellows & Co. Chemists St. John. N.B.; vertical on front; flask; 8" **3.00-4.00**

same as above except *ABM* **3.00-4.00**

Fellow's Laxative Tablets; 2½"; clear or amber **4.00-6.00**

Fellow's Syrup of Hypophosphits; deep indentation on lower trunk on face of bottle; oval; 7¾"; aqua **4.00-6.00**

Dr. M.M. Fenner, Fredonia, N.Y., St. Vitus Dance Specific; ringed top; 4½"; aqua **10.00-15.00**

Dr. M.M. Fenners Peoples Remedies; vertical on front; *U.S.A. 1872-1898* on side; *Fredonia, N.Y.* on opposite side; graduated collar; rectangular; 6"; amethyst **3.00-6.00**

Ferro China Melaro Tonico; lion embossed on three-sided bottle; tapered top with ring; green . . . . . **25.00+**

Ferrol the Iron Oil Food; one side *Iron & Phosphorus;* other side *Cod Liver Oil;* 9¼"; amber **8.00-10.00**

B.W. Fetters Druggist; *Phila. Pat. Aug. 1, 1876;* beer bottle shape; 8¾"; blue green........**10.00-12.00**

B.F. Fish, San Francisco, Fish Hair Restorative; 7¾"; aqua....................**4.00-10.00**

Dr. S.S. Fitch & Co., 714 Broadway N.Y.; pontil; 3¼"; aqua....................**10.00-20.00**

Dr. S.S. Fitch; on side; *707 Broadway N.Y.* on opposite side; sheared collar; rectangular; beveled corners; pontil; 3¾"; aqua..............**25.00-30.00**

Dr. S.S. Fitch, 701 Broadway N.Y.; pontil; 1¾"; aqua....................**8.00-20.00**

same as above except 6½"..........**16.00-22.00**

same as above except tapered top; oval....................**16.00-22.00**

Dr. S.S. Fitch, 714 Broadway N.Y.; vertical on front; oval; 6½"; aqua..............**25.00-30.00**

Five Drops; on side; *Chicago USA* on opposite side; rectangular; 5½"; aqua............**2.00-4.00**

Flagg's Good Samaritans Immediate Relief, Cincinnati, O.; pontil; five panels; aqua; 3¾"..........**10.00+**

A.H. Flanders M.D., N.Y.; on back; amber; 9"....................**65.00-70.00**

Fletchers Vege-Tonic; on front panel; beveled corner; 2½" square; amber; roof shoulder; under bottom *DOC;* 8½"....................**10.00-15.00**

Flippins; clear; 6½"....................**2.00-4.00**

R.G. Flower Medical Co.; amber; 9", $6.00-10.00

The Flowers Manufacturing Co.; clear; 6¼"..**4.00-6.00**

Foley & Co.; clear or amethyst; 5½"........**2.00-4.00**

Foley & Co., Chicago, Foley's Kidney Pills; 2½"; aqua....................**2.00-4.00**

Foley & Co. Chicago, U.S.A.; sample bottle; *Foley's Kidney Cure;* round; aqua; 4½"........**8.00-10.00**

Foley's Cream; on one side; *Foley & Co. Chicago, U.S.A.* on opposite side; square; 4¼"; clear....................**2.00-4.00**

Foley's Honey and Tar, Foley & Co., Chicago, USA; vertical on front; rectangular; sample size; 4¼"; aqua....................**2.00-4.00**

Foley's Honey & Tar; *Foley's & Co. Chicago;* 5¼"; aqua....................**4.00-8.00**

Foley's Kidney Pills, Foley & Co. Chicago; on front vertically; round; 2½"; clear............**3.00-4.00**

J.A. Folger & Co., Essence of Jamaica Ginger, San Fra.; tapered top; 6¼"; aqua............**8.00-10.00**

J.A. Folger & Co. Essence of Jamaica Ginger, San Francisco; vertical on front in oval slug plate; graduated collar; oval; 6"; aqua........**4.00-6.00**

Dr. Robt. B. Folers, Olosaonian N.Y.; beveled corners; tapered top; 7¼"; aqua............**15.00-25.00**

The Forbes Diastase Co.; *Cincinnati, O.;* 7⅝"; amber....................**10.00-20.00**

same as above except clear..........**8.00-12.00**

B. Fosgates Anodyne; round; flared top; 4½"; aqua....................**4.00-8.00**

same except ringed top; 5"..........**4.00-6.00**

H.D. Fowle, Boston; 5½"; aqua blue........**4.00-8.00**

Dr. Fragas; *Cuban Vermifuge* on two other panels; eight panels; aqua; 3¾"............**4.00-6.00**

Franco American Hygenic Co.; *Perfumer Chicago* other side; clear; 3"....................**2.00-4.00**

Fraser; cobalt; 4½", $4.00-8.00

Fraser & Co.; amber; 5"..................**2.00-4.00**

French Eau De Quinnine Hair Tonic, Atlanta; label; 10½"; clear....................**8.00-10.00**

J.H. Friedenwald & Co.; *Balt. Md., Buchen Gin For All Kidney & Liver Troubles; Friedenwalds Buchen Gin* on other side; 10"; green............**8.00-12.00**

Frog Pond Chill & Fever Tonic; cobalt; 7"..**8.00-12.00**

The Froser Tablet Co.; label; clear; 5¾".....**4.00-6.00**

Fruitola; on side panel; *Pinus Med. Co., Monticello, Ill., U.S.A.* on other side; rectangular; 6½"; aqua....................**2.00-4.00**

F.S. & Co. 229; two under bottom; 4".......**2.00-3.00**

Dr. Furber's Cordial of Mt. Bolm; flat ring top; 7¾"....................**8.00-12.00**

G.F.P. for Women; on side *L. Gerstle & Co.,* other *Chattanooga, Ten.,* amber....................**6.00-9.00**

Galled Armpits & Co.; one side *For Tender Feet;* other side *Turkish Foot Bath;* 7½"; aqua.......**4.00-6.00**

Gargling Oil, Lockport, N.Y.; tapered top; 5½"; green....................**6.00-8.00**

Garrett Drug Co.; *R.W. Garrett Mgr., Will Point, Texas;* 4⅛" and 5¾"; clear....................**1.00-2.00**

D.H. Geer & Son, Boston, Mass., Stump of the World Trademark; 9½"; aqua, 10.00-20.00

Gilbert Bros. & Co.; *Baltimore Md.;* 7¾"; green....................**4.00-6.00**

J.A. Gilka; *9 Schutzen str. 9* on back pour spout; plain bottom; amber; 9½" **60.00-70.00**

J.A. Gilka; two men with club and crown on bottom; black; 9" . . . . **25.00 +**

Girolamo Pagliano; on front and back in large vertical letters; rectangular; beveled corners; 4⅜"; apple green **15.00-25.00**

M.H. Gleeson & Brother; *Apothecaries, Boston,* aqua, oval flask shape, 8½" **10.00-15.00**

Glover H. Clay Co., N.Y.; on the front panel; rectangular; amber; 5" **1.00-2.00**

Glover's; *412* under bottom; amber; 5", $2.00-4.00

Glover's Imperial Mange Medicine; on the front of panel; 6½ fl oz., *H. Clay Glover Co.* on the left side; *N.Y.* on the right side; rectangular; amber; 6¾" **6.00-8.00**

Glover's Imperial Canker Wash., H. Clay Glover D.V.W., New York; vertical on front; rectangular; 5¼"; amber **3.00-6.00**

Glover's Imperial Mange Medicine 6½ Fl. Oz. New York, H. Clay Glover; on front and sides; rectangular; *ABM;* 7"; amber **3.00-4.00**

Glover's Imperial "Mange Remedy," H. Clay Glover D.V.S., New York; on front and sides **3.00-4.00**

Glycerole; on side slot; aqua; applied ring at top; 6¼" **1.00-2.00**

Glycothymoline 1 Lb. Net; amethyst; 8¼"; oval **3.00-5.00**

Glycothymoline 3 Fl. Oz.; around shoulder; amethyst; oval; 4" and 4¾" **2.00-3.00**

Glyco Thymoline; slanted lower right to top left; square; *ABM;* 4½"; clear **2.00-3.00**

S.B. Goff's Oil Liniment, Camden, N.J.; on front and side; rectangular; 5¾"; aqua **3.00-4.00**

S.B. Goff's Cough Syrup, Camden, N.J.; on front and opposite side; rectangular; 5¾"; aqua **3.00-6.00**

J.P. Goldberg, Jackson's Original American Med.; Indian with bow & arrow; pontil; 9" **10.00-15.00**

Golden's Liquid Beef Tonic; circular under bottle; in center of the circle, in round sunken panel, *C.N. Crittenton, Prarr, N.Y.;* champagne type bottle; green; 9½"; ring top **4.00-8.00**

Gombaults J.E., Caustic Balsam; on front panel; *The Lawrence Williams Co., Sole Props For The U.S. and Canada* on the left and right side of panels; aqua; 6½"; rectangular **4.00-8.00**

Goode's Sarsaparilla, W.S.G. Goode; *Practical Pharmacist, Williamsville, Va.* **10.00-20.00**

V.V. Googler; clear; 5" **2.00-4.00**

Goose Grease Liniment, Mfg. G.G.L. Co. of Greensboro, N.C.; ring top; picture of a goose on it; 7¼"; aqua **4.00-8.00**

W.J.M. Gordon Pharmaceutist, Cincinnati, Ohio; on three lines; blob top, 7½"; blue green . . **10.00-15.00**

Gouraud's Oriental Cream; *New York* on one side; *London* on the other; 4¼"; clear **1.00-2.00**

Gra Car Certosa of Pavia; 9½"; aqua **10.00-20.00**

Grace Linen; around shoulder; monogram on bottom; round; 2¼"; aqua **2.00-3.00**

Grahams No. 1 Hair Dye Liquid; 3½" **8.00-12.00**

Grand Union E.T.A. Co., Grand Union Tea Co.; on each side; 5¼"; clear or amber **2.00-6.00**

A.C. Grant, Albany, N.Y., German Magnetic linament; beveled corners; pontil; 5"; aqua **10.00-25.00**

Granular Citrate of Magnesia; kite with letter inside it; ring top; 8"; cobalt **10.00-30.00**

same except 6" **10.00-30.00**

Gray's Celebrated Sparkling Spray & Exquisite Tonic; blob top; clear **4.00-6.00**

Gray's Elixar, Gray Lab; 7¼"; amber **4.00-6.00**

Gray's Syrup of Red Spruce Gum; on opposite sides; sunken panels; rectangular; *ABM;* 5½"; aqua **3.00-4.00**

Dr. T.W. Graydon, Cincinnati, O., Diseases of the Lungs; vertical on front in slug plate; square collar; 5⅞"; light amber **4.00-8.00**

Great English Sweeny; vertical on front in sunken panel; *Specific* on side; *Carey & Co.* on opposite side; rectangular; 6"; aqua **3.00-6.00**

L.M. Green; other side *Woodbury, N.J.;* clear or amethyst; 4¼" **2.00-3.00**

S.L. Green, Druggist; *Camden, Ark., 3 iv* on shoulder; ring top, under bottom, *W.T. & Co., U.S.A.,* amber, 3" **2.00-4.00**

Drs. E.E. & J.A. Greene, N.Y. & Boston; 7½"; aqua **4.00-8.00**

Drs. E.E. & J.A. Greene; aqua; 7½" **4.00-8.00**

Drs. E.E. & J.A. Greene; on side; *New York & Boston* on opposite side; square collar; rectangular; 7½"; aqua **2.00-4.00**

Greever-Lot Speich Mfg. Co.; clear; 6¼" **2.00-3.00**

Dr. Gren's Sarsaparilla; rectangular, aqua, double ring top, 9¼" **14.00-19.00**

Grimault & Co.; clear; 6½" **4.00-6.00**

Groders Botanic Dyspepsia Syrup; *Waterville, ME* on side; *U.S.A.* other side; aqua; 8¾" **6.00-8.00**

Grove's; *Tasteless Chill Tonic, Prepared By Paris Med. Co., St. Louis* on the front panel; clear or amethyst; oval; 5¾" and 5⁵⁄₁₆" **2.00-3.00**

Dr. Grove's; on other side *Philadelphia,* on front *Anodyne for Infants,* ring top, aqua, 5¼" **9.00-12.00**

S. Grover Graham, Dyspepsia Remedy, Newburgh, N.Y. USA; vertical on front; rectangular; 6⅛"; clear **2.00-4.00**

Gun Oil; vertical in sunken panel; rectangular; 4¾"; clear **3.00-4.00**

Gurrlain; other side *Eau Lustrale;* open pontil; 6¼"; raspberry color, $4.00-6.00

H.H. Hackendohl; *Milwaukee, Wis* in 2 lines (Scrip); under bottom, *Pat. June 17-88-S.B.;* ring top, clear, 5½" **8.00-10.00**

Hagan's Magnolia Balm; on front of panel; milk glass or clear; rectangular; 5" **4.00-8.00**

Hagar's Nervina Tonic, The Great Blood Medicine; label; double band collar; 8¾"; light apple green **3.00-6.00**

Hair Balsam; olive green; blob top **4.00-6.00**

Hair Health, Dr. Hays; on opposite sides in sunken panels; rectangular; 6¾"; amber **3.00-4.00**

same as above except *ABM* **2.00-3.00**

Hair Restorative Depots; vertical on front in sunken panel; *Professor Woods* on side; *St. Louis & New York* on opposite side; rectangular; sunken panels; 7"; aqua **20.00-40.00**

Leon Hale; clear or amethyst; 6" **2.00-4.00**

Leon Hale; clear or amethyst; 5", $2.00-3.00

E.W. Hall; aqua; 3½" **2.00-4.00**

R. Hall & Co., Prop. Dr. Barnes, Essence of Jamaica Ginger; 5"; aqua **8.00-12.00**

Hall's Balsam for the Lungs; vertical on front; fancy arch panels; sunken panel; rectangular; 7¼"; aqua **10.00-12.00**

Hall's Balsam For the Lungs; on the front panel; *John F. Henry & Co.* on side; *New York* on opposite; rectangular; aqua; 7¾" and 6⅝" **10.00-12.00**

Hall's Catarrah Medicine; vertical; round; *ABM;* 4½"; clear **2.00-3.00**

Hall's Hair Renewer, Nashua, N.H.; label; *S&D 112* under bottom; 7¼"; aqua **8.00-12.00**

Hall's; on one side; *Hair Renewer* on opposite side of panel; this bottle is prettier than Ayer's Hair Vigor; rectangular; peacock blue; 6½" **10.00-30.00**

Hall's Sarsaparilla; vertical on sunken arch panel; *J.R. Gates & Co.* on side; *Proprietors, S.F.* on opposite side; rectangular; 9¼"; aqua **15.00-25.00**

Halsey Bros. Co., Chicago; 6¾"; amber, $4.00-6.00

Hamilton's Old English Black Oil; vertical on three panels; eight vertical panels; 6¾"; aqua . .**3.00-4.00**

Hamlin's Wizard Oil, Chicago, USA; aqua; 5¾"; rectangular **1.00-3.00**

Hamlin's Wizard Oil, Chicago, Ill. USA; on front and sides; rectangular; sunken panels; 6¼"; aqua **2.00-3.00**

same as above except 8" **2.00-3.00**

Hampton's; amber; 6½" **8.00-10.00**

Hance Brothers & White; *Phila. U.S.A.* in back; amber; 7" **2.00-4.00**

Hancock Liquid Sulphur Co.; *Baltimore Md.* on side; clear **3.00-4.00**

Hand Med. Co. Philadelphia; on front; oval; 5⅛"; aqua **2.00-3.00**

Hansee European Cough Syrup, R.H. Hansee Pro, Monticello, N.Y.; vertical on front in sunken panel; rectangular; 5¾"; amethyst **2.00-6.00**

Harlene for the Hair; in 4 lines, ring top, on one side sample, same on other, aqua, 3" **9.00-12.00**

Harper Headache Remedy, Wash., D.C.; 5"; clear **4.00-8.00**

Dr. Harrisons Chalybeste Tonic; 7¾"; teal blue **10.00-20.00**

Dr. Harter's Iron Tonic; label; amber; 9" **8.00-15.00**

Dr. Harter's Iron Tonic; 9¼"; amber **10.00-12.00**

Dr. Harter's Lung Balm; on front; clear **4.00-8.00**

E. Hartshorn & Sons, Established 1850, Boston; vertical lettering on slug plate; rare flask shape; aqua **2.00-6.00**

Hartshorn & Sons Established 1850, Boston; on center front; rectangular; 6¼"; clear **4.00-6.00**

same as above except 4⅞" **4.00-6.00**

Dr. Hastings Naphtha Syrup; on front; *London* **other side; aqua; pontil; 6½", $10.00-25.00**

Haviland & Co. New York, Charleston & Augusta; pontil; tapered top; 5¾"; aqua **10.00-30.00**

L.F.H.H. Hay Sole Agent; on shoulder; *L.F. Atwood* on base; 6½"; aqua **2.00-4.00**

R. Hayden's; *H.V.C.* on other side; light blue; 4½" **4.00-6.00**

Dr. Hayden's; *Viburnum* on back; aqua; 7" . . .**2.00-4.00**

Dr. Hayes; three stars on bottom; clear **2.00-4.00**

Dr. Hayne's Arabian Balsam, E. Morgan & Sons, Providence, R.I.; on four consecutive panels; twelve panels; band collar; 4¼"; aqua **2.00-4.00**

Dr. Hay's; amber; 6" **2.00-6.00**

Hay's; on side; *Hair Health* on opposite side; label on back *adopted April 1, 1912;* ABM; 7½"; amber **6.00-8.00**

Caswell Hazard & Co.; 7½"; 2¾" x 2¾" square; cobalt **6.00-8.00**

Caswell Hazard & Co; in 3 lines near top; in center in a circle *Omnia Labor Vincit;* under this in 4 lines *Chemists, New York & Newport;* 3¾"; square; beveled corner; short neck; 7½"; cobalt **6.00-8.00**

Health Nurser; 6⅓"; clear or amber **10.00-20.00**

Health Specialist Sproule; clear; 8¼″ **4.00-6.00**

Healy & Bigelow's Indian Oil; 5¼″ tall; 1¼″ round;
aqua **4.00-6.00**

Healy & Bigelow; reverse side *Indian Sagwa;* 8¾″;
aqua **6.00-8.00**

Heceman & Co.; on front of panel; on one side
Chemists; other side *New York;* 3″ x 2″ body; 6½″
neck; 3¾″; aqua **4.00-8.00**

Heceman & Co.; vertical in large letters on front;
Chemists on side; *New York* on opposite side; rectangular; 10½″; aqua **2.00-4.00**

G.M. Heidt & Co.; aqua; 9½″ **6.00-8.00**

H.T. Helmbold; *Philadelphia* on side; *Genuine Fluid Ex-*
tracts on front; side mold;
aqua; 7¼″ **8.00-10.00**

H.T. Helmbold's Genuine Preparation; pontil; aqua;
6½″ **20.00-40.00**

H.T. Helmbold; *Philadelphia* other side; *Genuine Fluid*
Extracts front side; side mold; aqua;
6½″ **8.00-10.00**

Hemoglobine Deschiens; 7¾″; cobalt **10.00-15.00**

Henry's Calcined Magnesia, Manchester;
pontil; 4¼″ **10.00-15.00**

Henry's Calcined Magnesia, Manchester; vertical on all
four sides; rolled lip; 4¼″; clear **6.00-8.00**

Henry's Three Chlorides; amber; 7¼″,
$4.00-6.00

The Herb Med. Co., Springfield, O.; reverse side
Lightning Hot Drops No Relief No Pay; 5″;
aqua **4.00-8.00**

Herb Med Co., Weston, W.Va.; 9½″; aqua . . **8.00-10.00**

Herbine; *St. Louis* on the left side; *Herbine Co.* on the
right side; rectangular; 6¾″; clear **1.00-3.00**

Herrings Medicine Co., Atlanta, Ga; label;
clear; 7¾″, $2.00-4.00

H. 82; under bottom; 7¼″; green **2.00-4.00**

H; on bottom; amber; 4″ **1.00-2.00**

E.H. Co.; aqua; 3½″ **4.00-6.00**

H.H.H. Medicine; *The Celebrated* one side; *D.D.T. 1869*
other side; aqua **4.00-10.00**

Hiawatha Hair Restorative, Hoyt; long neck; 6¾″; light
green **10.00-20.00**

Hicks & Johnson; *C.L.C. Co-2* under bottom; clear;
6½″ **3.00-5.00**

**Hicks' Capudine; three different sizes;
amber, $2.00-8.00**

Hicks' Capudine; amber; 5¾″ **3.00-5.00**

Hicks' Capudine Cures All Headaches & Cold Etc.;
5¾″; amber **6.00-10.00**

Dr. H.H. Higgins Sarsaparilla; *Romney Va.;* pontil; 10″;
aqua **20.00-40.00**

Dr. H.R. Higgins; in back *Romney Va.;* on one side, *Sar-*
saparilla; other side *Pure Extract;* pontil; tapered top;
10″; aqua **30.00-45.00**

Hill's; vertical on front; *Hair Dye No. 1* on back; square;
oval sides; 3¼″; aqua **2.00-3.00**

Hillside Chem. Co.; on bottom; amber; 7½″ . . **2.00-6.00**

Himalya; ring top; 7½″; amber **3.00-6.00**

**Hinds Honey and Almond Cream, A.S. Hinds Co.,
Portland, Maine USA, Improves The Complexion,
Alcohol;** *7%* on front and sides; rectangular; 2⅞″;
clear **3.00-4.00**

A.S. Hinds; *Portland, Me* other side;
clear; 5½″ **2.00-4.00**

Hobo Med. Co.; *Beaumont, Texas Registered*
Trademark; *HB* on the front panel in a diamond;
8⅛″; rectangular; clear; screw top **2.00-5.00**

Hoffman's Anodyne; label; rectangular; square collar;
5″; clear **2.00-3.00**

Hoff's German Liniment; *Goodrich & Jennings, Anoka,*
Minn. vertical on three panels; twelve vertical panels;
ring collar; 5¾″; aqua **4.00-6.00**

Hoff's Liniment; *Goodrich Drug Co., Anoka, Minn.* vertical on 3 panels; 12 vertical panels; ring collar;
ABM; 7″; aqua blue **3.00-6.00**

Hoffman's; in center in large letters, *Great Find Trade*
Make in 3 lines on front, one ring in neck, ring top,
aqua, 6¼″ **7.00-10.00**

Dr. J.J. Hogan; *next to post office, Vallejo, Cal* in circle;
W.T. & Co. U.S.A. under bottom; ringed top; 7¼″;
cobalt blue . . . . **20.00 +**

Holland; aqua; 3½″ **15.00-30.00**

Holland Drug Co.; *Prescriptions A Specialty, Holland, TX*
on the front; on the bottom *USP;* rectangular; 4¾″;
amethyst **1.00-2.00**

Hollis Balm of America; cylindrical; square collar; 5″;
aqua **6.00-8.00**

**Holman's Natures Grand Restorative J.B. Holman,
Prop.;** *Boston, Mass.* pontil, olive
green **225.00-275.00**

Holtons Electric Oil; on bottle vertically; round; 3¼″;
amethyst **2.00-4.00**

Holton's Electric Oil; vertical on bottle; cylindrical;
square collar; 3¼″; clear **3.00-6.00**

**The Honduras Co's Compound Extract Sarsaparilla,
1876;** 10½″; aqua **15.00-30.00**

Honduras Mountain Tonic Co.; fancy writing in sunken panel; double band collar; 9″; aqua....**10.00-20.00**

Hone Deure; on one panel; *Colours* on back panel; six panels; flared top; 2¾″; clear; t.p. pontils; small bottles **6.00-12.00**

Hoods Sarsaparilla; aqua; 8¾″...........**4.00-6.00**

Hood's; machine made; 8½″; clear.........**2.00-4.00**

Hood's Tooth Powder; clear; *C.I. Hood & Co., Lowell, Mass;* 3½″........................**6.00-8.00**

W.H. Hooker (sic) & Co. Proprietors, New York, U.S.A.; vertical on front in sunken panel; *For the Throat and Lungs* on side; *Acker's English Remedy* on opposite side; 5¾″; cobalt blue.....**10.00-15.00**

same as above except **N.&S. Americars;** 6½″........................**8.00-12.00**

same except round; and **Acker's Baby Soother;** aqua........................**6.00-8.00**

W.H. Hooper & Co.; *Proprietors New York, U.S.A.* in 3 lines in sunken panel; on one side in sunken panel *Acker's English Remedy;* on other *For the Throat & Lungs;* 5¾″ tall; 1½″ neck; ring top; cobalt........................**6.00-10.00**

G.W. House Clemens Indian Tonic; ring top; 5″; aqua........................**40.00-80.00**

The Howard Drugs & Medicine Co.; *Prepared By, Baltimore, Md., Frixie Hair Oil* in sunken panel on front in script, 6 lines; 2¼″ x 1″ x 4″; clear or amethyst........................**2.00-4.00**

same size as above except *Rubifoam For the Teeth, Put Up By E.W. Hoyth & Co., Lowell Mass* in 6 lines, not in sunken panel........................**2.00-4.00**

Hughel's Dander-Off Hair Tonic Dandruff Remedy; all on front side; square bottle; 6¼″; clear...**4.00-8.00**

Humphrey's; *Humphrey's Homeophathic* on back; clear; 3½″........................**2.00-4.00**

Humphrey's Marvel of Healing; clear or amethyst; 5½″........................**2.00-4.00**

Humphrey's Marvel Witchhazel; machine made; clear; 5½″........................**2.00-4.00**

R.H. Hurd Prop.; *No. Berwick, Me. U.S.A. Backer's Specific;* 4½″; clear................**8.00-15.00**

Hurley; clear or amethyst; 5″.............**2.00-3.00**

Husband's Calcined Magnesia, Phila.; vertical on all four sides; square; sheared collar; 4¼″; aqua........................**2.00-6.00**

Husband's Calcined Magnesia, Phila; square; sheared lip; 4½″; clear or amber................**4.00-6.00**

I.G.Co.; under bottom; 7″; aqua...........**8.00-10.00**

Imperial Hair/Trade Mark; shield with crown in center; *Regenerator* vertical on front; *Imperial Chemical Manufacturing Co.* on side; *New York* on opposite side; rectangular; beveled corners; square collar; 4½″; light green......................**6.00-10.00**

India Cholagogue; vertical on front; *Norwich, Conn. U.S.A.* on side; *Osgood's* on opposite side; rectangular; beveled corners; machine made; 5½″; aqua........................**2.00-4.00**

same as above except *New York* embossed on side; not machine made; 5⅜″; aqua.........**3.00-6.00**

Dr. H.A. Ingham's Vegetable Pain Extract; 4½″; aqua........................**4.00-6.00**

Iodine; machine made; 2¼″; amber.......**2.00-4.00**

I.R.; label; fancy bottle; graphite pontil; 6½″; aqua........................**10.00-20.00**

Ischirogeno O Battista Farmacia Inglese Del Cervo— Napoli; 7″; amber..................**10.00-15.00**

J & J; under bottom; sheared top; cobalt; 2½″........................**2.00-4.00**

Jackson Mfg. Co., Columbus, O.; ring top; 6¼″ clear........................**4.00-6.00**

Jacob's Pharmacy; other side *Atlanta, Ga., Compound Extract Pine Splinters;* 7½″; clear........**2.00-4.00**

Jacob's Pharmacy; *W.T. & Co. C. U.S.A.* under bottom; amber; 6″, **$6.00-10.00**

St. Jacob's Oel, The Charles A. Vogeler Company, Baltimore, MD. U.S.A.; vertical around bottle; cylindrical; 6⅝″; aqua.....................**3.00-6.00**

same as above except amethyst........**3.00-6.00**

Jad Salts, Whitehall Pharmacy Co., N.Y.; label; screw cap; 5¾″; clear, **$2.00-4.00**

Jamaica Ginger; label; clear; 5¾″..........**2.00-4.00**

Jamaica Ginger Fruit Cordial, Manufactured By C.C. Hines & Co.; Boston, Mass.; on two sides; square; 6½″; clear........................**4.00-8.00**

Jaques; aqua; 4½″......................**3.00-4.00**

Dr. D. Jaynes Tonic Vermifuge, 242 Chest St., Phila; on front; aqua; 5½″; rectangular.........**2.00-3.00**

Dr. D. Jaynes Expectorant; on front panel; on back *Philada* on each side three panels; short neck; 6¾″ aqua; pontil......................**10.00-25.00**

Dr. D. Jaynes Expectorant; vertical on front in sunken panel; *Twenty Five Cents* on side; *Quarter Size* on opposite side; rectangular; square collar; 5¼″; aqua........................**2.00-4.00**

Dr. D. Jaynes; *Half Dollar* on one side; *Half Size* on other side........................**2.00-8.00**

Dr. D. Jaynes; pontil; aqua; 7″..........**10.00-20.00**

Jaynes & Co., Boston; screwtop; 9½″; amber........................**4.00-8.00**

T.E. Jenkins & Co., Chemists, Louisville, KY.; graphite pontil; 7″; aqua..................**10.00-20.00**

Johnson's American Anodyne Liniment; around bottle; aqua; 4½″ or 6½″..................**4.00-6.00**

Johnson's American Anodyne Liniment; vertical; round; 4¼″; aqua..................**2.00-4.00**

same as above except 6½″.............**2.00-4.00**

Johnson's Chill and Fever Tonic; clear; 5¾″........................**2.00-4.00**

Johnson & Johnson Oil; label; *C1637* under bottom; aqua; 5″........................**2.00-4.00**

S.C. Johnson & Son, Racine, Wis.; under bottom; clear; 3″ **2.00-4.00**

Dr. E.S. Johnson Blood Syrup, Farmington, ME; vertical on front in oval slug plate; large square collar; oval; 9⅝″; aqua **6.00-8.00**

Dr. Johnson's Horse Remedies Prepared by New York Veterinary Hospital; vertical on front in slug plate; oval; flared collar; 6¾″; aqua **4.00-8.00**

Dr. Jones' Australian Oil; *Not To Be Taken* on each side; amber; 5″ **8.00-10.00**

Dr. Jones' Liniment; aqua; 6¾″ **2.00-4.00**

J.P.L.; under bottom; 7½″; aqua **4.00-8.00**

L.E. Jung; machine made; amber; 11″ **4.00-8.00**

Junket Colors; with monogram on one side; *Little Falls, N.Y. Chas. Hansen's Laboratory;* square; 3½″; aqua **2.00-4.00**

Kalium; 5½″; clear, $8.00-10.00

Kalo Compound for Dyspepsia, Brown Mfg. Co., Greenville, Tenn; (N's in TENN. are backwards) all on front in oval end of sunken panel; rectangular; square collar; 9½″; amethyst **10.00-20.00**

Ka:Ton:Ka, the Great Indian Remedy; on opposite sides; rectangular; graduated collar; 8¾″; aqua **10.00-20.00**

Keasbey & Mattison Co.; aqua or amber; 3¼″ **2.00-6.00**

Keasbey & Mattison Co.; light blue; 3½″ **2.00-4.00**

Keasbey & Mattison Co. Chemists, Ambler, Pa.; on front; light blue; 5″; rectangular **2.00-3.00**

Keasbey & Mattison Co, Ambler, Pa.; on front; smoky blue; round; 5¾″ **2.00-4.00**

Keasbey & Mattison, Philadelphia; around shoulder; cylindrical; ring collar; 6″; cobalt blue **4.00-10.00**

The Keeley Remedy Neurotene; *Discovered by Dr. L.E. Keeley Dwight;* 5⅝″; clear **8.00-15.00**

Dr. Kellings Pure Herb Med.; pontil; 6½″; green **10.00-25.00**

J.W. Kelly & Co.; *C* in a triangle on bottom; clear or amethyst; 6″ **4.00-6.00**

Kemp's; *O.F. Woodward* on side; *Leroy, N.Y.* on other side; light blue; 5½″ **2.00-4.00**

Kemp's Balsam; vertical on front; sample size; heavy glass; unusual flask shape; band collar; 2⅞″; aqua **2.00-5.00**

Kemp's Balsam for Throat and Lungs, Leroy, N.Y., O.G. Woodward; front and sides; rectangular; square band collar; 5¾″; aqua **2.00-4.00**

Kendall's Spavin Treatment; on shoulder; *Enosbury Falls, Vt.* on base; amber; 5½″; twelve panels **3.00-5.00**

Dr. Kendall's Quick Relief; vertical on front in sunken panel; rectangular; double band collar; 5″; aqua **2.00-4.00**

Dr. Kennedy's; aqua; 9″; side mold **2.00-6.00**

Dr. Kennedy's Favorite Remedy, Kingston, N.Y. U.S.A.; vertical on front in sunken panel; 7″; clear **2.00-4.00**

Dr. D. Kennedy's; on side; *Favorite Remedy* on front; *Kingston, N.Y. U.S.A.* on opposite side in sunken panels; graduated collar; rectangular; 8¾″; amethyst **2.00-4.00**

same as above except aqua **2.00-4.00**

Dr. Kennedy's Liniment, Rheumatic Liniment, Roxbury, Mass; 6¼″; aqua **8.00-10.00**

Dr. Kenney's; on other side; aqua; 9″ **4.00-8.00**

Keystone Drug Co.; *So. Boston Va.;* tapered; 9″; clear or amber **4.00-10.00**

Mrs. E. Kidder Cordial; marked vertically *Mrs. E. Kidder Dysentery Cordial, Boston;* round; open pontil; 8″; aqua **10.00-15.00**

Kidney Bottle Pills; label; kidney shape; ring top; 5½″; clear **15.00-25.00**

E.J. Kieffer & Co.; round back; clear or amethyst; 6½″ **2.00-6.00**

E.J. Kieffer's; amber; 6½″ **4.00-6.00**

Killinger; on front; aqua; 7⅞″; square **3.00-4.00**

Dr. Kilmer's; *Swamp Root Kidney Liver and Bladder Remedy, Binghampton, N.Y., U.S.A.* on front; aqua; 7″; rectangular **2.00-4.00**

Dr. Kilmer's; aqua; 7″ **4.00-6.00**

Dr. Kilmer's; *Swamp-Root, Kidney & Bladder Remedy* on front; *Binghampton, N.Y.* on left; aqua; rectangular; 8″ **3.00-5.00**

Dr. Kilmer's; *Swamp-Root, Kidney Remedy, Binghampton, N.Y.;* sample bottle; aqua; round; 4¼″ **5.00-8.00**

Dr. Kilmer's U & O Anointment, Binghampton, N.Y.; on front; round; 1¾″; aqua **2.00-4.00**

Dr. Kilmer's; clear, machine made; 7¼″, $2.00-4.00

Kina; *Laroche* on back; aqua; 7¾″ **2.00-4.00**

Dr. Kings New Discovery; on front; *Chicago, Ill* on side; *H.E. Bucklem & Co.* on right side; rectangular; 4½″; aqua **2.00-4.00**

Dr. Kings New Discovery for Coughs and Colds; on front panel; clear; rectangular; 6¾″ **3.00-4.00**

Dr. Kings New Life Pills; on front; clear; square; 2½ **2.00-3.00**

Kinney & Co.; clear or amethyst; 3″ **4.00-6.00**

S.B. Kitchel's Liniment; aqua; 8¼″ **4.00-8.00**

Klinker's Hair Tonic, Cleveland; vertical on front in fancy panel; ring collar; ring on neck; three ribs on side; base crown shape; fancy shape; 6″; clear **4.00-8.00**

Knapps; aqua; 4″ **2.00-4.00**

Kobole Tonic Med. Co., Chicago, Ill; 8½″; milk
glass. **15.00-35.00**

same as above except amber or aqua . . **10.00-20.00**

Dr. Koch's Remedies, Extracts & Spices; on one side
Dr. Koch Vegetable Tea Co., other *Winona, Minn.;*
9″; clear. **3.00-4.00**

Kodel Nerve Tonic, Free Sample; under bottom *E.C.
Dewich & Co., Chicago;* wide ring top; 3¼″;
aqua. **2.00-4.00**

Knapps; aqua; 4″ **2.00-4.00**

Kobole Tonic Med. Co. Chicago Ill; 8½″; milk
glass. **15.00-35.00**

same as above except amber or aqua . . **10.00-20.00**

Dr. Koch's Remedies, Extracts & Spices; on one side
Dr. Koch Vegetable Tea Co.; other *Winona, Minn.;*
9″; clear. **3.00-4.00**

Kodel Nerve Tonic, Free Sample; under bottom *E. C.
Dewich & Co. Chicago;* wide ring top; 3¼″;
aqua. **2.00-4.00**

Koken, St. Louis, U.S.A., 10 Fl. Oz.; on front; 7″; clear;
round **1.00-2.00**

Koko For the Hair; clear; 4¾″ **2.00-6.00**

Kola-Cardinette; on each side; *The Palisade Mfg. Co.,
Yonkers, N.Y.* under bottom; amber; 9″ . . **6.00-10.00**

Koning Tilly; in vertical line; sheared top; round; ¾″;
aqua **4.00-6.00**

Konjola Mosby Med. Co., Cincinnati, U.S.A.; on front;
Konjola on left and right panels; clear; 8¼″; rectangular; screw top. **1.00-2.00**

Dr. Wm Korong Hair Coloring Mfg. Chemist; *Louisville,
KY.* with *teaspoon* on each side, *3ii* on shoulder,
Simplex in scrip, clear, double ring
top, 4½″ **9.00-12.00**

The Krebs-Oliver Co.; amber; 5¾″,
$2.00-6.00

Kuhlman's Knoxville Tenn.; *W.&T. Co. U.S.A.* under
bottom; 4½″; clear. **3.00-4.00**

Kutnow's Powder; vertical on front in large letters; rectangular; large square collar; corner panels; 4¾″;
aqua **2.00-4.00**

LA America; clear or amethyst; 5½″ **3.00-6.00**

L.B.Co.; 11½″; clear. **4.00-6.00**

Lacto-Marrow Co.; other side *N.Y. U.S.A.;* clear or
amethyst; 9¼″; side mold. **3.00-6.00**

Lactopeptine, New York; clear or
amethyst; 4″ **4.00-6.00**

Lactopeptine For the Digestive Ailments; around cross;
dark green; 3″; sheared top. **4.00-8.00**

LA-CU-PIA; under bottom; aqua; four-part
mold; 8¼″ **2.00-6.00**

Laine Chem Co.; amber; 5½″ **2.00-4.00**

Laine Chem Co.; amber; 4″ **2.00-6.00**

Laine Chem Co.; amber; *341* under
bottom; 6½″ **2.00-6.00**

Geo. L. Laird & Co.; in horseshoe shape; *Oleo-Chyle* in
vertical line; cathedral type bottle; ring top; 6¾″;
blue **25.00-50.00**

Lake Shore Seed Co., Dunkirk, N.Y.; vertical on front in
large sunken panels; rectangular; ring on neck; 5½″;
aqua **2.00-4.00**

Langley & Michaels, San Francisco; vertical on front in
round sunken panel; round graduated collar; 6¾″;
aqua **4.00-8.00**

Lanman & Kemp; one side; other side *N.Y.;*
aqua; 6″ **3.00-4.00**

Lanman & Kemp; aqua; *Cod Liver Oil*
one side; other side *N.Y.;* 10½″,
$6.00-8.00

Lanman & Kemp; aqua; 8½″ **2.00-6.00**

Larkin Co., Buffalo; 6″; clear. **2.00-4.00**

Larkin Co.; clear or amethyst; **2.00-4.00**

**Larkin Soap Co., Modjeska Dermabalm, Modjest
Derma-Balm;** on three sides; square; flared lip;
4¾″; clear. **4.00-6.00**

**Laughlius & Bushfielo Worm Power, Wheeling, Va.
1850;** pontil; 3¼″; aqua. **10.00-20.00**

A.J. Laxol, White, New York; in two indented panels on
front; oval back; triangular; round band collar; 7″;
cobalt blue. **5.00-10.00**

Laxol; 2½″ neck; 7″; triangular; cobalt blue . . **6.00-10.00**

L-C 1903; on bottom; blue; sheared top; 4″ . . . **3.00-6.00**

John P. Lee; clear; 4½″ **2.00-4.00**

Legrande's Arabian Catarrh Remedy, N.Y.; on front;
flask type bottle; 9½″; aqua. **6.00-10.00**

Lehn & Fink, New York; on bottom; amber; seven-part
mold; 7¼″ **4.00-6.00**

Dr. H.C. Lemke's; on other side; aqua; 10″ . . **7.00-15.00**

Lemon Elixir; under bottom; paper label reads *Dr. H.
Moyey's Lemon Elixir Herb Compound, Atlanta, Ga.;*
7¼″; aqua. **4.00-8.00**

Leonardi's; on one side, other *New York, N.Y.* front
Golden Eye Lotion, relieves without pain all in
sunken panels, aqua, 4½″ **9.00-12.00**

same except *Tampa, Fla*. **9.00-12.00**

same except *A.B.M.*. **5.00-8.00**

S.B. Leonardi & Co; amber; 8¼″ **8.00-12.00**

Jarabe De Leonardi; *5* under bottom;
aqua; 5½″ **2.00-4.00**

Leonardi's Blood Elixir; *The Great Blood Purifier, Tampa, Fla.* all in 4 lines, beveled corners, ring top,
amber, 8¼″ **14.00-19.00**

same except *New York and Tampa, Fla*. **14.00-19.00**

Leonardi & Co.; *Pharmacists, Jackson Black, Tampa, Fla.* all in 3 lines, oval, thin tapered top, clear, 4¾″ x 6¾″ **9.00-12.00**

Leonardi, Jarabe; *De Para Latos Creasotado, Leonardi's Cough syrup creosated, New Rochelle, N.Y.* all in 4 lines, ring top, clear and aqua, 5¼″ **5.00-7.00**

same except *New York And Tampa, Fla* . . .**5.00-7.00**

Leonardi's Worm Syrup; *The Great Worm Killer, S.B. Leonardi & Co. N.Y. & Tampa, Fla* in 4 lines square ring top, aqua, 5 1/16″ **5.00-8.00**

same except *Prepared only by S.B.L. & Co. & New York,* aqua, 4¼″ **5.00-7.00**

W.F. Levera; on side, *Cedar Rapids, Iowa* on opposite side, amber, 5½″ **2.00-6.00**

Lewis & Co.; 7½″; amber **2.00-4.00**

J.A. Limcricks Great Master of Pain, Rodney, Mass.; pontil; tapered top; 6¼″; aqua **15.00-30.00**

Dr. Lindsey's Blood Searcher, Dr. J.M. Lindsey, Greensburg, Pa. 1850; *sold (by) agent Robert Emory Sellers & Co., Pittsburg, 1880;* 8½″; clear **12.00-24.00**

Dr. Linicks Malz Extract; vertical on front; ring collar; square; shaped like pickle jar; 6″; clear . . .**3.00-8.00**

Linim; 5¾″; clear **8.00-10.00**

Liniment or Oil of Life 16 Oz.; on front in sunken arch panel; *C.C. Taylor* on side; *Fairport, N.Y.* on opposite side; rectangular; graduated collar; 10½″; clear **4.00-8.00**

same as above except 5⅞″ **4.00-8.00**

Lippman's Liver Pills; aqua; 2¼″ **2.00-4.00**

Liquid Franconia, Leroy, N.Y.; *O.F. Woodward* on front and sides; rectangular; 4¼″; amethyst **2.00-4.00**

Liquid Peptonoids, Arlington Chemical Co., Yonkers, N.Y.; sunken in arched panel; square; 7⅝″; amber **2.00-4.00**

Liquid Opdeldoc; cylindrical; two-piece mold; square band collar; 4½″; aqua **8.00-12.00**

Liquozone; 8″ tall; 3″ diameter; amber **2.00-4.00**

Liquid Veneer; under bottom; 6¼″; clear or amber **2.00-6.00**

Listerine; near shoulder; at bottom *Lambert Pharmacal Co.* in 2 lines three sizes; clear or amethyst **2.00-4.00**

same except machine made **2.00-3.00**

Little Giant Sure Death To All Kinds of Bugs; *Every bottle warranted, Little Giant Co., Newburgport, Mass;* 8½″; aqua, $8.00-10.00

Live & Let Live Cut Rate Drug Co.; *Chattanooga, Tenn.;* 3½″; clear **4.00-6.00**

L.L.L.; in front; ring top; 7¾″; aqua **4.00-8.00**

Log Cabin Extract; label; *Rochester, N.Y. Pat'd Sep. 6 1889;* 6¼″; amber **40.00-50.00**

London; pontil; light green; 5½″ **8.00-12.00**

L.O.R. Co.; around an eye; tapered top; 4¾″; cobalt **15.00-30.00**

Lord's Opdeldoc; with embossed man breaking and tossing away his crutches, on front in arched panel; oval; square collar; 5″; aqua **8.00-12.00**

Lorentz Med. Co.; amber; 4″ **4.00-6.00**

Don Lorenzo; same on reverse side; 10″; dark olive, $10.00-20.00

J.M. Lotridge; *W.T.Co.* under bottom; clear; 6¼″ **2.00-4.00**

The Louis Daudelin Co.; clear; 8¾″ **2.00-4.00**

Louit Freres & Co. Bor Deaux; on front, mustard barrel, 3 rings at base and shoulder, crude ring collar, amethyst, graphite pontil, 4¾″ **11.00-15.00**

Lufkin Eczema Remedy; label; clear; 7″, $4.00-6.00

Lundborg, N.Y.; 8⅝″; teal blue **3.00-6.00**

Luyties; 7″; amber **4.00-8.00**

Lyman Astley-Cheyenne, Wyo.; in a circular panel; 7″; aqua **8.00-15.00**

Dr. J.B. Lynar & Son; *Logansport, Ind.; J.B.L.* in seal on shoulder; 6″; clear **3.00-6.00**

Dr. J.B. Lynas & Son; clear or amethyst; 6″ . .**3.00-6.00**

Lyon's; pontil; aqua; 6¼″ **8.00-12.00**

Lyon's; aqua; 6¼″ **3.00-6.00**

Lyon's Laxative Syrup, Lyon Med. Co.; reverse *Louisville, Ky.;* 6¼″; clear **2.00-4.00**

Lyon's For the Hair, Kat Hairon, New York; on front, back and sides; sunken panels; rectangular; pontil; 6⅛″; aqua **25.00-35.00**

Lyon Mfg' Co.; *Mexican Mustang Liniment* on back; aqua; 7¾″ **8.00-10.00**

Lyon Mfg' Co.; same as above except 7½″ . . .**4.00-6.00**

Lyric 3 — Y; under bottom; machine made; clear or amethyst; 4½″ **1.00-2.00**

Lysol; amber; 3½″ **2.00-4.00**

J.J. Mack & Co., San Francisco, Dr. A.E. Flints Heart Remedy; 7½″; amber **8.00-12.00**

Mack Drug Co., Prop's N.Y., Dr. Flints Remedy; flat ring top; 7½″; amber **8.00-12.00**

Macon Medicine Co.; *Guinns Pioneer Blood Renever* on other side, amber, 11″ **9.00-13.00**

Madame M. Yale Fruitcura Womans Tonic; reverse side *Chicago & N.Y.;* 9″; aqua **6.00-8.00**

Maggi #2; rectangular; tapered neck; 6″ amber **4.00-8.00**

Magnesie Calcinee; 8″; clear glass painted brown **10.00-20.00**

J.J. Maher & Co. Proprietors, Augusta, Maine; 8½″; amber **4.00-6.00**

P.H. Mallen Co. Chicago; under bottom *W.T.Co. U.S.A.;* 9″; amber **4.00-6.00**

The Maltine Mfg. Co.; *#3* under bottom; 7½″; amber **8.00-10.00**

The Maltine Mfg. Co. Chemists, New York; in 5 lines on front; various numbers under bottom; amber or brown; 6½″; short neck **4.00-6.00**

Malydor Mfg. Co., Lancaster, O. U.S.A.; on front; large beveled corners; one corner is sunken; 5″; amethyst **3.00-6.00**

Mansfield Medicine, Co. N.Y.; and *Memphis* on front; *Proprietors S. Mansfield* on each side; tapered top; 5½″; aqua **8.00-10.00**

S. Mansfield & Co.; reverse side *Memphis;* 5¾″; aqua **6.00-8.00**

Chas. Marchand; amber; 4″ **2.00-4.00**

Chas. Marchand; 8½″; clear or amethyst **3.00-6.00**

Marchand's; amber; 5½″ **2.00-4.00**

J.B. Marchisi M.D.; aqua; 7½″, $4.00-6.00

Marine Hospital Service 1798 U.S. 1871; around a crossed anchor and staff; near base *1000 c.c.;* ringed top; 9¼″; clear **15.00-20.00**

Marine Hospital Service; aqua; 5½″ and other sizes **10.00-20.00**

Marshall's; aqua; 4¾″ **2.00-5.00**

Dr. Marshall's Catarrh Snuff; on opposite sides in large letters; rectangular; round band collar; 3⅜″; aqua **4.00-6.00**

Wm. J. Matheson & Co. Ltd; sheared top; 3½″; clear **2.00-6.00**

Mathis Quarter Dollar Family Liniment; aqua; 4¼″ **2.00-4.00**

C.B. Mathis; aqua; 4″ **4.00-6.00**

Mathis Quarter Dollar Family Liniment, B. Mathis, Toms River, N.J.; in 7 lines on front; oval; aqua; 4″ **2.00-6.00**

Mazon Parfum; vertical on front; square; 4″; aqua **2.00-4.00**

J.O. McCann; clear; 2¾″ **2.00-4.00**

McCannon & Co., Winona, Minn. vertical on front in sunken panel; rectangular; double band collar; 7⅛″; aqua **2.00-4.00**

McCombie's Compound Restorative; pontil **20.00-25.00**

McCormick & Co.; clear; 3¾″ **2.00-4.00**

Drs. McDonald & Levy; *Sacramento City, Calif;* 4¾″; aqua **5.00-10.00**

McElrees Wine of Cardui; on side; *Chattanooga Medicine Co.* on opposite side; sunken oval panels; graduated collar; 8½″; clear **4.00-6.00**

McFadden The Druggist, Senatobia, Miss.; 5¾″; clear or amber, $2.00-6.00

McKesson & Robbins; amber; 3″ **2.00-4.00**

McKesson & Robbins; in 2 lines; amber; 2¼″ square; 1⅞″ wide **2.00-4.00**

Doctor McLane's, American Worm Specific; round; pontil; 4″ **8.00-15.00**

Dr. McLean's Liver & Kidney Balms; St. Louis, Mo.; 8¾″; aqua **8.00-10.00**

McLean's Strengthening Cordial; graphite pontil; 9¼″; aqua **15.00-25.00**

Dr. McLean's Liver & Kidney Balm, St. Louis; 9″; aqua; oval flask **2.00-4.00**

Dr. J.H. McLean's Volcanic Oil Liniment; on the front; 4″; square; aqua **3.00-6.00**

Dr. J.H. McLean's; aqua; sheared top; ten panels; 3½″ **2.00-6.00**

McMillan & Kester, Ess. of Jamacia Ginger, S.F.; all on front; flask; graduated collar; 6¾″; aqua **4.00-8.00**

McMillan & Kester, Ess. of Jamaica Ginger, S.F.; 6″; aqua **8.00-15.00**

Dr. McMunn's Elixir of Opium; pontil; round; 4½″; aqua **8.00-15.00**

Dr. McMunns Elixir of Opium; vertical around bottle; cylindrical; square collar; 4½″; aqua **3.00-6.00**

Furst McNess Co., Freeport, Ill.; vertical on front in sunken panel; rectangular; ring and band collar; ABM; 8½″; aqua **2.00-3.00**

same as above except 6¼″ **2.00-3.00**

M.C.W. 10½″ OZ.; under bottom; amber; 7½″, $2.00-3.00

M.C.W. 43; under bottom; round; amber; 3″ . . . **2.00-4.00**

M.D. U.S.A.; in center of bottle; ring top; 9½″; amber . . . . **8.00-15.00 +**

Meade & Baker; clear or amethyst; 3½″ **3.00-6.00**

Meade & Baker; clear; 4¼″ **4.00-10.00**

Medicine, plain; square; aqua; applied top; kick-up; pontil; 9¾″ **8.00-12.00**

Medicine, plain; round; cobalt; 3″ round; 7½″ .**4.00-6.00**

Medicine, plain; twelve-sided; round; 1¼″x2½″;
   pontil **7.00-10.00**

Medicine label; 4″; clear **2.00-3.00**

Medicine label; pontil; aqua; 6¾″ **6.00-8.00**

Medicine label; amber; 8″ **2.00-3.00**

Medicine label; cobalt; 4½″ **4.00-6.00**

Medicine label; clear or amethyst; *W* on
   bottom; 6″ **2.00-4.00**

Medicine label; clear or amethyst; 5″ **1.00-2.00**

Medicine label; aqua; pontil; 6½″ **6.00-12.00**

**Medicine label; amber; 7¼″,
$2.00-3.00**

Medicine label; free-blown; pontil; 3″; ⁹⁄₁₆″ diameter;
   clear **8.00-12.00**

Medicine label; 6″; kick-up; cobalt **2.00-4.00**

Medicine label; amber; 7¼″ **2.00-4.00**

Medicine label; 5¾″; cobalt **4.00-6.00**

Medicine label; pontil; aqua; 5¼″; 1½″
   diameter **6.00-12.00**

Medicine label; aqua; pontil; 2¼″ round **6.00-12.00**

Medicine label; clear; pontil; 2¾″ **5.00-8.00**

Medicine label; 7½″; light blue; small kick-up . .**2.00-6.00**

Medicine label; *W* under bottom; clear; 4½″ . . .**1.00-2.00**

M; plain medicine label; 8½″; amber **2.00-4.00**

Medicine label; three-cornered bottle;
   clear; 4″ **2.00-3.00**

Medicine label; aqua; 4¾″ **2.00-3.00**

**Medicine label; three-part mold;
aqua; 6¼″, $2.00-6.00**

Medicine label; cobalt; 5½″ **2.00-6.00**

Medicine label; *B* under bottom; aqua **2.00-4.00**

Medicine label; aqua; 6¼″ **2.00-3.00**

Medicine label; clear; 4½″ **2.00-3.00**

Medicine label; twelve panels; aqua; 4½″ **2.00-3.00**

Medicine label; *400* under bottom; 6¼″
   amber **2.00-4.00**

Medicine label; *5* on bottom; aqua; 8″ **1.00-2.00**

Medicine label; *17* on bottom; 7¾″; amber **2.00-4.00**

Medicine label; amber; 9″ **4.00-6.00**

Medicine label; free-blown; pontil; 9¾″;
   aqua **10.00-20.00**

   also *Pat. March 1893, St. Louis, Mo.* under bottom;
   clear; 7½″ **2.00-6.00**

Medicine label; aqua; 1¾″ **2.00-4.00**

Medicine label; clear; 2½″ **2.00-4.00**

Medicine label; amber; *2423* under
   bottom; 8″ **2.00-4.00**

Medicine label; *933* on bottom; amber; 8¾″ . . .**2.00-4.00**

Medicine label; amber; nine-part mold; machine made;
   7½″ **2.00-6.00**

Medicine label; clear or amethyst; 5″ **2.00-4.00**

**Medicine label; clear; numbers on
bottom; 4″, $2.00-3.00**

Medicine label; pontil; clear or
   amethyst; 3½″ **4.00-7.00**

Medicine label; three-part mold; clear; 5¾″ **2.00-3.00**

Medicine label; clear; 4″; pontil **4.00-6.00**

Medicine label; *W.T.Co. U.S.A.* under bottom; cobalt
   blue; 5¾″ **4.00-8.00**

Medicine label; three-part mold; cobalt
   blue; 9½″ **4.00-6.00**

Medicine label; clear; 4¾″ **1.00-2.00**

Medicine label; *171* under bottom; aqua; 5″ . . .**1.00-2.00**

Medicine label; aqua; 6″ **1.00-2.00**

**Medicine label; *E.L.& Co.* under bot-
tom; amber; 7″, $2.00-4.00**

Medicine label; round back; clear or amethyst;
   6¾″ **2.00-4.00**

Medicine label; clear or amethyst; 8½″ **6.00-10.00**

Medicine label; front has sunken panel, other side flat;
   14 under bottom; amber;
   7¾″ x 2½″ x 2½″ **2.00-4.00**

Medicine label; amber; 7″ **2.00-4.00**

Medicine label; cobalt; 3″ **2.00-4.00**

Medicine label; numbers under bottom;
   cobalt; 7½″ **4.00-8.00**

Medicine label; ringed top; 4½″; milk glass . . .**6.00-8.00**

Medical Dept. U.S.N.; reverse side *50c.c.;* 4″; clear or
   amber **8.00-15.00**

   same as above except 8½″ **8.00-15.00**

C.W. Merchant Chemist, Lockport, N.Y.; in vertical
   lines; tapered top; 5¾″; amber **8.00-10.00**

**C.W. Merchant, Lockport, N.Y., Oak Orchard Acid
   Springs;** tapered top; 9¼″; dark
   green **20.00-40.00**

The Wm. S. Merrell Co.; label; amber; machine
   made; 7¾″ **3.00-4.00**

The Wm. S. Merrell Co.; *FGN* on bottom; machine made; amber; 7¾"..................2.00-4.00

The Merz Capsule Co.; clear; 3¾"; twelve panels...........................2.00-3.00

T. Metcalf & Co.; clear; 8", $4.00-6.00

Mrs. S. Mettlers Medicine; 6½"; aqua......4.00-6.00

Mexican Mustang Liniment; in 3 vertical lines; round; 4½"; aqua; pontil..................10.00-20.00
same except no pontil.................2.00-4.00

Mexican Mustang Liniment; on back; clear; 7½", $6.00-8.00

A.C. Meyer & Co., Balto., MD U.S.A. Dr. J.W. Bulls Cough Syrup; 6½"; aqua.............4.00-6.00

John Meyer Chemist, Mt. Clemens, Mich.; 9½"; amber.................................6.00-10.00

Meyers Mfg. Co.; vertical on side; shaped like a miniature pop bottle; crown top; 4"; amethyst...........................3.00-4.00

Dr. Miles Nervine; on the front panel; aqua; 8¼"; rectangular.........................2.00-3.00

Dr. Miles Restorative Nervine; on the front panel; rectangular; aqua; 8¼"; old bubbles........3.00-5.00

Dr. Miles Medical Co.; on the front panel; 8¼"; aqua; rectangular.........................2.00-3.00

Dr. Miles Medical Co.; vertical in sunken panel on front; label on reverse side; *Dr. Miles Alterative Compound,* picture of man with diagram of blood veins; double band collar; rectangular; *ABM;* 8¾"; aqua...............................3.00-6.00

Dr. J.R. Millers; on side; *Balm* on opposite side; arch panels; rectangular; square collar; 4¾"; clear..................................3.00-6.00

Minards Liniment, Boston; seven vertical panels on front half; back plain; round; round band collar; 5⅛"; amethyst..........................2.00-6.00

Minards; clear or amethyst; 5"............2.00-6.00

Minards Liniment; six panels; round back; clear or amethyst; 6".........................3.00-6.00

Minute Oil Med Co. Ltd. New Orleans; aqua; 10¼"................................30.00-40.00

Mitchell's; cobalt; on side *Eye Salve*.........2.00-6.00

M.J. & Co.; amber; 8", $4.00-8.00

Moe Hospital, Sioux Falls, So. Dak.; vertical on front; side panels show scales; oval back; fluting on back; 8¼"; amethyst.....................4.00-8.00

Montecatini Salts, Italy; amber; 4".........2.00-6.00

George Moore; clear; 5¾".................2.00-6.00

Dr. J. Moore's Essence of Life; vertical around bottle; cylindrical; pontil; 3¾"; aqua..........15.00-25.00

Moore's Liver-Ax; aqua; 7".................3.00-5.00

Moore's Revealed Remedy; 8¾"; amber....8.00-10.00

Dr. Moreno; aqua; 8"; side mold; *W.T. & Co. 5 U.S.A.* under bottom........................6.00-8.00

E. Morgan & Sons, Sole Proprietors, Providence, R.I.; (E left out of Providence); twelve panels; on shoulder *Dr. Haynes Arabian Balsam;* 7½"; aqua......10.00 +

Morley Bros; label; aqua; 7"..............2.00-6.00

Morning Call-C Lediard, St. Louis; 10½"; olive, amber................................4.00-6.00

H.S. Morrell, N.Y.; pontil; tapered top; 5¾"; aqua..................................15.00-25.00

Morses Celebrated Syrup; vertically; oval; long tapered neck; graphite pontil; 9½"; aqua.......10.00-20.00

Morton & Co.; clear or amethyst; 5½".......2.00-3.00

Morton & Co. Tampa, Fla. W.T. & Co.; 4½"; clear or amber................................3.00-4.00

Moxie Nerve Food, Lowell, Mass; thick embossed line, graduated collar, round, aqua, 10"......9.00-12.00

Moxie Nerve Food, Trade Mark Registered, Moxie; on front and back; round; crown top; 10¼" aqua..................................5.00-10.00

Moyers Oil of Gladness, Bloomsburg, Pa; vertical on front in sunken panel; graduated collar; 5⅝"; aqua...............................4.00-8.00

Muegge Baker, Oregon; *Muegge's* on reverse shoulder; 8"; green, $8.00-10.00

H.K. Mulford Co., Phila; 7¼"; amber........4.00-8.00

Munyon's; in one sunken side panel; other *Paw-Paw;* in front on top a tree; two board lines with *Munyon's Paw-Paw;* plain back; amber; 10"; long tapered top...................................8.00-12.00

Munyon's Germicide Solution; side mold; green; 3¼". **3.00-6.00**

Munyon's Germicide Solution; green; 3½". . . **4.00-8.00**

Murine Eye Remedy Co., Chicago U.S.A.; round; 3½"; clear. **3.00-4.00**

Murphy Brothers, Portland; on front in oval end panel; rectangular; square collar; 4⅞"; aqua **2.00-3.00**

Sir J. Murray's Re-Carbonated Patent Magnesia; vertical on front; crude band and small band collar; oval; 7½"; light green. **4.00-8.00**

Natrium; clear; 4¾", $8.00-10.00

Nelson Baker & Co.; amber; 9". **3.00-4.00**

Nerve & Bone Liniment; round bottle; old type mold; aqua; 4¼". **4.00-6.00**

Nervine; *Prepared by the Catarrhozone Co., Kingston, Ont.* vertical on front in oval sunken panel; rectangular; square collar; 5¼"; amethyst. . .**6.00-10.00**

Newbros Herbicide Kill The Dandruff Germ; ring top; 5½" clear or amber. **4.00-6.00**

The New York Pharmacal Association; in 2 lines in a sunken panel on one side; on other side *Lactopeptine;* in front *The Best Remedial Agent In All Digestive Disorders;* 6" body; 1½" neck; 2¾" square; round corners; cobalt. **10.00-12.00**

N.Y. Medical; reverse side *University City;* 7½"; cobalt. **10.00-20.00**

North; pontil; 6¼". **8.00-20.00**

Norton; clear or amethyst; 5". **1.00-2.00**

Noyes, Granular Effervescent Magnesia Sulphate; vertical on front; rectangular; corner panels; square collar; 6" aqua. **4.00-6.00**

Nuco-Solvent Dr. Griffin; 5¼"; aqua. **4.00-8.00**

Nyal's Emulsion of Cod Liver Oil; amber; 9". **2.00-4.00**

Nyal's Liniment; 7"; amber; ring in neck. **2.00-4.00**

N.Y. Pharmacal Association; in 2 vertical lines; 8½"; cobalt. **5.00-8.00**

The Oakland Chemical Co.; amber; 4¾". **2.00-4.00**

The Oakland Chemical Co.; amber; 5¼". **3.00-6.00**

Od Chem. Co., New York; in 2 lines; 6¾"; amber. **1.00-2.00**

ODOJ; under bottom; milk glass; *M632* on one panel; 4½". **8.00-12.00**

O.K. Plantation; triangular; amber; 11". . . . . . .**200.00 +**

OL. Amygdal; clear; 5¾". **8.00-10.00**

Old Dr. Townsend's Sarsaparilla; pontil; green. **20.00-30.00**

Old Drug Store Apothecary Jars; open pontils, round, glass stoppers, 10½". **9.00-12.00**

Oldridge Balm of Columbia For Restoring Hair; 6¼"; aqua. **40.00-80.00**

Oleum, Dr. Peter's; in back, tree in center of it *P-B* under it *1783-1880,* on base *Trade Mark,* ring top, clear, 5⅞". **14.00-20.00**

Olive Oil; open pontil, no embossing, 10½". .**9.00-12.00**

Omega Oil Chemical Co., New York; in 3 lines at bottom; above bottom, a leaf with words *Omega Oil It's Green;* ring under this with *Trade Mark;* flared top with ring; under bottom, various numbers in circle; light green; 4½". **3.00-6.00**

Omega Oil It's Green, Trademark; all inside of leaf embossed on front; *The Omega Chemical Co. New York* at base on front; sheared collar; 6"; clear. **2.00-4.00**

same as above except 4½". **2.00-4.00**

same as above except *ABM:* thread top; 6". **2.00-3.00**

Omega Oil; vertical on front; cylindrical; 3¼"; aqua. **2.00-3.00**

Opium bottles, in different sizes; 1 drop to ½ ounce; most are clear, some amethyst. **3.00-8.00**

Opium; 2½"; aqua. **4.00-8.00**

Oriental Condensed Coffee, Trade Mark, Oriental Tea Company, Boston, Mass.; vertical on front in slug plate; square collar; oval; 6½"; aqua. **4.00-6.00**

Oriental Cream, Gourand's, New York; on flat front panel and sides; corner panels; flared lip; rectangular; 5½"; clear. **4.00-6.00**

Otis Clapp & Son; 7½"; amber, $6.00-10.00

C. Owens; clear; 2½". **1.00-2.00**

Owl; *J.B. Co., P.C. Co.* in diamond shape on bottom; clear; 3½". **4.00-6.00**

Owl Drug Co.; clear; 5¼". **2.00-6.00**

The Owl Drug Co. San Francisco; on bottom; double wing owl on mortar on front; 8⅜"; clear. .**4.00-10.00**

Owl bottle; double wing owl on mortar; thread top; rectangular; 3⅝"; clear. **2.00-4.00**

The Owl Drug Co.; on back; double wing owl; rectangular; square collar; *ABM;* 5¾"; clear. .**2.00-4.00**

same as above except 4". **4.00-8.00**

The Owl Drug Co.; on back; single wing owl; hair tonic type bottle; ring collar; tapered neck; round; 7"; amethyst. **4.00-6.00**

Owl Drug Store; embossed owl in center; 1½" x 2³⁄₁₆"; diamond and *2* under bottom; clear. **4.00-6.00**

Ox; pontil; cobalt blue; 8½". **20.00-40.00**

Oxien Pills, The Giant Oxien; *Augusta, Me;* 2"; clear. **4.00-6.00**

Oxien Pills; *The Giant Oxien Co., Augusta Me.;* clear; 2". **2.00-6.00**

Ozomulsion; amber; 5½". **4.00-8.00**

Ozon Antiseptic Dressing; W.H. Duncan, Natures Pine Remedy; label; rectangular; square collar; *ABM;* 6½"; clear. **2.00-6.00**

The Ozone Co. of Toronto, Limited; same in back; double ring top; 7″; clear....................8.00-10.00

The Liquid Ozone Co.; *8* under bottom; amber; 8″, $8.00-10.00

Paines Celery Compound; 10″; aqua.......8.00-10.00
same as above except amber...........4.00-8.00
Palace Drug Store; clear; 4½″............2.00-4.00
Palace Drug Store; clear or amethyst; 6″.....3.00-4.00
The Palisade Mfg. Co.; *Yonkers, N.Y.* on bottom; clear or amethyst; 7¾″....................6.00-10.00

The Palisade Mg. Co., Yonkers, NY.; under bottom; amber; 7¼″, $4.00-6.00

Jas. Palmer & Co. Philada.; one side *Wholesale;* other side *Druggists;* 5″; aqua...............4.00-6.00
Palmolive Shampoo, B.J. Johnson, Toronto, Ont. Canada; on front and back; rectangular; ring collar; ABM; 7¼″; clear....................3.00-4.00
10 Panel; 4″; bluish....................4.00-6.00
Pa-Pay-Ans Bell; ring top; amber...........3.00-4.00
Pa-Pay-Ans Bell; *(Orangburg, N.Y.)*.........6.00-8.00
John D. Park; *Cincinati, O., Dr. Cuysotts Yellow Dock & Sarsaparilla* in five vertical lines on front; 8½″ body, 2″ neck; tapered top; 2¼″ x 4¼″; graphite pontil; aqua....................25.00-50.00
John D. Park, Cincinnati, O., Dr. Wistars Balsam of Wild Cherry; 7½″; aqua..............8.00-12.00
Parke Davis & Co.; label; amber; 5½″.......4.00-6.00
Parke Davis & Co.; label; *343* under bottom; amber....................3.00-6.00
Parke Davis & Co.; label; black glass; 3½″...4.00-6.00
Parke Davis & Co.; label; *P.D. & Co. 274* under bottom; amber; 5¼″....................2.00-4.00
Parker; on one side; *New York* other side; *17* under bottom; amber; 7″....................2.00-4.00
Parkers Hair Balsam, New York; on front and sides in sunken oval panels; rectangular; *ABM;* 7½″; amber....................4.00-8.00
Parkers Hair Balsam, New York; on front and sides; rectangular; 6½″; amber............3.00-4.00
Dr. Park's Indian Linament, Wyanoke; 5⅜″; clear....................6.00-8.00

Paul Westphal; clear or amethyst; 8″.......4.00-8.00
Pawnee Indian Ta-Ha; *price 25¢, Jos. Herman Agt.* 8½″; aqua....................10.00-15.00
Pawnee Indian, Too-Re; vertical on front in sunken panel; plain sides and back; rectangular; 7¾″; aqua....................8.00-10.00
PD & Co.; under bottom; amber; 3¼″.......2.00-3.00
P.D. & Co.; 119; under bottom; amber; 4″....2.00-4.00
P.D. & Co.; under bottom; amber; 3¾″......2.00-3.00
P D & Co.21 S; under bottom; machine made; amber; 2½″....................2.00-3.00
P D & Co.; *334* under bottom; amber; 4¾″...2.00-4.00
Pearl's White Glycerine; cobalt; 6¼″.......6.00-10.00
Ebenezer A. Pearl's Tincture of Life; vertical on front in sunken panels; rectangular; 7¾″; aqua...3.00-6.00
Pease's Eye Water; *Newman, Ga.;* 4¼″; aqua....................2.00-4.00

Prof. W.H. Peek's Remedy; *N.Y.;* 8″; amber, $6.00-8.00

Dr. H.F. Peery's; on back *Dead Shot Vermifuce;* 4″; amber....................2.00-4.00
Dr. H.F. Peery's; clear or amethyst.........4.00-6.00
Wm. Pendelton; *Rockland, Me.* vertical on three panels; twelve panels; square collar; 4⅜″; aqua...2.00-4.00
Peoples Chemical Co., The Scientifically Prepared Red Cross; with cross embossed in circle, *Beef Wine & Iron Providence, R.I.* all on front; flask shape; flared collar; 7½″; clear.........4.00-8.00
Peperazine Effervescente Medy; in 3 vertical lines; amber; 6¼″, 2¾″ x 1¼″..............2.00-4.00
Peptenzyme; cobalt; 2½″.................4.00-6.00
Peptenzyne; at slant on front in sunken panel; 3¼″; cobalt blue....................3.00-4.00
Pepto-Mangan Guide; six panels; 7″ aqua....6.00-8.00
Dr. Peter's Kuriko; on one of the panels; *Prepared By Dr. Peter Fahrney & Sons, Co., Chicago, Ill. U.S.A.* on the other side; amethyst; 9″; square; paneled....................2.00-4.00
Peter Moller's Pure Cod Liver Oil; label; clear; 5¾″....................4.00-6.00
Dr. J. Pettits Canker Balsam; vertical on front; flask shape; 3¼″ clear....................4.00-8.00
Dr. Pettit's Eye Water; *Buffalo, N.Y.* on front, amethyst and clear, ring top, scale on back, 3″....9.00-12.00
Pfeiffer Chemical Co., Phila & St. Louis; on back; aqua; 6″....................2.00-6.00
Phalon's Chemical Hair Invigorator; pontil; clear; 5½″....................8.00-20.00
Dr. O. Phelps Brown; vertical on one panel; ring collar; square; wide mouth; 2¾″; aqua........3.00-4.00

John H. Phelps Pharmacist, Phelps Rheumatic Elixir; *Scranton Pa.* 5½"; clear, $2.00-4.00

Phillips Emulsion Cod Liver Oil, New York; vertical on front in sunken panel; rectangular; 9¼"; amber...................................3.00-6.00

C.H. Phillips, N.Y.; 9½"; amber..........6.00-8.00

Phillips' Emulsion; (N backwards); amber; 9½".....................20.00-30.00

Phillips Emulsion; #1 under bottom; sample; 4¾".......................8.00-10.00

Phillips Emulsion; amber; 7½"...........2.00-6.00

Phillips Milk of Magnesia; 7"; light blue......3.00-6.00

Pholon's Vitalia; same on reverse side; sunken arched panels; rectangular; flared lip; 6⅜"; amethyst.......................4.00-6.00

Phosphocyclo-Fer; on back, label; *Depose* **on bottom; 4½", $4.00-6.00**

Dr. Geo. Pierce's; on front; on back *Indian Restorative Bitters;* on side *Lowell, Mass;* aqua; 7½", 9", and other variants; pontil................40.00-60.00

Dr. Pierce's Golden Med. Disc.; on the front panel; *Buffalo, N.Y.* on the left side; *RV Pierce, M.D.* on the right side; rectangular; 8¼"; aqua.......2.00-4.00

R.V. Pierce, M.D.; on one side of panel; *Buffalo, N.Y.* on opposite side of panel; aqua; rectangular; 9⅛".....................1.00-2.00

Dr. Pierce's Anuric Table For Kidneys and Backache; on the front; aqua; round; 3½".........1.00-2.00

Dr. Pierce's Favorite Prescription; on the front panel; *Buffalo, N.Y.* on left side; *R.V. Pierce, M.D.* on right side; aqua; rectangular; 8½"...........2.00-4.00

Dr. Pierces, Anuric; embossed inside of kidney, *Tablets for Kidneys and Backache* all on front; cylindrical; 3"; clear.......................4.00-6.00

L. Pierre Valligny; La-Goutte-A-Goutte, New York, old type screw top, amber, rectangular, 5½".9.00-12.00

Pill Bottles; plain; oval; shear top; screw top; 2½"; clear...................................4.00-6.00

Pill Bottles; plain; oval; shear top; screw top; 1½"; clear...................................4.00-6.00

Pill Bottle; plain; 1¾"; aqua...............2.00-4.00

Pill Bottle; plain; 3½"; clear, amber........2.00-4.00

The Pillow-Inhale Co. Phila; 7½"; aqua.....4.00-8.00

Pineoleum for Catarrhal Conditions; on both front and back; conical; pewter neck and top; 6⅜"; amber...................................4.00-6.00

Pine Tree Tar Cordial, Phila.; on one panel; on another panel a tree and *patent 1859;* another panel *L.Q.G. Wisharts;* blob top; 8"; green..........30.00-50.00

Pine Tree Tar Cordial, Phila. 1859; with tree embossed; 8"; green.....................18.00-20.00

Pinex; on both sides; rectangular; 5¾"; aqua.2.00-3.00

Dr. Pinkham's Emmenagogue; tapered top; pontil; kick-up in base; 5"; light blue............30.00-50.00

Lydia E. Pinkham's; aqua; *C8* under bottom; 8¼".........................2.00-6.00

Pinkston & Scruggs Pharmacists, W.T. Co., O, U.S.A.; under bottom; 4½".....................2.00-4.00

Piperazine; gold; 5" or 6", $3.00-6.00

The Piso Company; in 2 lines in front sunken panel; on one side in sunken panel *Trade-Piso's-Mark;* on other side *Hazeltine & Co.;* under bottom, different numbers; green, clear; amber; 5¼".....2.00-6.00

Dr. S. Pitcher's; on the side panel; *Castoria* on the other side; rectangular; 5⅞"; aqua............2.00-4.00

Pitcher's Castoria; aqua; 6¼"..............2.00-6.00

Dr. W.M. Pitt's Carminative; aqua; 4".......3.00-5.00

Dr. W.M. Pitt's Carminative; clear or amethyst; 4".......................3.00-6.00

Plain medicine bottle; twelve panels; broken pontil; body 3"; neck 1"; clear...................6.00-10.00

Plain label; clear; 4¾"...................8.00-10.00

Plain label; clear; 4¾", $6.00-8.00

Dr. Planetts Bitters; iron pontil; amber; 9¾".......................40.00-50.00

Planks Chill Tonic Co.; *Chattanooga Tenn.;* 6½"; clear or amber....................................4.00-6.00

Planters Old Time Remedies; one side *Chattanooga Tenn.;* other side *Spencer Med. Co.;* aqua.4.00-8.00

Platt's Chloride; quart; clear or amethyst.....4.00-6.00

Pluto Water; under bottom, a devil and Pluto; round; light green or clear; 3¼" and other sizes..2.00-4.00

P.M.F.S. & Co.; on bottom; amber; 2¼".......2.00-3.00

Pompeian Massage Cream; 2¾"; clear or amber...................................3.00-4.00

Pompeian Massage Cream; on front; barrel shape; *ABM;* 2¾"; clear...................3.00-4.00

Pond's Extract; label; *1846* under bottom; 5½".......................2.00-4.00

Pond's Extract Catarrh Remedy; 5¾"; cobalt....10.00+

Pond's Monarch Liniment; on front in sunken panel at slant; rectangular; 6½"; aqua..........3.00-6.00

Porter's Pain King; on opposite sides; sunken panels; rectangular; 6¾"; clear...............3.00-4.00

Porter's Pain King; same as above except *ABM*...................................2.00-3.00

Dr. Porter, New York; vertical on front; rectangular; 4¼"; aqua.........................3.00-6.00

Porter's; *Pain King* on other side; *G.H.R.* under bottom; clear or amethyst; 7"..................3.00-6.00

Posen; *Wronkerstr. No. 6;* amber; 10", $10.00-20.00

Potter & Merwin; on front; plain back; on one side *St. Louis,* on other *Missouri;* beveled corner; roofed shoulder; aqua; tapered top; 5½".......6.00-8.00
same except pontil..................10.00-25.00

PP; (back to back) label; cobalt; 2½".......4.00-8.00

Preston & Merrill, Boston 1871; 4¼"; clear..2.00-4.00

Preston of New Hampshire; on front; mold threads; sheared collar; glass stopper with metal cup cover; 3½"; merald green.................2.00-4.00

Protonuceln; (sic); amber; 2⅞"............2.00-4.00

Proonuclein; amber; 2"; sheared top.......3.00-4.00

W.M. Prunder's Oregon No. 7138; (embossed child's head with ribbon wreath) on center: *Registered March 25th 1879, Blood Purifier, Wm. Prunder & Co.; Portland, Ore* all on front in slug plate; ring and flared collar; oval; 7½"; amber.......10.00-18..00

The Purdue Frederick Co., New York; 8"; clear or amber...............................3.00-4.00

Pure Cod Liver Oil, Byne Atwood, Provincetown, Mass.; vertical on front; oval; 7"; aqua....3.00-6.00

Pure & Genuine Four Fold Liniment, R. Matchetts; on front and sides; rectangular; 5¼"; clear...2.00-4.00

Pynchon; at base on front; *Boston* on opposite side at base; oval; 4¾"; aqua.................6.00-10.00

Q Ban; machine made; amber; 6¾"........2.00-4.00

Del Dr. Rabell; reverse side *Emulsion;* 9½"; aqua.................................4.00-6.00

Racine de Guimauve; cut glass; 9¼"; blue, $15.00-30.00

RACINE de GUIMAUVE

R.R.R. Radway & Co., New York, Entd. Accord. To Act of Congress; on flat front panel and opposite sides in large letters; rectangular; 6⅜"; aqua.................................4.00-8.00

Radway's; on side; *Sarsaparillian Resolvent* on front; *R.R.R.* on opposite side; *Entd. Accord. to Act of Congress;* sunken panels; rectangular; 7¼"; aqua.............................10.00-15.00

Ramon's Nerve & Bone Oil, Brown Mfg. Co. Proprietors; vertical on front in sunken panel; *Greenville, Tenn.* on side; *New York, NY* on opposite side; rectangular; 5¾"; aqua................4.00-6.00

Ramon's Nerve & Bone Oil; *Brown Mfg Co. Proprietors;* on one side *Greenville Tenn.;* other *St. Louis;* tapered top; 5¾"....................2.00-6.00

Rawleigh; in vertical script; under it in ribbon, *Trade Mark;* 7⅝"; clear or amethyst..........3.00-4.00

W.T. Rawleigh Med. Co.; *Freeport Ill* other side; clear; 8¼"....................................4.00-6.00

Rectangular; almost square; no embossing; pontil; 2½"; aqua.................................4.00-6.00

same as above, concave corner panels; crude flared lip; pontil; 5¼"; aqua..................4.00-6.00

Red Cross Family Liniment; label; *Cooperative Drug Mfg., Jackson, Tenn.;* 5½"; clear.......2.00-4.00

Red Cross Pharmacy, W.T. CO. U.S.A.; *Savannah* (sic) *Ga.;* 5½"; clear....................10.00-12.00

Redington & Co. Essence of Jamaica Ginger, San Francisco; vertical on front; 5½"; aqua...4.00-6.00

Reed & Carnrich, Jersey City, N.J.; in 3 slanting lines; in back *Peptenzyme;* 2¾" x 2½"; 8½" tall; cobalt; ring top............................10.00-12.00
same, two smaller sides.............8.00-10.00

Reed & Carnrich; same except 4½".......10.00-12.00

Reed and Carnrick Pharmacists, New York; in 5 lines on front panel; 7½"; amber............4.00-6.00

Reed & Carnrick, N.Y.; on bottom; amber; 4¾".........................2.00-6.00

Reed & Carnrick, N.Y.; dark blue; 6¼", $15.00-25.00

Reed & Carnrick, New York; *Peptenzyme* on back; cobalt; 4½".........................6.00-8.00

Reese Chemical Co., Blood & System Tonic; ring top; 3¾"; green........................8.00-12.00

Reid's; aqua; 5½".........................3.00-5.00

Renne's; aqua; 5"........................2.00-3.00

Reno's New Health Uterine Tonic; in center a lady head. *Prepared only by S.B. Leonardi & Co., New York, N.Y.* all in 8 lines on front, ring top, 7½" aqua...............................14.00-19.00

Reno's New Health; or *Woman's Salvation, Prepared only by S.B. Leonardi & Co. Tampa, Fla.* all in 7 lines, 7½" aqua....................14.00-19.00

Renwar; on each side, ring top, cobalt, 6"...**7.00-10.00**

Resinal Balto. Md. Chemical Co.; under bottom; milk glass; 3¼"..................**3.00-5.00**

Restorff & Bettman N.Y.; six panels; 4¼"; aqua..................................**4.00-6.00**

Rexall; *3VIII* on shoulder; rectangular; flared lip; 6½"; emerald green.......................**4.00-6.00**

C.A. Richards; amber; 9½"..............**10.00-25.00**

Rich-Lax; label; 7½"; aqua, $8.00-10.00

F.A. Richter & Co. Manufacturing, Chemists, New York; with embossed anchor, vertical on front; anchor on side; *Pain Expeller* on opposite side; rectangular; 5" aqua.....................**4.00-6.00**

Ricker Hegeman or Hegenak Drug Stores; in center; 5½"; cobalt......................**10.00-20.00**

Riker's Compound Sarsaparilla; vertical in sunken panel on front; beveled corners; rectangular; sunken panels on all sides; 10"; aqua blue.....**30.00-40.00**

C.B. Rinckerhoffs, Price One Dollar; on side, *Health Restorative, New York;* tapered top; 7¼"; olive**85.00+**

The River Swamp Chill and Fever Cure; with alligator in center; *Augusta Ga.;* 7"; clear or aqua**10.00-40.00**

James S. Robinson, Memphis, Tenn.; 7"; clear...................................**4.00-6.00**

Roche's Embrocation for the Whooping Cough, W. Edwards & Son; on consecutive panels; flared lip; 5"; clear...........................**6.00-8.00**

Roderic's Wild Cherry Cough Balsam; flared collar; *ABM;* 5½"; clear...................**2.00-3.00**

same as above except amber; 4½".....**2.00-3.00**

Ron-Bre; amber; 6½"...................**2.00-4.00**

Root Juice Med. Co.; aqua; 9"...........**2.00-4.00**

Root Juice Med. Co., label; clear or amethyst; 6".......................**4.00-6.00**

Dr. Rose's; *Philadel* on other side; pontil; aqua.............................**8.00-15.00**

Roshton & Aspinwall, New York; on back *Compound Chlorine Tooth Wash;* flared top; pontil; 6"; golden olive.........................**200.00-300.00**

Round; crude ring collar; cylindrical; whittled effect; pontil 5¾"; aqua blue.....................**4.00-7.00**

V. Roussin, Druggist, Muskegon, Mich.; 7¼"; clear...................................**4.00-6.00**

Rowlands Macassai (Oil); pontil..........**8.00-15.00**

Royal Foot Wash, Eaton Drug Co.; *Atlanta, Ga.*...................................**4.00-8.00**

Royal Gall Remedy; machine made; dark amber; 7½"......................**8.00-10.00**

Royal Germetuer; same on reverse side; one side *Kings Royal Germetuer Co.;* other side *Atlanta Ga. U.S.A.;* 8½"; amber..................**18.00-25.00**

Rubifoam for the Teeth, Put Up E.W. Hoyt & Co., Lowell, Mass.; all on front; oval; 4"; clear....................**3.00-4.00**

Rush's; on one side; *Remedy* on reverse; other two sides *A.H.F. Monthly;* double ring top; 6"; aqua.........................**4.00-10.00**

Rush's; vertical on front in small rectangular panel; *Lung* on side; *Balm* on opposite side; *A.H. Flanders, MD.* on back side; sunken panels; rectangular; 7"; aqua.........................**12.00-15.00**

Rushton's; *F.V.* on back; *Cod Liver Oil* on side; *N.Y.* other side; ice blue; 10½"...........**8.00-12.00**

Russ's Aromatic; side panel *Schnapps;* other side *N.Y.;* 8"; dark olive........................**15.00-30.00**

John Ryan Citrate of Magnesia, Savannah, Ga.; on front in four lines; 7"; aqua; short neck; round.**12.00+**

Dr. Sages; on one side; on other side *Buffalo; Catarrah Remedy* on front; on back *Dr. Price Propr.;* all on sunken panels; 2¼"; *#1* under bottom....**4.00-8.00**

Salvation Oil, AC Meyer & Co., Baltimore, MD.; in 4 lines in a sunken panel in front; round sides; under bottom, letter *D;* 2¼" x 1"; rectangular...**4.00-6.00**

Salvation Oil, A.C. Meyer & Co., Trade Mark, Baltimore, MD. USA; all on front; arched panel; rectangular; 6¾"; aqua..................**3.00-6.00**

Salvation Trade Mark Oil, A.C. Meyer & Co. Balt. Md. U.S.A.; ring top; 6¾"; aqua...........**3.00-6.00**

Sammy's Medicine; reverse side *Baltimore Md. U.S.A.;* under bottom *S.R. Scoggins;* front side *Reaches Through the Entire System;* 7"; sky blue..**4.00-8.00**

Sand's Sarsaparilla, New York; pontil; 6¼"; aqua, $15.00-25.00

Dr. Sanford, New York; on each side; aqua; 7½".........................**4.00-8.00**

Sanital De Midy; clear; twelve panels; 2¾"...**2.00-4.00**

The Sanitas Co.; label; aqua; 9", $3.00-6.00

Sanitol; *For the Teeth* on other side; clear; 4½".........................**4.00-6.00**

Dr. R. Sappington; reverse side *Flaxseed Syrup;* ring top; 7½"; aqua.....................**4.00-6.00**

A. Sartorius & Co. New York; on front; round; 2¾";
clear **2.00-3.00**

Sassafras; under it an eye cup; *Eye Lotion, Sassafras Eye Lotion Co., Maugh Chunk Pa.;* 6"; cobalt
blue **10.00-15.00**

Save; label; tan; 2¼" **1.00-2.00**

Saver; three-sided; amber; 3½" . . . .**25.00 +**
same as above except aqua; 4½" . . . .**25.00 +**

E.R. Schaefer's; round back; clear; 4" **2.00-4.00**

Scheffler's Hair Colorine, Best In The World; on front; rectangular; beveled corners; 4¼"; clear . .**3.00-4.00**

Schenbs Pulmonic Syrup; pontil **10.00-15.00**

Dr. Schenck's Pine Tar for Throat and Lungs; vertical in oval sunken end panel; rectangular; square collar; 6⅛"; aqua **7.00-10.00**

Schenck's Pulmonic Syrup, Philada.; on four panels; eight vertical panels; 5¾"; aqua **4.00-6.00**

Schenck's Syrup; vertical on front; oval end sunken panel; 6¼"; aqua **3.00-6.00**

Schenck's Syrup, Philada.; on 3 panels; eight vertical panels; 7¼"; aqua **15.00-30.00**

Hendrick Walter Schiedam, Aromatic Schnapps; 7"; olive **15.00-40.00**

Schlotterbeck & Fuss Co., Portland Me.; vertical on front in sunken panel; rectangular; sheared collar; 5"; amber **2.00-3.00**

Schutzen Str. No. 6; *J.E. Gilke* on back panel; 10", **$20.00-30.00**

Scott's Emulsion; *Cod Liver Oil* on one side; *With Lime Soda* on other side; aqua; various sizes . . .**2.00-4.00**

S. & D.; 8 under bottom; amber; 6" **2.00-4.00**

S & D 83; 2 under bottom; sheared top;
amber; 3½" **2.00-4.00**

S & D 2S; under bottom; amber; 4½" **1.00-2.00**

S & D 100; under bottom; sheared top;
clear; 2½" **2.00-4.00**

S & D 73; under bottom; amber; 6¼" **2.00-4.00**

S & D 83; under bottom; amber; 3½" **1.00-2.00**

Seabury; cobalt; sheared top; 3¾" **2.00-6.00**

Seabury; sheared top; amber; 3¾" **4.00-8.00**

R.N. Searles; on side; *Athlophoros* on opposite side; rectangular; 6¾"; aqua **3.00-6.00**

Shake; label; amber; 6" **2.00-4.00**

Shaker Fluid Extract Valerian; on front and back; square; 3¾"; aqua **8.00-10.00**

Dr. S.&H. and Co.; *P.R. Registered* on base; amethyst or aqua; round; 9¼" **4.00-10.00**

Sharp & Dohme; *Baltimore Md.* under bottom; amber; 5¾" **2.00-4.00**

Sharp & Dohme; three corners; round back; 3½"; cobalt **2.00-4.00**

Shecuts Southern Balm for Coughs, Cold 1840; 6¾"; aqua **20.00-40.00**

Wm. H. Shepard, Marblehead, Mass; label; aqua; 9" **4.00-6.00**

J.T. Shinn; clear; 4¾" **2.00-4.00**

S.H.K.C. Ext. P.C.; clear or amethyst; 4" **2.00-4.00**

Dr. Shoops Family Medicines; *Racine Wisc.;* aqua; ring top; 5½" **4.00-6.00**

Shores; label; clear; 9½" **4.00-6.00**

Short Stop for Coughs, H.M. O'Neil, N.Y.; vertical on front in sunken panel; 4"; aqua **2.00-3.00**

Shultz; *Dr. Shultz* on other side; aqua; 6½" . . .**4.00-6.00**

Shuptxine; in script, *Druggist, Savannah, Ga.* in 2 lines on front flat panel; top *31V;* panel each side; round blank back; under bottom *Pat 18/17 C.L.Co., Freen;* 5¼" tall; 2" x 1¼" **8.00-12.00**
same as above, 3½" tall; 1½" x ¾" **8.00-12.00**
same as above, 2½" tall; 1⅛" x ¾" . . .**10.00-14.00**

The Silburt Co., Trademark; *Cleveland, Sixth City,* clear, 4¼" long **5.00-8.00**

Simmons; 7"; aqua **3.00-5.00**

Simmons Liver Regulator; in 3 sunken panels on front; *Philadelphia* on side; *Macon, Ga.* on opposite side; *J.H. Eeilin & Co.* vertical on back; rectangular; 9"; aqua **4.00-6.00**

Dr. Simmons Squaw Vine Wine Compound; vertical lines; tapered top; 8½"; aqua **4.00-6.00**

Dr. M.A. Simmons Liver Medicine; *St. Louis;* 5¾"; aqua **4.00-6.00**

Dr. Simon Randall's; amber; 9", **$12.00-20.00**

Dr. T.J. Simpson's; aqua; 7¼" **6.00-10.00**

C. Sines; one side; *Phila Pa.* reverse side; front side *Tar Wild Cherry & Hoar Hound;* pontil; 5"; aqua **8.00-10.00**

Siphon Kumy Sgen Bottle For Preparing Kumyss From Reed & Carrick, N.Y.; 8¾"; cobalt **10.00-30.00**

S.J.S. for the Blood; on one side *L.G. Gerstle & Co.;* other side *Chattanooga, Tenn.;* 9"; amber, **$10.00-20.00**

52

Skabcura Dip Co.; *Chicago U.S.A.;* 5″; aqua . . **4.00-6.00**

Skeyhan' Pharmacy, Rockford, Ill; all in 3 lines on front, on shoulder *3/V,* on bottom *C.L.M. & Co.* 2½″, clear **7.00-10.00**

Skoda's Sarsaparilla; on side *Skoda's;* opposite side *Discovery* with *Belfast, Me,* on indented panel; front indented panel marked *Concentrated Extract Sarsaparilla Compound;* back panel has label; 9″; amber **10.00-20.00**

same as above except *Wolfville* on one side; *Nova Scotia* on other side **100.00-200.00**

Skoda's Wolefirlle Discovery; 9″; aqua **20.00-30.00**

Dr. Sledge's Horehound Pectoral; Horehound Pectoral; in indented front panel; *Memphis, Tenn* one side; *Dr. Sledge's* other side; graphite pontil; 7¼″; aqua **12.00-25.00**

Sloan's Liniment; clear or amethyst; 7″ **3.00-6.00**

Slocum's Coltsfoot Expectorant; on bottom; flask or oval shape; 2¼″; aqua **2.00-3.00**

Slocum's Expectorant Coltsfoot; under bottom; aqua; 2¼″ **2.00-4.00**

T.A. Slocum Co. Mfg., Chemists, N.Y. & London; with anchor seal; one side reads *For Consumption;* other side *Lung Troubles;* beveled corners; long collar; 9½″; aqua **8.00-10.00**

T.A. Slocum Mfg. Co., Psychine Consumption, 181 Pearl St. N.Y.; 8½″; aqua, $2.00-6.00

Mfg. Slough, Elliman's Royal Embrocation for Horses; double ring top; 7½″; aqua **8.00-10.00**

Smith's Bile Beans; clear; 1¾″ **2.00-3.00**

Smith Green Mt. Renovator; *E. Ga. Vt.* 6⅝″; olive amber; stoddard glass . . . . **200.00 +**

Dr. Smith's Worm Oil; 4″; aqua **2.00-4.00**

T.B. Smith Kidney Tonic, Cynthiana, KY.; 10½″; aqua **8.00-12.00**

Solomons Co; in script; *Branch Drug Store, Bull St., Savannah Ga.,* in 3 lines, in front; under bottom *WTCo, U.S.A.* in 2 lines; 7″; aqua or amethyst **2.00-4.00**

same only different sizes **2.00-4.00**

same only cobalt **4.00-8.00**

Solomons & Co., Savannah, Ga.; 6″; aqua . . **4.00-10.00**

A.A. Solomons & Co., Druggists Market Squae; (misspelled *Square);* aqua; 3¾″ **8.00-12.00**

Sozondont; on each side; clear; 2½″ **2.00-4.00**

Sparklene; *Registered* on back; amber; 5″ **2.00-4.00**

Sparks Perfect Health; *for Kidney & Liver Diseases,* 3 lines in sunken panel on front; round; aqua; 4″ **3.00-6.00**

Spencer Med. Co.; on one side sunken panel; front, *Nubian Tea* and *Trade Mark,* other side panel, *Chattanooga Tenn.;* amber; square; 4″ **2.00-6.00**

Spencer Med Co.; one side panel; on other *Chatt. Tenn.; Nubian Tea* in sunken panel on front; golden; 4″ **2.00-6.00**

P.H. Spillane, Pharmacist, Cohoes, N.Y.; *W.T. Co.* under bottom; clear; 5″ **2.00-4.00**

Spirit of Turpentine, Franklin, Ohio; label; *Pat April 21, 1896* under bottom; clear; 8¾″ **4.00-6.00**

Spith San Francisco Pharmacy; 11th & Railroad Avenues, flared lip 5¼″ **5.00-7.00**

E.R. Squibb 1864; round; 6″; green **4.00-8.00**

Dr. L.R. Stafford Olive Tar; label; directions, *J.R. Stafford* on side; *Olive Tar* opposite side; rectangular; double band collar; 6″; clear **3.00-4.00**

J.R. Staffords Olive Tar; on opposite sides; rectangular; 6″; aqua **2.00-3.00**

Standard Oil Co.; vertical on front; *Cleveland O.* on one side; *Favorite* on opposite side; rectangular; 6¼″; amethyst **2.00-3.00**

Staphylase Du Dr. Doyen; clear; 7½″ **2.00-6.00**

Stein & Co. Apothecarier, Jersey City; *M-W U.S.A.* under bottom; clear or amethyst; 5⅜″ **2.00-4.00**

Steelman & Archer, Philadelphia, PA.; on front; rectangular; 5½″; clear **3.00-6.00**

R.E. Stieraux Pills; on front in form of circle about the size of a half dollar; 1¾″; clear **2.00-3.00**

A. Stone & Co.; inside screw top; ***3 Philada*** **on screw top; aqua; 7½″, $10.00-25.00**

Strauss, Springfield Ave., N. High St. Neward, N.J.; 5¼″; clear **2.00-4.00**

Strontium; 7½″; aqua **4.00-6.00**

F.E. Suire & Co., Cincinnati; reverse side ***Waynes Duiretic Elixir;*** **8″ amber, $10.00-15.00**

Sulpho Lythin; amber; 3″ **2.00-3.00**

Sultan Drug Co.; *St. Louis & London* on other side; amber; 7¼″ **4.00-6.00**

Sutherland Sisters Hair Grower, New York; all 7 sisters on front in a sunken panel; *Sutherland Sisters* on the side; *New York* on opposite side; rectangular; *ABM:* 5¼″; clear **4.00-8.00**

The E.E. Sutherland Medicine Co.; aqua; 5½″ **2.00-3.00**

Sutherland Sisters Hair Grower; 6″; aqua **4.00-8.00**

L.B. Sutton; amber; 5½″ **2.00-4.00**

Swaim's; other panels; *Panacea, Established 1820 Philada;* aqua; 7″ **8.00-10.00**

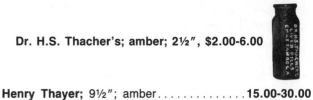

Dr. H.S. Thacher's; amber; 2½", $2.00-6.00

Swaim's; other panels; *Panacea, Phila;* pontil; olive; 8", $50.00-100.00

Swift's; cobalt blue; 9" **10.00-20.00**

Dr. Sykes; *Specific Blood Medicine, Chicago, Ill;* 6½"; clear **1.00-3.00**

Syr; Rhoead; cobalt blue; pontil; 8½" **20.00-25.00**

Syrup of Thedford's Black Drought; vertical on front in sunken panel; rectangular; *ABM;* clear **2.00-3.00**

Dr. Taft's Asthmalene N.Y.; on the front panel; aqua; rectangular; 3½" **2.00-4.00**

Henry Thayer; 9½"; amber **15.00-30.00**

Thomas Electric Oil; vertical on front in sunken panel; *Internal & External* on side; *Foster Milburn Co.* on opposite side; rectangular; 4¼"; clear **4.00-6.00**

Dr. S.N. Thomas Electric Oil; vertical on front; *External* on side; *Internal* on opposite side; *Northrup & Lyman, Toronto, Ont.* on back; double band collar; rectangular; 5½"; aqua **8.00-15.00**

Thompson's Herbal Compound, New York; label; 6¾"; clear or aqua **2.00-4.00**

Dr. Thompson's Sarsaparilla, Great English Remedy; on front indented panel; *Calais, Me. U.S.A.* side; *St. Stephens, N.B.* opposite side; rectangular; 9"; aqua **10.00-20.00**

Tangin; same on reverse side; 9"; amber, $10.00-12.00

Thompson's; *Philada* other side; *Diarrhea syrup* on back; aqua, $4.00-6.00

Tarrant & Co.; clear; 5¼" **3.00-6.00**

Taylor's Drug Store; clear or amethyst; 4" . . .**2.00-4.00**

Taylor's Drug Store; clear; 4¾" **4.00-6.00**

Taylor's Essence of Jamaica Ginger; 5½"; clear **8.00-12.00**

Teaberry for the Teeth & Breath; 3½"; clear **6.00-8.00**

Teinture D'Fotida; 5½"; amber **20.00-25.00**

Teissier Prevos A Paris; graphite pontil; 7½"; blue **50.00-70.00**

A Texas Wonder, Hall's Great Discover; *For Kidney, Bladder Troubles, E.W. Hall, St.Louis, Mo.;* 3½"; clear **2.00-4.00**

Dr. Thacher's; *Liver and Blood Syrup, Chattanooga, Tenn.* on the front panel; rectangular; 7¼" and 8¼"; amber **2.00-5.00**

Dr. Thacher's Liver and Blood Syrup; on the front; *Chattanooga, Tenn.* on one of the panels; *Sample* on the opposite panel; amber; rectangular; 3½" **2.00-4.00**

Dr. H.S. Thacher's Diarrhea Remedy, Chattanooga; on one of the panels; amethyst; square; 3⅜" **2.00-5.00**

Dr. Thacher's Vegetable Syrup, Chattanooga, Tenn.; on the front; amethyst; 7"; rectangular **1.00-2.00**

Dr. H.S. Thacher's Worm Syrup; on the front panel; *Chattanooga, Tenn.* on other panel; aqua; 4¼"; square **1.00-2.00**

Dr. Thacher's; olive; 3¼" **3.00-6.00**

Dr. Thacher's; *Chattanooga Tenn.* on side; aqua; 3¼" **3.00-4.00**

Dr. Thompson's; *Eye Water, New London, Conn.;* aqua; round; 3¾"; pontil **10.00-20.00**

Thurston & Kingsbury Tak Flavoring Extract, Bangor, Maine; vertical on front in oriental style letters; *Finest Quality Full Strength;* 5"; clear **3.00-4.00**

Dr. Tichenor's; aqua; *Antiseptic* on other side; 3¾" **4.00-8.00**

Dr. Tichenor's; on one side of panel; *Antiseptic* on the other side; rectangular; aqua; 5⅞" **1.00-2.00**

Dr. G.H. Tichenor's Antiseptic Refrigerant; one side *Sherrouse Medicine Co.;* other side *Ltd.; New Orleans La.;* 5¾"; aqua **8.00-10.00**

Tikheel; light blue; 6½" **4.00-6.00**

Tilden; under bottom; amber; 5" **2.00-4.00**

Tilden; amber; 7½" **2.00-4.00**

Claes Tilly; aqua; 3¾" **2.00-4.00**

G De Koning Tilly; oil; 1"; aqua **2.00-4.00**

Tippecanoe; amber, clear, aqua; 9" **60.00-80.00**

Tippecanoe; misspelled *Rochester* under bottom; 9"; amber **60.00-80.00**

Dr. Tobias, New York; aqua; 8" **4.00-8.00**

Dr. Tobias Venetian Horse Liniment, New York; on front and back; rectangular; 8¼"; aqua . . .**4.00-8.00**

Toka; reverse *Blood Tonic;* 8½"; aqua, $8.00-12.00

T. Tomlinson; aqua; 10½" **6.00-8.00**

Tonicio Oriental Para El Cabello; in 3 lines on sunken
panel on front; on one side _New York;_ on other _Lan-man Y Kemp,_ both in sunken panels, under bottom
_#34;_ 6"; aqua; flat collar; ringed neck **4.00-8.00**

To-Ni-Ta Lorents Med. Co. Trade Mark; around
shoulder; bitters label; amber; 9¾" **10.00-20.00**

R.E. Toombs Jr.; clear or amethyst; 5¼" **2.00-4.00**

Tooth Powder; label; 2"; milk glass **6.00-10.00**

Dr. Townsend; reverse _Sarsaparilla, 1850;_
9½" **60.00-100.00**

Dr. Townsend; _Sarsaparilla_ on other sides; pontil; 9½";
amber **60.00-150.00**

A. Trasks; _Magnetic Ointment_ on back; aqua; 2½" or
3¼" **4.00-6.00**

M. Tregor Sons, Baltimore Md., Wash. D.C.; E.R.B.;
8"; clear **4.00-8.00**

J. Triner, Chicago; on one panel; six panels; 5¼";
clear **8.00-10.00**

**Truax Rheumatic Rememdy, Ben O. Aldrich, Keene,
N.H.;** label; clear **3.00-5.00**

**Dr. Trues Elixir, Established 1851, Dr. J.F. True & Co.
Inc.;** _Auburn, Me.; Worm Expeller, Family Laxative_
on front and opposite side in sunken panel; rectangular; _ABM;_ 5½"; clear **3.00-4.00**

same as above except 7¾" **2.00-4.00**

**H.A. Tucker M.D., Brooklyn N.Y. Mo Diaphortic Com-
pound;** on front; ring top; 5½"; aqua **4.00-6.00**

J. Tucker, Druggist; reverse _Mobile;_
pontil; 7½"; aqua, **$18.00-20.00**

Nathan Tucker M.D.; _Star & Shield Specific for Asthma,
Hay Fever and All Catarrhal Diseases of the Res-
piratory Organs_ all on front; round; 4";
clear **4.00-6.00**

Turkish Foot Bath, Galled Armpits & Co; **4.00-8.00**

Turkish Liniment; 4¾"; aqua **2.00-4.00**

Robt. Turlington (Turlington misspelled); on one side
June 14, 1754; other side _London;_ back side _By the
Kings Royal Pat. Granted to;_ 2¾";
aqua **10.00-20.00**

Robt. Turlington; _By The Kings Royal Patent Granted
To_ on back; aqua; pontil; 2½" **15.00-30.00**

same except no pontil **6.00-10.00**

Turner Brothers, _New York, Buffalo, N.Y., San Francisco Cal._ on front; graphite ponti; tapered top; 9½";
amber . . . . **75.00+**

Tussicon; in one line vertical; ring top,
clear, 5" **7.00-10.00**

Dr. Tutt's; _New York_ on other side; _Asparagine_ on front;
aqua; 10¼" **6.00-10.00**

Dr. S.A. Tuttle's, Boston Mass.; on vertical panels;
twelve vertical panels; 6¼"; aqua **3.00-6.00**

Tuttle's Elixir Co., Boston, Mass; on two vertical
panels; twelve panels; 6¼"; amethyst **3.00-4.00**

Udolpho Wolfe's; on front panel; on back
Aromatic Schnapps in 2 lines; right side
plain; left _Schiedam;_ 2¼" square; beveled
corners; 1½" neck; golden amber,
$8.00-12.00

same except 9½"; light amber **4.00-6.00**

same except olive **12.00-25.00**

Udolpho Wolfe's; _Aromatic Schnapps_ on back;
Schiedam on side; other side plain;
olive; 8" **10.00-20.00**

Udolpho Wolfe's; _Aromatic Schnapps Schiedam_ on 2
sides; green; 7½" **12.00-18.00**

Udolpho Wolfe's; _Schiedam Aromatic Schnapps_ on 3
panels; yellow; 8" **10.00-25.00**

Dr. Ulrich; aqua; 7½" **4.00-8.00**

Uncle Sam's Nerve & Bone Linament; aqua . .**4.00-6.00**

Union Drug Co.; _Union Makes Strength_ (shield) _San
Francisco, Cal._ in slug plate, oval, fancy, clear,
flared lip, 6¼" **5.00-8.00**

U.S. Marine Hospital Service; clear; 5" **6.00-8.00**

U.S.A. Hospital Dept.; in a circle; flared top; oval; 2½";
cornflower blue **55.00-80.00**

United States Medicine Co.; _New York_ in 3 lines, flat
ring top, clear or amethyst, 5½" **7.00-10.00**

Van Antwerp's; clear; 6½" **2.00-4.00**

**Van Scoy Chemical Co., Serial #879, Mt. Gilead, O.
U.S.A.;** 6"; clear **3.00-4.00**

**Van Scoy Chemical Co., Serial No. 8795, Mt. Gilead,
O. U.S.A.;** 6"; clear **2.00-4.00**

Vanstans; aqua; 2" **2.00-4.00**

Van Vleet & Co.; _W.T. Co._ on bottom;
amber; 10" **6.00-8.00**

Dr. Van Werts Balsam; vertical on front in sunken panel;
Van Wert Chemical Co. on side; _Watertown, N.Y._ opposite side; beveled corners; 5¾";
aqua **4.00-6.00**

Vaseline; _Chesebrough New York,_ in 3 lines; 2½"; clear
or amethyst **2.00-4.00**

Vaseline; dark amber; 3"; machine
made, **$2.00-4.00**

Vasogen; amber; 3¼" **2.00-6.00**

Vicks; on one side; on other _Drops;_ cobalt; screw top;
machine made; 1⅞" tall, 1¼" wide, ½" thick; very
small **2.00-4.00**

Vin-Tone the Food Tonic; amber; 8¾".....**8.00-10.00**

The Charles A. Vogeler Company;
aqua; 6¼".........................**4.00-8.00**

The Charles A. Vogeler Co., St. Jacobs Oil, Baltimore, Md. U.S.A.; round; 6¼".............**4.00-6.00**

J.C. Wadleigh, Delights Spanish Lustra; tapered top; 6"; aqua.........................**4.00-6.00**

Dr. R.B. Waites, Local Anesthetic, Safe, Reliable, Non-Secret; vertical around bottle; ring collar; round; 3"; clear..........................**4.00-6.00**

Dr. R.B. Waite's Local Anaesthetic; *Safe Reliable Non-Secret, The Antecolor Mfg. Co., Springville, N.Y. U.S.A.;* 2¾"; clear...................**4.00-6.00**

Wait's Wild Cherry Tonic; *The Great Tonic* on back; amber; 8½", **$10.00-15.00**

Wakefields Black Berry Balsam; vertical on front; rectangular; 5"; blue aqua.................**3.00-4.00**

Wakelee's Camelline; vertical on front; rectangular; beveled corners; 4¾"; cobalt blue.......**6.00-8.00**
same as above except amber..........**3.00-4.00**

Walker's Tonic, Free Sample; 3⅜"; clear..**15.00-30.00**

Henry K. Wampole & Co.; clear or amethyst..**3.00-4.00**

Henry K. Wampole & Co.; clear or amethyst; 8¾".....................**3.00-6.00**

Henry K. Wampole & Co. Inc.; clear or amethyst; *408* on bottom; 8½".................**2.00-4.00**

Henry K. Wampole & Co. Inc.; 8½"; clear or amber......................**2.00-4.00**

Henry K. Wampole & Co. Inc. Philadelphia, PA. U.S.A.; on flat front panel; rectangular; 8¼"; amethyst.........................**3.00-4.00**
same as above except *ABM*............**2.00-3.00**

Dr. Wards Trade Mark; with line through it: *The J.R. Watkins Med. Co.* on side; *Winona, Minn.* on opposite side; 8¾"; amber...............**3.00-6.00**

W.R. Warner & Co.; clear; 2¼"............**2.00-4.00**

Warner & Co.; round bottom; sheared top; 2¾"; clear..............................**3.00-6.00**

Wm. R. Warner & Co. Philadelphia; in a race track circle in center; *W&C* on front; 6" body, 1½" neck, 2¼" square; square corners; under bottom *#67;* cobalt...........................**8.00-10.00**

Wm. R. Warner & Co.; label; amber; 5¼"....**2.00-4.00**

W.R. Warner & Co.; clear; 2½"............**3.00-6.00**

W.R. Warner & Co.; *Phila* on back; aqua; 8"; three-part mold...........................**2.00-6.00**

Wm. Warners & Co., Philada.; vertical on front; round; 4"; clear..........................**2.00-3.00**

Warners Safe Remedy; machine made; amber; 9".........................**8.00-15.00**

Warren's Mocking Bird Food; round; sheared top; 7"; aqua.........................**8.00-15.00**

Washingtonian Sarsaparilla; label; pontil; aqua.........................**10.00-15.00**

Watkins Chill Tonic; label; picture of J.R. Watkins and *Watkins Trade Mark;* embossed on opposite sides; *ABM;* 8½"; clear....................**3.00-4.00**

Watkins Dandruff Remover and Scalp Tonic; on side; *J.R. Watkins Co. Winona, Minn. USA.* on opposite side; rectangular; beveled corners; *ABM;* 6¾"; clear...............................**3.00-4.00**

Watkins Trialmark; 8½"; aqua, **$2.00-6.00**

The J.R. Watkins Co; in a sunken panel; 7¹/₁₆"; clear, amber...............................**2.00-4.00**
same except machine made............**1.00-2.00**

J.R. Watkins Med. Co.; clear or amethyst; 5¼".............................**2.00-4.00**

J.R. Watkins Medical Co.; 5¼"; clear or amber...............................**2.00-4.00**

The J.R. Watkins Medical Co.; *Winona Minn. U.S.A.* other side; round bottom; clear; machine made; 3¼".........................**4.00-6.00**

Watson's Pharmacy, Homer, N.Y.; *W.T. Co. U.S.A.* under bottom; 4¾"; clear or amethyst....**2.00-4.00**

Web's A No. 1 Cathartic Tonic; reverse side, *The Best Liver Kidney & Blood Purifier;* amber, **$15.00-30.00**

Webster Little; *W.T.Co.M U.S.A.* under bottom; clear; 4¾"...............................**2.00-6.00**

Weedon Drug Co.; *515 Franklin St. Tampa, Fla.* in 2 lines; regular medical bottle; clear or amethyst.........................**2.00-4.00**

Dr. T. West; clear; 5".................**2.00-4.00**

W.D. Co. 6A; under bottom; amber; 6".......**2.00-4.00**

J.B. Wheatleys Compound Syrup, Dallasburgh, Ky.; graphite pontil; 6"; aqua.............**40.00-70.00**

Wheeler's Tissue Phosphates; in 2 lines in a sunken panel; 2½"; square; 3 panels plain; beveled corners; 9"; under bottom monogram *WBYU* or other letters; aqua.........................**4.00-8.00**

**Wheelock Finlay & Co., Proprietors, Dr.Wilhoft's An-
tiperiodic or Fever & Ague Tonic, New Orleans;**
5"; clear **2.00-4.00**

A.J. White; on other panels; *Design Pat 1894* on bottom;
green; 7" **8.00-10.00**

Dr. White's; on other side *Dandelion Alternative,* applied
top, aqua, 9⅝" x 3¼" x 2" **7.00-10.00**

White & Co.; *Proprietors, New York;* 9½";
amber **10.00-20.00**

White's Cream; 5¼"; aqua, $2.00-3.00

**White's Liniment, White & Jones Proprietors, Blaine,
Maine;** vertical around bottle; ground top for glass
stopper; 5"; clear **3.00-4.00**

Whitehurst; vertical on center front; flask shape; 3½";
aqua **2.00-3.00**
same as above except *ABM* **2.00-3.00**

White Wine and Tar Syrup; vertical on front in sunken
panel; *Warners* on side; *Coldwater, Mich.;* 7";
aqua **3.00-4.00**

Williams Magnetic Relief; on one side *A.P. Williams;*
other side *Frenchtown N.J.;* 6¼"; aqua . . .**4.00-6.00**

Wilson Fairbank & Co.; 10" **8.00-12.00**

J.H. Wilson; reverse side *Brooklyn, N.Y.;* front side
Wilsons Carbolated Cod Liver Oil; 8";
aqua **10.00-12.00**

The Wilson Laboratories; machine made;
clear **2.00-4.00**

Winchester Crystal Cleaner; label; 6¼";
clear **4.00-6.00**

**J. Winchester, N.Y., Dr. J.F. Churchills, Specific
Remedy For Consumption, Hypophosphites of
Lime & Soda;** tapered top; 7¼"; aqua **4.00-6.00**

Wingfield; clear or amethyst; 5½" **2.00-4.00**

Mrs. Winslow's Soothing Syrup; *Curtis & Perkins,
Prop.,* aqua O.P. 5" **17.00-23.00**

Mrs. Winslow's Soothing Syrup; *Curtis & Perkins Proprietors,* in four vertical lines; 5¼"; short neck; small
round bottle; aqua **2.00-4.00**
same as above except pontil **2.00-4.00**

**Mrs. Winslow's Toothing Syrup, Curtis & Perkins Pro-
prietors;** 5"; aqua **10.00-15.00**

Winstead's; *Lax-Fos* on other side; amber;
7¼" **2.00-4.00**

Wintersmith; amber; 9¼" **6.00-8.00**

Wintersmith; amber; 8½" **3.00-5.00**

L.Q.C. Wishart's; pine tree trademark on one side; *Pine
Tree Tar Cordial Phila* on other side; different sizes
and colors **25.00-50.00**

Dr. Wistar's Balsam of Wild Cherry, Cinc. O.; 5½";
aqua **4.00-8.00**

Dr. Wistar's Balsam of Wild Cherry, 1848-1896; six
panels; pontil; clear or aqua **10.00-25.00**

Dr. Wistar's Balsam of Wild Cherry Philada.; on five
consecutive panels; eight panels in all; 5";
aqua **4.00-6.00**

Dr. Wistar's; same as above, 5⅝" **5.00-10.00**

**Dr. Wistar's Balsam of Wild Cherry, Seth W. Fowler &
Sons, Boston;** on six consecutive panels; 3⅝";
aqua **4.00-8.00**

Wolfe's; *Schnapps* on one panel; *X* under bottom;
amber; 8" **15.00-25.00**

Wolfstirns Rheumatic & Gout Remedy, Hoboken, N.J.;
vertical on front; rectangular; 5"; aqua **3.00-4.00**

That Wondrous Liniment; on front vertical; *A
Schoenhelt* on side; *San Jose, Cal.* on opposite side;
rectangular; beveled corners; 4¼"; aqua . .**5.00-8.00**

Wood's Pine Syrup Compound; aqua; 5¾" . .**3.00-5.00**

N. Wood & Son; on one side panel; *Portland, Me.* other
panel; clear or amethyst; 5¾" **6.00-8.00**

Woodard Clark & Co. Chemist, Portland Co.; 6¼";
clear or amber **2.00-4.00**

The Wright Rapid Relief Co.; 5¾"; clear **8.00-12.00**

Wright's Condensed Smoke; label with directions; *ABM;*
9½"; amber **2.00-3.00**

W T CO.; under bottom; amber; 3¼" **6.00-10.00**

W.T. Co. 4 U.S.A.; under bottom; aqua; 7¾" .**2.00-3.00**

W.T. Co. 9; under bottom; aqua; 2½" **1.00-2.00**

W.T. Co. 3; under bottom; amber; 4¾" **1.00-2.00**

W & T 50; under bottom; clear; 6½" **1.00-2.00**

**W.T.U.D.Co. 16; under bottom;
amber; 8", $8.00-10.00**

Wyeth; amber; 6¼" **2.00-3.00**

Wyeth 119 6; under bottom in sunken panel; 1¾" x
1¹³⁄₁₆"; 3⅝" tall; clear, amethyst **3.00-6.00**

Wyeth; under bottom; clear or amethyst; 3½" .**2.00-4.00**

Wyeth; under bottom; amber; 3¼" **1.00-2.00**

Wyeth & Bro, Philada; in a circle; saddle type flask;
under bottom *226A;* amber; 7½", 1½"
neck **2.00-4.00**
same except cobalt blue **4.00-8.00**

Wyeth & Bro.; saddle type flask; 7½"; amber .**4.00-8.00**

John Wyeth; clear; 3" **1.00-2.00**

John Wyeth & Bro., Beef Juice; on front; round; 3½";
amber **2.00-4.00**

John Wyeth & Bro.; *Pat May 16th 1899* under bottom;
cobalt; 6½" **8.00-15.00**
same except 3½" **10.00**

John Wyeth & Brother; *Philadelphia, Liquid Extract
Malt;* 9"; squat body; amber **4.00-8.00**

John Wyeth & Brother, Phila. 1870; round; 9″;
blue **10.00-20.00**

John Wyeth & Brother; saddle shape;
clear; 7¾″, **$3.00-6.00**

John Wyeth & Bro., Take Next Dose AT; around base
of neck; *Pat. May 16;* cap shows hours 1 to 12;
square; 5¾″; cobalt blue **5.00-8.00**
same as above except *ABM* **5.00-6.00**

**Dr. Wynkcops Katharismic Honduras, Sarsaparilla,
N.Y.;** 10½″ **20.00-40.00**

X-Lalia, Boston, Mass; clear or
amethyst; 7¼″ **4.00-6.00**

Yager's Sarsaparilla; 8½″; golden amber .. **10.00-15.00**

Madame M. Yale Co., N.Y. & Chicago U.S.A.; on each
side *La Freckla;* 6½″; clear **4.00-8.00**

Ben Lee Young; clear; 3½″ **2.00-4.00**

Ben Lee Young; clear; 3½″ **2.00-4.00**

Yucatan Chill-Tonic; label; embossed *Yucatan Chill-
Tonic Improved, Evansville, Ind.;* 6¼″;
clear **4.00-6.00**

Zipps; in fancy letters; *Cleveland, O.;* 5½″;
clear **3.00-4.00**
same except amber **4.00-8.00**

Zoa-Phora; c. 1900 .... **4.00-6.00**

Zoa-Phora, Woman's Friend; in front; on side
Kalamazoo, Mich. USA; ring top; 7½″; blue
green **3.00-6.00**

Zollick Hoffers, Anti-Rheumatic Cordial; Phil., tapered
top, pontil, 6½″ **17.00-23.00**

Poison

The colors of poison bottles were likely to be ghast-
ly shades of blues and browns. Bottles were likely to
be shaped as coffins or long bones and have ominous
embossments of human skulls resting on crossbones.
Containers were also likely to have ribbed or quilted
surfaces so that they could not be mistaken for
medicine bottles even when people would grasp about
in the dark.

The skull and crossbones was once a Christian
symbol. When eighteenth-century pirates used it on
their flags, it came to mean death; and this negative
meaning soon became associated with poisons.
Legislation to prevent the accidental intake or use of
poisons was adopted by the State of New York in 1829.
The word "poison" was to be inscribed somewhere on
all such containers. As early as 1853 the American
Pharmaceutical Association recommended national
laws be adapted to identify such substances. The
American Medical Association suggested in 1872 that
poison containers be uniformly identifed by their rough
surface on one side and the word "poison" on the
other. Yet between the years 1870 and 1930 a variety
of poison containers continued to be manufactured. In
the 1930's it became known that the many shapes and
colors of poison containers intrigued and attracted
children; and efforts directed at uniformity in packaging were then made.

John H.B. Howell of Newton, New Jersey, designed the first safety closure in 1886. However, such
closures did not become popular until simple bottle
designs for poisons were stressed in the 1930's. Most
poison bottles range in size from one-half ounce to sixteen ounces, though some are larger than sixteen
ounces. Most of the containers were cobalt blue though
some manufacturers used amber or green. Use of clear
glass for poison bottles is very rare.

Acid; round; clear or green; 6⅜″ **3.00-4.00**

Amber; vertical ribs all around; rectangular; ring collar;
ABM; 3¼″ **5.00-8.00**

Sp. Ammon Ar.; label; clear; 9½″ **10.00-15.00**

Baltimore, Md.; under bottom; 3″; amber **3.00-4.00**

Betul-OI, W.T. Co. U.S.A.; under bottom;
clear; 4¼″ **3.00-5.00**

Bowkers Plrox; *670-2* under bottom; clear or amethyst;
4½″ **3.00-5.00**
same as above, except 8″ **14.00-19.00**

Bowmans; in script; *Drug Stores* on side panels; ribs;
5¼″; cobalt; hexagonal **30.00-45.00**

Browns Rat Killer; under it, *C. Wakefiled Co.;* 3″; aqua;
applied lip **7.00-11.00**

Brown; three-sided; *ABM;* 4½″ **3.00-5.00**

Carbolic Acid; *3 oz.* on each side, poison crosses all
around it; ring top; 5″; cobalt **20.00-30.00**
same as above, except no *Carbolic
Acid;* 8½″ **32.00-45.00**

The Clarke Fluid Co., Cincinnati; *Poison*
on side; *8 to 64 oz.* graduated measure
on other side; clear or amethyst; quart
size, **$20.00-30.00**

C.L.C. Co. Patent Applied For; under bottom; 2¾″;
cobalt **5.00-8.00**

C.L.C. & Co. Patent Applied For; under bottom; emerald green; hexagonal; ½ ounce to 16 ounces **22.00-30.00**

same as above, except cobalt **30.00-45.00**

Cobalt blue; seven concave vertical panels on front half; ¼ oz. at top on front; square collar; oval; *ABM;* 2⅞" **4.00-6.00**

Cocaine Hydrochlor Poison; label; triangular; 5"; amber; vertical ribs; ring top **12.00-17.00**

Crossbones & star; 2¼"; snap-on top; amber **22.00-30.00**

Curtice Bros Preserves; *Rochester, N.Y.;* clear or amethyst; 7"; four-part mold **14.00-19.00**

Dagger; on front; square; 5"; aqua; pouring lip **12.00-17.00**

D D D; clear or amethyst; 3¾" and 5½" **5.00-8.00**

D.D. Chemical Co., N.Y. Sample; on front of panel; amber; 5"; square **2.00-3.00**

Dead Stuck; *Non-poisonous, won't stain* in small letters, *For Bugs* on same line but small letters, in center a bug, on each side *Trade Mark,* under it *Gottlieb Marshall & Co., Cersal, Germany, Philadelphia, Pa.* in 3 lines; under bottle *X;* aqua; 7" tall, 3½" x 1½" **20.00-30.00**

Depose; on bottom; four-cornered; 4⅛" tall, 1¾" x ½" neck; label reads *Riodine Organic Iodine 50 capsules* **6.00-9.00**

Finlay Dicks & Co Distributors, New Orleans, La, Dicks Ant Destroyer; sheared top; clear or amethyst; 6½" **12.00-15.00**

DPS; below skull and cross on front; *Poison* on each side; cross on four sides; ring top; cobalt **10.00-15.00**

Durfree Embalming Fluid Co.; *8 to 64 oz.* graduated measure; clear or amethyst; ½ gallon . . .**16.00-23.00**

Durfee Embalming Fluid Co.; clear or amethyst; 8¾", $17.00-24.00

Ecorc:Quinquina Pulv; 5¾"; clear; painted brown; pontil **15.00-22.00**

Eli Lilly & Co.; *Poison* on each panel; amber; 2"; four other different sizes **7.00-10.00**

E.R.S. & S.; under bottom; vertical ribbing on all sides; space for label; double ring top; 4½" square cobalt **15.00-22.00**

Evans Medical Ltd, Liverpool; label; *Chloroform B.A., Poison;* number and *U.Y.B.* under bottom; *ABM;* amber; 6½" **5.00-8.00**

Extrait Fl; De Quinquina; 6½"; amber **15.00-22.00**

Ferris & Co. Ltd., Bristol; near base; *poison* in center; vertical ribbing; wide ring top; aqua; 7½" **11.00-15.00**

Fortune Ward Drug Co.; *Larkspur Lotion Poison, 119 Maderson, Memphis, Tenn.* on label; on each side *for External Use Only;* ring top; 5½"; amber **7.00-11.00**

Frederia; vertical; flask type; hobnail cover; clear; ½ pint **50.00-70.00**

The Froser Tablet Co.; *St. Louis—N.Y.; Brooklyn, Chicago; Sulphate poison tablets;* label; 5¾"; *ABM;* clear **5.00-8.00**

F.S. & Co. P.M.; on base, *Poison* vertically, surrounded by dots; two sides plain; rectangular; amber; 2¾"; ring top **11.00-16.00**

J.G. Godding & Co., Apothecaries, Boston, Mass.; in 3 lines in center; ribs on each side; ring top; 4⅛"; hexagon; cobalt **18.00-25.00**

Grasselli Arsenate of Lead; *Poison;* on shoulder; different sizes **50.00-65.00**

HB Co; under bottom within an indented circle; glass top ornaments with *Poison* around half of bottle; nobs and lines; very few lines or nobs in back; 6½"; cobalt **7.00-10.00**

same as above except smaller; 3¾" **5.00-8.00**

same as above except plain bottom **4.00-6.00**

Hobnail Poison; collared neck; made using double gather; attributed to N. England; clear; 6" **60.00-80.00**

Ikey Einstein, Poison; on each side of it; rectangular; 3¾"; ring top; clear **18.00-25.00**

Iodine, Poison Tinct.; machine made; 2¼"; amber **4.00-6.00**

Iodine Tinct; no embossing on bottle, but stopper on glass tube is embossed; *The S.H. Wetmore Co./Pat. Aug 19, 1919;* square; ring collar; *ABM;* light amber; 3½" **4.00-7.00**

JTM & Co.; under bottom; 1¼" slim letters *Poison;* label reads *Miliken's Tri-Sept. Bernays No 2 Unofficial Poison* on two panels; tablet container; amber; 3" **6.00-9.00**

J.T.M. & Co.; under bottom; three-cornered; *Poison* on one side; amber; 10"; two plain sides; ring top **100.00-135.00**

Lin, Ammoniae; label; 6¾"; green **18.00-25.00**

Lin Bellad; label; 7¾"; green **26.00-37.00**

Lin Bellad; label; 7"; cobalt **55.00-75.00**

Lin Belladon; label; 7"; green; under bottom *Y.G. Co.* **18.00-25.00**

Lin Saponis; label; 6¾"; green **18.00-25.00**

Liq. Arsenic; label; 5¾"; green **18.00-25.00**

Liq. Hyd; Perchlor Poison; label; 9"; green **22.00-33.00**

Liq. Morph. Hydrochl Poison; label; 4½"; cobalt **33.00-46.00**

Liq. Strych. Hyd; label; 6"; green **18.00-25.00**

Lray Poison; label; embossed ribs on edges; amber; 3½" **14.00-20.00**

Edward R. Marshall Co.; *Dead Stuck Insecticide;* 9"; green **30.00-45.00**

McCormick & Co.; Registered Trade Mark., Balto, Md., Patented; three-sided; cobalt; 4" **7.00-10.00**

same as above except *July 8th 1882* **8.00-11.00**

McCormick & Co., Baltimore; three-sided; clear or amethyst; 3¾" **6.00-9.00**

McCormick & Co., Balto; in a circle; in center a fly or bee, under it *Patent Applied For;* triangular; 1½", 2¾" tall; cobalt; ring top **6.00-9.00**

Melvin & Badger, Apothecariers, Boston, Mass; ribbing on side; ring top; 7½"; cobalt **100.00-130.00**

R.C. Millings Bed Bug Poison; *Charleston, S.C;* clear; 6¼"; shoulder strap on side **12.00-17.00**

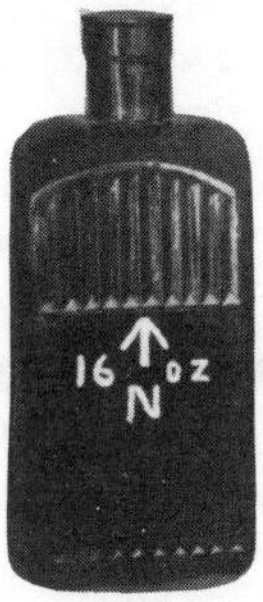

N 16 Oz; poison label; cobalt; 6½", $25.00-38.00

N 8 Oz; poison label; cobalt; 6" **12.00-17.00**

Norwick; on base; coffin shape; *Poison* vertical down center of front, also horizontal in back on shoulder; 7½"; covered with diamond embossed; amber **12.00-17.00**

same as above except cobalt; *ABM* **12.00-17.00**

same as above except *Bimal* **27.00-36.00**

The Norwick Pharmacy Co. Norwick, N.Y.; label; *M* under bottom; 3½"; *ABM;* cobalt **11.00-16.00**

Not To Be Taken; in center vertically; vertical wide ribbing on sides; rectangular; 6¾"; cobalt; ring top **11.00-16.00**

Not To Be taken; in center of bottle on each side in 3 vertical lines; *#12* under bottom; 7¾"; cobalt **45.00-65.00**

same as above except in 2 lines *Poison, Not to Be Taken;* cobalt **45.00-65.00**

same as above except emerald green, clear **17.00-25.00**

01. Camphor Forte; label; crystal glass; 5"; amber **25.00-35.00**

01. Eucalypti; label; crystal glass; 6½"; amber, $26.00-35.00

01. Sinap. Aeth.; label; crystal glass; 5"; amber **26.00-35.00**

Orge Monde; label; cut glass; blue **27.00-35.00**

Owl Poison Ammonia; label; three-cornered; 5¼"; cobalt **30.00-40.00**

The Owl Drug Co.; *Poison* other side; three-cornered; 8"; cobalt **100.00-130.00**

The Owl Drug Co.; in script on shoulder; on side vertically *Poison,* on other owl sitting on top of a mortar; different sizes; cobalt; ring top **6.00-25.00**

Poison Bottle; on one side; irregular diamond shape; ridges on 3 corners; amber; 4 sizes **5.00-8.00**

some have *Poison* on 2 sides **7.00-10.00**

some machine made **4.00-6.00**

Poison; on one panel; nobbed on 3 sides; *16* on bottom; round back; 3⁹⁄₁₆"; also 4 other sizes . . . **10.00-15.00**

Poison; on each side panel; no round back; four-cornered; 3 sides nobbed, other plain; 2¾"; amber **6.00-9.00**

Poison; on each side panel; round back; 3 sides nobbed; 4 different sizes; machine made; amber **6.00-8.00**

Poison, Tincture Iodine; under a skull and crossbones; ¼ on one side of skull, *Oz* on other; oval; 5 panels on front; under bottom *At 1-7-36;* 2¼" tall, ¾" x 1"; amber **9.00-13.00**

Poison; on each side; amber; *P.D. & Co.* on bottom; 2½" **6.00-9.00**

Poison; plain; different sizes; cobalt **6.00-15.00**

Poison; label; dark blue; 8" **6.00-8.00**

Poison; ribs in front; black back; 13½"; cobalt; *90* under bottom **85.00-115.00**

Poison; casket type; hobnail finish; amber; 3¼" **80.00-100.00**

Poison; *Use With Caution* on other side; cobalt; 8¾", $18.00-25.00

Poison Do Not Take; (N in Not backward); *DCP* under bottom; 4¼" **20.00-28.00**

Poison; label; cobalt; 8" **25.00-35.00**

Poison; machine made; ground top; clear; 13½" **17.00-26.00**

Poison; *12* under bottom; *Not To Be Taken* on side; cobalt; 7¾", $45.00-60.00

Poison; label; three-cornered; *74* under bottom; cobalt; 2½" **4.00-6.00**

Poison; label; cobalt; 5" **18.00-25.00**

Poison; flask; made rough to avoid a mistake in the dark; sheared top; ½ pint; aqua **130.00-170.00**

same as above except pontil; green **50.00-85.00**

Poison; on each side panel; *WRW & Co.* under bottom; amber; 2¾" **4.00-6.00**

X; around *Poison* in one panel; *X* around plain side *1 oz. use with caution;* diamond shape with letter D under bottom; ring top; 3¼"; cobalt **20.00-30.00**

Poison; label; dark blue; 8" **12.00-18.00**

Poison; label; 3½"; cobalt or amber **7.00-10.00**

Poison; label; 3¼"; cobalt **9.00-13.00**

Poison; skull; _Pat. Applied For_ **on bottom rim;** _S_ **under bottom; ceramic reproduction; 3½"; cobalt, $25.00-50.00**

Poison; clear; 6½"; embossed picture of rat on front; machine made **7.00-10.00**

Pyrox Bowker Insecticide Co., Boston & Baltimore; cream crock; glass top; 7½" **10.00-15.00**

Rat Poison; horizontal on round bottle; 2½"; clear or amethyst **18.00-26.00**

Rddes, 7073; under bottom; 6½"; three-cornered with ribs or ridges; ring top; aqua **18.00-26.00**

Reese Chemical Co., Cleveland, Ohio; _For External Use Only, etc.;_ rectangular; 5½"; sides ribbed; flat and ring top; cobalt, green, clear **16.00-24.00**

Rigo; embossed on base; vertical on left panel; _Use with Caution;_ in center _Not to be Taken;_ right usage extreme with stars all around bottle; ring top; cobalt **30.00-40.00**

Roman Inc.; vertical in script in center; ribbed on each side; hexagonal; ring top; 5¼"; emerald green **20.00-28.00**

S & D 173; under bottom; _ABM;_ poison label; 2½"; cobalt **17.00-25.00**

Sharp & Dohme; on one panel; _Phila_ on other panel; label; _X126-1_ under bottom; three-cornered; cobalt; 2" **9.00-12.00**

Sharp & Dohme/Baltimore; on 2 panels; six vertical panels; bulbous shoulder; ring collar; amber; _ABM;_ 2½" **4.00-6.00**

Sharp & Dohme; on one panel; _Baltimore, Md.;_ three-cornered; 3½"; cobalt **6.00-9.00**

Sharp & Dohme; on one panel; other _Phila;_ label reads _Ergotole D & D;_ three-cornered; 2"; cobalt; under bottom _X-126-1_ **9.00-12.00**

Skull & crossbones on each of six vertical panels, also _Gift_ embossed on each panel, (_gift_ means poison in German); aqua or clear; flared collar; 8⅛" **13.00-18.00**

Skull; _Poison_ on forehead; crossbones under bottom; 2" round, 3" tall, 1" neck; ring top; cobalt; _Pat. Appl'd For_ on base in back **100.00-200.00**

Spirits; silver and milk glass; 9" **25.00-35.00**

Sol. Trypaflavin; _1 + 49;_ crystal glass; 5"; amber **23.00-32.00**

Syr:Hypoph: Co.; 9"; green **21.00-29.00**

Syr:Fer:Pa;Co.; 7"; cobalt **48.00-62.00**

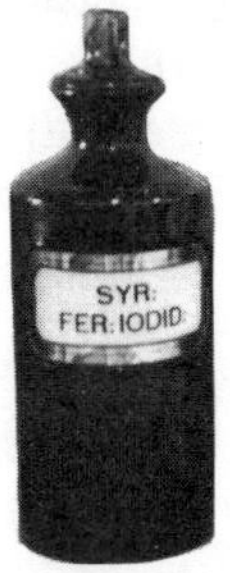

Syr:Fer:Iodid; 7"; cobalt, $75.00-100.00

Teinture de Cochenille; label; 7½"; amber **14.00-20.00**

F.A. Thompson & Co. Detroit; on front; _Poison_ on sides; ribbed corner; coffin type; ring top; 3½" **35.00-48.00**

Tinct Celladon, Poison; round bottle; vertical ribbing; aqua and green **32.00-45.00**

Tincture Iodine; in 3 lines under skull and crossbones; square; flat ring and ring top; amber; _ABM_ **6.00-9.00**

same as above except _BIMAL_ **9.00-13.00**

same as above except 2¾" **6.00-9.00**

Tinct. Aconiti.; label; 6"; green **18.00-26.00**

Tinct; Aconiti; label; 7¾"; green; _Y.G.Co._ under bottom **25.00-34.00**

Tinct. Camph: Co.; Poison; label; 9"; green, $22.00-30.00

Tinccт. Chlorof. et Morph. Co.; label; 7¾"; green **25.00-34.00**

Tinct. Conii, Poison; label; 6"; cobalt **32.00-43.00**

Tinct. Ergotae. Amm; _Y.G.Co.;_ under bottom; 7¾"; green **25.00-34.00**

Tinct. Iodi Mit.; label; 7¾"; green **25.00-34.00**

Tinct. Lobeliae Aeth; label; 6"; green **17.00-24.00**

Tinct. Nux Vom; label; 6"; green **17.00-24.00**

Tinct. Opll; label; 6"; green **17.00-24.00**

Tinct. Opll; _Poison_ on base; 7"; cobalt **35.00-46.00**

Tincture; Senegae; label; under bottom numbers _6_ _U.G.B.; ABM;_ amber; 6" **10.00-15.00**

Trilets; vertical; other side _poison;_ triangular; 3½"; cobalt; ribbed corner; _ABM_ **7.00-10.00**

same as above except _Bimal_ **12.00-17.00**

Triloids; on one panel of triangular bottle; _Poison_ on another; the other plain; corners nobbed; number under bottom; 3¼"; cobalt **6.00-9.00**

Tri-Seps; _Milliken Poison;_ one ribbed side; two for label; under bottom in sunken panel _JTM & CO.;_ ring top; 1½" x 2" tall, ¾" neck; 1¼" letters _Poison_ on side **6.00-8.00**

U.D.O.; on base; _Poison_ vertically on 2 panels; triangular; 5¼"; ring top; cross stitch around _Poison;_ cobalt **18.00-25.00**

same as above, except 8½" **22.00-32.00**

Vapo-Cresolene Co.; vertical on one panel with four rows of nail heads; _Patd. U.S. July 1794 Eng. July 23, 94_ on next panel with nail heads; square; double band collar; aqua; _ABM;_ 5½" **5.00-8.00**

same as above except clear; 4" **5.00-8.00**

same as above except S is reversed; dated _July 23, 94_ **10.00-20.00**

Victory Chemical Co.; *Quick Death Insecticide, 148 Fairmount Ave. Phila. Pa. 8 oz.;* 7"; clear . . .**11.00-16.00**

W.R.W. & Co.; under bottom; *Poison* on each side; ribbed corner; rectangular; 2½"; ring top . . **12.00-17.00**

John Wyeth & Co. Phila; on front; oval; cobalt; 4"; cross around base and side; flat ring collar**6.00-9.00**

John Wyeth & Bros., Phila; in 2 lines on side; square; 2¼" **17.00-23.00**

Wyeth Poison; vertical in back; round ring base and top; 2¼"; cobalt. **10.00-15.00**

same as above, except amber **6.00-9.00**

Soda

On a May afternoon in 1886, "Doc" Pemberton of Atlanta, Georgia, patiently stirred a mixture in a three-legged pot in his back yard. When at last it was ready, he sampled it and thought that he had been successful. Just to be sure he took a portion to Willis Venable, the proprietor of Jacob's Drug Store. Venable added ice and tap water to the syrup, tasted it and liked it, and agreed to sell it as a headache cure. Only one drink of Coca-Cola was consumed that day, but now over ninety-five million drinks of it are downed daily. "Doc" Pemberton was never able to cash in on the worldwide success of the new drink and made only fifty dollars in the first year of its existence.

Business did improve, however, after that hard first year when it was discovered that the addition of carbonated water made the drink taste better. Pemberton, unaware of the reverberations his discovery would cause, died in 1888, four years before a corporation was formed to manufacture the drink on a larger scale. The recipe for Coca-Cola was and still is a guarded secret and has never been exactly copied.

It occurred to Joseph A. Biedenharn in 1894 that if he could put Coca-Cola in bottles he could sell a great deal more of the beverage. He loaded the containers on his truck and peddled the drink, already a favorite of the rural people when they came to town, throughout the countryside around Vicksburg, Mississippi.

Alex Samuelson is credited with designing the familiar "Coke" bottle in 1915. A supervisor of the Root Glass Company in Terre Haute, Indiana, he studied drawings of cola nuts, the brown, bitter-tasting oval seeds from which Coca-Cola syrup was made. The result was the "hobble skirt" or "Mae West" bottle adopted by the Coca-Cola company in 1916. Though it resembled the cola nut in shape, it was dubbed "hobble skirt" after its similarity to a ladies' fashion fad of the day. Except for a minor trimming in the middle, the bottle has remained the same. Prior to 1916, a variety of shapes can be found.

Many people attempted to cash in on the rising popularity of Coca-Cola by mixing their own cola drinks. The most successful of these was Caleb D. Bradham of New Bern, North Carolina, who began producing Brad's Drink in 1890. In 1896, he changed its name to Pep-Kola and two years later to Pipi-Cola. It was not until 1906 that it finally became known as Pepsi-Cola.

Ever since it was discovered that some mineral springs contained natural carbonation, people had been trying to duplicate nature. It was a task assigned to sixteenth-century scientists, but Joseph Priestley, the English scientist who discovered oxygen, is credited with carbonating water in 1772. He hastily proclaimed the medicinal values of carbonated water, which were proved false. Small quantities of soda water were sold by Professor Benjamin Silliman of Yale in 1806. By 1810 a New York fountain sold homemade seltzers as sure cures for overweight. Flavored soda appeared in 1881, five years before Pemberton made his Coca-Cola, when a drink called Imperial Inca Cola was marketed. In the years that followed, many other flavored sodas—strawberry, orange, lemon, grape— were manufactured and sold.

Most of the early soda bottlers made their own products and sold them in the immediate area. It was not until the turn of the nineteenth century that the local plants began to expand. Many early soda bottles can be found with pontil scars—a pontil is a rod that holds the bottle at the bottom while it is eased away from the blowpipe at the neck. Most soda bottles, however, however, are unscarred.

In the days of sailing vessels, they often served as ballast; more than just dead weight, they could be sold for a profit at the destination. The flat bottoms made upright stacking impossible, which was the precise intention since they were stopped with cork. Cork expands when moist, thereby securely locking the contents within. If the cork was allowed to dry, it was quite likely that it would be expelled with a loud "pop," hence the nickname for soda.

One of the most popular bottles among collectors today is the John Ryan bottle. In addition to soda, John Ryan bottled ale, beer, bitters and cordials in containers that ranged in color from amber and aqua to cobalt blue and lime green. Ryan's first plant was built in Savannah, Georgia, in 1852 and others quickly followed in Atlanta, Augusta and Columbus. Prior to 1883, most of the bottles were embossed without a date with the exception of those that bore the dates 1852, 1859 and 1866.

A.B. Co., Alliance, O.; Hutchinson type; 6½"; aqua **8.00-15.00**

Abilena #1; under bottom; amber; label; 6" . . .**4.00-6.00**

The Acme Soda Water Co. Pittsburg, Registered; reverse side *W.A.S. Co.* in hollow letters; 6½"; aqua or clear. **8.00-20.00**

Alabama Bottling Co.; aqua; *A* under bottom; 7½"; in back—a bird in a circle *This Bottle Prop. of A.B.Co. Not To Be Sold* **8.00-15.00**

Alabama Grocery Co.; *Registered* on shoulder; clear; 8" **2.00-4.00**

Ala Cola; aqua, 7¾" **2.00-6.00**

Alexandria Bottling, Indiana; 7½"; aqua **8.00-12.00**

Alpha; *B.H.A.* in back; light green or aqua; 6" **2.00-4.00**

Alvan Valley Bottle Works, Everett, Wash.; 8½"; aqua **4.00-6.00**

H. Aman, Cheyenne, Wyo.; in a circle; Hutchinson type; 6½"; aqua **10.00-20.00**

The A.M. & B. Co., Reg. Waco Texas & St. Louis, Mo.; reverse side, *We Pay for Evidence Conv. Thieves For Refilling Our Bottles;* 8½"; aqua **8.00-10.00**

America Soda Works, Trade Mark, Portland, Or.; 7¾"; green **4.00-6.00**

Amos Post; *Not To Be Sold* on back base; clear or amethyst; 7¾", $8.00-15.00

Aqua Dist & Bot Co.; aqua; 8½" **4.00-6.00**

Arizona Bottling Works; *A* under bottom; *This Bottle Must Be Returned* on base; aqua; 7" **4.00-6.00**

Arter & Wilson, Manuf; *Boston* in 4 vertical lines, tapered top, graphite pontil, light green, 7" **60.00-80.00**

Artesian Bottling Works, Dublin, Ga.; in sunken circle; with ribs; bottom; or ten panels; *C.C.Co.* on one panel; 7"; aqua **4.00-6.00**

Augustin Vitale, Providence, R.I. A.V.; monogram all in slug plate on front; blob top; 9¼"; clear . . .**4.00-6.00**

Austin Ice & Bottling; *Reg. Must Not Be Sold* on back; *71* under bottom; 7¼"; aqua **4.00-8.00**

Wm. Aylmer Fargo, O.J.; 7"; blue **6.00-12.00**

B; large letter, tapered top, *(Belding, Cal.),* aqua or clear, 7½" **17.00-23.00**

B; on front; gravitating stopper made by John Matthews; *N.Y. Pat. Oct. 11, 1864* on bottom; 7¼"; blue aqua **4.00-8.00**

Babb & Co., San Francisco, Cal; in 3 lines; graphite pontil; 7½"; green **20.00-50.00**

Daniel Bahr; light blue; *D.B.* in back; 7½" **4.00-6.00**

John C. Baker & Co.; aqua; 7½" **4.00-8.00**

J. Ed Baker; clear; 9½" **3.00-8.00**

J. Ed Baker, 417 Washington St. Newburgh, N.Y.; on front slug plate; 7⅛"; aqua **4.00-6.00**

The Property of Mrs. J. Ed Baker, Newburgh, N.Y.; on front in oval slug plate; blob top; 9"; clear **4.00-8.00**

John S. Baker Soda Water T.B.I.N.S.; eight-sided; 7½"; green **4.00-8.00**

Barclay Street; in center *41, N.Y.;* applied lip; 7"; green **10.00-20.00**

Barth, Elias; in ¼ moon letters, under it in 2 lines *Burlington, N.J.,* blob top, squat type bottle, aqua, 7" **17.00-23.00**

Bartlett Bottling Work; 6½"; clear or amethyst **8.00-10.00**

Bartow Bottling Works; aqua; *root* under bottom; 7½" **2.00-6.00**

F. Bauman, Santa Maria, Cal.; in a circle; *Soda Works* in center; 7¼"; aqua **4.00-8.00**

Bay City Pop Works M.T. Registered Bay City, Mich.; on front in slug plate; *This Bottle Not To Be Sold,* on opposite side; blob top; quart; 8¾"; apple green **5.00-10.00**

Bay City Soda Water Co., S.F.; star symbol; 7"; blue **10.00-15.00**

B. & C., S.F; applied lip; 7¼"; cobalt **25.00-35.00**

R.M. Becker's; aqua; *B* under bottom; 6½" . .**2.00-6.00**

R.M. Becker; aqua; *B* on bottom; 7¼" **4.00-6.00**

R.M. Becker's Hygeia Bottle Works Trade Mark; in a shield; *B* on the bottom; crown top; 7½"; aqua **4.00-8.00**

M.O. Bennett, Cheyenne, Wyo.; 7½"; aqua **8.00-20.00**

same as above except in arched panel; Hutchinson; 6½"; aqua **4.00-6.00**

The Bennington Bottle Co., No. Bennington, Vt; in a sunken panel; under bottom *E.S. & H.;* ten-sided base; 7¾"; clear or amber **10.00-15.00**

Belfast Cochran & Co.; on front and back of tear drop bottle; 7/16" size letters; aqua; 9¼" **8.00-12.00**

Belfast & Dublin; *Cantrell, Cochrane;* see that cork is branded around bottles on bottom; pop type; 9½"; aqua; round bottom **4.00-6.00**

Belfast; round bottom; 9¼"; aqua **3.00-6.00**

Belfast; plain flat bottom; 9"; aqua **2.00-4.00**

Belfast Ross; round bottom; 9¼"; aqua **3.00-5.00**

Belfast Ross; plain; 9½"; aqua and clear **3.00-5.00**

C. Berry & Co. 84 Levett St. Boston, Registered; on shoulder in oval slug plate; crown top; 9⅜"; emerald green **4.00-6.00**

C. Berry & Co. 84 Leverett St., Boston; in oval slug plate; crown top; 9½"; clear **2.00-4.00**

same as above except 9¼"; amber **2.00-4.00**

same as above except blob top; 9"; clear **4.00-6.00**

Samuel Beskin, Fishkill Landing, N.Y.; on front in oval slug plate; blob top; 9⅜"; aqua **4.00-6.00**

Bessemer Coca-Cola; aqua; 6½", $100.00-200.00

Beverage; plain; 6¼"; aqua; opalescent; pop type **3.00-5.00**

Beverage; plain; 9"; Belfast type; aqua **3.00-4.00**

Beverage; plain; clear; aqua 3.00-4.00

Biedenharn Candy Co.; *B* under bottom; aqua; 7¼", $4.00-8.00

Biedenharn Candy Co.; *BCC* under bottom; aqua; 7¼" 40.00-60.00

Weiss Bier; under bottom *Carl Hutten, N.Y.;* blob top; 7¼"; aqua 8.00-12.00

Big 4 Mf'g. Co.; *1120* and 3 dots under bottom; aqua; 7¾" 4.00-6.00

Big Hollow Letter "B"; applied crown top, light green, 8½" 7.00-10.00

E.L. Billings, Sac. City, Cal.; reverse *Geyser Soda;* blob top; 7"; blue 8.00-10.00

Chas. Binder; *C.B. Mongroft C.B.* on back; *C.B.* bottom; aqua; 7" 4.00-8.00

Birmingham Bottling Co.; aqua; 7", $100.00-200.00

R.W. Black Bottler, Oklahoma, Texas; in slug plate; panel base; Hutchinson; 6¾"; aqua . . . . .40.00 +

Blackhawk Ginger Ale; dark green; 6½" 2.00-6.00

J.A. Blaffer & Co. New Orleans; squat type; blob top; 6½"; amber 10.00-20.00

T. Blauth, 407 K. St., Sacramento, Calif., Bottling Works; 6¾"; aqua .4.00-6.00

Bludwine Bottling Co.; aqua; 7½"; machine made 4.00-6.00

Bludwine; clear or amethyst; 8", $2.00-4.00

Bluff City Bottling; in horseshoe shape; in center of horseshoe *Co. Memphis, Tenn.;* on bottom, on one panel, *B.G.Co.* in very small letters and next to it *199;* aqua 3.00-6.00

Boardman; blue; ground pontil; 7½" 25.00-30.00

Geo Bohlen; *Brooklyn;* in a round slug plate in center *358 Hart St.;* blob top; 7¼"; aqua 4.00-6.00

Bolen & Byrne; in a dome shape under it *East 54th St. N.Y.;* reverse *T.B.N.T.B.S.;* 7¾"; aqua . .10.00-20.00

Bolen & Byrne; opposite side *N.Y.;* aqua; 8¼" . . .12.00 +

Bolen & Byrne, New York; round bottom; aqua; 9" 4.00-8.00

Boley & Co. Sac. City, Cal., Union Glass Works, Phila; 7½"; cobalt .10.00-20.00

Boley & Co.; *Sac City, Calif* in 2 lines, blob top, graphite pontil, cobalt, 7¼" 50.00-65.00

Boley & Co. Sac. City, Cal.; in slug plate; reverse *Union Glass Works, Phila;* graphite pontil; blob top; 7¼"; cobalt 20.00-40.00

The Bonheur Co., Inc. Syracuse, N.Y.; in script; clear; 7½"; *14 fl. ounce* on bottom; under bottom diamond shape figure; machine made 2.00-4.00

Bonode 5; 6¾"; clear or amber 4.00-6.00

Borello Bros. Co., Fresno (B.B.Co.); on bottom; crown top; 7¾"; lt. aqua blue 2.00-6.00

R. Bovee, Troy, N.Y.; 7½"; clear 8.00-12.00

Bowling type bottle, applied crown top, light green and dark green, 9" 24.00-33.00

same except blob top, aqua 17.00-24.00

W.H. Brace, Avon, N.Y.; on front in slug plate; blob top; 9¼"; aqua 4.00-6.00

C.W. Brackett & Co. 61 & 63 Andrew St. Lynn, Mass; on front in oval slug plate; 9⅛"; clear 4.00-6.00

H. Brader & Co.; *Penalty For Selling This Bottle, XLLR Soda Work, 738 Broadway, S.F.* on eight-panel bottle; blob top; 7¼"; aqua 10.00-20.00

Brieg & Schaffer, S.F.; picture of a fish under it; 6½"; aqua 4.00-12.00

Bremekampf & Regal, Eureka, Nev.; 7¼"; clear or aqua 6.00-10.00

Brenham Bottling Work; 8¼"; aqua 4.00-8.00

W.E. Brockway; in hollow letters; *New York;* graphite pontil; squat type; blob top; 6¾"; blue green 25.00-40.00

Brown Bros Chemists, Glasgow; round bottom; blob top; 9½"; aqua 4.00-8.00

H.L. & J.W. Brown; in hollow letters; *Hartford, Ct.;* squat type; tapered top; 7"; olive 10.00-30.00

I. Brownlee; in dome shaped lines; under it, *New Bedford;* in back *T.B.N.S.;* blob top; blue . . .10.00-30.00

J. Brunett; big hollow letter *A*, big *B*; aqua; 7", $8.00-12.00

The Brunner Bottling Co. 669 to 673 Grand St., Brooklyn, N.Y., 1889, Aug.; blob top; 7½" 8.00-10.00

Fillippo Bruno & Co. 298-300 North St. & 50 Fleet St., Boston, Mass; on front in oval slug plate on shoulder; 8⅞"; clear 4.00-6.00

R.W. Budd; aqua; 7¼" 4.00-6.00

Burke; *E & J* under bottom; amber; 7½" **4.00-6.00**

Henry Burkhardt; *H.B.* under bottom; aqua; 6¾" **4.00-6.00**

W.H. Burt, San Francisco; blob top; graphite pontil; 6½"; aqua **30.00-40.00**

W.H. Burt, San Francisco; 7½"; aqua **4.00-8.00**

Burt, W.H.; *San Francisco,* in 2 lines, blob top, graphite pontil, dark green, 7¼" **70.00-90.00**

Butel & Ertel, Tipton, Ind.; *B & E* under bottom; aqua; 6¾" **4.00-6.00**

J.G. Byars; in center; *1882 No. Hoosick, N.Y.;* reverse *T.B.N.T.S.;* 7"; aqua **8.00-12.00**

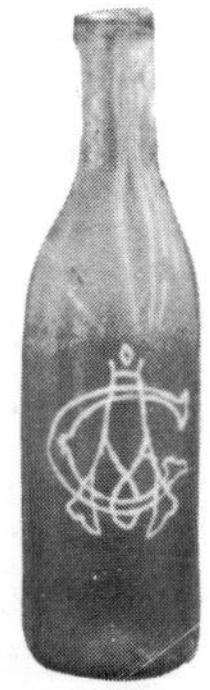

C.A.; aqua; 10", $6.00-8.00

Calhoun Falls; in center; *Bottling Works, Calhoun Falls, S.C.;* 7½"; clear or amber **6.00-8.00**

California Bottling Work, T. Blauth, 407 K St., Sacramento; 7"; clear **8.00-15.00**

California Soda Works; eagle in center; 7"; aqua **4.00-10.00**

California Soda Works; with an arrow under it; *H. Ficken, S.F.;* in back an embossed eagle; blob top; 7"; green **10.00-20.00**

Calvert Bottle Works; *Calvert, Texas;* aqua; soda water; 7¼" **2.00-4.00**

Camden Bottling Company; clear; 8" **6.00-8.00**

Camel Bottling Works; clear; 7" **4.00-6.00**

D. Camelio Co., 10 Lewis St., Boston, Mass.; on shoulder in oval slug plate; 8⅞"; clear **4.00-8.00**

Campbell & Lyon; aqua; 9" **4.00-6.00**

Canada Dry; *14 / Ginger Ale Incorporated* under bottom; carnival glass; crown top; machine made; 10½" **10.00-15.00**

P. Canterbury, Galveston Texas; blob top; 6¼"; aqua **4.00-8.00**

M.J. Cantrell, Yonkers N.Y., M.J.C.; monogram; 6½" or 11½"; amethyst or clear **4.00-8.00**

Cantrell & Cochrane's; *Aerated Water, Dublin & Belfast;* 8¾"; aqua; round bottom **3.00-6.00**

Cantrell & Cochrane's; *Aerated Waters, Dublin & Belfast* runs up and down; round bottom; 8¾"; aqua **4.00-6.00**

Cantrell & Cochrane; *Belfast & Dublin Medicated Aerated Water* around bottle; round bottom; aqua; 9¼" **6.00-10.00**

Cantrell & Cochrane; *Belfast & Dublin* around bottle; round bottom; aqua; 9" **6.00-10.00**

Capital S.W. Co.; aqua; 6½" **4.00-6.00**

N. Cappelli, 327 Atwells Ave., Providence, R.I. Registered; on front; blob top; 8¼"; clear **4.00-8.00**

Caproni Bros. Co. Prov., R.I. Registered; written inside of shield; blob top; 9¼"; clear **4.00-8.00**

Carbonating Apparatus Company, Buffalo, N.Y. Reg.; marble inside bottle; clear **8.00-12.00**

Cardova Bottling Works; aqua; 6¾" **6.00-8.00**

M. Carney & Co. Lawrence, Mass.; with *MC & Co.* mono. all inside of slug plate circle; blob top; 9¼"; clear **4.00-8.00**

E. Carre, Mobile, Ala.; 7¼"; aqua **6.00-8.00**

Owen Casey Eagle Soda Works; on front; *Sac City* on back; blob top; 7¼"; aqua blue **4.00-8.00**

Hugh Casey Eagle Soda Works, 51 K St., Sac., Cal.; 7¼"; aqua **10.00-20.00**

Owen Case Eagle Soda Works; 7¼"; dark blue **8.00-12.00**

Caswell & Hazard & Co., New York, Ginger Ale; in vertical line; round bottom; blob top; 9"; aqua **8.00-12.00**

C.B. Soda; *Quality Coca Cola Bottling Co.* on back; aqua; machine made; *St. Louis* on bottom; 8" **2.00-4.00**

C.C., Portland, Org., T.M. Reg., T.B.N.T.B.S.; 7½"; amber **6.00-10.00**

C.C.S. & M. Co., 1118 Toll 26 Royal St., New Orleans; crown top; 8"; aqua **4.00-6.00**

C.C.S. & M.F.; aqua; 8" **6.00-8.00**

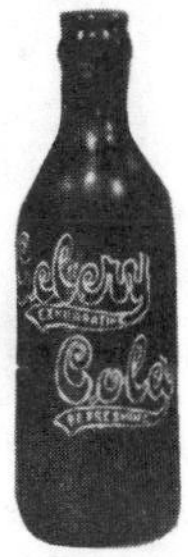

Celery Cola; *C* under bottom; amber; 7½", $8.00-20.00

Celery Cola; clear or amethyst; 7½" **2.00-4.00**

Central City Bottling Co.; clear or amethyst; 7¾" **2.00-4.00**

Central City Bottling Co.; on back *Bottle Not To Be Sold;* clear or amethyst; 7¾"; (note misspelling) **8.00-15.00**

Central City Bottling Co.; (note misspelled *Selma*); *Bottle Not To Be Sold* on back; 7¾"; clear **10.00-20.00**

Chadsey & Bro.; 2" hollow letters, N.Y.; blob top; graphite pontil; 7½"; cobalt **25.00-40.00**

Chcro-Cola; *Savannah, Ga.* on back; aqua; 7½" **3.00-6.00**

Checotah Bottling Works Checotah I.T.; 7¼"; light blue **100.00-200.00**

Chero Cola Bott. Co.; raised square X pattern; *Tyler, Texas;* aqua; 7⅝" **1.00-2.00**

Chicago Bottling Co.; *Root* on bottom; aqua; 7" **4.00-8.00**

Christian Schlepegrell & Co.; eight panels; ground pontil; blue; 8¼" **35.00-50.00**

The Cincinnati; on shoulder; under it in horseshoe letters *Soda Water & Ginger Ale Co.* in center; aqua **8.00-10.00**

The City Bottling Co.; on label; marble in center of neck; aqua; 7¼", $6.00-8.00

City Bottling Works, Cleveland, Ohio;
aqua; 7"..........................**8.00-10.00**

City Bottling Work, Detroit, Mich; in back *G. Norris & Co.; A&D.H.G.* on base; blob top; 7¾";
blue.............................**10.00-20.00**

City Ice & Bottling Works; aqua; 7½".......**4.00-6.00**

C & K; in hollow letters; *Eagle Soda Work, Sac. City;*
blob top; 7"; cobalt..................**20.00-40.00**

C. Clark; ground pontil; green; 7½".......**20.00-25.00**

Charles Clark; ground pontil; green; 7¾"...**20.00-25.00**

Cleburne Bottling Work; *Cleburne, Tex.;* paneled trunk;
7¼"; wire "pop" stopper..............**4.00-8.00**

Clinton Bottling Works; aqua; 8"..........**6.00-8.00**

Clysnic; under bottom; green; 7½", $2.00-4.00

G.B. Coates, G.B.C.; monogram, *Lynn, Mass.* in a slug plate; 8½"; clear.....................**2.00-4.00**

M.H. Cobe & Co. Bottlers, Boston; in large letters on front; clear; 8⅛"......................**4.00-6.00**

Coca Cola; bottle (Christmas Coke); *Patd. Dec. 25, 1923, Zanesville, Ohio* on bottom; *ABM;* crown top; 7⅝";
aqua.................................**4.00-8.00**

Coca Cola Co., Seattle, Wash.; 8½"; clear or aqua.................................**4.00-6.00**

Coca Cola Ideal Brain Tonic Summer & Winters Beverage For Headache and Exhaustion; all on label; 9½"; clear.................**50.00-100.00**

Coca Cola, Toledo, Ohio; 7"; amber......**8.00-15.00**

Coca Cola Bottling Works, Topeka, Kan.; 6";
aqua.................................**4.00-8.00**

Coca Cola, Buffalo, N.Y.; clear or amethyst; 7¾".............................**6.00-8.00**

Daytona Coca Cola Bottling Co.; clear or amethyst;
8½".............................**6.00-10.00**

Coca Cola; *Wilmington N.C.* around bottom of bottle;
under it small letters *D.O.C. 173;* aqua; 7¼";
clear.................................**2.00-4.00**

Coca Cola Macon Ga.; *Property of the Coca Cola Bottling Co.* on back; aqua; 7¾".........**4.00-6.00**

Coca Cola Bottling Co., Rome, Ga; *Trade Mark Reg.* on back; *This Bottle Not To Be Sold* on base; clear;
7½".................................**4.00-6.00**

Coca Cola Macon; (reverse N), *Ga;*
aqua, 7"......................**8.00-15.00**
same as above with different towns
in U.S.A....................**2.00-4.00**

Coca Cola; in center of bottle; under it *Trade Mark Registered;* around bottom of bottle *Waycross, Ga.;* on back, in small letters, *O.B.Co.;* aqua;
clear; 7¼"....................**2.00-4.00**
same as above with different town in
U.S.A........................**2.00-4.00**

Coca Cola Bottling Work; *6¼ Flu ozs* on lower trunk;
also in center of shoulder; clear or aqua; 7¼" or
various sizes.........................**2.00-4.00**
also in amber; vertical arrow, under it the name of
different towns; some have only
Coca Cola.........................**8.00-20.00**
also machine made..................**4.00-8.00**

Coca Cola; on crown top; 7¼"; amber; under the bottom
S B & G Co. #2; diamond shape label....**4.00-6.00**

Coca Cola; name on shoulder in center, also on trunk;
7¾"; aqua, clear....................**2.00-4.00**

Coca Cola Bottling Co.; *Charleston, S.C.* on front of
shoulder; other side *Trade Mark Registered;* under
the bottle *Root;* aqua or clear; 7¼"......**2.00-4.00**

Coca Cola; (not in script) in center; clear or
aqua; 8½".........................**4.00-6.00**

Coca Cola; around bottom base *Trade Mark Registered;*
around shoulder *Portland, Oregon, this bottle never
sold;* amber; 7½"....................**3.00-6.00**

Coca Cola; in ½ circle; under it *Berlin, N.H.;* slim bottle;
green; around bottom *Contents 7 fl. oz.;* 8¾";
machine made.......................**2.00-4.00**

Property of Coca Cola Bottling Co.; on small embossed
bottle; 7¾"; aqua; four square panels; six panels
above shoulder.....................**2.00-4.00**

Property of Coca Cola; 6 stars on shoulder; *Tyler,
Texas* on bottom; square; aqua; 7¾".....**3.00-4.00**

Coca Cola; on 2 sides of sample bottle; *Clear Soda
Water;* 2½".........................**1.00-2.00**

Coca Cola Bottling Co.; *Property of Waco, Drink
Delicious Bludwine For Your Health Sake;* sunken
middle; aqua; *7 flu. ozs.;* 7½"..........**2.00-4.00**

Coca Cola; some bottled in pottery and pop bottles or
Hutchinson with diamond shape labels in
1900's.............................**7.00-15.00**

Coca Cola Bottling Co.; *Lakeland, Fla.* in a circle; above
it in script, *Indian Rock Ginger Ale;* on bottom panel,
7 fluid oz.; ten pin type; about 1908;
aqua; 8½".........................**3.00-6.00**

Coca Cola; 6"; amber, $8.00-20.00

Coca Cola; on back shoulder *Trade Mark Registered;*
aqua; 3¾" round; *root* on bottom; semi-round
bottom.............................**5.00-8.00**

Coca Cola; clear or amethyst; 7¾"; semi-round bottom **4.00-6.00**

Coca Cola; amber; 6"; *S.B. &G. Co.* on bottom **40.00-80.00**

Coca Cola; aqua; 7" **4.00-8.00**

Coca Mariani, Paris France; 8½"; green **4.00-8.00**

Cochran & Co.; tear drop shape; *Belfast* **on back; 9", $6.00-10.00**

Cod Soda; embossing; *Star Brand Super Strong* with star at base on front; marble closure; 9¼"; aqua **4.00-8.00**

L. Cohen New York; *This Bottle is Reg. Not To Be Sold* on back; *2* under bottom; aqua; 7½" **4.00-6.00**

Cole's Soda; by *N.J. Cole, So. Acton, Mass.;* 7"; clear or amber **8.00-10.00**

Comanche Bottling Works; aqua; 6¾" . . **200.00-400.00**

Comstock Cove & Co. 139 Friend St., Boston; on front; *C.C. & Co.* in large letters on back; blob top; 7"; aqua **6.00-10.00**

F.A. Conant., 252 Girod St. N.O.; graphite pontil; blob top; 7¼"; olive **30.00-45.00**

Concord Bottling Co., Concord, N.H.; 6½"; aqua **8.00-10.00**

Jas. Condon., Walden, N.Y., C.J.; monogram; *Cont. 7 oz.,* 6¾"; amethyst or clear **4.00-8.00**

Conklin Bottling Work, Peekskill, N.Y.; on front in arched shape slug plate; blob top; 7⅛"; aqua . **6.00-8.00**

Connor & McQuaide; aqua; 8"; on back *C & S* **4.00-8.00**

Connor & McQuaide; aqua; 6½" **4.00-6.00**

Consumers; *C* under bottom; aqua; 7¾" **2.00-6.00**

Consumers B.B. Co.; amber; 9", $3.00-6.00

H. Cortes, Galveston, Texas; 7"; clear **4.00-8.00**

H. Cortes & Bro. Texas Bottling Work, Galveston, Texas; in back *Belfast Ginger Ale & Soda Water;* blob top; aqua **10.00-12.00**

H. Cortes & Co. Prop; *Texas Bottling Works, Galveston, Texas; A & D.H.C.* around base; Hutchinson; 8"; aqua **4.00-8.00**

Coscroul James; *Charleston, S.C.* in a circle; in center of circle *& Son;* in back *this bottle not to be sold;* aqua; 8¼" **2.00-4.00**

J. Cosgrove; aqua; 7" **4.00-6.00**

Cottan & Magg; (C & M mono.); *Boston, Mass* on front; 7½"; aqua **4.00-6.00**

John Cotter; aqua; 7¾" **4.00-6.00**

Cottle Post & Co., Portland; blob top; 7½"; blue **15.00-25.00**

Cottle Post & Co.; in center an eagle; under it, *Portland, Org.;* blob top; 7¼"; green **10.00-20.00**

John Coyle, Newburgh, N.Y.; inside of circular slug plate on front; *This Bottle Not To Be sold* also on front; blob top; 9¼"; clear **4.00-8.00**

C.R. Cramer & Jacky; in a dome line under it, *Phillipsburg, Mon.;* 6¾"; aqua **4.00-8.00**

W.A. Crawley, Clarksdale, Miss.; 7½"; clear **8.00-10.00**

C.W. Crell & Co.; ground pontil; blue green; 7", $25.00-35.00

M. Cronan, 230 K St., Sacramento; on front; *Sac. Soda Works* on bottom; 6¾"; green aqua **6.00-10.00**

M. Cronan, 230 K St., Sacramento, Soda Works; blob top; 6½"; aqua **4.00-6.00**

Crown Bottling & Mfg. Co.; aqua; 6½" **6.00-8.00**

Crown Bottling & Mfg. Co., Ardmore I.T.; with crown in center; aqua **100.00-200.00**

Crown Bottling Works, Delaware O.; in a circle; 6¾"; light green **8.00-10.00**

The Crown Cork & Seal Co. Baltimore; crown top; sample; clear; 3¾" . . . . **10.00+**

Crystal Bottling Co., Charleston, W.Va.; panel base; 7¼"; aqua **4.00-10.00**

Crystal Bottling Works; *C.B.W.* under bottom; aqua; 7½" **3.00-6.00**

Crystal Bottling Works; *C.B.W.* **under bottom; aqua; 7¾", $2.00-6.00**

Crystal Soda Works, Honolulu, H.I.; Hutchinson; 7"; aqua **10.00-25.00**

Crystal Soda Works, Honolulu, H.I.; 6¾";
aqua **15.00-30.00**

Crystal Soda Works Co., S.F.; 7¼"; aqua or light
green **4.00-8.00**

Crystal Spring Bottling Co., Barnet, Vt.; clear or
amber; 7¼" **4.00-6.00**

Crystal; (*Soda* in center) **Water Co.;** in back, *Pat. Nov.
12-1872, Taylors U.S.P.T.;* blob top; 7½";
blue **4.00-8.00**

A.W. Cudworth & Co., S.F.; 7¼"; aqua **4.00-6.00**

Culver House Pure Natural Lemonade Speciality; in
back *Registered Trade Mark* with house in center;
9"; golden amber . . . .**25.00 +**

Cunningham & Co., Phila; blob top; 7";
aqua **4.00-8.00**

T. & J. Cunningham, Phila; blob top; 7";
green **15.00-30.00**

John Cuneo; *269* under bottom; aqua; 9" **4.00-6.00**

Dr. Dadirrians Zoolak; vertical around neck on 2 lines;
7¼"; aqua **4.00-6.00**

M. D'Agastino; aqua; *1223* under bottom;
7¼" **4.00-6.00**

Dannenburg Bros. C.C.T.M.R.; in center *Goldsboro,
N.Y.;* 7¾"; clear or aqua **8.00-10.00**

**E. Dannenburg, Authorized Bottler of C.C. Wilson-
Goldsboro, N.C. U.S.A.;** in a circle on the base
T.B.N.T.B.S.; 8"; clear or amber **8.00-15.00**

C. Davis., Phoenixville; in slug plate; squat type;
graphite pontil; 7"; green **20.00-45.00**

Davis & Worcester; *E.HE Co. No. 3* on base; green
aqua; 6½" **8.00-15.00**

J. Day & Co.; in 2 lines; blob top; 7¾";
aqua **8.00-12.00**

Deacon Brown Mfg. Co. Montgomery, Ala.; on base
T.B.N.T.B.S.; 8¾"; aqua **2.00-4.00**

Deamer; in hollow letters; *Glass Valley* in back; *W.E.D.*
in hollow letters; blob top; 7¼"; aqua **3.00-6.00**

H.E. Dean., Great Bend, Kans.; Hutchinson; 7"; clear or
amber **4.00-8.00**

**W. Dean; small kick-up pontil; blue
green; 6½", $15.00-25.00**

Wm. Dean; 7¾"; pale blue **8.00-12.00**

Dearborn, 83 3rd Ave., N.Y.; blob top; 7";
green **25.00-40.00**

Deis & Tibbals, Lima, Ohio; Hutchinson; 7";
aqua **4.00-6.00**

E.T. Delaney & Co.; in center; *Bottlers Plattsburg, N.Y.;*
7"; aqua **8.00-15.00**

H. Delmeyer; in center, *1861 Brooklyn;* ; in back *XX;* in
hollow letters, *Porter;* squat bottle; blob top; 6½";
aqua **10.00-15.00**

Delta Mf'g. Co.; *Delta* in a triangle under bottom; aqua;
7¼" **6.00-8.00**

DeMott's Celebrated Soda; or *Mineral Water;* in back,
Hudson County, N.J.; 7¼"; cobalt . . . .**25.00 +**

G.V. DeMott's; graphite pontil; 7½"; green . . . .**25.00 +**

De Mott's Porter & Ale; squat type; blob top; 6½";
green **20.00-35.00**

H. Denhalter, Salt Lake City, UT; in 4 lines; Hutchinson; 6½"; aqua **15.00-30.00**

H. Denhalter & Sons; in a dome-shaped line; in center
Salt; under it, *Salt Lake City, UT.;* 7";
aqua **4.00-10.00**

D.G.W.; script type letters; blob top; 7¼";
aqua **8.00-10.00**

Diamond Soda Work Co., S.F., Trade Mark; *D* in diamond; Hutchinson; 6"; aqua **8.00-10.00**

Diehl & Danbury, Memphis, Tenn.; *D* under bottom; *D*
in back on shoulder; aqua; 6½" **6.00-8.00**

John Dietze, Winona, Minn; on front inside of slug
plate; crown top; 8⅛"; aqua **2.00-4.00**

J. Dinets, Superior Soda Water, Chicago; in panel; six
panels; graphite pontil; 8"; blue **25.00-40.00**

Distilled & Aerated Water Co., Mitchell, S.D.; 3½";
aqua **10.00-20.00**

Distilled Soda Water Co. of Alaska; 7½";
aqua **6.00-12.00**

Distilled Soda Water of Alaska; in a sunken panel; ten-
sided; Hutchinson; 7¼"; aqua **10.00-20.00**

Dixie Carbonating Co.; thick bottom; clear or amethyst;
9" **4.00-6.00**

Dixie Carbonating Co.; back shoulder *Trade Mark,
Augusta, Ga.;* 8"; clear or amethyst **4.00-6.00**

Dixie Carbonating Co.; aqua; 8" **4.00-6.00**

Henry Downes; aqua; 7½"; on back *The City Bottling
Works of New York* **4.00-6.00**

Dooly, Cordele, Ga.; panel base; 7"; clear or
amber **7.00-10.00**

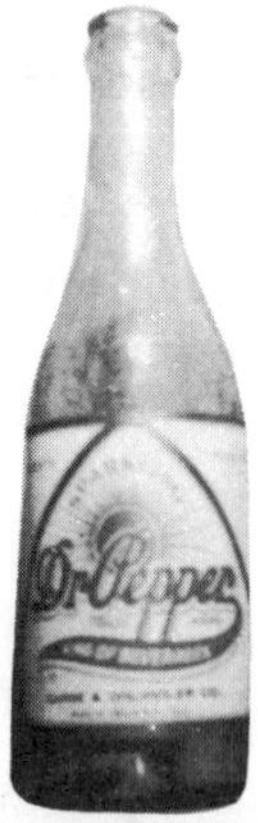

Dr. Pepper; label; aqua; 7", $2.00-4.00

Dr. Pepper King of Beverage; *Reg. Dallas Bottling Co.,
Dallas, Tx.;* amethyst; 8¼" **3.00-5.00**

Dr. Pepper; in script; under it *King of Beverages;* on
shoulder *Registered;* on base *Artesian Mfg. & Bot.
Co. Waco, Tex.;* clear, amethyst **4.00-6.00**

D.S. & Co., San Francisco; blob top; 7"; cobalt
blue **10.00-15.00**

E. Duffy & Son; 7"; green **30.00-40.00**

Francis Dusch, T.B.N.T.B.S. 1866; blob top; 7¼";
blue **10.00-15.00**

**Dutchess Brand Beverages Made in Verbank Village, 7
oz.;** on front; 8½"; amethyst **2.00-4.00**

James N. Dyer, Catskill, N.Y.; *This Bottle Not To Be Sold;* 6½"; aqua 4.00-10.00

Dyottville Glass Works, Phila; squat type; graphite pontil; 6¼"; green 30.00-60.00

Eagle symbol in a circle; marble closure; 8"; aqua, $8.00-10.00

Wm Eagle, N.Y. Premium Soda Water; paneled; blob top; graphite pontil; 7¼"; cobalt 70.00-90.00

W. Eagle, Canal St., N.Y.; reverse side, *Phila. Porter;* blob top; squat type; 6¾"; dark green . .35.00-55.00

Eagle Bottling Works; *D* under bottom; clear; 7¾" 4.00-6.00

Eagle Bottling Works, Birmingham, Ala; eagle symbol; crown top; 8"; aqua 6.00-8.00

Alex Easton, Fairfield, Iowa; in a circle; Hutchinson; 6½"; aqua 4.00-6.00

E.B. Co., Evansville, Ind.; *B* under bottom; panels around bottle; aqua; 7" 4.00-6.00

G. Ebberwein; *Savannah, Geo.* on front; *Ginger Ale* vertical on back; short neck; 7¾"; amber . .18.00-20.00

Eel River Valley Soda Works; in center; *Springville, Cal.;* 7"; aqua 6.00-8.00

El Dorado; tapered top; 7¼"; aqua 4.00-10.00

Electric Bottling Works, West Point, Miss.; Hutchinson; 6¾"; aqua, $4.00-8.00

Electro Brand; *Jackson Tenn* on back; *R.O. Co.* under bottom 3.00-6.00

Elephant Bottling Company; *D.O.C. Co.* on base; *D* under bottom; aqua; 8" 4.00-6.00

Elephant Bottling Co.; *D* under bottom; aqua; 7¾" 4.00-6.00

Elephant Steam Bottling Works; *D* under bottom; 6¼" 4.00-8.00

Elliott, Trenton, N.J.; blob top; 7¼"; aqua 10.00-15.00

El Reno, B.W.; 7¼"; aqua 6.00-12.00

Elsberry Bottling Works, Elsberry, Mo; on front in oval slug plate; *ABM;* crown top; 8" 2.00-4.00

G.L. Elwick, Lincoln, Neb.; light blue; 6¾" . . .3.00-4.00

Emmerling; amber; 9½" 2.00-4.00

Empire Soda Works, Vallejo, Cal; crown top; 6½"; aqua 4.00-6.00

Empsorrs; in fancy script; tall blob top; panel base; 9¼"; amber 4.00-10.00

F. Engle; big *E* in back; aqua; 7½" 8.00-12.00

Ensley Bottling Works, Ensley, Ala.; crown top; 7½"; clear or aqua 2.00-4.00

Enterprise Bottling Works, Davis & Co. Prop. Lincoln, Il; on panels; ten panels; 6¼"; aqua . . .10.00-12.00

Epps-Cola; *John C Epping, Louisville, Ky, Reg 7 Fluid Oz* around bottle; *E* under bottom; snap-on top; 8"; aqua 8.00-10.00

C. Erne's City Bottling Works, 348 & 350 Pienville St. N.O., T.B.N.T.B.S.; blob top; 8¼" 8.00-10.00

John M. Ertel; *B & E* under bottom; clear; 6¾" 4.00-6.00

J. Esposito, 812 & 814 Washington Ave., Kaca Kola; Hutchinson; 7¾" 4.00-8.00

Charles Euker; reverse *T.B.N.T.B.S., 1866, Richmond, Va.;* blob top; 7"; light blue 10.00-15.00

Eureka Bottling Works, Ft. Smith, Ark.; the words *Stolen From* are at the top; Hutchinson; 7"; aqua 10.00-12.00

Stolen From Eureka Bottling Works; 6¾"; aqua 30.00-40.00

Henry Evers; aqua; 7½" 8.00-12.00

James Everado, New York; clear or amethyst 4.00-6.00

F.A.B.; in a large horseshoe symbol, with *Galveston* inside; 7½"; aqua, $6.00-8.00

M. Fairbanks & Co., Howard St. Boston, Mass.; on front; large *F & Co.* on back; aqua 4.00-8.00

F.B.W., Fairfield, Iowa; tenpin type; blob top; 6½"; aqua 8.00-12.00

J.A. Falsone; clear or amethyst; 6¾" 2.00-4.00

S.H. Farnham; in center; *American Fla. Westernly, R.I.* vertical; 7½"; aqua 8.00-15.00

J.E. Farrell, Main St., Cold Spring; on front in oval slug plate; 9⅛"; clear 3.00-6.00

Feigenson Bros., Reg. Detroit, Mich; on front in oval slug plate; 6⅛"; aqua 4.00-8.00

Feihenspan P.O.N. Trademark Agency, Newburgh, N.Y.; in oval slug plate; crown top; 9¼"; aqua 2.00-4.00

H. Fellrath, Peoria, Ill; reverse side; at base, *SB & Co.;* Hutchinson; 7"; aqua 8.00-15.00

Ferber Bros. Phoebus, Va.; 7¼"; aqua 4.00-12.00

E.M. Ferry, Essex, Conn.; blob top; 9¼"; clear 4.00-6.00

C.P. Fey & Co.; 7½″; light blue . . . .**40.00 +**

S.C. Fields Superior Soda Water; eight panels; ground pontil; 7¼″; cobalt, $60.00-80.00

B.H. Fink; *J* intead of *F;* in back *To Be Returned;* ground pontil; 7¼″; blue green **30.00-60.00**

Henry Finks Sons; *Harrisburg, Pa.;* clear or amethyst; 9½″ **4.00-8.00**

Fleming Bros., Meadville, Pa.; in 4 lines; 6½″; aqua **4.00-10.00**

J.C. Fox & Co., Fox T.M., Seattle, Wash.; 7½″; aqua **4.00-8.00**

Wm. Freidman, Champion Soda Factory, Key West, Fla., T.B.N.T.B.S.; 6½″; clear or amber . .**4.00-6.00**

J. Furla Bottling Co.; aqua; 6½″ **8.00-15.00**

Gadsden; in center, *Bottling Works, Gadsen, Ala;* 6¾″; clear **4.00-8.00**

Gaffney & Morgan, Amsterdam, N.Y.; in a circle; panel base; 7½″; aqua **8.00-10.00**

C.H. Gahre Bottler, Bridgetown, N.J.; aqua; 7″ **8.00-12.00**

Gallitzin Bottling Co.; *326* under bottom; aqua **4.00-6.00**

Gallitzin Bottling Co.; amber; 9½″, $4.00-6.00

Galveston Brewing Co.; *Guaranteed Pure, Galveston Tex.;* aqua; 7¾″; round **2.00-4.00**

Henry Gardener Trade Mark, West Bromwish; 7½″; emerald green **4.00-8.00**

Geo. Gemenden; *Savannah Ga.* on front; Eagle, Shield and Flag on back; improved pontil; 7¼″; green; blob top **35.00-85.00**

William Genaust, Wilmington, N.C.; in a circle; blob top; reverse side *T.B.N.T.B.S.;* 9¼″ aqua**4.00-10.00**

Geyser Soda; in back *Natural Mineral Water, From Litton springs, Sonoma Co. Calif;* blob top; 7″; aqua **10.00-20.00**

Ghirard Ellis Branch, Oakland; 3 lines on front; blob top; 7¾″; blue **10.00-15.00**

Chas. Gibbons, Philad.; in a horseshoe shape; reverse a star; long neck; blob top; 8″; amber . .**20.00-40.00**

T.W. Gillett, New Haven; eight panels; graphite pontil; 7½″; blue . . . .**75.00 +**

Globe Bottling Works; *Savannah, Ga.,* in a circle in center on bottom; in back *This Bottle Is Never Sold;* clear; 8½″ **3.00-6.00**

G.M.S. Co.; crown in center, *Registered; Alliance, Ohio;* panel base; 7⅜″; aqua **6.00-8.00**

Golden Gate Bottling Work; in a horseshoe; under it *San Francisco;* 7¾″ **8.00-10.00**

Golden West S. & E. Soda Works, San Jose, Cal.; four-piece mold; 8⅜″; aqua green **4.00-6.00**

John Graf, Milwaukee; panel base; reverse *T.B.N.T.B.S.;* 8½″; blue **7.00-10.00**

John Graf; on other panels *This bottle never sold, Please Return, When Empty, To The Owner, Cor. 17th & Greenfield Ave., Trade Mark The Best What Gives,* **$10.00-30.00**

John Graf, Milwaukee, Wis.; on front; reverse *T.B.N.T.B.S. The Best What Gives* trade mark; eight panels on base; 6⅜″; aqua green **4.00-8.00**

Gramercy Bottling Works, Gramercy, La; Hutchinson; 7½″; clear or aqua, $4.00-8.00

Grant & Upton; in a horseshoe shape; under it, *Columbus, Ohio;* 6½″; aqua **8.00-12.00**

J & J Grantham; star under bottom; *Kiner Bros Ltd* on back; green; 8″ **15.00-20.00**

John Granz, Croton Falls, N.Y.; on front; *T.B.N.T.B.S.* on reverse side; blob top; 7½″; aqua **4.00-8.00**

Grape Products Co. Walkers; on bottom; clear or amethyst; 11″ **2.00-4.00**

Grattan & Co. Ltd.; 9″; aqua **6.00-8.00**

Great Bear Springs, Fulton, N.Y.; round bottom; 12″; aqua **10.00-20.00**

Greenwood Bottling & Supply Co.; Greenwood, S.C.; in a circle; crown top; 7½″; aqua **6.00-8.00**

Geo. Grubel, Kansas City, Kansas; in 3 lines; Hutchinson type; 6¾″; aqua **10.00-20.00**

G.T.B.; under bottom; marble in center; aqua; 7¾″, $3.00-6.00

Guyette & Company, Detroit, Mich; Registered; in center; *G* under bottom; 6¾″; cobalt . . . **30.00-50.00**

H; in hollow letter, also *SAC.* with hollow *P;* 7″; clear or aqua **4.00-8.00**

The Property of the Haas Co; in half circle in center; monogram *THCo,* on each side *Trade Mark;* under circle *Registered Chicago;* under bottom monogram *THCo;* aqua; on back *This Bottle is Never Sold;* 7″ **4.00-8.00**

Habenicht Bottling Works; *Columbia, S.C.* in sunken panel; aqua; 9″ **4.00-6.00**

Habenicht; next line *Bottling Work; Columbia, S.C.* in round sunken circle; 9½″; blob top; amber **4.00-6.00**

Haight & O Brien; graphite pontil; aqua; 7½″ **20.00-30.00**

H. Hall, Hilltown; *Ireland & New York* at base in 3 lines; in center a hand in shield; under it *Trade mark;* tapered top; semi-round; 9″; aqua **8.00-10.00**

Hanigan Bros; *Denver, Colo* on back; aqua; *H.B.* on bottom; 7″ **4.00-6.00**

Hanigan Bros.; *Denver, Colo.* vertical letters; Hutchinson; 6½″; clear or amethyst **8.00-20.00**

Hanne Brothers; *This Bottle Not To Be Sold* in back; clear; 7½″ **6.00-8.00**

Hanssen Bros., Grass Valley, Cal.; in center *G.W.B.,* 7¼″; aqua **6.00-8.00**

C.J. Hargan & Co., Memphis, Tenn.; blob top; 6¾″; aqua **10.00-15.00**

P. Harrington, Manchester, N.H., P.H.; monogram all inside slug plate; blob top; 9¼″; clear **3.00-6.00**

J. Harrison; in center *197 Fulton, N.Y.;* reverse *Phila XXX Porter & Ale;* squat type; 6½″; green **20.00-30.00**

C. Hartmen, Cleveland, O.; light blue and blue green **8.00-12.00**

F. Harvey & Co.; *This Bottle Not To Be Sold* on back; amber; 8½″, **$4.00-6.00**

J. Harvey & Co.; in hollow letters; *65½ Canal St. Providence, R.I.;* graphite pontil; tapered top; 7¾″; green . . . . **35.00 +**

J. Harvey & Co.; in hollow letters; *65½ Central St. Providence, R.I.;* blob top; graphite pontil; 7½″; green **20.00-40.00**

J. & J.W. Harvey, Norwich, Conn.; reverse hollow letter *H;* graphite pontil; blob top; 7¾″; green **20.00-40.00**

Harvey & Bro.; in a dome shape; under it *Hackettstown, N.J.;* in back, hollow letter *H;* 7″; green **20.00-35.00**

Hawaiian Soda Works, Honolulu, T.H.; 7½″; aqua **8.00-15.00**

Hayes Bros.; *This Bottle Never Sold* in back; 7″ **4.00-6.00**

J.S. Hazard, Westerly, R.I.; reverse side *XX* in hollow letters; blob top; 7¼″; aqua **8.00-15.00**

H & D; in raised letters 1½″ tall under this in 2 lines *Savannah, Geo;* squat bottle; aqua; 7″; blob **10.00-15.00**

Headman, Phila; reverse *F.W.H.* in hollow letters; graphite pontil; 7¼″; green **30.00-60.00**

MC. Heald & Co. (M.C.H. Co) Lynn, Mass.; inside of slug plate on front; crown top; 7½″; amethyst **2.00-4.00**

Heatly Bros., Mangum, O.T.; Hutchinson; 6⅜″; clear **100.00-200.00**

Heatly Bros., Mangum; *This Bottle Not To Be Sold* reverse side; 6¾″; aqua . . . . **50.00 +**

John Hecht, Brooklyn, N.Y.; 1862; aqua; 7½″, $10.00-15.00

J.J. Heinrich & Co.; *J.J.H.* under bottom; aqua; 7¼″ **4.00-8.00**

John Heinzerling, Baltimore, Md.; 7½″; aqua **6.00-8.00**

Geo. N. Hembdt, Monticello, N.Y., Reg.; on front in slug plate; 6¾″; aqua **4.00-6.00**

Hempstead Bottling Work; *Hempstead Tx.* in a circle; amethyst; 8″; fluted bottom **2.00-4.00**

Hennessy & Nolan Ginger Ale, Albany, N.Y.; in panels; reverse *H. & N.* monogram; *1876;* blob top; 7¼″; aqua **10.00-12.00**

Ed Henry, Napa, Cal.; monogram in center; 6¾″; aqua **4.00-6.00**

Geo Henry; aqua; 7½″ **8.00-12.00**

F.T. Heller; aqua; 7½″ **4.00-8.00**

Herancourt Brg. Co.; amber; 8¼″ **4.00-6.00**

J.C. Herrmann, Sharon, Pa.; Hutchinson; 9″; aqua **8.00-10.00**

Hewlett Bros., Salt Lake City, Utah; reverse *T.B.N.T.B.S.;* 6½″; aqua **4.00-8.00**

T.E. Hickey, Providence, R.I.; 6¼″; aqua **4.00-8.00**

E. Higgins, Oroville; in 2 lines; blob top; 7″; aqua **10.00-15.00**

O.G. Hille & Co.; *w.b.* under bottom; aqua; 7″ **8.00-10.00**

E. Hinecke; *Louisville, K.Y. H* under bottom; 7″; aqua **8.00-10.00**

Hippo Size Soda Water; *Prop. of Alamo Bottling Wks., San Antonio, Tx., Nov. 2-1926;* clear; 9½″; picture of hippopotamus **2.00-4.00**

Hire's; on bottom; old crown top; 9¾″; aqua . . **2.00-4.00**

H.L. & J.W. Hartford, Conn.; 6½″; amber **4.00-8.00**

Hobart Bottling Works; aqua; 5½″ **25.00-35.00**

Hoffman Bros., Cheyenne, W.; aqua . . . . **35.00 +**

71

Lawrence L. Holden, Fall River, Mass.; written at an angle; fancy; blob top; 9¼"; clear **4.00-8.00**
same as above except amber; 8½" **4.00-8.00**
Holdenville Bottling Works; 7½"; aqua **8.00-15.00**

Holihan Bros; clear or amethyst; 9¼", $4.00-6.00

Holland Rink Bottling Works, Butte, Mont.; in a sunken panel; Hutchinson; 6½"; aqua **10.00-20.00**
Holland Rink, Butte, Mont.; in center, *Bottling Works;* 6¾"; aqua **8.00-10.00**
Home Brewing Co., Richmond, Va.; (1895); 6¾"; aqua **8.00-12.00**
R.A. Horlock Co., Navasota, Texas; 8¼"; clear or amber **4.00-8.00**
Houck & Dieter Co., Douglas, Ariz; Hutchinson; 6"; aqua **10.00-15.00**
Houck & Dieter; in one of the six cathedral panels; *Company* in one; *El Paso* in another; *Texas* in another; two blank panels; under bottle *H&D Co.;* applied crown top; 8"; aqua **5.00-7.00**
Houck & Dieter; *H & D Co.* on bottom; aqua; 8" **4.00-10.00**
Houppert & Worcester; aqua; 6½"; *H & W.* under bottom **4.00-6.00**
L. House & Sons, Syracuse, N.Y.; 7"; aqua . . **4.00-8.00**
J.F. Howard; *Haverhill, Mass.* around the lower part of the trunk; round; fluted around; clear; 7¼" **1.00-2.00**
John Howell; hollow letters under it, *Buffalo, N.J.;* blob top; 7"; aqua **8.00-15.00**
Hoxsie, Albany; *Xosi* in back; blob top; 6½"; aqua **6.00-10.00**
Hulshizer & Co.; Premium; all on panels; graphite pontil; 8½"; green **60.00-80.00**
Hunt & Co.; *Trade Mark,* in 2 lines; *Hunt & Co.* in script inside a square below; word *Hinckley* below; in back near base, *Dan Hylands Ld Sole Marke, Barnsley;* 2½" at base to pinch shoulder; neck tapers to applied top; also in neck a pinch; inside of neck a marble; 8¾"; aqua **6.00-8.00**
same as above except no pinch in neck; 6½"; 1¾" at base; (Japan); light green **6.00-8.00**
Huntington; machine made; 7½"; amber **6.00-10.00**
Hutchinson Soda Bottling Works, Hutchinson, Minn; 7"; aqua **8.00-20.00**
E.L. Husting, Milwaukee, Wis; vertical on side; 6½"; aqua **4.00-6.00**
Hyde Park, St. Louis; crown top; 9¾"; amber **2.00-4.00**
Hygeia Bottling Works; aqua; 6¾" **4.00-6.00**
Hygeia Soda Works, Kahului, H.; in 3 lines; star under bottom; 7¼" . . . . **25.00 +**

Hygenic Distilled Water Co.; in horseshoe shape lines under it, *Brooklyn & Far Rockaway L.I.;* in back *H.D.W. Co.* interlocking hollow letters; 7"; aqua **8.00-12.00**
Imbescheid & Co.; in center, *Registered Jamaica* plain mass all in a circle; on base *Registered,* in back *T.B.N.T.B.S.* under bottom *Kare Hutter, 33 N. N.Y.* blob top, aqua, 9" **18.00-25.00**
Imperial Bottling Works, Portland, Oregon; 7¾"; aqua **6.00-12.00**
Ingall's Bros., Portland, Me; squat type; 7"; green **10.00-20.00**
Ingall's Bros., Portland, Me., Belfast Ale; vertical lines, round bottom; 8¼"; aqua **6.00-8.00**
Italian Soda Water Manufactor, San Francisco; in a horizontal line; reverse *Union Glass Works, Phila;* graphite pontil; 7½"; emerald green **40.00-80.00**
Iron City; *11* on bottom; *96* on base; aqua; 6½" **4.00-6.00**
IUKA; *C* in center of diamond shape under bottom; clear or amethyst; 6½" **100.00-300.00**

Jackson Bottling Works, Jackson, Tenn.; 8"; aqua, $4.00-6.00

J.L. Jacobs, Cairo, N.Y.; in a round sunken panel; 7"; green **8.00-10.00**
J.L. Jacobs, Cairo, N.Y.; reverse side, *This Bottle Not To Be Sold;* blob top; 7¾" **8.00-10.00**
The James Bottling Co.; aqua; 6¾" **6.00-8.00**
Jefferson Bottling Works, Jefferson, Texas; 7½"; aqua **6.00-8.00**

F.W. Jessen Bottling Works; amber; 9½", $3.00-6.00

J.L. & C. LDC 1449; under bottom; aqua; 9½" **2.00-4.00**
Johnson & Bro. Delta, Pa.; 6¾"; olive . . . **20.00-30.00**
same as above, only aqua **4.00-8.00**
Johnson & Corbett, Socorro, N.M.; in a circle; Hutchinson; 7"; aqua **15.00-30.00**
S.N. Johnson Bottling Work, Laredo, Tex.; blob top; 7½"; aqua **8.00-10.00**

Johnston Bros; *J* on bottom; clear; 7½".....**6.00-8.00**

Johnston & Co., Philada; squat type; blob top; 7"; green, $45.00-55.00

D. Johnston, Atlantic City, N.J.; in back; *J* in hollow letter; blob top; 7"; aqua.............**8.00-15.00**

A. Jones; aqua; 6¾"....................**4.00-8.00**

Geo. Jones; aqua; 7"....................**4.00-6.00**

Geo. Jones, Fonda, N.Y.; on front; *G-J Co.* on monogram on back; 7¼"; clear.........**4.00-8.00**

Daniel Kaiser, Keokuk, Iowa, P.A. & Co.; in 4 lines; 7½"; aqua.......................**10.00-20.00**

G. Kammerer; *A.G.W.L.* on base; aqua; 7", $4.00-8.00

Kanter Bros; aqua; 6½"..................**6.00-8.00**

Nick Karl, Gloversville, N.Y.; on front in oval slug plate; *This Bottle Not To Be Sold* on back; 9¼"; aqua........................**4.00-8.00**

John Karsch & Sons, Evansville, Ind.; Hutchinson; 6½"; aqua.........................**4.00-8.00**

K.B. LD 7-122-1; under bottom; aqua; 7½"...**2.00-4.00**

Keenan Mfg. Co., Butte Mt.; in a circle; ten panels at base; Hutchinson; 7¼"; aqua........**10.00-20.00**

P. Kellett, Newark, N.J.; squat type; graphite pontil; 6¾"; green....................**25.00-35.00**

P. Kellett, Neward, N.J.; reverse *K, 1857;* 7½"; green.........................**20.00-30.00**

Keryer & Co., Est. 1851, Belfast; in center; in center of *Trade Mark* a five-leaved flower; round bottom; aqua; tapered top; 9½"..............**8.00-12.00**

Kia-Ora T.M. Reg. Beverages Lemon Orange & Lime Made From Real Fruit Juice, O-T Ltd. Inc., S.F., Cal.; 11"; clear or amber.............**8.00-10.00**

H.B. Kilmer N.Y.; *Philada Porter & Ale* in back; graphite pontil; green; 6½"................**35.00-45.00**

George Kimmerer, Canajoharie, N.Y.; on front in oval slug plate; 9½"; aqua..................**3.00-6.00**

Kinsella & Hennessy, Albany, N.Y.; blob top; 6¾"; aqua.........................**10.00-12.00**

Kinsella & Hennessy; in a dome shape under it, *Albany;* blob top; 7½"; aqua.................**8.00-10.00**

G.A. Kohl, Lambert, N.J.; in back, *K* in hollow letter; graphite pontil; 7½"; green.............**25.00-50.00**

Chas. Kolshorn & Bro. Savannah, Ga; blob top; aqua; 8".........................**4.00-6.00**

C.L. Kornahrens; aqua; 7½"; *C.L.K.* in back..**6.00-8.00**

C.L. Kornahrens; *Charleston S.C.* in circle; *Trade Mark* in center; in back *This Bottle Not To Be Sold;* 7¾"; aqua.........................**4.00-6.00**

C.L. Kornahrens; in horseshoe shape; under it *Charleston, S.C.;* blob top; 7"; aqua.....**4.00-6.00**

C.L. Kornahrens; blue; 7⅜"............**20.00-30.00**

Kroger Bros., Butte, Mt; in a slug plate; 6¾"; aqua................................**14.00-16.00**

Kroger Bros., Butte, Mt.; in a circle; Hutchinson; 8"; aqua................................**15.00-30.00**

H.O. Krueger, Grand Forks, N.D.; 7½"; aqua................................**6.00-10.00**

A. Krumenaker; *New York* in a slug plate circle; in center, 2 lines, *512 & 514 West 166th St.;* under it *Registered;* in back *This Bottle Not To Be Sold;* blob top; 7¼"; aqua....................**4.00-6.00**

Henry Kuck, 1878; *Savannah Ga.* in 4 lines on front; 7½"; green; blob top.................**10.00-20.00**

same as above, no date.............**6.00-10.00**

Henry Kuck; *Savannah Ga* in a slug plate on front; blob top; short neck; 7½"; aqua...........**8.00-10.00**

Henry Kuck; *Savannah, Ga.* in 3 lines; green; 7"; blob top...........................**6.00-10.00**

same except no *GA*................**8.00-15.00**

The John Kuhlmann Brewing Co.; Ellenville, N.Y.; on front in oval slug plate; 6¾"; aqua......**4.00-6.00**

J.H. Kump; in hollow letters, *Memphis, Tenn.;* blob top; 7½"; aqua.......................**4.00-10.00**

L & V; in large hollow letters, blob top, pontil, aqua and green, 7"...........................**60.00-80.00**

Le Laghtleben-Hackensack, N.J. Registered; slanted on front; blob top; 9¼"; aqua..........**4.00-8.00**

J. Lake; in hollow letters, *Schenectady, N.Y.;* semi-round bottom; graphite pontil; 8"; cobalt.....**20.00-40.00**

Lancaster Glass Works, N.Y.; graphite pontil; 7¼"; blue................................**20.00-40.00**

Lancaster Glass Works, N.Y.; reverse in center *XX;* blob top; graphite pontil; 6¼"; aqua....**40.00-80.00**

Lancaster Glass Works, N.Y.; (reverse N in *Lancaster*); graphite pontil; 7½"; cobalt blue, $35.00 +

F. Lanckahr, Higginsville, Mo.; 6¼"; aqua................................**4.00-10.00**

A. Landt, Livingston, Mt.; 7"; aqua...........**35.00 +**

Laramie Bottle Works, Laramie, Wyo; crown top; 6½"; aqua................................**4.00-8.00**

Large, Kansas; reverse side on base, *A. & D.H.C.;* 7"; blue.............................**10.00-20.00**

Laurel Club, Boston; clear; 10"..........**4.00-6.00**

Lawrence & Shaver, Georgetown, Wash.; 8¼"; aqua................................**4.00-6.00**

Lawes & Co.; *Belfast Ginger Ale* around bottle; aqua................................**6.00-8.00**

L. & B.; in hollow letters; blob top; graphite pontil; 7¼"; green.............................**25.00-45.00**

L & B; in 2" hollow letters; blob top; 7"; aqua.**3.00-6.00**

Lebanon Bottling Works; aqua; 7½" **4.00-6.00**

Julius Liebert; *C 4* under bottom; aqua; *This Bottle Not To Be Sold* in back; 9½" **4.00-8.00**

Lime Cola; on both sides; aqua; under bottom *Duro-glas 9-47-G999;* machine made, **$2.00-4.00**

J.A. Lindsey; a harp on back; *33* under bottom; aqua; 7" **7.00-10.00**

J.A. Lindsey; clear or amethyst; 6¾" **4.00-6.00**

L. Lindy, Savannah; in sunken panel; under it, *Union Glass Works Phila* in 2 lines; cobalt blue; slug plate; improved pontil; 6½" **8.00-20.00**

Life Preserver; clear; 7", **$6.00-10.00**

C.C. Little, Greenfield, Mass; 7¼"; aqua . . .**6.00-12.00**

Locke & Beltz Bottlers, Brownsville, Pa.; in a slug plate; 7"; aqua **4.00-6.00**

Lodi Soda Works; 6¼"; aqua **4.00-6.00**

Andrew Lohr; 6½"; aqua; ridge on back mold; *C & C LIM* on base **6.00-8.00**

J A Lomax; *J.L.* under bottom; cobalt; 7¼" . . . . . .**20.00 +**

J.A. Lomax, Chicago; reverse *T.B.M.B.R.;* 7"; cobalt **30.00-60.00**

Longmont Bottling Works, Longmont, Colo; 6¾"; clear **4.00-10.00**

Los Angeles; in center, a star and *Soda Works;* crown top; 6½"; clear **4.00-6.00**

Los Angeles Soda Co.; in a dome shape line under it *Mineral Water Factory;* reverse side *H.W. Stoll;* blob top; 6¾"; aqua **8.00-15.00**

Los Banos; in center, *L & B Soda Works;* crown top; 6½"; clear **4.00-6.00**

John S. Low; aqua; 7" **6.00-10.00**

Henry Lubs & Co.; *1885, Savannah Ga.;* green; 7½"; blob top, **$8.00-15.00**

Henry Lubs & Co.; *1885, Savannah Ga* in a sunken circle; short neck; aqua; blob top **8.00-12.00**

Lyman Astley, Cheyenne, Wyo; 7"; aqua . . .**4.00-10.00**

Macon Medicine Co.; *Guinns Pioneer Blood Renerver* on other side; amber; 11" **8.00-10.00**

Macks Beverage San Angelo, Texas; 7½"; light green **4.00-6.00**

George E. Madden; aqua; 7" **4.00-6.00**

M. Madison, Laramie, W.T.; blob top; 7"; aqua **35.00-50.00**

Magnolia Bottling Co.; *Paso, Texas; Contents 7 fl. oz.* around bottom and shoulder; crown top; 7⅝"; aqua **2.00-4.00**

Thos Maher; in small letters on slug plate; ground pontil; 7½"; dark green **15.00-30.00**

same, except larger ½" size letters **15.00-30.00**

Thos Maher; 6¾"; green; slug plate, **$30.00-40.00**

Thos Maher; slug plate; dark green; 7" **15.00-20.00**

Manuel Bros. New Bedford, Mass; on front in slug plate; blob top; 9¼"; amethyst **4.00-8.00**

Marble bottle, Japan; two round holes on shoulder; green; 7½" **6.00-8.00**

Marble teardrop type bottle; aqua; 9¾" **8.00-15.00**

The Mar-Cola Co.; aqua; 7¾", **$4.00-6.00**

Marion Bottle Works; in center *M & B* monogram, *Marion, N.C.,;* 6½"; aqua **8.00-15.00**

A. Marotta, 249-251 North St., Boston, Mass.; 9¼"; clear **4.00-6.00**

Marquez & Moll; ground pontil; aqua; 7¼" . . . .**15.00 +**

Marthis & Co.; aqua; 8" **2.00-4.00**

C.H. Martin & Co., Soda Works, Avon, Wash; 7¼"; aqua **4.00-6.00**

B. Marsh & Son, Detroit, Mich; ten panels; blob top; 7½"; aqua **30.00-60.00**

Mason & Burns, Richmond, Va. 1859; blob top; 7"; dark green **10.00-25.00**

S.M. Matteawan, N.Y.; S.M.M.; monogram on back; ten panels at base; 6¼"; clear **4.00-8.00**

Mayfields, Celery-Cola, J.C. Mayfield Mfg. Co. Birmingham, Ala.; 6¾"; aqua **10.00-20.00**

M.B. & Co.; 145 W. 35th St., N.Y., 1862; blob top; 7¼"; aqua **8.00-12.00**

J.W. McAdams Trade Mark; in center of a bunch of grapes, *Richmond, Va.*; panel base; 7"; aqua **8.00-10.00**

M. McCormack; *W.McC & Co.* on back; amber; 7" . . . . **15.00 +**

S.E. McCreedy, Providence, R.I.; in a circle; panel base; Hutchinson; 6¼"; aqua **10.00-25.00**

McGee, Benicea; in 2 lines, blob top, plain bottom, 6¾" **45.00-60.00**

Thos. McGovern, Albany, N.Y.; blob top; 7½"; aqua **4.00-10.00**

J. McLauglin; 7½"; green **20.00-30.00**

McMahons Well's, Ft. Edward, N.Y.; T.B.N.T.B.S.; blob top; 7½"; clear or amber **6.00-8.00**

McMinnville Bottling Works; *This Bottle Not To Be Sold* in back; amber; 7½", **$4.00-6.00**

Dan McPalin, Park City, Utah; in a circle; Hutchinson; 6½"; clear or amber **5.00-10.00**

Meehan Bros., Barberton, Ohio; in script; 6½"; aqua **8.00-12.00**

Meincke & Ebberwein; in horseshoe shape in center *1882;* under it in 2 lines *Savannah, Geo; Ginger Ale* vertical on back; amber; short neck; 8¼"; blob top **15.00-30.00**

Memphis Bottling Works, R.M. Becker; 7½"; aqua **6.00-8.00**

Joseph Mentze, Milton, Pa; blob top; 7¼"; aqua **8.00-15.00**

Mercer Bottling Co.; *This Bottle Is Registered Not To Be Sold* on back; aqua; 9½" **6.00-8.00**

Merrit Moore Jr. Bottler; *This Bottle Not To Be Sold* on back; clear or amethyst; 7" **4.00-8.00**

Merritt & Co., Helena, Mont.; blob top; 7¼"; aqua **8.00-10.00**

Mexota; *Root* under bottom; 11½" **4.00-8.00**

A.W. Meyer 1885, Savannah, Ga; in 4 lines on front; short neck; 8"; green; blob top **15.00-30.00**
same except aqua **8.00-15.00**

John P. Meyer, Freehold, N.J.; on front in oval slug plate; 9"; clear **4.00-8.00**

Miami Bottling Works; clear or amethyst; 7½" **4.00-6.00**

Miguel Pons & Co. Mobile; blob top; graphite pontil; 7½"; teal blue **20.00-40.00**

A.H. Miller; aqua; 6½" **4.00-6.00**

C. Miller; aqua; 9¼" **4.00-6.00**

Millers Bottling Works; aqua; *M* under bottom; 8" **2.00-4.00**

Miller, Becker & Co. M.B. & Co. Cleveland, Ohio; apple green; blob top; 6¾" **4.00-6.00**

Milwaukee Bottling Co., N. Platte, Neb.; in a sunken panel; Hutchinson; 7¼"; aqua **10.00-20.00**

M. Mintz, M.M.; in center *Gloversville, N.Y., Registered;* blob top; 8"; clear **4.00-6.00**

Mirrians; on shoulder; graphite pontil; 7¼"; cobalt **20.00-40.00**

Mission Orange Dry Reg.; under bottom; black glass; 9½", **$2.00-6.00**

J.M. Moe, Tomahawk, Wis; in 3 lines; Hutchinson; 5¾"; clear **12.00-15.00**

C.A. Moeller; *Karl Hutter 33 n New York* under bottom; aqua; 9¼" **6.00-10.00**

Chas Mohr & Son; *5¢ for return of bottle, Mobile Ala;* 7"; clear **4.00-8.00**

Montana Bottling Co., Butte City Mon.; blob top; 6¾"; clear or aqua **10.00-20.00**

Monroe Cider & Vinegar Co. Eureka, Cal.; 7¼"; clear or aqua **4.00-8.00**

Morgan & Bro. 232 W. 47th St., N.Y.; reverse, *M.B. Trade Mark;* blob top; 7"; aqua **10.00-15.00**

Morley C. Victoria, B.C.; in 4 lines vertical, blob top, 6½" **55.00-75.00**

Morrill G.P.; in 2 lines, blob top, plain bottom, aqua, 7" **25.00-34.00**

T. & R. Morton, Newark, N.J.; in 3 lines; squat type; graphite pontil; 6¾"; green **40.00-60.00**

L.C. Moses Bottler, Parsons, Kansas and Bartlesville; crown top; aqua . . . . **25.00 +**

Mount Bottling Co.; *This Bottle Not To Be Sold* on back; *3* under bottom; aqua; 9½" **6.00-8.00**

C. Motel; aqua; 7"; big *M* on bottom **6.00-8.00**

Moxie; 6¾"; aqua or clear **8.00-20.00**

E. Moyle; aqua; 7¼" **4.00-8.00**

Edward Moyle, Savannah, Ga.; on front; *Ginger Ale* vertical on back; amber; 7½" **18.00-20.00**

E. Moyle, Savannah, Ga; in sunken circle; blob top; 7¼"; *1880;* aqua **4.00-6.00**

Moyle, Savannah, Ga.; sunken circle, blob top, 1880, aqua 7¼" **7.00-10.00**

John E. Muehleck, Nelliston, N.Y.; on front in arch slug plate; *T.B.N.T.B.S.* on reverse side; 6¾"; aqua **4.00-6.00**

Muff Co.; label; marble in center of neck; aqua; 7¼" **6.00-8.00**

Jas. Mulholland, South Amboy, N.J.; on front in oval slug plate; reverse side, *T.B.N.T.B.S.;* 9½"; blue aqua **4.00-8.00**

B.J.E. Mullens; eagle in center; *Standard Grade Bottling Work, Albany, N.Y.* in script; crown top; 9¼"; aqua **4.00-8.00**

T.F. Murphy, Brookfield, Mass; on front in slug plate; blob top; 9¼"; aqua **3.00-6.00**

P.C. Murray, Monticello, N.Y.; on front in slug plate; 7"; aqua **6.00-8.00**

Muskogee Bottling Works Muskogee, I.T.; 6¾"; aqua **100.00-200.00**

N.A. Pa.; (star under it), *Woods* (star under it), *Soda*; in back, *Natural Mineral Water;* blob top; 7¼"; blue . . . . **25.00+**

National Dope Co.; aqua; 8" tall; 2¼" diameter **6.00-8.00**

National Dope Co.; aqua; 8" **4.00-6.00**

Otis S. Neale Co., Howard St., Boston, Registered 1893; with *OSN* monogram, all on front; blob top; 9¼"; amethyst **4.00-8.00**

Nerve Pepsin Co.; *Trade Mark Registered* on shoulder; clear; 8", $4.00-6.00

Neumann & Funke, Detroit, Mich.; Hutchinson; 7"; aqua **4.00-10.00**

Nevada City Soda Works; *L. Seibert* in 4 lines, blob top, plain bottom, aqua, 7" **32.00-43.00**

New Alamaden/Mineral Water, W & W, 1870; same on reverse in large letters; blob top; 7½"; aqua **4.00-8.00**

New Castle Bottling Co., Mt. Kisco, N.Y.; on front in oval slug plate; 9"; amethyst **4.00-6.00**

Newton Bottling Works; aqua; 8" **2.00-4.00**

No. Main St. Wine Co., 208-212 No. Main, St., Providence, R.I.; with *H* in center inside of slug plate; blob top; 9¼"; clear **4.00-6.00**

G. Norris & Co., City Bottling Works, Detroit, Mich.; 6¼"; cobalt **25.00-60.00**

same as above except aqua **6.00-8.00**

Northern Coca-Cola Bottling Works Inc., Massena, N.Y.; seltzer bottle type with pewter nozzle; 9¼"; cobalt . . . . **35.00+**

Nova Kola; *This Bottle Not To Be Sold* on base; clear or amethyst; 7¾" **3.00-6.00**

Oakland Pioneer Soda Work Co.; Trade Mark; (embossed bottle inside of O); 8¼"; blue aqua **4.00-6.00**

Oakland Steam Soda Works Inc.; in center in a wheel; on base, *Bottle Not To Be Sold* **4.00-12.00**

Occidental Bottle Works, Occidental, Cal.; *O.B.W.;* monogram; 6¾"; aqua or clear **4.00-8.00**

Odiorne's; clear; 8½" **2.00-4.00**

O'Keefe Bros. Bottlers, Matteawan, N.Y. Registered; on front; *O.K.B.* monogram on back; ten panels at base; 6½"; aqua or clear **4.00-8.00**

same as above except 9¼" **6.00-8.00**

O.K. Soda Works; in 3 lines; 7"; aqua **4.00-8.00**

Olsen & Co., Memphis, Tenn.; blob top; 7½"; cobalt **40.00-80.00**

D.L. Ormsby; in 2" hollow letters; graphite pontil; blob top; 7½"; cobalt **35.00-50.00**

E. Ottenville, Nashville, Tenn.; Hutchinson; 6¾"; blue **25.00-50.00**

E. Ottenville; *McC* on base; *25* under bottom; cobalt; 6" **30.00-60.00**

Ozark Fruit Co., Memphis, Tenn; in a circle; panels around base; 7½"; aqua **8.00-10.00**

same except crown top **4.00-8.00**

Ozo-Ola The Happy Drink; clear; 7½" **2.00-4.00**

J. Pabst & Son, Humilton, Ohio; in a circle; 6½"; aqua **8.00-15.00**

Pacific & Puget Sound Soda Works, Seattle, Wash.; 7"; aqua **10.00-15.00**

Pacific Bottling Works, Pacific, Mo.; *ABM;* 8"; aqua **2.00-4.00**

Pacific Soda Works, Santa Cruz.; *R;* in a hollow letter in center **3.00-6.00**

D. Palliser, Mobile, Ala.; 6¾"; aqua **4.00-8.00**

D. Palliser; *Arthur Christian 1875 Pat. April 13* under bottom; glass plunger for stopper; aqua . . **8.00-10.00**

D. Pallisier; (Palliser, misspelled); aqua; 7½" **15.00-30.00**

D. Palliser; aqua; 7½" **6.00-8.00**

D. Pallisers Sons; aqua; 7" **4.00-6.00**

D. Paliser; (Palliser, misspelled); aqua; 6¼", $12.00-16.00

Palmetto Bottling Works; clear or amethyst; 9¼" **6.00-10.00**

Parker; graphite pontil; blue; 5" **25.00-40.00**

E. Parmenter, Glenham, N.Y.; on front in crude slug plate; 9¼"; aqua **4.00-8.00**

E. Parmenter, Matteawan, N.Y.; on front in slug plate; *T.B.N.T.B.S.* reverse side; blob top; aqua . . **4.00-6.00**

Pearson Bros.; Hutchinson; 6"; aqua **4.00-8.00**

Pearson's Sodaworks; aqua; 7" **4.00-6.00**

Pepsi-Cola; in center in script, also on bottom; *7* on top of shoulder; clear or aqua; crown top; not machine made **4.00-6.00**

Pepsi Cola; in script; *Trade Mark* on top; *Memphis, Tenn* under it on slug plate; on back; *Registered; 2322* under bottom; amber; crown top; not machine made . . . . **25.00+**

Pepsi Cola; *Newberry, S.C., This Bottle Not To Be Sold* on back; 8" tall; 2¼" diameter; aqua **4.00-6.00**

Pepsi Cola; aqua; 8¾" **3.00-6.00**

Pepsi Cola; aqua; 7¾" **2.00-6.00**

Pepsi Cola; aqua; 8" **2.00-6.00**

Pepsi Cola, Albany Bottling Co., Inc.; amber;
8″ **6.00-15.00**

Pepsi-Cola, Norfolk, Va.; *This Bottle Not To Be Sold Under Penalty of Law* on back; cross under bottom;
amber; 8¾″ . . . . **25.00 +**

P.W. Perkins, Tannersville, N.Y.; 6½″;
aqua **4.00-10.00**

Perry Mfg. Co., Inc., Sonora, Ky.; reverse side on
base, *Reg. T.B.N.T.B.S.* 8¼″; aqua **3.00-6.00**

N.C. Peters, Laramie, Wyo; Hutchinson; 6″;
clear **4.00-8.00**

M. Peterson Soda Works, San Rafael, (Va. City, Nev.);
blob top; 7¾″; aqua **4.00-8.00**

John V. Petritz; in a dome; *Anaconda, Mont;* 6¾″;
aqua **8.00-10.00**

Henry Pfaff, El Paso; clear or amethyst;
8¼″ **15.00-30.00**

Henry Pfaff; clear or amethyst; 9¼″ **10.00-15.00**

Geo. Pfeiffer Jr.; in a dome; *Camden N.J.;* blob top;
7½″; aqua **10.00-20.00**

**Phillipsburg (Bottle Work in center) Phillipsburg.
Mont.;** reverse side *T.B.N.T.B.S.;* 6¾″;
aqua **8.00-10.00**

Phoenix Bottling Works; on 3 panels; other 7 panels
are blank; 6½″; light blue **2.00-8.00**

Phoenix Glass Work; in a circle, under it *Brooklyn;* blob
top; graphite pontil; 7¼″; aqua **20.00-40.00**

R.V. Pierce M.D., Buffalo, N.Y.; *C2 1182* under bottom;
aqua; 7″ **4.00-6.00**

Dr. Pierces Anurid Tablets; label; aqua;
3¼″ **4.00-8.00**

B. Pietz, Piqua, O; *This Bottle Never Sold* on back;
aqua; 7¾″ **10.00-15.00**

Pioneer Bottling Works; *P.B.W.* under
bottom; aqua; 7¾″, **$4.00-6.00**

Pioneer Soda Works; a shield with word *Trade* on one
side, *Mark* on the other; blob top; 7½″;
aqua **40.00-80.00**

Pioneer Soda Works, Gilroy; in large letters;
7⅝″ **4.00-6.00**

Pioneer Soda Water Co., S.F.; in center of a bear;
6½″; aqua **4.00-8.00**

Pioneer Soda Works, Smith & Brian, Reno, Nev; 6″;
aqua **8.00-20.00**

W. Pipe; sky blue; 7″ **8.00-15.00**

**Joseph C. Plante & Co., 631-635 Elm St., Manchester,
N.H.;** on front inside of slug plate; blob top; 9¼″;
amethyst **4.00-6.00**

Paul Pomeroy, Ludington, Mich; aqua; 7″ . . . **4.00-6.00**

P. Pons & Co.; large P on back; ground pontil;
aqua **30.00-50.00**

Pop bottle, label; aqua; 7″ **4.00-6.00**

C.M. Pope Bottling, Hollidaysburg, Pa.; blob top; 6¾″;
aqua **6.00-8.00**

Portland; picture of an eagle; above that, *Trademark,
The Eagle Soda Works, P.O.;* blob top; 7¼″;
aqua **8.00-15.00**

Post E.A.; in center a eagle, under it *Portland Org.,* all
in watermellow circle, blob top, plain bottom,
aqua **45.00-60.00**

Post Exchange Bottling Work, Fort Riley, Kan; in a circle; crown top; 7″; aqua **6.00-20.00**

Pratt Bottling Works; amber; 8″, **$4.00-8.00**

Prescott Bottling Works, Prescott, A.T.; in 4 lines;
6½″; aqua **30.00-80.00**

S. Priester & Bro., Houston, Texas; 7¼″;
aqua **8.00-10.00**

Purity Bottling & Mfg. Co.; clear or amethyst; *purity* on
bottom; 8″ **4.00-6.00**

M.T. Quinan; in horseshoe shape; in center, *1884;* under
it in 2 lines, *Savannah, Geo;* in back, 2″ monogram
MTQ; on top, *Mineral* and under, *Water;* under bottom, monogram *MTQ;* cobalt; 7¾″; blob top . . **25.00 +**

Quinan & Studer 1888, Savannah, Ga.; 7½″; aqua;
blob top **8.00-12.00**

Radium Springs Bottling Co.; machine made; *R* on bottom; clear; 7¾″ **2.00-4.00**

Randall; clear or amethyst; 5¼″ **2.00-4.00**

James Ray's Sons, Savannah, Ga; in center; *Hayo-Kola*
in sunken circle; blob top; clear; 8″ **4.00-6.00**

James Ray, Savannah, Geo.; in sunken circle; on back
in one vertical line, *GingerAle;* cobalt; 8″; blob
top **15.00-25.00**

**James Ray, Savannah, Ga.; in watermelon
circle on back, monogram** *JR;* 7½″; **dark
amber, $15.00-25.00**

James Ray, Savannah, Ga.; in watermelon circle on
back, monogram, *JR;* 7½″; aqua **15.00-25.00**

James Ray & Sons 1876, Savannah, Ga; in a sunken
circle on back, *This Bottle Registered, Not To Be
Sold;* under bottom, *B;* 7½″; clear or
amethyst **8.00-12.00**

James Ray, Savannah, Ga; in a sunken circle; aqua;
blob top; under bottom *C24;* 7½″ **6.00-10.00**

James Ray, Savannah, Ga; in a sunken circle on front; 7½"; blob top; aqua..................**4.00-8.00**

James Ray & Sons 1876; same except on back *RJ,* hollow letters......................**4.00-10.00**

James Ray; 8"; aqua...................**8.00-10.00**

James Ray; aqua; 7¼"...............**6.00-10.00**

Rayners Specialties; aqua; 7½"..........**6.00-10.00**

R.C. & T., New York; graphite pontil; aqua; 7½"...............................**35.00-45.00**

R Crown Soda Works; in large slug plate; *ABM;* 7⅛" aqua.............................**2.00-4.00**

Read's Dog's Head, London; on front around base; crown top; *ABM;* 9¼"; emerald green....**2.00-4.00**

P.H. Reasbeck, Braddock, Pa.; 7"; aqua.....**4.00-6.00**

Registered; in oval slug plate; *T.B.N.T.B.S.;* crown top; 9¼"; amethyst......................**2.00-4.00**

Richard & Thalheimer; clear or amethyst; *Dixie* on bottom; 7½"............................**6.00-8.00**

C.H. Richardson; in a dome shape under it, *Trenton, N.Y.;* 7"; green...................**10.00-25.00**

N. Richardson, Trenton, N.J.; graphited pontil; dark green; 7".........................**30.00-35.00**

The Richardson Bottling Co.; Mansfield, Ohio; in a circle; 6¾"; aqua..................**4.00-6.00**

Richmond Pepsi Cola Bottling Co., Richmond, Va; in a circle; slim shape; 9"; aqua...........**8.00-10.00**

W.R. Riddle, Philad.; reverse, large monogram; graphite pontil; blob top; 7½"; blue................**35.00+**

C.W. Rider, Watertown, N.Y.; 6¾"; frost green...**50.00+**

C.W. Rider, Watertown, N.Y.; Hutchinson; 7"; amber....................................**8.00-15.00**

Riggs & Dolan; clear; 7"...................**2.00-4.00**

T. & H. Rober, Savannah, Geo.; graphite pontil; 7"; green............................**20.00-30.00**

James M. Robertson, Philada; reverse side *T.B.N.T.B.S.;* blob top; 7¼"; aqua.......**4.00-8.00**

A.B. Robinson; in a dome under it *Bangor, Me.;* blob top; 7¾"; aqua......................**8.00-12.00**

A.B. Robinson, Bangor, Me; aqua; 7½"....**6.00-8.00**

A.R. Robinson; aqua; 7" tall; 2¼" diam......**4.00-6.00**

J.P. Robinson, Salem, N.J.; reverse side, hollow letter *R;* blob top; 6½"; green.............**10.00-25.00**

R.Robinson's; *402 Atlantic Av. Brooklyn N.Y.* on back; aqua; 7¼", $10.00+

Robinson, Wilson & Leagallse, 102 Sudsburys, Boston; blob top; 6⅜"; ice blue.......**8.00-12.00**

Rocky Mountain Bottling Co., Butte, Mont.; in large letters; 6⅜"; aqua..................**8.00-20.00**

The Rocky Mountain Bottle Works; aqua; 6¾".................................**4.00-6.00**

A.I. Roe; *Arcadia Fla.* on panel; *Coca Cola Bottling Co.* on bottom; clear; 7¾"; machine made....**2.00-3.00**

C. Roos; aqua; 7⅝", $4.00-6.00

Ross's Belfast; 9"; aqua.................**4.00-8.00**

Henry Rowohlt; *HR Trade Mark Registered* on back; aqua; 7½".............................**4.00-8.00**

R. & W. Las Vegas, N.M.; in a sunken panel; ten-sided base; Hutchinson; 7½"; aqua........**10.00-20.00**

John Ryan; in 2" letters around bottle; hollow letters under it *Savannah, Geo.;* ground pontil; 7"; cobalt...................................**20.00+**

John Ryan; in 2" hollow letters around bottle; under it *Savannah, Geo;* under it *1859;* cobalt; 7", $20.00+

John Ryan Savannah, Ga.; in vertical line; in back, also vertical line *Gingerale;* on shoulder, *1852 Excelsior;* amber or golden; 7½"...............**15.00-20.00+**

John Ryan; *1866* in front; in back *Excelsior Soda-works, Savannah, Geo.;* cobalt, olive, blue, green and red; 7¼".............................**10.00-25.00**

John Ryan; in small no. *1866;* blue; 7¼"........**15.00+**

John Ryan; cobalt; 7¾"; round; on front *J.R. S. 1852. T, Columbus, Ga.;* on back *This bottle Is Never Sold 1883;* on bottom *R*..................**10.00-25.00**

John Ryan 1866 Savannah, Ga.; on front; in back, 1" letters *Cider;* 7½"; amber..................**15.00+**

John Ryan Savannah, Ga.; in center of it, *1852;* blue; 7½"..............................**10.00-20.00**

John Ryan Savannah, Ga; in 3 vertical lines; round bottom; 8"....................................**20.00+**

John Ryan Jamaica Ginger; in vertical line; 6"; aqua....................................**6.00-8.00**

Ryan Bros; *Gravitating Stopper Made By John Mathews N.Y. Pat. 11, 1864* in a circle under bottom; aqua; 7".........................**15.00-20.00**

John Ryan, Savannah, Geo.; reverse *XX, Philadelphia Porter;* squat shape; blob top; 6½"; green..........................**35.00-50.00**

same as above except long tapered, blob top; graphite pontil; 6¾"; cobalt..........**50.00-75.00**

John Ryan Excelsior Mineral Water Savannah, Ga.;
reverse side *This Bottle Never Sold, Union Glass Works, Phila;* graphite pontil; 7½";
cobalt............................**50.00-75.00**

John Ryan Excelsior Mineral Water, Savannah, Ga.;
reverse side *U.G.W.P. T.B.N.T.B.S.;* blob top;
graphite pontil; 7¼"; blue...........**50.00-75.00**
same as above except no pontil; blob top; peacock
blue............................**35.00-50.00**
same as above except on base *1859;* and graphite
pontil; cobalt.....................**50.00-75.00**
same as above except no pontil......**35.00-50.00**

John Ryan; in 2" hollow letters; *Savannah, Ga. 1859;*
7½"; cobalt......................**50.00-75.00**
same as above except no date; graphite
pontil.........................**50.00-75.00**

John Ryan; in 1" hollow letters; *Phila. XX Porter & Ale;*
squat type; 6¼"; blue..............**35.00-60.00**

John Ryan, Savannah, Geo.; reverse side *XX
Philadelphia Porter;* squat type; 5¾";
cobalt..........................**60.00-80.00**

John Ryan 1866 Savannah, Ga.; reverse side in 1"
hollow letters, *Cider;* blob top; 7½"; blue or
amber..........................**40.00-80.00**

John Ryan; in 1" hollow letters; *Philadelphia, 1866;*
reverse side *XX Porter & Ale;* squat type;
green..........................**40.00-80.00**

John Ryan 1852, Augusta & Savannah, Ga.; reverse
Philadelphia XX Porter & Ale; blob top; 6¾";
cobalt..........................**40.00-80.00**

John Ryan, Savannah, Ga.; in a circle in center *1852;*
blob top; aqua.....................**35.00-50.00**
same except amber.................**40.00-80.00**

John Ryder, Mt. Hollow, N.J.; blob top; 7";
aqua...........................**10.00-25.00**

Rye-Ola Bottling Works; *Doc 1166* on base; clear or
aqua; 8".........................**4.00-6.00**

St. James Gate, Dublin; machine made;
amber...........................**2.00-4.00**

**St. Petersburg Bottling Work; clear or
amethyst; 8", $2.00-6.00**

**Salinas Soda Works, Steigleman, Salinas, Cal.; Bottle
Never Sold;** 7⅞"; aqua...............**4.00-6.00**

Salsa Diablo; on panels around bottle;
clear; 6¾".......................**4.00-6.00**

Sammis & Heintz, Hemstead, L.I.; 7¼";
aqua...........................**8.00-10.00**

San Anselmo Bottling Co., San Rafael, Cal.; 6¾";
aqua...........................**8.00-20.00**

H. Sanders, Savannah, Ga.; 8½"; amber..**20.00-30.00**

John L. Sanders; *This Bottle Not To Be
Sold* on back; aqua; 7", $4.00-8.00

San Francisco Glass Works; blob top; 7⅛";
aqua............................**8.00-12.00**

San Jose Soda Works, A.J. Henry, San Jose, Cal.; all
on front; 8¼"; light blue.............**4.00-6.00**

San Jose Soda Works; (K missing in works); blob top;
7½"; aqua.......................**20.00-30.00**

Santa Barbara Bottling Co.; in center, *Santa Barbara,
Cal.;* 7"; aqua....................**4.00-8.00**

Sapula Bottling Works; 7¼"; clear........**8.00-12.00**

Sass & Hainer, Chicago, Ill; *C & I* on back;
aqua; 7¼"......................**6.00-10.00**

C.L. Schaumloleffel, Trenton, N.J. Reg., T.B.N.T.B.S.;
crown top; 7½"; aqua.................**6.00-8.00**

Schenk's; *Syrup Philada* on other panels;
clear...........................**8.00-15.00**

P. Schille; fancy script *Sp; Columbus Ohio;* Hutchinson;
7"; aqua........................**4.00-6.00**

P. Schille; in center; monogram *S.P.* under it; *Columbus,
O.* 6¾"; aqua....................**4.00-8.00**

**C. Schiners & Co., Sacramento, Cal. Capital Soda
Works;** Hutchinson; 6½"; aqua........**6.00-12.00**

A. Schmidt Bottler; aqua; 6¾"............**4.00-6.00**

F. Schmidt, Leadville, Colo.; Hutchinson; 6¼";
aqua............................**4.00-8.00**

Schoonmaker & Wilklow; in center; *Ellenville, N.Y.* in a
sunken circle; blob top; 7½"; aqua......**8.00-10.00**

Alex Schoonmaker, Ellenville, N.Y.; in an oval slug
plate; 6¾"; clear...................**4.00-8.00**

Carl H. Schult; top vertical line; in center *C-P;*
monogram *M-S;* 3 lines *Pat. May 4 1868 New York;*
tenpin type; 8½"; aqua..............**8.00-10.00**

Frank Scutt Bottler, Verband Village, N.Y. 702; inside
of slug plate; crown top; 7½"; amethyst...**2.00-4.00**

John Seedorff; ground pontil; blue; 7½"...**20.00-50.00**

Seitz Bros., Easton, Pa.; large *S* on reverse side; blob
top; graphite pontil; 7½"; cobalt...........**50.00**

**Seitz Br. Co.; large *S* in back; amber; 7¼",
$6.00-8.00**

Seitz Bros., Easton, Pa.; large *S* on reverse side; blob
top; 7¼"; green......................**25.00+**

Seitz Bros; large *S* on back; blue green; 7"..**10.00-15.00**

F. Setz, Easton, Pa; on back; ground pontil; green; 7¼" **25.00-35.00**

7 Up; crown top; brown; squat type bottle; 6", **$4.00-8.00**

E.P. Shaw's; label; marble in center of neck; aqua; 7¼" **6.00-8.00**

E. Sheehan 1880, Augusta, Ga.; blob top; *Return This Bottle* reverse side; 9"; aqua **8.00-10.00**

E. Sheehan 1880, Augusta, Ga.; blob top; 7¼"; amber **30.00-60.00**

E. Sheehan 1880, Augusta, Ga.; in an oval slug plate; reverse side *R.T.B.;* 7½"; cobalt . . . .**100.00 +**

E. Sheehan, Augusta, Ga.; blob top; 7½"; amber **18.00-20.00**

E. Sheehan, 1880, Augusta, Ga.; blob top; 7¼"; green **18.00-25.00**

E. Sheehan, 1880 Augusta, Ga.; reverse side *R.T.B.;* 8¼"; amber **18.00-25.00**

Sheridan Bottle Work, Sheridan, Ark; Hutchinson; 6"; aqua **8.00-20.00**

Sheyenne Bottling, Valley City, N.D., Stevens & Co. Prop; 6¼"; aqua **10.00-12.00**

Shiner Bottling Works, Shiner, Tex.; in a circle slug plate; 6½"; aqua **4.00-8.00**

Sinalco; *C* in a triangle and *8* under bottom; snap-on; machine made; amber; 7½" **2.00-6.00**

Sioux Bottling Works, Watertown, S.D.; 7"; clear **4.00-8.00**

Sip Drinks Tastes Like More; around base *Sip Bottling Corp;* reverse side, a hand with crossed fingers and embossing reading *Make This Sign;* crown top; 7½"; clear **8.00-10.00**

A.P. Smith; ground pontil; 7¼" **25.00-35.00**

B. Smith Reg. Poughkeepsie, N.Y.; in a slug plate; blob top; 9¼"; clear **4.00-6.00**

D. Smith, Yonkers, N.Y.; on front in shield slug plate; *T.B.N.T.B.S.;* 9"; aqua **4.00-8.00**

D.H. Smith, Yonkers, N.Y.; in shield slug plate; blob top; 11½"; clear **4.00-8.00**

John J. Smith, Louisville, Ky.; 6¼"; aqua **10.00-20.00**

Smith & Co.; panels around base; blue **25.00-35.00**

Smith & Co.; seven panels; ground pontil; green **30.00-40.00**

Smith & Sweeney, Middletown, N.Y.; on front in oval slug plate; blob top; 7"; aqua **4.00-8.00**

Soda, label; graphite pontil; 7½"; green **15.00-20.00**

Soda, plain; blob top with sunken circle; under it, *Registered;* aqua; 7½" **4.00-6.00**

Soda, label; *1589 C* on bottom; aqua; 7½" **2.00-4.00**

Soda, label; clear or amethyst; 7½" **2.00-4.00**

Soda, label; aqua; 9"; marble in neck **4.00-8.00**

Soda, label; tear drop; flat top; aqua; 8½" . . .**8.00-10.00**

Soda, label; dark amber; 7½" **8.00-12.00**

Soda, label; small kick-up; dark green; 7½" . . .**2.00-4.00**

Soda, label; *This Bottle Not To Be Sold* on back; aqua; 9¼" **2.00-4.00**

Soda, label; *Reg. This Bottle Not To Be Sold* on back; anchor under bottom; clear or amethyst; 7½" **4.00-6.00**

Soda Water Bottling Co., Property of Coca Cola, Pat'd June 1, 1926, Memphis; on 4 panels on center; 6 panels on neck with stars; *ABM;* 9¾"; green **2.00-6.00**

Solano Soda Works, Vacaville, Calif; in 4 lines; 6¾"; aqua **4.00-10.00**

A. Solary; aqua; 7", **$4.00-8.00**

South McAlister Bottle Works; *South McAlister, Ind. Ter.;* aqua; 7" **100.00-200.00**

Southern Bottling Co., Atlanta, Ga; 6¼"; aqua **3.00-6.00**

Southern Phosphate Co., Columbus, Miss; clear; 8" **4.00-6.00**

Southern Phosphate Co.; aqua; 8" **3.00-6.00**

The Southwestern Bottling Co., Tulsa; crown top; 7¾"; aqua . . . .**25.00 +**

Southwick & Tuppes, New York; on 8 panels; graphite pontil; 7½"; green . . . .**35.00 +**

Squeeze; clear or amethyst; *Ybor City Fla* on bottom; 8"; machine made **2.00-6.00**

Standard Bottling & Extract Co.; aqua; 9¼", **$2.00-4.00**

The Standard Bottling & Mfg. Co.; clear; *#20* on bottom; 6½" **4.00-6.00**

The Standard Bottling & Mfg. Co.; clear or amethyst; 8" **2.00-4.00**

Standard Bottling Co.; machine made; a star on bottom; aqua **2.00-4.00**

Standard Bottling Co., Atlanta; reverse side *This Bottle To Be Returned;* Hutchinson; 8"; aqua . . .**8.00-20.00**

Standard Bottling Co., Peter Orello Prop. Silverton, Colo.; 6¾"; aqua **6.00-10.00**

Standard Bottling Works, Minneapolis, Minn.; 6¼";
amber **8.00-12.00**
Star under bottom; aqua; 9½" **2.00-6.00**

Star Bottling Works, Anadarko O.T. T & M; Hutchinson; 7" aqua **100.00-200.00**

Star Bottling Works, Houston, Texas; written in a circle
around a large star; tear drop shape; blob top; 8"
aqua . . . .**50.00 +**

Star Mail Order House; *243* under bottom; clear or
amethyst; 12¼" **8.00-12.00**

M & M Star Bottling Co., Oskaloosa, L.A.; 6¾"; clear
or aqua **6.00-8.00**

Star Soda Works, Grible & Co; in a circle in center;
Nevada City; 7"; clear **4.00-8.00**

**E.B. Starsney; clear or amethyst; 8¼",
$2.00-4.00**

Steam Bottling Works, Shawnee, Okla., I.T.; 7";
clear **100.00-200.00**

Steinke & Kornahrens; on one panel; *Charleston S.C.*
other panel; 8 panels; dark olive; ground pontil;
8½" **35.00-50.00**

H. Stewart, 253 Room St., N.O.; blob top; graphite pontil; 7½"; aqua . . . .**25.00 +**

Stillman Bottling Co., 42 Stillman St., Boston; in a
slug plate; blob top; 9¼" **4.00-6.00**

Peter Stonitsch; aqua; 9" **4.00-6.00**

**Strawhorn & Slago, Registered, Greenwood, S.C.
T.B.N.T.B.S. & Must Be Returned;** crown top; 7¾";
aqua **6.00-10.00**

P. Stumpf & Co.; *This Bottle Not To Be
Sold* on back; amber; 8½", **$20.00-30.00**

J.P. Sullivan, Santa Rosa; blob top; 6½";
aqua **4.00-6.00**

Summers & Allen, Alexandria, Virginia; in 3 vertical
lines; 7½"; aqua **4.00-8.00**

Sunset Bottling Works; aqua; 7" **8.00-10.00**

Superior Bottling Work, Superior, Wash.; 6½";
aqua **8.00-20.00**

Superior Soda Water, J.F. Miller, Davenport, Iowa;
blob top; fancy shoulder; 5 panels;
blue **40.00-50.00**

Superior Soda Water; other side; ground pontil; blue;
7½" **30.00-60.00**

Supreme Bottling Co., Waukesha, Wis; on front in a
slug plate; 6¼"; aqua **4.00-8.00**

Swidler & Bernstein, Chicago; *S.B.* under bottom; aqua;
6½" **6.00-8.00**

Albert H. Sydney, Providence, R.I. Ahs; monogram all
inside of slug plate; blob top; 9¼"; clear . .**4.00-8.00**

Syphon Corp. of Florida; *Bottle Made in Czechoslovakia*
under bottom; emerald green; 9" **10.00-20.00**

Tampa Bottling Works; pale green; 8" **4.00-8.00**

Tampa Cider & Vinegar Co.; aqua **4.00-6.00**

The Tampa Pepsi Cola Bottling Co.; semi-round bottom; 6"; aqua **6.00-8.00**

Tango-Cola, Richmond, Va. Reg.; star around neck;
7½"; clear **4.00-8.00**

B.F. Tatman, Owensboro, Ky; in center on 3-4" panel;
other panels are plain; semi-round bottom;
aqua **4.00-8.00**

Taylor Soda Water Mfg. Co., Boise, Ida.; panel base;
6¾"; clear **8.00-15.00**

**Taylor, Erie, Pa. Reg.; around bottle; large
/ under bottom; aqua; 6¼", $4.00-6.00**

C. Taylor, Erie, Pa.; around bottle; large *T* under bottom; aqua; 6¼" **4.00-6.00**

Taylor & Wilson; aqua; 8½"; round bottom . .**8.00-12.00**

Tear drop (or sunbeam); 8½"; aqua; there are 3 or 4 different sizes **4.00-8.00**

Tear drop shape; crude blob top; 8"; dark
olive **50.00-60.00**

W.Z. Thomas, Niles, Ohio; in a circle; T.B.N.T.B.S. on
the base; Hutchinson; 8¼"; clear **4.00-6.00**

Thornton & Co.; in ¼ moon letters under it in 2 lines,
Hudson, N.Y., blob top, aqua **17.00-23.00**

Tolle Bottling Works; in center big *T; Litchfield, Ill;*
6½"; clear or amethyst **6.00-8.00**

C.A. Tolle; in a circle in the center; a big *C* in center;
Registered Litchfield, Ill; 6½"; aqua **4.00-8.00**

Tonopah Soda Works, Tonopah, Nev.; in 3 lines; Hutchinson; 6"; clear **8.00-12.00**

Towne's; aqua; 7" **4.00-6.00**

Trinidad Bottling Works; clear or amethyst;
6¾" **2.00-6.00**

Tri State Bottling Co.; *D.O.C. 1209* around base in
back; 7½" **8.00-12.00**

Try-Me Beverage Co.; machine made;
clear; 9" **1.00-2.00**

T. & S. Port Townsend Soda Works, P.T.W.T.; 6¼";
aqua **25.00-50.00**

T S, Savannah, Geo; in 3 lines; on back, *This Bottle Is
Never Sold;* emerald green; improved pontil; 6½";
blob top **8.00-15.00**

Tucson Bottling Works, Tucson, Ariz., I.P.G.Co.;
crown top; 7¼" **3.00-6.00**

Tuskaloosa Bottling Works, C.C. Simpson MGA.. Tuskaloosa, Ala; reverse *T.B.N.T.B.S.;* Hutchinson; 6¾″; aqua **4.00-8.00**

T. & W.; in hollow letter under it *1875;* reverse side *141 Franklin St. N.Y.;* blob top; 6½″; aqua . .**10.00-15.00**

Twitchell; aqua; 7½″ **8.00-15.00**

G.S. Twitchell; in center, hollow letter *T;* under it *Phila;* reverse hollow letter *T;* blob top; 7″; green **10.00-30.00**

Twitchell, Philada; in center, hollow letter *T;* same on back; green; 7½″ **20.00-35.00**

Tyler Bottling Works; aqua; 7¼″ **2.00-4.00**

Tyler Union Bottling Works, T.B.N.T.B.S., Tyler, Tex.; panel base; 7″ clear or amethyst **6.00-8.00**

U.C.B. Co.; *Contents 8 Fl. Oz.* under bottom; clear; machine made; 8″, **$2.00-4.00**

Wm. Underwood & Co., Boston; around base; amber or aqua; 7½″ **10.00-15.00**

Union Beverage Co., Jitney-Cola, Knoxville, Tenn.; *6½ Flo. Oz.* on shoulder; 7¾″; amber **4.00-8.00**

Union Bottling Co., Wilmington, Del., Registered; 7½″; aqua **8.00-12.00**

Union Bottling Work; in dome shape; under it *Victor, Colo.;* 6¾″; aqua **8.00-20.00**

Union Glass Work, Phila; blob top; graphite pontil; 7″; green **10.00-30.00**

Union Soda Water Co.; *W & C* under bottom; *This Bottle Never Sold Please Return* on back; aqua; 7½″ **3.00-6.00**

United Glass Ltd. England; map of world and *1759-1959;* these bottles were dropped in the ocean in 1959 with maps, etc. sealed inside to commemorate the Guinness Brewing Co., bicentennial; machine made; amber; 9″ **6.00-8.00**

A. Urmann; *649* under bottom; aqua; 7¼″ **6.00-8.00**

Property of Valley Park Bottling Works, Valley Park, Mo.; on front; *ABM;* 7½″; aqua **2.00-4.00**

Vancouver Soda Works, Vancouver, Was; star and trade mark in a sunken panel; Hutchinson; 7¼″; aqua **10.00-15.00**

Vernon & O'Bryan; *X* under bottom; aqua **4.00-6.00**

John Vickery, Ennis, Texas; *Registered* on shoulder; *62* under bottom; aqua; 8¼″ **2.00-6.00**

Vicksburg Steam Bottling Works; *P* under bottom; aqua; 6¾″ **4.00-6.00**

Vig-O; *T.E. McLaughlin, Lynchburg, Va;* aqua; 9½″ **2.00-4.00**

Vincent & Hathaway, Boston; reverse side, hollow letters *V. & H.;* 7″; aqua **10.00-15.00**

Vincent Hathaway & Co., Boston; blob top; round bottom; 7¼″; aqua **4.00-10.00**

Virginia Fruit Juice Co.; machine made; clear or amethyst; thick bottom; 7½″ **2.00-6.00**

Viva Bottling Works; *This Bottle Not To Be Sold* on base; *CS6G Co* under bottom; clear; 9″ . .**2.00-4.00**

Vogels Beverages, Sylacauga, Ala.; 6¾″; aqua **2.00-6.00**

Vogel Soda Water Co., St. Louis, Mo.; squat; crown top; 7¼″; aqua **8.00-10.00**

Albert Von Harten, Savannah, Ga.; in 2 vertical lines; in back; same except one line *Ginger ale;* 7″; dark green; blob top **12.00-15.00**

Albert Von Harten, Savannah, Ga.; in 2 lines; on back *Ginger Ale;* 7″; 2″ neck; blob top; green **10.00-20.00**

Von Harten & Grogan, Savannah, Ga.; on front; dark green; 7¼″; blob top, **$12.00-18.00**

Wabash Bottling Works, B.F.Heilman, 702 Wabash, Ind.; *ABM;* crown top; 7⅝″; light blue **2.00-4.00**

Wagoner Bottling Works; panel base; 7″; aqua . . .**10.00+**

Wainscott's Distilled Waters, Winchester, KY; in a circle; 7¼″; aqua **8.00-12.00**

H.S. Wartz & Co., 78, 80 & 82 Leverett St. Boston, Mass; in oval slug plate; blob top; clear . . .**4.00-8.00**

Weacle Vestry, Varick & Canal St.; *Prem Soda Water* on back; graphite; pontil; cobalt; 7½″ . . .**15.00-60.00**

Webb & Riley, Joliet, Ill. Trade Mark; Hutchinson; 7″; aqua **4.00-8.00**

Webbs; *London* on back; amber; 9½″ **10.00-15.00**

Joseph Weber; aqua; 7¼″; *J.W.* inside cloverleaf **8.00-12.00**

R.B. Webster; *New York Ginger Ale* around bottle; 7½″; aqua . . . .**10.00+**

A. Wegener & Sons, Detroit, Mich; in oval slug plate; 6⅜″; aqua **4.00-6.00**

H. Weigel; big *W* under bottom; aqua; 6¾″ . . .**4.00-6.00**

J.W. Welch; *This Bottle Not to Be Sold* on back; *4-X* under bottom; aqua; 9¾″ **8.00-10.00**

Geo. Weller, Schenectady; blob top; 7½″; aqua **8.00-10.00**

R. Weller; in center *176 Spring St., Saratoga N.Y.;* reverse *T.B.N.T.B.S.;* blob top; 7½″; aqua **8.00-15.00**

Chas. Westerholm & Co., Chicago, Ill. Trademark W. Co.; in a monogram on front; blob top; 6½″; aqua **2.00-6.00**

Western; in center a deer head and trade mark; under it *Soda Work, P.O.;* 6¾″; aqua **8.00-10.00**

W.F. & S.; star in the center and *MIL;* Hutchinson; 6¾″; aqua **4.00-12.00**

Hiram Wheaton & Sons; *Registered* on bottom rim; *19* under bottom; 7½″ **4.00-6.00**

H. Wheaton & Sons Trademark, New Bedford, Mass. Reg.; 7½″; aqua **6.00-10.00**

Wheeler Bros., Waukesha Soda Water Co., Waukesha, Wis; in a slug plate; blob top; 6½″; light green **4.00-6.00**

Wheeler & Co. Ud Cromac Spring; in line around base of round bottom bottle; under it *Belfast;* under bottom big *W;* in center a wagon wheel; between top spoke *E.R.;* on bottom of wheel between spokes *&Co.;* under wheel *Registered;* aqua; 9½"; blob top **6.00-10.00**

White Spring Co.; light aqua; 8" **3.00-5.00**

W.P. White; clear or amethyst; 7" **6.00-8.00**

Williams Bros., San Jose; in oval slug plate; crown top; 7⅝"; light aqua **2.00-6.00**

S.M. Williams, Matteawan, N.Y.; *SMW* monogram on reverse side; 10 vertical panels; blob top; 6½"; clear **4.00-8.00**

Willits Soda Works, Willits, Cal; crown top; 7¾"; aqua **4.00-6.00**

C.C. Wilson, Marked Tree, Ark.; 7"; clear **4.00-8.00**

Henry Winkle; in a dome shape; *Sac. City;* blob top; graphite pontil; 7¼"; aqua **10.00-20.00**

Winkler, Aug; *S.B.* in center, large letters *Doa Works,* all in circle, blob top, aqua, 6¾" **22.00-29.00**

Herman Winter; in ½ circle; *Savannah, Ga* under it; in back *This Bottle Not To Be Sold* in 3 lines; aqua; 8¼"; round; blob top **8.00-15.00**

Herman Winter; in a horseshoe shape; under it *Savannah, Ga.* 8"; blob top; aqua; 3" diameter . .**6.00-8.00**

A.J. Wintle & Sons, Bill Mills, Nr Ross, T. Turner & Co. Makers, Dewsbury; 6¼"; golden . . .**8.00-15.00**

Jacob Wirth & Co. Inc.; *JW* monogram; *Prov., R.I.* in a diamond slug plate; 9¼"; clear **4.00-10.00**

Wiseola; star under bottom; clear or amethyst; 8¼", $3.00-6.00

Wiseola Bottling Co., star under bottom; clear; 7" **6.00-8.00**

The P.H. Wolters Brewing Co.; *This Bottle Never Sold* in back; aqua; 9½" **2.00-4.00**

By Wootan Wlls Co.; (written vertically on bottle), *Wootan Wells, Texas;* Hutchinson; 6½"; aqua **4.00-8.00**

W. & P. Co.; in ½" letters; blob top; 7"; aqua **8.00-12.00**

W.S. Wright; under bottom; *Pacific Glass Works;* blob top; 7½"; green **10.00-30.00**

Wright's; *Coca Cola* on back; amber; 7" **8.00-20.00**

W.T. & Co.; star under bottom; aqua; 7¼", $25.00 +

W. & W.; in large letters; *Burlington, Iowa;* blob top; 6¾"; aqua **8.00-10.00**

X.L.C.R.; in ¼ moon letters, under it in 2 lines *Soda Works, San Francisco, Ca.* blob top aqua, 7" **40.00-55.00**

Yale Bottling Co.; in center 268½ *Wooster St., New Haven, Conn.;* 7¾"; aqua **4.00-12.00**

Yetter & Moore; clear or amethyst; 8" **4.00-6.00**

J.H. Yetter; aqua; 7½" **15.00-20.00**

Philip Young & Co. Savannah, Ga; on front; on back, eagle, shield and flag; improved pontil; 7½"; green; blob top, $15.00-30.00

Mrs. B.Z. Zimmerman, New Brunswick, N.J.; in a circle; under it *T.B.N.T.B.S.;* 6⅛"; clear or amethyst **4.00-8.00**

Otto J. Zipperer; *This Bottle Is Never Sold* on back; amber; 8½" **8.00-20.00**

Mineral Water

Before it became stylish for wealthy folk to flock to the seashore or retreat to the mountains, America's nobility gathered at resorts established around the healthful, sparkling waters of mineral springs. They bathed in it, drank it, and because that somehow wasn't enough, they took it home with them in bottles.

Mineral water had been sought for its medicinal properties since ancient times. The Greek physician Hippocrates described the value of mineral waters in 400 B.C. The traditional appeal of the healing waters was maintained through the generations, and by the eighteenth century, the European leisure class was congregating in large numbers at health spas. In America, practical Yankees designed less elaborate spas than their European counterparts. Still, they were resorts complete with hotels, gambling, horse racing and other diversions reserved soley for those who could afford them. The rich could frolic in the cure-all waters, while the less fortunate could only dream of its wonderful taste. However, that was remedied in 1767 when a Boston spa began to bottle its waters. It was followed in 1800 by a spa in Albany and in 1819 by one in Philadelphia.

Competition soon developed among the spas. Claims of the healing virtues of the various bottled mineral spring waters often were as extravagant as those of their medicine cousins.The sparkling waters purportedly cured rheumatism, diabetes, kidney and urinary diseases, gout and nervous disorders. Doctors recommended it to their patients.

European immigrants to America were so convinced of the powers of these salted waters that they imported their favorite brands from the "old country." These arrived in crudely fashioned pottery bottles. The first American bottles were unadorned, but made of glass. Glassmaking had, after all, been the first industry in the New World. The first commodity produced by the earliest glasshouse in Jamestown in 1608 was probably a bottle.

Development of a spa was likely to be a successful commercial venture. George Washington had a speculative eye on Saratoga Springs in Saratoga County, New York, and in August of 1783 attempted to invest in it. His attempt to purchase failed, and several years later the springs were opened to the public. But the cooling, curing mineral waters found there were not bottled until 1820 when the Reverend Mr. D.O. Griswold, who slyly chose to stamp his bottles with the pseudonym "Dr. Clarke," began to market the water. Just 30 years later over seven million bottles were needed annually to keep up with the demand for Saratoga Springs water.

Promoters of mineral water were quick to capitalize on stories about its properties. Since a mineral spring was located near the Gettysburg, Pennsylvania, Civil War battlefield, it was only natural that Gettysburg Katalysine Spring Water be bottled. Its bottling was prompted by the story that many soldiers wounded in that battle had been cured by the spring waters.

Following the Civil War, at a time when sales of mineral water began to drop, excessive boasts began to appear that lithium, an alkali metal supposedly with healing properties, was in the water. An investigation after the passage of the Pure Food and Drug Act in 1907 found only infinitesimal traces of lithium in the bottled water. "Lithia Water" abruptly disappeared from bottle labels.

Bottled spring water began to replace mineral water in the late nineteenth century. Most of the collectable bottles were closed with cork and are from the 1850-1900 period.

Abilena Natural Cathartic Water; on the bottom; 11½"; amber or brown. **4.00-8.00**

Abilena Natural Cathartic Water; on bottom; blob top; 10⅛"; amber. **8.00-10.00**

Aderondack Spring, Wesport, NY; tapered top with reg. plain bottom, qt. Eme. green **30.00-50.00**

Aderondack Spring, Whitehall, N.Y.; mineral water tapered top & ring emerald green, pt. . . **35.00-50.00**

Aetna Mineral Water; 11½"; aqua. **4.00-6.00**

Aetna Spouting Spring; in horseshoe letters in center; *A & E* in block letters; *Saratoga, N.Y.;* pint; aqua. **60.00-150.00**

Akesion Springs; *Owned By Sweet Springs Co. Saline Co.* Mo.; 8"; amber, $10.00-15.00

Albert Crook; *Saratoga Co. N.Y.* in a circle; through center of it *Paradise Spring;* tapered top; six rings; pint; green or aqua. **60.00-80.00**

Alex Eagle; in center, *1861 Mineral Water;* tapered top; 7¼"; aqua. **8.00-15.00**

Alhambra Nat. Mineral Water Co., Martinez, Cal; applied top; 11¼"; aqua. **8.00-12.00**

Alleghany Spring, Va.; amber. **10.00-20.00**

Allen Mineral Water; horizontal letters placed vertically on bottle; blob top; 11½"; golden amber. **8.00-12.00**

Allen Mineral Water; big ring top; 7½" **8.00-15.00**

American Kissinger Water; in vertical lines; tapered top and ring; pint; aqua. **25.00-65.00**

American Mineral Water Co., New York, M.S.; monogram all inside slug plate; *This Bottle Not To Be Sold* at base; blob top; 9¼"; aqua. . . **8.00-10.00**

Artesian Ballston Spa; green. **20.00-30.00**

Artesian Spring, Ballston, N.Y.; same on back; green; 8", $15.00-30.00

Artesian Spring Co.; in center an *S* super-imposed over an *a;* under it *Ballston, N.Y.* tapered top & ring pt. emerald green. **25.00-45.00**

Artesian Spring Co., Ballston, N.Y.; *Ballston Spa. Lithia Mineral Water* on back; dark aqua; 7¾". **25.00-30.00**

Artesian Water; pontil or plain; *Dupont* on back; dark olive; 7¾". **50.00-100.00**

Astorg Springs Mineral Water, S.F. Ca.; blob top; 7"; green **8.00-15.00**

John S. Baker; *Mineral Water, this bottle never sold* on panels; blob top; eight panels; pontil; aqua **20.00-40.00**

Bartlett Spring Mineral Water, California; in a slug plate; blob top; 11⅝″; aqua **8.00-15.00**

Batterman H.B.; in ½ moon circle, in center, *1861,* under it in 2 lines *Brooklyn, N.Y.,* tapered top, ground pontil *(C1860),* aqua, 7½″ **20.00-50.00**

Bauman, N.; Pottsville, Pa; in 4 lines, slug plate, *(C1860)* ground pontil, tapered top and ring, green, 7½″ **50.00-85.00**

Bear Lithia Water; aqua; 10″ **4.00-8.00**

J. & A. Bearbor, New York Mineral Water; 8 panels; star on reverse side; graphite pontil; 7¼″; blue **20.00-45.00**

Bedford Water; label in back; aqua; 14″ **4.00-8.00**

Bitterquelle Saxlehners Janos; on bottom; 10½″; whittle mark or plain; avocado green; ring top . **4.00-6.00**

Blount Springs Natural Sulphur; cobalt; 8″ . . . . . . **15.00 +**

Blue Lick Water Co., Ky; mineral water bottle, double ring top, pontil, pt. amber **85.00-130.00**

J. Boardman & Co. Mineral Water; 8 panels; graphite pontil; 7¾″; cobalt **30.00-80.00**

Boley & Co., Sac, City, Cal; reverse side *Union Glass Work, Phila.* slug plate; blob top; graphite pontil; 7½″; blue **50.00-75.00**

J. Born Mineral Water, Cincinnati; reverse hollow *B, T.B.N.T.B.S.;* blob top; 7¾″; green **8.00-20.00**

J. Born Mineral Water, Cincinnati; in 3 lines; reverse side large *B* and *T.B.N.T.B.S.;* blob top; 7½″; blue **30.00-40.00**

Bowden Lithia Water; under it a house and trees; under that *Lithia Spring Ca.;* blob top; aqua . . . **12.00-20.00**

Brown Dr; N.Y.; in 1 line, vertical big *B* in back, tapered top, pontil *(c. 1850),* green, 7½″ **40.00-85.00**

Buckhorn Mineral Water; label; aqua; 10¼″, **$8.00-10.00**

Buffalo Lick Springs; clear or amethyst; 10″ . . **3.00-6.00**

Buffalo Lithia Spring Water; aqua; 10½″ . . . **8.00-12.00**

Buffalo Lithia Gin; clear or amethyst; 10¼″ **8.00-12.00**

Buffalo Luthis' Water; *Natures Materia Medica;* lady sitting with pitcher in hand; under it, *Trade Mark;* round; 11½″; aqua; ½ gallon **6.00-12.00**
same with whittle effect **7.00-14.00**

Bythinia Water; 10¼″; tapered top; amber **4.00-8.00**

Cal. Nat. Mineral Water, Castalian; around shoulder; 7¼″; amber **6.00-8.00**

California Natural Seltzer Water; reverse side picture of a bear, *H.&G;* blob top; 7¼″; aqua **10.00-20.00**

W. Canfield; *Agt. for S.H.G.;* graphite pontil; squat; blob top; 6¼″; green . . . . **15.00-35.00 +**

Cantrell, Thos J.; *Ballfast, Medicated aerated water,* all in 5 vertical lines, blop top, round bottom, aqua, 9¼″, *(c1900)* **10.00-20.00**

Carlsbad L.S.; sheared collar; cylindrical; ground top; 4″; clear **3.00-6.00**

Carlsbad L.S.; on bottom; short tapered top; quart; 10¼″; green **6.00-10.00**

Carters Spanish Mixture; pontil; 8½″ **30.00-60.00**

C.C. & B. San Francisco; in 2 lines; reverse side *Superior Mineral Water;* ten-sided base; blob top; graphite pontil; 7″; blue **35.00-80.00**

Champion Spouting Spring; amber; 7¾″ . **75.00-100.00**

Chaplain Spring, Highgate, Vt.; mineral water, tapered top & ring, emerald green, qt. **40.00-65.00**

Chase & Co. Mineral Water, San Francisco, Stockton, Marysville, Cal.; in 6 lines; graphite pontil; blob top; 7¼″; green **35.00-65.00**

City Bottling Work; under it a girl seated; *Mt. Vernon, O.;* tapered top; 11″; clear **15.00-30.00**

C. Clark; on front; *Mineral Water* on back; dark olive; 7″; ground pontil **25.00-75.00**

John Clarke, New York; around shoulder; three-piece mold; pontil; 9¼″; olive, $45.00-60.00

John Clark, N.Y. Spring Water; 7″; green; . **40.00-60.00**

Lynch Clark, N.Y.; aqua **30.00-40.00**

Clark & White; in U; under it *New York;* in center *C Mineral Water;* 9¼″; olive green **15.00-30.00**

Clark & White; in horseshoe; in center big *C;* in back, *Mineral Water;* 9½″; olive green **10.00-25.00**

Clarke & Co., N.Y.; in 2 lines; tapered top and ring; 7¾″; pontil; blue green **35.00-55.00**

Clarke & White; wide mouth; dark olive; 7″ x 3¾″ diameter, $30.00-90.00

Clarke & White; green; 7½″ **15.00-30.00**

Clarke & White; olive; 8″ **15.00-30.00**

C. Cleminson Soda & Mineral Water, Troy, N.Y.; blob top; 7¼″; blue **12.00-20.00**

Columbia Mineral Water Co., St. Louis, Mo; 7¼″; aqua **4.00-6.00**

Colwood, B.C., Hygenic Mineral Water Works; blob top; crock; white and brown; 8″ **8.00-12.00**

Congress & Empire Spring Co.; *Hotchkiss Sons & Co. New York, Saratoga, N.Y.* large hollow letters; *CW* in center; 7" olive **50.00-75.00**

Congress & Empire Spring Co., Sarotoga, N.Y.; reverse side *Congress Water;* 7¾"; dark olive **20.00-40.00**

Congress & Empire Spring Co.; in horseshoe shape; big *C* in center; above it *Hotchkiss Sons;* under the big *C, New York, Saratoga, N.Y.;* pint; 7¾"; under bottom 2 dots; green; wood mold **15.00-30.00**

Congress & Empire Spring Co; in a horseshoe shape; in center of it a big *C* in a frame; under it, *Saratoga, N.Y.;* tapered and ring top; 7¾"; emerald green, $35.00-55.00

Congress & Empire Spring Co.; on back *Empire Water;* dark green; under bottom a star; 7½" tall; 3" diameter **15.00-30.00**

Congress & Empire Spring Co., New York, Saratoga; olive green; 7½" **15.00-30.00**

Congress & Empire Spring Co., in U; under it *Saratoga, N.Y.;* in center of big *C, Mineral Water;* 9¼"; blue green **10.00-20.00**

Congress Spring Co., Saratoga, N.Y.; dark green; quart; tapered top and ring **25.00-35.00**

Congress Spring Co.; in horseshoe shape; in center large *C;* under it *Saratoga, N.Y.;* in back *Congress Water;* quart; 7¾"; dark green **15.00-30.00**

Congress Springs Co. S.S.N.Y.; in a circle; under the bottle in center *#4;* old beer type; wood mold; blue green; 9½" **8.00-10.00**

Congress Springs Co.; in horseshoe shape; in center a *G, Saratoga, N.Y.;* emerald green; 8"; tapered top and ring **25.00-50.00**

Congress Water; in 2 lines; tapered and ring top; green; 8" **25.00-50.00**

Conner, C.; in ½ moon letters; in back also *Union Glass Works, Phila.,* tapered top with ring, pontil, green, 7½" **40.00-85.00**

P. Conway Bottler, Phila; reverse side *No. 8 Hunty, 108 Filbert, Mineral Water;* blob top; cobalt; 7¼" **10.00-30.00**

Coopers Well Water; *BCOO* on back base; aqua; 9¾", $20.00-30.00

Corry Belfast; in 2 hollow letters lines, ver. tea drop bottle, blob top, aqua, 9½" **10.00-25.00**

Couley's Fountain of Health, No. 38 Baltimore's Baltimore; symbol of a fountain in the center; tall whiskey bottle shape; pontil; 10"; aqua **15.00-25.00**

Courtland Street 38 N.Y.; *T. Weddle's Celebrated Soda Mineral Water* on back; graphite pontil; cobalt; 7½" **30.00-60.00**

Cowleys Fountain of Health; pontil; aqua; 9½" **10.00-40.00**

Crown; on shoulder; 8½"; olive green; beer type bottle **6.00-8.00**

Crystal Spring Water; in horseshoe shape; under it, *C.R. Brown Saratoga Spring, N.Y.;* quart; 9½"; green **60.00-90.00**

Crystal Spring Water Co., N.Y.; around base; aqua; 9½" **4.00-8.00**

Dearborn, J & A; in ¼ moon letters under it *New York,* in back *"D"* tapered blob top, pontil, blue, 7½" **60.00-85.00**

Deep Spring; 3-part mold; *C* in a diamond under bottom; amber; 12¾" **12.00-18.00**

Dobbs Ferry Mineral Water Co., Dobbs Ferry, N.Y.; 6½"; aqua, $8.00-15.00

Dobbs Ferry Mineral Water Co. White Plains, N.Y.; all inside slug plate; *Contents 7 oz. Registered* on front at base; 8"; amethyst and clear **4.00-6.00**

D.P.S. Co.; *Rochester, N.Y. U.S.A.* 3½"; amber **2.00-3.00**

Eagle Spring Distillery Co.; on front; rectangular; 7"; amethyst **3.00-4.00**

Eagle's W.E., Superior Soda & Mineral Water; all in 4 lines in black large *W.E.,* pontil, blob top, blue, 7½" (c.1856) **80.00-100.00**

G. Ebberwein; *Savannah, Geo* in 3 lines on front; on back between words *Mineral Water,* monogram *EGB;* under bottom monogram *E;* light blue; 7½"; blob top **12.00-20.00**

same except aqua . . . . **10.00 +**

same except amber or dark blue **10.00-30.00**

same except short neck; 8"; vertical in back *Ginger Ale* **12.00-30.00**

same except amber **15.00-30.00**

Elk Spring Water Co., Buffalo, N.Y.; on front in oval slug plate; blob top; ½ gallon; clear **4.00-10.00**

C. Ellis & Co., Phila; short neck; graphite ponti; 7"; green **20.00-40.00**

Empire Spring Co.; *E* in center, *Sarotoga, N.Y., Empire Water;* 7½"; green, tapered top and ring **20.00-30.00**

Empire Water; pint; star under bottom; green **10.00-20.00**

A.C. Evans Sup[R] Mineral Water, Wilmington, N.C.; written vertically; graphite pontil; 7½"; green **40.00-80.00**

Excelsior Springs, Mo; *Roselle* under bottom; clear or amethyst; 8".......................**2.00-4.00**

Excelsior, Spring, Saratoga, N.Y.; plain bottom, tapered top & ring, (C1870) emerald green, qt...**40.00-50.00**

The Excelsior Water; blue; 7"; ground pontil.....**35.00 +**

The Excelsior Water; on 8 panels; blob top; graphite pontil; 7¼"; green.................**30.00-50.00**

Farrel's Mineral Water, Evansville, Ind.; graphite pontil; 7½"; aqua.......................**15.00-30.00**

Franklin Spring, Mineral Water; *Ballston, Spa Saratoga Co. N.Y.* mineral water bottle, emerald green pt......................**95.00-125.00**

Friedrichshall, C. Oppel & Co.; on the bottom; label; blob top; 9"; green.................**6.00-10.00**

J.N. Gerdes; *S.F. Mineral Water;* **blob top; green; 7½", $4.00-8.00**

J.N. Gerdes S.F. Mineral Water; vertical on 4 panels; eight panels in all; blob top; 7⅛"; aqua blue............................**18.00-30.00**

Gettysburg Katalysine Water; *X* under bottom; green; 10"......................**20.00-25.00**

Geyser Spring, Saratoga Spring, State of N.Y.; light blue; 7¾".......................**20.00-30.00**

Geyser Spring, Saratoga Springs; in horseshoe; in center *State of New York;* in back vertically *The Saratoga Spouting Spring;* 7¾"; about a quart; light blue............................**25.00-30.00**

Gilbeys Spey Royal; label; three dots and number under bottom; golden amber; 8", $10.00-15.00

Glacier Spouting Spring; in horseshoe shape; letters under it *Saratoga Spring, N.Y.* in back a fountain; pint; green; *Glacier* misspelled.....**100.00-150.00**

Glendale Spring Co., This Bottle Not To Be Sold; blob top; 7"; aqua......................**8.00-12.00**

Granite State Spring Water Co., Akinson Depot, N.H., Trade Mark; embossed; two Indians taking water from stream and large granite rock; crown top; 10"; aqua..................................**4.00-8.00**

Great Bear Spring; *Fulton N.Y., This Bottle Is Loaned and Never Sold* on bottom; aqua; 11½"..**8.00-10.00**

Charles S. Grove & Co. Sparkling Mineral Water, No. 30 Canal St., Boston; in a diamond shape; reverse side *T.B.N.S. Deposit on Same, Refund When Returned;* 7½"; aqua.................**14.00-18.00**

Guilford Mineral Spring Water; blue green; 9¾", $20.00-35.00

Guilford Mineral, Spring Water,Guilford, VT; tapered top with ring, yellow green, qt........**55.00-95.00**

Guilford Mineral Spring Water; green.....**10.00-20.00**

Guilford & Star Spring; green or amber....**10.00-15.00**

Guilford Mineral Spring Water; in side of a diamond in center; also *G.M.S.;* under it *Guilford, Vt.;* short neck; 10"; dark green................**20.00-40.00**

Hanbury Smith; light olive; 8".............**6.00-8.00**

Hanbury Smith's Mineral Waters; 7¾"; dark green........................**15.00-30.00**

Harris; amber; 9¼".....................**4.00-8.00**

Harris Albany Mineral Waters; graphite pontil; tapered top; 7¼"; aqua.....................**8.00-12.00**

Dr. Hartley's Mineral Water, Phila.; in front; in back *Improved Patent;* pontil; flared top; 6¾"; light emerald green...........................**40.00-75.00**

Hathorn; amber; 9¼".....................**15.00-25.00**

Hathorn Spring; in horseshoe shape; under this, *Saratoga, N.Y.;* dark amber; under bottle a "drop" and a letter *H;* 7½"; round...........**20.00-35.00**
same except bottom plain; very dark green.........................**15.00-30.00**

Hathorn Water, Saratoga, N.Y.; paper label; 9½"; amber........................**4.00-6.00**

Headman; in a dome shape under it *Excelsior Mineral Water;* reverse *F.W.H.* in hollow letters; graphite pontil; 7¼"; green.....................**25.00-40.00**

Heckings Mineral Water; green..........**20.00-30.00**

High Rock Congress Spring, Saratoga, N.Y.; mineral water bottle, tapered top & ring, qt., yellow olive (c1870).........................**50.00-65.00**

Highrock Congress Spring; aqua........**10.00-40.00**
same except amber.................**15.00-30.00**

Holmes & Co. Mineral Water; ground pontil; 7½"; blue.............................**20.00-60.00**

Holmes & Co.; graphite pontil; *Mineral Water* **in back; light blue; 7¼", 25.00-65.00**

Honesdale Glass Works, Ap ("Pa" backwards); *Mineral Water* in back; aqua; 7½"............**18.00-22.00**

Honesdale Glass Works, Pa; in a dome shape; reverse side *Mineral Water;* graphite pontil; blob top; green **40.00-60.00**

J. Hopkins, Phila; pontil; short neck; dark aqua **20.00-35.00**

Horan P., 75, West 27th St., N.Y.; all in 4 lines, pontil, *(C 1860)* blob top, green, 7½" **40.00-75.00**

Hubener, J.; in ¼ moon letters under it *New York,* in back, *mineral water* big *H,* tapered top, pontil, blue, 8", *(c1850)* **50.00-90.00**

Hygeia Water; *Cons. Ice Co., Memphis, Tenn.* around base; 9¾"; aqua **4.00-10.00**

Hyperion Spouting Spring; in a horseshoe shape; tapered top and ring; pint; aqua **40.00-60.00**

Improved Mineral Water; short tapered top; graphite pontil; 7½"; cobalt **25.00-50.00**

Improved Mineral Water; blob top; graphite pontil; 6¼"; blue **20.00-40.00**

Indian Spring; in center; Indian head under bottom; 10½"; aqua **10.00-15.00**

Iodine Spring, L, South Hero, Vt.; qt. golden amber, tapered top, with ring **120.00-185.00**

Jackson Napa Soda; on front; in back *Natural Mineral Water, Jacksons TB.I.N.S.;* 7½"; aqua . . **10.00-20.00**

Jackson's Napa Soda Spring; on front; reverse side *Natural Mineral Water;* blob top; 7½"; aqua **8.00-12.00**

Johnston & Co. Phila; in large block letters; on back large fancy 2" *J;* tapered top; 6¾"; sea green **16.00-35.00**

Jubilee Spring Water Co.; *101* under bottom; *5 pt* on back; aqua; 11½" **10.00-20.00**

J. Kennedy, Mineral Water, Pittsburg; in 3 lines on back; script letters *J.K.;* graphite pontil; blob top; 7½"; green **35.00-40.00**

Kissinger Water; dark olive; 6¼" **25.00-35.00**

Kissinger Water Patterson & Brozeau; tapered top; 7"; olive **15.00-20.00**

D.A. Knowlton; in a dome shape; undr it *Saratoga, N.Y.;* tapered top; 9½"; olive **30.00-50.00**

Knowlton; D.A. Saratoga, N.Y.; in 3 lines, *(C1850)* tapered top & ring, em green pt **40.00-50.00**
same except amber **100.00-200.00**
same except blue **100.00-200.00**

R.T. Lacy, New Kent Co., Va. Prop. Belmont Lithiawater; in a circle in center 2 men turning a hand drill; under that *Deus Aquam Creavit Bibamus* and *AD 1877;* 10"; blue green **15.00-30.00**

J. Lamppin & Co. Mineral Water, Madison, La.; in back *Madison Bottling Establishment;* graphite pontil; blob top; 6½"; blue green **40.00-80.00**

Liviti Distilled Water Co., Pasadena, Ca.; around base in small letters; crown top; *I.P.G. Co. 841 Liviti* on bottom; round; ABM; tapered neck; 7¾"; aqua **4.00-6.00**

J.A. Lomax, 14 & 16 Charles Place, Chicago; four-piece mold; 9¾"; amber **10.00-20.00**

Lynch & Clark, New York Mineral Water; tapered top & ring pontil, olive amber, pt **75.00-120.00**

Lytton Spring; in center a pelican; *Sweet Drinks* under it; in 3 lines *P.M.H. Co., San Francisco, C.H.B.;* 6½"; aqua **12.00-15.00**

Macnish & Son, Jamaica; in 2 lines, semi-round bottom, applied crown top, aqua, 9½" **10.00-15.00**

Madden Mineral Water Co.; label; aqua; 7", **$8.00-10.00**

Maduro, IL. Canal Zone; all in a water mellow circle, marble bottle, applied top, aqua, 9¼" . . **10.00-20.00**

Magee's; aqua; 10½" **8.00-15.00**

Magnetic Spring; amber **20.00-35.00**

Magnetic Spring, Henniker, N.H.; tapered top & ring, qt. Go. amber plain bottom *(C1868)* **65.00-85.00**

J. Manke & Co. Savannah; in 2 lines; in back *Mineral Water;* blob top; 7"; aqua **10.00-15.00**

Massena Spring, Water, Mineral Water; tapered top & ring, emerald green, qt **50.00-85.00**

Frederick Meincke; in horseshoe shape; in center of horseshoe *1882;* under it, in 2 lines, *Savannah, Geo.;* on back 2" monogram *F.M.;* on top of it *Mineral Water;* under it *Water;* cobalt; 7¾"; under bottom is monogram *M* **30.00-75.00**

Meincke & Ebberwein; *Savannah, Geo.* in horseshoe shape; in center *1882;* on back monogram between words *Mineral Water, M & E;* under bottom, monogram *ME;* cobalt; blob top **30.00-50.00**

Merchant, Lockport, N.Y.; plain bottom tapered top & ring, emerald green, qt **40.00-60.00**

Micuelpiris Mineral Water, No. 334 Royal St., N.O.; ground pontil; 7½"; aqua **20.00-35.00**

Middletown Healing Spring; amber **15.00-30.00**

Middletown Spring, Vt.; amber **15.00-20.00**

J. & D. Miller, Marietta, Ohio; reverse side *Mineral Water;* blob top; 7½"; aqua **8.00-20.00**

Mills Seltzer Spring; under bottom *M;* blob top; 7½"; aqua **12.00-20.00**

Mineral Water; tapered top; graphit pontil; 7¼"; green **20.00-40.00**
same as above except cobalt **30.00-65.00**

Mineral Water; tapered top; 6 panels; improved pontil; dark green; 7" **12.00-18.00**

Mineral Water; label; light green; 10¾" **4.00-8.00**

Mineral Water; ground pontil; 7¼"; green, $30.00-40.00

Mineral Water; label; green; 6½" **10.00-12.00**

Mineral Water; label; dark olive; pontil; 6" . . **15.00-20.00**

Mineral Water; in 2 lines on front; 7½"; blob top;
  aqua **5.00-10.00**
  same except pontil **15.00-40.00**

Minnegue Water; _Bradford Co., Pa.;_ 8"; aqua; tapered
  top and ring **15.00-30.00**

Missisquoi; _A_ in center; _Spring_ on reverse side, also an
  Indian woman carrying a baby; olive **40.00-80.00**

Missisquoi; olive; 9¾" **20.00-35.00**

Murtha & Co.; in front running ver. in back _mineral water_
  in 2 lines running ver., tapered top, pontil, green,
  7½" (c. 1842) **60.00-80.00**

Napa Soda, Phil Caduc; reverse _Natural Mineral Water;_
  tapered neck; blob top; 7½" **20.00-35.00**

Natural; in center; a man with sleeping cap and handkerchief around neck; under it _Mineral Water;_ blob top;
  7½" **10.00-20.00**

New Almaden; in a horseshoe shape; under it _Mineral
  Water;_ blob top; 6¾"; aqua **8.00-12.00**

New Almaden Mineral Water, W & W; on panels; 10
  panels; tapered top; blob top; graphite pontil 7½";
  green **20.00-50.00**

N.Y. Bottling Co., N.Y.; star on shoulder; _10 Cts.
  Deposit_ on back; _This Bottle is Loaned, 10¢ Will Be
  Paid For Its Return_ under bottom;
  aqua; 12" **6.00-8.00**

Oak Orchard Acid Spring; in shoulder _H.W. Bostwick
  Agt., No. 574 Roadway, N.Y.;_ on bottom _From F.
  Hutchins Factory Glass, Lockport, N.Y.;_ 9"; light
  amber **20.00-35.00**

O.K. Bottling Co., _O.K.;_ in center _526, 528, 530, W.
  38th St., N.Y.;_ reverse side Indian holding a flag;
  10¾"; aqua **10.00-25.00**

**O'Keefe Bros. High Grade Mineral Water, Matthewan,
  N.Y.;** with monogram; crown top; 7¾";
  amethyst **4.00-8.00**

Olympia Water Co.; in a dome shape; under it _Mineral
  Wells, Tex.;_ blob top; several different sizes;
  aqua **10.00-20.00**

**Olympia Water Co., Mineral Wells, Tex;
  aqua; 9½", $8.00-15.00**

Original Calif. Mineral Water Co.; _Sweetwater Springs,
  San Diego, Calif;_ 11"; aqua **10.00-12.00**

E.O. Ottenville; large _E.O._ on front; reverse _Ottenville,
  Nashville, Tenn._ 9¼"; amber **25.00-30.00**

P; on base, round bottle, blob top,
  aqua, 9¾" **6.00-10.00**

Pablo & Co.; _Mineral Water Factory_ on back; aqua;
  7½" **12.00-15.00**

Pacific Congress Water; on bottom; crown top; four-
  piece mold; 8¼"; aqua **6.00-8.00**

Pacific Congress; in horseshoe shape; under it _Water;_
  applied top; 7"; light blue **10.00-20.00**

B. Page Jr. & Co.; _Pittsburgh, Pa_ other side; side mold;
  aqua; 7½" **15.00-25.00**

**Paraiso Mineral Water Bottled By P. Stegelman,
  Salinas, Cal;** on front; 4-piece mold; crown top;
  8¼"; aqua **4.00-8.00**

Paris, Miguel, Mineral Water, No. 334, Royal St. N.O.;
  all in 5 lines in back big _P,_ blob ring top, pontil,
  aqua, 7½" (c. 1850) **40.00-60.00**

Patterson & Brazeau, Vichy Water, N.Y.; dark green,
  6¾" **6.00-10.00**

Pavilion & United State Spring Co.; dark olive; 7¾"
  tall; 3" diameter **70.00-100.00**

P.H. Crystal Spring Water Company N.Y.; around base;
  crown top; tenpin shape; 9¼"; aqua **4.00-10.00**

Poland Water; aqua **20.00-35.00**

Priest Natural Water; aqua **6.00-10.00**

Prist Napa; _A Natural Mineral Water Recarbonated At St.
  Helena From The Priest, Mineral Spring, Napa Co.,
  Calif;_ applied crown; 7¼"; aqua **4.00-8.00**

Pure Natural Waters Co., Pittsburg, Pa; inside fancy
  shield, with house embossed in center; crown top;
  ABM; 12¼"; aqua **4.00-6.00**

The Puritan Water Co., N.Y.; aqua; 12¼" **4.00-8.00**

Quaker Springs, I.W. Meader & Co. Saratoga Co. N.Y.;
  all in 3 lines, tapered top & ring, plain bottom, green
  and teal blue, qt (c.1880) **90.00-120.00**

R.C. & T.; in hollow letters under it New York, tapered
  top, pontil, green, 7½", (c.1853) **60.00-85.00**

Rockbridge Alum Water; aqua; 9½" **10.00-20.00**

Round Lake Mineral Water; amber 7¾",
$75.00-100.00

Rutherfords Premium Mineral Water; ground pontil;
  dark olive; 7½" **45.00-55.00**

Rutherford & Ka; on shoulder; 3-piece mold; graduated
  collar; 10½"; olive amber . . . . **30.00 +**

John Ryan; _Excelsior Mineralwater, Savannah_ in front;
  back _Unionglass Work, Phila, This Bottle Is Never
  Sold;_ cobalt; 7"; improved pontil **25.00-50.00**

St. Regis Massena Water; green **10.00-15.00**

San Francisco Glass Works; tapered neck; blob top;
  6⅞"; sea green **20.00-30.00**

San Souci Spouting Spring; in a horseshoe shape; in
  center a fountain and _Ballston Spa, N.Y.;_ tapered
  top and ring; pint; aqua **25.00-125.00**

Saratoga; under it a big _A,_ under it _Spring Co., N.Y.;_
  tapered top and ring; olive green; 3¾" x 9";
  round . . . . **20.00 +**

Saratoga Red Spring; green, 7½" **30.00-55.00**

Saratoga Seltzer Spring; olive green; 8"; quart; tapered
  top and ring **25.00-35.00**
  same except pint; 6¼" **25.00-75.00**

Saratoga Spring; honey amber; 9¾" **20.00-30.00**

Saratoga Vichy Spouting Spring; in a horseshoe shape; in center a hollow letter *V;* under it *Saratoga, N.Y.;* tapered top; 7½"; aqua **25.00-40.00**

Seven Springs Mineral Water Co. Goldsboro, N.C.; 8"; aqua **4.00-8.00**

Shasta Water Co.; *Mineral Water Co.;* 10½"; amber **4.00-8.00**

E.P. Shaw & Co. Ltd. Wakefield; paper label; 5"; green **4.00-8.00**

Shoco Lithia Spring Co., Lincoln, Neb.; crown top; 7¾"; aqua **2.00-6.00**

S. Smiths, Knickerbocker Mineral & Soda Water, N.Y.; pontil; 7"; green **25.00-50.00**

Sparkling Londonberry Spring Letha Water, Nashua, N.H.; label; 11⅝"; green **2.00-6.00**

Star Spring; aqua **8.00-10.00**

Steinike & Weinlig Schutz Marke; embossed hand holding some tools; *Seltzers* in large letters on back; three-piece mold; blob top; 9¾"; emerald green **8.00-12.00**

Stoddard Magnetic Spring, Henniker, N.H.; amber **60.00-80.00**

Summit Mineral Water, J.H.; in 3 lines; blob top; 7½"; green **8.00-15.00**

Sunset Spring Water, Catskill Mt., Hames Falls, N.Y.; on base *This Bottle Loaned Please Return;* 13"; aqua **8.00-10.00**

Syracuse Springs; different sizes, amber . . .**38.00-50.00**

Taylor; *never surrenders* in 3 lines, slug plate in back, *Union Glass Works, Phila.* in 2 lines, tapered top, pontil, blue, 7¼" (c.1850) **110.00-140.00**

Thompsons; in center *Premium Mineral Waters;* tenpin shape; reverse side *Union Soda Works, San Francisco;* blob top; 7½" aqua **10.00-15.00**

Tolenas Soda Springs; reverse side *Natural Mineral Water;* tapered neck; blob top; 7"; aqua blue **7.00-12.00**

Triton Spouting Spring; in horseshoe shape; in center block letter *T,* under it, *Saratoga, N.Y.;* pint; green **75.00-125.00**

Tweddles Celebrated Soda or Mineal Water; reverse side *Courtland Street,* in center *#38,* under it *New York;* tapered top; graphite pontil; 7½"; cobalt **30.00-60.00**

Underwood Spring, Falmouth Foreside, Me; on front in oval slug plate; crown top; 8⅞" **4.00-8.00**

Ungars Ofner Bitterwasser; green; 9½" **4.00-8.00**
same as above with no embossing **2.00-4.00**

Union Glass Works, Phila.; under it *Superior Mineral Water;* panel base; blob top; graphite pontil; 7½"; blue **30.00-50.00**

Union Spring; green; 8" **50.00-10.00**

Ute Chief of Mineral Water; *Maniton, Colo. U.T.* on base; crown top; clear or purple; 8" **4.00-6.00**

Varuna Mineral Water Wells; in a horseshoe shape; *Richwood, Ohio,* under it *I. Miller, Prop. T.B.N.S. and must be returned;* 6½"; clear **10.00-20.00**

Vermont Spring Saxe & Co.; green **10.00-20.00**

Veronica Medicinal Spring Water; 10½"; amber **4.00-10.00**

Veronica Mineral Water; around shoulder; 10¼"; square; amber, clear **6.00-10.00**
same as above except *ABM* **4.00-8.00**

Veronica Mineral Water; on square shoulder; square; 10½"; amber **6.00-10.00**

Vichy Etat; label; reverse side embossed *Establishment Thermal De Vichy;* 6¾"; cobalt **15.00-20.00**

Vichy Water Cullums Spring, Choctaw Co., Ala; 7¼"; dark olive **30.00-40.00**

Vichy Water, Patterson & Brazeau, N.Y.; vertically on front; pint size; 6¾"; dark green **8.00-15.00**

Washington Spring; picture of Washington's head; pint; 6¼"; emerald green **75.00-110.00**
same except quart; 8¼" **70.00-100.00**

Weller Bottling Works, Saratoga, N.Y.; blob top; aqua **15.00-35.00**

G.W. Weston & Co.; **10.00-20.00**

G.W. Weston & Co. Mineral Water, Saratoga, N.Y.; amber **20.00-50.00**

Whelan Troy; embossed tulips; Hutchinson; 7½" **10.00-12.00**

D.J. Whelan; *Mineral Water* on back; aqua; 7½" **8.00-12.00**

White Sulphur Water; blue green; 8¾" **4.00-8.00**

Witter; *Witter Medical Spring* under bottom; amber; 9½" **4.00-8.00**

Witter Spring Water; *Witter Medical Springs Co.* under bottom; amber; 9½" **4.00-8.00**

Witter Springs Water, W.M.S. Co., San Francisco; around shoulder and bottom; 9¼"; amber **8.00-12.00**

W.S.S. Water; machine made; *9-2-8 O.I* with diamond shape under bottom; green; 5½" **1.00-2.00**

XXX ($\frac{X}{XX}$) in 2 lines; blob top; graphite pontil; 7"; green **15.00-30.00**

Adam W. Young, Canton, Ohio; in slug plate; squat shape; graduated collar; 9¼"; aqua **4.00-8.00**

Zarembo Mineral Spring Co., Seattle, Wash.; blue; 7½"; tapered top **10.00-20.00**

Ale and Gin

Ale and gin were both alcoholic beverages that the average person could afford. Ale could conveniently be made at home, while gin could be produced cheaply and was therefore affordable. Early ale bottles were usually of pottery and nearly always from England. The first ones had a matte surface, while later examples are shiny. The home brewer of ale in the early seventeenth century was aware of the hazards of cork closures: If the corks became dry, the carbonation would expel them from the bottles and the contents would be ruined.

Francisco de la Boe, a Dutch doctor seeking a medicinal compound to treat kidney disease, discovered gin in the mid-seventeenth century. The product was sold as medicine and soon the druggists, who knew a good thing when they tasted it, devoted full-time work to the distillation of gin. By the end of the eighteenth century it was a favorite drink throughout most of Europe.

The shape of gin bottles has not varied a great deal since the seventeenth century. Their square bodies allowed twelve to be packed in a special wooden case, and they came to be called case bottles. The first case bottles were octagonal in shape, however. Early case bottles had particularly short necks, while the later ones had long, stretched necks. Many case bottles in this country were imported from Holland. Because English and American glasshouses made use of Dutch craftsmen, it is difficult to differentiate between Dutch, English and American bottles.

Most of the case bottles with tapered collars can be dated to the nineteenth century. Plate molds began to be used in bottle making in the late 1800's; such molds were designed to hold plates with lettering or designs on them to be easily transferred to the bottle. Some case bottles are embossed with animals, people and stars.

Case bottles range in size from a half-pint to the multiple-gallon container. Though they vary in size, most have the traditional shape. The early bottles are crudely made and have pontil scars.

Abmyersam; *Rock Rose, New Haven, Md;* 9⅛"; dark green 4.00-6.00

A & D.H.C.; yellow amber; 9½" 8.00-18.00

A.H.; in seal; roll top; 11⅜"; green amber . . **30.00-60.00**

A.I.; with an anchor in seal on shoulder; honey amber; 8¾" **40.00-90.00**

Ale, label; dark green; 9½"; turn mold 2.00-6.00

Ale, label; olive; 8½"; turn mold; kick-up 2.00-4.00

Ale, label; green; 6"; kick-up 2.00-6.00

Ale, label; *1716 A* under bottom; olive; 9½" . . . 2.00-4.00

Ale, label; 9½"; aqua 2.00-6.00

Ale, label; aqua; kick-up; 8" 2.00-3.00

Ale, label; aqua; *Root* under bottom; 11¾" 2.00-4.00

Ale, label; dark olive; 9½"; turn mold 6.00-12.00

Ale, label; amber; ground pontil; 11¼" . . . . 20.00 +

Ale, label; amber; 8¾" 8.00-12.00

Ale, label; light green; small kick-up pontil; 9" 8.00-10.00

Ale, label; olive; kick-up; 7½" 6.00-12.00

Ale, label; olive; kick-up with broken pontil; 12" 15.00-35.00

Ale, label; olive; kick-up pontil; three-part mold; 8¾" 15.00-20.00

Ale, label; amber; pontil; 9" 20.00-24.00

Ale, label; milk glass; 11" 10.00-20.00

Ale, label; five dots under bottom; small kick-up; black 10" 4.00-8.00

Ale, label; light aqua; 9½" 2.00-6.00

Ale or wine, label; 3-part mold; *B* under bottom; dark olive; 10" 4.00-6.00

Ale or wine, label; kick-up; dark olive; 9½" 2.00-4.00

Ale or wine, label; kick-up; dark olive; 10", $2.00-4.00

Ale, plain; 7¼"; free-blown; 2" diameter; pontil; crude top **10.00-15.00**

Ale, plain; aqua; free-blown; kick-up; pontil; light-weight bottle; 9½"; very crude top; 2¾" diameter **12.00-20.00**

Ale, plain; free-blown; aqua; kick-up; pontil; 8½"; 2¼" diameter; crude top **10.00-15.00**

Ale, plain; quart; 6"; 3" neck; very crude applied top; pontil in kick-up; very light blue **10.00-20.00**

Ale, plain; 8 panels; graphite pontil; 7"; green **18.00-25.00**

Ale, plain pottery; 8½"; brown and white 3.00-4.00

Ale, plain pottery; 8½"; white 2.00-4.00

Ale, plain; 11½"; white; pottery 3.00-4.00

S. Alvares; on seal; clear; 11½"; kick-up 3.00-5.00

Ameliorated Schiedam Holland Gin; 9½"; amber **15.00-25.00**

Antediluvian Luyties Brothers New York; small kick-up; olive; 12", $6.00-8.00

ASCR; in a seal; olive; kick-up; 10½"; pontil or plain **50.00-150.00**

Asparagus Gin, The Rothenberg Co.; on front in circle; slug plate, *S.F. Calif.;* same shape as a Duffy malt; graduated collar; 10⅛"; aqua **10.00-20.00**

Avan Hoboken & Co.; on front; seal on shoulder *AVH;* case bottle; 11¼"; olive **28.00-35.00**

Baird Daniels Co. Dry Gin; tapered and ring top; 9"; aqua 8.00-10.00

same as above except *Mistletoe Dry Gin;* 8½"; clear or amethyst 8.00-10.00

same as above except *Coronet* under bottom; aqua 8.00-10.00

Bart E.L.; in old English type on one line; on the other, *Dry Gin;* 8½"; light green **2.00-4.00**

Bass' Pale Ale; label; three-part mold; amber; 9½" **2.00-6.00**

B.B. Extra Superior; whiskey; amber; 10½" **12.00-18.00**

B.C.W.; dark olive; pontil; 9", $60.00-175.00

Benedictine; dark green; 8¾"; kick-up; *F22* on bottom **6.00-8.00**

Bergomaster; *Geneva Gin, Cobb Hersey Co., Boston* on round label; also ship on bottom of label; case type; 10½"; olive **8.00-12.00**

Bergomaster; *Geneva Gin, Cobb Hersey Co.* (no label); case type; 10½"; olive **6.00-10.00**

Berry Bros.; *323 E. 38th St. N.Y.* in circle on front; aqua; 11¼" **2.00-4.00**

Big 6 gin, Original; tapered top; 6½"; clear or amethyst **4.00-8.00**

Bill & Dunlop; dark olive; 11½" **15.00-25.00**

Black bottle; beer or ale; three-part mold; kick-up with one dot; 4½" body; 2" neck; 7¾"; crude top; bottom 3"; dark olive **8.00-12.00**

Black bottle; 4¾" body; 2" neck; 3" bottom; 3-part mold; kick-up; dark olive **8.00-12.00**

Black bottle; 5½" body; 2½" lady's leg neck; improved pontil; 2¾" bottom; crude top **8.00-12.00**

Black bottle, beer or ale; 3-part mold; 6½" body; 3" neck; 2½" bottom; dark olive **8.00-12.00**

Black glass; plain; 3-part mold; 7¾"; kick-up **4.00-10.00**

Black glass; *C.W. & Co.* under bottom; 3-part mold; kick-up **4.00-10.00**

Blake Bros Pale Ale, Langport; label; *P & R B* under bottom; 3-part mold; olive; 9½", $8.00-10.00

Blankenheym & Nolet; on front, ½" letters; case bottle; 9½"; olive **15.00-30.00**

Blankenheym & Nolet; dark olive; 7½" **15.00-25.00**

Blankenheym & Nolet, 1912; 9½"; green or amber **10.00-20.00**

same as above except 8½"; brown or amber **10.00-20.00**

same as above except 7⅛"; brown . . . . **15.00 +**

same as above except 9⅜"; clear **8.00-15.00**

same as above except 9½"; green . . . . **15.00 +**

Bouvier's Buchu Gin; on front; on back, *Louisville, Ky;* square fancy shoulder and neck; purple **10.00-14.00**

Dr. C. Bouvier's Buchu Gin; vertical in 2 lines; 11¾"; fancy quart bottle **4.00-6.00**

Bouvier's Buchu Gin; 11¾"; clear or amethyst **2.00-4.00**

Bouvier's Buchu Gin; clear; 6"; machine made **1.00-2.00**

Bower & Tuft's; *New Albany, Ind.* around bottom in 10 panels; *L & W* under bottom; dark amber; 9½", $25.00-35.00

E.J. F. Brands; (ale) in seal; case type; ribbed sides; tapered top; 9½" . . . . **45.00 +**

B.R.P. Co.; mold-blown; tapered top; 8⅞"; green or amber **20.00-30.00**

Bungalow; gin label; tapered top; 10½"; amber **20.00-35.00**

C.A. & C. Dos Vinhos Do Porto; vertical; 11¾"; whittle mold; olive, amber **4.00-8.00**

Carl Mampe, Berlin; ale; small kick-up; tapered top **10.00-20.00**

Case bottle; with 2 dots under bottom; crude applied top; 9½" **15.00-30.00**

Case bottle; plain; broken pontil; curved bottom; dark olive; 10"; short neck **35.00-45.00**

Case bottle; plain; curved bottom; dark olive; crude applied top; full of bubbles; short neck; 9¼" **15.00-30.00**

Case bottle; plain; clear; 9"; long neck; on front, sunken circle **10.00-15.00**

Case bottle; plain; 10½"; 5 dots under bottom; short neck; crude top; olive **15.00-30.00**

Case bottle; plain; 10½"; short neck; crude top; olive **15.00-30.00**

Case bottle; plain; 9½"; small kick-up; dark olive **15.00-30.00**

Case bottle; plain; 9½"; milk glass; roof type shoulder; 2" neck and top; 1¼" deep circle under bottom **40.00-50.00**

Case bottle, plain; curved or plain bottom; dark olive; tapered top; short neck; 10" **20.00-45.00**

Case bottle, plain; curved or plain bottom; dark olive; tapered top; short neck; 3⅞" **40.00-80.00**

Case bottle, plain; curved or plain bottom; brown-olive, light olive; tapered top; short neck; 10" **15.00-30.00**

Case bottle; label; black; 8" **10.00-15.00**

Case gin, label; green; 10"; cross on
    bottom **15.00-25.00**

**Case gin, label; pontil; 10"; black,
$10.00-20.00**

Case gin, label; dark olive, green; 9" **10.00-15.00**

Case gin, label; green; 8½" **4.00-8.00**

Case gin; much larger . . . . **10.00 +**

E.P. Cawet; in seal; deep kick-up; light
    green; 12" **4.00-6.00**

Richard Chambery; turn mold; kick-up; aqua;
    12½" **4.00-8.00**

P. Chapman; inside screw top; *N & Co. 2401* and a
    spike under bottom; green; 9" **8.00-12.00**

Chinese letters; under bottom; label; crown top; ale;
    8¾"; green **8.00-10.00**

S. Cobbs; in seal; ale; squat bottle; slim ring near top;
    6½"; olive **70.00-110.00**

Roger Comerback 1725; in a seal; pontil; blue
    green; 7" **100.00-200.00**

**Crown seal, label; kick-up; aqua; 11",
$2.00-4.00**

C.S. & Co.; under bottom; 3-part mold; olive;
    10" **6.00-8.00**

C.W.&Co.; under bottom; kick-up; dot in center; 3-part
    mold; 5" body; 2" bob neck type; 3" bottom; dark
    olive **8.00-12.00**

John De Kuyper & Son; olive; 10¼" **10.00-15.00**

De Kuyper Gin; label; 10½"; dark amber . . . **20.00-30.00**

De Kuyper, L.G. Co.; square face gin; 7⅜"; dark
    green **8.00-12.00**

Demijohn, sample label; 4"; clear or
    amethyst **3.00-8.00**

Demijohn; olive; 12" **4.00-12.00**

Demijohn, label; cobalt; 12" **25.00-30.00**

Demijohn; pontil; dark green;
    16½" x 6½" x 8" **25.00-35.00**

De Mondariz V.H.P. Acuar; around shoulder; snap-on
    top; olive; machine made; 8½" **4.00-6.00**

Double Eagle Seal; kick-up on bottom; turn mold; ring
    top; 9¾"; light green **10.00-15.00**

Drews Doppel Kronenbier; squat bottle; ale; 8"; dark
    amber **25.00-30.00**

D^R K; in center of a circle with *Introduced On Merit*
    around edge of circle; on bottom, *Established D^R K
    1851* inside a circle; applied top; quart size;
    amber **20.00-40.00**

D-Sears; in a seal; ale; tapered collar; 10½";
    olive **20.00-30.00**

Dub & G; in seal; olive; 8¼" and 6½" **80.00-125.00**

**Dunmore or squat, label; different
sizes and heights; dark olive,
green; pontil; free-blown,
$85.00-200.00**

J. & R. Dunster; on front panel; tapered top; 9½"; olive
    green **20.00-60.00**

F. Dusch, Richmond, Va., T.B.I.N.S.; reverse side *XXX
    Porter;* squat type; 6¾"; aqua . . . . **25.00 +**

Dutch Onions; ale; free-blown; open pontil; olive . . **45.00 +**

Dyottville Glass Works, Phila.; under bottom; 3-part
    mold; olive **10.00-15.00**

Dyottville Glass Works, Phila.; *5* under bottom; 3-part
    mold; amber; 11" **8.00-12.00**

W. Eagle, Canal St, NY; (missing period after N);
    Philadelphia Porter 1860 on back; ice
    blue; 7" **20.00-25.00**

Emon Coll; in seal; kick-up; olive; 11½" . . . **15.00-30.00**

D.H. Evans, St. Louis; ale; 3-piece mold; tapered top
    and ring; quart; black glass **20.00-40.00**

**F; under bottom, label; amber; 6",
$4.00-8.00**

Fabricade Gijon; under bottom; dark
    olive; 11" **4.00-8.00**

F.C.G. Co., Lou., Ky; under bottom; 12";
    amber **8.00-12.00**

FES & Co. Gin; aqua; 9¾" **10.00-20.00**

Finest Old Windmill Gin; tapered top; 10½";
    clear **15.00-30.00**

Flora Temple Harness Trot 219; horse on front; amber; 8½″, $90.00-100.00

Garnet Dry Gin; clear; 8¾″ **6.00-10.00**

Ginebra De La Campana; in center a bell in seal; dog bottle; a Star of David on base; *Trade Marca Registrada;* tapered case gin; 9⅛″; green **50.00-80.00**

Gin, label; free-blown; open pontil; wide collar; 11″; green **15.00-30.00**

Gin, label; free-blown; flared lip; open pontil; 13″; amber green **15.00-30.00**

Gin, label; free-blown; roll lip; pontil; 15½″; green or amber **40.00-60.00**

Gin, label; free-blown; improved pontil; 8½″; dark green **20.00-60.00**

Gin, label; 9½″; clear or amethyst **2.00-3.00**

Gin, label; green; 10½″ **6.00-8.00**

Gin, plain; clear; 3¼″ **2.00-3.00**

Golden Spray; clear or amethyst; 9½″ **4.00-6.00**

Gordon's Dry Gin; on front; on one side *England;* the other *London;* under bottom in sunken circle a wild boar; 8½″ or 8⅝″; green or clear; seam to top **4.00-6.00**

same, except seam to top ring; the boar is a little different; amber **6.00-8.00**

Graves Gin; label; 6″; clear **4.00-6.00**

HDB & C; roll lip; 6¼″; green or amber **20.00-40.00**

P.F. Heering; amber; 11″ **12.00-20.00**

P.F. Heering; on a seal; amber; 10¼″ **30.00-45.00**

P.F. Heering; on ribbon shield; kick-up; double ring top; dark green; 8¾″ . . . . **60.00 +**

J.H. Henkes, Delshaven; tapered top; 8½″; green **20.00-30.00**

J.H. Henkes; tapered top; 10⅜″; green **25.00-35.00**

Highest Medal, Vienna 1873; in circle; head in circle; 8¼″; green **30.00-60.00**

I.C. Hoffmann; in seal; kick-up; dark olive; 9″ **50.00-150.00**

P. Hoppe, Schiedam; in seal; flared top; improved pontil; 9⅜″; dark green . . . . **35.00 +**

same as above; 9½″; green . . . . **25.00 +**

A. Houtman & Co., Schiedam; same on reverse side; roll lip; 11″; amber green . . . . **25.00 +**

H.T. & Co. London & N.Y.; under bottom; *Capacity 24½ oz* on shoulder; sheared top; aqua **4.00-8.00**

Herman Jansen, Schiedam Holland; in seal; 9⅜″; dark green . . . . **25.00 +**

Javoi; *908* under bottom; dark olive; 8″ **8.00-12.00**

C.A. Jourde Bordeaux; dots under bottom; olive; 10½″ **6.00-8.00**

Juniper Berry Gin, Bottled By Quinine Whiskey Co., Louisville Ky.; wide ring top; 10″; aqua **10.00-20.00**

Juniper Leaf gin; case type; 10½″; amber **18.00-30.00**

Kaiserbnauerei, Bremen; vertically in ¾″ letters; 9¼″; olive; inside screw top **10.00-15.00**

Key seal; dark olive; 9½″ **40.00-95.00**

E. Kiderlen; dark olive; 5¾″ **30.00-60.00**

H.B. Kirk & Co. N.Y.; *Bottle Remains The Property of* in back; right face; amber; 11″ **4.00-6.00**

same as above, except left face **4.00-6.00**

A.B. Knoll Registered Erie, Pa.; amber; 9½″ **4.00-6.00**

Koppitz Melchers; Detroit, Mich; *A B & Co.* under bottom; aqua; 9½″ **4.00-6.00**

L.M.G. Co.; in seal; flared top; improved pontil; 9½″; brown, green **30.00-60.00**

London Jockey; N in London is backward; *Club House Gin* on one side; man riding a horse on back; dark olive; 9¾″, $100.00-150.00

same except N is correct **40.00-80.00**

Long Neck Porter; free-blown; open pontil; olive **25.00-50.00**

P. Loopuyt & Co. Distillers, Schiedam; dark olive; 9½″ **15.00-30.00**

Lotharingen; pontil; dark olive; 10″ x 18″ **100.00-175.00**

L & T Gin; anchor on front; olive; 9″ **60.00-80.00**

Madison Original Ale; *John Femnell Louisville, Ky.* on front; tapered ring top; star under bottom; 7⅛″; amber **8.00-15.00**

The Maltine M'F'G Co., New York; amber; 6″ **10.00-15.00**

V. Marker & Co.; semi-script; tapered top; 9⅜″; green or amber **20.00-30.00**

J. Mebus; in seal; olive; 9¾″ **25.00-55.00**

Meder & Zoon; swan with *W.P.* in center, all in a seal; 9¼″; amber or green **15.00-35.00**

J. Meeus; anchor with *J.M.* over it; improved pontil; 9¾″; clear or amber **20.00-60.00**

L. Meeus, Antwerp; key in center; 10¼″; green, brown **30.00-60.00**

V. Meier, Indianapolis, Ind.; dark amber; 8¾″ **25.00-30.00**

Melcher Gin; label; dark olive; 10¾″ **10.00-20.00**

J.J. Melcherswz Cosmopoliet; on top; *J.J. Melcherswz* under; in center, a man holding a bottle; on base *Schiedam;* case type short neck; tapered top; dot under bottom; dark olive; 10″ **40.00-50.00**

Monk label; amber; 10" **40.00-80.00**

Nathan Bros, 1863, Phila.; amber; 9½" **50.00-60.00**

A.C.A. Nolet, Schiedam; 8⅞"; greenish
brown **20.00-35.00**

I.A.I. Nolet, Schiedam; 8¼"; dark green,
amber **20.00-40.00**

Nolets Mistletoe Brand; dark green,
amber **40.00-60.00**

Palmboom; with palm tree; in a seal *Ilyes & Co.,
Schiedam;* improved pontil; 11"; green . . **25.00-50.00**

P & C; tapered top; 11¾"; green **20.00-40.00**

J.J. Peters; on one side; *Hamburg* other side; sunken panel under bottom; green; 8½" x 3¼" x 3¾", $15.00-30.00

J.J.W. Peters; tapered top; figure of dog on one side;
7¾" x 2½" x 2½"; green **25.00-50.00**

J.J.W. Peters, Hamburg; on bottom; dog figure; tapered
lip; two-piece mold; oval; 7¾"; amber . . **25.00-50.00**
same as above except 8¼"; dark
amber **25.00-60.00**

J.J.W. Peters; in vertical line; tapered lip; case type; dog
figure; 10½" x 3¼" x 3"; green **50.00-100.00**

P.G. & Old Bristol; seal; pontil; dark olive;
9" **75.00-175.00**

Philantrop; *only imported by Lrucipsoila Demerara Mein;*
crown over head; 10¾"; amber, green . . **40.00-60.00**

G.W., Porter, XX Porter & Ale; hollow *P* on reverse
side; tapered top with ring; 7¼"; light
green **35.00-60.00**

Posen, Wronkerstr, No. 6, Hartwig Kantorowic; eagle
under bottom; 10"; amber **30.00-60.00**

P.S.; in seal; ale; double ring top; pontil; 10";
olive **40.00-95.00**

James Ray, Savannah, Ga.; in front; in back, *XX Ale;* 4"
body, 2¾" neck; blob top; aqua **18.00-25.00**

T.M. Reeve 1732; in a seal on shoulder; square; refined
pontil; olive; 10½" **65.00-175.00**

Relyea, Carter & Co's; on one side *Royal;* other side
Schiedam Schnapps; olive; 9½" **60.00-100.00**

Roman bottle; teardrop catcher; free-blown;
aqua; 4" **60.00-100.00**

Roman bottle, teardrop catcher; pontil;
aqua; 4½" **60.00-100.00**

Ross's Irish Gin; label; 3-part mold; quart;
aqua **4.00-6.00**

Royal Champi; dark olive; 8¾" **25.00-35.00**

Rucker Dry Gin; *1* under bottom; aqua; 9" . . **6.00-8.00**

R.W.; in a seal on shoulder; squat body; ale; long neck;
6¼"; olive **40.00-85.00**

John Ryan, Savannah, Ga.; 2 dots under *a,* in front; *XX
Philadelphia Porter* on back; cobalt; 6½"; improved
pontil **30.00-60.00**

John Ryan; in 1" letters around bottle; ½" letters under
John Ryan, *XX Porter & Ale, Philada;* blue; 7¾";
ground pontil **40.00-100.00**

John Ryan 1866; in 1" hollow letters around bottle; ½"
under J.R. *XX Porter & Ale, Philada;*
blue; 4¾" **40.00-100.00**

John Ryan 1866 Savannah, Ga.; in front; *Philadelphia
XXX Star* on each side of *Ale* on back; squat body;
blue; 7¼" **40.00-80.00**

John Ryan 1866 Savannah, Ga; in front; *Philadelphia
XXX Star* on each side of *Porter* on back; squat
body; blue; 7¼" **30.00-50.00**

John Ryan Porter & Ale, Philada, XX 1859; graphite
pontil; cobalt; 7" **40.00-80.00**

Sample, label; square; 6"; free-blown; black
glass **40.00-50.00**

Sargent 1830; (reverse 3 on front); dark
amber; 8½" **50.00-150.00**

Seahorse Hollands Gin; tapered top; 3 dots under bottom; 9⅝"; green **40.00-60.00**

St. Angeline; *#1136* under bottom; dark amber; 11", $40.00-95.00

St. Dominic; indentation in back for label; dark olive;
9¼" **15.00-25.00**

T.C.C.R.; in a seal at the base; 3-piece mold; 11"; dark
green **20.00-30.00**

A Theller; label; *Theller Arnold* under bottom; dark olive;
8¾" **6.00-10.00**

Vandenburgh & Co.; bell in a seal on shoulder of bottle;
case gin; avocado or olive, crude
top; 11" **50.00-100.00**
same except 9" **50.00-100.00**

Vandenburgh & Co.; bell with ribbon in center; flared
top; 8⅞"; dark amber **30.00-80.00**

Vandenburgh & Co.; bell with ribbon in center; improved
pontil; 9"; green or amber **40.00-100.00**

J. Vandervalk & Co., Rotterdam; 9½";
green **30.00-60.00**

Vanderveer's Medicated Gin, Or Real Schiedam
Schnapps; flared top; 8½"; amber **10.00-20.00**

Van Dunck's Genever, Trade Mark; *Ware & Schmitz* in
back; amber; 9" **100.00-175.00**

S. Van Dyke, Amsterdam; cross in center; 10¼"; dark
green **20.00-25.00**

H. Van Emden Posthoorn Gin; *M* in a ring under bottom; clear or amethyst; 10⅝" **8.00-12.00**

J.H. Vangent, Schiedam; tapered top; 3 dots under bottom; 9⅜"; brown **20.00-25.00**

A. Vanpraag & Co's. Surinam Gin; 9¾"; dark
green **40.00-50.00**
same except dark amber **40.00-60.00**

V.G.&C; flared top; pontil; 10"; green or
amber **30.00-65.00**

VH & C; under bottom; dark olive; 9½" **15.00-20.00**

**Vhoytemaec; vertical; case bottle; 9", 2¼"
x 2¼"; short neck; tapered top; dark olive,
$18.00-25.00**

V.H.P.; *Aquas De Mondariz* around shoulder; 3-part
mold; olive; 6½" **30.00-65.00**

VIII; pontil; dark olive; 9" **45.00-100.00**

Daniel Visser & Zonen, Schiedam; tapered top; 9";
amber **30.00-40.00**

Warners Imported; *B Gin* in back; sky blue;
9" **20.00-30.00**

**Watson Biltonpark; olive; 9",
$50.00-100.00**

Weiss Bier; on front; *Karl Hutter, N.Y.* on bottom; blob
top; 7¼" **4.00-10.00**

R. White & Sons Ld. London; around a *W* on bottle top;
on bottom *J* in a shield; whittle mark; dark olive;
10¼" **12.00-16.00**

Woodman's; pontil; 3-part mold; black glass;
8" **90.00-100.00**

Beer

Beer was consumed in Mesopotamia several thousand years ago, and each medieval monastery had its own brewery. The beverage sailed on the *Mayflower* with the Pilgrims in 1620, and George Washington and Thomas Jefferson brewed their own beers at home. It was as common a drink one hundred years ago as it is today.

Most of the first beer in America was tapped from barrels in taverns. The first bottles were made of pottery; those imported from England between the years 1860 and 1890 were recycled by American breweries. Bottled beer often served as ballast on sea vessels.

By the end of the Civil War, most American cities boasted at least one brewery. By 1870 most beer bottles followed a standard pattern—they were usually glass, contained a quart of beer and were closed with cork. The embossing of brewery names and emblems was not popular until after 1870.

C. Conrad and Company, a wholesale for Adolphus Busch in St. Louis, sold the original Budweiser bottle from 1877 to 1890. The Budweiser name was a trademark of C. Conrad, but in 1891 the company sold it to the Anheuser-Busch Brewing Association. By that time, Adolphus Busch, founder of the brewery, had already established two companies to make beer bottles. In addition to providing bottles for Budweiser, they supplied other breweries from about 1880 to 1910.

Herman F. Graw, a German immigrant to the United States, had hopes of establishing the country's largest brewery. To aid him in the quest of his dream, he shrewdly married a brewer's daughter in New York,

in 1871. By 1899 his Buffalo Brewery established in Sacramento, California. Unfortunately, his venture never attained the desired proportions and folded in 1929. His bottles were brown and were embossed with the trademark of a horseshoe and buffalo.

David Nicholson of St. Louis manufactured ordinary beer under the pretentious but intriguing title, "Liquid Bread—A pure Extract of Malt." To further enhance salability, he bottled it in cobalt blue glass.

Nineteenth-century Americans found it difficult to avoid connecting available products with one's general well-being. Hoff's Malt Extract was advertised as a beer to be drunk in order to maintain good health. The bottle's label insists that the brew is a "remedy recommended by European physicians for complaints of the chest, dyspepsia, obstinate cough, hoarseness, and especially consumption."

Closures on beer bottles were greatly improved by the invention in 1891 of the crown cork closure by William Painter of Baltimore. The same type of closure is used on beer bottles today.

When production of beer was resumed after Prohibition ended in 1933, use of green glass in the bottles was discontinued since it was believed that the color let in too many of the sun's harmful rays. Bottle shapes took their traditional form, minus embossing, which was replaced by paper labels. Today, many of the bottles have been replaced by aluminum cans.

ABC Co.; aqua; 9½" **2.00-4.00**

A.B.C.M. Co.; *E27* on bottom in circle;
aqua; 11½" **1.00-3.00**

A.B.G.M. Co.; *C13* under bottom; aqua; 9½" . .**2.00-4.00**

A.B.G.M. Co.; *S4* under bottom; aqua; 10" . . .**3.00-4.00**

A.B.G.M. Co.; in a circle under bottom; in center *E27;*
aqua; 11¼" **4.00-6.00**

A.B.G.M. Co.; under bottom; aqua; 9¾" **2.00-6.00**

Aberdeen Brewing Co., Aberdeen, Wash.; 9¼"; blob
top; amber; clear **3.00-6.00**

AB6G; *4* under bottom; aqua; 9½" **2.00-4.00**

A,661,2; under bottom; aqua; 9½" **2.00-4.00**

Acme Brewing Company; aqua; 9½" **6.00-8.00**

Alabama Brewing Co., Birmingham, Ala.; 9½";
aqua **4.00-8.00**

American Brewing & C.I. Co., Baker City, Ore.; crown
top; 11¼"; amber **3.00-6.00**

**Anheuser Busch Inc; amber; machine
made; 9½", $1.00-2.00**

Arnas; under bottom; amber; round; 8" **2.00-3.00**

Aroma; *F* under bottom; amber **2.00-6.00**

Augusta Brewing Co., Augusta, Ga.; around outside of
circle; in center of circle a large *A* with bottle shape
embossed over *A;* crown top; 9¼";
aqua **4.00-10.00**
same except 7" **4.00-6.00**

The Baker Co., Dayton, Ohio; on front in oval slug
plate; blob top; quart; 11½"; amber **4.00-6.00**

Beadleston & Woerz; *Excelsior Empire Brewery* in a circle; in center of it 2 ladies, eagle, monogram, *New
York, This Bottle Not To Be Sold;* 9"; round;
aqua **2.00-4.00**

Becher & Co. Bottle Beer, Lancaster, O.; blob top;
10½"; aqua **4.00-8.00**

The George Bechtel Brewing Co.; *This
Bottle Not To Be Sold* on back; aqua; 9",
$8.00-10.00

Beer; amber; *A.B.G.M. Co.* in center *K 17* all under bottom of bottle; 9½"; opalescent **2.00-6.00**

Beer; brown; 11½" **2.00-3.00**

Beer; green; 11¼" **2.00-3.00**

Beer; label, plain; amber, 8½" **2.00-4.00**

Beer; label; plain; light amber; 8¾" **2.00-4.00**

Beer; label; *M.G.Co.* under bottom; amber;
9¼" **2.00-4.00**

Beer; label; star under bottom; amber; 7¾" . . .**4.00-8.00**

Beer; label; dark green; 9", $4.00-8.00

Beer; label; cobalt; 9¼" **15.00-25.00**

Beer; label; on bottom, / inside ring; clear or amethyst;
9½" **2.00-4.00**

Beer; label; *Root 8* on bottom; amber; 9½" . . .**2.00-4.00**

Beer; label; crown top; 11½"; amber **2.00-4.00**

Beer; label; lady's leg neck; 12"; amber **4.00-6.00**

Beer; label; blob top; 9½" **4.00-8.00**

Beer; label; pontil; 10½"; aqua **14.00-18.00**

Beer; milk glass; wine type; crown top;
10¼" **8.00-12.00**

Beer; plain; 8¾"; amber **2.00-4.00**

Beer; plain; 11½"; amber **2.00-4.00**

Beer; plain; 11¼"; blue, light green **2.00-4.00**

Beer; plain; 11¾"; blue **2.00-4.00**

Berghoff; on shoulder; *Ft. Wayne, Ind* at base; crown
top; *ABM;* aqua **2.00-3.00**

Berghoff, Fort Wayne, Ind.; blob top; amber . . . . . .**4.00 +**

B. 42; on bottom; dark green; turn mold; 9½" .**3.00-6.00**

Bierbauer Brewing Co., Cana-Joharie, NY; on front in
slug plate; blob top; aqua; 9⅜" **3.00-6.00**

Blatz, Milwaukee; on shoulder; olive; 9¼" **2.00-4.00**

Blatz, Old Heidelberg; stubby bottle; amber . .**8.00-15.00**

Blatz, Pilsner; amber; 10½" **3.00-4.00**

Blatz, Val Brewing Co., Milwaukee; on shoulder in a
star *VB;* under bottom *V.B. & Co. Milw.;* blob top;
amber; 12" **4.00-8.00**

**Bohemian Lager Beer, Bodie Bottling Work, Bodie,
Cal;** crown top; aqua **4.00-10.00**

Born & Co., Columbus, Ohio; in a diamond shape; blob
top; quart; amber **4.00-6.00**

Bosch Lake, Linden, Mich.; on front; *T.B.N.T.B.S.* on
bottom; blob top; 12"; amber **4.00-6.00**

Bosch Lake, Linden, Mich. T.B.N.T.B.S.; on bottom;
blob top; 12"; amber **4.00-8.00**

Bosch Lake Linden, Mich; blob top; quart;
amber **3.00-4.00**

R. Bovee; large block outline of a *B; Troy, N.Y.;* reverse
T.B.N.T.B.S., N.B.B. & Co.; 12"; aqua **4.00-8.00**

Buffalo Brewing Co., Sacramento, Cal; in form of circle,
horseshoe with buffalo jumping through; blob top;
quart; 12"; amber **8.00-10.00**

Buffalo Brewing Co., S.F. Agency, BB Co.; monogram; crown top; 9⅛″; amber 8.00-10.00

E & J Burke; *E & B* on bottom (cat); *ABM;* 8″; amber 2.00-4.00

C.W. Burr, Richmond, Va.; in a circle; reverse *T.B.N.T.B.S.;* blob top; 9¼″; aqua 4.00-8.00

Cairo Brewing Co.; on shoulder; amber; 9″; round; wire-porcelain stopper 3.00-5.00

same as above except aqua 3.00-6.00

Camden City Brewery; amber; 9″; various numbers on bottom 2.00-6.00

Canton, Ohio; star under bottom; 9¾″; aqua 8.00-10.00

Cas-Car-Ria Bottle; with *45* in a circle; 9½″; amber 8.00-10.00

CB Co.; monogram in circle; under it, *Chattanooga, Tenn.;* 11½″; light amber 2.00-4.00

CB Co.; monogram near shoulder; under it *Chattanooga, Tenn.;* 11¼″; amber 2.00-4.00

The Central Brand Extra Lager Beer; label; aqua; 9¼″, $2.00-4.00

Chas Joly; *Phila* on back; amber; 9¼″ 8.00-10.00

Chattahoochee Brewing Co.; *This Bottle Not To Be Sold, Phoenix City, Ala.* on back; aqua; 9½″ 6.00-8.00

Chattahoochee Brewing Co., Columbus, Ga.; aqua; 9½″ 6.00-8.00

Chattahoochee Brewing Co., Brownsville, Ala.; aqua; 9½″, $6.00-8.00

Chattanooga Brewing Co.; aqua; 9½″; *C* on bottom 4.00-6.00

Claussen Brewing Ass'n. Seattle, Wash.; crown top; 9½″ 2.00-4.00

Claussen Sweeney Brewing Co.; blob top; 10½″; aqua 4.00-6.00

The Cleveland & Sandusky Brewing Co.; under bottom *M;* in center of bottle *C.S.B.C.* monogram; blob top; 9″; aqua .3.00-4.00

Cobalt blue beer; label; graduated and flared band collar; 9¾″ 8.00-12.00

The Connecticut Breweries Co.; *The Connecticut, Bridgeport, Conn.* in a circle; in center *Breweries Co.;* 9½″; blue green 2.00-3.00

same except *Registered* on shoulder 2.00-4.00

C. Conrad & Co.; *Original Budweise, U.S. Patent no. 6376;* under bottom *CCCO;* short tapered top with ring; 9¼″; aqua 8.00-12.00

Consumers Ice Co.; *Hygeia Water, Memphis, Tenn.* around lower bottom; round; tapers to small neck; 10″ tall; base 4¼″; porcelain-spring stopper 2.00-5.00

The Cook & Bernheimer Co.; on one side; other side *Refilling Of This Bottle Prohibited;* on the bottom, *C&B Co. Bottling;* 2¼″x4″; amber 4.00-10.00

The Cook & Bernheimer Company; *Refilling Of This Bottle Prohibited* other side; amber 10.00-12.00

Cook Bock Beer; label; amber; 9¼″ 2.00-4.00

Cooks 500 Ale; label; aqua; 9½″, $2.00-6.00

Crown on shoulder; label; applied lip twisted neck; deep grooves; three-piece mold; iron pontil; 8½″; dark olive 10.00-20.00

Crystal Brewage, Baltimore, Md. U.S.A.; 10½″; amber 4.00-8.00

C 6 Co.; / on bottom; aqua; 9¼″ 2.00-4.00

Dallas Brewery; machine made; amber; 7½″ . .2.00-4.00

Dallas Brewery; clear or amethyst; 9″ 4.00-6.00

Dayton Breweries; amber; 9½″ 6.00-8.00

Diamond Jims Beer; label; aqua; 9¼″ 2.00-6.00

Diehl, Defiance, Ohio; wine type; blob top; 9½″; amber 6.00-10.00

Dixie Brewery, Phenix; (sic) **City, Ala.;** aqua; 9½″ 8.00-15.00

Du Bois; blob top; 8″; amber 4.00-6.00

Dubuque Brg. & Malting Co.; *Dubuque, IA* under bottom; amber; 8¾″ 6.00-8.00

Dukehart & Co.; *Maryland Brewery, Baltimore* on front, 3 lines; squat body; long neck; 8″; amber; round 8.00-12.00

Eagle Spring Distillery Co.; on front; rectangular; 7″; amethyst 3.00-4.00

E.B. Co., Escanaba, Mich.; 8½″; amber 4.00-6.00

E.B. & Co. Ld 11614; on bottom; aqua; 12″ . . .2.00-6.00

The Ebling Brewing Co., New York, USA; on front; crown top; 9¼″; aqua 3.00-6.00

same as above except blob top 4.00-6.00

The John Eichler Brewing Co., New York, Registered; (written fancy) on front; blob top; 9"; aqua **4.00-6.00**

El Dorado Brewing Co., E.D.B. Co.; monogram, *Stockton, Ca.;* crown top; 4-piece mold; quart; 12"; amber **10.00-12.00**

El Paso Brewery; amber; 8" **4.00-6.00**
same as above except aqua **8.00-15.00**

Engel & Wolf's No. 26 & 26, Dillwyn St., Phila; applied lip; graphite pontil; 7¾"; blue green **10.00-20.00**

Enterprise Brewing Co., S.F., Cal.; vertical on front; 4-piece mold; quart; blob top; 11¾"; light amber **10.00-12.00**

C.H. Evans & Sons Ale; on shoulder; crown top; 9"; amber **2.00-4.00**

Excelsior; *M* under bottom; 9¾"; aqua, $8.00-15.00

Excelsior Lager Bier From Valentine Blatz Bottling Dept. Chicago; in a circle; blob top; *T.B.I.N.S.* on reverse side; 9"; aqua **8.00-10.00**

Falstaff Lemp. St. Louis; inside of shield; crown top; 9"; aqua **3.00-6.00**

Fee Bros., Rochester, N.Y. Bel Isle; *8 fl. oz.* 6" **4.00-6.00**

John E. Feldman, Richfield Springs, N.Y.; in oval slug plate; blob top; 9¼"; clear **4.00-6.00**

F.H.G.W.; *4* under bottom; amber; 10" **2.00-3.00**

F.H.G.W.S.; tapered top with ring; blob neck; 12" **4.00-8.00**

Finley Brewing Co. Toledo, O.; under bottom; trade mark, an *F* in a diamond on shoulder; blob top; quart; aqua **4.00-6.00**

Finley Brewing Co., Toledo, O.; *Trade Mark* on top of a diamond shape in center of which is an *F,* all on bottom; 10¾"; aqua **4.00-6.00**

The Florida Brewing Co., Tampa, Fla; in sunken panel; aqua; under bottom *F.B.Co.;* 6¾" **2.00-4.00**

The Foss-Schneider Brewing Co.; 7½"; aqua **4.00-6.00**

The Foss-Schneider Co.; in a horseshoe shape; under it *Brewing Co., Cincinnati, O.;* crown top; 11"; aqua **4.00-6.00**

J. Gahm & Son Trade Mark; (mug with J.G. monogram) *Boston, Mass* on front; blob top; 9"; amethyst **4.00-6.00**
same as above except old crown top **4.00-6.00**
same as above except amber; *ABM* **4.00-6.00**

Gallitzin Bottling Co.; *326* under bottom; clear; 10" **4.00-6.00**

Gallitzin Bottling Co.; aqua; 9½" **2.00-4.00**

Galveston Brewing Co.; *Guaranteed Pure, Galveston Tex.;* aqua; 7¾"; round **2.00-4.00**

Galveston Brewing, Galveston, Tex.; reverse *T.B.N.T.B.S.;* 9½"; aqua, $4.00-6.00

G-B-S; (with arrow); *Baltimore, Md., Trade Mark* on the shoulder; clear; 9¼"; round; porcelain wire top **2.00-3.00**

Geo. Ch. Gemunden, Savannah, Geo.; in a circle in center; *Lager Beer* on back, *This Bottle Is Loaned Only* in 3 lines; blob top; 8" **8.00-12.00**

Georgia Brewing Association; aqua; 9¾" **4.00-8.00**

The Germania Brewing Co.; aqua; 7½" **6.00-8.00**

A. Gettleman Brewing Co.; *Pure Malt & Hops, Milwaukee;* round; hand holding hops; amber; 9¼" **4.00-8.00**

Great Seal Styron, Beggs & Co., Newark, Ohio; round; 9"; clear **4.00-6.00**

Charles S. Grove Co.; *78 & 80 Merrimac Street Boston, Sparkling Lager Beer,* with CSG Co. monogram all inside of diamond-shaped panel on front; blob top; 9"; clear **4.00-6.00**

Gutsch Brew. Co.; *13* under bottom; red or amber; 8½", $8.00-20.00

A. Haas Brewing Co, Houghton, Mich; in circle on front; blob top; large size; *Registered* at base; 12"; amber **3.00-4.00**

A. Haas Brewing Co.; written fancy at slant; blob top; 9½"; amber **3.00-6.00**

Hack & Simon; aqua; 9½" **2.00-6.00**

The John Hauck Brewing Co.; *Cincinnati O;* on the bottom *A.B. Co.;* round; 11⅜"; clear or amber **4.00-6.00**

Henninger; machine made; amber; 11½" **4.00-6.00**

Heustis' E.M.; *Main St., Charleston, Mass.; This Bottle Not To Be Sold, Registered;* 9"; aqua; round **2.00-4.00**

H.G. Co.; on base; tapered top; blob top; 9½";
    amber 4.00-8.00

Home Brewing Co., Richmond, Va.; on shoulder;
    number under bottom; aqua; 9½" 4.00-6.00

Home Brewing Co., Indianapolis; blob top;
    clear 4.00-10.00

Hoster Co, O; *665* and mark under bottom; amber;
    11¾" 8.00-10.00

Hoster's; in script, *Columbus, O.; Weiner Beer;* blob top;
    quart; amber 2.00-4.00

    same as above except 7½"; dark
    amber 8.00-10.00

Houston Ice & Brewing Co.; crown top; *ABM;* 7¾";
    aqua 8.00-10.00

Hudson, N.Y., Evans Ale; on shoulder; crown top; *ABM;*
    10"; amber 2.00-3.00

A. Hupfel's Son's; *161 St. & 3rd Ave. New York;* blob
    top; 9⅜"; amber 3.00-6.00

    same as above except crown top; 9" 3.00-4.00

Independent Br'g Ass'n; on bottom in circle form with
    big *E* and building on top and small *B* at bottom of
    E; 11¼"; amber 4.00-6.00

Independent Brewing Co. of Pittsburgh; on front;
    crown top; 9"; light amber 3.00-4.00

    same as above except *Pittsburgh* misspelled
    Pittsbrugh .10.00-15.00

Ind. Br'g. Assn., Marion; in a circle; 9½";
    amber 2.00-8.00

Indianapolis Brewing Co.; *R.C. Co.* under
bottom; 7¼"; amber, $8.00-20.00

Indianapolis Brewing Co., Indianapolis, Ind.; angel
    holding a glass of beer, sitting on a wheel on world,
    USA, all on front; 9½"; aqua 6.00-12.00

Iroquois Brg. Co, Buffalo; inside of circle, *Indian Head*
    in center; crown top; *ABM;* amber 3.00-6.00

Jackson & Co.; hop leaves with *B* in center, *Yonkers,*
    N.Y. on front; *1904* on bottom; blob top; 9½";
    clear 3.00-6.00

Jacob Jackson; 803 & 805 *Dickinson St., Philada;* blob
    top; reverse *T.B.N.T.B.S.;* 9½"; aqua 4.00-8.00

The Kansas City Breweries Co.; on front; crown top;
    9"; amber 3.00-4.00

Kaufman Bev. Co., Cincinnati, O. USA.; 7";
    clear 4.00-8.00

A.W. Kemison Co.; in horseshoe shape; blob top; blob
    neck; 7¾"; amber 4.00-8.00

Kessler Malt Extract; squat body; crown top;
    amber 4.00-6.00

Koppitz-Melchers Brewing Co.; trademark star in
    center; *Reg. Detroit Mich.* in a circle slug plate; blob
    top; 11¼"; aqua 4.00-8.00

M. Kress, Redwood City, T.B.N.T.B.S. 15.00-30.00

The Kress Weiss Beer Co.; amber; 7¼",
$4.00-6.00

C.A. Krueger; *D.O.C. 36* under bottom; amber;
    9¾" 6.00-8.00

K.S.; monogram, *Kuebeler Strong, Sandusky, Ohio;* blob
    top; 7½"; aqua 4.00-6.00

    same as above except 11" 4.00-10.00

K.S.; monogram on front; crown top; *ABM;* 9";
    aqua 2.00-3.00

The John Kuhlman Brewing Co. Ellenville, N.Y.; aqua;
    7" 10.00-25.00

John Kuhlman Brewing Co., Ellenville, N.Y.; on front in
    oval slug plate; crown top; 9¼"; aqua 3.00-6.00

Lake Erie Bottling Works, Toledo, Ohio; in a circle;
    10½"; aqua .4.00-10.00

Large aqua bottle; round blob-top; *This Bottle Loaned*
    Not Sold, Six Pints; near base, place for large label;
    13¼" 4.00-6.00

Leechen Beer, Germany; label; amber; 9¼" . .2.00-6.00

Leisy; *Peoria, Ill* on back; amber; 9½" 4.00-6.00

Lemp; *AB Co.* under bottom; aqua; 9½" 2.00-3.00

Lexington Brewing Co., Lexington, Ky.; blob top; *S.B.*
    & Co. under bottom; 12"; amber 4.00-8.00

Limp, St. Louis; in a shield; blob top; 8¾";
    amber 4.00-8.00

D. Lutz & Son Brewing Co., Allegheny, Pa; on front in
    oval slug plate; blob top; 9¾"; aqua 4.00-6.00

Malzbier Beer German; 8½"; amber,
$2.00-6.00

The Maryland Brewing Company;
    amber; 9" 8.00-10.00

Massachusetts Breweries Co., Boston; crown top;
    9½"; amber 2.00-3.00

M. Mayer; *This Bottle Not To Be Sold* in back; *5* under
    bottom; aqua; 9" 4.00-6.00

McAvoy Brewing Co., Lager Beer, Chicago; blob top;
    9½"; aqua 4.00-8.00

D.W. McCarthy, D.W. McC.; monogram; *Stockton, Cal.*
    on front; blob top; four-piece mold; quart; 12";
    amber 10.00-15.00

    same as above except 9½" 8.00-10.00

McLyman & Brady, Toledo, Ohio; blob top; 11½";
    aqua 4.00-8.00

George Meyer Beer; aqua; 9″ 8.00-15.00

George Meyer, Savannah, Ga.; 7½″; aqua, $8.00-15.00 +

C. & J. Michel Brewing Co., Lacrosse, Wis; reverse side *B.N.T.B.S.;* blob top; 7½″; amber . . .8.00-10.00

Miller Becker Co.; on back *Send Me Home When I Am Empty;* on base *This Bottle Not To Be Sold;* machine made; aqua; 11½″ 2.00-6.00

Mineral Spring Beer; label; aqua; 9″, $2.00-4.00

Mobile Brewery, Mobile, Ala; 10″; aqua 8.00-10.00

The Christian Moerlein Brewing Co., Cincinnati, O.; in a circle; in center of circle monogram *M;* aqua; 9½″ 2.00-4.00

The Christian Moerlein Brewing Co., Cinti., O.; in 4 lines; amber; fifth; blob top; blob neck . . .7.00-10.00

Moffats-Ale Brewery-Inc.; on both sides; large *M* on bottom; *ABM;* crown top; 9⅜″; grass green 3.00-4.00

Munchner Bavarian Type Beer; aqua; 9¼″ . . .2.00-6.00

National Lager Beer, H. Roltrbacher Agt., Stockton, Cal. H.R.; monogram all on front; 4-piece mold; blob top; amber; 11½″ 6.00-10.00

same as above except pint size 4.00-12.00

same as above except 8″ 4.00-12.00

Nebraska Brewing Co., Omaha, Neb.; in a circle; amber; 9″ 6.00-8.00

same except clear 3.00-6.00

same except red or amber 10.00-15.00

T.L. Neff's Sons; case bottle trade mark on back; aqua; 11″ 8.00-10.00

Dyson Nelson; *Trade Mark;* round; aqua; 6¾″; inside screw; 2.00-6.00

Oakland Bottling Co., Oakland, Cal.; around shoulder; blob top; 9″; amber 4.00-8.00

O.B. Co.; under bottom; label; amber; 9¾″ . . .3.00-6.00

Oconto Brewing Co.; blob top; amber 4.00-10.00

The Property of Ohlsson's Cape Brewery; inside screw cap 10.00-15.00

W. Olmsted & Co.; on one side; reverse *New York;* roof type shoulders; on roof in front *Constitution;* pontil; 10½″ 40.00-85.00

Pabst Brewing Co. of Milwaukee; amber; 12″, $4.00-8.00

Pabst; *Milwaukee, Trade Mark,* crown top; 9¼″; amber 4.00-8.00

Pabst, Milwaukee; in circle in center, leaves and in circle big *P, Trade Mark* under it; on bottom *Registered, This Bottle Not To Be Sold;* amber; 9¼″ 3.00-4.00

The Palmedo Brewing Co, Charleston, S.C.; in a circle in center, large monogram *P;* 7¾″; aqua . .2.00-4.00

same except no *P;* 9½″; crown top; aqua .2.00-4.00

C. Pfeiffer Brewing Co., C.P.B. Co., Detroit, Mich, in circle on shoulder; blob top; 9¼″; amber . .4.00-6.00

Phoenix Brewing Co.; an eagle with trade mark under it, *Victoria, B.C.;* tapered top; 8¼″; amber 10.00-15.00

Piel Bros; *This Bottle Not To Be Sold* on back; 9″; clear 4.00-6.00

Piel Bros, P.B.; and arrow shield, *East New York Brewery,* all on front; crown top; 9¼″; amber 4.00-6.00

same as above except dark aqua 4.00-6.00

Piel Bros; above *P.B.* inside of circle; under that *East New York Brewery;* aqua; 9″ 2.00-4.00

Pittsburgh Brewing Co.; crown top; 12¼″; amber 4.00-8.00

Robert Portner Brewing Co.; amber; 7¼″ . .10.00-20.00

Prospect Brewery, Chas Wolter's Phila.; reverse *T.B.N.T.B.S.;* blob top; 8″; amber 10.00-15.00

same as above except 7¼″ 8.00-10.00

W.O. Putnam; clear; 9½″ 4.00-6.00

Rahr's Beer, label; amber; 9¼″ 2.00-6.00

John Rapp & Son, S.F., Cal.; on front; blob top; quart; 11½″; light amber 6.00-10.00

same as above except 9½″ 8.00-10.00

same as above except 8¼″ 4.00-8.00

R.C. & A; reverse *New York;* tapered top; 9″; cobalt blue 20.00-30.00

Reno Brewing Co., Reno, Nev.; tapered top; 10¾″; amber 4.00-8.00

Rose Neck Brewing Co. Richmond, Va.; embossed star; round; crown top; 9¾"; aqua **4.00-8.00**

Rosessle Brewery, Boston, T.B.T.B.R.; on front; *Premium Lager* on back; crown top; 9"; aqua **3.00-6.00**

Roth & Co.; in center monogram, letters *RCO, San Francisco* in a circle; tapered top; 10¼"; amber **8.00-12.00**

Royal Red; *Not To Be Refilled, No Deposit No Return,* on base; *ABM;* 9½"; red **8.00-12.00**

Rubsam & Horrmann Brewg. Co.; in horseshoe shape in center; *Staten Island, N.Y., Registered;* in 4 lines on back near bottom *This Bottle Not To Be Sold;* blob top; under bottom *KH, 1906;* aqua; 9" **4.00-6.00**

Jacob Ruppert Brewer, New York; on shoulder in circle; crown top; 9¼"; yellowish green or amber **3.00-4.00**

John Ryan; *All XXX Star 1866;* blob top; 8¼"; cobalt **20.00-30.00**

Sakura Beer; on base; foreign writing on back; 11¼"; dark amber **10.00-20.00**

Santa Clara County Bottling Co., San Jose; 4-piece mold; ½ pint; 7¾"; light amber **4.00-8.00**

F. & M. Schaefer Mfr'g. Co. New York; around base on front; crown top; 9"; aqua **2.00-4.00**

The Schaefer-Meyer Bro. Co. Trade Mark Louisville, KY; in a shield; 11"; amber **8.00-10.00**

Schnells Beer; label, *Schells Brewing Co., New Ulm, Minn.;* 9½"; amber **2.00-4.00**

Phil Schewermann Brewery, Hancock, Mich.; *T.B.N.T.B.S.* on bottom; 12"; amber **4.00-6.00**

same as above except quart size **4.00-6.00**

Schlitz, Milwaukee; under bottom; tapered top; 5½"; amber . . . . **35.00+**

Jos Schlitz Brewing Co.; 7½" **2.00-4.00**

Schlitz Brewing Co.; *124* on bottom; amber; 9½", 6.00-10.00

C. Scneer & Co; in horseshoe letters, under it *Sacramento, Cal.;* blob top; blob neck; 7½"; amber **8.00-15.00**

Chas Seiler, Milwaukee, Beer; in 2 lines on front; on back *Empty Bottle to Be Returned;* blob top; aqua; 8" **4.00-6.00**

G.B. Selmer, California Pop Beer; reverse *Pat. Oct. 29 1872;* tapered top; 10½"; amber **30.00-50.00**

Smith Bros. Brewers, New Bedford, Mass.; inside of slug plate; *To Be Washed and Returned* on front also; blob top; clear **4.00-6.00**

Southern Brewing Co.; 9½"; machine made; green, $2.00-3.00

L. Speidel & Co., Boston, Mass.; *Hop Leaf and B* on center front; *Registered LS Co.* monogram on back; blob top; 9"; clear **4.00-6.00**

Springfield Breweries Co., Boston Branch, Boston, Mass., Trade Mark, S.B. Co.; monogram; blob top; 9"; clear **4.00-6.00**

Stettner & Thomas, Weiss Beer Brewers, St. Louis.; blob top; 9½"; amber **10.00-15.00**

St. Mary's Bottling Works, St. Mary's, Ohio; in a circle; quart; blob top; aqua **4.00-8.00**

John Strohm, Jackson, Cal., J.S.; monogram on front; 4-piece mold; 7¾"; light amber **8.00-10.00**

Peter Stumpf; *This Bottle Not For Sale* on back; amber; 8½" **8.00-10.00**

Teikoku Beer; Japanese writing on back; graduated collar and ring; 11¾"; amber **4.00-6.00**

Terre Haute Brewing Co.; 9½" tall; 2½" diameter; *R.G.Co.* on bottom; aqua **4.00-6.00**

Geo. A. Ticoulet Sac.; on front; 4-piece mold; 7¾"; amber **8.00-12.00**

Toledo Brewing & Malting Co.; amber; 9½" . . **2.00-6.00**

John Tons, JT; monogram; *Stockton, Cal.* on front; 4-piece mold; blob top; quart; 11½"; amber **6.00-10.00**

S.A. Torino; gray snake around bottle; *Red Eye, Red Tong;* 12¼"; clear **10.00-15.00**

same as above except aqua **8.00-12.00**

Trommer's Evergreen Br'y; aqua; 9¼" **2.00-6.00**

Union Brewing Co., Ltd., Beer, Tarrs, Pa.; on bottom *Union Made C & CO;* 8"; brown **8.00-10.00**

United States Brewing Co. Chicago, Ill; 9"; aqua **4.00-8.00**

Va. Brewing Co.; 9¾"; aqua **4.00-6.00**

A.G. Van Nostrand, Charlestown, Mass.; inside of ribbon, *Bunke Hill Lager, Bunker Hill Breweries, Est. 1821 Reg.;* 9¾"; amber **20.00-30.00**

C.J. Vath & Co., San Jose; on front in slug plate; blob top; 12"; amber **8.00-12.00**

Victoria Brewing Co.; on base *Not To Be Sold, Victoria, B.C.;* 9½"; amber **4.00-8.00**

same except red amber **6.00-10.00**

The Wacker & Birk Brewing Co., Chicago; reverse *T.B.N.T.B.S.;* 9½"; aqua **4.00-6.00**

Sidney O. Wagner; on shoulder; crown top; 11¼"; amber **4.00-6.00**

The J. Walker Brewing Co., Cincinnati, Ohio; in a circle; 11¼"; amber **3.00-8.00**

Henry K. Wampole & Co., Philada.; around shoulder; graduated collar and ring; 8½"; light amber **4.00-6.00**

Washington Brewing Co.; trade mark with picture of eagle; *Reg. Wash D.C.;* 9¼"; aqua **8.00-16.00**

West End; written fancy; *Brg. Co. Utica, N.Y.;* crown top; *ABM;* 9½"; amber **2.00-4.00**

W.F. & G.P. Mil; under bottom; clear; 9¼", **$3.00-6.00**

W.F. & S.; on bottom; crown top; 9½"; aqua . . **2.00-3.00**

W.F. & S Mil; under bottom; aqua; 9" **2.00-4.00**
same except *#39* and amber **2.00-4.00**

Wiedemann; *0179* under bottom; amber; 9½" **6.00-8.00**

Wisconsin Select Beer; aqua; 9¼" **2.00-6.00**

The P.H. Wolters Brewing Co.; *This Bottle Never Sold* in back; aqua; 9½" **2.00-6.00**

Wunder Bottling Co., W.B. Co.; monogram, *San Francisco, Cal.,* on front; 7⅝"; amber **4.00-8.00**
same as above except *Oakland* **4.00-8.00**

Y; under bottom, label; 9¾"; amber **4.00-6.00**

Yoerg Brewing Co., St. Paul, Minn.; 9½"; aqua **2.00-6.00**

Geo. Young California Pop Beer; reverse *Pat. 29th 1872;* 10½"; amber **30.00-50.00**

Theo. Young; with large stars, hop leaves, buds, in a monogram, *T.Y. Union Ave., 165th & 166th St. N.Y.,* all on front; crown top; 9"; amber **4.00-6.00**

Flasks

During the 1800's the equivalent of the sayings and sentiments expressed on today's automobile bumpers were the embossed whiskey flasks. These containers picked sides in Presidential campaigns, ironically warned of the evils of their contents and kept the new spirit of nationalism that followed the War of 1812 within reach of the common man by putting American eagles on his favorite whiskey flasks.

The earliest American flasks were probably from the Pitkin glasshouse built in 1783 near Hartford, Connecticut. The first were free-blown, or made without the aid of a mold. By 1850 there were four hundred design varieties. These containers have black graphite pontil marks caused by the coating of the pontil with powdered iron to enable the bottle's bottom to be broken away without damaging the glass. The several hundred additional types of flasks made between the years 1850 and 1870 have no such markings due to the invention of the snapcase, a spring device which cradled the bottle in the finishing process.

Flasks were immediately popular. In addition to carrying a "message" they also contained whiskey, a combination that was simply unbeatable. Glassmakers realized that such containers brought profits and nearly every glasshouse in the country was producing them. Plagiarism of mold designs by rival companies was common.

Thomas W. Dyott, a poor English immigrant who worked his way up from a boot polisher to the owner of the Philadelphia and Kensington Glass Works, manufactured several popular flasks. In recognition of his own triumphant career, he produced a flask with his portrait embossed on one side and Benjamin Franklin's on the other. Another of Dyott's flasks honors the French general, Lafayette. The general was beloved by the American people as a champion in the struggle for human liberty. He received tumultuous welcomes wherever he appeared when he visited the United States in 1824. Dyott, always with an eye on publicity, personally presented Lafayette with a flask that same year.

The Masons were literally builders of the nation, and were strong politically as well, despite growing anti-Mason sentiment. Many Masonic flasks appeared with emblems of the order on one side and the symbolic American eagle on the reverse. Public opinion was enraged against the Masons when William Morgan of Batavia, New York, who threatened to make public secrets of the order, was mysteriously abducted. The incident caused the formation of an anti-Mason party, but public anger eventually subsided.

George Washington was a popular subject for flasks, despite the belief that he had ambitions to be king of America. Upon his death in 1799, the press chose to eulogize him as the "Father of his Country." At first he appeared on the flasks as a soldier in uniform, but as his accomplishments as first President became more apparent in retrospect, he was shown on whiskey flasks in a classic portrait pose. Not a few citizens pointed out the inconsistency of having a likeness of the father of one's country appear on a whiskey bottle.

Even the Temperance people had a flask of sorts—it bore the inscription, "Use me, don't abuse me."

Singer Jenny Lind, "the Swedish Nightingale," was also honored on a flask. She was brought to the U.S. by P.T. Barnum for a two-year tour in 1850 and was enthralled with America. The people were enthralled with her, too, paying as much as $650 a ticket to hear her sing.

Flasks extolled the qualifications of Presidential candidates John Quincy Adams and Andrew Jackson in the elections of 1824 and 1828. Adams was elected in 1824 and by 1828 was publicized as an aristocratic man of privilege. Jackson, who was popularized as a friend of the common man, was elected in 1828.

An echoing cry of gold and easy fortune in the Colorado mountains prompted many men, unemployed by the depression of 1857, to pack a pick ax and head toward Pike's Peak. Of the approximate 100,000 who set out for the region in the spring of 1858, half soon turned back, according to *Harper's Weekly*, "deluded and suffering . . . retracing their steps back to quiet farms in the West." The magazine reported them to be in a "starving condition, barefooted, ragged and penniless." Nevertheless, flasks bearing the slogans "For Pike's Peak" and "Pike's Peak or Bust" appeared in 1859.

John Q. Adams; in a circle; eagle facing to right; on base *J.T. & Co.;* beaded edge; sheared top; pontil; pint; green.....................**500.00-800.00 +**

A.G.W.L.; under bottom; saddle flask; amber; ½ pint, 8.00-15.00

All Seeing Eye; star and large eye in center; under it *A.D.;* in back, six-pointed star with arms; Masonic emblem; under it *G.R.J.A.;* pontil; sheared top; pint; amber...........................**185.00-200.00**

Anchor flask; double ring; ½ pint, quart; amber or clear................................**10.00-30.00**

Aquamarine; pint......................**20.00-40.00**

Baltimore Glass Works; aqua; very thin glass; pontil; on back a stack of wheat, $100.00-200.00

Baltimore Monument; and under it *Balto.,* door with step railing; in back sloop with pennant flying, sailing to right, above it *Falls* below point; half pint 3 ribbed on side, plain top, pontil, aqua quart c. 1840.........................**85.00-125.00**
same as above except plain bottom...**65.00-100.00**

B.P. & B; ½ pint; yellow green...........**30.00-40.00**

Bridgeton, New Jersey; around a man facing to left; in back a man facing to the left with *Washington* around it; ribbed sides; sheared top; pontil; pint; aqua...........................**100.00-200.00**

Calabash; hunter and fisherman; quart; aqua...........................**30.00-40.00**

Cannon and Capt. Bragg; pint; aqua.....**200.00-400.00**

Cannon and clasped hands; pint; aqua....**60.00-100.00**

Cannon Flask; cannon and balls lengthwise of flask, cannon balls at left of wheel in foreground, rammer and swab beneath. A rammer leans against cannon in front of right wheel. In horseshoe circle around cannon—*Gen. Taylor Never Surrenders* * * Vine and grapes form a frame, in center of it—*A Little More Grape Capt Bragg;* vertically ribbed with heavy medial rib, plain top, pontil, puce, half pint, aqua...........................**200.00-400.00**

Chapman P., Balt., Md; soldier with a gun, on front; a girl dancing on a bar in back; sheared top; pint; aqua...........................**100.00-150.00**

Clasped hands and cannon; pint; aqua....**45.00-110.00**

Clasped Hands: Eagle Flask (c. 1860-75) Union 13 stars, clasped hands, eagle above banner mark, *E, Wormer & Co. Pittsburgh;* aqua, quart.**45.00-100.00**

Clasped Hands; Eagle Flask (c. 1860-75) one with eagle and banner, above oval marked *Pittsburgh, Pa.;* other cannon to left, flag and cannonballs; aqua, pint.................................**40.00-85.00**

Clasped Hands; Flask (c. 1860-75) One with eagle and banner, above oval marked *Pittsburgh, Pa.;* other cannon to left, flag and cannonballs; aqua, pint.................................**40.00-85.00**

Columbia; Eagle Flask (c. 1820-50) Columbia with Liberty Cap facing left; 13 stars, half moon circle around bust; in back eagle facing right under eagle *B&W;* plain top, pontil, yellow, pint........**150.00-300.00**
same as above except aqua, c. 1830..........................**165.00-285.00**

Corn For the World; amber; 8¼".......**200.00-400.00**

Corn for the World; in half moon around ear of corn, in back design on large oval panels; Baltimore Monument and under it *Baltimore;* the step railing of the entrance door facing left; round top, golden yellow, quart, pontil c. 1835.............**200.00-300.00**
Same as above except for the door is facing right, half pint smooth edge, sheared top, pontil, aqua, c. 1840.........................**85.00-125.00**

Corn and Balt. monument; quart; citron...**100.00-200.00**

Cornucopia; pint; emerald green...........**30.00-50.00**

Cornucopia; designs on oval panels, beading on edges and at top, inverted cornucopia coiled to left and filled with produce; in back large circular, in center of it large geometric star, around it 8-petaled rosette, under it palm plain top, pontil, light blue green, half pint...........................**900.00-1500.00**

Cornucopia; flask, cornucopia coiled to the left and filled with produce; urn in back with 6 bars and filled with produce; pontil, plain top, light amber, half pint...........................**40.00-60.00**
Same except aqua.................**60.00-70.00**

Cornucopia and eagle, ½ pint; aqua.....**100.00-300.00**
same as above except inverted cornucopia......................**150.00-300.00**

Cornucopia and urn; olive; pint. **40.00-50.00**

Cornucopia and urn; ½ pint; amber. **40.00-50.00**

Cornucopia and urn with twig; open pontil; ½ pint; olive or amber. **60.00-80.00**

Cunningham, Pittsburgh, Pa.; Indian, hunter and eagle **50.00-110.00**

Delicate powder blue; ½ pint. **20.00-40.00**

18 diamond quilted flask; 6¼"; green. **80.00-90.00**

Dog in center; in back man in uniform on a horse; pontil; sheared top; quart; aqua. **90.00-110.00**

Double eagle (eagles lengthwise); open pontil; olive green. **80.00-100.00**

Double eagle; pint; aqua. **100.00-125.00**

Double eagle; pint; light green. **80.00-100.00**

Double eagle; *Stoddard, N.H.;* pint; olive or amber. **80.00-100.00**

Duck flask; picture of a duck in water; under duck *Swim;* above duck *Will You Have a Drink*; pint; aqua. **90.00-125.00**

American Eagle; facing left, shield with bars on breast, above eagle 13 stars, 3 arrows in right talons, branch in left, back big bunch of grapes and smaller one at right, above it two large leaves, quart, aqua, fine vertical ribbing, pontil, plain top, c. 1835. . . . .**65.00-80.00**

Eagle; facing left, shield with 8 vertical bars on breast, 4 arrows in left claw, large branch in right talons, branch in left, back big bunch of grapes and smaller one at right, above it 2 large leaves, quart, aqua, fine vertical ribbing, pontil, plain top, c. 1835. . . . .**60.00-80.00**

Eagle; facing left, ribbon held in beak with 5 stars extending to the right, below eagle large stellar motif, same in back, all in designs on oval panels, quart, corrugated horz, with vertical rib, aqua, plain top, pontil c. 1845. . . . .**85.00-125.00**

Eagle and Cornucopia; half pint, pontil, aqua. **100.00-185.00**

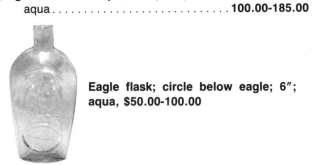

Eagle flask; circle below eagle; 6"; aqua, $50.00-100.00

Eagle; facing to right resting on a shield and rock pile; pint; aqua. **60.00-110.00**

Eagle and Masonic flask; large eagle with rays over head and *Ohio* in a circle under eagle; under that *J. Shepard & Co.;* on shoulder *Zanesville;* reverse Masonic arch; ornaments under arch; pontil; pint; green, amber or olive. **125.00-225.00**

Eagle; resting on arrows and olive branch with ribbon in beak; an oval panel under eagle; *Cunningham & Co., Pittsburgh, Pa.;* ring neck; quart; olive green. **100.00-130.00**

Eagle and clasped hands; pint; aqua. **30.00-50.00**

Eagle and cornucopia; ½ pint; clear. **100.00-150.00**

Eagle and Dyottville G.W.; pint; aqua. **80.00-100.00**

Eagle and flag; pint; aqua. **90.00-125.00**

Eagle and girl on bicycle; *A & DHA;* pint; aqua. **40.00-80.00**

Eagle, Masonic; pint; blue green. **90.00-175.00**

Eagle and stag; ½ pint; aqua. **90.00-175.00**

Eagle and tree; pint; aqua. **40.00-90.00**

Eagle Tree; flask, eagle head turned to left; shield with 8 vertical bars on breast; large olive branch in right, etc.; in back large tree in foliage; plain top, pontil, aqua, Kensington Glass Works, common flask, pint. **85.00-125.00**

Eagle; head to the left, wing partly up, large shield with 6 bars on breast, above eagle Liberty, eagle stands on wreath branches, in back in 4 lines *Willington Glass Co. West Willington, Conn.,* quart, tapered top, plain base, dark olive green c. 1860. . .**60.00-100.00**

Eagle; on oval panels, 25 sun rays in half circle around eagle head, 8 vertical bars on shield. End of olive branch and arrows under claws in oval frame with 23 small pearls around. *T.W.D.;* in back full sailing to right. U.S. flag at reas., waves beneath frigate and in semi-circle beneath Franklin, pint, 3 vertically ribbed on side, sheared top, pontil, aqua c. 1830. . . . .**85.00-126.00**

General Jackson; Eagle Flask, Jackson three-quarter view facing left in semi-circle above bust; in back eagle head turned to right, laurel branch in eagle's beak, nine stars above eagle. Eagle stands on oval frame with inner band of 16 large pearls, J.R. in oval frame below eagle; in semi-circle below oval frame—Laird. Sc. Pitts; edge horizontal beading rib; plain top, pontil, aqua, pint. **800.00-1000.00**

Flask, plain; amber; ½ pint. **4.00-8.00**

Flask, plain; ½ pint; bulbous neck; 6¾". **3.00-5.00**

Flask, plain; ½ pint; bulbous neck; 7". **4.00-6.00**

same as above except clear. **3.00-5.00**

same as above except 7". **4.00-6.00**

Flask, label; 6"; pontil; very pale olive, $35.00-65.00

Flask, label; dark olive; 5½". **20.00-50.00**

Flask, label; ribbed base; clear; 6¾". **8.00-12.00**

Flask, label; amber; 7½". **8.00-10.00**

Flask, round label; amber; 6½". **8.00-12.00**

Flask, label; pontil; clear; 6¾". **10.00-20.00**

Flask, plain; sheared top; pontil; pint; green. **100.00-150.00**

Keene P & W Sunburst Flask; (c. 1814-30) olive amber, half pint. **175.00-200.00**

same as above except clear. **100.00-150.00**

Flora Temple; pint; aqua. **150.00-200.00**

Flora Temple; handle pint; puce or amber. **150.00-200.00**

Florida Universal Store Bottle; clear; pint. . . .**2.00-6.00**

Frank Tea & Spice Co.; *Turpentine, Cinti;* aqua; 5⅜" **4.00-8.00**

H. Frank, Pat'd. Aug 6th 1879; under bottom; 2 circles in center; reverse plain; ring top; ribs on sides **20.00-40.00**

H. Frank, Pat. Aug. 6, 1872; all on bottom; circular shaped flask; 2 circles in center on front; reverse side plain; wide rib on sides; ring neck; pint; aqua **25.00-50.00**

Franklin & Franklin; quart; aqua **100.00-125.00**

Gen. MacArthur and God Bless America; ½ pint; purple or green **8.00-10.00**

G.H.A.; *Concord, N.H. 1865;* ½ pint; aqua . . **10.00-20.00**

Girl For Joe; girl on bicycle; pint; aqua **40.00-80.00**

Granite Glass Co.; in 3 lines; reverse *Stoddard, N.H.;* sheared top; pint; olive **100.00-150.00**

Guaranteed Flask; clear or amethyst; 6¼", $2.00-6.00

Guaranteed Full; 6½"; clear **4.00-8.00**

History flask; label; aqua; side panels; 7¼" **10.00-20.00**

Hunter and dog; pint; puce **200.00-300.00**

Iron pontil; double collared; pint **20.00-40.00**

Isabella G.W.; sheaf of wheat; pint **60.00-110.00**

Jenny Lind; with wreath; reverse picture of glass works; above it *Fislerville Glass Works;* wavy line on neck; pontil; tapered top; quart; aqua **85.00-100.00**

same except *S. Huffsey* **30.00-60.00**

Jenny Lind Lyre; pint; aqua **90.00-100.00**

Keene; Masonic; tooled lip; pontil; pint . . . **100.00-200.00**

Keene; sunburst; green **200.00-300.00**

Lafayette and eagle; amber **60.00-70.00**

Lafayette and eagle; *Kensington;* open pontil; pint; aqua **90.00-125.00**

Lafayette and Dewitt Clinton; ½ pint; olive, amber **100.00-200.00**

Lafayette and liberty cap; pint; aqua **90.00-110.00**

Lafayette; large bust in uniform, face slightly to the right, *General La-Fayette* in three-quarter circle around bust, back, on edges, *Republican Gratitude-Kensington Glass Works, Philadelphia,* under eagle facing left in oval frame *T.W.D.* pontil, pint, aqua, c. 1830 . . . . **250.00-385.00**

Lafayette and Masonic; ½ pint **100.00-200.00**

L.C. & R. Co.; on bottom, eagle in a circle; reverse plain; ½ pint clear **20.00-40.00**

Legendary Grandfather; broken swirl pattern; reddish amber **90.00-100.00**

Liberty & Union; in 3 lines; in back *Baltimore Monument;* in above semi-circle *Baltimore* entrance to door is without step railing; edges smooth, plain lip, pontil, yellow olive, pint **2000.00-3000.00**

Louisville G.W.; and eagle; ½ pint; aqua . . **50.00-100.00**

Louisville Glass Works; aqua; 7½", $75.00-100.00

Lowell R.R.; ½ pint; olive, amber **100.00-125.00**

Lyndeboro, L.G. Co.; *Patent* on shoulder; pint; aqua **10.00-20.00**

Lyndeboro, L.G.Co.; quart; golden amber . . **25.00-35.00**

Man with a gun and bag; reverse side running dogs; double ring top; pint; aqua **90.00-125.00**

Man with a gun and bag and a feather in hat; reverse side grape vine, with bunches of grapes and leaves; ribbed sides; sheared top; pontil **40.00-80.00**

Marked double eagle; pint; olive or amber . . . **40.00-80.00**

Masonic Arch; pillars & pavement, no stars etc. pint, 2 rings at shoulders, fine horizontal corrugations around flask, etc., sheared tapered top, pontil O., amber in back eagle head turning left, shield with bars and tiny dots on breast, 3 arrows in its left claw, olive branch in right, plain ribbon above head, plain oval frame below eagle, c. 1825 . . . . **750.00-1100.00**

Masonic Arch; pillars & pavement, 6 stars surrounding quarter moon & without comet at right of pillars; eagle facing left. No shield on breast, etc. under it in plain oval frame *KCCNC* pint, O. amber, one single vertical rib, sheared top, pontil, c. 1825 . . . . **85.00-125.00**

Masonic; Eagle Flask (c. 1814-50) pillars and pavement, except 6 stars surrounding quarter moon and without comet to right of pillars in back, eagle facing to left, KCCNC in oval frame, mold work error, should read *Keene;* olive amber, pint **200.00-300.00**

Masonic and eagle; *J.F.B.;* pint **200.00-300.00**

Masonic and eagle; pint; olive or amber . . . **90.00-125.00**

Masonic and eagle; pint; blue-green **100.00-150.00**

Masonic and Eagle; pint, pontil, green . . . **300.00-650.00**

Monument and corn; in a circle under this, *Baltimore;* reverse side a large ear of corn; quart; aqua **90.00-125.00**

same as above except amber **100.00-160.00**

Mounted soldier and dog; quart; citron . . . **100.00-200.00**

Pike's Peak Historical Flask; Penn. (c. 1859-70). Ring top; eagle prospector to right, under it *For Pike's Peak,* yellow amber, pint **200.00-400.00**

Pikes Peak; man with pack and cane walking to left; reverse eagle with ribbon in beak in oval panel; pint; aqua **60.00-90.00**

same except several colors **60.00-100.00**

For Pike's Peak; reverse side, man shooting a gun at a deer; 9½"; aqua, $20.00-40.00

For Pike's Peak; old rye; pint; aqua......**30.00-40.00**

Pikes Peak; traveler and hunter; pint; olive, amber..........................**300.00-395.00**

Pittsburgh; double eagle; pint; citron....**150.00-200.00**

Pittsburgh; double eagle; pint; aqua......**20.00-30.00**

Pittsburgh, Pa.; in raised oval circle at base, with an eagle on front; back same except plain for label; pint; aqua; applied ring at top; 7½", $35.00-60.00

Pitkin type; pint; light green.............**30.00-60.00**

Pottery flask; figure of a man and horse; same on reverse side; pint.................**210.00-225.00**

Quilted pattern flask; sheared top; pontil; ½ pint; reddish brown, amber, green, olive amber....**300.00-400.00**

same except amethyst.............**300.00-400.00**

same except white bluish cast......**110.00-175.00**

Quilted poison flask; ½ pint; olive green...**80.00-120.00**

Railroad; Eagle Flask (c. 1830-48). amber, pint............................**100.00-150.00**

Railroad Flask; on oval panels, horse drawing long cart on rail to right. Cart filled with barrels and boxes, under it *Lowell* and above it *Railroad,* in back eagle facing left. Shield with 7 vertical & 2 horizontal bars on breast, 3 arrows in eagle's left claw, olive branch in right, 13 large stars surround edge, half pint, 3 ver. ribbed on side, sheared top, pontil, O. amber c. 1860.........................**85.00-150.00**

Railroad Flask; design on oval panels, crude locomotive to left on rail, embossed *Success to the Railroad,* reading around locomotive back but the line connecting the tender with rear wheel shows a slight break and E in success carries a convex dot attached to the upper bar, pint, 3 vertically ribbed on side, sheared top O. amber, c. 1830......**85.00-125.00**

Ravenna Glass Works; in 3 lines; ring top; pint; yellow green..........................**60.00-125.00**

Ravenna Glass Works; Star Flask (c. 1857-60), Ohio; aqua, pint....................**90.00-125.00**

Ravenna; in center; anchor with rope; under it *Glass Company;* ring top; pint; aqua........**90.00-125.00**

Ravenna Travelers Companion; pontil; quart; amber..........................**150.00-300.00**

Rehm Bros.; *Bush & Buchanan Sts & O'Farrel & Mason Sts,* in a sunken circle; ribbed bottom; 2 rings near shoulder; coffin type; metal and cork cap; ½ pint; clear or amethyst....................**6.00-10.00**

Ribbed flask; fluted base to shoulder; sheared top; pontil; ½ pint; aqua....................**100.00-160.00**

same except yellow or amber.......**125.00-200.00**

Sailing vessel and *Columbia Jubilee;* pint; amber..........................**60.00-90.00**

Sailor bottle; dancing sailor on back; amber; 7½", $40.00-80.00

Scroll; aqua; one star; 7"; smooth base.......**6.00-8.00**

same as above except two stars.......**20.00-40.00**

Scroll; ½ pint to quart; one star; clear, aqua or amber; pontil.........................**40.00-80.00**

same as above except two stars.......**40.00-80.00**

Scroll; 9"; aqua, $200.00-300.00

Scroll; open pontil; pint; aqua............**20.00-30.00**

Scroll; *M.C.* on side in script; pint; blue or aqua.........................**30.00-50.00**

Scroll; *D.C. Mott;* ½ pint................**20.00-30.00**

Scroll; pint; green.....................**40.00-60.00**

Scroll; banded neck; aqua..............**30.00-40.00**

Scroll; quart; aqua....................**60.00-90.00**

Scroll; pint; iridescent blue.............**80.00-125.00**

Scroll; 2½ quart; aqua................**100.00-125.00**

Scroll Flask; Penn. (c. 1845-60) aqua, 2½ quart.........................**200.00-300.00**

same except deep sapphire blue, quart.......................**1000.00-2000.00**

Scroll Flask; (c. 1845-50); deep golden amber, pint.........................**200.00-300.00**

Scroll Flask; scroll decoration framing acanthus leaves. Diamond motif at center, four-petaled flower motif at top and leaf motif at base same in back, pint, vertical medial rid, pontil D, aqua sheared top, c. 1850........................**600.00-900.00**

Scroll; large heart-shaped frame with elaborate scrolls, one 8-pointed star on shoulder, in center 6-pointed star, same in back, pint, pontil, plain top, blue aqua, c. 1850........................**40.00-80.00**

Scroll Flask; (c. 1845-60); blue-green,
pint **200.00-400.00**
Same except yellow-green, pontil **300.00-400.00**

Scroll Flask; (c. 1845-60); sapphire blue,
pint **600.00-1000.00**

S.G. Co. and anchor; on bottom; aqua; 6¼" . **8.00-15.00**
same as above except amber **6.00-12.00**

Sheaf of wheat and grapes; open pontil; ½ quart;
aqua **85.00-110.00**

Sheaf of Wheat; *Westford Glass Co. Conn.,* pint, red
amber, double top collared, plain base,
c. 1860 . . . . **50.00-70.00**

Sheaf of Wheat; *Westford Glass Co.* Pictorial flask
GX111-36, pint, amber, double ring top, plain base,
GX11-36, Conn. c. 1865 . . . . **65.00-85.00**

Soldier-Dancer Flask; *Md. (c. 1830-52) Chapman,* below
dancer; *Balt. Md* under soldier; yellow green,
pint **200.00-300.00**

South Carolina Dispensary; with palm tree; pint;
aqua **30.00-65.00**
same except ½ pint; amber **40.00-100.00**

Spiral flask; spiral to the left; pontil; sheared top; ½ pint;
amber **185.00-285.00**
same except spiral to the mint; pint;
green **110.00-175.00**

Springfield G.W. and Cabin; ½ pint; aqua . . **40.00-60.00**

Spring Garden; in center; anchor; under it *Glass Works;*
reverse side, log cabin with a tree to the right; ring
top; ½ pint; aqua **95.00-200.00**

Spring Garden Glasswork Flask; Md. yellow olive,
pint **200.00-300.00**

Stag and tree; pint; aqua **40.00-60.00**

Star; Cornucopia Flask: designs oval panels banded at
top; sides by same on edge; inverted cornucopia
coiled to left and filled with produce; in back large
circular in center, star-shaped design with six ribbed
points and in center circle with small 8-petaled
rosette; under it medallion modified symmetrical
palm motif rising from pointed oval with hatching;
plain top, pontil horizontal beading edges, light blue
green, half pint **1000.00-2000.00**

**Star with a circle around it on shoulder; ½
pint; light amber; saddle flask, $15.00-35.00**

Stoddard double eagle; *Granite Glass Co., Stoddard,
N.H.;* pontil; pint; golden amber **80.00-90.00**

Stoddard, N.H.; in panel under eagle facing left; reverse
same except blank panel; sheared top; pontil; pint;
amber **60.00-125.00**
same except tapered top; olive green . **60.00-125.00**

Strongman and two gentlemen; ½ pint;
clear **60.00-120.00**

S.T.R.A.; in a five point star; reverse plain; ring; collared
top; ½ pint; amber **50.00-110.00**

Success to the Railroad; with a horse and a cart on rail
around it; same on reverse side; sheared top; pontil;
pint; olive or aqua **110.00-225.00**

Success to the Railroad; around a horse and cart on a
rail; in back an eagle with wings spread; also an arrow and a branch; 17 stars around this; sheared lip
and pontil; ½ pint; amber **150.00-200.00**

Success To R.R.; eagle; pint; olive **80.00-125.00**
same except pint; aqua **100.00-125.00**
same except pint; olive green or
amber **80.00-100.00**

Summer and winter flask; ½ pint; aqua **60.00-80.00**
same except quart **60.00-80.00**

Success to Railroad; *Flask N.H.* (c. 1830-50) *Keene
Glassworks;* olive amber, pint **100.00-150.00**

Sunburst flask; pint; olive, amber or light
green **60.00-100.00**

Sunburst Flask; *Conn.* (c. 1813-30), olive amber, pontil,
half pint **60.00-100.00**
same except olive green **200.00-300.00**

Sunburst Flask; large elliptical sunburst (4⅛"x2½") 24
rounded rays rounding downward to surface of flask
and forming ellipse, back same, pint, horizontal cor-
rugation extends around side at base and around
upper part between neck and squared and concave
shoulder (3 ring) sheared top, pontil, olive green c.
1820 . . . . **350.00-450.00**

Vertically Ribbed Sunburst Flask; (c. 1810-50), light
blue-green, half pint **150.00-200.00**
same except ½ pint; aqua or green . . **100.00-200.00**

Sunburst flask; pint; aqua **60.00-80.00**

Sunburst; *Keene;* pint; olive or amber **100.00-150.00**

Sunburst; *Keene P & W;* pint; olive or
amber **100.00-150.00**

Sunburst; *Keene;* ½ pint; amber **100.00-150.00**

Swirled Pitkin; amber **100.00-125.00**

Swirled Pitkin; pint; blue green **40.00-80.00**

Taylor, Genl; Facing right in half moon circle, bust in
uniform, back *Falls Point* in semi circle above monument, under it *Balto.,* pint, ver. 3 ribbed, with many
heavy medal rib, aqua, pontil, plain top, *Maryland* c.
1850 . . . . **70.00-110.00**

Taylor & Ringgold; pint; aqua **40.00-80.00**

Travelers; in center a sunflower; under it *Companion;* in
back *Ravenna;* in center sunflower; under it *Glass
Co.;* sheared top; pint; amber **90.00-110.00**

Travelers Companion and sheaf; quart;
amber **80.00-100.00**

Travelers Companion and star; ½ pint;
aqua **40.00-60.00**

**Union; side mold; ball and cannon on
back; 7½"; aqua, $60.00-100.00**

Union; clasped hands in shield; eagle with banner on
reverse side; pint **30.00-60.00**

U 2266; on bottom; clear or amethyst; 5" **2.00-3.00**

Violin flask; curled ornaments in a heart shape, with a panel with 2 stars and a *C;* reverse same except no C; collared neck; pint; green........**90.00-175.00**

Warranted Flask; clear or amethyst; 7½"....**6.00-10.00**

G. Washington; prune color; pontil; 10½", $85.00 +

Washington and Albany; ½ pint; aqua.....**90.00-125.00**

Washington General; in three-quarter moon circle above bust facing left, in back eagle facing right, *E Pluribus Unum* above sun rays; *T.W.D.* in oval frame near base, vertically ribbed and inscription *July 4, A.D. 1776, Kensington Glass Works, Phila.,* three star above *1776,* pint, aqua, pontil, plain top........**150.00-250.00**

Washington; (c. 1810-52); bust facing left; falls above bust below point; back Baltimore Monument; under it *Balto;* plain top, pontil, c. 1835, aqua, pint........**110.00-300.00**

Washington; in half moon circle above bust, in back eagle facing left; *B.K.* in oval frame near base, *P.T.,* edge, vertical ribbin, pontil, plain top, yellow green........**40.00-60.00**

Washington; above bust in three-quarter circle, *The Father of His Country,* in back, *I have endeavour, D. Do My duty* above bust in three-quarter circle, quart, plan edge, plain top, aqua........**50.00-100.00**

G. Washington and A. Jackson; pint; olive green........**100.00-125.00**

G. Washington and T. Jefferson; pint; dark amber........**100.00-150.00**

G. Washington and sheaf of wheat; pint; aqua........**100.00-125.00**

G. Washington, and Z. Taylor; open pontil; aqua; pint........**30.00-40.00**

G. Washington and Z. Taylor; quart; green........**40.00-80.00**

same except aqua........**30.00-50.00**

same except pint; green........**30.00-50.00**

G. Washington and Z. Taylor; Washington in a circle; over it *The Father of His Country;* reverse Taylor in a circle; over it *Gen. Taylor Never Surrenders;* sheared top; pontil; quart; aqua........**60.00-120.00**

Washington-Taylor; (c. 1820-40) no inscription around Washington bust facing right; in back *Baltimore X Glass Works,* (r omitted); in center Taylor facing right; heavy vertical medial rib with narrow rib each side and two narrow ribs forming out edge of each panel; plain top pontil, deep puce, quart........**800.00-1000.00**

Washington-Taylor Flask; Washington bust facing left without queue; in back Taylor facing left in uniform; smooth edge, deep yellow green, tapered top and ring quart........**200.00-400.00**

Washington-Taylor Flask; (c. 1860-75); *Dyottville Glass Work;* Washington facing left; Taylor facing left, in uniform, 4 buttons on coat; light blue, quart........**200.00-300.00**

Washington Bust; in back tree, Calabash flask, quart, aqua sloping collared with ring, vertical fluting, pontil, c. 1850........**40.00-80.00**

Washington Flask; (c. 1840-60) *Father of His Country* around bust; back plain, *N.Y.;* plain top, light green, pint........**60.00-100.00**

Washington-Taylor; (c. 1833-60); Washington facing left; back, Taylor facing left; deep blue-green, quart........**200.00-400.00**

Washington; Bust, Washington in half moon circle above bust, back Gen. Z. Taylor in half moon circle above bust, quart, smooth edge, aqua, plain top, c. 1850........**50.00-85.00**

Washington; facing left in half moon circle above bust; in back *Baltimore Glass Works* in three-quarter around monument, side 3 ribbed, pontil, plain top, pale blue-green, c. 1840........**165.00-200.00**

Washington-Taylor; Washington facing left; in back Taylor facing left; deep sapphire blue, pint........**200.00-300.00**

same except yellow green, plain back, double ring top........**100.00-150.00**

Washington; facing right in three-quarter moon circle *Bridgetown, New Jersey,* above bust, unknown bust facing right, in three-quarter moon circle; above bust *Bridgetown, New Jersey* side 3 ribbed with heavy medial rib, deep wine, quart pontil, plain top c. 1830........**800.00-1200.00**

Washington; facing right in half moon circle bust, back Jackson facing left - half moon circle bust, half pint, pontil, plain top, *Coventry Glass Work, Conn.* c. 1840, olive amber........**85.00-115.00**

Washington; facing right, *Falls;* above bust below point, buck *Balto,* below *Monument,* pontil, plain top, quart, aqua, c. 1840........**125.00-185.00**

Westford; Eagle flask, eagle head turned to left, shield on breast, eagle stands on large laurel wreath, above eagle Liberty; in back *Westford Glass Co. Westford, Conn.;* double ring top, pontil, olive amber, half pint........**75.00-100.00**

Wheeling, Va.; a bust facing to the right; in a horseshoe shape *Wheat Price & Co., Wheeling, Va.;* reverse a building; around it *Fairview Works;* sheared top; pontil; green........**350.00-450.00**

Westford Glass Co.; in ½ circle; under it *Westford, Conn.;* reverse side a stack of wheat; pint; green........**50.00-100.00**

Whiskbroom; 7½"; clear........**10.00 +**

Whiskey flask; quilt design; 8"; clear or amethyst........**8.00-10.00**

Willington; Eagle flask (c. 1860-72), bright green, pint........**85.00-110.00**

Willington; *Willington Glass Co., West Willington, Conn.* on 4 lines; reverse eagle and shield; under it a wreath; on shoulder *Liberty;* amber, pint........**60.00-199.00**

Willington Glass Co., West Willington, Conn.; on 4 lines; reverse eagle & shield; under it a wreath; on shoulder *Liberty;* pint; amber........**60.00-100.00**

Will You Take A Drink? Will A Duck Swim?; pint; aqua **125.00-200.00**

Winter and summer flask; tree with leaves and a bird on right side; above it *Summer;* reverse side tree without leaves and bird; above it *Winter;* tapered top; quart and pint; aqua **60.00-110.00**

same as above with *Summer* on front and *Winter* on back **40.00-90.00**

Zanesville City Glass Works; in oval panel; reverse plain; ring top; amber **60.00-110.00**

same except aqua **40.00-60.00**

Zanesville Ohio, J. Shepard Co.; *S* is backwards; reverse side *Masonic;* with pontil; aqua **100.00-200.00**

Spirits

Dr. Billy J. Clark, a physician, managed to attract a group of concerned citizens to a meeting in 1808 at Moreau, New York. Before the gathering adjourned, forty-four had placed their signatures on a document vowing to ''use no rum, gin, whisky, (sic) wine or any distilled spirits . . . except by advice of a physician, or in the case of actual disease.'' The American Temperance Movement had begun.

The great majority of Americans did not pledge to avoid the evils of spirits, however, and their favorite beverages were bottled in increasing numbers. They believed that the Irish had the right idea when they gave us the word ''whiskey'' from a Gaelic phrase meaning ''water of life.'' Irish tradition claims that it was St. Patrick himself who taught them the art of distilling.

In 1860, E.G. Booz of Philadelphia manufactured a whiskey bottle in the shape of a cabin. His name, the year 1840, the phrase ''Old Cabin Whiskey,'' and the company address were proudly embossed on the bottle. Many claim that this bottle accounts for the origin of the phrase ''bottle of booze''; others insist that the colloquial ''booze'' actually comes from the word ''bouse,'' a word for liquor in the seventeenth century.

The Booz bottle is credited with starting the practice of embossing brand names onto spirits bottles. Dedicated drinkers could order their favorite by name, an innovation that added a certain amount of distinction to alcohol consumption. Jack Daniel was a popular brand. As a child, young Jack exhibited an independent nature. He ran away from home and managed to obtain a full partnership in a distillery. By 1866, just three years later, he owned his own whiskey company in Tennessee. His enterprise was a success, and Jack Daniel whiskey is still produced today.

Other spirits bottles are found in the figural shapes of cannons, clocks and barrels. These and other figurals are the most sought-after bottles today. At the turn of the century until Prohibition began in 1920, small bottles—called nips—were given away by tavern owners to their steady customers, especially during the holiday season. All liquor bottles after the repeal of prohibition in 1933 bore the inscription, ''Federal Law Forbids Sale or Re-Use Of This Bottle.'' That practice was discontinued in 1964.

The making of wine is an art that has been passed down through generations from antiquity. Wine bottles usually hold a pint of liquid. The one- to ten-gallon capacity containers used to transport or store wines were called carboys or demijohns. Carboys were so durable that they were also used to store corrosives; demijohns had characteristic long necks. Both types of containers were reusable and weighed thirty to forty pounds.

The shapes of wine bottles came to be associated with certain wine types by the mid-nineteenth century. Seal bottles were also popular, especially among the wealthy. Family crests and coats-of-arms were stamped on these bottles in the finishing process. The practice dwindled in the late 1800's after invention of the plate molds which eliminated the hand stamping. Though some wines today still use seals to identify the contents, paper labels have largely replaced them.

Acker Merrall; label; *A9* under bottom; amber; 11'' **6.00-8.00**

Adam-Booth Co.; in center anchor lean-to toward left, *Sacramento, Cal.* all in a circle, tapered top and ring, clear, 12'' **32.00-45.00**

F.P. Adams and Co.; *Boston, Mass., USA* under bottom; decanter with handle; ring top; clear **10.00-25.00**

Adams, Taylor & Co.; *Full Qt. Registered* on back; clear; 12½'' **12.00-15.00**

Adams, Taylor & Co.; *Boston, Mass., Royal Hand Made Sour Mash Whiskey;* clear; quart **10.00-15.00**

Agcs Co.; birds or eagle all around bottle on base; clear; 12'' **8.00-15.00**

AGW; on base; cefrin type; aqua; quart **4.00-8.00**

Alameda Company; *Tremont and Bromfield Streets, Boston* on front written in slug plate; flask; ring collar; side bands; amethyst; 8'' **4.00-8.00**

Alameda; same as above except ½ pint; monogram on center; 6⅛'' **4.00-8.00**

Alcohol; on label, also *Brandy;* square bottle; clear; 8¼'' **2.00-4.00**

Alderney Old Rye Whiskey; around a cow; *Chris Gallagher, 806 Lombard Street, Philadelphia;* 7½'' **10.00-20.00**

Almaden Vineyards; green; 10'' **1.00-2.00**

Ambrosial B.M. & EAW & Co.; in a seal on shoulder; pontil; amber; 9'' **100.00-200.00**

Americus Club; amber; 7½" **4.00-8.00**

Americus Club Pure Whiskey; clear or
amethyst; 9½" **6.00-10.00**

Ametgan Therapeutic Co.; green; 8" **10.00-25.00**

Amidon's Union; *Ginge Brandy Registered;* in center
lady with long hair; clear or amethyst;
11¾" **6.00-8.00**

E.L. Anderson Distilling Co.; *Newport, Ky* on front in
circle; round; tapered; graduated top and
ring; clear. **8.00-10.00**

Andresen & Son; *Western Importers, Minneapolis, Minn.
& Winnipeg* on back; amber;
5" x 4¾" x 3" **200.00-400.00**

Angelo Myers; clear or amethyst; 6½" **2.00-4.00**

Arcade Grocery Co.; whiskey; clear; quart . . . .**10.00 +**

Aronson J.; in center full-measure, *Seattle, Wash.,* all in
a circle, applied ring top, amber,
10½" **25.00-34.00**

Aronson J. Seattle, Wash.; all in a circle, double rings
top and neck (union oval flask), amethyst,
½ pt. **14.00-19.00**

Aspasia; tan and white crock; 10" x 9" . .**200.00-225.00**

Baileys Whiskey; clear or amethyst; 9¾" **8.00-10.00**

Banjo; label; lavender camphor glass; 10" . .**20.00-30.00**

The Bantam Cock, Northampton; under bottom *64
H.32;* aqua. **25.00-30.00**

same as above except clear. . . . .**15.00-25.00 +**

Bar bottle; label; clear; 10¾" . . . .**10.00-25.00 +**

Bar bottle; fancy; plain rib on bottom; clear;
10¼" **8.00-12.00**

Bar bottle; clear cut glass type; plain; quart;
10¾" **18.00-25.00**

Bar bottle; label; red; 10¾" **25.00-50.00**

Bar bottle; label; pontil; dark amber; 10¼" . .**20.00-30.00**

Barclay; amber; 12" **34.00-60.00**

Barclay 76; machine made; amber; 12" **8.00-12.00**

Barkhouse Bros. & Co.; *Golddust, Ky., Bourbon, John
Van Bergen, Sole Agents;* amber;
quart . . . .**50.00-100.00 +**

A. Bauer & Co.; *Pineapple Rock & Rye,
Chicago, USA;* under bottom *Design
Patented;* clear; 9¾", $10.00-15.00

same as above except amber; 8½" **8.00-10.00**

B & B; clear or amber. **2.00-4.00**

B.B. Extra Superior Whiskey; in center a hand holding
playing cards; blob neck; amber; 4½" . .**10.00-20.00**

Sol. Bear & Co.; *Wilmington, North Carolina;* ring top;
clear or aqua; 6" x 2½" x 1½" **8.00-10.00**

Beech Hill Distilling Co.; *B* under bottom;
amber; 12" **8.00-10.00**

same as above except letters closer together and
longer neck **10.00-20.00**

Belfast Malt Whiskey For Medicine Use; in a circle;
aqua; 11". **20.00-50.00**

Belle of Nelson; label; whiskey; top *one full quart; M.M.*
under bottom; clear; 12" **4.00-6.00**

Belsinger & Co. Distillers; *Guar. Full Qt.* on back; clear;
10"; **6.00-10.00**

Benedictine; liquor crescent above shoulder; olive
green **12.00-18.00**

same as above except machine made. . . .**2.00-4.00**

Bernard Conaty Co., Inc. Providence, R.I.; *TBNTBS* on
base; letters and number under bottom;
smoke; 9". **6.00-10.00**

Bernheim Bros and Uri, Louisville, Ky; on seal; amber;
9½" **10.00-25.00**

E.R. Betterton & Co.; amber; 11",
$20.00-50.00

E.R. Betterton & Co.; *Distilleries Chattanooga, Tenn.* in
3 lines in sunken panel in back; raised panel plain;
flask; 3 ribs on each side; 20 ribs around neck;
under bottom a diamond with letter *Y;* brown; ½
pint. **4.00-8.00**

E.R. Betterton & Co.; *White Oak* on back; *C* in diamond
under bottom; amber; 12" **15.00-20.00**

George Bieler & Sons, Cincinnati; on base; *Brookfield
Rye; B* in center; clear; 9¼" **10.00-15.00**

George Bieler & Sons, Cincinnati Rye; fancy fluted
neck; ring top; clear; 9½" **8.00-15.00**

A.M. Bininger & Co.; *Distilled in 1848* around base; pontil; 8". **100.00-200.00**

A.M. Bininger & Co.; *Kentuckey (sic)* on
front; *No. 19 Broad St. N.Y., Biningers
Old Kentuckey Bourbon 1849 Reserve
Dist. in 1848* on side; amber; 9¼",
$60.00-90.00

Binswanger & Bro.; *Simon W.L.Co., St. Joseph, Mo.* on
front; whiskey; clear or amethyst; 6¾" **2.00-4.00**

Binswanger & Bro.; *Simon* in horseshoe, *W.L. Co. St.
Joseph, Mo.* under it; flask; clear. **2.00-4.00**

Black and White Whisk y; *E* left out of whiskey; 3-part
mold; olive; one 10½"; other 11½" **10.00-20.00**

G.O. Blake; clear or amethyst; 12⅝″ **8.00-12.00**

G.O. Blake's Ky. Whiskey; aqua; 12½″ **8.00-10.00**

Bluthenthal & Beckart/Atlanta "B & B" Cincinnati/High Grade Liquors; vertical in slug plate; flask; clear; ½ pint; 6½″ **4.00-6.00**

Bluthenthal & Bickart; clear or amethyst; 6¼″ **2.00-4.00**

Bob Taylor Whiskey; *Jos A. Magnus & Co.; Cincinnati O. U.S.A.;* lion and arrow monogram on back; amber; 9½″, $75.00-95.00

C.T. Bond, Merchant & Trader, New Albany, Miss.; on back eagle in circle, *C.T. Bond;* golden amber; 6¼″ **100.00-200.00**

W.E. Bonney; in center of barrel-shaped bottle; 2 rings encircling bottle; 3 rings on top and bottom; stands up on one side; aqua; 2½″ tall; 3″ long x 1½″ wide **4.00-8.00**

Bonnie Bros.; on top of circle; *Louisville, Ky.* on bottom; in center circle *Bonnie & Twiges;* whiskey; clear; quart; 6½″ **4.00-5.00**

Bonnie Bros.; in circle; foliage and *Bonnie* in center; *Louisville, KY.* on front; rectangular; amethyst; ½ pint; 7″ **4.00-6.00**

E.C. Booz's; broad sloping collar; smooth with circular depression; *Old Cabin Whiskey* on one roof; on back roof *1840;* short neck on front door; 3 windows on back; plain on one side; *120 Walnut St.,* 2 dots under *St.; Philadelphia* on other side; *E.C. Booz's Old Cabin Whiskey* on another side . . **200.00-350.00**

same as above except no dot under *St.;* very short neck with large round collar; smooth with circular depression; pale green **200.00-300.00**

same as above except reproduction or machine made **2.00-6.00**

Bourbon; in center; over it inside a diamond *131 F;* amber; 3″ round bottle; 7½″ body; 2¾″ neck with a handle from neck to shoulder **20.00-50.00**

Bourbon Whiskey; bitters; 1875; amber; 9¼″ **90.00-100.00**

same as above except puce **100.00-150.00**

John Bowman and Co.; *Old Jewell Bourbon, San Francisco;* amber **150.00-350.00**

same except flask **310.00-375.00**

S.W. Branch; amber; ½ gallon; 9½″ **15.00-20.00**

The Henry Brand Wine Co.; *Toledo, Ohio;* crown top; hock wine shape; amber; 14″ **4.00-8.00**

Brandy, Chicago Fancy; clear or amethyst; 11¾″ **4.00-6.00**

Brandy, Chicago Fancy; ruby red; 11¾″ . . . **8.00-12.00**

Brandy; crescent on shoulder; amber; 10″ **3.00-6.00**

Brandy; no crescent; clear or amethyst; 9¼″ . . **4.00-6.00**

Brandy, plain; amber; 9¼″ **2.00-4.00**

Brandy, plain; amber; 8½″ **2.00-4.00**

Brandy, plain; olive; 12″ **2.00-4.00**

Brandy, plain; olive; 11½″ **2.00-4.00**

Brandy, plain with crescent; green; 11½″ **2.00-3.00**

Brandy, plain; blob neck; red amber; 10½″ . . . **3.00-5.00**

Brandy; square type with crescent on shoulder; amber; 10″ **3.00-6.00**

Brandy, plain; square type; clear or amethyst; 9¼″ **4.00-6.00**

Brandy, plain; square type; amber **2.00-4.00**

Brandy, plain; beer type; amber; 8½″ **2.00-4.00**

Brandy, plain; round; lady's leg neck; olive green; 12″ **2.00-4.00**

Brandy, plain; round; lady's leg neck; olive green; 11½″ **2.00-4.00**

Brandy, plain; crescent; round; amethyst or clear; 11⅝″ **1.00-3.00**

Brandy, plain; crescent; round; clear or amethyst; 12″ **1.00-3.00**

Brandy, plain; beer type; blob neck; olive green; 9¾″ **2.00-4.00**

Brandy, plain; round; short neck; amber; 11½″ **2.00-4.00**

Brook Sunny; *the Pure Food Whiskey;* left medallion *Grand Prize St. Louis 1904;* right medallion *Gold Med. St. Louis 1904;* clear or amethyst; 10¾″ **10.00-20.00**

Brook Sunny; *the Pure Food Whiskey;* with 2 shields on front, *Grand prize, St. Louis 1904* on one side, *Gold Medal St. Louis 1904* other side; clear; 10¾″ **15.00-25.00**

Brookville Distilling Co. Cincinnati, O. USA; in circle; *Distilleries* in center; *Guaranteed full quart* on back; fluting on neck and shoulders; graduated top and ring; amethyst; 9⅞″ **8.00-12.00**

Brown's Catalina; tapered; barber type neck; amber; 11″ **15.00-25.00**

Brown-Forman Co. Distillers Louisville, KY; on front; flask; double band collar; clear; pint; 7½″ **4.00-6.00**

Brown-Forman Co.; Louisville, KY; machine made; clear or amethyst; quart **4.00-8.00**

Brown-Forman Co.; on one line; *Louisville, Ky* on shoulder; whiskey; clear or amethyst **2.00-4.00**

Brown-Forman Co, Distiller, Louisville, KY; flask; clear; ½ pint; 6¼″ **4.00-8.00**

Brown Thompson & Co.; on one line; *Louisville, KY.* on shoulder; beer type; lady's leg neck; opalescent; amber; 11″ **4.00-8.00**

Sursh Brown; label; *R.B.J. & Co.* under bottom; clear; 8″ **10.00-20.00**

Brownsville Fruit Distilling Co.; *Native Wine Maker, Brooklyn, N.Y.;* clear; 13¼″ **10.00-12.00**

Buffalo Old Bourbon; *George Dierssen & Co. of Sacramento, Calif;* clear; quart **100.00-125.00**

Buffalo Spring; with buffalo in center; *Stomping Ground, Ky. Co.;* 7″ **4.00-12.00**

Bureau The; in center crown, *Portland, Or.* all in a circle, pumpkin seed flask, double ring top, amethyst or clear, pt **70.00-90.00**

Sir R. Burnett & Co. Trade Mark; between *Co.* and *Trade* is a circle with a crown in it on top of shoulder; under it *This Bottle Not To Be Sold But Remains Property of Sir R. Burnett & Co. London, England;* under the bottom *B & Co.;* in center of bottom *K B 57;* whiskey; clear or aqua; 12″ **10.00-25.00**

Sir R. Burnett & Co.; aqua; 8½″ **6.00-10.00**

Sir R. Burnett/& Co./London/England Trade Mark; (crown): *This Bottle Is Not To Be Sold But Remains Property of;* bulbous neck; gloppy square and ring top; round; aqua; 11¾″ **10.00-25.00**

Burns & O'Donohue; amber; 10¼″ **8.00-15.00**

Burrow Martin & Co.; *Norfolk, Virginia;* round ring top; clear or aqua; 6″ **8.00-15.00**

Cahn, Belt & Co.; clear; 8½″ **4.00-6.00**

Cahn, Belt & Co.; clear; ½ pint; 7″ **2.00-4.00**

Caledonia Whiskey; B.C. Distillery Co. L.T.D. New Westminister B.C.; oval shape; graduated top; emerald green; quart **4.00-6.00**

Callahan Whiskey; clear or amethyst; 12⅛″ . . . **5.00-6.00**

Callahan/Whiskey/J. Callahan & Company; (written fancy) *Boston, Mass/Reigstered;* round; amethyst; 12⅛″ **4.00-8.00**

J.F. Callahan & Company/Boston, Mass; at slant; clear; ½ pint; 6⅝″ **4.00-6.00**

John F. Callahan, Bottled Only By Boston, Mass; round; slug plate; graduated top and ring; amethyst; 11″ **8.00-12.00**

D. Canale & Co.; *Memphis, Tenn. Old Domnick Bourbon* other side; clear or amethyst; 11″, **$10.00-15.00**

T.F. Cannon & Company/Boston, Mass/Guaranteed Full Pint; all in slug plate; *12 Devonshire St.* on side; *28-30 Exchange St.* on opposite side; rectangular; clear; pint; 8″ **8.00-10.00**

Carlson-Bros; in center *wholesale and retail* in 3 lines, *Astoria,* are all in a circle, applied ring top, clear, ½ pint **16.00-23.00**

Cartan, McCarthy & Company, San Francisco, Calif. Full Quart; with monogram at top, all vertically; rectangular; graduated top and ring; amber; 10¾″ **15.00-30.00**

Cascade; clear; 9½″ **8.00-15.00**

J.W. Cashin Family Liquor Store; clear or amethyst; 6¼″ **4.00-8.00**

Caspers Whiskey; cobalt; 10½″ . . . . **75.00+**

Cedarhurst; *Cont. 8 oz.* on back shoulder; amber; ½ pint; 7″ **6.00-8.00**

Century Liquor & Cigar Co.; *B-8* under bottom; amber; pint **6.00-10.00**

Champagne; cylindrical; 2″ indented bottom; pale green; 11⅞″ **5.00-8.00**

Champagne, plain; kick-up; opalescent; green; 12″ x 10″ x 9″ **1.00-3.00**

Champagne, plain; green; 4¼″ **4.00-6.00**

Champagne, plain; kick-up; dark green; 8″ . . . **4.00-8.00**

Chapin & Gore, Chicago; *Hawley Glass Co.* under bottom; amber; 8¼″, **$65.00-100.00**

Chapin & Gore; diamond shape on back for label; amber; 8¾″ **60.00-90.00**

Henry Chapman & Company; *sole agents, Montreal* in circle; pumpkin seed type; inside screw; *Patent 78* on screw cap; amber; 5¼″ **40.00-50.00**

Cheatham & Kinney; *W. Mc & Co.* under bottom; aqua; 8¾″ **10.00-20.00**

Chesleys Jockey Club; in center a jockey and running horse, under it *Whiskey* all in a circle, tapered top and ring, amber, 12″ **170.00-230.00**

Chestnut bottle; kick-up; handle; ring around top neck; squat; amber; 2″ neck; 4″ body; 3″ x 4″ **18.00-25.00**

same as above except larger; amber . . . **15.00-30.00**

same as above except machine made **4.00-8.00**

same as above except clear or blue **10.00-20.00**

Chestnut bottle; kick-up; ring around top; pontil; blue; 4″ body; 2″ neck **40.00-60.00**

Chestnut bottle; 25 ribs; Midwestern; l.h. swirl; sheared top; green; 7½″ **60.00-80.00**

Chestnut bottle; 24 vertical ribs; sheared neck; attributed to Zanesville; golden amber; 5¼″ **90.00-150.00**

Chestnut bottle; light vertical rib plus 18 r.h. swirl ribs; sheared neck; attributed to Kent; green **60.00-70.00**

Chestnut bottle; 16 vertical ribs; sheared neck; 6½″ **80.00-90.00**

Chestnut bottle; swirl tooled top; pontil; green; 5¾″ . . . . **50.00-100.00+**

same as above except deep amber; 5¼″ **95.00-110.00**

Chestnut bottle; long outward flared neck; bluish aqua; ½ pint **30.00-60.00**

Chestnut bottle; diamond; ¼″ ground off top; attributed to Zanesville; yellow green; 10″ . . . . **20.00+**

Chestnut bottle; aqua; 5½″ **40.00-60.00**

Chestnut bottle; 12 diamonds quilted over 24 vertical ribs; tooled mouth; clear; 5¾″ . . . . . . **100.00-200.00+**

Chestnut bottle; diamond; yellow green or clear; 5¼″ **20.00-30.00**

Chestnut bottle; sixteen ribs; sheared neck; mantua; 6¼″ **60.00-80.00**

Chestnut bottle; sixteen ribs; l.h. swirl; mantua; aqua; 6½″ **60.00-80.00**

Chestnut bottle; kick-up; ring around top; pontil; amber;
6″ **15.00-20.00**
same as above except clear **15.00-30.00**
Chestnut bottle; kick-up; squat body; handle ring around
neck; light amber; 6″ **8.00-10.00**
same as above except machine made;
clear **4.00-8.00**
Chevaliers Old Castle Whiskey; *San Francisco;* spiral
neck; aqua or amber; quart **100.00-200.00**
Chicago Fancy Brandy; label; amber; 12″ . . . **8.00-15.00**
Chicago Fancy Bottler Brandy; ribs on shoulder and
bottom; clear or amethyst; 11¾″ **4.00-8.00**
Chicago Fancy Bottler Brandy; ribs on shoulder and
bottom; ruby red; 11¾″ **15.00-30.00**
Cigar bottle, cigar-shaped; amber; 7½″ **6.00-18.00**
Cigar bottle; cigar-shaped; amber; 5½″ **6.00-18.00**
Clarke Bros & Co.; amber; 11½″ **4.00-8.00**
Clown bottle; (front and back of bottle pictured); frosted
clear or amethyst; 17″ **85.00-95.00**
Coca Mariani; on one line; *Paris* on line near shoulder;
liquor; whittle mold; green; 8¾″ **2.00-6.00**
Coca Mariani Paris; in 2 lines; whittle effect; short body;
long neck; green; 8½″ **3.00-5.00**
Coffin type; all basket weave except neck; clear or
amethyst; ½ pint **6.00-10.00**
Coffin type; 2 rings on shoulder; checker type body except neck; in center on front; a circle for label; clear;
amethyst; 5″; 1¾″ at bottom **6.00-10.00**

Cognac Castillon; *Depose* under bottom; curved back; clear; 6½″,
$5.00-10.00

Geo. Cohn & Co.; amber; 4½″ **4.00-6.00**
George Cohn & Company; *Louisville, Ky.;* blob neck;
amber; 4¾″ **10.00-12.00**
Congress Hall Whiskey Blend; *The Fleischmann Company, Cincinnati, USA;* amber; 11″ **10.00-25.00**
same as above except dark amber **20.00-35.00**
Cook & Bernheimer Co.; *Mount Vernon Pure Rye* on
one side; amber; 6″ **10.00-15.00**
Cooper & Co.; *Portobello (Scotland)* all in a circle under
bottom, 2 pts. mold, small kick up, double ring top,
black, 9¼″ **16.00-23.00**
Very Old Corn; *From Casper Winston, North Carolina,
Louist Price Whiskey House; write for private terms;*
fancy with handle and glass top **40.00-80.00**
Cowie & Co. Ltd.; clear; 8¾″ **10.00-20.00**
S. Crabfelder & Co.; amber; 7″; 4″ x 2″ **6.00-8.00**
Creamdale; *Hulling, Mobile, Alabama, Cincinnati, Ohio;
Refilling of This Bottle Will Be Prosecuted By Law*
under bottom; amber; 11¼″ **10.00-15.00**
Cream of Kentucky "Thee" Whiskey; clear;
11¼″ **20.00-25.00**
Creame De Menthe; gold claws; green;
11″ **10.00-20.00**

The Crigler & Crigler Co.; clear or amethyst;
4½″ **4.00-6.00**

Crigler & Crigler Distillers; *Full Qt. Union
Made* other side; clear or amethyst; quart,
$6.00-8.00

Crigler & Crigler Distillers, Covington, KY; vertical on
one panel; *Full Quart Union Made* on next side;
square body; lady's leg neck; graduated top and
ring; amethyst; 10⅛″ **10.00-20.00**
**Get The Best, Order Your Whiskey From J. Crossman
Sons;** *New Orleans, La.;* amber; quart . . . **8.00-10.00**
Crown; label; whiskey pinch bottle; machine made;
amber; 8½″ **6.00-8.00**
Crown Distilleries Co.; around monogram *Crown & Co.*
in center; inside screw thread; amber;
10″ **4.00-6.00**
Crown Distilleries Company; under bottom, *Sample
Whiskey;* round; clear or amethyst **3.00-4.00**
Crown Distilleries Company; in circle; *Crown & Shield,
CD Co.* monogram, on center; *S.F. Whiskey;* inside
threads; embossed cork; round; amber;
11¼″ **15.00-20.00**
same as above except reddish amber;
quart **4.00-8.00**
Cuckoo; clear or amethyst; 11¾″ **15.00-25.00**
Cuckoo; (bird, branches, leaves on center) *Whiskey/M.
Burke/Boston/Trade Mark;* flask; clear;
½ pint; 6½″ **10.00-20.00**
Cuckoo/Whiskey/M. Burke/Boston/Trade Mark; all with
embossed cuckoo bird in branches and leaves; *Full
MB. Quart* on back; graduated top; round; amethyst;
12″ **20.00-30.00**
Curner & Company; *80 Cedar Street, New York;* 3-part
mold; olive, amber; 11½″ **35.00-50.00**
Cutter, J.H.; *Old Bourbon* under it a crown, around it
bottled by A.P. Hotaling & Co. all in a watermelon
circle, tapered top and ring, amber, 12″ . **35.00-47.00**
Cutter, J.H.; *Old Bourbon, A.P. Hotaling & Co. sale
agents* all in 5 lines on shoulder a crown, tapered
top and ring, chip mold, light amber,
11¾″ **240.00-290.00**
J.H. Cutter Old Bourbon; *A.P. Hotaling & Company,
Portland, Oregon;* pewter screw cap; round top;
amber **100.00-300.00**
J.H. Cutter Old Bourbon; *A.P. Hotaling & Co., Portland,
Oregon;* quart . . . . **30.00-50.00 +**
J.H. Cutter Old Bourbon; *Moorman Mfg. Louisville, KY.;
A.P. Hotaling & Company;* amber;
quart **60.00-80.00**
J.H. Cutter Old Bourbon; *E. Martin & Company;* amber;
quart **90.00-125.00**
J.H. Cutter/Trade Mark; (star and shield) */E. Martin &
Company/San Francisco, Cal.* in circle; slug plate;
graduated top; round; amber; 11″ **10.00-15.00**

J.H. Cutter Old Bourbon; *by Milton J. Hardy & Company, Louisville, Ky.;* barrel in center; amber; 12″ **90.00-125.00**

J.H. Cutter Old Bourbon; *Louisville, KY.;* amber; quart. **20.00-50.00**

J.H. Cutter Old Bourbon; barrel and crown in center; *C.P. Moorman Mfg., Louisville, Ky., A.P. Hotaling & Co.;* amber; quart **60.00-80.00**

Cutter Hotaling; coffin type; 1886; amber . . **75.00-100.00**

Dallemand & Co. Inc.; *Chicago* around bottom; brandy; fancy; blob neck; amber; 11¼″ **3.00-6.00**

Dallemand & Co.; *Cream Rye* around bottom; fancy shoulders; amber; 2¾″ **3.00-4.00**

Dallemand & Co. Chicago; *Design Pat 21509 Apr. 26, 1892* under bottom; amber; 11″, $10.00-12.00

B.B. Davis & Company, New York, Contents 8 Fl. Ozs; flask; graduated collar and ring; amethyst; ½ pint; 6¾″ **4.00-8.00**

Davis' Maryland; label; *Guaranteed Full Pint* in back; *Davis & Drake;* clear; 8½″ **4.00-6.00**

Peter Dawson Ltd, Distillers; on bottom; graduated and flared collar; concave and convex circles (thumb prints) around shoulder and base; green; 11¾″ **4.00-6.00**

Deep Spring; *Tennessee Whiskey;* amber; quart; 7″ **10.00-15.00**

De Kuyper's Squareface; Who DeKuyper's Nightly Takes, Soundly Sleeps and Fit Awakes; on 2 panels; vertical at slant; vase gin shape; *ABM;* thread top; grass green; 7⅞″ **10.00-15.00**

R. Denner Wine & Spirit Merchant; *Bridgewater;* in 3 lines on one side shoulder; crock with handle; coffin flask type; ring top; short neck; tan and cream; 8½″ tall, 2¼″ x 3″ **25.00-60.00**

Devil's Island Endurance Gin; clear or amethyst; pint **4.00-6.00**

De il's Island; V missing from Devil's; clear; 9″, $10.00-12.00

Diamond Packing Co., Bridgeton, N.J.; *Pat. Feb. 11th 1870* on shoulder; aqua; 8″ **8.00-12.00**

Diamond quilted flask; double collar; very light aqua, almost clear; quart; 9″ **10.00-20.00**

Diehl & Ford; *Nashville, Tennessee* around bottle each letter in a panel; light amber; 9″ . . . . . . **10.00-25.00+**

Dip mold wine; kick-up; pontil; dark amber . . . **5.00-10.00**

J.E. Doherty Company, Boston, Mass; written vertically; flask; clear; ½ pint; 6¾″ **4.00-6.00**

J.E. Doherty Co./Boston, Mass; on shoulder; *Regist. Full Qt.* on back; 3-piece mold; graduated top; lady's leg neck; amethyst; 11″ **6.00-10.00**

N.F. Doherty, 181-185 Cambridge St., Boston, Guaranteed Full Pint; vertically in slug plate; rectangular; graduated collar and ring; amethyst; pint; 8¾″ **4.00-8.00**

Neil Doherty; *176 North St. Boston* in circle; in center of circle *Wine & Liquors;* strap flask; light amber; 9⅝″ **5.00-8.00**

Donaldson & Company Fine Old Madera, Madcira House, Founded 1783; label; aqua; quart; 12¼″ **4.00-8.00**

Dreyfuss-Well & Company, Distillers, Paducah, KY, USA; clear; ½ pint, $4.00-6.00

Dreyfuss-Weil & Co.; clear or amethyst; 6½″ **2.00-6.00**

D.S.G. Company; under bottom; light amber; 7¾″ **20.00-30.00**

Duff Gordon Sherry; 3-part mold; aqua; 12″ **7.00-10.00**

The Duffy Malt Whiskey Co.; *Rochester N.Y.U.S.A.* on front in watermelon circle; in center monogram *D.M.W. Co.;* under bottom *pat'd Aug 24-1886;* different number or letter on bottom; round; amber; 10¼″ **3.00-6.00**

same as above except ½ pint or pint . . . **20.00-30.00**

same as above except miniature **10.00-20.00**

same as above except machine made **2.00-3.00**

The Duffy Malt Whiskey Company; *Baltimore, Md. U.S.A.* in a circle monogram; in center of circle *D.C.O.;* under bottom *Pat. Aug. 24-86, Baltimore Md.;* some have letters or numbers; amber; approximate quart **4.00-8.00**

same as above except machine made **2.00-4.00**

same as above except approx. pint **10.00-20.00**

same as above except machine made; approx. pint **8.00-10.00**

same as above except approx. ½ pint . . **10.00-20.00**

same as above except machine made; approx ½ pint **8.00-10.00**

same as above except sample **8.00-10.00**

The Duffy Malt Whiskey Co.; *Baltimore Md., U.S.A.* in watermelon circle; in center of circle monogram *D.M.W. Co.;* under bottom *Pat. Aug. 24 '86, Baltimore Md.* ½″ ring around neck; amber **8.00-15.00**

The Duffy Malt Whiskey Company; *Patd Aug. 1886* in back; plain bottom; amber; 10½″ **25.00-60.00**

Dukehart & Co.; amber; 4″ **15.00-25.00**

Durham; amber; 11½″ **100.00-250.00**

Durkin Wholesale and Retail Wine and Liquor; *Hill and Sprague Street, Spokane, Washington* in front; tapered; ring top; 13½″ **15.00-30.00**

James Durkin Wine & Liquors; *Wholesale & retail, Durkin Block, Mill & Spragne, Spokane, Washington, Telephone Main 731; 32 ounce* on front; blob neck; tapered top and ring; amber; 11⅜″ **8.00-12.00**

Dyottville Glass Works, Phila; on bottom; gloppy graduated and flared lip; round; green; quart; 11½″ **10.00-30.00**

Dyottville Glass Works, Phila; green; 6½″ **30.00-50.00**

Dyottville, Gass Works Phila; all in a circle, under bottom, tapered and ring top, black, 11½″ **35.00-48.00**

Eagle Liqueur Distilleries; olive; 7¾″, **$40.00-50.00**

National's Eagle Blended Whiskey; label; light amber; 4½″ **4.00-6.00**

F.H. Earl, Spring St., Newton N.J.; *Full Qt.* on shoulder; light green; 7½″ **4.00-8.00**

Edgemont Whiskey Blend; label; *The I. Trager Co., Cincinnati, Ohio;* clear; 8″ **8.00-12.00**

Edgewood; in gold lettering; clear; quart; 11″ **15.00-20.00**

Edgewood; panels on shoulders and base; clear or amethyst; 11″ **15.00-20.00**

Weiss Eichold Liquor Co.; sheared top; 3 dots on bottom; clear or amethyst; 7″ **6.00-8.00**

Elixir De Gullie; in center *G* all in seal, dip mold, sheer top, applied ring, deep kick-up, green, 6½″ **60.00-80.00**

Elk Run Br'g Co. Punx'y, Pa.; golden amber; 9½″, **$6.00-8.00**

Erie Club; clear or amethyst; quart or fifth; 11″ **8.00-12.00**

Essence of Jamaica; label; clear or amethyst; 5″ **8.00-10.00**

same as above except 7½″ **10.00-12.00**

N.J. Ethridge; *Macon, Ga., pure old Winchester rye whiskey,* label; clear; 6½″ **8.00-12.00**

Eureka; clear or amethyst; 7¾″ **4.00-8.00**

Evans & O'Brien; *1870 Stockton;* amber or green **80.00-150.00**

Everett-Liquor Co., Everett, Wash.; all in a circle, applied ring top, amber, 11″ **30.00-40.00**

Farmville Dispensary, Farmville, Va.; in a circle; *Registered Full Pint;* ring collar; and below it tapered ring top; clear or amethyst **8.00-15.00**

Farmville Dispensary, Farmville, Va. Registered Full Pint; clear; pint flask; 8″ **8.00-12.00**

Farrell; *A Merry Christmas and a Happy New Year,* label; sheared top; clear or amethyst; 4½″ **6.00-15.00**

Fred Ferris, Elmira, N.Y.; amber; 6¾″ **8.00-10.00**

John F. Fitzgerald Whiskey; clear or amethyst; quart **6.00-12.00**

same as above except ½ pint **8.00-10.00**

Fleming's; *Bottled Expressly For Family & Medicinal Purposes* in back; *1 Qt.* on side; clear or amethyst; 8½″ **20.00-25.00**

Fockinr, Wynard, Amsterdam; all under bottom, sheer top and applied ring, black, 9½″ **32.00-42.00**

James Fox; *Full* under bottom; clear or amethyst; 9½″ **15.00-30.00**

Fraiellt Branca, Milano; in crude blob seal on shoulder; 2 ring collar; turn mold; green; 14″ **25.00-50.00**

The Purdue Frederick Co, New York; inside of oval circle; *PF Co.* monogram in center; oval flask; amethyst; pint; 8″ **4.00-6.00**

Friedman Keiler & Co.; *Distillers and Wholesale Liquor Dealers, Paducah, Ky; 1* under bottom; amber; 12″ **8.00-10.00**

Friedman Keiler & Son; amber; 12″, **$8.00-12.00**

Jos Fuhrer & Sons; *3701 Butler Street, Pittsburgh, Pa.;* tapered top; clear or amethyst; 9½″ **8.00-15.00**

Gaelic Old Smuggler; on bottom; round; square and ring collar; fat neck; olive green; quart; 10″ . . .**8.00-10.00**

Gagle Glen Whiskey; *29 Market Street, San Francisco, Werle & Willow* **15.00-30.00**

Gahn, Belt & Co.; clear or amethyst; 8″ **4.00-6.00**

Gannymede; amber; 7½″ **4.00-8.00**

Garrett & Co.; clear, 6½″ **6.00-9.00**

Garrett & Co.; *Established In 1835* on top; in center eagle and shield with *American Wines;* on each side of it *St. Louis, Mo. Norfolk, Va.;* at bottom *Registered Trade Mark, Refilling Prohibited;* fancy; clear or amethyst; quart; 12″ **4.00-8.00**

same as above except amber **12.00-18.00**

same as above except sample with *Norfolk, Va.;* 4¾″ **4.00-8.00**

Garrett & Co.; 2 types crown top—14"; applied top—12"; clear or amethyst; 14" **4.00-6.00**

same only 12" **6.00-8.00**

Garrett Williams Co.; clear; 6½" **4.00-6.00**

Gellert, J.M.; in center *230 Washington St. Portland, Oregon,* bulb neck and applied tapered top, amber; 10¾" **70.00-90.00**

C.R. Gibson, Salamanca, New York; in shield; amber; pint **8.00-12.00**

Old Joe Gideon Whiskey; amber; 11½", $20.00-40.00

Old Joe Gideon; amber; ½ pint **6.00-10.00**

Gilbert Bros. & Co. Baltimore, Md; on front; oval; graduated collar and ring; thick glass; aqua; pint; 8¼" **6.00-8.00**

H & A Gilbey Ltd; aqua; 12" **3.00-6.00**

J.A. Gilka; vertically; *J.A. Gilka/Berlin* vertically on side; *This Bottle D* vertically on corner panel; *Not To Be Sold* on corner panel; *Schutzen Str. No. 9* on side; graduated collar and ring; light amber; quart; 9¾" **20.00-30.00**

J.A. Gilka Berlin; on side; *J.A. Gilka* on back; *Schutzen Str. No. 9* on opposite side; same as above except embossing; gloppy collar; red amber; quart; 9¾" **20.00-30.00**

W. Gilmore & Son, Pavilion, N.Y.; kick-up; teal blue; 10¼" **10.00-15.00**

Ginocchio & Co.; in center *Importers 287 - First St.* in 2 lines, *Portland,* all in a circle, pumpkin seed flask, clear, pt. **110.00-135.00**

Glenbrook Distilling Co/Boston, Mass; vertically; oval flask; aqua; ½ pint; 6¾" **4.00-6.00**

Glenbrook; on bottom; flask; amber; ½ pint; 6¾" **4.00-6.00**

same as above except aqua **4.00-6.00**

The Glendale Co.; 3-part mold; clear or amethyst; 12" **8.00-12.00**

I. Goldberg Distiller; five panels; clear; 13¼" **10.00-12.00**

I. Goldberg; on one panel; next panel *171E Broadway;* next *Houston or Clinton St., 5th Ave. cor, 115th St.;* next *New York City, Brooklyn;* next *Graham Ave. cor. Debevoise St. Pitkin cor. Rockaway Ave.;* 3 panels blank for label; under bottom different number; on shoulder *I. Goldberg;* and *Est. 1873;* 12¼" **20.00-30.00**

I. Goldberg; on one panel; next *Distiller;* next *171-E Broadway;* next *Houston cor Clinton St.;* next *5th Ave cor 115th St. New York City;* 3 panels blank for label; plain shoulder; amber; 12¼" **15.00-20.00**

I. Goldberg; vertically on 1 panel; *171 E. Broadway* on next; *Houston Cor Clinton St. 5th Ave. cor 115th St.* on next panel; *New york City, Brooklyn* on next panel; *Gram Cor Debevoise Pitkin cor Rockaway Ave;* on next panel; 8 large vertical panels; graduated collar; amber; quart; 12½" ...**30.00-40.00**

Golden & Co. San Francisco, Cal.; inside of circle; *Net Contents One Quart Full Measure* on front; round; graduated collar and ring; amber; 11¾" **15.00-25.00**

Golden Cream 1878 Whiskey; *Weiss Echold Liquor Co., Mobile, Ala, Proprietors;* clear or amethyst; 8½", $8.00-10.00

Golden Cream; 7 panels; clear; fifth **8.00-12.00**

Golden Gate Co. Baltimore Celery Rye; *Pat Apl. For* under bottom; clear; quart **4.00-8.00**

same as above except amethyst **4.00-8.00**

Golden Hill; on base; *#2* under bottom; 2 ring top; amber; 4½" **8.00-10.00**

Golden Wedding; *Jos. S. Fench & Co. Schenley Pa,* label; whiskey sample; 4" **8.00-10.00**

Goldie—Klenert Co, Stockton, Cal; in slug plate; graduated collar; round; clear; quart; 11¼" **4.00-8.00**

Gold Thimble Scotch Whiskey; *Black Bros Glasgow;* pinch bottle; amber; 8½" **15.00-25.00**

Goldtree Bros; in slug plate; *1880; San Luis;* amber; quart **200.00-400.00**

Morris T. Gombert, Houston; clear or amethyst; 6" **8.00-10.00**

Geo. H. Goodman; *B* on bottom; clear or amethyst; fifth **6.00-10.00**

Gordons Dry Gin, London, England; square with wide beveled corners; boar on bottom; graduated and flared collar; aqua; quart; 8⅝" **4.00-8.00**

same as above except oval back; old **2.00-6.00**

same as above except ABM **2.00-6.00**

G.P.R.; whiskey label; clear or amethyst; 7½" **2.00-6.00**

G.P.R.; *Baltimores G. Gump & Sons* on shoulder; clear; 10¾" **8.00-10.00**

S. Grabfelder & Co.; */* on bottom; amber; 5¾" **4.00-6.00**

S. Grabfelder & Co.; *99a* on bottom; amber; 7" **6.00-8.00**

S. Grabfelder & Co.; *J* on bottom; amber; 7¼", $6.00-10.00

S. Grabfelder & Co.; clear or amethyst; 6" . . . 3.00-6.00

Graffing & Co. N.Y.; under bottom; boy and girl climbing trees; clear; 12¼" 20.00-30.00

C.E. Granger, Wine & Liquors, Sunbury, Ohio; double collar; bottom—*AMF & Co;* clear; ½ pint; 6½" 8.00-15.00

C.E. Granger, Wines & Liquors; double collar; flask; under bottom—*AMF & Co. warranted full measure;* clear; ½ pint; 6½" 8.00-12.00

E.E. Gray & Co./Importers/Boston, Mass; vertically; *Full Quart Registered* on back; round; graduated collar; 7 rings; amethyst; quart; 12½" 8.00-12.00

Great Seal Styron Beggs & Co. Newark O.; clear or amethyst; 6" 4.00-6.00

Great Seal; clear or amethyst; 6", $2.00-6.00

Green & Clark Missouri Cider; *Registered, Aug. 27, 1878* in vertical lines under bottom; *A. B & M Co.;* blob top; amber; 9½" 10.00-15.00

Greenbrier Whiskey; label; *The Old Spring Distilling Company, Cinncinnati;* H2 under bottom; clear; 11" 4.00-6.00

B.S. Greil & Co. Cincinnati, Ohio; clear or amethyst; pint 10.00-15.00

The Grim Reaper; *Sandemong Cherry Black* on back; *Royal Doulton China* under bottom; black; 10½" old 25.00-30.00

same as above but new 10.00-15.00

Guaranteed; on ribbon; *Full Pint* under ribbon at top; long graduated collar with ring; rectangular; 8¾" 4.00-6.00

Guaranteed Full; amber; 6½" 4.00-8.00

Guitar Whiskey; label; amber; 15" 8.00-12.00

H; on bottom; whiskey label; clear or amethyst; 6½" 2.00-4.00

L. Haas & Co. Toledo, O.; label; horseshoe seal; clear; 12½" 4.00-6.00

Haig & Haig; clear; 8" 4.00-8.00

same as above except amber 10.00-15.00

Hall, Luhrs & Co. Sacramento; monogram on the front pumpkin seed; amethyst; 6¾" **8.00-20.00**

Ham on shoulder; shape of a whole ham; screw top; sheared top; amber; 6¼" tall, 3½" wide **20.00-40.00**

Handled whiskey jug; Chestnut type; amber; 7⅝" **10.00-25.00**

Handmade Sour Mash; clear; 4½" **4.00-8.00**

same as above except amber **8.00-12.00**

Hannis Distlg Co.; *Pat April 1890* under bottom; amber; 8¾" **20.00-30.00**

I.W. Harper; with like-new wicker; name shows through window in wicker; graduated collar; light amber; quart; 9¾" **15.00-30.00**

I.W. Harper; *Medal Whiskey* in center; gold on front; anchor in gold; rope around neck; 3" pottery; very light tan; 4" square tapering to 3½" on shoulder **20.00-40.00**

I.W. Harper; whiskey; amber; 9½" **8.00-15.00**

/I.W. Harper; clear or amethyst; 4¼" **10.00-30.00**

Adolph Harris and Co.; *San Francisco;* amber; quart **30.00-40.00**

Adolph Harris & Co.; (deer head) *San Francisco;* cylindrical; amber; fifth **70.00-85.00**

Albert H. Harris N.Y.; label; turn mold; amber; quart **4.00-8.00**

Harvard Rye; with interlocking *HR,* inside of rectangle; slug plate; vertical panels on neck and shoulder; fancy; graduated collar; round; amethyst; quart; 12" **4.00-8.00**

Harvard Rye; with interlocking *HR* monogram in center; rectangular; double band collar; heavy glass; clear pint; 7½" **4.00-8.00**

Harvard Rye; clear or amethyst; 7½", $8.00-10.00

The Hayner Distilling Co.; *Dayton, Ohio & St. Louis Mo. Distillers;* W on bottom, also *Nov. 30th 1897;* whiskey; amethyst; 11½" **6.00-14.00**

The Hayner Distilling Co. Dayton, St. Louis, Atlanta, St. Paul, Distillers; *Design Patented Nov. 30th, 1897* under bottom; amber; 11½" **8.00-10.00**

Hayner Rich Private Stock Pure Whiskey; in back *H.W. Distillers, Troy, Ohio;* under bottom, *Distillers, Pat. Nov. 30th 1897-F* clear; 11½" **6.00-8.00**

The Hayner Whiskey Distillers, Troy, Ohio; *Design Patented Nov. 30th, 1897* on bottom; fluting around base 1" high, also on shoulder and neck; graduated collar and ring; round; *ABM;* clear; quart; 11½" **4.00-8.00**

Hayner Whiskey Distillery, Troy O.; lower trunk and paneled shoulder; *Nov. 30th 1897, F* on bottom; round; amethyst **6.00-14.00**

Hayners Distilling Co. Dayton, Ohio, USA, Distillers & Importers; in circle; *Design Patented Nov. 30th, 1897* on bottom; 14 fancy vertical panels on shoulder and neck; 14 vertical 1″ panels around base; graduated collar and ring; amethyst; liter; 12″ **4.00-8.00**

W.H. Heckendorn & Co.; label; *2* under bottom; 3-part mold; golden amber; 12″ **7.00-10.00**

Edward Hefferman; in center, *Reg. Full Pint* at top, *88 Portland St. Boston, Mass* all on front in slug plate; rectangular; light green; pint; 8½″ **3.00-6.00**

W.H. Hennessey, 38 to 44 Andrew St. Lynn, Mass; vertically; slug plate; rectangular; graduated collar and ring; amethyst; ½ pint; 6¾″ **4.00-8.00**

Here's A Smile To Those I Love; clear; 5½″ **10.00-15.00**

Here's A Smile To Those I Love; clear or amethyst; 5½″, $14.00-18.00

Here's Hoping—; clear; 8″ . . . .**10.00 +**

Hewonts Squeal; hog bottle **15.00-35.00**

Highcliff Whiskey Cini O; label; amber; ½ pint **4.00-6.00**

Hock Wine; label; sheared top and ring; red ground pontil; mold; 14″ **10.00-20.00**

same as above except old; teal blue; 11½″ **4.00-8.00**

same as above except old; teal blue; 14″ **4.00-10.00**

same as above except old; red amber; 11½″ **3.00-6.00**

same as above except old; light amber; 7″ **4.00-8.00**

same as above except old *ABM;* light amber; 14″ **3.00-6.00**

same as above except old *ABM;* green; 13½″ **2.00-4.00**

Hofheimer's Eagle Rye Blend; (large eagle embossed on shield) *M. Hofheimer & Co. Norfolk, Va;* rectangular; clear; ½ pint; 6″ **4.00-8.00**

Hofheimer's Eagle Rye Blend; clear or amethyst; 6″ **4.00-6.00**

Holberg Mercantile Co.; amber; 11″ **10.00-12.00**

Hollands; in gold letters; around it gold circle; glass top with *H;* fancy; 9½″ . . . .**50.00 +**

Hollywood Whiskey; round; graduated collar and ring; amber; quart; 11″ **10.00-20.00**

same as above except golden amber . . .**15.00-30.00**

Hollywood Whiskey; amber; 12″ **8.00-12.00**

Hollywood Whiskey; kick-up; amber; 11¼″ . .**8.00-12.00**

Holton, Chas. F.; in center in hollow letters *Hover lap C., Olympia, W.T.* all in a circle *Shoo Fly Flask, Pt.,* clear, ring top **135.00-165.00**

Home Supply Co.; wine label; 3-part mold; amber; 11¼″ **4.00-8.00**

Home Supply Co.; whiskey label; 3-part mold; amber; 11¼″, $4.00-8.00

Honest Measure; clear; 4¾″ **6.00-8.00**

Honest Measure; *half pint* on shoulder; saddle flask; amber; ½ pint **4.00-8.00**

same as above except clear **2.00-4.00**

same as above except clear; pint **4.00-6.00**

W. Honey Glass Works; under bottom; amber; 7½″ **15.00-30.00**

Hotaling Co. The A.P.; in center a crown, under it *Portland, Or., sole agents* all in a watermellow circle, applied top, amber, 11″ **225.00-285.00**

Hotel Donnelly, Tacoma, (Miniature); 3″, Pu top, clear **18.00-24.00**

Hotel Worth Bar, Fort Worth, Texas; inside screw; amber; 6″ **50.00-100.00**

Huber Kuemmel Liqueur, B.S. Flersheim Merc. Co.; label; amber; 10″, $8.00-15.00

H.W. Huguley Co., 134 Canal St. Boston; *Full Quart* on back; round; graduated collar and ring; amethyst; 12″ **4.00-8.00**

H.W. Huguley Co.; clear or amethyst; 11¾″ **8.00-10.00**

Hurdle Rye; clear panels; neck; letters etched; 3″ **8.00-15.00**

Huber Kuemmel Liqueur, B.S. Flersheim Merc. Co.; label; amber; 10″ **8.00-15.00**

H.W. Huguley Co., 134 Canal St. Boston; *Full Quart* on back; round; graduated collar and ring; amethyst; 12″ **4.00-8.00**

H.W. Huguley Co.; clear or amethyst; 11¾″ **8.00-10.00**

Hurdle Rye; clear panels; neck; letters etched; 3″ **8.00-15.00**

The Imperial Distilling Co.; *Kansas City, Mo* in center; *IDCO;* fancy shoulder; clear; 4″ **8.00-12.00**

Imperial; in ribbon; *Pint* on back in ribbon; oval; aqua; 9" **4.00-6.00**

Imperial; in back; aqua; ½ pint; 7¾" **10.00-20.00**

Imperial Wedding Whiskey Blend; label; clear or amethyst; 8" and other sizes, $6.00-10.00

Importers; vertically; flask; clear; ½ pint; 6½" **3.00-6.00**

G. Innsen & Sons, Pittsburgh; under bottom; green; quart **18.00-20.00**

Jack Cranston's Diodora Corn Whiskey; *Jack Cranston Co., Baltimore, Md.* in back; *U* blank seal; clear; 12" **8.00-15.00**

Jack Daniel's Gold Medal Old No. 7; clear; 7¾" **18.00-25.00**

James Buchanan & Co. Ltd.; ½ ring on each side; *106* under bottom; dark green; 7¼" **10.00-20.00**

Jesse Moore-Hunt Co.; amber; 11¾" **10.00-15.00**

J.M. & Co. Boston, Mass; in slug plate; oval flask; aqua; 10" **4.00-6.00**

Johann Maria Farina No. 4, Julicrsplatz No. 4; clear or amethyst; 4" **3.00-6.00**

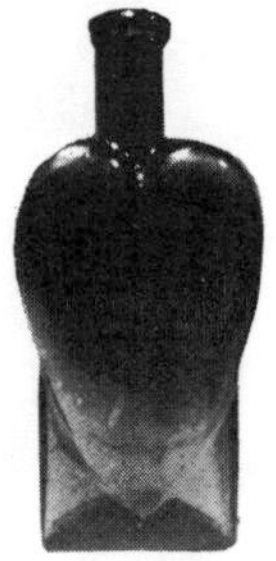

John Hart & Co.; on each side; amber; 7¼", $25.00-35.00

W.L. Johnson Kentucky; pontil; amber; 8¼" **65.00-75.00**

W.H. Jones & Co. Established 1851; (shield with bear) *Importers/Hanover and/Blackstone Sts/Boston, Mass* all on front; flask; light green slug plate; pint; 8¾" **10.00-20.00**

W.H. Jones and Co.; clear; 9½" **8.00-15.00**

Jug; round base; bulbous neck; light green; gallon; 13½" tall, 5¾" across **10.00-20.00**

L.E. Jung & Co. Pure Malt Whiskey, New Orleans, LA; amber; 10¾" **8.00-12.00**

J & W Hardie Edinburgh; on bottom; 3-piece mold; large square collar; emerald green; 10¼" **4.00-6.00**

J & W.N. & Co.; under bottom; aqua; 11" **2.00-4.00**

same as above except clear; 10" **3.00-5.00**

Kane, O'Leary & Co; in center *221 & 223*, under it *Bush St. S.F.* inside of square box enclosing tapered top and ring, amber, 12" **170.00-230.00**

Kelly & Kerr; *222 Colleges St., Springfield, Mo.; C.W. Stuart's;* machine made; clear, amber or aqua; quart **4.00-6.00**

Kelly & Kerr; *222 College St., Springfield, Mo.;* machine made; clear or aqua **2.00-4.00**

Kentucky Gem, S.M. Copper Distillers, Whiskey; *T.G. Cockrill, San Francisco;* quart **200.00-400.00**

Keystone Burgundy; tapered top; amber; 8¾", $35.00-40.00

Keystone; whiskey label; clear or amethyst; 7½" **10.00-15.00**

King Bee; 10 panels; clear; 11¾" **10.00-20.00**

Kirby's; *222 Colleges St., Springfield, Mo. 1870;* quart; clear or aqua **4.00-12.00**

H.B. Kirk & Co.; amber; 11⅛" **8.00-15.00**

Remains the Property of H.B. Kirk & Co. N.Y.; on back; 3 Indian heads embossed in circle on shoulder; trademark in ribbon; *Registered U.S.* on front; graduated collar and ring; round; amber; quart; 11¼" **10.00-20.00**

Henry Klinker, Jr.; *The Owl, 748-10th ave., SE corner 51st Street, N.Y.* in circle under it; *Full Measure;* double collar; under bottom—*LCMG, 182 Fulton Street, N.Y.;* amber; 1½ pint **8.00-10.00**

C.F. Knapp, Philadelphia; pig slope; clear or amethyst; 3¼" x 2" **20.00-40.00**

Chateau Lafiete 1896; in circle; blob seal on shoulder; crude band collar; kick-up; green; 12" **4.00-8.00**

Lake Drummond Pure Rye, J & E Mahoney; rectangular; clear; ½ pint; 6½" **4.00-8.00**

Lake Keuka Vintage Co., Bath, New York Winery No. 25; same shape and design as a Hayner Whiskey; graduated collar and ring; amethyst; 12" **6.00-10.00**

Lambe & Denmarke Fine Whiskey; *Arkansas City, Ark.;* under bottom, *L.C. & R Co.;* tapered top and ring; fancy bottom; clear or aqua; 8" **10.00-20.00**

Langert Wine Co.; *422 Sprague Ave. Spokane, Wash.* all in a circle, applied ring top, amethyst and clear, qt **12.00-17.00**

John Latreyte; under bottom *C Pat'd, April 1, '84;* clear or aqua; 7¼" **10.00-12.00**

Leipps; in script; *Chicago;* tapered top; amber; 4½" **8.00-12.00**

Licking Valley Co.; clear, quart size **10.00-15.00**

Lilienthal, Cincinnati, San Francisco & New York, 1885; yellow amber **100.00-200.00**

Lilienthal Distillers; coffin type with crown; amber **100.00-200.00**

Lilienthal Co.; flask; amber . . . . **100.00-200.00 +**

Los Angeles Co., 51 & 53 Summer St., Boston, Mass., La Co.; monogram; flask; ring collar; amethyst; ½ pint **7.00-10.00**

Louisville, KY. Glass Works; aqua; 8¾", $40.00-65.00 +

Lyndebors; *L.G. Co.* on base; cylindrical; honey amber......................**20.00-30.00**

Lyons, E.Y. and Raas; *San Francisco, California;* cylindrical; clear or amethyst............**10.00-15.00**

Mackenzie & Co. Fine Tawny Port, Medal of Honor S.F. 1915; label on front and back; round and flared band collar; slight bulbous neck; emerald green; 11½"............................**4.00-6.00**

Jos Magnus & Co.; embossed dragon and *Cincinnati, Ohio;* rectangular; square collar; clear, ½ pint; 6"........................**4.00-6.00**

Jos. A. Magnus & Co.; clear or amethyst; 6½"................................**4.00-8.00**

J & E Mahoney Distillers, Portsmouth and Alexandria, VA.; rectangular; flask; clear; 6¼"......**4.00-8.00**

Mailhouse Rye; clear or amethyst; 8¼".......**100.00 +**

Mallard Distilling Co.; Baltimore and New York, Patent Applied For; sunken sides; ½ pint; 6¼"..**3.00-6.00**

Mallard Distilling Co.; clear or amethyst; pint..................................**2.00-4.00**

Man's face figural whiskey bottle, label; clear or amethyst; 7½", $20.00-35.00 +

Isaac Mansbach & Co.; in a dome shaped line; under it, *Fine Whiskeys, Philadelphia;* square; flat collar; ring; amber; quart......................**10.00-20.00**

Isaac Mansback & Co.; *Philadelphia* other side; *Millionaires Club Whiskey* around shoulder; amber; 4¾"..................................**10.00-15.00**

Isaac Mansbach & Co.; in back; *Millionaire Club* on shoulder; amber; 4½"..................**6.00-8.00**

The J.G. Mark's Liquor co. Wholesale; on back; clear or amethyst; 9".....................**15.00-25.00**

The J.G. Marks Liquor Co.; 3 barrels trademark in back; clear or amethyst; 9¼"........**15.00-25.00**

Marriage bottle; crock; black, white, blue, tan; 8¾"..............................**20.00-50.00**

Martini Cocktails, For Martini Cocktails Use Only Martini Vermouths; champagne shaped; sand blasted or etched lettering; *ABM;* green; 12½"....**4.00-6.00**

May & Fairall Grocers, Baltimore; 3-piece mold; slug plate; amber; quart; 11¼"............**10.00-15.00**

Mayse Bros. Distillers Rye; with seal; clear or amethyst; 10"...................**25.00-50.00**

McAvdy Brew Co.; amber; 8½"...........**4.00-6.00**

McDonald & Cohn; *San Francisco, Cal.;* amber; quart............................**8.00-12.00**

McKnights; amber; 10½"................**6.00-8.00**

same as above except clear; 9¼".......**4.00-6.00**

John A. McLaren; in center; *Perth Malt Whiskey, Perth, Ont;* saddle flask; *193* under bottom; 2-ring top; 8"......................**10.00-15.00**

Meridith's Club Pure Rye Whiskey; *East Liverpool, Ohio;* white; 7¼"..................**10.00-15.00**

Merry Christmas Happy New Year; quilted back; sheared top; clear; 6", $25.00 +

Merry Christmas & Happy New Year; in center; clear or amethyst; 5".....................**10.00-20.00**

Merry Christmas & Happy New Century; in back a watch with Roman letters and *B / Co.* in center; pocket watch type; milk glass.........**15.00-25.00**

Mexican drinking bottle; clear; 10" tall, 7" round............................**6.00-12.00**

Meyer Pitts & Co.; clear or amethyst; 6".....**2.00-4.00**

H. Michelsen; in center; on top *Bay Rum;* under it *St. Thomas;* clear or amethyst; fifth.........**5.00-6.00**

I. Michelson & Bros; clear or amethyst; 11"................................**8.00-12.00**

Midland Hotel; *Kansas City, Mo;* panels on neck; clear; 3"..................................**4.00-8.00**

Milk glass; 7¼"......................**20.00 +**

J.A. Miller, Houston, Texas; clear or amethyst; ½ pint..........................**8.00-10.00**

M & M T Co.; clear or amethyst; 3¼", 4.00-6.00

J. Moore Old Bourbon; amber; 12".......**25.00-50.00**

J. Moore; amber; 11"...................**25.00-50.00**

Jesse Moore & Co. Louisville, Ky; *Ringdeer Trade Mark; Bourbon & Rye; Moore Hunt & Co.; sole agents;* flask; amber...............**200.00-400.00**

Jesse Moore & Co. Louisville, KY.; outer circle; *C.H. Moore Bourbon & Rye* center; *Jesse Moore Hunt Co./San Francisco* at base; graduated collar and ring; quart; 11½"...................**15.00-30.00**

same as above except golden amber; 11¾"............................**15.00-30.00**

G.T. Morris; a bunch of flowers on back; amber, 12"............................**100.00-200.00**

Moses in bulrush; clear or amethyst; 5"...**40.00-100.00**

Mount Vernon; machine made; amber; 8¼"................................**8.00-10.00**

Mount Vernon Pure Rye Whiskey; in 3 lines; back *Hannis Dist'l G Co., Full Five* in 2 lines; 2 more lines *Re-Use of Bottle Prohibited;* under bottom *Patented March 25 1890;* amber; 3¼" square, 4¼" tall, neck 4" **10.00-20.00**

same as above except sample; 3¼" **10.00-20.00**

same as above except machine made **2.00-4.00**

Mulford's Distilled Malt Extract; embossed, *J.F. Mulford & Co., chemists, Philadelphia;* amber; 8¾" **4.00-6.00**

Munro, Daluhinnil, Scotland; *reuse of bottle prohibited* in 5 lines on front; in back, *House of Lords, whiskey,* 2½" x 2½" square, blob neck, double ring top, improved pontil, dr. aqua, 12½" **33.00-41.00**

Murphy The; in center, *Wine & Liquor Co. 308-310 Pike St. Seattle, Wash.* all in a circle, applied ring top, amber, qt. **55.00-75.00**

Murray Hill Maryland Rye; *Sherbrook Distilling Co., Cincinnati,* **label; clear or amethyst; 6", $6.00-8.00**

John Murray (JM) Rye Whiskey; label only; flask; amber; ½ pint; 7" **4.00-6.00**

Angelo Myers; clear or amethyst; 6¼" **4.00-8.00**

H.C. Myers Company/New York, N.Y./And/Covington, Ky., Guaranteed Full ½ pint; all on front; flask; amethyst; 6⅜" **4.00-8.00**

Neals Amb Phth; in seal on shoulder; cobalt blue; 9⅛" **40.00-80.00**

Newman's College; *San Francisco and Oakland;* round like football; amber; 4¼" **15.00-25.00**

Nixon & Co. J.C.; in center *Seattle, W.T.* all in a circle; flask; amber, ½ pt **100.00-150.00**

O'Hare Malt, H. Rosenthal & Sons; *#1* under bottom; amber; 10¾" **8.00-12.00**

O'Hearn's Whiskey; **#1919 under bottom; side mold; inside screw; amber; 10¼", $15.00-30.00**

Ohio; expanded swirl bottle; 24 rib pattern; vertical over swirl to left; club shaped; deep blue aqua; 7¾" **50.00-75.00**

Old Ashton; clear; 8½" **5.00-10.00**

The Old Bushmills Distilling Co., Limited Trademark; *pure malt, established 1734;* 10" to
1903 . . . . **6.00-10.00**
1915 up **4.00-6.00**

Old Charter Whiskey, Louisville, Ky.; label; amber; 11¾" **4.00-6.00**

Old Duffy's 1842 Apple Juice, Vinegar Sterilized 5 Years; around shoulder; amber; 10" **4.00-8.00**

Old Edgemont Whiskey; label; clear; ½ pint; 6½" . . . . **8.00+**

Old Edgemont Whiskey, The I. Trager Co. Cincinnati, Ohio; label; clear; ¼ pint; 5" **8.00-10.00**

Old Family Wine Store; (diamond design)/*Established 1857/Jos. Cleve & Co/19821 Cambridge St. Boston* in slug plate; narrow flask; ring collar; clear; ½ pint; 6½" **6.00-8.00**

Old Henry Rye; in script; ring top; clear or aqua; 9½" **8.00-10.00**

Old Hudson; pinch bottle; clear; 6½" **20.00-30.00**

Old Irish Whiskey; (trademark—shield and crown); *This Is the property of Mitchell & Co. of Belfast, Ltd, Imperial Pint,* all on front; flask shape; graduated collar and flared band; *ABM;* aqua; 9½" **3.00-4.00**

Old Irish Whiskey; *Imperial Pint* on back; aqua; 10" **10.00-20.00**

Old J.H. Cutter V.F.O. Rye, Louisville Ky.; label; clear or amethyst; 11" **4.00-6.00**

Old Joe Gideon Whiskey Bros.; *F* under bottom; 11½" **10.00-20.00**

Old Kaintuck Bourbon; clear; 3¾" **6.00-10.00**

The Old Kentucky Co.; clear or amethyst; 11" **8.00-12.00**

Old Port Haley Whiskey; *Swope & Mangold, Dallas, Texas;* clear or aqua; quart **15.00-25.00**

Old Prentice Whiskey; **label; in back embossed** *J.T.S. Brown & Sons, Distillers, Louisville, Ky.;* **clear; 11", $4.00-6.00**

Old Quaker; *1234* under bottom; clear; 6½" . . **3.00-6.00**

Old Servitor Distributing Co. N.Y.; amber; 11" **4.00-6.00**

The Old Spring Distilling Co.; clear or amethyst; 8½" **6.00-10.00**

Old Spring Whiskey; clear or amethyst; 9¼" **10.00-12.00**

Old Time; *First Prize Worlds Fair 1893;* clear; 9½" **10.00-20.00**

Oppenheim; *Fine Whiskey, Atlanta, Ga;* **amber; 8", $10.00-20.00**

The Orene Parker Co.; clear or amethyst; 11¼″ **8.00-10.00**

E. Otlenville, A.G.D.H. Co.; in back *E.O. Nashville, Tenn;* tapered top; amber; 9″ **10.00-25.00**

J.W. Palmer, Nelson County Ky. Whiskey; in 4 lines; in back *Compliments of J.W. Seay, Savannah, Ga.;* pottery jug, with handle; brown and tan; 3″ **15.00-35.00**

Parker Rye; in front of squat bottle; ribs under bottom; 6 panels on neck; flat top; clear; 1½″ neck; 3¼″ **4.00-6.00**

Parker Rye; 6 panels; fancy; clear; 1¾″ neck; 1½″ body **6.00-10.00**

Parole; amber; 10½″ **60.00-90.00**

Patent; on shoulder; 3-part mold; round; amber; 10½″ **2.00-4.00**

Patented April 3d, 1900; at base on concave panel; oval back; 2 rings on neck; unusual shape; amber; ½ pint; 6½″ **3.00-6.00**

Patterson's Liquor Store; *Wapakoneta, Ohio;* flask; clear; 6½″ **8.00-12.00**

Patterson's Liquor Store; *Wapakoneta, Ohio* in a circle; lined at bottom; clear; 6¼″ **8.00-15.00**

Paul Jones 1908 N8; under bottom; amber; pint **4.00-6.00**

Paul Jones Bourbon, Louisville, Ky.; in seal; amber; quart **10.00-15.00**

Paul Jones Pure Rye, Louisville, Ky; on blob seal; round; amber; 9¼″ **8.00-14.00**

same as above except *Whiskey* **8.00-14.00**

same as above except *Old Monongahela Rye* **10.00-18.00**

Paul Jones & Co.; in script on curved 1½″ x 3″ panel on one side; front and back of bottle curved; off center neck; light green; 6½″ to top, 4½″ to curved shoulder **15.00-35.00**

Paul Jones; (enameled) ground pontil; clear **20.00-30.00**

Paul Jones Whiskey; label; amber; quart . . . **10.00-15.00**

Paul Jones Whiskey; amber; 4″ **6.00-8.00**

Paul Jones & Co.; *718* in diamond shape under bottom; machine made; amber; 12″, $6.00-8.00

Paul Jones 1905 22; under bottom; amber; 9″ **4.00-8.00**

Paul Jones Pure Gin, Louisville, Ky; in seal; green; 9½″ **15.00-20.00**

Paul Jones Pure Rye, Louisville Ky; in circle; small kick-up; amber; 5¾″ **10.00-15.00**

Pearsons/Pure Old/Malt Whiskey; at top; *Redington & Co./Pacific Coast Agents* at base; round; graduated collar; clear; quart **4.00-6.00**

Pedro; *1880;* glop top; amber; quart **60.00-80.00**

S.F. Petts & Co./Importers/Boston/U.S.A./Registered; horizontally; round; graduated collar and ring; amethyst; 12½″ **6.00-8.00**

Picnic flask or pumpkin seed; there are many different sizes and colors, some embossed, some not **3.00-10.00**

S.N. Pikes Magnolia, Cincinnati, Ohio; *The Fleischman;* clear or amethyst; 12¼″ **10.00-15.00**

Pikes Peak Old Rye; aqua; pint **40.00-50.00**

Pikesville Rye; clear; 4″ **4.00-6.00**

same as above except *Patented* under bottom **5.00-8.00**

Planter Rye, Registered Ullman & Co., Ohio; amethyst; ½ pint **10.00**

Planter Mary Lou Rye; *Ullman & Co. Cincinnati;* ground top; clear; 5½″ **6.00-10.00**

Planter Mary Lou Rye; *Ullman & Co., Cincinnati;* clear; 5½″ **8.00-10.00**

Pond's Rock & Rye with Horehound; R missing in Rock, E missing Rye; aqua; 10″ **10.00-20.00**

Preacher Whiskey; curved bottle; 3″ round sides; off-center neck; clear or amethyst; ½ pint; 6½″ **15.00-30.00**

P & SP; under bottom; 3-part mold; dark olive; 9½″, $8.00-12.00

same as above except 11½″ **18.00-30.00**

Pumpkin seed; small; on back and front, sunburst pattern; clear or amethyst; 5″ **14.00-18.00**

Pumpkin seed; plain; clear or amethyst; all sizes **5.00-10.00**

Pumpkin seed picnic flask; double band collar; amethyst; 5½″ **3.00-6.00**

Pumpkin seed; amethyst; 6″ **4.00-6.00**

Pumpkin seed, label; amber; 4″ **10.00-20.00**

same as above except dark aqua; 4½″ **20.00-40.00**

Pure Malt Whiskey, Pride of Canada; tapered top; amber; 10½″ **10.00-20.00**

Quaker Maid Whiskey; girl in center of label; *S. Hirsch & Co. Kansas City, Mo.;* fancy shoulder; clear; 3½″ **8.00-20.00**

Quaker Maid Whiskey; *Patented* under bottom; clear or aqua; quart **10.00-15.00**

Quarterback Rye Whiskey; *S. Silberstein, Philadelphia, Pa.;* clear; quart **15.00-30.00**

Queen Mary Scotch Whiskey; amber; quart **15.00-30.00**

Queensdale Whiskey; label; amber; quart **2.00-3.00**

Quinine Whiskey Co. Louisville, Ky; on bottom; amber; 5¼", $6.00-12.00

F.R. Quinn; *This Bottle Not To Be Sold* on back base; aqua; 11½" **6.00-10.00**

W.J. Rahily Co.; on back shoulder; 3-part mold; clear or amethyst; 11" **4.00-6.00**

Fred Raschen Co. Sacramento, Cal; in form of circle; *F.R. Co.* monogram; round; graduated collar and ring; amber; quart; 12" **10.00-20.00**

Fred Raschen, Sacramento, Cal.; amber; quart **15.00-25.00**

RCV NP; on shoulder, on top a crown; 3 pt. mold; applied top; kick up; dark green, 9½" **20.00-40.00**

Rebecca At The Well; pontil; clear or amethyst; 8" **30.00-65.00**

Records and Goldborough, Baltimore, Md; vertically on slug plate; rectangular; ring colar; clear; pint; 6" **4.00-6.00**

Red Chief; *Fort Hood, Indiana, Ballina Rye;* clear; 12" **10.00-15.00**

Red Top; with *Top* on shoulder; *R.D. Westheimer & Sons* on bottom; under bottom, different numbers; flask; extra ring on bottom of neck; amber; ½ pint **4.00-6.00**

Registered Honest One Pint; at top half; rectangular; graduated collar and ring; amethyst; pint and ½ pint **3.00-4.00**

Registered; clear or amethyst; 8" **6.00-8.00**

E. Remy; champagne; cognac; machine made; *A.R.* on bottom; green; 4" **1.00-2.00**

Rheinstrom Bros. Proprietors; on other side, *Mother Putnam's Blackberry Cordial;* amber; 11" **10.00-25.00**

J. Rieger & Co. Kansas City, Mo; clear or aqua; 11½", $6.00-10.00

W.R. Riley Distilling Co. Kansas City, Mo.; clear; quart **8.00-10.00**

H.H. Robinson, Boston; label; *Guaranteed Full Pt* on back; clear or amethyst; 8¾" **2.00-4.00**

Roma California Wine, Pride of The Vineyard, R.C.W. Co.; monogram all on front; *ABM;* thread top; amber; 12⅛" **2.00-3.00**

L. Rose & Co.; rose & vine bottle; applied crown; tapered; aqua; 7½" **4.00-10.00**

Rosedale Ok Whiskey; *Siebe Bros. & Plagermann, San Francisco;* clear or amber; quart **20.00-40.00**
amber **100.00-200.00**

Rosskam Gerstley & Co.; *Old Saratoga Extra Fine Whiskey* on back; *Philadelphia* in seal; small kick-up; clear or amethyst; 9¼" **8.00-12.00**

Rosskam Gerstley & Co.; *Monogram No. 6* clear; 8¼" **20.00-40.00**

Rosskam Gerstley & Co.; clear; 9½" **10.00-25.00**

Ross's Brand; aqua; 14¼" **10.00-12.00**

Roth & Co., San Francisco, California; pocket flask **10.00-12.00**

Roth & Co., San Francisco; amber; quart . . **30.00-60.00**

Roxboro Liq. Co.; clear or amethyst; 8" **6.00-8.00**

Aqua De Rubinat; aqua; 11" **2.00-4.00**

Chas. Rugers, Wine & Liquors, Houston, Texas; *#181* under bottom; amber; 6" **8.00-10.00**

Rum; 5 rings; clear; 3¾" **4.00-6.00**

Rusconi, Fisher & Co., San Francisco; in 3 lines, back full quart on shoulder; inside threads top; flask type bottle; amber, 11" **20.00-40.00**

Rye; 3-part mold; clear; 11" **8.00-10.00**

Rye; ground pontil; silk glass; hand painted; 11" **18.00-30.00**

Rye; decanter; gold trim; clear; 9¼", $25.00 +

Safe Whiskey; aqua; 9¼" **40.00-50.00**

Sailor's flask; crock; tan and brown; 8¼" . . **75.00-85.00**

St. Jacobs; 10½" **6.00-8.00**

St. Jacobs Malt Whiskey, Cincinnati O. U.S.A.; amber; 9¾" **8.00-10.00**

St. Thomas Double Distilled Bay Rum, St. Thomas, V.I.; label; *ABM;* 10⅛" **4.00-6.00**

St. Thomas Bay Rum; on bottom; *St. Thomas, V.I. USA;* graduated ring collar; emerald green; quart; 11" **4.00-6.00**

L.A. Chrten, St. Thomas, D.W.I. Bay Rum; all on label; graduated collar and ring; slight bulbous neck; emerald green; 11½" **3.00-4.00**

Sallade & Co.; aqua; 8" **4.00-8.00**

M. Salzman Co., New York; label; same in back with *Purity* above all; *Old Doctrine Club Whiskey;* quart; 11¼" **4.00-8.00**

The Sam'l Lehman Co., Cincinnati, Ohio; amber; 11½" **12.00-18.00**

Thos. D. Samuel, Wholesale Liquor Dealer; *11 East 5th Street, Kansas City, Mo;* 8¾" **4.00-12.00**

T.W. Samuels Bourbon Whiskey; label; clear; 11" **4.00-8.00**

Saw Palmetto; *Genuine Vernal Buffalo N.Y.* on other sides; clear or amethyst; 10" **6.00-12.00**

S.B. Co. Chicago; in back; clear; 3" **8.00-10.00**

S.B. & Co.; under bottom; amber; 12" **2.00-4.00**

S.B. & G. Co.; under bottom; aqua; 8" **2.00-6.00**

S.C. Dispensary; under monogram *SCD;* under bottom *C.L.F.G.C.O.;* with palm tree also; clear; ½ pint, pint, quart **20.00-30.00**

Daniel Schaeffer's Log Cabin Whiskey **40.00-60.00**

Schlesinger & Bender, Pure Wine & Brandies, San Francisco, Cal.; amber; quart **50.00-100.00**

Barney Schow; *Wholesale & Retail Wine & Liquors, Willits, California;* net contents, 8 oz.; screw cap; amber; 6" **25.00-30.00**

Schutz-Marke; *Eigenthym Von A. Schenk Altona* **in back; amber; 11½, $10.00-15.00.**

Schwarz Rosenbaum & Co.; *B* under bottom; amber; 11½" **8.00-12.00**

Scotch; label; clear; 10" .... **8.00 +**

G.B. Seely's Son; clear; 11" **8.00-12.00**

Shea-Bacqueraz Co., San Francisco, Cal.; vertically; round; graduated collar and ring; dark amber; quart; 11½" **10.00-20.00**

A.A. Sheaffers; label; 3-part mold; amber; quart **4.00-6.00**

Sheehan's Malt Whiskey; with monogram in center; *Utica, N.Y.;* same shape as The Duffy Malt; round; graduated collar; amethyst; 10½" **4.00-8.00**

Sheffield Co, New York; amber; 9¾" **10.00-15.00**

Shell figural; whiskey; sheared top; clear or amethyst; 5" **30.00-65.00**

S.H.M. Superior; *Old Bourbon;* quart **100.00-200.00**

Shoe fly or coffin flask; graduated collar and ring; clear; pint and ½ pint **3.00-6.00**

Shoe figural, label; dark purple; 6" x 3½" x 1¼", $65.00 +

Shoomakers; *1331 Famous Resort, Pa. Avenue, Washington, D.C.; Registered Full Pint;* side strap; ring top; clear; quart **10.00-20.00**

S.I.G.W.; *1* under bottom; aqua; 12" **2.00-4.00**

Silver Leaf Pure Rye Whiskey; *Virginia, Carolina Co., owners, Richmond, Virginia, U.S.A.;* clear; ½ pint **8.00-10.00**

Silver Leaf Rye; *Virginia, Carolina Grocery Co., Richmond, Virginia;* under bottom; *B.R. G. Co.;* clear or amethyst; 6¼" **8.00-10.00**

Simon Bros.; horseshoe seal on back shoulder; clear; 10" **4.00-8.00**

Simon Bros; plain seal on back; clear or amethyst; 13" **8.00-12.00**

SM & Co.; ground pontil; amber; 11" **60.00-90.00**

Thos. L. Smith & Sons/Boston, Mass; on shoulder; three-piece mold; bulbous neck; round; graduated collar and ring; amethyst; quart; 12¼" **4.00-8.00**

Sol. Bear & Co.; clear or amethyst; 13¾" .. **10.00-12.00**

South Carolina Dispensary; clear; 9¼" **15.00-25.00**

South Carolina Dispensary; aqua; 9½" **40.00-85.00**

Southern Comfort; clear; 11½" **1.00-2.00**

Southern Liquor Co., Dallas, Texas; in a circle; tapered top; clear or amethyst; 10½" **7.00-15.00**

William H. Spears Old Pioneer Whiskey; bear in center; *A. Feukhauser & Co.,* sole agents, San Francisco; amber; quart **100.00-200.00**

Jared Spencer; flask; flared top; green; pint **1,000.00-2,000.00**

R.A. Splaine & Co., Haverhill, Mass.; on shoulder; *It Pays To Buy the Best* written on shoulder on opposite sides; 3-piece mold; round; graduated collar and ring; amethyst; quart; 11½" **6.00-8.00**

S.S.T. Patent; amber; quart **6.00-10.00**

Star in center with stars circling; clear; 4¾" ... **6.00-8.00**

Star whiskey label; saddle strap; amber; pint, $4.00-6.00

Stein Bros. Chicago; on bottom; round; graduated rows of beads swirled around on shoulder; graduated band and ring collar; amethyst; quart; 11¾" **6.00-10.00**

C.B. Stewart, Atlanta, Georgia; double top; clear; pint **8.00-12.00**

C.B. Stewart, Atlanta, Georgia; clear or aqua; pint **4.00-8.00**

Stoddard; label; wine; iron pontil; olive or amber; 8½" **10.00-20.00**

Stone Brook; turn mold; amber; 9½" tall, 4" diameter **4.00-8.00**

Old Henry Whiskey; Straus Gunst & Co., Richmond, Va.; panels on shoulder; clear or amethyst; 11" **10.00-20.00**

Straus Gunst & Co., Proprietors, Richmond, Virginia; amber; ½ pint **10.00-20.00**

Strauss Bros. Co., Chicago, U.S.A.; deep green;
12¼" **8.00-10.00**

Strauss Pritz & Co.; sheared top; clear or amethyst;
5½" **4.00-8.00**

The Strauss Pritz Co.; clear or amethyst;
6¼" **4.00-6.00**

C.W. Stuarts; amber; quart. . . . .**10.00 +**

Swans G.; *The-owl, 5160 Ballard Ave. Ballard, Wash.* all
in a circle; double ring top and neck flask; clear and
amethyst, ½ pint. **8.00-15.00**

Louis Taussig & Co./San Francisco/New York; vertically on one side; *Union Made; C.B.B.A. Branch No. 22*
on opposite side; square; graduated collar; clear;
scant quart; 10¼" **4.00-8.00**

LT & CO; inside of circle; *Patented Feb. 4th, 1902* on
bottom; oval front paneling; ribbed; panels at base
on back; rectangular; graduated collar and ring;
amber; quart; 10½" **4.00-8.00**

Louis Taussig, Main Street, San Francisco; flask;
amber. **100.00-200.00**

Taylor & Williams; clear or amethyst; 3¼" **4.00-6.00**

Taylor & Williams; side strap; clear; 6½" **2.00-3.00**

Taylor & Williams; in a horseshoe shape; under it *Louisville,
KY;* in center *Whiskey;* ring top; clear or amethyst; 4¾"
round **4.00-6.00**
same as above except 11⅜" **4.00-10.00**

Tea cup; *Old Bourbon; Shea Bacqueraz & Co., San
Francisco;* amber; quart **100.00-300.00**

Teakettle Old Bourbon; *San Francisco;* amber;
quart. **100.00-200.00**

Texas; flask; tapered top; whiskey; clear; quart; 11" tall,
1¾" neck, 8" wide at center, 4" x 3" at
bottom **8.00-10.00**

Jas. Tharp's Sons; in center; *Wine & Liquor,
Washington, D.C.;* saddle flask; ring top; amber;
7¾" **15.00**

A. Theller; on shoulder; under bottom of bottle, in a circle, *Theller Arnold;* applied top; kick-up; dark olive;
9½" **4.00-6.00**

Theodore Netter; *1232 Market St. Phila., Pa;*
cobalt; 6" **50.00-100.00**
clear **15.00-25.00**

Tokj; in seal; small kick-up; clear; 11" **4.00-8.00**

Tonsmeire & Craft, Mobile, Alabama;
amber; 11", $10.00-20.00

The I. Trager Co.; amber; 12" **8.00-10.00**

The I. Trager Co., Cincinnati, Ohio; inverted V instead
of A in Cincinnati; amber; 12" . . . .**20.00 +**

The I. Trager Co.; ring top; amber; ½ pint. . . .**4.00-6.00**

The I. Trager Co.; amber; 8½" **2.00-6.00**

The I. Trager Co.; amber; ½ pint. **3.00-6.00**

Trost Bros; clear; 6½" **4.00-6.00**

Tucker Ala; on one panel; 4 running legs in circle on
back panel; amber; 9¼" . . . .**60.00 +**

**F.G. Tulledge & Co., Pure Pop Corn Whiskey, Cincin-
nati, Ohio;** clear; quart. **4.00-8.00**

Two Fish Whiskey; clear or amethyst;
7½" **75.00-150.00**

Ullman & Co.; *Planter Rye Registered* on back; clear or
amethyst; 6¼" **6.00-8.00**

Union Made C.B.B.A. of US & C Trademark; in circle;
flask; clear; pint; 8¾" **3.00-6.00**
same as above except ½ pint. **4.00-8.00**

**Union Square Company, 239 Union St., Lynn, Mass.
Guaranteed Full ½ Pint;** all in slug plate; rectangular; clear; 7" **2.00-3.00**

N.M. Uri & Co.; *B* on bottom; amber; 4¾" tall; 1½"
diameter **6.00-8.00**

N.M. Uri & Co. Louisville, KY.; amber; 5¾" . .**6.00-8.00**

U.S. Mail; clear; 5½" **12.00-18.00**

W.B. Vail; golden amber; 11½" . . . .**12.00 +**

Varwig & Son, Portland, Ore.; monogram in center; *Full
Measure;* round; graduated collar and ring; amber;
12¼" **20.00-30.00**

L. Vereterra Oviedo; on bottom; ring top; 12" .**2.00-4.00**

**The North Vernon Distilling Co., Distillery Office Cin-
cinnati, O;** round; ten fancy vertical panels on neck
and shoulder; graduated collar and ring;
amethyst **6.00-8.00**

VI; on base; whiskey label; pontil; clear;
5¼" **10.00-15.00**

Vieux Cognac; 3-part mold; small kick-up; old top; aqua;
8¾" **4.00-8.00**

Vinol; *Private Mold Pat April 18,1898* under bottom;
amber; 6½" **6.00-8.00**

Violin, plain back; different colors & sizes **8.00-10.00**

Violin, label; plain back; different colors &
sizes **15.00-20.00**

Violin, label; amber; 8½" **15.00-25.00**

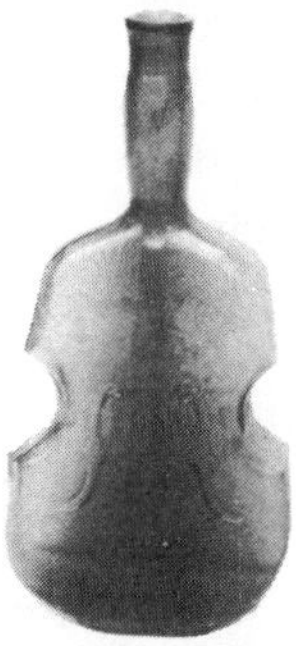

**Violin, label; music score on back pon-
til; different colors; 9¾", $10.00-15.00**

Violin; in back; musical score; plain bottom; many colors;
various sizes. **6.00-10.00**

Walkers Kilmarnook Whiskey 1807; on bottom; square;
square band and ring; *ABM;* emerald green;
10¼" **4.00-8.00**

Walters & Co. Baltimore; on back base; amber;
11¾" . . . .**25.00 +**

Walters Brothers & Co.; *115-6-7 Front Street, San Francisco;* red; quart. **75.00-100.00**

Warranted; flask; dark amber and golden amber; pint or
½ pint. **4.00-8.00**

Warranted; flask; light aqua; pint and ½ pint. .**3.00-6.00**

Warranted; flask; side bands; double band collar; amber;
pint and ½ pint. **4.00-8.00**

Warranted; flask; side bands; double band collar;
amethyst; pint and ½ pint. **4.00-8.00**

Louis Weber, Louisville, KY; *H.W.M. Colly & Co. Pittsburg* under bottom; 3-part mold; olive; 10". . . .**25.00 +**

Edward Weiss; *leading West End Liquor House; corner
of West and Calvert, Annapolis, Md.;* ring top; clear
or aqua; 6". **4.00-6.00**

West Bend Old Timers Lager Beer; label; aqua;
9¼". **2.00-4.00**

West End Wine & Spirits Co.; *Full Qt.
Registered* on back; amber; 12¼",
$60.00-90.00

Ferdinand Westheimer & Sons, Cincinnati, USA; in circle; rectangular; graduated collar and ring; amber; ½
pint **3.00-4.00**

Ferdinand Westheimer & Sons; amber; 6". . .**6.00-8.00**

Ferdinand Westheimer & Sons; amber;
9½". **10.00-15.00**

W.F. & S.; under bottom; aqua; 9½". **2.00-4.00**

Wharton's Whiskey; *Witter Glass Work Glasboro N.J.*
under bottom; amber; 10". **200.00-400.00**

**Whiskey decanter; inlaid with silver;
crystal glass; clear or aqua; 11¼",
$8.00-15.00**

Whiskey; ½ barrel shape; in front a rooster in center; in
1¾" x 2¾" panel *A Merry Christmas and a Happy
New Year;* in center of panel *M.C. & H.N.Y.* and a
woman in an old dress holding a glass while sitting
on barrel; ½ pint; 1¾" neck; 4" body. .**20.00-30.00**

Whiskey; ribs on shoulder and bottom; clear or amethyst;
fifth. **4.00-6.00**

Whiskey; ribs on shoulder and bottom; clear or amethyst;
fifth; 4½". **6.00-8.00**

Whiskey, plain; 3¼" round; 4½" body tapering to a blob
neck 4¼"; ring around top and bottom of body with
plain seal on shoulder; amber; quart. . . .**12.00-20.00**

Whiskey, plain; side strap or shoe fly, Union oval; light
green, clear or amber; ½ pint. **6.00-12.00**

same as above except pint. **6.00-12.00**

same as above except quart. **6.00-12.00**

Whiskey, plain; turn mold; emerald green; quart;
11¼". **8.00-12.00**

Whiskey, plain, with ribbed shoulder; various numbers
under bottom; clear or amethyst; quart. . . .**2.00-4.00**

same as above except pint. **2.00-4.00**

Whiskey, plain, with ribbed shoulder; with various
numbers under bottom; amber pint. **4.00-8.00**

same as above except quart. **4.00-8.00**

Whiskey, plain; turn mold; kick-up; pontil; light olive;
11½" tall, 2½" diameter. **10.00-16.00**

Whiskey, plain; 3-piece mold; round; amethyst;
11". **4.00-6.00**

Whiskey, plain; round; tapered shoulder; amethyst;
9⅞". **2.00-4.00**

Whiskey, plain; green; fifth. **8.00-12.00**

**Whiskey, label; sheared top; also pewter
top; clear; 6", $6.00 +**

Whiskey, label; aqua; 6½". **6.00-10.00**

Whiskey, label; milk glass; sheared top; 8". .**10.00-15.00**

Whiskey, label; seal on shoulder; *H999* on bottom; 11½"
tall, 2½" diameter. **6.00-8.00**

Whiskey, label; 3-part mold; whittle mark; a dot on bottom; aqua; 11½" tall, 3" diameter. **6.00-10.00**

Whiskey, label; clear or amethyst; 8". **2.00-6.00**

Whiskey, label; small kick-up; turn mold; red amber;
10½". **3.00-6.00**

Whiskey, label; clear or amethyst; ½ pint. . . .**2.00-6.00**

Whiskey, label; shallow kick-up; turn mold; amber;
8¼". **6.00-10.00**

Whiskey, label; amber; 6¼". **2.00-6.00**

Whiskey, label; clear; 10" tall, 4" diameter. . . .**3.00-6.00**

Whiskey, label; 3-part mold; clear or amethyst;
11". **4.00-6.00**

Whiskey, label; sample; *B* on bottom; amber;
4". **2.00-4.00**

Whiskey, label; sample; round; amber; 4½". . .**2.00-4.00**

Whiskey, label; sample; amber; 4½". **2.00-4.00**

Whiskey, label; sample; round; amber; 5". **4.00-6.00**

Whiskey, label; sample; round; amber; 4⅞". . .**2.00-4.00**

Whiskey, label; sample; round; *#4* on bottom; amber;
5½". **2.00-4.00**

Whiskey, label; press glass; clear or amethyst;
6½". **4.00-6.00**

Whiskey, label; amber; 10". **10.00-20.00**

Whiskey, label; 2 stars under bottom; clear;
6½". **2.00-4.00**

Whiskey, label; sample; kick-up; amber; 4½". .**4.00-6.00**

Whiskey, label; sample; amber; 3¾". **2.00-4.00**

Whiskey, label; sample; 3-part mold; dark amber; 5¾" **4.00-6.00**

Whiskey, label; sample; dark amber; 5¼" **2.00-4.00**

Whiskey, label; sample; *B* under bottom; dark amber; 5¾" **2.00-4.00**

Whiskey, label; sample; kick-up; light amber; 5⅛" **4.00-6.00**

Whiskey, label; turn mold; small kick-up; dark amber; 10" tall, 3½" diameter **6.00-8.00**

Whiskey, label; machine made; amber; 6¾" . . .**2.00-4.00**

Whiskey or bitters, label; amber; 9" **8.00-15.00**

Whiskey, label; brown crock; 6½", $6.00-8.00

Whiskey, label; sample; amber; 5½" **4.00-6.00**

Whiskey, label; amber; 9" **3.00-5.00**

Whiskey, label; amber; quart **4.00-6.00**

Whiskey, label; diamond shape with # under bottom; amber; 5" **2.00-4.00**

Whiskey, sample or medicine; clear; 3" **2.00-4.00**

Whiskey, label; 2 dots under bottom; amber; 4" **2.00-3.00**

Whiskey, label; sample; sheared top; 4" **3.00-6.00**

Whiskey, label; light gold; 6½" **2.00-6.00**

Whiskey, label; amber; 12" **3.00-8.00**

Whiskey or bitters, label; nine rings top and bottom; graphite pontil; amber **50.00-75.00**

Whiskey, decanter; *E.B. & Co. Lp Reg. No 709209 1886* under bottom; 7" **8.00-10.00**

Whiskey, decanter, label; clear; 10" **10.00-20.00**

Whiskey, decanter, label; *1 Qt.* on shoulder; clear or amethyst . . . .**20.00 +**

Whiskey, decanter; painted with gold and other colors; 10½", $40.00-60.00

Whiskey, label; olive; 3½" **15.00-25.00**

Whiskey, label; dark green; 8¼" **40.00-70.00**

Whiskey, label; clear; 3½" **4.00-6.00**

Whiskey, label; pontil; amber; 7¾" **45.00-90.00**

Whiskey, label; pontil; amber; 5½" **25.00-50.00**

Whiskey, label; turn mold; small kick-up; clear; 11½" **2.00-4.00**

Whiskey, label; 3-part mold; olive; 8¾" **8.00-10.00**

Whiskey, label; pontil; aqua; 9" **70.00-90.00**

Whiskey, label; sheared top; clear or amethyst; 9½" **8.00-10.00**

Whiskey, sample; plain; amber; 4½" **2.00-4.00**

Whiskey, sample; plain; clear or amethyst; 3½" **2.00-4.00**

Whiskey, sample; plain; clear; 4¼" **2.00-4.00**

Whiskey, sample; plain; clear; 4½" **2.00-4.00**

Whiskey, sample; plain; clear; 4" **2.00-4.00**

Whiskey, sample; plain; *506* under bottom; olive; 3¾" **2.00-4.00**

Whiskey, sample; plain; *506* under bottom; amber; 3½" **2.00-4.00**

Whiskey, sample; plain; clear; 3¾" **2.00-4.00**

Whiskey, sample; plain; seal; clear; 3¾" **4.00-6.00**

Whiskey, sample; plain; *2* under bottom; clear; 3¾" **4.00-6.00**

Whiskey, sample; plain *5* under bottom; clear; 4½" **4.00-6.00**

Whiskey, sample; plain; clear; 3¾" **2.00-4.00**

White Rye; label; clear or amethyst; 11¾" **2.00-6.00**

William Whiteley Leith; *Reuse of Bottle Prohibited* in back; *Whiteleys Leith Scotch Whiskey;* applied top; aqua; 8½" **15.00-35.00**

same as above except double ring top . . .**8.00-20.00**

Wine, decanter; clear; 8¼" **4.00-8.00**

Wine, decanter; leather cover; Italy machine made; lion head with ring in mouth; 2 small lion heads, $8.00-12.00

Wine, label; cobalt; 12" . . . .**35.00 +**

Wine, label; amber; 4" **8.00-10.00**

Wine, label; clear or amethyst; 11" **4.00-8.00**

Wine, label; aqua; 12" **10.00-15.00**

Wine label (fish); French wine; aqua; 11", $20.00-30.00

Wine, label; also with wicker; green; 9" **1.00-2.00**

Wine tester; turn mold; green; 8½" **4.00-8.00**

Wine, label; clear; 11" **2.00-4.00**

Wine, label; kick-up; aqua; 7¼" **2.00-4.00**

Wine, label; kick-up; clear; 4" **4.00-6.00**

Wine, label; *WT* under bottom; carnival glass;
10½" **4.00-6.00**

Wine, label; machine made; clear; 8" **2.00-4.00**

Wine, label; 200 to 300 yrs. old; pontil; blue green; 5½"
tall, 3½" diameter **50.00-75.00**

Wine, label; 3-part mold; kick-up; pontil; whittle mark;
light green; 14½" tall; 5" x 4" **18.00-35.00**

Wine, label; kick-up; olive; 13" **2.00-6.00**

Wine, label; very crude; free blown; kick-up; olive;
11½" **8.00-15.00**

Wine, label; pontil; small kick-up; light aqua;
9¾" **8.00-15.00**

Wine, label; small kick-up; amber; 11¼" **4.00-6.00**

Wine, label; aqua; 7¼" **3.00-6.00**

Wine, label; small kick-up; turn mold; dark green;
12" **2.00-6.00**

Wine, label; pontil; double collar; olive green;
9" **25.00-60.00**

Wine, plain; lady's leg; kick-up; light green body 7"; neck
6½" **35.00-75.00**

Wine, plain; turn mold; olive green; 8", 9½" or
11½" **2.00-4.00**

Wine, plain; turn mold; green; 9¾" or
11¼" **2.00-4.00**

Wine, plain, turn mold; jade green; 9¾" or
11¼" **2.00-4.00**

Wine, plain; *P* on bottom; 3-part mold; aqua;
12" **2.00-6.00**

Wine, plain; turn mold; aqua; 12½" **2.00-4.00**

A.J. Wintle & Son; *Pint Imperial* on shoulder; dark olive;
8" **4.00-10.00**

W.M.; in circle on shoulder; *Whyle & MacKay* on back;
3-part mold; aqua; 8¾" **4.00-8.00**

Wolters Brothers & Co.; *115-6 Front Street, San Francisco;* red, quart **40.00-60.00**

Wood Pollard & Co/Boston, Mass; slanted on front
lower left to upper right; *Full Quart* on front; blob
seal on back; round; bulbous neck; graduated collar
and ring; amethyst; 12½" **6.00-10.00**

Wormer Bros., San Francisco; embossed vertically;
flask; clear **15.00-20.00**

Wormer Bros.; in semicircle; *San Francisco* in horizontal
lines; flask; clear **50.00-100.00**

same as above except *S.F.* instead of *San
Francisco* **15.00-20.00**

Wormer Bros., San Francisco; *Fine Old Cognac;* double
rolled collar; flask; amber **80.00-90.00**

Wormer Bros., S.F.; *Fine Old Cognac 1872;* double rolled collar; flask; amber **80.00-90.00**

Wood Pollard & Co/Boston, Mass; slanted on front
lower left to upper right; *Full Quart* on front; blob
seal on back: round; bulbous neck; graduated collar
and ring; amethyst; 12½" **6.00-10.00**

Wormer Bros., San Francisco; embossed vertically;
flask; clear **15.00-20.00**

Wormer Bros.; in semicircle; *San Francisco* in horizontal
lines; flask; clear **50.00-100.00**

same as above except *S.F.* instead of *San
Francisco* **15.00-20.00**

Wormer Bros., San Francisco; *Fine Old Cognac;* double
rolled collar; flask; amber **80.00-90.00**

Wormer Bros., S.F.; *Fine Old Cognac 1872;* double rolled collar; flask; amber **80.00-90.00**

Wright & Taylor Distillers Louisville, KY; in large letters
on one side on shoulder; *Full Quart Registered* on
opposite side; large base; round; graduated collar
and ring; amber; 9" **5.00-10.00**

Wright & Taylor; *Full Quart Registered on back; A B Co.*
under bottom; amber; 10½" **8.00-12.00**

Wyeth & Bro.; saddle flask; amber; 7½" **4.00-8.00**

John Wyeth & Bro.; amber; 9" **6.00-8.00**

Jno. Wyeth & Bro.; amber; 9" **6.00-8.00**

Xeres; in seal on shoulder; dip mold; applied ring; kick
up; olive green, 10½" **40.00-60.00**

Ye Old Mossroff Bourbon; label on panel; *R.S. Roehl-
ing, 1 Schutz, Inc. Chicago;* cabin shape; amber;
9½" **8.00-12.00**

Zeller Schwarze Katz; on base in center; *Golden Cat* on
round base; under bottom *AC* and misc. numbers;
machine made; green; 13¼" **8.00-10.00**

same as above except a monkey wrapped around
bottle **8.00-10.00**

Zwack; label sea; *Zwack* around shoulder; each letter in
a flower; amber; 4¼" **8.00-10.00**

Food

Milk in the nineteenth century was not hidden from the public in plastic gallon jugs or shrouded behind cardboard container walls. Catsup did not come in tiny individual squeeze packages. Milk, pickles and condiments were all bottled in glass. While a large portion of bottles manufactured today are for containing food, the burgeoning plastic industry is replacing many of them.

Peppersauce bottles were fashioned in the shape of a Gothic cathedral with arches and windows on each side. The connection between the peppersauce and the cathedral design is not apparent; most were manufactured between 1860 and 1890, and the earlier bottles are pontil scarred. These bottles came in shades of green, while tomato sauce bottles appeared in clear glass.

Mustard jars came in a variety of shapes. Differences include varying numbers of rings around the jar and differing sizes of jar mouths. Colors used were the practical, easy-to-produce bottle green or clear.

Older mustard jars have pontil scars, and some are embossed, as are some chili sauce bottles. One chili sauce bottle bears a Maltese cross.

Cooking oil bottles were tall and slim in shape; most were produced after 1890. A few are embossed, though most embossing was dropped at the turn of the century because paper labels were much cheaper.

Though round bottles traveled better in shipments because they could withstand more pressure, pickle or chutney bottles resisted the laws of physics and were large and square in shape. Spice bottles, too, could not travel exceptionally well due to their concave front and back panels. Both the early pickle and spice bottles have pontil scars.

Worcestershire sauce, originally made in Worcester, England, was a common flavoring in demand by household gourmets in the last century. The sauce bottles are quite common and easy to find, particularly the Lea and Perrins brand. Most are in shades of green.

Henry J. Heinz began to manufacture "good things for the table" in 1869. The company began production on a small scale; the goal was to give consumers confidence in the purity of foods not preserved in the home. One innovation was to use clear glass to show that there were no impurities in the product. The company's first bottled product was horseradish. It was a success, and the company began to bottle catsup in 1889. Both products are seen in familiar bottles in supermarkets today.

Before effective glass packaging techniques, milk came directly from the family cow or from a churn or milkcan. A Brooklyn milkman was reported to have been delivering milk in bottles to the steady customers on his route as early as 1878. The ancestor of the present-day milk bottle was not invented, however, until 1884 by Dr. Harvey D. Thatcher, a druggist in Potsdam, New York. Thatcher's first milk bottle was embossed with a Quaker farmer milking his cow while seated on a three-legged stool. The words "Absolutely Pure Milk" were tamped into the glass on the bottle's shoulder. Today, waxed cardboard and plastic containers have largely replaced glass milk bottles.

The Abner Royce Co.; *The Abner Royce Co. Pure Fruit Flavor, Cleveland, Ohio* in back; clear; 5¼" **2.00-6.00**

The Abner Royce Co.; aqua; 5½" **3.00-6.00**

A.E.B.B., Pure Olive, Depose France; aqua; 10" **2.00-3.00**

A.G. 5 & Co.; *4-Patented April 5, 1898;* clear; quart **40.00-60.00**

Alart & McGuire Trademark "OK" Pickles; amber; 7" **6.00-8.00**

Alart & McGuire N.Y.; under bottom; aqua; 5" **4.00-6.00**

Alexis Godillot Jeune; *Bordeaux* on back panel; 8 panels; green; 6¼" **8.00-14.00**

American Grocery Co. Pat App. For N.Y.; under bottom; clear; 10" **2.00-8.00**

Anchor; screw top; clear or amethyst; quart; 9" **30.00-45.00**

The A-1 Sauce; aqua; 7¾" **4.00-6.00**

The A-1 Sauce; aqua; 11" **4.00-6.00**

Armour and Company, Chicago; in 4 lines on cathedral type panels; round corner; lady's leg neck; milk glass; 5¼" **6.00-12.00**

Armour & Co. Packers, Chicago; under bottom; milk glass; 2¼" **2.00-3.00**

Armour & Co.; aqua; 4" **2.00-4.00**

Armour & Co.; milk glass; 5¼" **8.00-20.00**

Armour's Top Notch Brand, Chicago; under bottom; clear or amethyst; 5¾" **2.00-3.00**

A-10; under bottom; clear or amethyst; 8" **2.00-4.00**

Babblin Brook; milk bottle; clear; pint **2.00-4.00**

Baby Top; two-face milk bottle; *Brookfield* on other side; *1 qt. liquid 2 Reg. Sealed 157* on base; clear **15.00-35.00**

Baker's; aqua; 4¾", $2.00-4.00

Baker's Flavoring Extracts, Baker Extracts Co.; on one side *Strength & Purity;* on the other side *Full Measure;* machine made; clear **1.00-2.00**

Banquiet Brand Charles Gulden. N.Y.; on slug plate; flared lip; amethyst; 5⅛" **3.00-4.00**

Barrel mustard, plain; 2 rings on top, 3 on bottom; amethyst or clear; 4½" **2.00-3.00**

Barrel mustard, plain; 3 rings on top and bottom; clear or amethyst; 4½" **2.00-3.00**

B.B.G.Co. 326; under bottom; clear or amethyst; 8" **1.00-2.00**

B.B.G.Co. 78; on bottom; clear or amethyst; 7½" **2.00-3.00**

B & Co. Ld. B, 13; under bottom; aqua; 8½" . **2.00-3.00**

B C Co.; clear or amethyst; 4½" **3.00-6.00**

Becker's Pure Horse-Radish, Buffalo; aqua; 4¼" **4.00-8.00**

B.F.B. Co. 109 2845; on bottom; aqua; 8" **2.00-3.00**

B & FB Co. 2445; under bottom; aqua; 8" **2.00-3.00**

Bireley's Trademark Reg. Hollwood, Cal.; milk bottle; clear; 5¼" **4.00-6.00**

Bishop & Company; under bottom; clear or amethyst; 5½" **4.00-6.00**

Bishop & Company; on bottom; fourteen vertical panels; ring at base; catsup; amethyst; 9¾" **2.00-4.00**

same as above except 7⅝" **2.00-4.00**

A. Booth & Co. Balt.; label; *Oyster Cocktail Catsup Salad Dressing* under bottom; clear or amethyst; 7½" **2.00-4.00**

same as above except 6" **10.00-15.00**

Bordens Condensed Milk Co.; milk glass; clear or amethyst; 4½" **4.00-8.00**

Breast pump; sheared top; clear; 4" **2.00-6.00**

H.B. Brooks; amber; 10¼", $40.00-65.00

same as above except clear **4.00-10.00**

B-33; on bottom; aqua; 5" **1.00-2.00**

Burnett's Standard Flavoring Extracts; in sunken panel; aqua; 5¼" **2.00-3.00**

Burnett's Standard Flavoring Extracts; long neck; medicine bottle type; clear or amethyst; 4½" **1.00-2.00**

same as above except 5⅝" **1.00-2.00**

BWCA; in monogram; 8 panels; clear or amethyst; 10" **4.00-8.00**

Joseph Campbell Preserve Co.; clear or amethyst; 8" **2.00-4.00**

Candy Bros. Mfg. Co. Confectioners; label; aqua; 12", $8.00-15.00

Cannon bottle; amber or olive; 9½" **20.00-30.00**

Caper, plain; green; 6½" **6.00-8.00**

same as above except machine made **2.00-3.00**

Caper bottles; several different sizes and colors; some embossed, some not **6.00-12.00**

Capers; 8 indented panels in neck; 2-ring top; 3 sizes **8.00-18.00**

Don Carlos cylinder; *Pat. June 19, 1894 N.Y.* under bottom; clear; 5¼" **4.00-8.00**

Carnation's Fresh Milk; *Chicago Sealed 1 qt.;* milk bottle; amber **1.00-2.00**

Cathedral pickle, label; light blue; 9½" **15.00-20.00**

Cathedral; ground pontil; blue green; 8½" **50.00-150.00**

Catsup, plain; clear or amethyst; 7½" **1.00-2.00**

Catsup; 10 panels; amethyst or clear; 8" or 9¾" **2.00-4.00**

Catsup; 10 panels; top and bottom panels alternate; clear or amethyst; 10" **2.00-4.00**

Catsup; 2 mid-sections; 10 panels; clear or amethyst; 8" **3.00-5.00**

Catsup, plain; tapered body; ring at shoulder; tapered neck; ring top; clear, amethyst; 7½" **3.00-6.00**

Catsup, plain; clear or amethyst; 10" tall; 2½" diameter **4.00-6.00**

Catsup, label; *1600* on bottom; clear or amethyst; 10" **1.00-2.00**

Catsup, label; clear or amethyst; 9¾" **3.00-6.00**

Catsup, plain; clear or amethyst; 9" **3.00-5.00**

Catsup, plain; clear or amethyst; 8½" **4.00-6.00**

Catsup, label; *403* on bottom; clear or amethyst; 7½" **2.00-3.00**

Catsup, label; aqua; 8", $3.00-6.00

Catsup, plain; clear or amethyst; 8½" **3.00-6.00**

Catsup, label; clear or amethyst; 10½" **4.00-6.00**

Catsup, label; swirl design; clear or amethyst; 8" **4.00-6.00**

Catsup, label; *10F* under bottom; clear or amethyst **4.00-6.00**

Catsup, label; clear; 9½" **2.00-4.00**

Catsup and preserve bottles; embossed **2.00-4.00**

C B B; under bottom; aqua; 8" **6.00-8.00**

C.B.K; and *1233* on bottom; aqua; 7¼" **2.00-3.00**

C B W; under bottom; clear or amethyst; 10¼" **4.00-6.00**

C & D; under bottom; aqua; 7¾" . . . . **8.00 +**

Central Mfg. Company; clear or amethyst; 5" **2.00-4.00**

Champagne Catsup; round; screw top; amethyst or clear; 7½" **3.00-5.00**

Champagne Catsup; applied top; one ring; amethyst; 9¾" **3.00-5.00**

Champion Vermont Maple Syrup; label; clear or amethyst; 8½", $3.00-6.00

Champion's Vinegar; aqua; 14½" **10.00-40.00**

Champion's Vinegar; aqua; 15½" **15.00-25.00**

R.C. Chances Sons, Table Talk Ketchup, Phila; label; clear or amethyst; 9¼" **4.00-6.00**

Cherry, label; *B* under bottom; clear; 4½" **1.00-2.00**

Cherry, plain; *33* and a star on bottom; clear or amethyst; 6¼" **2.00-4.00**

Cherry pickle, plain; clear or amethyst; 6" **2.00-3.00**

The C.I. Co. Ltd; *This Tradedmark Registered, Maple Sap & Boiled Cider Vinegar;* on front, *East Ridge, NH;* 3 rings near base; flint shoulder; tapered neck and ring top; cobalt; 11½" **15.00-30.00**

The J.M. Clark Pickle Co. Louisville, Ky.; round; clear; 5" **4.00-10.00**

N.L. Clark & Co. Peruvian Syrup; aqua; 8½" **4.00-8.00**

Condiment; plain milk bottle type; clear or amethyst; 6½" **2.00-3.00**

same as above except vase type bottle; 4" **2.00-3.00**

Cottage Cheese; 10 panels; clear or amethyst; 4½" **4.00-6.00**

Courtenay & Co.; *A & P* under bottom; clear or amethyst; 7" **4.00-6.00**

Courtenay & Co.; clear or amber; 7" **2.00-4.00**

C.R.B.; under bottom; label; aqua; 8" **2.00-4.00**

Crown; under bottom; pickle label; 14" . . . .**20.00+**

Cruikshank Bros & Co.; *Allegheny Pa.* under bottom; clear or amethyst; 8" **2.00-3.00**

C.S. & Co. LD5302; on bottom; 8 panels; aqua; 6½" **2.00-6.00**

Curtice Brothers Co.; *1613* under bottom; clear or amethyst; 8" tall, 2¼" round **2.00-4.00**

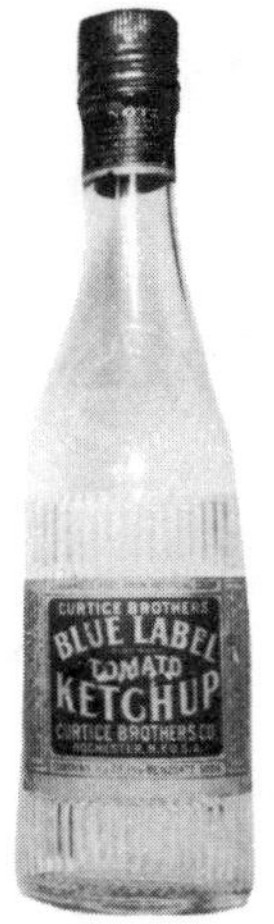

Curtice Bros.; machine made; clear or amethyst; 10", $2.00-4.00

Curtice Bros. Co.; *Preserves* on the shoulders; ridges all around; round; amethyst or clear; 7¼" **2.00-4.00**

Curtice Brothers Co. Preserves Rochester, NY; in circle on tapered neck; 8", 10½" or 12¼" . .**2.00-6.00**

Curtis Bros. Preserves; clear; 10½" or 12½" **8.00-10.00**

George M. Curtis, Pure Olive Oil; clear; 17" . .**2.00-4.00**

Geo M. Curtis, Pure Olive Oil; slim; round . . .**1.00-2.00**

Curtis & Moore; clear or amethyst; 10" tall, 2¼" x 2¼" **6.00-10.00**

Davis OK Baking Powder; round; aqua; 4½" **2.00-4.00**

Dawson's Pickles; 10 panels; clear or amethyst; 7½" **2.00-4.00**

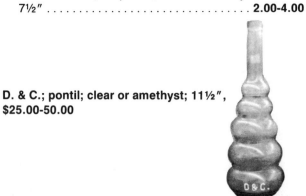

D. & C.; pontil; clear or amethyst; 11½", $25.00-50.00

D & Co.; mustard; clear or amethyst; 4½" **2.00-3.00**

Dixie; under bottom; clear; 7¾" **2.00-6.00**

Dodson & Hils Mfg Co.; aqua; 8" **2.00-4.00**

Dundee; gray **6.00-8.00**

J. Dupit Bordeaux Elixir De Soulac Les Bains; amber; 3" **10.00-20.00**

A. Durant & Fils Bordeaux; round; aqua and blue; 7⅛" **2.00-4.00**

same as above except no embossing; fancy **2.00-4.00**

E.R. Durkee & Co., N.Y.; pontil; aqua; 4½" **10.00-20.00**

E.R. Durkee & Co. Challenge Sauce; sample; amethyst; 4" **4.00-6.00**

E.R. Durkee & Co. Salad Dressing, N.Y.; vertically; *Bottle Patented April 17, 1877* on bottom; round; amethyst; 6½" **1.00-3.00**

E.R. Durkee & Co. N.Y.; round; screw top; amethyst; 3½" **1.00-2.00**

E.R. Durkee & Co., Salad Dressing, N.Y.; round shoulder; *Patented April 17, 1877* on the bottom; round; clear; 4½" or 7¾" **1.00-2.00**

E.R. Durkee & Co., New York; in vertical lines; clear or amethyst; 5", 6¾" or 8¼" **2.00-3.00**

E.R. Durkee and Co.; sheared top; 8 panels; clear or amethyst; 4" **4.00-8.00**

E.R. Durkee & Co.; clear or amethyst; 6" **3.00-6.00**

E.R. Durkee & Co.; clear or amethyst; 7" **3.00-4.00**

E.R. Durkee & Co.; clear or amethyst; 4" tall; 1½" diameter **2.00-6.00**

E.E. Dyer & Co. Extract of Coffee, Boston Mass; graphite pontil; green; 6" **25.00-50.00**

E.H.V.B.; graphite pontil; 6 panels; light blue; 9½" **25.00-50.00**

Eiffel Tower Lemonade; *G. Foster Clark & Co. Manufacturer* on opposite side; clear; 2¾" **3.00-4.00**

Charles Ellis Son & Co. Phila; aqua; 6" **2.00-4.00**

Eno's Fruit Salt; *W* on bottom; 7" tall, 1½" x 2½", $4.00-8.00

Eskay's; *pat. J11-93 Albumenized 163 Food* on bottom; sheared top; amber; 7½" **4.00-8.00**

Eskay's; *pat July 93 Albumenized 179 Food* on bottom; machine made; amber; 7½" **2.00-4.00**

Evangeline Peppersauce; *Made in St. Martinville, La. U.S.A.* on one side panel; 12 panels; tiny screw top; 5¼" **2.00-3.00**

Extract Tabasco; under bottom; clear; 4¾" . . .**2.00-3.00**

F; in center of bottle; refined pontil; clear; 5" . .**4.00-8.00**

Fancy Olive Oil; small base with 5 rings; 6 rings at shoulder; long bulbous neck; aqua; 7" . . .**8.00-10.00**

F.G.W.; under bottom; clear; 7¾" **4.00-6.00**

J.A. Folger & Co.; *Golden Gate High Grade Flavoring Extracts 2 oz Full Measure* on front panel; rectangular; amethyst; 5½" **2.00-3.00**

Folgers Golden Gate Flavoring; on panel; rectangular; amethyst; 5¼" **1.00-2.00**

Forbes Delicious Flavoring Extracts; *Made By Forbes Bros. & Co. St. Louis* on front panel; rectangular; clear; 4¾" **1.00-2.00**

4N; under bottom; clear or amethyst; 9¾" **2.00-4.00**

The Frank Tea & Spice Co.; machine made; clear; 5½" **2.00-4.00**

Frank Tea & Spice Co, Cincinnati O.; *Jumbo Peanut Butter, Made from No 1 Spanish and No 1 Va. Peanuts, Salt Added, 5 oz;* embossed head of elephant; round ridges on bottle; clear **1.00-2.00**

Louit Freres & Co. Bordeaux; mustard barrel; 3 rings at base and shoulder; crude ring collar; open pontil; amethyst; 4¾" **4.00-8.00**

same as above except graphite pontil **4.00-10.00**

G.A.J.; under bottom; sheared top; 7" **2.00-4.00**

Garretts Food Products; *Garrett & Co. Inc. Monticello, N.Y., St. Louis Est. U.S. Pat. Off.;* round; green; 10½" and 12⅛" **4.00-8.00**

Gebhardt Eagle; on the side panel; *Chile powder* on the opposite panel; *Eagle* embossed on the front with *Trademark;* screw top; rectangular; clear or amethyst; 3½" or 5½" **2.00-4.00**

The M.A. Gedrey Pickling Co.; aqua; 9¼" . . .**4.00-6.00**

Gibbs; *B* on bottom; clear or amethyst; 8¼", $2.00-3.00

Goldberg-Bowen & Co.; *Sierra Madre Olive Oil San Francisco, Cal;* shaped like a gin bottle; flared collar; bulbous type neck; amethyst; quart; 11¼" **3.00-4.00**

Golden Tree Pure Syrup; crown top; aqua; 11¼" **2.00-4.00**

The Graduated Nursing Bottle; clear; 6¾" . .**8.00-15.00**

Grape juice, plain; aqua; 6" **2.00-4.00**

Grapette Products Co. Camden Ark.; under bottom; *ABM;* clear; 7¼" **2.00-4.00**

Grary & Co.; stag head on shoulder; *Worcestershire Sauce* on side; a stag on neck; clear or amethyst **4.00-6.00**

Charles Gulden; clear or amethyst; 4¾" **2.00-4.00**

Chas. Gulden, New York; on bottom; pickle jar; 4 large bulbous rings; flared collar; clear; 5½" **3.00-6.00**

Chas. Gulden; *16* under bottom; aqua or clear; 8½" **6.00-8.00**

Chas. Gulden, New York; 4 rings on base; 3 on shoulder; mustard barrel; amethyst; 4⅝" **3.00-4.00**

Chas. Gulden, N.Y.; under bottom; clear; 4¼", $2.00-6.00

Chas. Gulden, N.Y.; under bottom; clear or amethyst; 4¼" **2.00-4.00**

H; under bottom; clear; 4½" **2.00-6.00**

Halford Leigestershine; aqua; 7⅛" **2.00-3.00**

Hananc; aqua; 6" **2.00-4.00**

Thomas L. Hardin Co.; clear or amethyst; 7" **3.00-6.00**

Geo Harm; *This Bottle To Be Washed and Returned, Not To Be Bought or Sold* on back; clear; quart **8.00-12.00**

H.J. Heinze Co. No. 37 Gothic Horseradish; aqua; 6" **2.00-4.00**

H.J. Heinze Co.; on bottom; also large notch on bottom; 18 panels; round; clear; 8¾" **2.00-5.00**

H.J. Heinz Co.; patent on the bottom; 8 panels; amethyst; 9¼" **2.00-4.00**

H.J. Heinz Co. 69 Patd.; under bottom; clear; 6", $4.00-6.00

H.J. Heinz Co.; *122 Patd* under bottom; 10 panels; clear or amethyst; 4¾" **2.00-4.00**

H.J. Heinze Co.; *7 Patented* and an *X* on bottom; clear or amethyst; 8¼" **4.00-8.00**

Heinz; clear or amethyst; 6" **3.00-6.00**

Heinz; *No. 28* under bottom; aqua; 7¼" **2.00-3.00**

Heisey Relish; label; 8 panels; lead glass; clear or amethyst; 4" **4.00-8.00**

Herb Juice; on panel; rectangular; clear; 8⅜" **2.00-4.00**

Hill's; label; machine made; *L.B. Co.* monogram on back; aqua; 11" **8.00-12.00**

Hires Improved Root Beer; panel *Mfg. by The Charles Hires Co.;* panel, *Philadelphia Pa. U.S.A.;* panel, *Make Five Gallons of a Delicious Drink;* aqua; 4¾" **3.00-6.00**

Holbrook & Co.; *P.B.* on bottom; aqua; 7½" . . **3.00-4.00**

Holbrook & Co.; aqua; 4½" **8.00-12.00**

Holbrook & Co.; *R.B.B.* under bottom; aqua; 8¾" **8.00-10.00**

Honey; clear or amethyst; 8" **5.00-8.00**

Honeywell; sauce type bottle; rolled lip; concave panels; front and back; 3 concave on sides; open pontil; aqua; 6¾" **6.00-8.00**

Horlick's Trademark, Racine, Wis., Malted Milk M.M. U.S.A. 1 Gal.; round; clear; 10¾" **1.00-3.00**

Horlick's; twice on shoulders; round; screw top; clear; 2¾" **1.00-2.00**

Horlick's; clear or amethyst; 5" **2.00-4.00**

Horlick's; aqua; different sizes **2.00-4.00**

Horton-Cato Mfg Co, Detroit, Mich; in 3 lines; 3 round panels; on bottom *T.P.;* clear; 5½" **2.00-6.00**

Horton-Cato Co.; clear; 7" **3.00-6.00**

Horton-Cato & Co., Detroit; reverse side *Crown Celery Salt;* **gold; 8",** **$15.00-25.00**

Horton-Cato Mfg. Co., Detroit, Mich; under bottom; clear; 6" **3.00-6.00**

J.W. Hunnewell & Co.; on side; *Boston* on opposite side; 3 concave panels; aqua; 1½" **4.00-6.00**

same as above except aqua green **4.00-6.00**

H.W. P. 394; under bottom; sheared top; clear; 6" **6.00-8.00**

Hyman Pickle Co., Louisville, Ky; under bottom; yellow; 8" **6.00-10.00**

India Packing Co., Portland, Org.; moon in center; aqua; 6" **10.00-20.00**

Jelly, label; *Patented June 9-03 June 23 03* under bottom; clear; 3½" **2.00-3.00**

Jelly, label *2* under bottom; clear or amethyst; 4¾" **2.00-4.00**

Jelly, label; sheared top; 2¼" **2.00-4.00**

Jelly, label; *Patented June 9-03 June 23 03* under bottom; clear or amethyst; 2½" **2.00-4.00**

Joslyn's Maple Syrup; 8 sides; ground lip; aqua; 8" **5.00-10.00**

J.P.S.; under bottom; clear or amethyst; 7¼" . **2.00-3.00**

J.P.S.; under bottom; pickles; green; 6" **4.00-6.00**

J.P.S.; under bottom; green; 6" **4.00-6.00**

J.P.S.; under bottom; clear or amethyst; 5" . . . **4.00-6.00**

J. Wm Junkins Catsup, Baltimore Md.; clear or amethyst; 8" **8.00-10.00**

Kelloggs; on base; oval; clear; 4¼", 6" or 7" . **1.00-2.00**

Kepler; on 4 sides on shoulder; tapered bottle; ring top; under bottom *Snowhill RW&Co, London;* green; 1¾" x 2¼"; 5¼" tall; 1¼" neck **6.00-10.00**

same except no *Kepler* on shoulder; 7½" tall; 2¼" x 3¼" **10.00-15.00**

Karl Kiefer Pat; in glass lid to fit pickle bottle; round; amethyst or clear; 6" **3.00-4.00**

Kitchen Bouquet; on bottom; round; *ABM;* aqua; 5¾" **2.00-3.00**

LAM A & F; under bottom; green; 9¼" **15.00-35.00**

Lamp candy bottle; aqua; 3" **4.00-8.00**

Lea & Perrins; *J10D,S* on bottom; aqua; 11½" **4.00-6.00**

same as above except 8½" **2.00-4.00**

same as above except 7¼" **2.00-3.00**

Lever Bros. Co. New York; label; amber; 10" **2.00-4.00**

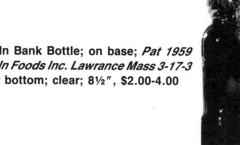

Lincoln Bank Bottle; on base; *Pat 1959* **Lincoln Foods Inc. Lawrance Mass 3-17-3 under bottom; clear; 8½", $2.00-4.00**

Lipton; number on bottom; aqua; 8½" **2.00-6.00**

Joshua Longfield; *North of England Sauce* around shoulder; aqua; 7" **4.00-8.00**

Long Syrup Refining Co., S.F. Ca.; wine color; 4¾" **4.00-8.00**

Lundborg; clear or amethyst; 2½" **2.00-4.00**

E.G. Lyons & Raas Co.; clear or amethyst; 4" **4.00-6.00**

M; under bottom; amber; 6½" **4.00-8.00**

Mander Weaver & Co.; cream crock; 4" **8.00-10.00**

Mansfield Dairy; clear; quart **4.00-10.00**

SGDG Grand Marnier; on back; snap on; machine made; light amber; 6", $6.00-15.00

D. Maurer & Son; under bottom; 3" **1.00-3.00**

F.E. McAllister's; aqua; 7" **3.00-6.00**

McCormick & Co. Spice Grinders, Baltimore; 8 panels; sheared top; clear or amethyst; 3¾" **2.00-4.00**

McCormick & Co., Extracts, Spices & Etc., Baltimore Md.; clear; 4½" **4.00-8.00**

McCormick & Co., Baltimore; triangular; clear; 3½" **3.00-6.00**

McCormick & Co.; clear or amethyst; 4¾" **3.00-6.00**

McCormick & Co.; clear; 5¼" **2.00-4.00**

McCormick & Co.; round; aqua; 5¼" **2.00-6.00**

McIlhenny Co., Avery Island La.; clear or amethyst; 8" **4.00-6.00**

McIlhenny Co., Avery Island La.; swirl pattern; clear; 8" **8.00-12.00**

Mellins Food, Free Sample; *P* on bottom; aqua; 3¾" **2.00-3.00**

Menley-James Limited; *N.Y., London* on bottom; milk glass; 1¾" **1.00-2.00**

Milk bottle; *HA* under bottom; clear, **$2.00-4.00**

Milks' Emulsion; *F.C.W.* under bottom; machine made; amber; 6¼" **2.00-3.00**

Milks' Emulsion; *#1054* under bottom; machine made; amber; 6¼" **2.00-4.00**

M&M; on one line; *T* in center; *Co.* on bottom line; pumpkin seed type bottle; clear; 3¾" **6.00-10.00**

Moutarde Diaphane/Louit Freres & Co.; mustard barrel; 3 rings at base and shoulders; crude ring collar; graphite pontil; amethyst; 5" **6.00-10.00**

same as above except clear **4.00-8.00**

Muskogee Who. Gro. Co.; clear; 8¼" **4.00-6.00**

Mustard, label; clear or amethyst; 4½" **2.00-3.00**

Mustard, label; small kick-up; six-part mold; clear or amethyst; 5½" **2.00-4.00**

Mustard, label; *Patented* under bottom; 12 panels; clear or amethyst; 4¾" **2.00-4.00**

Mustard barrel; plain; 3 rings at top and bottom; sheared top; clear or amethyst; 1¾" round, 4½" tall **4.00-8.00**

same as above except no sheared top **2.00-4.00**

My Wife's Salad Dressing; machine made; blue green; 8" **8.00-10.00**

Bibo Newman & Kenberg; *Bni;* monogram; *San Francisco, Cal;* round; ring collar; clear; 5¼" .. **4.00-8.00**

Nut House; figure of house and other writing; store jar; ball shape; clear **8.00-15.00**

Old Duffy's 1842 5 Year Old Apple Juice Vinegar; on top shoulder; *Duffy's* in diamond shape and *1842* in circle on neck; 8 panels; amber; 6¾" **15.00-30.00**

Olive oil; long neck; ring collar; graphite pontil; light aqua; 12½" **6.00-8.00**

Olive oil, plain; old flared lip; round with tapered neck; aqua; 11¼" **4.00-8.00**

Olive oil, plain; 3-part mold; flat ring top; under bottom, sunken circle; cobalt; 4¼" tapered body, 2½" neck **8.00-12.00**

Olive oil; amber; 1½" round, 6¼" tall, 2½" neck **3.00-4.00**

Olive oil; slim, bulbous neck; clear or aqua; 3 sizes; 7¼" to 12½" **6.00-10.00**

Olive oil, label; aqua; 7½" **2.00-6.00**

Olive oil; aqua; 10¼" **2.00-4.00**

Olive oil; free-blown; pontil; small kick-up; aqua; 10" **8.00-12.00**

Olive oil, label; clear; 6½" **2.00-3.00**

Olive oil, label; kick-up; aqua; 12¾" **6.00-12.00**

Olive oil, label; clear or amethyst; 8" **3.00-4.00**

Olive oil aqua; 10" **3.00-6.00**

Olive oil, label; clear or amethyst; 5½" **2.00-3.00**

Olive oil, label; free-blown; pontil; aqua; 13½" **15.00-20.00**

Olive oil, label; free-blown; pontil; aqua; 10" **10.00-25.00**

Olive oil, label; applied ring top; deep kick-up; aqua; 9½" **4.00-8.00**

J.M. Oliver & Sons; on blob seal; olive oil; aqua; 7" **4.00-8.00**

F.A. Osten's Pure Salad Oil; 8-ring top; long neck; flared bottom; aqua **5.00-10.00**

Parker Bros.; vertically; on shoulder; *London Club Sauce;* crude top; round; aqua; 7¼" **4.00-6.00**

Paskola's, The Pre-Digested Food Co., Trademark; embossed *Pineapple;* amber; 6" **4.00-8.00**

Peppermint; marble in center of neck; aqua; 7¼", $8.00-12.00

Peppersauce; 20 rings around bottle; round; space for label; clear or aqua; 6¼" **6.00-12.00**

Peppersauce; 22 rings around bottle; space for label; oval; clear or aqua; 7" **6.00-12.00**

Peppersauce; cathedral; gothic arch in lower half of 6 panels; 2 windows in upper half of each panel; aqua; 8½" **12.00-18.00**

Peppersauce; clear; 8" **6.00-12.00**

Peppersauce, label; 4¾" **2.00-3.00**

Peppersauce, label; *X* on bottom; aqua; 9" **8.00-12.00**

Peppersauce; clear or amethyst; 6½" tall, 1½" square .... **10.00+**

Peppersauce, label; clear or amethyst; 6½" **1.00-2.00**

Peppersauce, label; aqua; 7" **2.00-6.00**

Peppersauce, label; aqua; 10½" **8.00-12.00**

Peppersauce, label; 24 rings clear; 8¼" **6.00-12.00**

Peppersauce, label; *NYMM* and monogram under bottom; aqua **8.00-15.00**

Peppersauce, label; leaded glass; clear or amethyst; 7¼" **4.00-6.00**

Peppersauce, label; swirl pattern; clear or amethyst; 8½" **4.00-6.00**

Peppersauce; 15 rings; cathedral type; *G.C.O. Pat. Sept 26, 1875* on base; double ring top; aqua; 8½″ **10.00-20.00**

Peppersauce, label; *C & B* on base; clear or amethyst; 7½″ **8.00-15.00**

Peppersauce, label; clear; 12½″ **4.00-6.00**

Peppersauce, label; amber; 7¾″, $10.00-15.00

Peppersauce, label; *D.E.* under bottom; aqua; 8″ **4.00-8.00**

Pepsine Chapoteaut; 10 panels; clear or amethyst; 3½″ **2.00-4.00**

Peptogenic Milk Powder; around shoulder; machine made; tin measure top; amber; 5¾″ **4.00-6.00**

Phoenix Brand; machine made; clear; 6″ **3.00-5.00**

Pickle bottle; cathedral; square; four gothic panels; applied ring and lip; aqua; 11½″ **30.00-50.00**

Pickle; cathedral; cobalt; 5½″; ½″ square . . **25.00-50.00**

Pickle, plain; paneled corner; tapered neck; yellow; 7¼″; 2½″ square **10.00-15.00**

same except no panel; under bottom *Pat Apr 4 1882, Heinz 16* in circle; aqua **2.00-6.00**

Pickel, label; clear or amethyst; 13½″ tall, 3¾″ square **6.00-10.00**

Pickel, label; machine made; *165* under bottom; clear or amethyst; 7″ **2.00-3.00**

Pickle, label; pontil; aqua; 10″ **25.00-35.00**

Pickle, label; broken pontil; aqua; 7¼″, $50.00-85.00

Pickle, label; kick-up; pontil; aqua; 8½″ **10.00-20.00**

Pickle, label; *W.T. & Co.* under bottom; aqua; 6¼″ **1.00-2.00**

Pickel, label; aqua; 8¼″ **2.00-6.00**

Pickle, label; aqua; 6½″ **2.00-4.00**

Pickle, label; green; 11″ **6.00-8.00**

Pickle, label; clear or amethyst; 6¾″ **6.00-10.00**

Pickle, label; small kick-up; aqua; 9″ **4.00-8.00**

Pickle, label; clear or amethyst; 7½″ **2.00-4.00**

Pickel, label; *Patented Aug. 20, 1901* under bottom; clear or amethyst; 7″ **1.00-2.00**

Pickle, label; *Pat Applied For #16* under bottom; clear; 11¼″ **4.00-6.00**

Pickle, label; *Pat July 11th 1893* under bottom; sheared top; clear; 7″ **4.00-6.00**

Pickle, label; *3* under bottom; aqua; 3½″ **4.00-8.00**

Pickle, label; sheared top; clear or amethyst; 5″ **3.00-5.00**

Pickle, label; sheared top; aqua; 12¾″ **25.00-35.00**

Pickle, label; aqua; 10½″ **4.00-6.00**

Pickle, label; clear or amethyst; 5″ **4.00-6.00**

Pickle, label; small kick-up; green; 7½″ **10.00-12.00**

Pickle, label; 8 panels; clear or amethyst; 6½″ **2.00-4.00**

Pickle, label; amber; 6¾″ . . . . **10.00 +**

Pickle, label; clear; 7″, $4.00-6.00

Pickle, label; clear or amethyst; 11″ tall, 2½″ x 3¼″ **4.00-8.00**

Pickle, label; green; 5½″ **2.00-8.00**

Pickle, label; 10 panels; clear or amethyst; 10¼″ **2.00-4.00**

Pickle; *AM* on bottom; clear **2.00-3.00**

Pickle, label; *Pat Apr. 20, 1901* on bottom; clear or amethyst; 8¼″ **2.00-4.00**

Pickle, label; *Pat. O.P. 1900* on bottom; clear or amethyst; 6″ **3.00-6.00**

Pickle, label; sunken bottom; aqua; 9″ tall, 2½″ diameter **2.00-6.00**

Pickle, label; aqua; 8½″ **6.00-10.00**

Pickle, label; pontil; aqua; 9″ **6.00-8.00**

Pickle, label; clear; 4½″ **3.00-4.00**

Pickle, label; broken pontil; aqua; 6½″ **8.00-10.00**

Pickle, label; improved pontil; amber; 10″ . . **30.00-40.00**

Pickle, label; cathedral design; blue green; 13½″ **50.00-75.00**

Pickle, label; sheared top; green; 3¼″ **2.00-5.00**

Pickle, label; small kick-up; amber; 7½″ **8.00-10.00**

Pickle, label; 4 side panels; pontil; aqua; 6¼″ **20.00-30.00**

Pickle, label; green; 8½″ **8.00-10.00**

Pickle, label; *Pat App. For* under bottom; aqua; 9¼″ **6.00-8.00**

Pickle, label; pontil; aqua; 7½″ **8.00-20.00**

Pickle, label; 3-piece mold; light blue; 12″ **4.00-8.00**

Pickle, label; aqua; 9″ **2.00-4.00**

Pickle, label; 10 panels halfway down; small kick-up; aqua; 12″ **4.00-8.00**

Pickle or cherry, label; *Pat. App. For* under bottom; clear or amethyst; 5″ **4.00-6.00**

Pickman's Chocolate; machine made; aqua . . **2.00-4.00**

E.D. Pinaud; aqua; 2¼″ **4.00-8.00**

Pin Money; clear; 5¼″ **4.00-8.00**

Planters; same in back; peanut figures on each corner; glass top with a peanut nob; clear **85.00-150.00**

Planters; same in back; square; glass top with peanut nobs; clear **20.00-50.00**

Planters Salted Peanuts; same in back; glass top with peanut nob; clear **15.00-40.00**

Planters; same in back on base; glass top with peanut nob; clear **15.00-40.00**

Planters; on shoulder; *Pennant 5c Salted Peanuts* on front; on each side a Planters Peanut Man figure; glass top with peanut nob; clear **50.00-100.00**

P/P Co.; under bottom; clear; 5″ tall; 1¾″ diameter **2.00-4.00**

Dr. Price's; clear or amethyst; 5¾″ **2.00-3.00**

Price-Booker Mfg. Co.; clear or amethyst; 8″ **2.00-6.00**

Pride of Long Island; clear or amethyst; 9¾″ **2.00-4.00**

Pompeian Brand Virgin Lucca Olive Oil; in 4 lines; aqua; 7½″ **2.00-4.00**

same as above except other sizes **2.00-6.00**

The Potter Parlin Co.; under bottom; sheared top; clear or amethyst; 4″ **4.00-6.00**

Primrose Salad Oil Western Meat Co.; vertically on one panel; aqua; 9½″ **3.00-4.00**

same as above except quart **4.00-6.00**

Pure Olive Oil S.S.P.; bulb shaped base; long neck; amethyst; 7¼″ **3.00-5.00**

Querus; pontil; aqua; 5¼″, $25.00-30.00

Radish, label; 8 panels; clear or amethyst **2.00-6.00**

Radish, label; 10 panels; clear; 4½″ **2.00-3.00**

Radish, label; square on bottom; clear or amethyst; 7″ **2.00-4.00**

Radish, label; *2* on bottom; sheared top; clear or amethyst; 10¾″ **3.00-6.00**

Radish, label; green; 5½″ **4.00-6.00**

Radish, label; clear or amethyst; 9½″ **2.00-3.00**

Radish, label; clear or amethyst; 5¼″ **2.00-4.00**

Radish, label; *Pat April 2nd 1901* under bottom; clear or amethyst; 5½″ **2.00-4.00**

Radish, label; ribbed base; clear or amethyst; 7½″ **2.00-4.00**

Radish, label; 8 panels; clear or amethyst; 86½″ **2.00-4.00**

Radish, label; *169* under bottom; clear or amethyst; 8¾″ **2.00-3.00**

Radish, label; clear or amethyst; 6″ **2.00-4.00**

Radish, label; clear or amethyst; 5¾″ **2.00-4.00**

Radish, label; *56S* in triangle under bottom; clear; 4½″ **2.00-3.00**

Red Snapper Sauce Co., Memphis, Tenn.; 6 sides; clear; 9½″ **4.00-10.00**

Red Snapper; clear or amethyst; 7½″ **3.00-4.00**

Restorff & Bettmann, N.Y.; under bottom; light green; 4½″ **2.00-6.00**

Restorff & Bettmann F.F., N.Y.; under bottom; mustard; aqua; 4½″ **8.00-12.00**

R.J. Ritter Conserve Co.; under bottom; clear; 8¼″ or 10½″ **4.00-6.00**

Rowat & Co.; same in back; light green; 10″ **8.00-10.00**

Royal Luncheon Cheese; milk glass; 2½″ **2.00-3.00**

Royal Luncheon Cheese; under bottom; milk glass; 3″ **2.00-3.00**

Salad dressing, label; clear or amethyst; 6¼″ . .**2.00-6.00**

M. Salzman Co., Purity Above All; *855* under bottom; amber; 10½″ **8.00-15.00**

Sauce; round; tapered neck; 16 concave vertical panels all around; aqua; 8″ **4.00-6.00**

Sauce; coffin shape; ring on base and top of neck; clear; 8¼″ **3.00-4.00**

Sauce; olive oil shape; round; tapered neck; graduated collar; pontil; aqua; 5¾″ **4.00-8.00**

Sauce; square; tapered neck; 16 rings; sunken panel on front; aqua; 8⅜″ **2.00-4.00**

Sauce; tapered neck; 23 rings; oval; sunken panel on front; *ABM;* aqua; 8″ **2.00-4.00**

Sauce; triangular; tapered neck; diamond shape down center on all 3 sides; crude collar; amethyst; 8¾″ **4.00-6.00**

Skilton Foote & Cos., Bunker Hill Pickles; light olive; 11½″ **20.00-50.00**

Skilton Foote & Cos., Bunker Hill Pickles; in outer ring; picture of pickle barrels, trees, fence, tower, all in center; round; aqua; 6⅜″ **4.00-8.00**

same as above except gold; 7½″ **12.00-15.00**

Snowhill B.W. & Co. London; on bottom; amber; 6½″ **2.00-4.00**

Societe Hygienique, No. 5 Rue J.J. Rousseau, Paris; vertically around bottle; cylindrical; graphite pontil; clear; 6⅜″ **6.00-8.00**

Strong Cobb & Co., Cleveland O.; *Pure Concentrated Flavoring Extracts* embossed; clear; 6½″ . .**4.00-6.00**

Tillmann's; in small panel at top; star with *T* in center in circular panel; *Oil* in square panel at base; square; aqua; 8″ **4.00-6.00**

Tabasco or dry food; wide mouth—2½″ opening; pontil; dark green; 7½″, $25.00-40.00

Tournades Kitchen Bouquet; clear or amethyst; 5¼″ **3.00-6.00**

Trappeys Tabasco Peppers; on center panel; vertical panels on upper and lower half; 4 large rings divide the panels crown top; oval; *ABM;* clear; 6¾″ **2.00-4.00**

William Underwood & Company; around bottom; aqua; 10″ **8.00-12.00**

U.S. Navy; pepper; 8 panels; aqua **25.00-50.00**

Valentines; amber; 3¼″ **3.00-6.00**

V.D.Co.; *Pat April 27, 1875* under bottom; aqua; 7" **8.00-12.00**

Vinegar, label; milk glass; 5½" **4.00-8.00**

Virginia Fruit Juice Co., Norfolk, Va.; in script on front; machine made; tenpin shape; clear or amethyst; 7½" **2.00-4.00**

M.T. Wallace & Co. Prop. Brooklyn N.Y.; *Brasst's Purifying Extract 1850;* pontil; aqua; 9½" . . . **25.00-50.00**

Wm. R. Warner & Co.; clear; 8¼" **4.00-8.00**

Warsaw Pickle Co.; aqua; 8¾" **10.00-15.00**

Waters Bros. Olive Oil and Extracts, Oakland, Cal.; round; light aqua; 11½" **4.00-6.00**

WDS N.Y.; graphite pontil; dark green; 8" . . **25.00-50.00**

C. Weisbecker, Manhattan Market, New York; pickle jar; corner panels; square; ring on neck; square collar; aqua; 6¼" **3.00-6.00**

Wellcome Chemical Works; under bottom; *Kepler* around top; machine made; amber; 6½" . . **2.00-4.00**

The J. Weller Co.; clear or amethyst; 7½" . . . **4.00-6.00**

Wells & Richardson Co.; *Cereal Milk* on each side; amber; 7¾" **8.00-12.00**

H. Wickert; aqua; 7¼" **6.00-8.00**

The Williams Bros Co.; pickle label; clear; 7½" **2.00-4.00**

Wood Cooper Pure Olive Oil, Santa Barbara, Ca; inside of crude blob seal on shoulder; band collar; round; aqua; 11" **4.00-6.00**

Fruit Jars

In 1795 the French army under Napoleon was deeply involved in military conflicts. A good food supply was often a determining factor in victory—and in how long victory and conquest would persevere. Napoleon, determined that an empire would be his, offered a goverment prize of twelve thousand francs (about four thousand dollars) to anyone who could invent an effective food preservation process. Nicolas Appert claimed the prize fourteen years late. His idea was incredibly uncomplicated: enclose the food in glass, seal it, then boil it to destroy bacteria. He put this theory in a book, which was translated and published in New York in 1812. The book was well-received in America, where people were always looking for better ways of living.

The public soon clamored for glass jars in which to preserve fruit. Thomas W. Dyott, a prominent American bottle maker, was promoting sales of his fruit jars by 1829 in Philadelphia. It was his advertising campaign that gave preserving bottles the name fruit jars.

The most common closure used during the first fifty years in the development of food preservation was cork sealed with wax. The process was improved in 1855 by Robert Arthur who invented an inverted saucer-like lid to be inserted into the jar to insure its airtight integrity. The Hero Glass Works of Philadelphia developed a glass lid in 1856.

The first significant improvement in the glass food jar and the sealing of its contents came with the patent on November 30, 1858, of a screw-type glass jar by John Landis Mason. The jars could be easily and tightly sealed, but they were not without disadvantage. The lids were made of zinc, and it was not healthy to have food exposed for long periods of time to that metal. But this problem was circumvented by the Hero company's development of a glass lid for Mason's jar in 1868, Mason transferred his patent rights on the jar to the Consolidated Fruit Jar Company, which subsequently let the rights expire. The competition was then opened and Ball Brothers of Muncie, Indiana, began distributing Mason jars on a national basis in 1880.

Meanwhile, Mason had gone to pursue other ideas—he invented a folding life raft, a soap dish, a brush holder and a sheet metal cap dye.

Use of a semiautomatic bottle-making machine in 1898 in Buffalo, New York, increased production of the Mason jars. The biggest impetus to the industry probably was the automatic bottle-making machine in 1903. John Landis Mason did not live to see his fruit jars attain national popularity—he died in poverty in 1902.

A.B.G.A. Mason Improved; green; quart **2.00-4.00**

A.B.G.A. Mason Perfect, Mason Made in U.S.A.; green; quart **2.00-6.00**

A & C, 1885; glass lid and wire clip; aqua green; quart **40.00-60.00**

ACME; in shield, stars; 1920; square wire lid; pint, ½ gallon **4.00-8.00**

Adler; on lid; clear or green; ½ pint, pint, quart, gallon **4.00-14.00**

Advance; 1885; glass lid with metal clamp; aqua; quart **25.00-60.00**

same as above except *Trademark, Pat. Apl'd For, J.W.* monogram; green; quart **15.00-30.00**

Agee Queen; 1925; clear; quart **14.00-18.00**

Agee; in script; *Utility Jar;* round, screw top, clear; pint **6.00-12.00**

Agee; in script; *Victory;* clear; quart **4.00-10.00**

Agee Lightning Fruit Jar; square; wire clamp; clear **8.00-12.00**

Agnew; 1876-1892; wax sealer; aqua; quart **20.00-30.00**

A.G.W.L.; 1865; *Pitts, Pa.;* wax seal; aqua . . **20.00-30.00**

Airtight; 1877; wax sealer; barrel shape; green; quart **60.00-90.00**

All Right; 1868; glass lid with wire clamp; green; quart **30.00-45.00**

Almy; glass cap; aqua; quart **25.00-40.00**

The Alston; metal lid and wire clip; clear; pint,
quart **20.00-30.00**

Amazon Swift Seal; glass lid with full wire bail; 1920;
blue; pint, quart, ½ gallon **6.00-10.00**

American Fruit Jar; 1885-95; aqua, green; several
sizes **20.00-40.00**

**Anchor; with figure of anchor; quart;
9″, $30.00-45.00**

Anchor Hocking; in center; an anchor with an *H* under
it; *Mason* under bottom; clear; 7″ **2.00-3.00**
same as above except with glass top; 1915; metal
band; clear or amethyst; quart **10.00-20.00**

Anchor Hocking Lightning; 1937; glass top; clear;
different sizes **4.00-6.00**

Anchor Hocking Mason; 1937; screw top; clear;
quart **2.00-4.00**

Anchor Mason's Pat.; screw top; clear; quart .**4.00-6.00**

Anderson Preserving Co.; 1920; screw top; clear;
quart **6.00-8.00**

Athorholt, Fisher & Co; 1875; wire clamp; clear;
quart **20.00-35.00**

Atlas Clover; in center, *Good Luck;* clear; 4¾ .**2.00-4.00**

Atlas E-Z Seal; 1896; wire bail and glass lid; amber;
green or clear; quart **10.00-20.00**

Atlas E-Z Seal; green or clear; 4½″ or 5¼″ . .**2.00-4.00**
same as above except green; 6¾″ or 7″ . .**2.00-3.00**

**Atlas; *Atlas E-Z Seal, Trade Mark
Reg.* on bottom; aqua; quart; 7¼″,
$2.00-6.00**

Atlas Good Luck; 1930; glass lid; full wire bail; clear; ⅓
pint, ½ pint, pint, quart, ½ gallon **6.00-8.00**

Atlas Good Luck; with cloverleaf; wire top; aqua or
amber; different sizes **10.00-15.00**

Atlas; with *HA* in center; *Mason;* clear; 9″ **1.00-2.00**

Atlas H-A Mason; 1920; glass insert; metal screw band;
clear; pint, quart **2.00-4.00**

Atlas H-A Mason; metal screw band; clear; ½
pint **2.00-4.00**

Atlas Improved Mason; 1890's; glass lid; metal screw
band; aqua or green **4.00-8.00**

Atlas Mason's Patent; 1900; zinc lid; blue green;
quart **10.00-20.00**

Atlas Mason's Patent Nov. 30; 1858; zinc lid; green; ½
gallon **4.00-8.00**

Atlas Mason's Patent Nov. 30th, 1858; screw top;
green; quart **3.00-4.00**

Atlas Mason's Patent; screw top; green;
quart **2.00-3.00**

Atlas Special; screw top; 1910; clear or blue . .**4.00-8.00**

Atlas Special Mason; 1910; zinc lid; wide mouth; aqua;
quart **2.00-8.00**

Atlas Strong Shoulder Mason; green or clear; 5⅛″ or
6⅞″ **8.00-10.00**

Atlas Strong Shoulder Mason; 1915; zinc lid; aqua;
green, clear or blue; pint, quart **6.00-10.00**

Atlas Wholefruit Jar; glass lid and wire bail; wide
mouth; clear; pint, quart, ½ gallon **4.00-8.00**

Atmore & Son; glass lid and metal screw band; wide
mouth; aqua, green; quart **15.00-19.00**

The Automatic Sealer; 1895; glass lid with spring wire
bail; aqua, green; quart **14.00-25.00**

Baker Bros; 1865; wax sealer; groove ring; green or
aqua; pint **30.00-40.00**

Ball; vaseline glass; screw top; pint, quart **4.00-6.00**

Ball; 1890; screw top; green; 3 sizes **5.00-10.00**

The Ball; 1890; screw top; green; quart **10.00-15.00**

Ball; in script, *Ideal;* wire top clamp; clear; 3″ or
4¾″ **4.00-6.00**

Ball; in script, *Ideal;* in back, *Pat. July 14, 1908;* wire top
clamp; green or clear; 3 sizes **3.00-4.00**

**Ball Ideal Patd July 14 1988; (error in
date); blue green; pint, $15.00-20.00**

Ball Ideal Pat'd July 14, 1908; wire and glass lid; aqua
or blue; quart; 7¼″ **4.00-6.00**

Ball Ideal Patd July 14, 1908; lid and wire; aqua or
blue; quart **2.00-4.00**

Ball Improved; aqua; pint **2.00-3.00**

The Ball Jar, Mason's Patent Nov. 30, 1858; screw-on
lid; aqua; quart **4.00-8.00**

Ball; in script, *Masons Patent 1858;* green; 3
sizes **2.00-3.00**

Ball; in script, *Mason;* clear or green; 6 sizes . .**2.00-6.00**

Ball Mason; aqua; quart **2.00-3.00**

Ball; in script, *Perfect Mason;* screw top;
6 sizes **2.00-4.00**

Ball Perfect Mason; clear; quart **2.00-3.00**

Ball; (printed) *Perfect Mason;* deep aqua; pint .**3.00-4.00**

Ball Perfect Mason; aqua; quart **2.00-3.00**

Ball Perfect Mason; no line under *Ball;* zinc lid; aqua;
pint, quart **3.00-4.00**

Ball Perfect Mason; 1900; zinc lid; vertical lines around
sides are cup and pint measurements; amber, olive,
blue or clear **25.00-35.00**

Baltimore Glass Works; 1865; aqua;
quart **40.00-80.00**

Banner Trade Mark Warranted; glass top; aqua;
quart **8.00-10.00**

Banner Widemouth Warranted; 1910; glass lid; full wire bail; wide mouth; blue; quart.........**6.00-12.00**

B.B.G.M. Co.; 1887; glass lid and metal screw band; blue, green or aqua; quart...........**30.00-50.00**

Beaver; 1897; glass lid and screw band; amber; green, clear or amethyst; pint, quart.........**12.00-25.00**

Beaver; *4* under bottom; amber; 7¼", $10.00-20.00

Beech Nut Trade Mark; with leaf; green; quart................................**4.00-6.00**

Bee Hive; zinc band and glass insert; blue..**20.00-30.00**

Bennett's; 1875; green; quart...........**35.00-40.00**

Bernardin Mason; zinc lid; clear; quart.....**25.00-30.00**

Best; zinc screw band and glass insert; wide mouth; green; quart....................**18.00-25.00**

The Best; 1875; glass stopper that screws into the neck; quart................................**18.00-30.00**

The Best Fruit Keeper; glass lid and wire clamp; green; quart................................**25.00-35.00**

Best Wide Mouth; zinc band and glass insert; aqua or clear..................................**2.00-4.00**

Boldt Mason Jar; zinc lid; blue green.....**10.00-20.00**

Borden's Milk Co.; 1885; hexagonal; metal band and glass insert; clear; pint.............**10.00-20.00**

Bosco Double Seal; glass lid and full bail; clear; quart..................................**4.00-8.00**

Boyd Mason; 1910; zinc lid; olive green; pint, quart..................................**4.00-8.00**

Boyd Perfect Mason; zinc lid; green; ½ pint, pint, quart..........................**4.00-6.00**

Braun Safetee Mason; zinc lid; aqua.......**3.00-5.00**

Brelle Jar; glass lid and wire clamp wide mouth; clear; quart................................**15.00-30.00**

Brighton; 1890; glass lid; metal wire clamp; clear, amber or amethyst; quart...............**35.00-60.00**

Geo. D. Brown & Co.; 1857; glass lid and heavy metal clamp; green; quart.................**20.00-40.00**

The Burlington; 1880; zinc band; clear or aqua; quart................................**20.00-40.00**

Burnham & Co.; 1865; iron lid; green; quart................................**60.00-100.00**

Canadian King; glass lid and full wire bail; clear; quart................................**4.00-8.00**

Canadian Sure Seal; metal lid and wire metal screw band; wide mouth; clear; quart.........**2.00-4.00**

Canton Domestic Fruit Jar; 1895; glass lid and wire bail; clear; quart, $20.00-30.00

Cassidy; 1885; glass lid and wire bail; clear..............................**35.00-50.00**

C.F.J. Co.; 1871; glass lid and metal band; green; quart................................**12.00-20.00**

C.G. Co.; 1890; screw lid; clear; quart.....**10.00-20.00**

A. & D. H. Chambers Union Fruit Jar, Pitts; clear; quart................................**8.00-10.00**

The Champion, Pat. Aug. 31, 1868; glass lid and top metal screw band; aqua; quart.......**25.00-35.00**

Clarke Fruit Jar Co.; 1886; glass lid and wire bail with lever lock clamp; aqua; quart.........**40.00-50.00**

Clarke Fruit Jar Co., Cleveland O.; *54* under bottom; aqua; 7¼".....................**20.00-30.00**

Clark's Peerless; 1882; wire bail and glass lid; blue; quart................................**10.00-20.00**

Climax; full wire bail and glass lid; green; pint................................**8.00-16.00**

Clyde Lightning; screw top; clear or green; quart................................**8.00-10.00**

Clyde Mason; 1880; screw top; green; quart................................**10.00-20.00**

Cohansey; 1870; glass lid and clamp; barrel shaped; aqua; quart.....................**18.00-20.00**

Cohansey Glass Mfg. Co.; *Pat Mch 20 77* under bottom; barrel shaped; aqua, $40.00-70.00

Columbia; glass lid with clamp; amber; quart................................**20.00-35.00**

Commonwealth Fruit Jar; glass lid and wire bail; green; quart................................**20.00-40.00**

Corona Jar Improved; beaded neck design; clear; all sizes................................**4.00-10.00**

Crown; 1890; glass lid and zinc screw band; aqua; quart................................**18.00-25.00**

Crown; 1870; glass lid and zinc screw band; aqua; all sizes................................**6.00-12.00**

Crown; glass lid and zinc screw band; all sizes................................**2.00-4.00**

Crown Mason; zinc screw band; white opal insert; round with vertical ribs on the sides; all sizes....**2.00-4.00**

Crystal Jar; clear or amethyst; 6½", $10.00-20.00

Crystal Jar C.G.; sheared top; clear; quart...**6.00-10.00**

Cunningham & Ihmsen; 1868; wax seal; cobalt blue; quart................................**40.00**

Cunningham's & Co; 1879; wax seal; aqua; quart................................**20.00-30.00**

The Daisy; in a circle; glass lid and wire bail; aqua; quart................................**8.00-20.00**

The Daisy Jar; 1885; heavy iron clamp; round; aqua; quart................................**25.00-45.00**

Dalbey's Fruit Jar; 1866; glass lid; round extending wax seal neck; deep aqua; quart.........**45.00-70.00**

The Dandy; 1885; glass lid and wire clamp; round and slender; light green; quart...........**20.00-30.00**

The Dandy; *Gilberds 9* under bottom; amber; 7½" **20.00-30.00**

The Darling; 1885; zinc screw band and glass insert; round tapering sides; aqua; quart **20.00-30.00**

Decker Dependable Food, Jacob E. Decker & Son, Mason City, Iowa; clear; quart **2.00-4.00**

Decker's Iowana; glass lid and wire bail; clear; quart **8.00-12.00**

Dexter; 1865; zinc band with glass insert; aqua; quart **20.00-40.00**

Diamond Fruit Jar; glass lid and full wire bail; clear; quart **4.00-10.00**

Dictator D.D.I. Holcomb Patented Dec. 14th, 1869; wax seal; blue; quart **15.00-30.00**

Dillon; 1890; wax seal; round; aqua; quart . . **20.00-30.00**

Dominion; 1886; zinc band and glass insert; round; clear; quart **25.00-40.00**

Dominion Widemouth Special; zinc lid; round; clear; quart **4.00-8.00**

Doolittle, The Self Sealer; glass lid; wide mouth; clear; quart **20.00-30.00**

Double Safety; glass lid and full wire bail; clear; quart **2.00-4.00**

Double Safety; in script; *Smalley Kiviare Outhank, Boston Mass.;* in center #4; clear; 7⅜" . . . **2.00-4.00**

Double Seal; in script; clear; 7¼" **2.00-4.00**

Drey Ever Seal; glass lid and full wire bail; clear or amethyst; quart **2.00-4.00**

Drey Improved Ever Seal; glass lid and full wire bail; round; clear; quart **2.00-4.00**

Drey Mason; screw top; round; aqua; all sizes **2.00-4.00**

Drey; in script, *Perfect Mason;* screw top; clear or green; several sizes **2.00-4.00**

Drey Perfect Mason; zinc lid; green; pint, quart **2.00-4.00**

Drey Square Mason; zinc lid; square; clear or amethyst; quart **1.00-2.00**

The Dunkley Celery Co., Kalamazoo; 4-piece mold; ground top; amethyst; quart **25.00-35.00**

The Dunkley Preserving Co.; 1898; glass lid, metal clamp; clear; quart **12.00-15.00**

Du Pont; screw top; round; aqua; quart **14.00-20.00**

Durham; glass lid and wire bail; round; aqua; quart **10.00-20.00**

Dyson's Pure Food Products; metal band; round; clear; quart **4.00-8.00**

Eagle; 1876; glass lid and iron thumbscrew to tighten; green; quart **50.00-85.00**

Easi-Pak Mason-Metro; screw top; clear **4.00-6.00**

Easy Vacuum Jar; 1895; glass lid; tall and round; clear; quart **15.00-25.00**

The Eclipse; 1868; wax seal; aqua; quart . . . **25.00-50.00**

Eclipse Wax Sealer; 1868; wax seal; green; quart **40.00**

Economy; metal lid and spring wire clamp; amethyst; pint, quart, ½ gallon **2.00-6.00**

Economy, Trade Mark; clear or amethyst; quart **2.00-4.00**

Economy, Trade Mark, Pat. June 9, 1903; clear or amethyst; quart **2.00-4.00**

E.G.Co.; (monogram) *Imperial;* clear; quart . . . **8.00-10.00**

Electric; glass lid and wire bail; round; aqua; quart **15.00-25.00**

Electric Fruit Jar; 1900-1915; glass lid and metal clamp; round; aqua; quart **25.00-35.00**

Electroglas N.W.; clear; quart **2.00-4.00**

Empire; in maltese cross; clear; quart **2.00-4.00**

Empire; 1860; glass stopper; deep blue; quart **50.00-60.00**

The Empire; 1866; glass lid with iron lugs to fasten it; aqua; quart **35.00-50.00**

Erie Fruit Jar; 1890; screw top; clear; quart **10.00-25.00**

Erie Lightning; clear; quart **4.00-6.00**

Eureka; 1864; wax dipped cork or other; extending neck; aqua; pint **20.00-30.00**

Eureka, Pat. Feb 9th, 1864, Eureka Jar Co., Dunbar, W.Va.; 1870; aqua; quart **25.00-50.00**

Everlasting Improved Jar; in oval; 1904; quart **4.00-6.00**

Everlasting Jar; 1904; glass lid and double wire hook fastener; round; green; pint, quart, ½ gallon **10.00-17.00**

Excelsior; 1880-1890; zinc screw band and glass insert; aqua; quart **20.00-27.00**

Excelsior Improved; 1890; green; quart **15.00-20.00**

Exwaco; clear or green; quart **10.00-20.00**

F.A. & Co.; 1860; glass stopper; green; quart **30.00-40.00**

Fahnstock Fortune & Co.; green; quart . . . . **20.00 +**

Family Fruit Jar; wire top; clear; quart **10.00-15.00**

Farley; glass lid and full wire bail; square; slender; clear; quart **4.00-6.00**

F.C.G. Co.; 1875; metal cap; amber or green; quart **35.00-50.00**

Federal Fruit Jar; 1895; glass lid and wire bail; olive green; quart **20.00-30.00**

Fhanestock Albree & Co.; pontil; sheared top; aqua; 7¼", $50.00-100.00

Fink & Nasse, St. Louis; green; quart **20.00-40.00**

Flaccus Co., E.C. Trade Mark; elk and floral design; milk glass **70.00-110.00**

W.L.J. Fleet Liverpool; glass stopper; aqua; quart **30.00-50.00**

Foster Sealfast; glass lid and full wire bail; clear or amethyst; quart **4.00-10.00**

Franklin Dexter Fruit Jar; 1865; zinc lid; aqua; quart **12.00-20.00**

Franklin Fruit Jar; 1866; screw-on lid; green; quart **20.00-40.00**

Fruit Grower's Trade Co.; wax dipped cork; oval; extending wax seal neck; green; quart......**10.00-30.00**

Fruit jar, label; graphite pontil; seal top; aqua; 9½", $80.00-150.00

Fruit jar, label; sheared top; 4¼"..........**4.00-6.00**

Fruit jar, label; pontil; clear; quart.......**100.00-150.00**

Fruit jar; ground pontil; blue green; 8¼", $50.00-100.00

Fruit jar, label; *4* under bottom; sheared top; black; 7".....................**60.00-150.00**

Fruit jar, label; graphite pontil; aqua; 10"..**90.00-150.00**

Fruit Keeper; glass lid and metal clamp; deep green; quart.....................**20.00-30.00**

The Gayner; glass lid and wire bail; clear; quart.....................**10.00-15.00**

The Gem; 1856; zinc band and glass insert; amber, aqua or green; quart...............**6.00-12.00**

Gem; 1868; zinc screw band and glass insert; green; quart.....................**10.00-12.00**

Gem; 1869; zinc screw band and glass insert; aqua; quart.....................**10.00-15.00**

The Gem, C.F.J.; monogram; 1882; wide zinc screw band and glass insert; aqua green; quart.....................**10.00-20.00**

Gem; 1884; zinc screw band and glass insert; green; quart.....................**10.00-20.00**

Gem; with maltese cross; aqua; quart.......**2.00-4.00**

Gem HGW; aqua; quart..................**2.00-6.00**

Gem Improved Made in Canada; clear; quart.....................**6.00-15.00**

Gem Improved; 1860; zinc band and glass insert; round; green; pint.....................**10.00-20.00**

The Gem, Pat. Nov. 26, 1867; clear; quart...**4.00-8.00**

Genuine Boyds Mason; 1900; zinc lid; green; quart.....................**6.00-8.00**

Genuine Mason; 1900; zinc; olive green; pint, quart.....................**20.00-25.00**

G.G. Co.; screw top; clear..........**6.00-10.00**

Gilberds; *Gilberds Improved Jar Cap Jamestown N.Y. Oct 13, 1885 Pat July 31, 82* on top; small kick-up; sheared top; aqua; quart...........**60.00-80.00**

Gilberds Improved Jar; 1885; glass lid and wire bail; aqua; quart.....................**35.00-44.00**

Gilberds Jar; 1884; glass lid and screw band; aqua; quart.....................**50.00-60.00**

Gilchrist; 1895; zinc lid and dome shaped opal liner; wide mouth; aqua green; quart.........**4.00-8.00**

Gilland & Co.; 1890; glass stopper; aqua; quart.....................**10.00-20.00**

G.J.; monogram; clear; quart............**10.00-20.00**

Glass screw-cap jar; *Pat Oct. 24, 1905;* six panels; *Warm Cap Slightly To Seal or Unseal* on top of cap; amethyst; 5".....................**4.00-8.00**

Glassboro; trademark; 1880-1900; zinc band and glass insert; light to dark green; 3 sizes......**15.00-24.00**

Glassboro Improved; 1880; wide zinc screw band and glass insert; aqua or pale green; quart..**20.00-25.00**

Glenshae G. Mason; (G in square); clear; quart.....................**2.00-4.00**

Globe; glass lid; metal neck band; top wire bail and bail clamp; amber, green or clear; quart....**10.00-20.00**

Glocker, Pat. 1911 Others Pending Sanitary; aqua; quart.....................**10.00-20.00**

Golden State S; in a triangle; *Pat. Dec. 20, 1910, Pat. Pending* under it; amethyst............**4.00-8.00**

Golden State; metal screw-on lid; wide mouth; clear; 4 sizes.....................**8.00-10.00**

Golden State Improved; thin metal screw-on lid; clear; 2 sizes.....................**6.00-10.00**

Good House Keeper's Mason Jar; 1935-1946; screw-on metal lid; clear; quart.................**2.00-4.00**

Good House Keeper's, R; in circle, *Wide Mouth Mason;* screw top; clear; quart.................**2.00-4.00**

Green Mountain G.A. Co.; wire clamp; aqua..**2.00-4.00**

G Square Mason; metal screw-on lid; clear; quart.....................**4.00-8.00**

Haines; 1882; glass lid and iron clamp; green; quart.....................**35.00-50.00**

Haines Improved; 1870; glass lid and top wire bail; aqua green; quart.....................**30.00-40.00**

Hamilton Glass Works; green; quart.......**10.00-20.00**

Hansee's Place Home Jar; *Pat. Dec. 19 1899* under bottom; aqua; 7".....................**20.00-30.00**

Harris; 1860; metal lid; deep green; quart...**50.00-60.00**

Harris Improved; 1875-1880; glass lid and iron clamp; green; quart.....................**40.00-50.00**

Haserot Company; 1915-1925; zinc lid; green; quart.....................**10.00-20.00**

The Haserot Company, Cleveland Mason Patent; screw top; green; quart.....................**2.00-4.00**

E.C. Hazard & Co. Shrewsbury N.J.; wire clamp; aqua; quart.....................**4.00-8.00**

Hazel; glass lid and wire bail; aqua; quart...**10.00-15.00**

Hazel-Atlas Lightning Seal; full wire bail and glass lid; green; quart.....................**10.00-12.00**

H. & D; 1915; glass top; metal band........**4.00-6.00**

Helme's Railroad Mills; amber; 7¾".......**8.00-15.00**

Helmes Railroad Mills; amber; quart.......**8.00-16.00**

The Improved Hero; glass top; metal band; green.....................**8.00-10.00**

Hero; with cross and lightning at top; green; quart.....................**8.00-16.00**

The Heroine; wide zinc screw band and glass insert; light green; quart.....................**18.00-20.00**

The High Grade; zinc screw-on top; clear . . . **12.00-20.00**

Holz, Clark & Taylor; 1878; screw-on glass lid; aqua;
quart **50.00-100.00**

Hom-Pak; metal lid; clear **2.00-4.00**

Hom-Pak Mason; 2-piece lid; clear; pint,
quart **4.00-8.00**

The Household;; in center *W.T. Co.;* under it *Fruit Jar;*
aqua; quart **8.00-10.00**

H & R; 1886; round wax sealer; blue; quart . . **8.00-16.00**

Hudson Bay; picture of a beaver on side coat of arms;
rawhide clamp top; square; clear; quart . . **8.00-12.00**

The Ideal; 1890; zinc lid; clear; pint, quart . . **10.00-20.00**

Ideal Wide Mouth Jar; flat metal lid; clear;
quart **2.00-4.00**

The Imperial; 1886; glass lid and wire clamp; green;
quart **15.00-25.00**

Imperial Improved Quart; glass lid and wide zinc screw
band; aqua or green; quart **8.00-10.00**

Improved Everlasting Jar; in a watermelon panel; under
bottom *Illinois Pacific Glass Co. S.F. Cal. Pat* in
center; amethyst; 6½" **4.00-8.00**

Independent; 1888; screw-on glass lid; clear or
amethyst; quart **25.00-30.00**

Independent Jar; 1882; screw-on glass lid; clear or
amethyst; quart **20.00-30.00**

Ivanhoe; glass lid and wire bail; clear; quart . . **8.00-10.00**

Ivanhoe; *4* under bottom; clear; 4¼" **4.00-8.00**

J. & B. Fruit Jar; 1898; zinc lid; light green; pint,
quart **12.00-16.00**

Jeannette; a *J* in a block under it, *Mason Home Packer;*
clear; quart **2.00-3.00**

Jewel Jar; wide zinc screw band and glass lid; clear or
amethyst; quart **2.00-4.00**

same as above except also made in
Canada **2.00-4.00**

J.G. Co.; monogram; zinc lid and domed opal liner; wide
mouth; green; quart **14.00-25.00**

Johnson & Johnson, New Brunswick, N.J. U.S.A.;
1890; ground top; square; amber; 4¼" or
6½" **4.00-8.00**

Johnson & Johnson, New Brunswick, N.J. U.S.A.;
cobalt blue **50.00-100.00**

same as above except amber **12.00-20.00**

Jug; glass ears with wire handle; round; amethyst;
gallon **6.00-10.00**

Kalamazoo, The Jay B. Rhodes; 1875; wax seal;
Kalamazoo, Mich; quart **6.00-10.00**

K.C. Finest Quality; in banner, *Mason;* square,
spacesaver style; zinc lid; clear or amethyst;
quart **6.00-10.00**

Keffers Glass; screw-on top; aqua; quart . . . **25.00-35.00**

Kerr Economy Trade Mark; *Chicago* on base; metal lid
and narrow clip band; clear or amethyst; pint,
quart **2.00-4.00**

Kerr Economy; in script, under it *Trade Mark;* under bottom *Kerr Glass Mfg. Co. Sand Spring, Okla;* clear;
3¾" **2.00-3.00**

same as above except *Chicago Pat.* under
bottom **1.00-2.00**

Kerr Glass Top Mason; flat metal lid; clear; pint,
quart **2.00-3.00**

Kerr Self Sealing, Trade Mark Reg.; in banner, *Pat.
Mason;* clear; quart **2.00-3.00**

same except indigo blue **4.00-8.00**

Kerr Self Sealing Wide Mouth Mason; base reads; *Kerr
Glass Mfg. Co. Sand Springs, Okla., Pat. Aug 31,
1915;* clear **2.00-3.00**

Kerr; in script, *Self Sealing Trade Mark* in a ribbon;
under it *Mason;* clear; 6¾" **1.00-2.00**

same as above except square; clear; 9" . . **1.00-2.00**

Kerr Self Sealing Trade Mark 65th Anniversary;
1903-1968 . . . . **4.00-8.00**

**Kerr Wide Mouth Mason; clear; ½
pint, $8.00-15.00**

KG; in oval; wire clamp; clear; quart **2.00-6.00**

The Kilner Jar; zinc screw band and glass insert; clear;
quart **6.00-8.00**

King; full wire bail and glass lid; clear or amethyst;
quart **8.00-10.00**

Kinsells True Mason; 1874; zinc lid; clear;
quart **6.00-8.00**

Kline Pat. Oct. 27, 1863; *A;* on glass stopper; aqua;
quart **10.00-20.00**

Kline A.R.; 1863; glass fitting lid and clamp; aqua;
quart **18.00-25.00**

Knight Packing Co.; screw top; clear; quart . . . **2.00-4.00**

Knowlton Vacuum Fruit Jar; with star in center; clear or
amethyst; quart **4.00-8.00**

Knowlton Vacuum Fruit Jar; zinc lid and glass insert;
blue; quart **16.00-25.00**

Knox Mason; zinc lid; clear; quart **2.00-4.00**

Kohrs; glass lid and half wire bail; clear;
quart **2.00-4.00**

Kygw Co.; on base; clear; quart **15.00-30.00**

Lafayette; 1864; wax dipped cork, with profile; aqua or
blue; quart **80.00-200.00**

Lamb Mason; zinc lid; clear; pint, quart **4.00-8.00**

The Leader; glass lid and wire clamp; amber;
quart **25.00-50.00**

Lee & Co., J. Elwood; zinc screw; amber . . . **8.00-10.00**

Legrand Ideal Co., L.I.J.; monogram; screw top; blue;
quart **8.00-20.00**

Leotric; in oval; glass lid; medium green;
quart **8.00-10.00**

Lightning Trade Mark Registered U.S. Patent Office;
Putnam 4 on bottom; lid with dates; aqua;
pint **4.00-6.00**

Lightning Trade Mark; *Putnam 199* on bottom; aqua; ½
gallon **4.00-6.00**

same as above except wire and lid; pint . . . **4.00-6.00**

Lightning Trademark; glass top; round; aqua;
6" **4.00-10.00**

same as above except *Putnam* on base; aqua; quart,
½ gallon **6.00-10.00**

same as above except amber; pint, quart,
½ gallon **12.00-20.00**

Lightning; *Putnam 824* under bottom; sheared top;
aqua **10.00-15.00**

Lindell Glass Co.; 1870; wax sealer; amber; quart **30.00-50.00**

Lockport Mason; zinc top; aqua; ½ gallon . . . **4.00-10.00**

Lockport Mason, Improved; zinc screw band; glass insert; aqua; quart **6.00-12.00**

Lorillard & Co.; on base; glass top; metal clamp; amber; pint **9.00-17.00**

P. Lorillard & Co.; sheared top; amber; 6¼", $10.00+

Lustre R.E. Tongue & Bros. Co. Inc. Phila.; in circle or shield; wire clamp; quart **2.00-4.00**

Lustre; glass top and wire bail; aqua **4.00-8.00**

L.& W.; 1860; wax sealer; green; quart **20.00-35.00**

W.W. Lyman; 1862; glass top and wire clamp; aqua; quart **25.00-30.00**

Lyon & Bossard's Jar; glass lid and iron clamp; aqua; quart **40.00-50.00**

Lyon & Bossard's Jar, East Stroudsburg Pa.; 1890; iron clamp; aqua; quart **80.00-125.00**

Macomb Potter Co. Pat. Applied For; on base; screw top; white crock **10.00-12.00**

The Magic Fruit Jar; 1890; glass top and iron clamp; amber; quart **50.00-70.00**

The Magic Fruit Jar; star in center; clear; quart **4.00-8.00**

Mallinger; zinc top; clear; quart **6.00-10.00**

Masnfield Improved Mason; clear; quart **2.00-4.00**

The Marion Jar; #5 under bottom; sheared top; aqua; quart, $10.00-20.00

The Marion Jar; 1858; zinc top; green; quart **8.00-12.00**

The Mason; zinc top; light green; quart **4.00-6.00**

Mason Fruit Jar; zinc lid; clear; quart **4.00-8.00**

Mason Fruit Jar; zinc top; clear; quart **4.00-12.00**

same as above except amber **35.00-50.00**

Mason Fruit Jar; zinc top; aqua; quart **8.00-12.00**

Mason Fruit Jar Patent Nov. 30th, 1858; zinc top; aqua; quart **10.00-20.00**

The Mason Jar of 1858; zinc top; aqua; quart **8.00-20.00**

Mason Keystone; clear; quart **2.00-4.00**

Mason Patent Nov. 30th, 1880; zinc top; clear; pint, quart **10.00-20.00**

Mason Patent Nov. 30th, 1858; with dots on letters hand painted with hot glass; screw top; green; quart **8.00-10.00**

Mason Pat. Nov. 30th, 1858; 1910; clear; quart **2.00-4.00**

Mason Porcelain; tan; quart **10.00-12.00**

same as above except black **100.00-200.00**

Mason; star design jar; zinc top; clear; pint . **10.00-20.00**

Mason's; sheared top; pale green; 7¼", 2.00-6.00

Mason's; *Pat Nov. 26-67* under bottom; aqua; 5½" **8.00-12.00**

Mason's; sheared top; black; 7¼" **110.00-300.00**

Mason's; swirled milk glass; 7¼" **75.00-100.00**

Mason's CG, Patent Nov 30, 1858; zinc lid; green; quart **8.00-14.00**

Mason's C-Patent Nov. 30th 1858; green; 7" **4.00-8.00**

Mason's Improved; zinc screw band and glass insert; aqua or green; pint **10.00-25.00**

Mason's Improved Butter Jar; sheared top; aqua; ½ gallon, $8.00-10.00

Mason's Improved; *Hero F J Co.* in cross above; zinc band and glass lid covered with many patent dates, earliest *Feb 12, '56;* aqua; quart **8.00-12.00**

Mason's Keystone; 1869; zinc screw band and glass insert; aqua; quart **10.00-20.00**

Mason's "M" Patent Nov. 30th 1858; green; 7" **4.00-8.00**

Mason's; under it *"M" Patent Nov. 30th 1898;* screw top; aqua; quart **6.00-8.00**

Mason's Patent 1858; zinc lid; amber or green; pint **20.00-30.00**

Mason's Patent 1858; zinc top; aqua; quart . . . **6.00-8.00**

Mason's Patent Nov. 30 1858; zinc top; amber or yellow; quart **6.00-12.00**

Mason's Patent Nov. 30, 1858; zinc top; aqua or green; pint **20.00-45.00**

Mason's Patent Nov. 30, 1858; zinc top; clear; quart **8.00-13.00**

Mason's; (cross) *Patent Nov. 30th, 1858; Pat. Nov. 26, 67,45* in center on bottom; blue or aqua; pint **6.00-8.00**

Mason's Patent Nov. 30th 1858, C.F.J. Co.; monogram; aqua; pint **4.00-6.00**

Mason's; under it an arrow, under that *Patent Nov. 30th 1858;* sheared top; quart **10.00-15.00**

Mason's; with flat type cross; *H.F.J. Co.* in each corner; *Patent Nov. 30th 1858;* ½" letters; sheared top; aqua; gallon **8.00-15.00**

Mason's Patent; zinc lid; aqua, green or clear; quart **4.00-8.00**

Mason's Patent, Nov. 30th 1858; 3 errors on M,P,N; reads *Asons Atent, Ov.;* aqua; quart **15.00-20.00**

Mason's Pat. Nov. 30th 1858; (backward S); *New Reproduction;* sheared top; amber; pint **10.00-20.00**

Mathia's & Henderson; glass lid and heavy wire clamp; clear; quart **15.00-25.00**

M.C.Co.; on base; screw top; amber; quart . .**10.00-20.00**

McDonald New Perfect Seal; wire bail and glass lid; blue; quart **8.00-12.00**

McDonald New Perfect Seal, Patent July 14, 1908; clear; quart **2.00-4.00**

Metro Easi-Pak Mason; threaded neck; clear; quart **2.00-4.00**

M.F.A.; metal screw-on top; clear; quart **8.00-16.00**

Michigan Mason; zinc top; clear; quart **10.00-20.00**

Mid West; wide zinc band and glass top; clear or amethyst; quart **2.00-6.00**

Miller's Fine Flavor; 3 bees in circle in center; aqua; quart . . . .**15.00 +**

Millville Atmospheric Fruit Jar; in back *Whitall's Patent June 18, 1861;* clamp **10.00-15.00**

Millville Improved; 1885; zinc lid and glass insert; aqua; quart **20.00-30.00**

Mission; a bell and trademark on each side, under it *Mason Jar, Made in Calif;* on bottom *Los Angeles Calif. Mfg. by W.J. Latchford Co.;* screw top; clear or green; 3 sizes **3.00-10.00**

Model Mason; 1910; zinc top; green; quart . . .**8.00-14.00**

John M. Moore; 1865-1875; glass top and heavy iron clamp; aqua; quart **50.00-85.00**

Moore's Patent, Dec. 3, 1861; glass top with cast iron clamp and screw; aqua or green; quart **35.00-65.00**

National; 1885; metal top; quart **25.00-40.00**

National Super Mason; 1870; glass top and iron clamp; clear; quart **18.00-35.00**

Newark; zinc top; clear; quart **8.00-15.00**

Newark Special Extra Mason Jar; **4.00-6.00**

Newark; zinc top; clear; quart **4.00-10.00**

New Gem; wide zinc top; clear; quart **2.00-4.00**

N Star; metal top and wax seal; blue; quart **10.00-20.00**

N.W. Electroglass Wide Mouth Mason; screw top; clear or amethyst; quart **2.00-4.00**

N.W. Electroglass Wide Mouth Mason; zinc top; clear or amethyst; quart **4.00-8.00**

OC; on base; glass top; wire clamp; quart **8.00-10.00**

Ohio Quality Mason; clear; quart **4.00-6.00**

Opler Brothers Inc., OB; monogram, *Cocoa and Chocolate, New York U.S.A.;* glass top; wire clamp; clear **4.00-6.00**

Osotite; in diamond; clear; quart **2.00-4.00**

Pacific Glass Works; zinc band and glass insert; green; quart **40.00-50.00**

Pacific Mason; zinc top; clear; quart **10.00-20.00**

Pacific S.F. Glass Works; 1880; green; quart **20.00-30.00**

Paragon, New; glass top and iron clamp; green; quart **35.00-40.00**

Patent Applied For; metal top and wax seal, extending wax seal neck; green; quart **10.00-20.00**

P.C.G. Co.; wax seal; aqua; quart **10.00-25.00**

The Pearl; zinc screw band and glass insert; green; quart **20.00-30.00**

Peerless; wax dipped cork; green; quart **50.00-60.00**

The Penn; metal cap and wax seal; green; quart **25.00-30.00**

Peoria Pottery; metal top and wax seal; glazed brown stoneware; quart **6.00-12.00**

Perfection; double wire bail and glass top; clear; quart **20.00-30.00**

The New Perfection; clear or amethyst; ½ gallon, $15.00-25.00

Perfect Seal; full wire bail and glass top; clear; quart **2.00-6.00**

Perfect Seal; in shield, *Made in Canada;* clear; quart **2.00-4.00**

Pet.; glass stopper; green; quart **40.00-50.00**

Pet.; glass stopper and wire bail; aqua; quart **25.00-30.00**

H.W. Pettit, Wesville, N.J.; under bottom; aqua; quart, $4.00-10.00

The Goragas Pierie Co., Phila., Royal Peanutene; sheared top; clear **8.00-10.00**

Pine Deluxe Jar; full wire bail and glass top; clear; quart **2.00-6.00**

Pine; (P in square) *Mason;* zinc top; clear; quart **2.00-6.00**

Porcelain Lined; zinc top; aqua; quart **12.00-20.00**
same as above except green; 2 gallon . .**10.00-15.00**

Potter & Bodine Philadelphia; glass top and clamp; aqua; quart **35.00-50.00**

Premium Coffeyville Kas.; wire ring and glass top; clear or amethyst; quart **15.00-30.00**

Premium Improved; glass top and side wire clips; clear; quart **10.00-15.00**

Presto; screw-on top; clear **2.00-4.00**

Presto Fruit Jar; screw-on top; clear **2.00-4.00**

Presto Glass Top; half wire bail and glass top; clear or amethyst; quart **2.00-6.00**

Presto Supreme Mason; threaded neck; clear; pint **2.00-4.00**

Presto Widemouth Glass Top; threaded neck; clear; quart **2.00-4.00**

Princess; fancy shield; glass top and wire bail; clear; quart **12.00-20.00**

Protector; flat zinc cap and welded wire clamp; aqua; quart **15.00-20.00**

Protector; *6* under bottom; sheared top; six panels; aqua, $10.00-20.00

The Puritan; glass top and wire clamp; aqua; pint **25.00-30.00**

Putnam Glass Works; on base; wax seal; green; quart **50.00-110.00**

The Queen; circled by *Pat. Dec. 28th Patd. June 16th 1868;* wax seal; green; quart . . . .**20.00 +**

The Queen; *Patd. Nov. 2 1869, #39* under bottom; clear; quart **20.00-30.00**

The Queen; 1875; zinc band; aqua or green; quart **16.00-22.00**

Queen Improved; shield design; glass lid and wire clamps; clear; quart **4.00-8.00**

Quick Seal; in circle; glass lid and wire bail; green, blue or clear; quart **2.00-4.00**

Quong Hop & Co., 12 oz. Net; glass lid and wire bail; Chinese writing; clear; pint **2.00-4.00**

Quong Yeun Sing & Co; half wire bail and glass lid; clear; pint **4.00-6.00**

Ramsey Jar; glass lid; 12-sided jar; aqua; quart **40.00-50.00**

Rau's Improved Groove Ring Jar; *1910;* wax sealer; pink; pint, quart **25.00-35.00**

Red Key Mason; *2* under bottom; clear or amethyst; 6½", $20.00-30.00

Red Mason's; embossed key, *Patent Nov. 30th 1858;* zinc lid; aqua or green; pint **10.00-14.00**

Reid Murdock & Co. Chicago; zinc lid; clear; quart **4.00-10.00**

Reliable Home Canning Mason; 1940's; zinc screw band and glass insert; clear; quart **2.00-3.00**

Reliance Brand Wide Mouth Mason; screw-on lid; clear; 3 sizes **2.00-4.00**

Root; 1925; clear; quart **2.00-6.00**

Root Mason; 1910; zinc screw-on lid; aqua, green or blue; quart **4.00-7.00**

Root Mason; 1925; clear; quart **2.00-6.00**

The Rose; 1920; screw-on lid; clear; 3 sizes **10.00-20.00**

Royal; sheared top; clear, $3.00-6.00

Royal of 1876; screw top; clear; quart **20.00-40.00**

Royal Trade Mark; with crown; glass lid and full wire bail; light green or clear; pint, quart, ½ gallon **4.00-8.00**

Royal Trade Mark Full Measure; *1900, Registered;* with crown; green; quart **2.00-4.00**

Safe Seal, Patd. July 14, 1908; clear; quart . .**2.00-4.00**

Safe Seal; 1935; glass lid and wire bail; aqua or clear; pint, quart **3.00-4.00**

Safety; 1900; full wire bail and glass lid; amber; pint, quart, ½ gallon **40.00-50.00**

Safety Seal Made in Canada; half wire bail and glass lid; clear; pint, quart **10.00-15.00**

Safety Valve Patd. May 32, 1895; with emblem in center on bottom; amethyst; pint **6.00-10.00**

Safety Valve Patd. May 21, 1895; midget jar; ground top; clear; 3¾" **25.00-30.00**

Safety Wide Mouth Mason, Salem Glass Works, Salem N.J.; zinc lid; aqua or green; quart, ½ gallon **8.00-14.00**

Samco; in center *Genuine Mason;* zinc screw band and opal insert; clear; all sizes **1.00-2.00**

Samco Super Mason; 1920; zinc screw band and opal insert; clear; all sizes **1.00-2.00**

Sampson Improved Battery; 1895; screw-on lid; aqua; quart **10.00-16.00**

Sanety Wide Mouth Mason; 1920; zinc lid; wide mouth; aqua; quart **12.00-19.00**

Sanford; 1900; metal screw band and glass insert; clear; quart **15.00-21.00**

Sanitary; 1900; glass lid and wire bail; aqua; quart **10.00-17.00**

San Yuen Co.; 1925; glass lid and half wire bail; clear; quart **6.00-10.00**

The Schaffer Jar, Rochester N.Y.; monogram S.J.C.; aqua; quart **15.00-20.00**

Schram; *Schram St. Louis* on bottom; clear or amethyst; 4" **6.00-8.00**

Schram Automatic Sealer; in ribbon; flat metal lid and wire clamp clear; all sizes **7.00-13.00**

The Scranton Jar; 1870-1880; glass stopper and wire bail; aqua; quart **40.00-50.00**

Sealfast; *sold by W.H. Vanlew, Dayton, Wash. Bakery & Grocery* in an oval; wire clamp top; green; 6¾" **10.00-20.00**

Sealfast; 1915; full wire bail and glass lid; clear or amethyst; all sizes....................**2.00-4.00**

Sealtite Trade Mark; green; quart..........**2.00-4.00**

Sealtite Wide Mouth Mason; flat metal top and screw band; green; quart...................**6.00-10.00**

Season's Mason; metal band and glass insert; clear; 3 sizes.............................**8.00-20.00**

Security; glass top and wire bail; clear; quart...................................**8.00-12.00**

Security Seal; half wire bail and glass top; green or blue; pint, quart.....................**6.00-10.00**

Selco Surety Seal; half wire bail and glass top; green or blue; pint, quart.....................**6.00-10.00**

Selco Surety Seal; in a circle, *Patd. July 14, 1908;* green; quart.........................**2.00-4.00**

Silicon Glass Company, Pittsburg, Penn.; wire bail and glass top; clear or aqua; quart........**10.00-18.00**

Simplex; glass screw top; clear; pint, quart..................................**10.00-25.00**

Sirra Mason Jar; zinc top; clear; pint, quart..................................**10.00-15.00**

Smalley; zinc screw band and milk glass insert; amber; quart...................................**15.00-20.00**

Smalley; zinc top; clear; quart.............**4.00-8.00**

The Smalley Fruit Jar, Sept. 23, 84; aqua; quart.............................**40.00-70.00**

Smalley Full Measure Quart; *Patented Dec. 1889, Apr. 1896, Dec. 1896* under bottom; sheared top; clear or amethyst, $4.00-6.00

Smalley Self-Sealer Wide Mouth; full wire bail and glass top; clear; pint, quart.................**6.00-8.00**

Smalley's Royal; Royal Trade Mark Nu-Seal; crown; clear; pint..........................**2.00-4.00**

J.P. Smith, Son & Co., Pittsburgh; clear; quart...................................**10.00-20.00**

Spencer; 1865; glass top and iron clamp; aqua; quart...................................**30.00-40.00**

Spencer's Patent; 1868; wax dipped cork; aqua; quart...................................**30.00-60.00**

Standard Mason Lynchburg; aqua; quart.....**2.00-6.00**

Standard; with ribbon and *Mason* inside; aqua; quart...................................**4.00-8.00**

Standard, W.C. & Co.; aqua...............**4.00-8.00**

Standard; wax sealer; aqua; quart.......**10.00-16.00**

Standard Mason; zinc top; light aqua or light green; pint, quart..............................**4.00-8.00**

Star; *6* under bottom; aqua; 6½".........**30.00-40.00**

Star; 1895; zinc band and glass insert; clear; quart...................................**15.00-20.00**

Star Glass Co., New Albany Ind.; aqua....**10.00-20.00**

Sterling Mason; zinc top; clear; pint, quart....**2.00-4.00**

Steven's; 1875; wax sealer; green; quart...**40.00-50.00**

A. Stone & Co. Phila; aqua...............**10.00-20.00**

Stone Mason Fruit Jar, Union Stoneware Co., Red Wing Minn; sand crock; ½ gallon......**10.00-15.00**

Stone Mason Fruit Jar; zinc top; white crock; quart...................................**6.00-12.00**

Suey Fung Yuen Co.; Chinese writing; clear; quart.....................................**4.00-8.00**

Sun; glass top and metal clamp; light green; quart...................................**25.00-30.00**

Supreme Mason; screw top; clear; quart.....**4.00-8.00**

Sure Seal; full wire bail and glass top; deep blue; quart.....................................**4.00-6.00**

Swayzee's Fruit Jar; zinc top; aqua; pint, quart...................................**8.00-15.00**

Swayzee's Improved Mason; blue or aqua; pint.....................................**4.00-6.00**

Swayzee's Improved Mason; zinc lid; green or aqua; pint.....................................**4.00-8.00**

Taylor & Co.; wire bail and glass top; aqua; quart...................................**6.00-11.00**

Telephone Jar; full wire bail and glass top; green; quart...................................**15.00-20.00**

The Telephone Jar, Trade Mark, Reg. Whitney Glass Works; clear; quart...................**2.00-6.00**

The Wide Mouth Telephone Jar, Trade Mark Reg; clear; quart..........................**2.00-6.00**

Texas Mason; *made in Tx by Tx* under bottom; clear; 6¾", $4.00-8.00

TF; monogram on base; clear; quart.........**2.00-4.00**

Tight Seal Pat'd July 14, 1908; half wire bail and glass lid; green or blue; all sizes.............**2.00-4.00**

Tropical Canners; metal top; clear; quart.....**2.00-4.00**

True Fruit; 1900; glass top and metal clamp; clear; quart...................................**12.00-16.00**

True Seal; glass top and wire bail; clear.....**8.00-10.00**

Union; 1865; wax seal and metal lid; extending neck, deep aqua; quart.....................**18.00-20.00**

Union Fruit Jar; 1866; wax seal and metal top; aqua; quart...................................**10.00-20.00**

United Drug Co. Boston Mass.; clear; quart..**2.00-4.00**

Universal; screw top; clear; quart..........**4.00-8.00**

Universal L.F. & Co.; clear; quart..........**2.00-6.00**

Vacu-Top; on base; flat metal lid and clamp; light green; quart..........................**15.00-30.00**

The Vacuum Seal; glass top; slender extending neck; clear; quart..........................**8.00-12.00**

The Valve Jar Co., Philadelphia; 1864; *Patent March 10th 1868;* screw top; aqua.........**50.00-100.00**

The Valve Jar; 1868; zinc screw-on top; aqua; quart...................................**20.00-30.00**

The Van Vliet; glass top and iron band with screw; aqua or green; quart....................**40.00-60.00**

Veteran; bust of soldier; clear; quart........**8.00-12.00**

The Victor; 1899; flat metal top and clamp; light green; quart...................................**8.00-12.00**

The Victor, Pat. Feb 20, 1900, M; monogram in circle and diamond; clear; quart...........**10.00-15.00**

Victory; 1875; flat glass top and side wire clips clear; quart **6.00-10.00**

Victory Hom-Pak Mason; clear; quart **2.00-4.00**

"W"; 1885; wax seal; green; quart **4.00-10.00**

W & Co.; on base; green; quart **10.00-20.00**

Geo. E. Wales; on base; glass lid and metal clamp; clear; quart **6.00-15.00**

Wallaceburg Gem; glass insert and zinc screw band; clear or amethyst; quart **4.00-8.00**

Wan-Eta Cocoa, Boston; zinc top; amber, blue; quart **10.00-15.00**

Wan-Eta Cocoa, Boston; ½ pint; 4¾" **8.00-12.00**

The Warsaw Salt Co.; in center, monogram *W.S.Co.* under it *Choice Table Salt Warsaw, N.Y.;* screw top; quart **8.00-12.00**

Wears Jar; glass top and wire clamp; clear; quart **8.00-16.00**

Weideman Boy Brand, Clev.; clear; quart . . . **8.00-10.00**

The Weir, Pat. Mar. 1st 1892; wire bail; crock; quart **6.00-12.00**

Weir Seal; white stoneware lid and wire bail; white; quart **6.00-8.00**

Western Pride; 1880; wax seal; clear; quart **40.00-50.00**

Wheaton; on base; clear; quart **2.00-4.00**

Wheeler; 1889; glass top and wire bail; aqua or green . . . . **40.00 +**

Whitall's; glass top and clip with screw tightener; green; quart **20.00-25.00**

Whitall's Patent, June 18, 1861; in form of circle; on back, *Millville Atmospheric Fruit Jar;* aqua; quart **15.00-29.00**

White Crown Mason; framed in circle and oblong; aqua; quart **2.00-4.00**

Whitney Mason Patd.; 1858 in a circle; clear; 9" **4.00-8.00**

Whitney Mason; 1858; zinc lid; aqua or light green; quart **24.00-32.00**

Wilcox; 1867; flat meal lid and clamp; green; quart **20.00-26.00**

Wills & Co.; 1880-1885; glass stopper and metal clamp; blue green **35.00-44.00**

Winslow Jar; 1870-1873; glass lid and wire clamp; green; quart **30.00-36.00**

Woodbury; 1884-1885; glass lid and metal band clamp; aqua; quart **18.00-26.00**

Woodbury Improved, WGW; monogram; *Woodbury Glass Works, Woodbury, N.J.* on bottom; aqua; quart **8.00-10.00**

Woodbury Improved; 1885; zinc cap; aqua; 3 sizes **20.00-30.00**

Woodbury; *Woodbury Glass Works Woodbury, N.J.2* **under bottom; aqua; 7",**
$20.00-25.00

Worcester; clear or amber; quart **25.00-45.00**

Joshua Wright, Phila; pontil; barrel type **150.00-300.00**

Xnox; in center, a block with K in middle, *Mason* under it; *Xnox* is an error, should read *Knox;* clear; quart **10.00-20.00**

Yelone Jar; 1895-1900; glass lid and wire bail; clear **10.00-14.00**

Yeoman's Fruit Bottle; 1855-1870; wax sealer; small mouth; aqua **30.00-40.00**

Pottery Bottles, Crocks and Jugs

When the best method known for making glass was blowing it by hand, it was recognized that the ancient process of taking wet clay from the earth and shaping and baking it was a more economical means of making containers. Pottery had several advantages: It kept beverages cooler, and it shielded the contents from harmful sunrays.

Pottery containers were being made in this country as early as 1641 by John Pride of Salem. The majority of early pottery bottles were imported, however, mostly from England. The bottles were primitive and since each was handmade, each was unique. The first settlers in Pennsylvania and Ohio were famous for their pottery—bottles, jugs and mugs of the fired clay held beverages, medicines, condiments and inks. Many early jugs were decorated with flowers, birds, people and, of course, the American eagle.

Chinese immigrants to the United States brought a variety of pottery containers with them. The Chinese worked hard and demanded little, and many were brought to help build the railroads. Others had been beckoned to California by the discovery of gold in 1848. Wherever they settled they formed their own community to maintain their traditions—often arousing the suspicions of American observers.

The Chinese contained their food and household items in earthenware jugs. Western Americans held the belief that these containers were burial urns in which the newcomers shipped the cremated ashes of their dead to China. In reality, the jugs contained pickles or vinegar. Another popular theory, possibly correct, was that the two-inch high medicine bottles held opium. Beverages were also stored in pottery—one Chinese whiskey was ninety-six proof.

Chinese bottles are often highly glazed and colorful, with the several colors running together. Some are embossed with Oriental characters, though most designs were impressed into the clay, rather than embossed.

After the discovery of the role of the microbe in disease-causing bacteria in the late 1800's, it seemed only logical that enterprising medicine sellers would attempt to blame every disease known to humanity on the organism and then invent cures to do away with it. One of the more infamous of these "cures" was marketed in pottery containers by William Radam, a Prussian immigrant living in Texas. He was granted a patent for his "Microbe Killer" in 1886. The Pure Food and Drug Act of 1907 put an end to his lucrative business. It was discovered that his "cure" was a simple combination of wine and water. Since the wine was only a fraction of one percent of the total contents. He was making a profit of twenty thousand percent.

Most household pottery jars were made in the nineteenth century. Jugs glazed on the inside are later than 1900. The advent of the automatic glassblowing machine in 1903 made glass bottles cheaper and easier to produce, and pottery began to decline in popularity. But pottery containers had inherent disadvantages anyway—it was difficult to determine how much of a substance remained in the jugs or if the insides were clean. Today a collector must exercise extreme caution when purchasing pottery or crocks as it is quit difficult to ascertain what is old and what is in fact new.

Alaskan Yukon 1909 Pacific Expo. of Seattle; flower on shoulder; jug; 2¾" **8.00-20.00**

P.H. Alders, Compliments of the Eagle Saloon, St. Joseph, Mo.; cream and brown; 3" **8.00-10.00**

Ale, label; tan; 8½" **8.00-10.00**

Ale, label; brown; 6" **2.00-4.00**

Allen & Hanbury's Ltd. Bynol Malt & Oil; black on prints, enormous amount of writing **12.00-17.00**

The Altmayor & Flatau Liquor Co., Fine Liquors, Macon Ga.; round; tan; 6½" **20.00-30.00**

American Stone Ware; in 2 lines, blue letters also near top a large 6, 14 x 13, gray, 13½" **25.00-34.00**

F.A. Ames & Co.; *Owensboro Ky* in back; flat; tan and brown; 3½" **8.00-12.00**

Anderson's Weiss Beers; 7¼" **3.00-6.00**

Armour & Company, Chicago; jug; pouring spout; white; 7¼" **10.00-20.00**

B. & J. Arnold, London England; *Master Ink;* dark brown; 9" **8.00-10.00**

B & H; cream; 3" **8.00-12.00**

Bass & Co. N.Y.; cream; 9½" **8.00-10.00**

Bean pot, label; light blue; 4¼" **2.00-4.00**

L. Beard; on shoulder, cream & blue, blob top, 8½" **16.00-22.00**

Bellarmine Jug; superb mask, 2 horseshoe decorations below mask, 13" **23.00-32.00**

Compliments of Beniss & Thompson, Shelbyville, KY; tan and brown; 3¾" **10.00-15.00**

Jas. Benjamin, Stoneware Depot, Cincinnati, O; blue stencil lettering; mottled tan; 9" **18.00-20.00**

same as above except tan; 13½" **15.00-20.00**

Biscuit Slip Glaze Stone Porter; blob top with small impressed ring for string. Firmly impressed towards base *J, Heginbotham, Kings Arms, Stayley Bridge.* Reserve has other letters impressed below shoulder which cannot be clearly deciphered; *UBL?T ??? ?EA Tody.* Towards base are a further possible 14 characters which cannot be deciphered. Mint State & early 1800's, 9½" **45.00-65.00**

Bitter, label; olive, brown trim; 10¼" **25.00-30.00**

B.B. Bitter Mineral Water, Bowling Green, Mo.; white; 5 gallon; 15" **20.00-25.00**

Black Family Liquor Store; stamped in blue glaze; brown and tan; gallon **10.00-12.00**

Black's Family Liquor Store, H.P. Black; *2042-43 Fresno* in blue glaze letters, 1 Gal. jug ivory and dark brown **25.00-38.00**

Blanchflower & Sons, Homemad; *4 Prize Medals, GT, Yarmouth, Norfolk,* cream with black, 6 sided lid **16.00-22.00**

Blue Picture Print Ginger Jar; picture extends entire circumference of jar, building and junk in sail, 3½" **22.00-33.00**

Blue Print Oinment Pot Beach & Barnicott; *successors to Dr. Roberts Bridport, Poor Man's Friend,* crisp print **11.00-15.00**

Blue Top & Print Cream Pot; *Golden Pastures, Thick Rich Cream, Chard,* picture of maid milking cow **12.00-17.00**

Boston Baked Beans; *HHH* on back; brick color; 1½" **2.00-6.00**

Boston Baked Beans; *OK* on back; brick color; 1½" **2.00-6.00**

Bowers 3 Thistles Snuff; cream color with blue lettering; 2 to 3 gallon, $10.00-30.00

Brownings Pale Ale, Lewes; sparkled biscuit glazed finish, string rim at neck. Cork closure, impressed; 8¾" **15.00-20.00**

Brownings Pale Ale, Lewes; potter's mark; *Stephen Green's Lambeth* **15.00-20.00**

Bryant & Woodruff, Pittsfield, Me; handled jug; blue gray; 7" **18.00-20.00**

Burgess, John & Son, Anchovy Paste, Warehouse 107 Stand; black print on white, 3½", curved shoulder type, print 2 x 2¾" **25.00-38.00**

Butter crock; no label; handle; blue-gray decoration;
4" **15.00-25.00**

Butter crock; no label; blue-gray decoration;
5¼" **12.00-15.00**

Bynol Malt & Oil, Allen & Hanbury's; black on white,
print 2¾" x 3¾", height lots of writing on this pot,
4⅕" **18.00-24.00**

California Pop; *Pat. Dec. 29, 1872;* blob top; tan;
10½" **60.00-70.00**

California Cough Balm; *dose teaspoon full, children ½,*
10-brown crock jug with handle, 3¼" . .**90.00-120.00**

Canning crock; inscribed *Hold Fast That Which is Good;*
dark brown; 6½" **18.00-20.00**

Canning crock; wax sealer; 6" **18.00-20.00**

Canning crock; wax sealer; reddish brown;
8" **10.00-12.00**

Canning crock; blue with a gray decorative design;
8½" **18.00-20.00**

Canning crock; mustard color; 7" **10.00-12.00**

Canning crock; maple leaf design in lid; caramel color;
6" **6.00-8.00**

Canning crock; brown; 5"; **8.00-10.00**

**Canning crock; wax channel; brown; 8½",
$10.00-12.00**

Canning crock; reddish brown, green on the inside;
6¾" **12.00-14.00**

Canning crock; crude; brown; 4" **6.00-8.00**

Canning crock; wax sealer; dark brown;
5½" **8.00-10.00**

Canning crock; wax sealer; tan; 5½" **8.00-10.00**

Canning crock; wax sealer; dark brown; 5½" . .**5.00-8.00**

Canning crock; wax sealer; dark brown; 6½" . .**5.00-8.00**

Canning crock; wax sealer; mottled gray; 5" . . .**4.00-6.00**

Canning crock; wax sealer; brown; 5½" **8.00-10.00**

Canning crock; barrel; dark brown; 5½" **8.00-10.00**

Canning crock lid; star design; dark brown;
8¾" **12.00-15.00**

Canning crock; dark brown; 7½" **8.00-10.00**

Canning crock; tan; 9" **10.00-12.00**

Canning crock; wax channel; brown; 7½" . . .**10.00-12.00**

**Casper Co. From The, Winston-Salem, Lowest Price
Whiskey House;** write for confidential list, tan-
crockery, blue letters, with wire handle,
9¼" **60.00-80.00**

18th Century Bellarmine; superb large decorative mark
approx. 2½" x 2½", large star decoration beneath
contained in oval with decorative border,
9¼" **225.00-300.00**

Geo. M. Chernauckas Buffet, Telephone Canal 1756;
1900 S. Union St., Corner 19th St. Chicago, large
hall, etc. in a square under it ½ gal. liquid measure,
gal. brown & white, black lettering,
8½" **40.00-55.00**

Chinese Crock Jug; vase; wide, flared mouth; black or
dark brown; 6" **6.00-8.00**

same as above; except with *Federal Law
Forbids* **2.00-4.00**

Chris Morley's; under it in a scroll, *Ginger Beer,* under it
Victorias B.C., brown and cream, inside screw,
7¾" **12.00-15.00**

Clark Bros.; *Pat. May 17, 1899,
Zanesville, Ohio;* brown; 7½",
$10.00-20.00**

Clark Bros. Grocers, Birmingham, Ala.; handle; jug;
white and brown; 10½" **12.00-15.00**

Commemorative Whiskey/Spirit Jug; *by Copeland
Spode* & bearing their marks on base. Underglazed
transfer in band around neck reads; *Coronation of
King George 5th & Queen Mary,* June 22, 1911.
Distillers, Edinburgh, 8½". Main body in royal blue
with 2" band at neck in grey, ¾" bottom ornamental
white embossed relief royal crown with 2 flags; the
left bearing portrait of King George V on background
of Union Jack & the right bearing Portrait of Queen
Mary on background of Royal Standard. Whole
measures approx. 3¾" x 3¾", reverse of jug;
Crowned Royal Coat of Arms surrounded by Garter.
Thistle to left top. Rose to right top. Shamrock either
side of base. Rose thistle & shamrock relief in white
around top of neck **60.00-75.00**

Compliments of M.A. Clauton, 26 Farm St.; brown and
tan; 3" **8.00-10.00**

Compliments of Martin Collins, Cartersville, Ga.;
brown and tan; 3" **8.00-12.00**

**Compliments of Columbia Liquor Company, Augusta,
Ga.;** handle; tan and brown; 3" **8.00-15.00**

Conner's Blood Remedy; cream; 6⅜" **8.00-10.00**

Compliments of J.R. Copeland, 781 24th St.; miniature
jug; brown and white, blue lettering;
5¼" **20.00-40.00**

Cook Fairbank & Co., Akron, Ohio; on shoulder, 11 x
6½" with handle, gray **8.00-15.00**

Cooper's Frank Seville Marmalade; black on white,
3¾", large print with lots of writing **2.00-6.00**

Cornish Mead Co., Ltd; Penzance, Cornwall, *One Pint
Two Tone Stone Jar With Handle,* underglaze Mary-
print on side; *The Honey-moon Drink, Ye Olde Mead
25%* proof, black top **10.00-20.00**

Cowden & Co., Harrisburg, Pa.; dark brown;
6½" **18.00-20.00**

Cramer's Kidney Cure, Albany N.Y.; N's are backward;
aqua; 4½" **10.00-20.00**

Crock bottle; gray; 10" **5.00-8.00**

Crock, label; cathedral type; brown and tan;
8½" **25.00-30.00**

Crock flask; red and brown glaze; 7½" **50.00-100.00**

Crock, label; brown, green and tan; 7" **8.00-10.00**

Crock, label; light gray; 6½",
$8.00-12.00

Crock, label; brown; 7" **8.00-10.00**

Crock with seal; *Amsterdam;* tan; 12" **8.00-10.00**

Crock, label; tan and cream; 6¾" **6.00-8.00**

Crock, label; tan and cream; 5½" **6.00-8.00**

Crock, plain; ring top; 2 tone, tan and cream;
8½" **2.00-4.00**

Crock, plain; *Kinney* on base; ring top; 2 tone, tan and
cream; 8½" **4.00-8.00**

Crock, plain; bottle type; tapered crown; cream and tan;
7½" **2.00-6.00**

Crock, plain; roof type shoulder; cream and tan;
8" **2.00-4.00**

Dr. Cronk's Sarsaparilla Bar; blob top; sand color;
9½" **10.00-20.00**

Crown Ginger Beer Co., Cleveland, Ohio; in a circle in
center; brown; 6¾" **6.00-12.00**

Crowous, J.W. Drug Co. 1 Lb. Mercury; *Dallas, Tex* in
4 lines, tan crock, ring top, 2¾" **35.00-48.00**

Cruiskeen Lawn; cream and
brown; 8", $4.00-10.00

Presented By P.J. Currin; A Merry Christmas and Happy New Year; pint jug; brown and tan with blue
stencil lettering; 6½" **15.00-20.00**

Dawson Salts & Water Co. Distributors Hamby Salts,
Iron and Lithia Water, Dawson Springs, Ky.; large
5 above; jug brown and white, blue lettering;
18" **20.00-25.00**

D.C.; gray; 11" **5.00-8.00**

same as above except tan; 10½" **4.00-6.00**

The D.C.L. Scotch Whiskey Distillers Limited, London,
Edinburgh, Glasgow, Gold Medals, Edinburgh;
1886; under bottom *Bengimark, Doulton, Shicon,
England* **30.00-60.00**

Deacon Brown Vinegar; in 3 lines, tan & brown,
3¼" **25.00-37.00**

Geo. A. Dickel & Co. Cascade Distillery, Hand Made
Sour Mash Tennessee Whiskey; white with black
lettering, blue bands; 9½" **15.00-18.00**

D.J. and Co., No 2A Lumber Street, N. York; 1795;
preserves crock; seal top; salt glaze; 5" . . . . . **100.00+**

A.P. Donaghho, Parkersburg, W.V.; canning crock; tan,
blue stencil; 8" **18.00-20.00**

A.P. Donaghho, Parkersburg, W.V.; written at a slant;
blue-gray stencil; 8" **18.00-20.00**

Doster-Northington Drug Co., Birmingham, Ala; jug
with handle; white and brown; 11" **12.00-15.00**

Doster-Northington Drug
Co., Birmingham, Ala;
brown and cream; ½
gallon, $15.00-25.00

Compliments of A J. Dresel, Second & Magnolia Ave.,
Louisville Ky.; brown and tan; 2¼" **20.00-40.00**

Dotrick Distilling Co.; Dayton, O. Motto Jug, *Eat, Drink
and Be Merry* in 3 lines, crock brown & cream with
hand, 5½" **38.00-50.00**

Drinkometer; in back; tan; 5" **4.00-8.00**

Eagle Liqueur Dis., Cincinnati O.; ring top; eagle and
shield in center; green; 2¼" **10.00-20.00**

Eelaarki, Adrsv. Schiedarn; crock with handle; ring
around bottom; tan; 4" **4.00-6.00**

same as above except 12" **4.00-8.00**

England Natoine; in 2 lines on base; 4 rings near
shoulder; spout; brick brown; 10" **4.00-8.00**

same as above except in all colors and sizes; some
with panels; some with plain tops **4.00-10.00**

Etruia Stone Chin; *2518* under bottom; syrup label; tan;
6" **10.00-20.00**

J.W.M. Field & Sons Wholesale Liquors, Owensboro,
Ky; cream; 3¼" **20.00-40.00**

Fockin, Wynand, Amsterdam; beer jug with handle; tan;
12" **8.00-15.00**

Football figural; whiskey label; brown;
3¾" x 2½" **10.00-15.00**

Fowlkes & Myatt Co. Cider Vinegar; miniature jug;
brown and white, blue lettering; 3" **20.00-40.00**

Franc, L. & Co.; *Toledo, Ohio, M.C. Kingon Hand Made
Sour Mash Whiskey* in a frame, blue letters, tapered
top & ring, 10½" **10.00-20.00**

J. Frieder; hand-painted picture; ring around bottom; tan;
12" **18.00-20.00**

same as above except *B. Frankfer* **18.00-20.00**

Frog; sheared top, coming out of mouth, green,
6½" **8.00-15.00**

same as above except *B Frankfer* **18.00-20.00**

G W Fulper & Bros. Flemington, N.J.; tan and blue
decorations; 11¼" **20.00-25.00**

Gallagher & O'Gara, Dealers in Fine Whiskey, Bessemer, Ala.; tan **8.00-10.00**

Galloway's Everlasting Jar; *Pat'd Feb. 8th Pat. Applied for 1870;* canning crock with wax sealer; gray; 7¾" **15.00-18.00**

Ginger pot; fancy decoration; no lettering; turquoise; 3½" **6.00-8.00**

Gold Tester; crock; 4" **2.00-4.00**

Charles S. Gove Company, Wholesale Liquor Dealers, Boston, Mass; jug with handle; brown top and cream base; 9" **12.00-15.00**

Compliments of H. Graff & Co., Fresno, Cal.; in 3 lines; jug with handle; letters stamped in blue glaze; ivory and dark brown; 3½" **15.00-25.00**

H. Graff & Co., Compliment of Fresno, Cal.; in 3 lines, blue glaze letters, cream brown, 3¼", with handle **17.00-24.00**

Grasselli Arsenate of Lead; poison crock; cream; 6½", $10.00-15.00

The O. L. Gregory Vinegar Co.; tan and brown; 3½" **20.00-40.00**

Hailwoods Manchester, Brown Top Cream Pot; outline picture of cow at center, height 4" **22.00-33.00**

Hammersley's Creamery, Blue Print Cream Pot; Broughton, 3 hammers pictured at center, 4" **17.00-24.00**

same but height 3" **26.00-38.00**

Happy Patty; with handle; brown and tan; 8½" **4.00-8.00**

I.W. Harper, Nelson Co., Ky.; cream; 3¼ **20.00-40.00**

Harper, I.W. Nelson Co., Kentucky; Wluses & many doz a ribbing etc. on front of jug with handle, tan neck, etc. ring top, cream, 7½" **75.00-100.00**

I.W. Harper, Gold Medal Whiskey; square base; long twisted neck; cobalt; 8¾" **25.00-75.00**

W.P. Hartley, Liverpool & London; London Tower in center; under it *Trademark Reg.;* 11 panels; tan; 4" **4.00-8.00**

Vincent Hathaway & Co.; blob top; tan; 9½" **5.00-8.00**

Hayner Lock, Box 290, Dayton, Ohio; white; 8" **15.00-20.00**

Helment Rye; blue lettering; cream; 3" **8.00-16.00**

Hessig-Ellis Drug Co., Memphis, Tenn; *1 lb. Mercury, Cream,* ring top **13.00-19.00**

Distilled By James R. Hogo, Jim Whiskey, Poplar Bluff, Mo; white and brown, blue lettering; 9¾" **18.00-40.00**

Compliments of Holdberg, Mobile and Cincinnati; brown and white; 3¼" **6.00-12.00**

E.J. Hollidge; label; cream; 6" **7.00-10.00**

Holloway's Family Ointment for the Cure of CTC; 8 lines (London), 1 x 1½" round crock, in back 7 lines, ring top **17.00-24.00**

Holloway's Ointment, Gout & Rheumatism; height 1½" **9.00-12.00**

J.W. Hooper & Bro. Groceries and Liquors Nashville, Tenn.; jug; tan with brown top and blue lettering; 8¼" **20.00-40.00**

Horton Cato Mfg. Co., Detroit, Michigan, Royal Salad Dressing; wide mouth jug; white and brown with black lettering; 10¼", $15.00-18.00

R.M. Hughes & Co.s; monogram, *Vinegar;* blue label; white; 9¼" **20.00-25.00**

Humphrey & Martin; tan and brown crock; 8¾" **25.00-40.00**

Ink crock; conical; light gray; 2¾" **4.00-8.00**

Ink crockery; round pouring lip; cream; 10¾" . .**4.00-8.00**

Ink crockery; round pouring lip; brown; 7¾" . . .**4.00-8.00**

Ink crock, plain; roof type shoulder; pouring lip; 6" **8.00-12.00**

Ink crock, plain; tan; 2¾" **4.00-8.00**

Ink crock, plain; no neck; round collar; brown; 1¾" round, 1¾" tall **6.00-8.00**

Ink crock, label; light gray; 5¾" **10.00-20.00**

Ink crock, label; tan; 2½" **4.00-8.00**

Ink crock, label; tan; 2½" **10.00-20.00**

Ink crock, label; tan; 2¾", $6.00-15.00

Ink crock, label; tan; 7" **6.00-8.00**

Ink crock, label; cream; 5" **4.00-8.00**

Ink pottery; light blue; short neck **6.00-8.00**

Ink pottery; some have embossing; brick brown; 10" **6.00-8.00**

Ink pottery; plain; conical; light gray; 2¾" around bottom, 2⅛" tall **4.00-8.00**

same as above except brown **4.00-8.00**

Ink pottery; plain; ring top; light brown; 1¾" round ¼" neck **6.00-8.00**

Jones Bros. & Co.; brown and tan; 3½" **2.00-6.00**

Jones Bros., Compliments of J. Carr Mfg's of High Grade Cider & Ving., Louisville, Ky.; tan and cream; 3½" **20.00-40.00**

Jordan & Stanley, Wine & Spirit Merchants, New Port, I.W., Spirit Jug, Cork Closure; brown top, light fawn bottom, incised across top front, handle at neck, round section jug with waist towards bottom third, 8"............................**18.00-26.00**

Jug; very crude bell shape; red and tan; 7"...**6.00-8.00**

Kabbenbeer Ltd., London, Patented One Litre Lidded Beer Jug; white glaze, handle at side, impressed below neck, *IL* base impressed *W,* black underglaze printed lid reads *This Jug is The Property of Kabbenbeer, Ltd. London, Patented.* Handle at side, brass thumb plate for opening lid, over center brass clip to keep lid closed, 9¼" hairline crack extends 3½" down from neck on one side only. Unusual brewery item. No other chips or damage except defect mentioned....................**12.00-40.00**

Kaehler Bros., Fresno Cal.; in a circle with a medicine trademark; ivory and brown; gallon.....**10.00-20.00**

Kan 2; in seal on shoulder, ring neck, ring top, handle, tan, 12", round....................**26.00-37.00**

James Keiller & Sons, Dundee Marmalade, London, 1862, Great Britain; gray; 4"...........**6.00-8.00**

Kennedy; tan and beige; 8½"............**8.00-10.00**

The Kintore; cream and brown; 8¼".......**4.00-10.00**

C.B. Kirby, Late R. Crook & Co., Hervey Street, Ipswich; tan and cream; two gallon, $15.00-25.00

J.W. Kolb & Son, 4471 St. Louis Ave., St. Louis, Mo.; jug; stamped letters dark brown and cream; 3¼"....................................**5.00-8.00**

Kutner Goldstein & Co., Return To; *Wholesale Grocers Fresno, Calif* in 4 lines in blue glaze letters, bucket type handle, 1 gal., cream...........**15.00-25.00**

Return to Kitner & Goldstein & Co., Wholesale Grocers, Fresno, Calif.; wire handle; cream; gallon............................**10.00-15.00**

Lambrecht; in script, *Butter;* white and blue lettering; 2⅞"....................................**5.00-8.00**

Little Brown Jug; engraved; brown pottery; 2¾"....................................**4.00-8.00**

Little Brown Jug 1876; dark brown; 3"....**15.00-30.00**

Liverpool; on base, brown and white, tapered top, 7¼"....................................**8.00-10.00**

Lymans Clare & Co., 384 & 386 St. Paul Street, Montreal; tan, blue incising; 6"...........**8.00-10.00**

Manchester, Hailwoods Pure Rich Cream; cream pot, stone color, creamery, Broughton, 4"....**8.00-15.00**
same but height 3¼"................**10.00-25.00**

Compliments of J.C. Mayfield Mfg. Co., Birmingham, Ala.; tan; 3¼"....................**8.00-12.00**

Mayfield Vinegar & Cider Co., Mayfield, Ky, The Family & Pickling Vinegar; cream; 3¼"....**20.00-40.00**

McComb Pottery; *Pottery Pat. Pend.* on bottom; canning crock; tan and brown; 6"............**15.00-18.00**

McComb Pottery & Co.; *Pat. Jan. 24, 1899;* canning crock; white; 7"....................**16.00-23.00**

Compliments of McDonnel, John A.; *269 Conception St.* in 4 lines, crock with handle cream, 3"....................................**20.00-45.00**

The Medenhall Hotel Baths, Claremore, Okla; *radium water from: Cures rheumatism, stomach trouble, exzema and other ailments,* letters in blue, 1 gal. jug, ivory and brown with handle..........**10.00-25.00**

Melchers, J.J. Wz-Schiedorm; *Honey Suckle, Old Gin* in 4 lines on base, tan, 12½ x 2¾" with handle, ring top....................................**8.00-15.00**

M.H. Melick, Roseville, Ohio; canning crock; gray; 8¼"....................................**10.00-12.00**

Mercury; tan and white crock; 5".........**20.00-40.00**

Mercury Spurlock Neal Co., Nashville, Tenn.; jug white and blue lettering; 3¼".............**20.00-40.00**

Meredith's Diamond Club Pure Rye Whiskey; white; 8", $25.00-50.00

Metropolitan Club, Freberg & Kahn Distillers; miniature jug; brown and white, blue lettering; 3¼"....................................**20.00-40.00**

Miller, C.J.; *Fine Whiskies, Vicksburg, Miss* in 3 lines, crock jug with handle, brown, tan, 7½", qt....................................**10.00-20.00**

Minn. Stoneware Co., Red Wing, Minn.; on bottom; wide mouth; reddish brown; 7"........**12.00-15.00**

Minn. Stone Ware Co. Safety Valve Pat.; canning crock; white and blue markings; 8½"...**15.00-18.00**

Christian Moerlein Brewing Co. Cin. O; in a circle on shoulder; *Trademark* on top of it in center; *Moerleins Old Jug Lager Run Beer* with fancy design around it; dark brown; 8"..........................**25.00 +**

Compliments of D. Monroe, SR.; *303-305 South 18th St.;* brown and tan; 3½"............**10.00-20.00**

Motto Jug ''As I Go Up The Hill of Prosperity, May I Never Meet A Friend''; *Dotrick Distillery Co., Dayton, O.,* brown and cream crock with handle, 4½"....................................**40.00-60.00**

Moutarde Dessauz Fils Orleans France; on back; cream; 4"....................................**4.00-8.00**

Mouth Wash; letters running bottom left to top right with 3 leaf clover, applied top, elephant stopper, pale blue, 5"....................................**11.00-15.00**

Wm. J. Moxley's Special Oleo-Margarine; *The Taste is the Test, Pat. 6-2-14;* white and black lettering, blue bands; 7½"....................**10.00-12.00**

Grape Juice Prepared by Myers Benton & Co., Cleveland; tan; 5½"....................**35.00 +**

N.K.A.; in a circle near shoulder, tan with handle, short neck, double ring top, tan, 11¼" **14.00-20.00**

D. Newman; tan and white crock; 7" **4.00-6.00**

Nordjausen Kornschnapps; tan and cream; 7½", $10.00 +

Compliments of Norton & Norton, Savannah, Ga.; brown and tan; 3¼" **8.00-10.00**

E. & L. P. Norton, Bennington, VA.; gray with blue decorative design; 8¾" **25.00-35.00**

E.B. Norton & Co. Worcester, Mass; handle; gray with blue decorative design; 14" **30.00-60.00**

John H. Oelkers, 730 S. Rampart St. N.O. La.; tan and brown; 4½" **10.00-20.00**

Old; in center a picture of a jug on it, *Rye, Jug;* tan, 3½" **28.00-39.00**

Old Continental Whiskey; miniature size; brown and tan; 3¼" **20.00-40.00**

same as above except cream **20.00-40.00**

Old Continental Whiskey; brown and cream; 3" **20.00-40.00**

Old Cutter Rye, A.E. Campbell Catering Co., Birmingham, Ala; tan; 3¼" **8.00-10.00**

Old Dexter Dis. Co., Butler, Kentucky; Dis. in a circle a flower in center in back *Pat. Aug. 11, 1919, The Old Dexter Jug Whiskey,* rib side, round jug with handle and vase bottom, 8" **40.00-60.00**

Old Jug, Bourbon, G. Hanneman, Portland, Ore.; in 4 lines, handle, silver-plated, pouring spout, 10½" **80.00-100.00**

Old Jug Lager; *The Fashionable Beverage of the Day Brilliant in Color, Absolutely Pure, Stimulating Rejuvenating, Truly Cultured, Veritable Luxury, Nashville, Tenn.;* all in ornate lettering; cream; 8¼" **4.00-8.00**

Old Nectar Rye; *R.P. Blalack, Mobile Ala;* cream; 3" **20.00-40.00**

Old Private Stock Pure Rye; in 2 lines, brown and gray crock with handle, double ring top, 3¼" **15.00-30.00**

Old Taylor; on side; reverse *S.H. Taylor & Sons Dist., Frankfort, Ky.;* tan; quart.............**10.00-25.00**

Oregon Import Company, Portland, Oregon; with handle, brown and cream crock, ½ gal....**15.00-30.00**

D.L. Ormsby, 1850; with star in a circle; reverse at base in shield *Patent Pressed W. Smith N.Y.;* twelve-sided; very crude; tan; ½ pint........**10.00-12.00**

Ottman Bros. & Co. Fort Edward, N.Y.; blue bird; gray with cobalt decoration; 11" **50.00-65.00**

J.W. Palmer; tan; 3" **20.00-40.00**

Pain & Baylor; tan and white; 7" **4.00-6.00**

Richard Pearce; tan; 7" **4.00-6.00**

Pewtress, S.L.; *Conn, #2, Blue Flower Dis.;* tapered ring top, same color....................**50.00-100.00**

G.W. Piper; cream; 7¼" **4.00-6.00**

Price & Bristol; on base, brown and white, tapered top, 7¼" **8.00-10.00**

M. Quinn, Wholesale Grocer, Kansas City, Mo.; wire handle with wooden grip; white with blue lettering; 10" **12.00-15.00**

Wm. Radam's Microbe Killer No. 1; handle on jug; white with blue lettering; 10¾" **20.00-25.00**

Randolph & Co.; brown and tan; 3" **20.00-40.00**

Theo Rectanus Co.; *Pure Old Hand Made Sour Mash Louisville;* brown and cream; 3¼" **20.00-40.00**

Reliable Middle Quality Fruit Preserves; gray with black lettering; 6" **12.00-15.00**

Jacob Richter Co., Fresno, Cal; *Best Wines & Liquors $5 per gal.* in 4 lines; brown and ivory; gallon **25.00-35.00**

H.E.N. Ross; in a circle; in a circle under it a cross and *Cross Flag;* under it in one line *Phein Preussen; Pottery* or *Crock* on shoulder; handle; tan; 12" tall, 3¼" round **4.00-10.00**

Royal Doulton Dewars Whiskey; with Scottish figure, crock jug, qt....................**40.00-58.00**

Russell, M.C. & Son; *Corner 3rd & Market Sts. Maryville, Ky* in a frame, brown and sand with handle, 6" **28.00-37.00**

Sainsbury's Bloater Paste; black or white, 3" **5.00-7.00**

Sanford's Inks, the Quality Line Pastes; jug with pouring spout; white with blue lettering; 10½" **20.00-50.00**

Satterlee & Mory, Ft. Edwards, N.Y.; gray with blue decorative design; 7½" **20.00-25.00**

James Scham; *Pat. July 13, 1909;* embossed *Sherwood;* canning crock; glass lid; white; 7½" **8.00-10.00**

Christian Schmidt, Shenandoah, Pa.; cream; 7" **8.00-10.00**

Comp. of H. Schroder, 401 & 403 Broughton; brown and tan; 3½" **8.00-10.00**

Fred L. Schwantz, Up-To-Date Grocer, Fine Liquor, 63 Beale St. Memphis, Tenn; jug; tan with brown top; 8½" **20.00-25.00**

Scotland Export Co. Ltd. Chivas Regal; tan; 12" **30.00-50.00**

Shuster, Ben J., Compliments of; *Salem, Ala* in 3 lines, beige and brown with handle, 3¾" **22.00-37.00**

B.J. Simond's; blob top; 10" **30.00-50.00**

Simplex Hektograph; *Composition for Hall's Patent Simplex,* large picture of hatted man blowing trumpet, very large print 3 x 3 inches, printed at rear with instructions *For Use*.............**18.00-25.00**

D.F. Smith & Snows; *Whitefoot, Pat. July 17, 66;* blob top; tan; 10" **30.00-50.00**

J.L. Smith; inside under lip; crude Southern pottery; brown; 11" **12.00-15.00**

Smoky Mt. 1880; vinegar jar; brown; 5", $15.00-30.00

Stout & Ginger Beer; tan and brown, 6″ a cross in center **4.00-8.00**

Comp. of Southern Gro. Co. 114 Bernard St.; brown and tan; 3½″ **20.00-40.00**

Soy Sauce; pottery jug; short neck; ring top; side spout; brown; 5″ **6.00-8.00**

Soyer's Perfect Sauce, Meadville, Pa; on front in 3 lines, crock with handle, ring top, 7½″ .. **10.00-15.00**

W.M. Spencer; *Clarks improved, Pat. May 19th 92, Zanesville, Ohio* on bottom; white with blue lettering; 9″ **18.00-20.00**

Stone Mason Pat'd Applied For; on shoulder; canning crock; tan and brown **12.00-15.00**

The Weir Stonewall Fruit Jar, Pat. 1892; tan and brown; 6½″ **10.00-15.00**

E. Swasey & Co., Portland, Me.; butter crock; white and brown; 3½″ **10.00-12.00**

Dr. Swett's Original Root Beer, Registered, Boston, Mass; brown and tan; 7¾″, $6.00-10.00

E.B. Taylor, Richmond Va.; at an angle; gray with blue stencil lettering; 8″ **18.00-20.00**

Thwaites Dublin; tan tapered top, short neck, 6¾″ **6.00-8.00**

Timothy White Co., Ltd. Extract of Malt & Cod Liver Oil; black on white, 5⅜″, print size 3½″x3¼″, crisply printed **8.00-15.00**

Tode Bros; *T.B.* and arrow through a ring on bottom; dark tan, $4.00-6.00

N.M.Uri & Co R.H. Parker; tan; 2¾″ **40.00-60.00**

Vase, label; 3½″ **3.00-4.00**

Vitreous Stone Bottling, J. Bourne & Son; *patentees Denby Pottery, near Derby P & J Arnold Sondon,* 4¼″x2½″, pouring lip, brown **14.00-20.00**

Vodoo face jug; *2* under bottom; gray; 6″ x 6″ **40.00-50.00**

Walkdens Copying Ink; salt glaze; 7½″ ... **50.00-100.00**

Waterlow & Sons, Limited; brown; 7½″ ... **10.00-12.00**

Wesson Oil; blue lettering; 5″, $10.00-12.00

Western Stoneware Co.; *Pat. Jan 24, 1899* on bottom; brown and tan; 7″ **12.00-15.00**

Weymans Snuff; on base; tan; 6¾″ **10.00-20.00**

same as above except cream **10.00-20.00**

Whiskey, label; tan and cream; 4″ **15.00-30.00**

N.A. White & Sons, Utica, N.Y.; blue iris flower on front; tan; 6¾″ **20.00-25.00**

White-Hall, W.H.; monogram; *S.P. & S. Co. Whitehall, Ill;* canning crock; 7″ **18.00-20.00**

Wing Lee Wai, Hong Kong; under bottom; *Chinese Rice Wine; Federal Law Forbids Sale Or Re Use of This Bottle* on back brown; 6″ **8.00-10.00**

Woapollinaris-Brannen; *M* with an anchor in center of the seal; under it *Cebry Kreuyber Ahr Weiler, Rhein Prausse;* under it *#65;* handle; tan; 12″ **14.00-18.00**

Comp. of Worrell & Foster, West End, Ala; tan and brown; 3¼″ **8.00-12.00**

X; on shoulder; brown pottery; 6½″ tall, 3¾″ diameter **4.00-6.00**

Wright & Greig, Glasgow; whiskey jug, 3½″ biscuit color, handle at neck, underglaze transfer; *Roderick Dhu, Highland Whiskey, Sole Proprietors; Wright & Greig, Glasgow,* bottom incised *C & F Glasgow,* transfer measures 4¼″ x 3½″ and is picture of Highland Chief in full dress against background of mountains **35.00-50.00**

Compliments of Mrs. J.M. Yockers, 500 Wilkinson St.; tan and cream; 3¼″ **20.00-40.00**

Ink

Ink has been a part of man's civilization, aiding it in organization and communication. The Egyptians and Chinese used it as early as 2500 B.C., and in the first century B.C., ink was made from mixing glue with coal. People of that era were fascinated by the cuttlefish, or ink fish, a clever creature that ejects a black fluid to conceal itself when endangered. The Romans managed to extract the liquid from the fish's pouch and use it as ink.

The first patent for the manufacture of ink was granted in England in 1792. The first American patent was granted to the firm of Maynard and Noyes in Boston in 1816. Since England and France were famous for their high quality inks, the first ink in the United States was imported. Most of the bottles were crudely fashioned of pottery, usually brown or white in color. The first American-made master bottles—bottles that contained a pint or quart of ink and were used primarily to store ink—were poor quality glass containing many bubbles and tears.

The ink industry in America had difficulty catching on partly because of a lack of effective writing instruments. Quills—feathers fashioned into pens by pointing and slitting the lower end—were used well in the 1850's, though other innovations preceded them. Peregine Williamson of Baltimore invented a metal pen in 1809, but it did not find widespread acceptance until 1858. In that year, Richard Esterbrook opened a factory to produce the pens in Camden, New Jersey. They were not an immediate success—they had to be dipped in the ink often which frequently resulted in messy ink spills at the writing tables. American engineering and ingenuity were set to work to come up with an ink bottle that would not topple. This resulted in over one thousand types of ink bottles, many designed not to tip. Umbrella-shaped ink bottles were a popular shape as were the teakettle shapes, complete with pouring spouts. Other shapes included turtles, barrels, shoes, buildings, boats, schoolhouses and cathedrals.

The first ink bottles were fancy since they adorned the writing table. D. Hyde of Reading, Pennsylvania, invented the fountain pen in 1830. Upon its commercial manufacture in 1884, the extravagance of fancy ink bottles became unnecessary since small and round or square ink containers could be conveniently placed in a drawer. Many ink bottles were embossed, and the paper labels, when used, were ornate.

The familiar Carter ink bottle was first manufactured by William Carter in Masachusetts in 1858. A few Carter bottles were of pottery, but they were expensive—particularly when so many broke in transit—and their manufacture was discontinued.

Alling's; sheared top and teapot spout; green;
2¼″ **10.00-20.00**

Alling's Ink; triangular; green; 1⅞″x2¼″ . . . **20.00-30.00**

Alonzo French; barrel; *Pat. March 1st. 1870;* aqua; 2″
tall, 2″ long **30.00-40.00**

Angus & Co.; cone; aqua; 3½″ **4.00-6.00**

Antoine Et Fils; straight top with pouring lip; brown pottery; 8⅜″ **6.00-8.00**

P & J Arnold; collar with pouring lip; brown;
9¼″ **10.00-12.00**

Arnold's; round; clear or amethyst; 2½″ **4.00-6.00**

A3; *Pat July 9, 1895* under bottom; aqua;
2¼″ **6.00-8.00**

B & B; pottery bottle; tan; 7½″ **4.00-8.00**

Bell; sheared top; clear or amethyst; 3″ **4.00-6.00**

Bell, label; crock; double ring top; tan **10.00-20.00**

Bertinguiot; sheared top; amber; 2″ **18.00-30.00**

Billing & Co.; *Banker's Writing Ink; B* in center; aqua; 2″
x 1½″ **4.00-10.00**

Billing & Co.; *Banker's Writing Ink; B* embossed in
center on bottom; aqua; 2″ **4.00-6.00**

Billings, J.T. & Son; sheared top; aqua;
1⅞″ **4.00-8.00**

Billings/Mauve Ink; near base; dome shaped; sheared top; aqua; 1¾″ tall, 2¹¹⁄₁₆″ deep base . . **10.00-20.00**

S.M. Bixby & Co.; aqua; 2½″ **10.00-20.00**

Bixby; on bottom; aqua; 2½″ **2.00-4.00**

Bixby; on bottom; clear or amethyst; 2½″, $2.00-3.00

Bixby; under bottom; ink or polish; *Patented Mch, 83* under shoulder; square base; round corners slanting upward so the bottle gradually becomes round; bulbous shoulder; amber; 4″ tall; 1⅜″
base **4.00-8.00**

same as above except plain, no *Bixby* **2.00-6.00**

Bixley Mushroom Ink; aqua; 2″ **15.00-20.00**

C. Blackman; green; 2½″ **10.00-20.00**

Boat shaped; plain; blue; 1¾″ **4.00-6.00**

same as above except clear **4.00-6.00**

Bonney Barrel Ink; aqua; 2½″ **10.00-20.00**

Bonney Cone Ink; *Bonney Premium French Ink, South Hanover, Mass;* aqua; 2½″ **30.00-50.00**

W.E. Bonney Ink, South Hanover, Mass; aqua;
2¼″ **8.00-10.00**

W.E. Bonney; aqua; 2½″ x 3″ x 1½″ **10.00-20.00**

J. Bourne & Sons Near Derby; on base; *Carter's Ink;* tan; 7″ **8.00-15.00**

J. Bourne & Son, Patentees, Derby Pottery Near Derby, P.J. Arnold, London, England; embossed near the base; pottery; round; pouring spout lip light brown; 9½″ tall, 3¾″ diameter **6.00-8.00**

Bourne Derby; crock; brown; 8½″ **4.00-6.00**

Brickett J. Taylor Ink; cylindrical; flared lip
4½″ **100.00-150.00**

D.B. Brooks & Co. Ink; blue green; 2⅛″ **8.00-12.00**

D.B. Brooks & Co.; amber; 2″ x 2½″ **10.00-20.00**

Bulldog head; milk glass; 4″ **10.00-20.00**

J.J. Butler; aqua; 2″ **6.00-8.00**

Calumbine Ink; between four pointed starts; ring top; aqua; 1¾″ x 1½″ x 1½″ **15.00**

Cardinal Bird Ink; turtle; aqua **60.00-70.00**

Cardinell Ink Ou Trade Mark, Montclair, N.J.; *Cardinell Erado Trade Mark Montclair, N.J.* on back; square; collar; *ABM;* amber; 1″ x 2⅛″ **2.00-4.00**

Carter; *#11* under bottom; aqua; 2½″ **2.00-6.00**

Carter; under bottom; milk glass; 3″ **6.00-10.00**

Carter Ink; *Made in U.S.A.* under bottom; tea kettle; clear; 2½″ x 4″, $60.00-110.00**

Carter Ink; clear or amethyst; 2¼″ **2.00-4.00**

Carter's; on bottom; double *V* band collar; ring on shoulder and base; round; aqua or amethyst; 2⅝″ **3.00-4.00**

same as above except *Carter's 7½ Made in USA* on bottom; aqua **4.00-6.00**

Carter's; on bottom; cone; large and small raised ring at base of neck; 2 round bands on collar; aqua; 2½" x 2⅞" **4.00-6.00**

Carter's; on lid; screw-on top; *13* embossed on bottom; clear; 1⅛" **4.00-6.00**

Carter's; cobalt; 6½", $6.00-8.00

Carter's; 8 panels; aqua; 1¾" **4.00-8.00**

Carter's; on shoulder; 3-part mold; ring collar and pouring lip; light green; pint **8.00-16.00**

Carter's; one ring tapers at neck; round base; amethyst; 2¼" **2.00-4.00**

Carter's; 3 dots close together under bottom; aqua; 2½" **2.00-6.00**

Carter's Full ½ Pint; on shoulder; applied ring; round; aqua; 6¼", $5.00-12.00

Carter's; on back; *Full ½ Pint* on bottom; *Pat Feb. 14-99;* 6" tall, 2½" round **4.00-10.00**

Carter's Full Quart; on top shoulder; under that *Made in U.S.A.;* aqua; 9½" **6.00-10.00**

Carter's Full Quart, Made In U.S.A.; around shoulder; *Pat. Feb. 14, 99* on base; round; applied lip; aqua; 9⅝" **8.00-15.00**

Carter's; *House Ink;* turtle; double door with 2 windows on dome near spout, *Ink,* and below that, *Carter's* **90.00-110.00**

Carter's Ink; plain 3-part mold; round; pouring lip; light green; ½ pint, quart; 10¼" tall, 3" bottom, 2¼" neck **8.00-16.00**

same as above except ring collar; 2-part mold **8.00-16.00**

Carter's Ink Made in U.S.A.; under bottom, label; aqua; 2¾" **4.00-6.00**

Carter's Ink Co.; 2 bottles, one in the shape of a man and one in the shape of a woman; woman has red blouse, red and white skirt, black shoes, yellow hair, and rolling pin in her left hand; man has tan trousers, blue jacket and red tie; 3⅝" . . **40.00-80.00**

Carter's Koal Blk Ink; label; machine made; clear; 2" **2.00-4.00**

Carter's Made In U.S.A.; on shoulder; also *Full Qt. Bulk Ink;* aqua; 9¾" **3.00-6.00**

Carter's; on base *Made in U.S.A. 1897;* round base; tapers at neck; one ring; green or aqua; 2½" tall, base 2⅜" **3.00-7.00**

same as above except brown **8.00-12.00**

Carter's/Non-Copying/Carmine/Writing/Fluid; imprinted on jug; *The Carter's Ink Co.;* seal, powderhorn, etc.; brown and tan glaze; gallon **15.00-30.00**

Carter's No. 1; on base; round; cobalt blue; 32 fluid ounces; 9½" **5.00-10.00**

Carter's No. 5 Made in U.S.A.; on bottom; machine made; clear or amethyst **2.00-4.00**

Carter's No. 5 Made in USA; on bottom; ring collar; large ring forms shoulder; cone; *ABM;* amethyst; 2½" **2.00-4.00**

Carter's #6 Made in USA; on bottom; round; ring collar; ring on shoulder and base; aqua; 2½" diameter, 3" tall **3.00-5.00**

Carter's #6½ Made in USA; on bottom; *16 Fluid Oz.* on shoulder; sheared type collar and ring on neck; bulbous shoulder; ring at base; round; *ABM;* amethyst; 3" diameter, 7½" tall **6.00-10.00**

Carter's #9 Made in USA; on bottom; double ring collar; step on shoulder; amethyst; 2" x 2" x 2" . . **2.00-4.00**

Carter's #9; on bottom; ring collar; *ABM;* square; clear; 2" **2.00-3.00**

Carter's 1897; on bottom; cone; wide and narrow raised rings; rings at base of neck; narrow, round band collar; aqua; 2½" **4.00-6.00**

Carter's 1897 Made in U.S.A.; under bottom; cone; aqua, $6.00-7.00

Carter's 1897 Made in U.S.A.; under bottom; cone; emerald **7.00-10.00**

Carter's Pencraft Combined Office & Fountain Pen Fluid; clear; 7½" **4.00-8.00**

Carter's Pro Writing Fluid; label; machine made; *G 11 Sk No. 1* under bottom; on shoulder, *32 Fl. Oz.;* cobalt; 9½" **8.00-15.00**

Carter's Ryto Permanent; *Blue-black ink for fountain pen and general use, The Carter's Ink Co.;* Carter embossed near base; *The Cathedral,* label; 9¾" **30.00-40.00**

Carter's 2 C-101; under bottom; cathedral type; in bottom of each window *Ca;* machine made; cobalt blue; 10" **20.00-40.00**

same as above except 8" **25.00-50.00**

Caw's Black Fluid Ink; light blue; 7¾" **20.00-25.00**

Caw's Ink; *New York* on one side; circle on top of shoulder with raised square on top of circle; clear, aqua or light blue; 2¼" x 1¾" **2.00-4.00**

Caw's Ink; aqua; 3½" x 2" x 2" **4.00-8.00**

Challenge; green; 2¾" **4.00-10.00**

Chase Bros.; *Excelsior Office Ink, Haverhill, Mass.;* label; under bottom *Feb. 15, 1885;* cobalt; 9" **8.00-15.00**

Clar-O-Type Cleaner; label; *Clar-O-Type* embossed on each side; *3* under bottom; cobalt; 2½" . . . **3.00-6.00**

Climax; on shoulder; machine made; square; curved bottom; clear; 3¾" **4.00-6.00**

The Club Ink Carter Hexagonal; 4-leaf clover; cobalt; 4 ounces **15.00-30.00**

Confederate hat ink well; copper and tin; 3¾" x 1½" **30.00-50.00**

Conqueror; label; blue or aqua; 2¼" **12.00-15.00**

Continental Jet Black Ink Mfg. Co., Philadelphia; label; 2 dots under bottom; clear **3.00-6.00**

Continental Ink; long tapered collar and pouring lip; aqua; 7¾" **8.00-10.00**

Coventry Geometric Ink; open pontil; amber; 1⅝" **60.00-70.00**

Cross Pen Co.; aqua; 2¾" **10.00-12.00**

Cross Pen Co. Ink; *Cpc;* trademark; aqua; 2¾" **8.00-10.00**

Apple Green Cross Pen Co.; embossed monogram; 2½" **8.00-10.00**

Currier & Hall, Concord, N.H. Pot Ink; brown; quart **20.00-40.00**

Currier & Hall Pottery Master Ink; 2-tone label **8.00-10.00**

Currier & Hall's Ink, Concord, N.H.; *1840,* label; 12-sided; open pontil; aqua; 2½" **40.00-60.00**

David's Electro Chemical Writing Fluid; label; *M 3* under bottom; machine made; cobalt blue, 9" **10.00-15.00**

David's Turtle Ink; green **20.00-40.00**

T. David's & Co.; aqua; 1¾" **4.00-6.00**

Thad David's Co. N.Y.; on bottom; amber; 2¾", $4.00-6.00

Thad David's Ink; beveled edges; slope shoulder; green; 1¾" square **4.00-8.00**

Thaddeus David's Co.; pinched pouring lip; clear; 6⅜" **10.00-15.00**

Thaddeus David's & Co.; label; *Writing Fluid, New York;* cream crock; 5¾" **25.00-35.00**

Davies; sheared top; *Patd Sept 4-80* under bottom; clear or amethyst; 2½" **25.00-40.00**

W.A. Davis Co.; in back; *U.S. Treasury* on front shoulder; clear or amethyst **8.00-12.00**

W.A. Davis; clear; 2¼" **3.00-5.00**

W.A. Davis Co/Boston, Mass/U.S.A.; embossed on shoulder; decorated cylinder with sixteen curved panels at top of body, and sixteen near base of body; base pedesta; flared; double rings at base of neck; mold lines end at base of neck; flared ring on lip; greenish aqua; 8" **8.00-15.00**

Diamond & Onyx; aqua; 9" **6.00-12.00**

Diamond & Onyx; aqua; 9¼" **2.00-6.00**

Diamond & Onyx; aqua; 3" **3.00-5.00**

Diamond Ink Co., Milwaukee; in a circle under bottom; pinch type bottle; in each pinch a diamond; round ring on shoulder; ring at base; clear; ½" neck **8.00-12.00**

Diamond Ink Co., Milwaukee; on base; *Patented Dec. 1st, 03; No. 622;* square; amethyst; 1⅝" **3.00-5.00**

Diamond Ink Co.; clear; 1½" **3.00-5.00**

Diamond Ink Co.; wash pen point; one large and small connected jar **8.00-15.00**

Doulton, Lambeth; pouring lip; brown pottery; 4½" **5.00-10.00**

Dovell's Patent; cone; blue; 2½" **3.00-6.00**

S.O. Dunbar; stopper or cork; aqua; 2½" **5.00-10.00**

S.O. Dunbar, Tarington; cone; 8-sided; open pontil; aqua **15.00-30.00**

S.O. Dunbar, Taunton; cone; 8-sided; open pontil; aqua **15.00-30.00**

S.O. Dunbar, Taunton, Mass; round; graduated collar; aqua; 5¾" tall, 2¾" diameter **8.00-10.00**

Earles Ink Co.; pouring lip; crock; beige; 6⅛" **4.00-10.00**

E.B.; inside threads; cone; clear or amethyst; 2⅛" **4.00-6.00**

Edison Fountain Pen Ink, Petersburg Va; under bottom *A.C.W. 232;* ring tip and neck; square; clear **6.00-10.00**

Esbins Indelible Ink; aqua; small bottle **4.00-6.00**

Estes, N.Y. Ink; pontil; aqua; 6¾" **10.00-25.00**

Farley's Ink; open pontil; olive or amber; 2" x 2" **85.00-100.00**

Farley's Ink; 8-sided; open pontil; aqua; 2" x 2" **60.00-70.00**

L.P. Farley Co.; sheared top; dark green; 2" **15.00-20.00**

Fine Black Writing Ink; label; pontil; aqua; 5" **10.00-20.00**

H.B. Forster; aqua; 7¾" **6.00-10.00**

Patent Fortschmitt, Canada; long metal cap with *P;* clear; 6" **20.00-40.00**

Fountain Ink Co., N.Y., USA; clear; 3½" **8.00-15.00**

Foxboro; clear; 2½" **2.00-8.00**

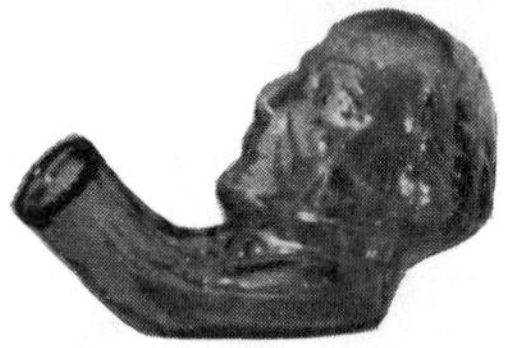

Franklin Ink; aqua; 4" long, 2" at tallest part, $15.00-50.00

French Ink Co., Hanover, Mass **30.00-50.00**

Fuller's Banner Ink, Decatur, Ill; aqua; 8" **10.00-20.00**

Gates; round; clear; 6" **1.00-2.00**

Geometric ink well; *Coventry Black Glass;* round open pontil; dark olive amber or olive green; 1½" x 2½" **75.00-125.00**

Glenn & Co.; round; clear; 1⅝" **8.00-10.00**

Glue or ink, label; clear; 2¾" **2.00-4.00**

Glue or ink, label; 8 panels; aqua **6.00-10.00**

G.M.W.C.A.A.S.; turtle; ink pen rest slot; oval; aqua **8.00-12.00**

Greenwood's; sheared top; under bottom *Patd March 22, 92;* tapered; clear or aqua green; 1½" **6.00-10.00**

Haley Ink Co.; aqua; 2¾" **6.00-8.00**

same as above except clear **4.00-6.00**

Haley Ink Co., Made In USA; 2 rings on shoulder; 4 rings on base; clear or amethyst; 6¾" . . **8.00-10.00**

same as above except brass spout; aqua **10.00-15.00**

Harris Ink; label; pontil; black glass; 10½" . . **10.00-15.00**

Harrison's Cola Ink 2; open pontil; aqua . . . **40.00-60.00**

Harrison's Columbian Ink; 8 panels; pontil; aqua; 2" **20.00-40.00**

Harrison's/Columbian/Ink; 8-sided squat; open pontil; aqua; 1¾" tall, 1¾" base **40.00-50.00**

Harrison's Columbian Ink; open pontil; cobalt; 1½" x 1½" **100.00-125.00**

Harrison's/Columbian/Ink; embossed vertically on 3 of 12 panels; *Patent* embossed vertically on 3 of 12 panels; *Patent* embossed on shoulder; iron pontil; aqua; 7½" x 4" **20.00-50.00**

Harrison's/Columbian/Ink; open pontil; aqua; 3⅛" x 1½" **40.00-60.00**

Chas. M. Higgins & Co.; aqua; 7½" **4.00-8.00**

Higgins Drawing Ink; under bottom; machine made; clear; 3" **2.00-4.00**

Higgins Inks, Brooklyn, N.Y.; on bottom; round; squat; clear; 3¾" **4.00-6.00**

same as above except *ABM* **2.00-3.00**

Higgins Inks, Brooklyn, N.Y.; round; amethyst or clear; 2" **2.00-6.00**

H.J.H. Writing Ink; *B.B.* on panels; sheared top; clear or aqua; 2½" **15.00-25.00**

Hogan & Thompson; *Phila;* cone; open pontil; aqua; 2" x ⅜" **50.00-75.00**

John Holland, Cincinnati; square bottle with rounded corners; ring top and neck; aqua; 2¼" **4.00-6.00**

Hooker's; sheared top; round; aqua; 2" **8.00-10.00**

House Ink; light blue; 2⅞" **4.00-6.00**

Hover, Phila.; on 2 panels; 8 panels; umbrella shape; aqua; 2" **25.00-50.00**

Hunt Mfg. Co. Speedball, U.S.A. Statesville, N.C.; embossed on bottom; cone; clear; 2¾" **2.00-3.00**

Hunt Pen Co. Speedball, U.S.A., Camden, N.J.; embossed on bottom; round; clear; 2¾" **2.00-3.00**

Igloo Ink; dome shaped; plain with neck on side; sheared top; panels on bases; aqua; 1¾" or 1¼" tall, 2" round **4.00-10.00**

same as above except cobalt **300.00-650.00**

Improved Process Blue Co.; aqua; 2⅜" **2.00-4.00**

Ink; ring around base, base of shoulder and neck; amber; 2⅝" x 1⅞" **2.00-6.00**

same as above except aqua or clear **2.00-4.00**

Ink; cone; ring collar; bulbous ring forms shoulder; ring on base of neck; amber; 2½" x 2½" **4.00-6.00**

Ink; square; *ABM;* cobalt blue; 2" x 2¼" **3.00-4.00**

Ink; round; cobalt blue; 2½" x 3" **4.00-6.00**

Ink; round; *ABM;* cobalt blue; 1⅞" x 2¾" **4.00-6.00**

Ink; cone type, yet not a true cone; base is cone shape with 2 large graduated flared bands on shoulder and neck; sheared collar; aqua; 3⅜" **4.00-6.00**

Ink; cone; honey amber; 2½" **4.00-15.00**

Ink; cone; aqua; 2½" **4.00-5.00**

Ink; cone; cobalt blue; 2½", $8.00-15.00

Ink; cone; amber; 2⅝" **8.00-15.00**

Ink; cone; light blue; 2¾" **6.00-8.00**

Ink; cone; plain; clear or amethyst; 2½" **2.00-3.00**

same as above except blue or amber **8.00-12.00**

Ink; cone; amethyst; 3" **4.00-8.00**

Ink; *design Patd. Feb 16th, 1886* under bottom in sunken circle; 5 different size rings on top of shoulder; one 1¼" ring on base; clear; 12¼" **6.00-10.00**

same as above except one ring near shoulder; green **6.00-10.00**

Ink; three-piece mold; crude graduated collar; ice blue; pint; 7⅜" **6.00-10.00**

Ink; ice cube shaped; solid glass; heavy; small well; metal collar; desk type; clear; 2" x 2" x 2" **3.00-4.00**

Ink, label; three-part mold; aqua; 2¾" **8.00-15.00**

Ink, label; black; 7½" . . . .**20.00+**

Ink, label; cone; ring shoulder; 2½" **4.00-8.00**

Ink, label; crock; tapered neck; brick red; 4" . . .**4.00-6.00**

Ink, label; aqua; 2¾" **3.00-6.00**

Ink, label; crock; green and white; 2½" x 2½", $4.00-8.00

Ink, label; clear; 2½" **2.00-4.00**

Ink, label; light blue; 2¾" **2.00-6.00**

Ink, label; tin box; 1½" **8.00-15.00**

Ink, label; dark aqua; 2¾" **3.00-6.00**

Ink, label; clear; 6½" **2.00-8.00**

Ink, label; clear; 2½" at base tapering to 2" at top **8.00-10.00**

Ink, label; wood; brick red; 3" **6.00-8.00**

Ink, plain; checked bottom; clear; 3" tall, 1¾" x 1¾" base, $8.00-12.00

Ink, label; aqua; 5¾" **4.00-6.00**

Ink, label; three-part mold; green; 9¼" **10.00-20.00**

Ink, label; sheared top; pontil; clear; 2" **20.00-40.00**

Ink, label; desk bottle; sheared top; clear or amethyst; 1¾" **4.00-6.00**

Ink, label; *Pat. Oct. 17, 1865* around bottom; clear or amethyst; 2¾" **10.00-20.00**

Ink, label; desk bottle; sheared top; clear or amethyst; 1½" **4.00-6.00**

Ink, label; clear; 1½" **4.00-8.00**

Ink, label; sheared top; panels on shoulder; clear or amethyst; 1¼" x 1½" x 1½" **25.00-50.00**

Ink, label; green; 2½" **75.00-110.00**

Ink, label; broken pontil; green; 7½" **10.00-20.00**

Ink, label; sheared top; aqua; ½" tall, 5½" long . . .**25.00+**

Ink, label; long square body; neck on end; clear; 3¾" x ¾" **10.00-15.00**

Ink, label; round; dark green; 2¼" **8.00-12.00**

Ink; pen rest on both sides at shoulder; sheared collar; amethyst; 2⅝″ x 2⅜″ x 2⅜″ **6.00-10.00**

same as above except aqua; 2″ x 2¼″ x 2¾″ **4.00-8.00**

Ink or glue; plain; heavy ring forms shoulder; slightly raised ring above at base of neck; conical; aqua; 2¼″ tall, 2½″ base **2.00-4.00**

same as above except brown or amber . . . **2.00-6.00**

same as above except green or blue **4.00-8.00**

same as above except cobalt **6.00-10.00**

Ink; plain has two deep rounded troughs on shoulder on either side of neck for pen rest; plain top; sunken bottom; clear or amethyst; 2¼″ x 2½″, neck ¾″ **8.00-10.00**

Ink; plain; ring encircling base; another forming shoulder; small ring on base of neck; round; clear; 2¼″ x 2″ **2.00-4.00**

same as above except different colors **6.00-8.00**

Ink; plain 2¾″ round bottom; trench from shoulder to shoulder ¾″ wide for clamp of some kind; flat ring; ring at bottom of neck; 1½″ ring top; ½″ neck; machine made; clear **2.00-4.00**

Ink; plain; round; inside of flower stand; 2 prongs on left top to hold pen; all metal is gold color; clear; 2½″ tall, 3½″ round **15.00-30.00**

Ink; plain; round; green, clear or amethyst; 2⅝″ **2.00-4.00**

Ink; plain; round bottom; green; 9″ **4.00-10.00**

Ink; plain; square top; on top and bottom fancy gold colored metal stand; round base; clear; 2″ **10.00-20.00**

Ink; plain; square; green or clear; 2″ **2.00-4.00**

Ink; square; squat; cobalt blue; 2⅜″ **4.00-8.00**

Ink; square; amethyst or aqua; 2½″ **2.00-4.00**

Ink; *2 oz.* on short neck; square; rounded corners; machine made; cobalt, clear or blue; 2″ x 2″ **2.00-4.00**

Ink well; sunken desk type; flat; round; *ABM:* clear; 3″ x 1½″ **2.00-4.00**

Irving; square; aqua; 2½″ **20.00-25.00**

J & IEM; imprinted in each panel; turtle with 6 panels; on base *Patd Oct 31, 1865;* under bottom *J;* aqua **20.00-40.00**

same as above except no patent date; amber **15.00-25.00**

same as above except cobalt **35.00-75.00**

same as above except *J & IEM* around bottle in ⅘″ ring **4.00-10.00**

Jasmine Ink Corp., Norfolk Virginia; square; labeled *Perfumed Jasmine Ink;* ABM; clear **2.00-4.00**

J. M & S Igloo Ink; early **10.00-15.00**

Johnson Ink Co., Willington, Conn.; fancy label; *Stoddard;* tapered and sheared top; dark green; 5⅞″ **20.00-30.00**

Keene Geometric Ink; open pontil; amber . . **75.00-85.00**

Keene Umbrella Ink; 8 sided, open pontil; green **35.00-45.00**

Keller; double ring top; clear or amethyst; 2½″ **4.00-8.00**

Keller Ink, Detroit; square; screw top; machine made; clear or amethyst **2.00-4.00**

The Robert Keller Ink Co.; clear; 9¼″ **6.00-8.00**

Kellers Ink; under bottom; clear; 1¼″ x 1½″; ½″ neck **10.00-15.00**

F. Kidder Improved, Indelible Ink; around bottle; square; aqua; 2½″ x 1½″ x 1½″ **25.00-30.00**

same as above except 5″ clear **20.00-25.00**

Kirkland Writing Fluid; ring on shoulder and base; aqua; 2¼″ x 1½″ **4.00-8.00**

L & B; monogram in center; cone; aqua; 2½″ **8.00-12.00**

Lake's; cone; aqua; 2½″ **15.00-20.00**

Levison's; machine made; clear; 7¼″, $6.00-8.00

Levison's Inks; amber; 2½″ **100.00-185.00**

Lochman's Locomotive Ink; train shaped; trademark, *Patd, Oct, 1874;* plain collar; aqua; 2³⁄₁₆″ x 2″ **25.00-50.00**

Lombard's Lilac Ink; diamond shape label; house type; clear; 2⅜″ **4.00-6.00**

Lyndeboro; rectangular; slots for 2 pens; aqua; 2¼″ **8.00-15.00**

Lyndeboro; rectangular; slots for 2 pens; green; 2¼″ x 2⅜″ **8.00-10.00**

Magnus; tan pottery; 4⅝″ **5.00-10.00**

Carl Mampe Berlin; amber; 2″ . . . . **15.00+**

Manchester Novelty Co.; aqua; 2⅝″ **10.00-14.00**

Mann's; label; *Design Patd Feb 16, 1886* under bottom; amber; 9¼″, $10.00-20.00

Massachusetts Standard Record Ink; on shoulder; clear; 7¾″ **10.00-15.00**

Maynard's Writing Ink; sheared top; amber case; 8 panels; umbrella type; dark green; 2″ . . . **30.00-50.00**

Jules Miette, Paris; sheared top; blue green; 2¾″ **30.00-50.00**

Mon-Gram Ink; round; clear or amethyst; 2½″ **4.00-6.00**

Moore; square or cylindrical; aqua; 2″ **4.00-8.00**

Moore & Son; sheared top; aqua or clear; 1⅝″ **6.00-10.00**

Moore J & IEM; igloo; round; 2½″ to 6½″; several other types and sizes **6.00-35.00**

M.S. Co.; *Sanford's #216* on bottom; clear **2.00-6.00**

Mt. Washington Glass Co.; *New Bedford, Mass; Bubble Ball Inkwell;* clear; 2" . . . **20.00-40.00**

My Lady Ink; on base; *Carbonine Ink Co.; N.Y.;* aqua; 1⅜" **6.00-10.00**

National Ink N.W.W. & Co.; label; clear; 2" . . . **2.00-4.00**

National Surety Ink; round; 2 rings on shoulder and base; *32 oz.* on shoulder; *ABM;* clear; 9" **4.00-10.00**

Naymard & Moyes, (sic) Boston; label; pontil; clear . . . . **35.00 +**

P. Newman & Co., Gilsum, N.H.; label; umbrella type; 8 panels; olive green; 1½" **30.00-50.00**

Nichols & Hall; label; house type; clear; 2⅞" **4.00-10.00**

Octagon Ink; mushroom shaped; pontil; aqua **20.00-30.00**

The Oliver Typewriter; round; clear; 2" **4.00-8.00**

1 X L; fancy ink; ring top; clear; 2½" **8.00-10.00**

Opdyke; barrel shaped bottle with 4 rings around it; opening in center; clear; 2" **10.00-12.00**

same as above except panels around bottom; ring top; *Opdyke* under bottom; clear; 2¼" . . **18.00-30.00**

Opdyke Bros. Ink; barrel with opening in center; ring top; aqua; 2½" x 2⅜" **15.00-30.00**

Opdyke Bros. Ink; barrel; *Patd March 11, 1870;* opening in center; aqua; 2½" x 2⅜" **18.00-30.00**

Palmer; round; sheared top; golden amber; 4¼" . . **45.00 +**

Parker; panels on shoulder; ring top; *ABM;* clear; 2½" **10.00-20.00**

same as above except *Parker's "Quink"* under bottom; *Made in U.S.A. #1; ABM;* 1½" **5.00-10.00**

Paul's Inks; *N.Y., Chicago* on back; cobalt; 9½" **12.00-20.00**

Paul's Safety Bottle & Ink Co. N.Y.; shoulder; squat; ring top; clear; 1⅜" **10.00-20.00**

Paul's Writing Fluid; *N.Y., Chicago;* flared neck; ring top; three-part mold; 5½" **10.00-20.00**

P.B.Co. Ink; round; aqua; 2½" **8.00-10.00**

Peerless; on 2 panels; 8 panels; umbrella type; bulbous shoulder; sheared top; clear or amethyst **10.00-20.00**

J.W. Pennell; embossed on 8 panels on base; round top; ring top; aqua; 2" **10.00-20.00**

Penn. Mfg. Work, Phila; 8 flat sides; white; 2½" **25.00-50.00**

Perry & Co., London, Patent; in 2 lines; on top ½" hole for ink and funnel hole for pen; flared ring bottom 3" to 2¼" top; sunken bottom; cream pottery; 3" round, 1¾" tall. **10.00-20.00**

Pitkin ink Keene; open pontil; dark aqua; 1¾" **100.00-150.00**

Pitkin Inkwell; 36-rib mold, swirls to left; flared lip; lime green; 1¾" x 2½" x 2¼" . . . . **200.00 +**

Pomeroy Ink, Neward, N.J.; label; 2 rings on base and shoulder; ring top; aqua; 2¾" **6.00-8.00**

G.A. Potter; pottery; tan; 9⅞" **6.00-10.00**

Raven's; label; *Design Patd Feb 16th 1886* under bottom; 7¾" **10.00-20.00**

Reading Ink Co., Reading, Mich., Superior Blue Ink; label; round; wide collar; flared top; aqua; 6³⁄₁₆" x 1⁹⁄₁₆" **8.00-12.00**

Reading Ink Co., Reading, Mich.; diamond shaped label; on base *Pat. April 18, 1875;* round; crude pouring lip; aqua; 6⅛" **8.00-15.00**

Reading Ink Co.; *Violet Ink,* label; crude cone with pronounced mold lines; 2¾" x 2⅝" **8.00-15.00**

Reads Inkstand & Ink; *Pat. Nov. 25, 1872;* ring top; aqua blue; 2" **18.00-25.00**

Safety Bottle & Ink Co. N.Y.; *Paul's pat.* on shoulder; diagonal swirls; sunburst pattern on base; clear; 2⅛" x 2⅜" **12.00**

Sanford Horse-Shoe Ink; *Sanford 21/7 Pat. Apl. for;* aqua **8.00-10.00**

Sanford/Inks/One Quart/and Library Paste; vertically; raised ¾" ring around base and shoulder; round; square collar and ring; ABM; amber; 3¾" diameter, 9⅜" tall. **4.00-8.00**

same as above except embossing on pouring cap, *Pat. Feb. 27, '06; 10½"* **8.00-16.00**

Sanford Mfg. Co.; *Pat. May 23, 1899* on bottom; clear or amethyst; 3" **3.00-4.00**

Sanford's Bellwood, Ill.; *Made in U.S.A. 44 CC.* embossed on bottom; metal screw-on top; red plastic; 1½" **4.00-6.00**

Sanfords Mfg. Co.; vertically in sunken panel; *1 oz* on next panel; *S.I. Co.* monogram on next panel; square collar; *ABM;* amethyst; 1½" x 2½" **3.00-4.00**

Sanford's Free Sample Never Sold; sheared top; 3½" **4.00-8.00**

Sanfords #6; on bottom; *1½ oz.* on one panel; large step on shoulder; double band collar; clear; 1¾" x 2¼" **2.00-3.00**

Sanford's #8; under bottom; light green; 2½" . **2.00-6.00**

Sanford's 9; under bottom; machine made; clear or amethyst; 2½" **3.00-4.00**

Sanford's 25-8; on bottom; aqua; 2½", $2.00-6.00

Sanford's #27; on bottom; machine made; clear; 2½" **2.00-3.00**

Sanford's #29 Pat App'd For; on bottom; boat shaped; clear; 2" x 2¾" x 2¼" **8.00-12.00**

Sanford's 30 Patent Applied For; on bottom; boat shaped; aqua; 2" tall, 2¼" x 1¾" base . . **8.00-10.00**

Sanford's #39; on bottom; large ring with deep grove at base and shoulder; step on shoulder; small and large ring collar; round; aqua or amethyst; 2" x 2⅜" **3.00-4.00**

Sanford's #39 3N; on bottom; aqua; 2½" **2.00-5.00**

Sanford's #88; bell shaped; sheared collar; amethyst; 2½" diameter, 3⅜" tall. **4.00-8.00**

Sanford's #89; somewhat conical; sheared collar; amethyst; 2¼" diameter, 2½" tall. **2.00-4.00**

Sanford's #98 Chicago, New York 1½ Oz.; on bottom; large ring on base and shoulder; 2 rings on collar; round; *ABM;* clear; 1¾" x 2½" **2.00-3.00**

Sanford's, Chicago, #187; under bottom; round; flared top; clear; 1½" x 1½" **10.00-15.00**

Sanford's #219; on bottom; large ring on base and shoulder; large ring and small ring collar; round; ABM; clear; 1⅞" x 2¼" **2.00-3.00**

Sanford's #276; on bottom; *S.I. Co.* monogram in sunken bull's-eye panel; rings at base of neck; *ABM;* 3 other plain bull's-eyes; clear; 1⅞" x 2⅝" **2.00-3.00**

Sanford's Premium Writing Fluid; label; *ABM;* amber; 9" **4.00-8.00**

Schlesinger's Hydraulic Ink; white and black crock, copper top; 6" **25.00-75.00**

Sheaffer's/Scrip/The Successor To Ink; embossed on metal plate in top of wooden cylinder; container for an ink bottle; wooden cylinder; container for an ink bottle; wooden threaded screw-on top; 3⅝" tall, 2⁷⁄₁₆" diameter. **4.00-6.00**

Shoe, label; clear; 6" long. **8.00-12.00**

Shoe with buckle; clear; 3⅞" **6.00-10.00**

Signet Ink; threaded for screw top; cobalt blue; 7¾" **16.00-20.00**

S.Sill - (cannot decipher balance); *Chester, Conn.;* blue label under bottom; 3¼" round ring at bottom and top; vase shaped; 4 different side holes to hold quill pens; in center top a bottle for ink; all wood; brown; 1¾" . . . .**15.00 +**

Sisson & Co.; sheared top; round; pale aqua green; 1⅝" **4.00-10.00**

Skrip; *tighten cap, tip bottle to fill the well* on metal top; *Pat'd 1759866* on bottom; ink well; screw-on top; clear; 2¾" **10.00-15.00**

S.M. Co 6; under bottom; aqua; 2¼" **6.00-8.00**

Sonneborn & Robbins; flared lip; cork stopper topped with brass; tan pottery; 5½" **6.00-8.00**

So. Stamp & Stationery Co., Mfg. Stationers, Richmond, Virginia; amber; 9½" **20.00-30.00**

Stafford's Commercial Ink; round; *Pat. Jan 13-85, S.M. Co.;* clear; 2" **8.00-10.00**

Stafford's Ink; in 2 lines, running vertically; 2 rings on shoulder and bottom; amber; 4¼" body, 2" neck. **6.00-12.00**

Stafford's Ink; green; 8" **10.00-15.00**

Stafford's Ink; round; aqua; 3" **4.00-6.00**

S.S. Stafford Ink, Made In U.S.A.; in 2 lines in a sunken panel; under it *This Bottle Contains One Full Quart;* 2 rings on bottom, 2 on shoulder; short neck; aqua; 2" **8.00-16.00**

same as above except 7" **8.00-16.00**

same as above except 6". **10.00-18.00**

same as above except 4¾" **10.00-18.00**

Stafford's Inks, Made In U.S.A.; pouring spout; cobalt blue; 6" **10.00-20.00**

Stafford's Ink SS, Made In U.S.A.; in sunken panel; under it, *This Bottle Contains One Full Qt.;* aqua or light blue; 9½" **5.00-8.00**

Stafford's No. 5, Pat Nov. 17, 1896, Nov. 22, 1892; on base; shoe shaped; aqua; 2½" neck, 3¼" **12.00-16.00**

Stafford's Vermilion Ink; 2 pen slots; aqua with blue label **8.00-10.00**

Stanford; square roof and 1½" chimney; ½" base; *Stanford's Fountain Pen Inks;* machine made; 2" x 2" **4.00-6.00**

Stanford's Blue Ink; label around body; ring on base, neck and shoulder; 2⅜" neck, 2" tall, 2" round, $4.00-6.00

Henry C. Stephens, Ltd.; pouring spout; dark brown; 9" **6.00-10.00**

Stoddard Master Ink; olive amber around pontil; 9⅜" **25.00-35.00**

Stoddard Umbrella Ink; 8-sided; open pontil; amber. **40.00-60.00**

Superior Ink; tan and brown; 2" **6.00-10.00**

Swift & Pearson; top and neck drawn out and shaped by hand; bulbous neck; dark green; 7⅝" **30.00-40.00**

Syr-Rhel Ink; pontil; cobalt; 8" **30.00-60.00**

Brickett J. Taylor Ink; cylindrical; flared lip; Keene; open pontil; 4½" **100.00-150.00**

Tea kettle; stars on 8 panels; metal top; cobalt; 2½", $100.00-200.00

same as above except no stars and long neck; clear; 6" **85.00-110.00**

same as above except no stars and short neck with 8 panels; metal top; blue. **85.00-125.00**

Tea kettle; place for 2 pens on top; *Pat. App for* and cloverleaf under bottom; aqua; 2" **30.00-50.00**

Tea Kettle Ink; label; 8 panels; 2½" sheared top; cobalt; 2" x 4" **85.00-125.00**

same as above except clear. **40.00-50.00**

same as above except neck is close to the 8 panels; metal top; aqua. **50.00-100.00**

Thomas; on bottom; cone; bulbous shoulder; double collar; amethyst. **4.00-8.00**

L.H. Thomas & Co.; clear or aqua; 2¼" x 3⅛" **2.00-4.00**

L.H. Thomas Chicago Co. #57; on bottom; double band collar; large and small ring on shoulder; large ring on base; round; aqua; 2½" **6.00-8.00**

L.H. Thomas Ink; aqua; 5¼" **10.00-15.00**

L.H. Thomas Ink; bell shaped; aqua; 2¾" . .**15.00-25.00**

L.H. Thomas Ink; *Pat. April 13, 1875* under bottom; aqua; 8" **10.00-15.00**

W.B. Todd; ring top; round; green; 2⅞" **5.00-10.00**

Travel Ink; label; with fitted hard leather case; 6 panels; aqua; 2" **8.00-10.00**

Turtle; plain rim around bottle at bottom; spout extends 1¹⁄₁₆" on side; sheared top; aqua; 1½" wide, 2⅛" tall. **4.00-8.00**

Turtle; aqua; 2" x 4", $25.00-60.00

Turtle; 12 lines lower half; granite; aqua....**20.00-40.00**

Umbrella ink; 8-sided; tapers into small round neck; open pontil; cledar; 2½" tall, 2½" base.....**10.00-25.00**

    same as above except brown.........**10.00-20.00**

    same as above except blue...........**7.00-14.00**

    same as above except no pontil.......**5.00-10.00**

    same as above except no pontil; brown or blue **6.00-10.00**

Umbrella ink; 6 panels; aqua or blue; 2½"...**4.00-10.00**

    same as above except with pontil......**15.00-30.00**

    same as above except smaller type....**15.00-45.00**

Umbrella ink; rolled lip; 8 vertical panels; aqua; 2⅝" **4.00-8.00**

Umbrella ink; rolled lip; open pontil; light emerald green; 2½" diameter, 2⅜" tall.............**35.00-45.00**

Umbrella ink; 8 vertical panels; rolled lip; whittled effect; open pontil; emerald green; 2⅜"......**40.00-50.00**

Umbrella ink, label; 12 panels; open pontil; aqua................**15.00-25.00**

Underwood; aqua; 3", $10.00-25.00

Underwood Inks; cobalt blue; 6½".......**50.00-100.00**

Underwood Inks; embossed; cylindrical; 2 pen rests on shoulder; flared lip, cloudy; mold line ends at base of neck; aqua; 1⅛" tall, 2⅛" base.......**10.00-20.00**

Underwood Inks; under bottom; circle or ring; tapered bottle; space for label; aqua; 3¼" x 2¼" **25.00-50.00**

John Underwood & Co.; cobalt blue; 9½"..**20.00-35.00**

Union Ink Co.; ring top; aqua; 2¼".......**10.00-20.00**

Union Ink Co./Springfield/Mass.; on sloping front; dome shaped; sheared top; aqua; 1½".......**15.00-30.00**

Union ink Co./Springfield Mass; aqua; 2"...**8.00-15.00**

Volgers Ink; label; house type; *T.C.V.* under bottom; ring top; clear; 2"........................**8.00-15.00**

Samuel Ward & Co.; sheared top; clear; 3" **10.00-20.00**

Ward's Ink; pouring spout; round; olive green; 4¾" **10.00-20.00**

Waterlow & Sons, Limited, Copying Ink; label; crock; brown; 7½", $8.00-10.00

L.E. Waterman Co.; squat band; *ABM:* aqua..**2.00-4.00**

E.Waters; aqua; 6½"....................**5.00-10.00**

Waters Ink, Troy, N.Y.; on panels; 6 panels; pontil; ring on shoulder and ring top; tapered; aqua; 2½" x 2" ....**10.00+**

J.M. Whitall; round; green; 1¾"...........**4.00-10.00**

Whittemore Bros & Co.; dark green; 9½"..**10.00-20.00**

Williams & Carleton, Hartford, Conn.; round; aqua................**15.00-20.00**

George W. Williams & Co.; *Hartford, Conn.;* cone; aqua; 2½" **15.00-25.00**

Woods, Portland, Maine Black Ink; tapered; ring top; aqua; 2½"........................**15.00-25.00**

Wright-Clarkson, Merc. Co. Duluth, Minn; on base; clear; 6½"....................**4.00-6.00**

Writewell & Co/Ink/Chemically Pure; label; cobalt blue; 7¼" x 2¹⁵⁄₁₆" **10.00-15.00**

Yale; *Dickinson & Co., Rutherford, N.J.;* amber; 1¾" **4.00-8.00**

Perfume, Cosmetic

The world's oldest known glass bottles are from Egypt and Mesopotamia and once contained cosmetics and medicine. Egypt's Eighteenth Dynasty in 3000 B.C. made perfumes in religious ceremonies and used them in embalming and religious celebration. Guests at banquets would be splashed with perfume.

Greeks esteemed perfume so highly that they arranged to meet their friends in perfume shops, rather than cafes or street corners, despite protests of the practice from Socrates. During the European Age of Extravagance of the eighteenth century, social custom required men to bring a trinket or small present to their lady when they came to call. The favorite of the women was a scent bottle.

One of the prime reasons for using perfume was to cover up personal body odors, since sanitary facilities were not what they are today. Martha Washington reportedly carried a small perfume bottle with her that she could discreetly slip into her glove. Her bottle was said to have been made by Caspar Wistar who owned the first successful American glasshouse. The plant was founded in New Jersey in 1739 and Wistar's work became known for its functional qualities.

Henry William Stiegel entered glassmaking in 1763. His bottles, in contrast to Wistar's simplicity, are decorative. They are of the pattern-molded and expanded variety-blown into a mold, then removed and finished to the desired shape by blowing. Stiegel's diamond-patterned perfume bottles are particularly ornate.

In the 1840's, Solon Palmer of Cincinnati, Ohio, began to manufacture and sell perfumes. A few had rather unusual names, Jockey Club and Baby Ruth among others. A greater availability of resources prompted his move to New York in 1871. By 1879 his products were familiar to all drugstores and are interesting to collectors because of the brilliant emerald green color of the glass.

Perfume bottles embossed with a child's face appeared around 1880. Known as Charley Ross bottles, they commemorate the abduction in 1874 of the youngest of seven children of a grocer in Germantown, Pennsylvania. Young Charley was only 4 years old and easily fooled by the 2 men who offered him candy. The father did not pay the ransom, and the child was never seen again. The case remained unsolved, but the father never gave up the search for his son. He advertised in major newspapers for people willing to help him locate information. Extra impetus was given in the five-thousand-dollar reward he offered. He encouraged the Charley Ross bottles to be produced to keep public conscience concerning the kidnapping alive.

Perfume was not only for ladies. Trade cards—advertisements usually with a full-color picture on one side and a product description on the other, often inserted in packages at the factory of mailed—were a popular form of proclaiming the virtues of the various products available. A trade card for Florida Water, a gentleman's after-shave fragance, boasted it to be "the richest, most lasting yet most delicate of all perfumes for use on the handkerchief, at the toilet and in the bath, delightful and healthful in the sick room, relieves weakness, fatigue, prostration, nervousness, and headache." The product was undoubtedly noticed when applied; it was about 75% alcohol.

In the mid-1880's, David H. McConnell, a door-to-door book salesman, began to entice his prospective customers by giving away free samples of perfume. His book sales increased, but he found that his customers were more interested in the perfume than in the books. Thus, in 1886 he established the California Perfume Company in New York City which later, in 1939, became know as Avon.

Demand for perfume and cologne increased at the turn of the century. The perfection of the automatic bottle-making machine in 1903 by Michael Owens helped supply keep pace with demand. Prior to that time, all bottles were expensive to make. A variety of products including hair balsam dyes, lotions, washes, unguents and oils were contained in bottles usually under 6″ in height. The perfection of the automatic bottle-making machine in 1903 by Michael Owens helped supply keep pace with demand. Prior to that time, all bottles were expensive to make. A variety of products including hair balsam, dyes, lotions, washes, unguents and oils were contained in bottles usually under 6″ in height. Fortunes were amassed, and still are today, through sales of these products.

Aubry Sisters; *Pat Aug 22, 1911* under bottom; milk glass; 1″ **1.00-2.00**

C.R. Bailey; aqua; 3½″ **2.00-6.00**

Baker's Perfume; ring top; clear; 3″ **3.00-4.00**

Baldwins Queen Bess Perfume; reverse side *Sample Baldwins Perfume,* label; ring top; 5½″ . . **8.00-10.00**

Barber bottle; milk glass; ring top; 4¾″ x 2½″ sunken panel on front of bottle for label; round; 9″ **10.00-20.00**

Barber bottle, label; clear or amethyst; 7¼″ . . . **6.00-8.00**

Barber bottle, label; milk glass; 12″ **12.00-20.00**

Barber bottle, label; clear or amethyst; 10½″ **8.00-12.00**

Barber bottle, label; aqua; 8″ **4.00-8.00**

Barber bottle, label; blue green; 8½″, $25.00-50.00

Barber bottle, label; aqua; 8½″ **6.00-8.00**

Barber bottle; plain; red; 3½″ **10.00-20.00**

Bay Rum; on one panel; barber bottle; 6 1¾″ panels; roof type shoulder; lady's leg neck; neck 3¼″; ring top; milk glass; body, neck and shoulder 4½″ tall **15.00-25.00**

Bell; plain; perfume; clear; 3″ tall, 2″ round . . . **4.00-6.00**

Boot; perfume label; clear or amethyst; 3½″ **10.00-20.00**

Bruno Court Parfumeur; green with gold neck; 5½″ **6.00-10.00**

Calif. Perfume Co.; fruit flavors on the front of panel; rectangular; amethyst; 5½″ **4.00-10.00**

Card Cologne or Opium Square; decorated; frosted; tapered **3.00-4.00**

C Co.; perfume; fancy shape; screw top; clear; 3¼″ **3.00-6.00**

Chapoteaut; reverse side *Paris; BL4063* on bottom; clear or amethyst; 2¾″ **2.00-4.00**

Chapoteaut; on back *Paris;* clear **2.00-3.00**

Christian Dior; clear; 4″ **6.00-8.00**

Christiani De Paris; perfume; fancy shape; thin flared lip; open pontil; aqua; 3⅜″ **25.00-35.00**

Clarke & Co.; *Woodard* under bottom; cosmetic; square; cobalt; 4¼″ **1.00-2.00**

C.L.G. Co.; under bottom; inside screw; clear or amethyst; 4¼″ **8.00-10.00**

C.M.; label; clear; 1¾″ **2.00-4.00**

Colgate & Co.; clear or amethyst; 6¼″ **3.00-6.00**

Colgate & Co. New York; in a circle; through center of circle *Perfumers;* clear or amethyst; 3⅝″ **2.00-3.00**

Colgate & Co.; *New York* on back; clear; 4¾″ **2.00-4.00**

Colgate & Co. New York; on bottom; fancy shape; 5 concave panels on side; step on shoulder; ring collar; amethyst; 5¼" **2.00-4.00**

Colgate & Co. N.Y. Coleo Shampoo; _X;_ on sides; flask; _AMB;_ amethyst. **3.00-4.00**

Colgate & Co. Perfumer 4 N.Y.; on bottom; machine made; clear; 4¼" **2.00-3.00**

Colgate & Co. Perfumers, New York; rectangular; long neck; amethyst; 3⅝" **3.00-4.00**

Colgate and Co. Perfumer's N.Y.; on one panel; rectangular; amethyst or clear; 3¾" **3.00-4.00**

Cologne; decorated trunk and shoulder; applied lip; 6 panels; amethyst or clear; 5¼" **3.00-5.00**

Cologne; cathedral type; ring top; 1¼" square at bottom; improved pontil; cobalt; 5¾", $50.00-100.00

Cologne, label; fancy shape; panels; milk glass; 7¼" **18.00-25.00**

Cologne, label; fancy shape; open pontil; flared lip; aqua; 4¾" **35.00-45.00**

Cologne, label; _603_ on bottom; clear or amethyst; 3" **2.00-3.00**

Cologne or peppersauce, label; 5 stars on 3 panels; light green; 7½" **10.00-15.00**

Cologne, label; pontil; cobalt; 8¾" **8.00-10.00**

Cologne; plain; round; clear or opalescent; 2¾" **1.00-2.00**

Cosmetic jar; round; cream; 2¼" tall, 1¾" base **3.00-4.00**

Cosmetic; plain; square; metal screw top; cobalt; 6" **1.00-2.00**

Cream, label; milk glass; 2¼" **1.00-2.00**

Cream, label; milk glass; 2" **1.00-2.00**

Cream, label; tan; 2" **2.00-3.00**

Cream, label; milk glass; 2" **2.00-3.00**

Cream, label; milk glass; 2½" **1.00-3.00**

Cream, label; tan; 2¾" **2.00-3.00**

Cream, label; milk glass; 2½" **2.00-3.00**

Cream, label; milk glass; 2¾" **1.00-3.00**

Cream, label; milk glass; 1¾", $2.00-3.00

Cream, label; tan; 3¼" **1.00-2.00**

Cream, label; milk glass; 2¾" **1.00-2.00**

Creme Simon; _J.S. 80_ under bottom; milk glass; sheared top; 2½" **2.00-4.00**

The Crown Perfumery Co.; amber; 2½" **2.00-6.00**

Crusellash; wood marks; aqua; 11½" **10.00-15.00**

Cutex; rectangular; frosted; 1½" x 1¾" x 2½" **2.00-3.00**

Daggett & Ramsdell; _Perfect Cold Cream, Trade Mark Made in U.S.A._ on base; round; screw top; clear; 2¾" **1.00-2.00**

Daysbrooks Detroit Perfumers; on top in a round design; _3_ on bottom; clear or amethyst; 6" **3.00-6.00**

Depas Perfume; clear; 4" **15.00-20.00**

Derwillo; on the front panel; _For The Complexion_ on the back; tapered to shoulders; square; clear; 3¾" **1.00-2.00**

De Vry's Dandero-Off Hair Tonic; label; clear; 6½" **8.00-10.00**

Doll; figural; perfume; clear; 2½" **15.00-25.00**

Dryden & Palmer; _D&P_ under bottom; clear; 7½" **4.00-6.00**

Eagle Brand Nova; milk glass; 1½" **2.00-3.00**

Marie Earle, Paris; under bottom; clear; 2¾" . .**6.00-8.00**

Eau Dentifrice Du Docteur, Jeau-Paris; in 4 lines; clear or amethyst; 3" **2.00-3.00**

Elcaya; milk glass. **2.00-3.00**

Empress Josephine Toilet Co.; milk glass; 6¼" **10.00-15.00**

Face cream, label; cream and black; 1½" **2.00-3.00**

Florida Water; label; clear; _568_ on bottom; 7¼" **2.00-4.00**

Florida Water; label; pontil; aqua; 8" **8.00-10.00**

Franco American Hygienic Co, Chicago; on front panel; _Toilet Requisites_ on left side; _Franco-American_ on the right side; rectangular; amethyst; 6" . . .**2.00-4.00**

Franco American Hygienic Co.; other side _Franco American Toilet Requisites;_ clear; 7" tall, 1½" x 1½" base. **2.00-6.00**

Frostilla; on front panel; _Elmira N.Y., U.S.A._ on side; _Fragrant Lotion_ on other side; clear; 4½" **4.00-6.00**

German enamelled bottle; on front, painted on panels; a girl drinking from a glass; in back; 5 lines in German script; on each side on a panel; flowers; 7 panels in all; pontil; small crude neck, around 1650; blue green; 5½" **100.00-200.00**

German enamelled bottle; hand painted; pontil; around 1650; blue green; 5½", $85.00-175.00

Gouraud's Oriental Cream; _New York_ on side; _London_ other side; machine made; 4¼" **1.00-2.00**

L.L.E. Grand; _P.L._ on bottom; clear; 3½" **3.00-6.00**

Grimault & CIE Paris; reverse side _Pharmacie, Dy;_ pontil; clear; 4" **4.00-8.00**

Guerlain Paris; *Depose* in back; clear; 6¾"...**4.00-8.00**

Gurrlain; *Eau Lustrale LUS* other side; broken pontil; raspberry; 6¼".....................**4.00-6.00**

Hagans Magnolia Balm; in 3 lines on front; beveled corners; ring top; milk glass; 5"........**8.00-12.00**

same as above except turned-under top; 4½".......................**8.00-12.00**

Hair Oil; label on back; amber; 10¼".....**35.00-45.00**

Harmony of Boston; on bottom; cold cream; 8 panels; screw top; amethyst; 2½"............**2.00-3.00**

Harrison's Columbia Perfumery; clear; 2¾"........................**75.00-125.00**

J. Hauel; reverse *Philadelphia;* on side *Perfumer;* square; flared lip; open pontil; aqua; 3"..........................**12.00-18.00**

H.B. & H. N.Y.; on shoulder; clear; 3½".....**4.00-6.00**

C. Heemstreet & Co., Troy N.Y.; 8 panels; ring top; pontil; blue; 7"......................**75.00+**

Hessig-Ellis Chemist, Memphis Tenn; *Q Ban For The Hair* on back; clear; 6½", $4.00-6.00

Hilbert's Deluxe Perfumery; flattened heart shape with long neck; clear; 3¼".............**4.00-8.00**

H.J.; perfume label; 2¼"..............**2.00-4.00**

Hogg & Co.; 3-cornered bottle; 8".......**8.00-12.00**

Holt's Nickel Cologne; in a sunken front panel; round; amethyst or clear; 2⅞"..........**2.00-4.00**

Homatropin; perfume dropper; blue; 2"....**8.00-12.00**

F Hoyt & Co. Perfumers, Phila.; in sunken panel; round; amethyst; 3"..............**2.00-3.00**

Hoyt's; clear; 3¼".....................**2.00-4.00**

Hubbard, Harriet, Ayer N.Y.; in a square with monogram; *3¾ ounces* on the trunk; square screw top; clear; 4¾".....................**1.00-2.00**

Hubbard, Harriet, Ayer N.Y.; cosmetic jar; milk glass; square; screw top; 1½" or 2½"........**1.00-2.00**

Richard Hudnut, N.Y.; monogram; *4 fl. ozs. Net;* rectangular; clear; 5¾".................**1.00-3.00**

Richard Hudnut, N.Y. U.S.A.; with eagle and monogram; tapered neck; round; clear; 5¾".......................**1.00-3.00**

Richard Hudnut Perfumer N.Y.; square; amethyst; 3" or 3½".......................**2.00-4.00**

Richard Hudnut; clear or amethyst; 3"......**3.00-5.00**

Richard Hudnut; machine made; clear; 4"....**2.00-3.00**

C.W. Hutchins Perfumer, New York; clear; 3¼"........................**2.00-4.00**

Hyacinthia Toilet Hair Dressing; crude applied lip; open pontil; rectangular; aqua; 6".........**10.00-20.00**

Imperial Crown Perfumery & Co.; clear; 5"..........................**4.00-6.00**

Ingrams Milkweed Cream; on shoulder; screw top; milk glass jar; white; 2¼"................**1.00-2.00**

Ingrams Shaving Cream; on shoulder; screw top; round; cobalt; 2¼".......................**1.00-3.00**

Jean Marie Farina Cologne; 6-sided; pontil; clear; 4⅝"..........................**25.00-35.00**

Jewelette Laboratories, Perfumers, Chicago; clear; 8".........................**6.00-10.00**

Juillet 1827, 28, 29, 30; perfume; shaped like a harp with a rooster at base; improved pontil double coated with a turquoise milk glass effect on the outside and a brilliant ultramarine effect on the inside; 5¼".........................**200.00+**

D. Kerkoff, Paris; tapered; footed; rectangular; amethyst; 3¼".......................**1.00-2.00**

Kerkoff; clear or amethyst; 5¼", $2.00-4.00

Kiken St. Louis; under bottom; label; clear or amethyst; 8¼".........................**4.00-8.00**

Dr. Koch's Toilet Articles, Winona Minn.; ring top; clear or amethyst; 5¼"...............**4.00-6.00**

Kranks Cold Cream; jar; milk glass; round; screw top; 2¾".......................**1.00-2.00**

G.W. Laird; milk glass; 4¾"..............**8.00-15.00**

Larkin Co; dark green; 3" tall, 1½" x 1¼" base, $2.00-6.00

Larkin Co.; under bottom; milk glass; 2"......**2.00-4.00**

L B; under bottom; clear or amethyst; 4".....**4.00-6.00**

Dr. H. Howard Levy; milk glass; 1".........**2.00-3.00**

L.H.; on bottom; shape of a slipper; perfume; improved pontil; flared lip; clear; 3½" long.......**25.00-35.00**

Lightner's Heliotrope Perfumes; lightning on back; in center, hollow letters *L.E.N. & Co. Detroit Mich.;* milk glass; 6½".........................**20.00-30.00**

Lightner's Maid of the Mist; lightning on back; in center, hollow letters *L.E.N. & Co. Detroit Mich.;* milk glass; 6½".........................**20.00-30.00**

Lightner's White Rose Perfumes; lightning on back; in center, hollow letters *L.E.N. & Co. Detroit Mich.;* milk glass; 6½"..................**20.00-30.00**

Lit. Piver Paris; under bottom; clear or amethyst; 3"..........................**1.00-2.00**

Lubin; clear; 3¼" tall, 1½" diam...........**2.00-4.00**

Lubin Parfumers Paris; pontil; clear; 3½"....**6.00-8.00**

Mack's Florida Water; tapered top; aqua; 8½"..........................**4.00-6.00**

Melba; label; machine made; clear; 4¾".....**2.00-4.00**

Mineralava Face Finish N.Y.; *Scotts Face Finish* on back; clear; 5¼".....................**4.00-6.00**

Monell's Teething Cordial, N.Y.; on 3 of 8 panels; aqua; 5″ tall, 1⅛″ round..............**3.00-6.00**

Morton, Carpenter Co., Colonite Boston, Mass.; square; amethyst or clear; 4″.........**2.00-4.00**

Murray & Lanman; machine made; aqua.....**2.00-4.00**

Murray & Lanman, Agua De Florida, New York; 6″ or 9″..................................**3.00-6.00**

Murray & Lanman, Agua De Florida, No. 69 Water St. N.Y.; pontil; aqua; 9″..............**25.00-50.00**

Murray & Lanman Druggists, Florida Water, New York; in 4 vertical lines; aqua; 5½″ body, 3¾″ neck...................................**4.00-6.00**

same as above except smaller bottle.....**4.00-6.00**

Newton, London; shape of a schoolhouse; flared lip; milk glass; 2⅝″.....................**40.00-80.00**

Theo Noel; aqua; 4½″.....................**2.00-6.00**

Nuit De Mone; around top; black glass; 3¾″..**4.00-6.00**

Obol; under bottom in sunken panel; front and back 1¼″ panels, plain; on each side 3 panels; 3-part mold with short round neck facing out; ½″ open on one side; milk glass; 4¼″ tall, 2⅛″ x ¾″....**6.00-12.00**

same as above except no writing; flat bottom; 2″...................................**6.00-12.00**

Oriental Cream; on side; *Gourands, New York;* square bottle with short neck; clear or amethyst; 5¼″..................................**2.00-3.00**

Oriza-Oil L. Legrand Paris; *Modele Exclush Depose* on back; clear; 5¼″.....................**2.00-4.00**

Palangie; *BL 2874* under bottom; clear; 5¾″..**2.00-4.00**

Palmer; in script, vertically on flat sides; some round bottles; emerald green; 4½″..............**4.00-8.00**

Palmer; metal crown, with *Salon Palmer Perfumer* and 2 stars; fancy shape; ribbed shoulders; emerald green; 5¾″..................................**8.00-12.00**

same as above except with rings instead of ribs; glass stopper; *Salon Palmer Perfumer* on shoulder; 4½″..................................**8.00-12.00**

Palmer; in script in center of bottle; ring top; 2″ round, 4½″ body, 2″ neck................**6.00-10.00**

same as above except oval; 7¼″.......**6.00-10.00**

Palmer; clear or amethyst; 3¼″............**2.00-4.00**

Palmer; clear; 2½″.......................**2.00-4.00**

Palmer; flat front, round back; blue green; 4¾″..................................**4.00-6.00**

Palmer; *C2* under bottom; oval shape; blue green; 5″, $6.00-10.00

Paris Perfume Co., Jersey City, N.J. Guaranteed Full 2 Oz.; ring top; clear or amethyst; 6″.....**2.00-4.00**

L. Pautauberge Pharmacieu, Paris; in 3 lines; on bottom *R 6, 5862;* beveled corners; cobalt; 2¼″ square base, 6″ body, 2″ neck..............**10.00-12.00**

P.D.; on base; aqua; 4¾″.................**30.00-40.00**

Perfume; fancy shape; 4 sides; round ribs on 3 sides; one plain ring; ring top; ring vase type body; 3¼″ tall, 2″ neck...................**7.00-10.00**

Perfume; fancy shape; clear; 3″.............**2.00-4.00**

Perfume; label; aqua; 6½″.................**8.00-12.00**

Perfume; label; clear or amethyst; 6¼″......**2.00-4.00**

Perfume; label; blue; 2¾″.................**2.00-4.00**

Perfume; label; fancy shape; clear; 3¼″......**2.00-4.00**

Perfume; label; clear; 6½″, $3.00-6.00

Perfume; label; clear; 5½″.................**2.00-4.00**

Perfume; label; clear or amethyst; 3″........**2.00-4.00**

Perfume; label; clear; 2¾″.................**2.00-6.00**

Perfume; label; various colored stripes around bottle; 2″...................................**6.00-8.00**

Perfume; label; clear or amethyst; 3″........**2.00-3.00**

Perfume; label; aqua; 6″...................**3.00-6.00**

Perfume; label; clear; sheared top; 2½″.....**8.00-10.00**

Perfume; label; pontil; clear or amethyst; 4″...**3.00-7.00**

Perfume; label; aqua; 7½″.................**4.00-6.00**

Perfume; label; clear or amethyst; 4¾″......**2.00-6.00**

Perfume; label; 8 panels; clear or amethyst; 1¾″..................................**2.00-4.00**

Perfume; label; pontil; aqua; 3¾″.........**10.00-20.00**

Perfume; label; clear; 5¼″.................**2.00-6.00**

Perfume; label; clear or amethyst; 5½″.....**10.00-15.00**

Perfume; label; pinch bottle; pontil; green; 6″..................................**20.00-40.00**

Perfume; label; golf frame around bottle with marble on each corner; aqua; 4″, $20.00-30.00

Perfume; label; flat front, round back; clear; 6½″..................................**2.00-6.00**

Perfume; label; pontil; clear; 12¼″.........**10.00-15.00**

Perfume; label; clear; 6½″...............**15.00-20.00**

Perfume; label; cut glass flower satin glass; sheared top; 5″...................................**8.00-10.00**

Perfume; label; clear; 4″...................**2.00-4.00**

Perfume; label; clear; 6½″.................**8.00-10.00**

Perfume; label; pontil; cobalt; 5″.........**35.00-45.00**

Perfume; label; snail design; machine made; satin, clear; 7½″..................................**4.00-8.00**

Perfume; label; flowers around bottle; square; milk glass; pontil; 5″........................**15.00-30.00**

Perfume; label; cobalt; 5½″..............**10.00-15.00**

Perfume; label; fancy shape; clear or amethyst; 3¼″..................................**2.00-5.00**

Perfume; label; fancy shape; clear or amethyst; 3¼″..................................**4.00-6.00**

Perfume; label; clear or amethyst; 3¾" **6.00-8.00**

Perfume; ½ bell shaped; clear or amethyst; 3" **5.00-10.00**

Perfume; 8 vertical panels; ring collar; glass stopper; improved pontil; clear; 3⅛" **8.00-12.00**

Perfume; fancy hand-painted gold-leaf design; open pontil; deep purple appears black; 6½" . . . **70.00-100.00**

Perfume; very ornate; fancy scroll work around gothic letter *M;* reverse side has blank oval area for label; flared lip; open pontil; clear; 4" **35.00-45.00**

Perfume; shaped like a clam shell; still has partial paper label with round mirror glued to label; very crude; open pontil; clear; 3½" **50.00-100.00**

Perfume; shaped like a woven basket with handles; small oval circle on front for paper label; open pontil; aqua; 2⅞" **25.00-35.00**

Perfume; figure of an Indian maiden sowing seeds on front; each side has a potted plant; fancy shape; fluted neck; clear; 4⅞" **15.00-25.00**

Perfume; violin or corset shaped; flared lip; open pontil; clear; 5⅜" **40.00-50.00**

Perfume; picture of an Indian holding a spear between gothic arches; open pontil; turquoise; 4" **30.00-40.00**

Perfumerie; clear; 3½" **2.00-4.00**

J. Picard; clear; 3¼" **2.00-3.00**

Ed Pinaud; clear or amethyst; 7" **4.00-6.00**

Ed Pinaud; aqua; 6" **3.00-6.00**

Ed Pinaud; clear; 3¾" **2.00-3.00**

Pinch bottle shaped; plain; light amber; 3½" body, 4½" neck **10.00-20.00**

same as above except smaller **2.00-6.00**

Pompeian Massage Cream; clear or amethyst; 2¾" **3.00-4.00**

Pompeian Mfg. Co.; machine made; clear or amethyst; 3¼" **2.00-4.00**

Pond's; milk glass; 1¾" **1.00-3.00**

Pond's Extract; *1846* on bottom; machine made; clear; 5½" **2.00-4.00**

Prepared By N. Smith Prentiss, Espirit De——, New York; perfume; fancy shape; picture of young girl with an armful of flowers on front; on reverse an embossed vase and plant; open pontil; flared lip; aqua; 5½" **40.00-50.00**

By N. Prentiss; reverse *28 John St. N. York;* one side *Bearsoil;* other side *Perfumes;* square; flared lip; open pontil; clear 2¾" **15.00-25.00**

Pumpkin seed; perfume; plain; clear or amethyst; 3¼" **2.00-4.00**

Pumpkin seed; label; side strap; clear or amethyst; 3½" **3.00-8.00**

Quentin; clear; 3" **1.00-3.00**

Q.T.; on base; perfume; monument shaped with round ball supported by eagles; flared lip; open pontil; clear; 5" . . . . **50.00+**

Ricksecker's; clear; 3½" **3.00-6.00**

Rieger's California Perfumes; crooked neck; clear; 3¼" **10.00-30.00**

R & M; shoe shaped; clear; 3½" **10.00-30.00**

Roger & Gallet; clear or amethyst; 4¾" **2.00-4.00**

Roger & Gallet Paris; on back; *8897 H.P.* under bottom; clear or amethyst; 5½" **4.00-6.00**

Roger & Gallet; clear or amethyst; 4¼" **2.00-6.00**

J. Roig; clear; 3¼" **2.00-4.00**

Charley Ross; picture of a boy; 4 sizes . . . . **50.00+**

C.H. Selick, Perfumer N.Y.; ring top; clear; 2⅝" **4.00-6.00**

Stiegel; perfume; teardrop shaped 16 swirls to the left; improved pontil; clear; 3⅛" **50.00-125.00**

T; *oz.* on shoulder; square; cobalt; 2¾" **4.00-6.00**

Toilet Water; on one panel of a six-paneled bottle; roof type shoulder lady's leg neck barber bottle; milk glass 3¼", $15.00-25.00

Toilet water; label; amber; 7¼" **4.00-6.00**

T.P.S. & Co., NY; on base; man's head figural; 3-part mold; metal cap; 7" **40.00-60.00**

Treville Paris; green; 8¼" **4.00-8.00**

Vail Bros; green; 3" **3.00-8.00**

Valentines; green; 2¾" **2.00-4.00**

Van Buskirb's; aqua: 5" **2.00-3.00**

Velvetina; *Velvetina Skin Beautifer Goodrich Drug Co. Omaha* on back; milk glass; 5¼" **8.00-12.00**

Vin De Chapoteaut Paris; clear or amethyst; 10½", $2.00-4.00

Violet Dulce Vanishing Cream; 8 panels; 2½" **2.00-6.00**

Vogn; in script; in 2 lines *Perfumery Co. New York;* case type body; seam end at collar; clear; 7¾" **3.00-6.00**

W.B. & Co.; under bottom; aqua; 3½" **4.00-6.00**

W. & H. Walker; clear; 8¾" **3.00-6.00**

White Rose; label; second label picture of a bird holding a note which reads *Faith and Love;* cucumber shaped; turquoise green; 4⅜" long **20.00-40.00**

Witch Hazel; milk glass; 9¼" **20.00-30.00**

Alfred Wright, Perfumer, Rochester, N.Y.; cobalt or amber; 7½" **6.00-8.00**

W.T. & Co. V; in center; *U.S.A.* under bottom; beveled corners; ring top; milk glass; 5" **6.00-10.00**

Miscellaneous

A variety of necessities and luxuries have been and continue to be contained in glass. Everything from milk for nursing babies to fire extinguishing materials to candy has been put in bottles.

Charles M. Winship of Roxbury, Massachusetts, patented the first United States nursing bottle in 1841. Nipples in the nineteenth century were of the makeshift variety—rags, sponges and wood often serving the purpose until the rubber type replaced them in the early 1900's. Many nursing bottles of the late 1800's were made to lay flat and a few types were embossed with reminders such as "Feed the Baby." By 1945 there were over 200 different kinds of nursing bottles in the United States.

Candy was popularly contained in figural glass bottles. One such container was in the shape of the Liberty Bell and was brought out at the Centennial Exposition in Philadelphia in 1876. Many from the last century were thought to be souvenir items since they bore the names of hotels and restaurants. Others were in the shape of railroad lanterns, horns, clocks, cars, planes, guns and battleships. Many converted into banks when empty.

Fire grenades—bulb-shaped bottles filled with carbon tetrachloride—were designed to be thrown and broken onto fires. Alanson Crane of Fortress Monroe, Virginia, was granted the first American patent for such an extinguisher in 1863. The most well-known maker of the product, the Harden Hand Fire Extinguisher Company of Chicago, was granted a patent on August 8, 1871, exactly 2 months before the Great Chicago Fire. Fire grenades were manufactured under various intriguing names including the Dash-Out, the Diamond, the Harkness Fire Destroyer, Hazelton's High Presure Chemical Firekeg, Magic Fire and the Y-Burn Winner. The invention of the vaporized chemical fire extinguisher replaced them in 1905.

Intricate little bottles with likenesses of stars of the stage, favorite politicians or scenic pictures pasted on their surfaces and covered with glass were customarily given by barbers to their regular customers in the nineteenth century. Most of them were personalized with the customer's name in gold lettering at the top. Brightly colored and found in a wide variety of surface patterns, these bottles contained such substances as witch hazel and perfumed alcohol. The majority of American bottles of this type were produced in Glassboro, New Jersey. Because of their beautiful nature, most are found in art collections today.

Samuel F.B. Morse received a patent for the telegraph in 1840. A means of insulating the telegraph wires was needed and inventor Ezra Conell suggested using glass. He designed hollow glass bell-shaped caps to fit over the pegs on the telegraph poles. Louis A. Cauvet, a carpenter from New York, further improved on the insulator by designing caps with threads to

secure the devices to the pegs in 1865. Most electric insulators used today are porcelain instead of glass but they have retained the bell shape.

Other types of interesting and collectable containers include bar bottles, shoe polish bottles, glue bottles, snuff bottles, blueing bottles, germicide bottles, cement bottles and oil bottles.

A, Made in Japan; milk glass; 2½", $4.00-6.00

Acid; plain; green; 6½" **2.00-3.00**
Acid; plain; green; 6½" **1.00-2.00**
Acid; plain; round; amber; 8" **1.00-2.00**
Acid; plain; round; gold; 12" **2.00-4.00**
Acid line; line around bottles; fire extinguisher; aqua or amethyst; 6" **1.00-2.00**
Agua Carabana; small kick-up; aqua; 9½" **2.00-4.00**
Airplane; figural candy container; clear; 4¼" long **10.00-15.00**
Alma Polish; on shoulder; *M & Co.* under bottom; aqua; 5" **2.00-4.00**
Ames; clear; 1¾" **2.00-4.00**
Ammonia; flask type; aqua; all sizes **1.00-4.00**
Apple bottle, label; machine made; clear frosted; 7" **2.00-6.00**
Appleby & Helmes, Railroad Mills; reverse side *Snuff, 133 Waters, New York;* flared top; amber; 4¾" **6.00-12.00**
Armers Top Notch Brand; *Chicago* under bottom; clear or amethyst; 5½" **2.00-4.00**
Arna's 23; under bottom; amber; 8" **4.00-6.00**
E. Arnstein, Chicago, Ill; clear; 3¾" **2.00-4.00**

F.B. Asbury, N.Y.; under bottom; large plain shield on front; amber; 12", $10.00-30.00

Avery Lactate Co., Boston Mass., U.S.A.; in center; picture of a woman with a bucket of milk on her head and a cow in back of her; 2 panels on each side; clear; 7" **8.00-12.00**

B; under bottom; label; clear or amethyst;
7½" **2.00-4.00**

B & B; under bottom; sheared top; amber;
3¾" **4.00-8.00**

Baby bottle; *ounces* on front; oval; *ABM;* clear;
5⅛" **2.00-6.00**

Baby bottle; *Ounces* on front; cylindrical; *ABM;* clear;
6⅞" **2.00-4.00**

Baby bottle; flask; *ABM;* amethyst; 7" **2.00-5.00**
same as above except 4½" **2.00-4.00**

H.A. Bartlett & Co. Philade; *Shoe Dressing* on bottom
rim; aqua; 4½" **8.00-10.00**

Beech Nut, Canajoharie N.Y.; on 1 line on shoulder; on
bottom *23 N 51;* under bottom *B N P Co., A, 16;*
machine made; aqua; 9½" **2.00-3.00**

Benton Holladay & Co.; shoe polish; aqua;
4½" **4.00-8.00**

B.F.B. Co. 2845; under bottom; aqua; 8" **2.00-4.00**

Biluk; aqua; 4" tall, 2¼" x 2¼" base **10.00-25.00**

Bixby; shoe polish; aqua; 3¾" **3.00-4.00**

Bixby; under bottle; round bottle tapering to round
shoulder; short neck; wide flared mouth; green; 4¼"
tall, 2½" bottom **6.00-10.00**
same as above except clear **2.00-4.00**

Bixby #15; on bottom; shoe polish; dark green;
4" **4.00-6.00**

Bixby 6-83; on front; on bottom *patented mch;* shoe
polish; conical; aqua; 3⅜" **3.00-4.00**

Bixby, Patented Mch, 6, 83; bulbous shoulders; flared
narrow collar; aqua; 4" **2.00-4.00**

S.M. Bixby & Co.; aqua; 4¼", $4.00-6.00

Bixby's French Polish; fancy lettering; aqua;
3½" **4.00-6.00**

Bluing, label; different numbers on bottom; clear or
amethyst; 4¾" **2.00-3.00**

The Boyle Needle Co., Chicago; on side *3 oz. full
measure;* machine made; clear; 6¼" **1.00-3.00**

Brain's; *Cardiff* on back; *SAB* under bottom; inside
screw top; machine made; amber; 10" . . .**4.00-10.00**

Brand Bros. Co. Eigenthumer Asetzlich Geschutzt; 3
sides; fancy shape; amber; 5" **20.00-40.00**

**Bryant's Root Beer, This Bottle Makes 5 Gallons, Mfg.
By Williams Davis Brooks & Co. Detroit, Mich.;**
amber; 4½" **4.00-8.00**

Bull Dog Brand Liquid Glue; around shoulder; crude
ring collar; aqua; 3½" **2.00-4.00**

Burn Olney Canning Corp.; catsup; clear;
8" **4.00-8.00**

Cala Nurser Baby Bottle; embossed in circular slug
plate; *ounces* on back; ring on neck; oval; *ABM;*
clear; 7⅛" **2.00-6.00**

Candy bottles shaped as telephone, train, gun,
phonograph or lantern; screw top; clear . .**8.00-10.00**

Car, figural; candy; clear; 4¾" **10.00-15.00**

Carbona Fire Extinguisher; label; *Carbona* under bottom; amber; 11" **15.00-25.00**

Caulk; square; clear; 1¾" **1.00-2.00**

Child's Fire Extinguisher, Utica N.Y.; aqua;
6½" **20.00-40.00**

Child's Fire Extinguisher, Utica, N.Y., Sulphuric Acid;
4 oz. line; aqua; 6¼" **20.00-40.00**

Christo Mfg. Co.; amber; 9½" **4.00-6.00**

Circle A Gingerale; on bottom; round; aqua; 7⅜" or
9¼" **2.00-4.00**

**Cleanfont Vented Nursing Bottle, Fox Fully &
Webster, New York & Boston;** *Patented Oct. 25,
1892* on bottom; ring top; Aladdin's lamp type; clear
or amethyst; 5½" **20.00-30.00**

C.L.G. Co. P; under bottom; clear; 3½" **2.00-4.00**

Clorox; machine made; nine-part mold; amber;
8" **2.00-8.00**

CM; under bottom; amber; 11½" **6.00-8.00**

Cohen Cook & Co. 229 Washington St. New York;
graphite pontil; aqua; 8¾" **25.00-50.00**

C 185; on bottom; label; amber; 3" **2.00-3.00**

C 1637; on bottom; label; aqua; 5" **2.00-3.00**

Cook & Bernheimer Co.; *Full Quart, Refilling of This
Bottle Prohibited;* under bottle *C&B
Bottling* **8.00-10.00**

R. Cotter & Co., Houston, Tex.; *I.X.L. Sarsaparilla &
Iodide Potassium* on reverse side; aqua;
9½" **15.00-30.00**

Cowdrey, E.T. Co.; in center; twirl top and bottom;
screw top and sheared top; 6¼" **8.00-15.00**

Crimault & Co.; clear; 6¼" **2.00-6.00**

Crowleys Milk Co. Beacon, N.Y.; in circular slug plate;
Liquid One Quart; large ring collar; *ABM;* clear;
9¾" **3.00-4.00**

C.W. & Co.; under bottom; kick-up; dot in center; 3-part
mold; dark olive; 5" body, 2" blob neck, 3"
bottom **8.00-12.00**

**Dairymen's League Co-Operative Association Inc.
Registered;** *Dairylea Reg. U.S. Pat. Off., One Quart
Liquid* on back; large ring collar; *ABM;* clear;
9½" **2.00-6.00**

Decanter; silver inlay; cobalt; 7",
$15.00-25.00

Decanter; whiskey label; fancy sides; wine color;
10½" **8.00-15.00**

Deimel Bros. & Co.; under bottom; clear or amethyst;
4¾" **2.00-8.00**

Design Pat'd, Feb. 16th 1886; under bottom in sunken
circle; 5 different sizes of rings on top of shoulder;
one ¼" ring on bottom (trunk); clear;
12¼" **6.00-10.00**

Detroit Creamery Co. Detroit, Mich Registered; *DC Co. 12 Oz. Liquid Sealed 48* on back; large ring collar; fourteen vertical ribs on shoulder; clear; pint; 5¼" **3.00-6.00**

F.W. Devoe & Co.; clear or amethyst; 3¼" ...**2.00-4.00**

Dog, figural; candy; clear; 3¾" **5.00-10.00**

Dog, figural; beverage; clear; 10" **4.00-8.00**

John T. Doyle & Co. New Haven, Conn., Bokaska Laundry Soap; clear or aqua..........**4.00-8.00**

Dunkley's Genuine; bulge at shoulder; screw top; round; amethyst; 6" **1.00-2.00**

D.W. & Co.; under bottom; aqua; 9½".....**2.00-4.00**

Dyson Nelson, Trade Mark; round; inside screw; aqua; 6¾" **2.00-6.00**

Eastman, Rochester, N.Y.; clear; 5" **2.00-4.00**

Eclipse; number on bottom dark amber; 4½", $3.00-4.00

Eclipse; machine made; aqua; 4½" **2.00-3.00**

Thomas A. Edison; in script; *Battery Oil;* clear; 4¼" **2.00-4.00**

E.G.; label; *D* under bottom; aqua; 8" **2.00-4.00**

E.G.L. Co., Boston; *The Samson Battery No. 1* on one side; sheared top; aqua; 5¾" x 4" x 4" ..**8.00-12.00**

Elgin Milkine Co.; sheared top; aqua; 5½" ..**6.00-10.00**

Charles Ellis & Son Co.; aqua; 7" **4.00-6.00**

Empire Nursing Bottle; *void* on one flat side; neck tapered; amethyst; 5¼" **2.00-3.00**

Carlo Erba; on 1 panel; on back *Milano;* beveled corners; 1¾" square; 6" **4.00-8.00**

same as above except 7½" **4.00-8.00**

Everett & Barron Co., Shoe Polish, Providence R.I.; oval; clear; 4¾" **1.00-2.00**

Everlasting Black Dye, Baltimore, Md.; *ABM;* cobalt; 4¾" **4.00-8.00**

E Z Stove Polish; *#14* on bottom; aqua; 6" ...**2.00-8.00**

Fair Acres Daisy, Most Modern Dairy in Nebraska, Phone 511; in circular slug plate; large ring collar; *ABM;* clear; 5½" **3.00-4.00**

Falk; in sunken panel; *Improved Fire Ext'r* **in 3 panels; on shoulder** *Pat. Appl'd For;* **green; 6½", $55.00-95.00**

Fire Extinguisher Mfg. Co., Babcock Hand Grenade; on round panels; *S. Des Plaines St. Chicago; non freezing;* ball shaped; fourteen rings around bottle; clear; 7½" **25.00-60.00**

This Bottle Loaned By F.W. Fitch Co.; on lower trunk; tapered neck; round; amethyst; 8" **2.00-4.00**

Five Drops; on one panel; *Chicago U.S.A.* on the other; rectangular; aqua; 5½" **2.00-3.00**

W & J Flett; aqua; 6¾" **15.00-20.00**

Flli Viahov, Pescara; clear; 11½" **30.00-50.00**

Florida Tropical; *405 FD.G. 2* under bottom; clear; 7½" **4.00-6.00**

Robt. H. Foerderer, Philadelphia, U.S.A.; aqua; 4½" **2.00-4.00**

Fox Trade Mark; clear or amethyst; 3¾" **2.00-4.00**

French Glass; shoe polish; aqua or blue; 4½" **2.00-4.00**

This Bottle Can Be Refilled At The Furst Co.; clear or amethyst; 3¼" **2.00-3.00**

Furst-McNese Co., Freeport Ill.; on front panel; rectangular; aqua; 8⅜" **2.00-3.00**

Gay Ola; in script, *Trade Mark Registered;* **clear or amethyst; 7½", $6.00-15.00**

Gillet's; *A & Dac* under bottom; aqua; 5½" ...**4.00-8.00**

Gilt Edge Dressing; *Pat. May 13, 1889* under bottom; clear **4.00-8.00**

Glue, label; sheared top; clear or amethyst; 3" **3.00-4.00**

Goofus glass; clear; 7" x 6½" **50.00-60.00**

Golden State Company Ltd. One Pint; *Golden State Brand* in shield on back; large *G.S.* on bottom; large ring collar; *ABM;* clear; 7¼" **3.00-6.00**

Mary T. Goldman, St. Paul, Minn.; on front panel; rectangular; 5½" **2.00-4.00**

B.F. Goodrich Co.; amber; 4½" **4.00-6.00**

B.F. Goodrich Co.; amber; 8", $10.00-15.00

Graduated nursing bottle; clear; 6½" **8.00-10.00**

Grand Union Company; clear; 5¼" **2.00-4.00**

Great Seal; aqua or amethyst; 5½" **2.00-6.00**

Grimault & Co. Injection Aumatico; clear; 6½" **4.00-6.00**

G.W.; under bottom; aqua; 5¾" **8.00-10.00**

Hagerty's Glass Works, N.Y.; under bottom; aqua; 6½" **10.00-20.00**

Hammer Dry Plate Co., St. Louis, Mo.; on panel; square; amethyst; 6¼".................**2.00-4.00**

Hand-blown; pontil on bottom; ⅝" applied sheared lip; round; long neck about 3½"; aqua; 8¾"............................**12.00-35.00**

Hand Mfg. Co.; on the shoulder, *Phila.* on lower front; oval with front panel; clear; 5¼"........**1.00-2.00**

Harden's; *HNS;* on large diamond monogram in front and back; hand grenade fire extinguisher with 4 large and 8 small diamond sides; round; light amber or golden; 3" neck.................**55.00-95.00**

Harden's; *HNS;* on large diamond monogram in front; hand grenade fire extinguisher with 2 plain diamonds and 8 small diamonds; cross on bottom; gold; quart.................................**55.00-95.00**

Harden's Star Hand Grenade; *Fire Extinguisher* in back; blue; 6¾"............................**65.00-110.00**

Harkness Fire Destroyer; ball shaped; 10 horizontal rings on body; 5 rings on neck; blue; 6¼"..................................**50.00-85.00**

E. Hartshorn & Sons; side mold; clear or amethyst; 5"......................................**3.00-5.00**

Hauthaways Lynn Burnishing Ink, Boston Mass.; label; shoe ink; amber; 7½"..............**10.00-15.00**

Hayward Hand Grenade Fire Extinguisher; around shoulder; cobalt; 6"................**50.00-85.00**

Hzen, Brown, Boston Mass; amber; 4¾"..**10.00-20.00**

Hazeltons High Pressure Chemical Fire Keg; amber; 11½"............................**55.00-95.00**

H.J. Heinz Co. #54; clear or amethyst; 8¼"..**2.00-4.00**

Helme's; amber; 4½".....................**4.00-6.00**

Helme's Railroad Mills; sheared top; amber; 3¼"......................................**4.00-8.00**

Herbine; one side *St. Louis;* other side *Herbine Co.;* aqua; 6⅜"............................**2.00-4.00**

Herbine Co., St. Louis; aqua; 6¾".........**3.00-5.00**

Hillcrest Farms, Fishkill, N.Y.; in outer ring; *HF* monogram; *One Pint Liquid;* 14 ribs around neck; amethyst; 7¼"......................**3.00-4.00**

A.S. Hinds; on sunken side; *Portland, Me* on other side of panel; rectangular; amethyst; 5¾".....**2.00-4.00**

Hires; under bottom; clear or amethyst; 9¾"..**2.00-4.00**

Hires Household Extract For Making Root Beer At Home; reverse side *Mfg. by the Charles Hires Co. Philadelphia, Pa. U.S.A.;* blue; 4½".....**6.00-10.00**

Holton's Electric Oil; vertically on bottle; round; amethyst; 3¼"........................**4.00-6.00**

Holy Water; *IHS* on back; clear; 6".........**4.00-8.00**

Honey barrel; 5¼", $25.00-40.00

Horlick's Corp. Malted Milk, Racine, Wisc.; 5½"......................................**4.00-6.00**

Horseshoe-shaped bottle; light amber; 4".....**4.00-8.00**

J.F. Howard, Haverhill, Mass.; around the lower part of trunk; round; fluted; clear; 7¼".........**1.00-2.00**

Hrrrol; green glass; painted black; 6¼".........**10.00 +**

Hubbard's Vegetable Germicide, Disinfectant and Deodorizer, Trade Mark J. Hubbard & Co. Boston, Mass; clear; 4¾".....................**4.00-8.00**

Hunt Mfg. Co.; machine made; clear; 2½"....**2.00-4.00**

Husbands; aqua; 4½".....................**3.00-6.00**

Hygienic Nursing Bottle, Prevents Sickness, Pat'd., Easily Cleaned Easily Filled, Graded Measure 1-8 oz.; clear; 6½".....................**8.00-10.00**

Hynson Wescott Dunning; square; clear; 2"..**1.00-2.00**

Imperial Polish Co.; label; aqua; 7¼".......**2.00-4.00**

India Cholagogue; *N.Y.* on left; *Osgoods;* on right; rectangular; aqua; 5¼".....................**3.00-7.00**

same as above except *Norwich, Conn.*.....**3.00-7.00**

Jennings Bluing; blob top; aqua; 7".........**4.00-6.00**

Alexis Codillot Jeune; on one cuved panel; *Bordeaux* on 1 of 4 1¼" x 1" curved tapered panels; curved corner panels; vase type blob neck; ring top; green; 9" tall, 1¾" mouth...................**7.00-12.00**

Johnston & Co.; in horseshoe, under it *Philada;* in back, big monogram *J;* aqua...............**10.00-20.00**

JSP; monogram in center of bottle; green; 9¼"......................................**4.00-8.00**

Keen Kutter, St. Louis, U.S.A., Trademark; on front; *E.G. Simmons, Simmons Hardware Co.* on left; *Keen Kutter Oil* on right; rectangular; clear; 4"..**2.00-4.00**

Keller Detroit; under bottom; clear or amethyst; 2½"......................................**3.00-4.00**

Kellerstrass Dis. Co.; *Reg. Dis., Kansas City, Mo.;* *U.S.A.* on bottle; round; tall ornate neck, amethyst; 12".....................................**6.00-16.00**

Kerosene bottle; metal and glass; aqua; gallon, $25.00-35.00

Wm. F. Kidder; clear; 5¾"..................**3.00-6.00**

Killinger; sqaure; aqua; 7⅞"...............**3.00-4.00**

Knapps Root Beer Extract, Trade Mark; man holding glass with both hands; yellow green......**4.00-8.00**

Koken, St. Louis, U.S.A., 10 Fl. Oz.; round; clear; 7"......................................**1.00-2.00**

Kutnow's Powder; aqua; 4¾"..............**6.00-10.00**

KY. C.W.; under bottom; aqua; 7"..........**3.00-6.00**

Ky Glass Works; under bottom; clear; 7"...**10.00-20.00**

Lake Carmel Dairy, Carmel, N.Y.; in circular slug plate; *One Quart Liquid; ABM;* clear; 9½".....**3.00-4.00**

Lake Shore Seed Co.; aqua; 5¾".........**4.00-6.00**

Larkin Soap Co.; clear; 3½"..............**2.00-4.00**

Laroche; small kick-up; aqua **2.00-4.00**

Reilly Leavy & Co, New York; on panel; flat corner; roofed shoulder; amber; 2″ neck, 2½″ square, 9½″ tall **6.00-10.00**

Ledyard Farm, Reg. N. Reading T.M.C.T.; seal in circle on shoulder; clear; 7¼″ **4.00-8.00**

P.C. Leidigh, Ashland, Pa.; *P.C.L.;* monogram; blob top; aqua; 9¼″ **4.00-8.00**

Lincoln Penny Bank; Lincoln figural; screw top; clear; 3½″ **10.00-15.00**

Liquid Veneer; under bottom; clear or amethyst; 6¼″ **2.00-6.00**

Loaf of bread figural; crude top; short neck; 3-part mold; big pontil; green; 6½″ tall, 10″ long, 6″ wide **25.00-50.00**

L S; in a diamond shape under bottom; light amber; 6″ **4.00-6.00**

Made in Lynchbor, No. 44; (backwards) *U.S.A.;* insulator; green **5.00-10.00**

M.M. Mackie Scott & Co.; row of dots on back; satin finish glass; 12½″ **8.00-10.00**

K.H. Macy & Co. N.Y.; snuff; clear **10.00-20.00**

Major's Cement; *This is Major's Leather Cement* on back; aqua; 3″, $3.00-4.00

Major's Cement Co.; *N.Y. U.S.A. This Is Major's and Rubber Cement* on other sides; aqua; 4¼″ **6.00-8.00**

E. Maluwitz; 3¾″ **4.00-8.00**

The Manola Co.; label; machine made; amber; 9½″ **2.00-4.00**

Martin & Martin; clear; 6″ **2.00-4.00**

W.E. Masten's Capital City Cla. Water, Albany, N.Y.; aqua; 9″ **8.00-10.00**

Mavis; under bottom; machine made; amber; 8″ **2.00-4.00**

W. McCully & Co.; under bottom; *Chicago* on back; olive; 10″ **8.00-10.00**

McHenry; amber; 10″ **6.00-10.00**

Libby McNeil, Chicago; clear; 8¼″ **30.00-50.00**

Melchior Bros. Chicago; sunken panel in back for label; clear or amethyst; 8″ **2.00-6.00**

Milk 3c Deposit; around base; clear; 8½″ . . . **8.00-10.00**

Frank Miller & Sons N.Y. Pat. Dec. 26, -76, Newtons; aqua; 5″ **10.00-15.00**

Frank Miller's Crown Dressing, N.Y. U.S.A.; *27* under bottom; aqua; 5″ **8.00-10.00**

Missouri Lumber & Mining Co.; *Grandin Mo.* on label; clear; 5¾″ **2.00-4.00**

Mo; aqua; 2½″ tall, 1½″ x ¾″, $2.00-4.00

Monogram on bottom; aqua; 8¼″ **2.00-4.00**

Mt. Washington Glass Co.; 19th century; opaque glass encrusted with gold, roses and pastel flowers; 12¼″ **100.00-300.00**

T.H. Muskopf; sheared top; clear or amethyst; 5½″ **4.00-8.00**

N; under bottom in a small kick-up; aqua; 9½″ **2.00-4.00**

N & B Co.; under bottom; amber; 7½″ **2.00-4.00**

Nelson Baker & Co.; amber; 12¾″ **8.00-12.00**

Newbro's; clear or amethyst; 7″ **2.00-4.00**

Newhouses Retail Department; in fancy letters in 2 lines, with 2 flower designs; *Louisville, WT & CO* under bottom; emerald green; 5¼″ **4.00-8.00**

Nonpareil Nurser; aqua; 5½″ **12.00-18.00**

Notox, Feb. 14, 1922; *#4* under bottom; inside screw top; amber; 7″ **4.00-8.00**

Nuline Products; almost all are machine made; reproduced from old molds such as *Cabin Bitters* and *Apple Bitters* **2.00-6.00**

Nursing bottle; in front, graduated scale of 1-8 ounces; under bottom *86* triangle with *T* and *#1;* clear or amethyst; 6¼″ **4.00-8.00**

Wm. F. Nye Oil; and a star under bottom; clear or amethyst; 2″ **3.00-4.00**

Old Dr. J. Townsends; other side *Sarsaparilla 1860;* graphite pontil; blue green; 9½″, $50.00-85.00

C. Oppel & Co. Friedrigh Shall; under bottom; olive; 9″ **6.00-8.00**

Oxolo; aqua; 8″ **6.00-8.00**

Packer 1870 West Brook's Pat.; around base; amber; 8½″ **50.00-85.00**

Paste; plain; conical; aqua; 3¼″ **2.00-6.00**

Paste; plain; 12 panels; conical; aqua; 3⅛″ . . . **2.00-4.00**

Geo. R. Patterson, Jeb-City; on back monogram *G.R.P.;* on each side *Trade Mark;* aqua; 7¼″ **2.00-4.00**

P.D. & Co.; under bottom *84;* round; short neck; green; 7½″ **4.00-6.00**

Peppermint; pontil; clear; 6½″ **15.00-30.00**

Perfection Bottle Co., Wilkes Barre, Pa.; *Patd. March 3-97* on base; aqua; 8½″ **15.00-25.00**

Persian bottle; pontil; olive; 6¾″ **30.00-60.00**

Persian water bottle; saddle flask; label; pontil; green; 9″ **35.00-75.00**

Pig figural; bank bottle; clear; 5½″ **4.00-8.00**

Pilden Co., New Lebanon N.Y.; St. Louis Mo.; label; clear; 8¼″ **4.00-6.00**

P.L.; under bottom; snuff; round corners; amber; 3″ x 2¼″ x 1½″ **8.00-10.00**

P.L. Co.; under bottom; snuff; beveled corners; amber **8.00-15.00**

P.L. Co.; under bottom; snuff; sheared top; amber; 4¼" 4.00-6.00

Pocket watch bottle, label; clear; 2½" 2.00-4.00

Polish; plain; light green; 5" 1.00-2.00

The Potter-Parlin Co.; under bottom *Cin;* ridge around bottom; vase type; sheared lip; clear 3.00-6.00

Pottery & Merwin; plain back; on one side *St. Louis;* on other *Missouri;* beveled corner; roofed shoulder; tapered top; aqua; 5½" tall; 2½" x 1½" .. 6.00-8.00
same as above except pontil 8.00-12.00

Prices Patent Candle Company, Toper Limited; in 5 lines on front; square; in center *A.Y. 46 and RD* with 2 lines under; cobalt blue 25.00-50.00

The Purdue Frederick Co.; saddle side strap; clear or amethyst; 8" 3.00-4.00

Reed's; *Reed's Patties Eugene O. Reed Co., Chicago* on back; cork top filler; clear; 11", $4.00-8.00

R G & Co.; clear; 4¾" 2.00-4.00

Rhum Vilejoint; embossed monogram and shield; emerald green; quart; 10" 10.00-20.00

J. Rieger & Co.; clear or amethyst; 4½" 2.00-6.00

Wisdom Robertine; in 2 vertical lines on front; cobalt; 5" 2.00-4.00

Rockford Kalamazoo Automatic and Hand Fire Extinguisher, Patent Applied For; cobalt; 10¾" 25.00-35.00

Roman bottle; tear drop; free-blown; pontil; aqua; 5" 35.00-85.00

E. Roome, Troy New York; pontil; square; dark amber; 4½" corner panels; 4¼" tall 40.00-100.00

L. Rose & Co. Ltd; on shoulder; rose vine on bottle; pale green; 11¼" or 14" 6.00-8.00

R & S 182B; under bottom; aqua; 9½" 2.00-6.00

Rumford Chemical Works; 8 panels; blue green; 5¾" 4.00-8.00

Rutard 85; under bottom; clear or amethyst; 8½", $10.00-12.00

Sauer's Extract; on each side in panels; clear or amethyst; 6" 2.00-4.00

Sawyer's; aqua; 5¾" 4.00-8.00

Carl H. Schultz, N.Y.; blue; 7½" 15.00-20.00

Scrubbs; *Fluid* on back; *D & M Reg No 592584* under bottom; aqua; 8" 8.00-10.00

S & D; under bottom; amber; 2¾" 2.00-4.00

Seamans, Poughkeepsie, N.Y. Dairy; *One Quart Liquid;* in circular slug plate; large *S* on back in circular slug plate; large ring collar; *ABM;* clear; 9½" .. 3.00-4.00

Seville Packing Co. N.Y.; preserves jar; green; 7" 4.00-8.00

Shamrock Oil; on one side *Cincinnati Ohio;* other side *C.B. Dodge;* aqua; 6½" 6.00-8.00

Shoe polish, label; aqua; 4¾" 2.00-3.00

Shoe polish, label; *782 4* under bottom; 4¼" .. 2.00-4.00

Shoe polish, label; *4* under bottom; clear; 3¼" 2.00-4.00

Shoe polish, label; aqua; 3¼" 1.00-2.00

Shoe polish, label; aqua; 4¼" 2.00-4.00

Simmons Hardware Co. Inc.; 3-piece mold; clear or amethyst; 5¼" 6.00-8.00

James P. Smith & Company; aqua; 4½" 2.00-6.00

James P. Smith N.Y. & Chicago; sheared top; clear; 5" 2.00-3.00

John J. Smith; aqua; 6¾" 3.00-6.00

Snuff, label; *#16* under bottom; beveled corners; amber; 4" x 2¼" x 1" 4.00-6.00

Snuff, label; pontil; light olive; 5¾" 40.00-80.00

Snuff, label; *#445* under bottom; beveled corners; amber; 4" x 2½" x 1" 4.00-6.00

Snuff, label; beveled corners; amber; 4¼" x 1¼" x 2¾" 4.00-6.00

Snuff, label; pontil; olive or amber; 4¼" 25.00-50.00

Snuff, label; machine made; amber; 2½" 1.00-2.00

Snuff; plain; round sunken circle under bottom; ring neck; golden amber; 1⅞" x 1¼", 1⅜" curved front and back 4.00-6.00

Snuff; plain; beveled corners; crude top; golden amber; 2½" square base, 4" tall 6.00-12.00

Snuff; plain beveled corners; very short crude neck; pontil; amber; 2½" square base, 4" tall 25.00-50.00

Snuff; plain; beveled corners; sunken *T* under bottom; very short crude neck; olive; 2¾" x 1¾", 4¼" tall 25.00-50.00
same as above except pontil; 6½" tall 35.00-75.00

Sorosis; aqua; 4" 2.00-3.00

Spalding's; *Glue* on back; aqua; 3¼" tall, 1½" diameter 2.00-6.00

Spalding's; *Glue* on back; crude; aqua; 1½" round bottom, 3¼" tall 2.00-4.00

The Specialty Co.; clear or amethyst; 5" 1.00-2.00

Sperm Sewing Machine Oil; *Will Not Gum* on one side; *Will Not Corrode* on other side; clear; 5½" 2.00-4.00

Spurr's Jamaica Ginger Flask, Boston Mass; label; clear or amethyst; 4¾", $8.00-10.00

Standard Oil Co.; label; *433* under bottom; clear; 6" 4.00-6.00

Frederick Stearns & Co.; *Detroit Mich* on side panel; 3-cornered bottle; amber; 10¼"........**8.00-10.00**

same as above except machine made....**2.00-4.00**

same as above except *F. Stearnes & Co.;* 6¼".................................**8.00-10.00**

same as above except 4¾"...........**8.00-10.00**

Stick Well Co.; on 3 panels; 6 panels in all; conical; aqua; 3"..............................**6.00-8.00**

Stick Well & Co.; clear; 3"..............**8.00-15.00**

Stoddard Snuff; beveled corners; open pontil; olive green; 4¾".....................**35.00-75.00**

John W. Stout & Co.; in a half circle; in center big *X* under it *New York;* globular body; tapered top; aqua; 4" neck; 8¼" tall..................**10.00-15.00**

Stovink Johnsons Laboratory Worcester Mass; clear; 4½"...**2.00-4.00**

Tappan; clear; 3¼".......................**4.00-8.00**

Tappan's; aqua; 5½".....................**2.00-4.00**

Tarrant & Co.; clear; 2¼"...............**2.00-3.00**

Thompson & Taylor, Shake Thoroughly, It Foams; aqua or clear.........................**4.00-6.00**

True Cephalick Snuff By the Kings Patent, 1848; pontil; 3½".........................**30.00-50.00**

T.W.C. Co. U.S.A.; on bottom; cobalt; 7½"..**8.00-12.00**

Van Duzers Essence Jamaica Ginger, New York; aqua; 6"...**4.00-8.00**

Vase; plain; green or clear; 8".........**2.00-6.00**

Venable & Heyman, 152 Chambers St. N.Y.; under bottom *Buckingham;* amber; 6".........**10.00-12.00**

Virtray; green; 6¼", $4.00-6.00

V02; under bottom; sheared top; clear; 6".....**2.00-6.00**

Wardles, London Superfine; open pontil; clear or amethyst.........................**10.00-20.00**

W.R. Warner & Co.; *Phila* on back; 3-part mold; aqua; 8".................................**2.00-6.00**

E. Waters Troy N.Y.; *Leather Varnish,* label; 4¾"..**45.00 +**

Weyman Bruton Co. Snuff; label; machine made; amber; 4¼".........................**2.00-3.00**

Wharton Chemical Co.; clear; 6½".........**4.00-6.00**

R. White; *R.B.R. 3213* on base; aqua; 8½", $8.00-12.00

Whittemore, Boston, U.S.A.; in sunken panel; ring top; aqua or clear; 5⅕" tall, 1⁷⁄₁₆" x 2¼".....**3.00-6.00**

Whittemore, Boston, U.S.A.; in sunken panel; aqua; 5½"...**2.00-4.00**

Whyte & Mackay; on back; *M & M* on front; 3-part mold; aqua; 9¾".........................**5.00-10.00**

Edward Wilder & Co., Wholesale Druggists, Louisville, Ky; reverse side *E.W. Sarsaparilla Potasil;* windows on panels; clear; 8½", $75.00 +

W. Wintersmith, Loisville, KY; in 2 vertical lines in a slug plate; amber; 5½"..............**40.00-80.00**

W.F. & Co.; amber; 9½"...................**2.00-3.00**

same as above except 8¼"............**3.00-4.00**

W.T. & Co.; on bottom; label; blue; 3½".....**2.00-4.00**

W.T. & Co.; Pat'd July 1, 91; letter *A* in center of bottom; cylindrical barrel in center *Fill Only to Here* around bottle; rings from base to neck; clear; 2½"...**2.00-4.00**

W.T. & Co., V; in center; *U.S.A.* under bottom; beveled corners; ring top; milk glass; 5".........**6.00-10.00**

Wyokoff & Co. Bluing; in circle *Union and Star;* aqua; 4¼"...**2.00-4.00**

X Bazin Succrto; 6 panels; sheared top; clear; 2¾"...**4.00-6.00**

Schroeder's ANTIQUES Price Guide

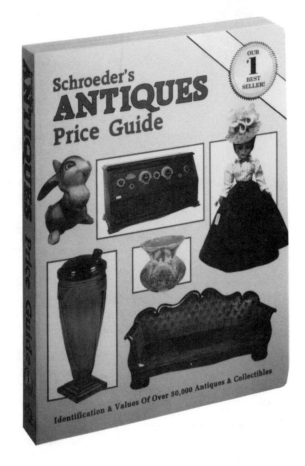

Schroeder's Antiques Price Guide is the #1 best-selling antiques & collectibles value guide on the market today, and here's why . . . More than 300 authors, well-known dealers, and top-notch collectors work together with our editors to bring you accurate information regarding pricing and identification. More than 45,000 items in almost 500 categories are listed along with hundreds of sharp original photos that illustrate not only the rare and unusual, but the common, popular collectibles as well. Each large close-up shot shows important details clearly. Every subject is represented with histories and background information, a feature not found in any of our competitors' publications. Our editors keep abreast of newly-developing trends, often adding several new categories a year as the need arises. If it merits the interest of today's collector, you'll find it in *Schroeder's*. And you can feel confident that the information we publish is up to date and accurate. Our advisors thoroughly check each category to spot inconsistencies, listings that may not be entirely reflective of market dealings, and lines too vague to be of merit. Only the best of the lot remains for publication. Without doubt, you'll find *Schroeder's Antiques Price Guide* the only one to buy for reliable information and values.

8½ x 11", 608 Pages   **$12.95**

COLLECTOR BOOKS
A Division of Schroeder Publishing Co., Inc.